Back to Nature

Back to Nature

The Green and the Real in the
Late Renaissance

Robert N. Watson

PENN

University of Pennsylvania Press
Philadelphia

Copyright © 2006 University of Pennsylvania Press
Printed in the United States of America on acid-free paper

10   9   8   7   6   5   4   3   2   1

Published by
University of Pennsylvania Press
Philadelphia, Pennsylvania 19104-4112

Library of Congress Cataloging-in-Publication Data
Watson, Robert N.
    Back to nature : the green and the real in the late Renaissance / Robert N. Watson.
        p.   cm.
    Includes bibliographical references (p.   ) and index.
    ISBN-13: 978-0-8122-3905-8
    ISBN-10: 0-8122-3905-9 (cloth : alk. paper)
    1. English literature—Early modern, 1500–1700—History and criticism.   2. Nature in literature.
3. Pastoral literature, English—History and criticism.   4. Philosophy of nature in literature.
5. Human ecology in literature.   6. Renaissance—England.   I. Title.

PR428.N39W39 2005
820.9'36'09031—dc22   2005042431

To my daughter,
Emma Cairns Watson

Contents

PART I

Introduction

The Green and the Real

Ecology, Epistemology, and Empiricism

This book is the offspring of two seemingly incompatible parents: one a desire to bring ecological advocacy into the realm of Renaissance literature (where it has usually been deemed irrelevant at best), the other a desire to articulate the intricate philosophical ironies of Shakespeare's *As You Like It*, Marvell's "Mower" poems, and seventeenth-century Dutch painting. They were brought together by a discovery that what looks to modern eyes like early environmentalist sentiment—what would later evolve into that sentiment—originally functioned as an analogy: civilization is to nature as perception is to reality. Pastoralism was part of a broad primitivism: the nostalgia that appears to concern a lost ecology also laments a lost epistemology. English literature and its cultural contexts during the era of Protestant power running roughly from the destruction of the Armada in 1588 to the Restoration in 1660, which I will be calling the late Renaissance, reveal that the familiar efforts to recover simple experience out in the fields or the wilderness, to re-immerse oneself in the natural order, were partly fueled by a craving for unmediated knowledge in any form. As the persistent references to the Garden of Eden suggest, the movement back to nature was partly a code for a drive back toward some posited original certainty—a drive baffled by paradox and by history, leaving the pastoralist merely posing with his back to nature.

Ecocriticism

Would anyone have bet on horticultural studies as a plausible heir to cultural studies at the forefront of literary criticism in English? Perhaps someone recalling the shift from the divisive Vietnam War protests of the 1960s to the generally cuddlier environmentalism of the 1970s could have foreseen that the next generation of scholars would look back penitently from the ivory tower toward the planted rather than the tented field.[1] In any case, ecocriticism seems to be booming in its test markets (British Romanticism and the literature of the American West), and now stands ready to push its way back into the Renaissance.[2] My goal is to move from the Lake District and Yosemite to Stratford-upon-Avon and Hull—or at least into the Forest of Arden and the fields of the mowers—with due respect for the complexities of literary experience. Though the ecocritical position-papers collected in *PMLA* (October 1999) seem wry and dubious about their ability to colonize Shakespeare, this book finds me in the Greens' camp—perhaps as a Trojan horse, however, since I read *As You Like It* as wry and dubious about the prospects for any authentic involvement with the natural world. Perhaps my view, too, can be historicized, as the critical heir to another form of retreat from the political crises of the late 1960s: the acknowledgment (via Eastern religion or psychedelia) that the mind is its own place and that engagement with the "real world" is a delusion rather than an obligation.

This greening of the literary-critical field generates political as well as philosophical discomforts—especially when regarded through the dark-rose lenses of much Cultural Materialist criticism. The color spectrum on which green and red stand far apart sometimes seems to describe the relationship better than the political spectrum on which they share the left side. Without pursuing the provocative suggestion that the Nazis were the most ecologically minded government of the modern Western world,[3] a critic may still feel swarmed by uneasy questions. Is scarcity (as environmentalists warn) a crucial objective fact about the natural environment, or (from a Marxist perspective) is scarcity itself manufactured to produce value and permit control? Is ecocriticism—like New Historicism, some might argue—mostly an effort of liberal academics to assuage their student-day consciences (and their current radical students) about their retreat into aesthetics and detached professionalism, by forcing literary criticism into a sterile hybrid with social activism? Is environmentalism generally an elitist discourse because it is not obviously relevant to the needs of most city dwellers, misguidedly paternalistic toward rural populations who are directly dependent on hunting, logging, or mining, and structurally unjust to inhabitants of technologically undeveloped societies which consume relatively little yet are being asked to bear the burden of preserving outposts of wilderness for the pastoral contemplation and escape of a patronizing Western aristocracy?[4]

To push the questioning a step further: is ecocriticism the latest resort of identity politics in the academy, a way for those excluded by the usual categories to claim victim status, either by identifying with an oppressed biosphere, in part or in whole, or else by imagining their suffering and extinction in an anticipated ecological catastrophe? Is sentimentality toward nature different from other forms of sentimentality? Is it an effort to have religion without coming to terms with religion's irrational and authoritarian demands, an effort to find an alternative locus for the sacred in an increasingly secular culture—a kind of neutral (if only because infinitely various and infinitely interpretable) object for collective worship, a low common denominator for our experience of Creation?

Is attempting to speak for animals, or trees for that matter, a progressive or an appropriative action? Is it in any way parallel to other efforts in cultural studies to give voice to those who have not been empowered to speak for themselves; or is the parallel I have just proposed itself an offense against social justice, since it echoes pernicious rhetoric associating a human underclass with the so-called "lower forms of life" and encourages a leap beyond issues of social justice that have not yet been effectively addressed? Am I wrong to give a Humane Society money that the human society could use? Do I allay or aggravate this concern by subordinating the environmentalist impulse to more abstract philosophical issues? My questions about ecocriticism in general thus circle back to my speculations about the origins of its current popularity: the search for a politically safe and aesthetically attractive version of late 1960s radicalism may look like a healthy adaptation at one moment, a sinister co-optation at another.

It would be wrong to sophisticate away the growing ecological and environmental mission, all the more wrong because it would be so convenient; wrong to let such important problems slide just because they are ethically and tactically complicated; wrong, also, not to think them through from many angles. If we can understand how some people came to care, in politically and intellectually responsible ways, about present and future life on this planet as a collectivity, we can hope to expand the ecologically minded community and its wisdom. That may in turn expand, in space and time, in however small and gradual a way, the niche in which life makes its beauties and finds its joys.

Overview

This book explores artistic responses to the nostalgia for unmediated contact with the world of nature—a common sentiment focused and magnified by a cultural moment in which urbanization, capitalism, new technologies, and the Protestant Reformation each contributed to anxieties about mediation and the lost sensual past. Behind late-Renaissance efforts to identify with fauna and even flora lies a tendency to view things-in-themselves as the primary object of knowledge and reverence. These anticipations of the Romantic and physicist eras, two hundred and four hundred years later, were already provoking skeptical critiques that alienated humanity from nature and discerned a fundamental indeterminacy in reality. The pursuit of empirical science forced one set of prominent Renaissance thinkers to confront epistemological doubts, while the multicultural upheaval associated with Renaissance humanism threatened to produce a cognitive crisis among another set of thinkers by revealing that the world is less observed than constructed, less an accessible reality than a contingency manufactured by a team of repressed solipsists.

Representation thus became a psychic as well as political crisis in early modern England. Indeed, anxieties about the arbitrary, prejudiced, and unstable character of perception—including both the eccentricities of individuals and the possibility of collective delusion—must have put special pressures on those (particularly in the Parliamentary movement) who were advocating a system of political representatives.[5] Constitutionalism seemed to imply a recognition that all the world is constituted. By the middle of the seventeenth century, both politics and epistemology were increasingly presumed to operate by consent rather than absolutism; that is, reality consisted of what was commonly perceived by human beings, and government consisted of their common interest. The agreement to settle for figurations and approximations of the individual material entity coincided with a similar agreement about the will of the individual citizen. The strenuous and approximate aspects of consensus made it an awkward ally for the dream of government by revelation. While activists, scientists, zealots, philologists, and travelers proclaimed that the rightful truth was ready to manifest itself spontaneously, a repressed fear whispered that it was ever more distant— was, perhaps, nowhere.

The consequent yearning takes many synergistic forms: theological (seeking a new earthly Eden as well as a simpler way to heaven), political (arising from urban afflictions, enclosure controversies, and the sentimental association of political movements with primitive English agriculture), economic (dreaming of a society either fully founded on gold or completely neglectful of it), philosophical (responding to the resurgence of skepticism), philological (attempting to recover a "pure" Latin and an idealized textual past), scientific (seeking a transparent descriptive rhetoric), psychoanalytic (recalling the symbiotic union of breast-feeding—rivers of milk were a pastoral commonplace),[6] painterly (wrestling with the implications of landscape and perspective), and poetic (arising from a sense of artistic belatedness, particularly in the rediscovered pastoral mode). The nostalgia for Eden, for the Golden Age, for an idealized collective-agrarian feudal England, and for a prelinguistic access to reality all come together (notably in Traherne's "Centuries") in fantasies of a liberating regression to garden and wilderness.[7] Titles of important works such as Edward Stillingfleet's *Origines Sacrae* (1662) and Matthew Hale's *Primitive Organization of Mankind* (1677) remind us how eager this culture remained, even as it became scientifically sophisticated, to found truth on some simple and original point— how much the discovery of truth, which for a modern scientific culture is the goal of progress, was then understood as a function of regress. The gaze was so persistently backward (toward ancient paganism and ancient Christianity alike), provoked by the multicultural explosion of the High Renaissance (including the diaspora of scholars, and the voyages of early colonialism and world trade), that I have preferred "late Renaissance" to "Early Modern" in my title.

From the moment of their conception, modern ecological and epistemological anxieties were conjoined twins. Their conjunction brings into alignment a number of important binary oppositions: human/animal, mind/body, self-consciousness/instinct, self/other, art/nature, word/thing, signifier/signified, Symbolic/Imaginary, Platonic shadow/Platonic form, fallen/unfallen consciousness, and even (to the extent that misogynist traditions blame women for alienating men from nature, or make women the repositories or captives of nature) man/woman.[8] Set in parallel series, these polarities conveyed a considerable cultural shock. When Marvell—the great ancestor of Wallace Stevens as a lyricist of self-consciousness—asserts in "The Garden" that "Two paradises 'twere in one / To live in paradise alone," the patristic resentment of Eve thinly covers the story of another fall, into Cartesian dualism, in which actual nature and perceived nature become distinct, because "a green shade" is never quite identical with the "green thought" that represents it in human consciousness. Renaissance man was post-lapsarian in (among others) a post-structuralist way. How valuable, how viable, is the "Paradise within thee" promised to Milton's Adam and Eve if it misrepresents a paradise that is lost—lost because it can only be misrepresented?[9]

None of this is to claim that these forms of mediation and alienation were entirely new, nor that any period in recorded history has been immune to regrets about a posited lost simplicity. The Middle Ages did not sit comfortably on a firm platform of direct realism. But some late-Renaissance societies nonetheless appear to struggle with a convergence of forces that together raised this familiar cultural problem to the level of crisis, a crisis indirectly narrated by the artists of those societies and formative of the ecological sympathies and epistemological anxieties that now dominate liberal intellectual consciousness, humanistic and scientific alike.[10] My definition of nature may seem to shift among several usages of the term: flora and fauna, the innate character of a being, and the totality of the physical universe. Similarly, my description of a skeptical crisis will sometimes blur the differences among the problem of establishing the existence of material bodies, the problem of discerning essences, and the problem of knowing other minds. My defense in both cases is that this jumbling is exactly what late-Renaissance culture was doing and what permitted it to imagine it could attack the epistemological problems through various forms of pastoral primitivism: "in the state of innocency in the first creation, *Man had perfect naturall knowledge of* all naturall things."[11] Humanity's lost touch with nature is fundamentally a problem of lost knowledge.

Recognizing this amalgamation of issues evokes something new and noteworthy from the individual artworks, which collectively suggest something important about the world that made them and the world we are making. My goal is to apply the stains and the lights that make visible this particular pattern in the grain of cultural history. Moving beyond traditional expositions of the art-nature polarity in this period,[12] I am suggesting homologies among the various causes of this intensified sense of loss and alienation, and suggesting dangerous synergies among the effects. Protestantism sought to restore a direct link between the Savior and the soul through direct reading of the Bible by the sinner, as opposed to the complicated institutional mediations associated with the Catholic version of Christianity; the idea that Protestantism claimed to be returning to the true origins of Christianity, scraping away the accretions which had grown on the Catholic Church like barnacles over time, is so central and so generally acknowledged then and now that I will not linger to offer examples. Peter Sterry, Oliver Cromwell's chaplain, demonstrates how the projects of returning to nature, returning to the origins of Christianity, and returning to Eden could be blended rhetorically into a single inspiring program of Platonist Protestantism: "as Paradise, so the *pure Image* of God in the Soul, seems to some not to be *lost* or destroyed, but *hid* beneath the ruins of the fall. Thus *Knowledg* springing in the Soul, seems to be a *remembrance*, the Life of all good, an awakening by reason of the primitive Image of pure Nature raising itself by degrees, and sparkling through the *Rubbish*, the confusions of the present state."[13] The radical Protestant sects reveal the way this regression toward the primitive church could become a regression toward a thoroughly primitivist absorption in nature. Even allowing for demagogic sensationalism behind reports of nudism among Picardians, Ranters, Adamists, and Quakers, the thematic persistence of such accusations suggest strong atavist and minimalist tendencies in the radical Reformation—a desire to manifest, so to speak, the thing itself.[14] The Ranters were said to believe that "when we die we shall be swallowed up into the infinite spirit, as a drop into the ocean . . . and if ever we be raised again, we shall rise as a horse, a cow, a root, a flower and such like."[15] This is atavism blended into atomism, with overtones of Pythagorean beliefs (about which Jonson's *Volpone*, Donne's *Metempsychosis*, and several of Shakespeare's best-known plays joke uneasily) that proposed a dizzying cycle of origins, back through various other species, for each human soul. The infinite regress pointed not to a Creator, but always further into a void—or at least toward an abysmally low common denominator. Like Darwinism later, Pythagorean metempsychosis was at best an equivocal force in promoting common respect for all forms of life, but it is interesting that resistance to the extreme and casual cruelties toward animals in the period is voiced mostly by Puritans such as Philip Stubbes, William Perkins, Thomas Beard, and George Wither.[16]

Meanwhile, human beings were also imposing new cruelties on each other. Sixteenth-century England was (many economic historians agree) the time and place where wage labor became dominant: segments of the feudal peasantry became a rootless proletariat for hire, alienating workers from their fields and their own bodies in the course of alienating work from product and ownership from object. New channels of money and status carried aristocrats from their country estates to court. Long before industrialism diverted them away from agriculture, capitalism took away Englishmen's proprietary relationship to the earth. Land, labor, and identity were a socio-economic Trinity pulled asunder. Money became an increasingly disturbing and dominant instance of the way that seemingly arbitrary signifiers could come between people and their material world, and periods of rapid inflation drove painfully home how unstable (and therefore contingent) that signification could be. Urbanization, as Barnabe Googe and other pastoralists complained, promoted not only a new kind of anonymity (which wage labor magnified), but also (as in the Hellenistic era) the pangs of alienation from a past more directly linked to the land—and family— that provided life.

Emerging nationalism in the late Renaissance drew heavily on fantasies of origins and of the almost autochthonic "natures" of different peoples. But personal identity—supposedly a truth based in both chief senses of "nature"— became elusive. If inward subjectivity was the rock on which both Montaigne and Descartes would build, outward seeming was therefore all the more opaque. Radical, iconoclastic Reformers such as Andreas Karlstadt argued that there were no external markers of grace. Implicit in this period's anti-theatrical polemics and sumptuary legislation alike was a suspicion that roles and clothes might misrepresent—and thereby alter—the essential nature, the true identity, of a person. Class, gender, even race were at risk of being disguised—which may have been the safe way of saying they were at risk of being exposed as merely costumes, merely constructed.[17] Blaise Pascal comments bitingly on the use of "red robes" to distinguish judges who otherwise have no judgment to distinguish them.[18] Slippage among name, personal appearance, and social place seemed intolerably threatening. The regulations and diatribes were a way of enforcing an illusion of order, not unlike Marvell's mower enforcing, in bad faith, the "pathetic fallacy" (to borrow a useful term from Ruskin's *Modern Painters*) that nature had neglected to sustain once the mower fell into misery. Even the sale of knighthoods and other supposedly hereditary or quality-specific honors by King James would have manifested this split between the nominal and the natural. The fears about lost stability of the social hierarchy and about lost comprehensibility of the material universe—the sociological and epistemological crises—thus inflected and amplified one another. Beneath practical concerns about the current limits of knowledge lurked proto-Kantian concerns about the nature and conditions of knowledge itself. The crises of identity and subjectivity contributed to a fear that representation was not only potentially but inherently a fraud—since (as Greenblatt's argument about self-fashioning suggests) there was also a burgeoning fear that there might be no essence of the self to express or return to, that disrobing after a day of social assertions might be another instance of the onion peeling down to nothing.[19]

Discomfort about how people dressed also reflected discomfort about how they undressed—and nowhere more clearly than in the theater. The fears of unstable selfhood that fueled the sumptuary laws conjoin with a fear of failed erotic teleology in the now-notorious attacks on cross-dressing that featured so prominently in the anti-theatrical tracts.[20] Though literary critics are somehow demographically fated to scoff at this moral indignation, there seems little question that audiences were significantly titillated by the blurring of gender when boys played women's roles. The plays often toy with this open secret, building toward a moment when the genitals would be exposed or involved; think of the tension surrounding the king's order to "Strip that boy" in *Philaster* (5.5), or less directly but with greater complications, the repeated delays in consummating Othello's marriage, and the mixed signals about his wedding sheets. While Othello is being made to wonder whether it is possible that he could ever have Desdemona's maidenhead, or whether it is instead all a cruel joke, audiences are nudged to wonder something similar for a different reason: they too are being cheated, teased with a consummation the playwright could never really give them. Think also about the many plays—especially Jonson's comedies such as *The Alchemist* and *Volpone*—that break off the villains' plot at the moment when the honest woman is finally about to be genitally violated; then consider what Jonson does with this theme in *Epicoene* where a final twist of gender surprises the audience and resolves the plot, and in *Bartholomew Fair* where the puppets finally do what Jonson had so often just barely refused to do: lift up the skirts of the players, only to show the lack underneath. A recent study asserts that the epistemology of cross-dressing on the London stage demonstrates "how in the early modern period sodomy functioned not as an identity, nor even as an activity, but as a site in which the failure of representation produces a desire that has no object."[21] An elusive object, anyway, or a fantastic one. The point of the dramatic tease is precisely that it will not, cannot, be resolved—which leaves gender and sexuality in the same maze of mediations, the same sense of lost contact with both fundamental and biological reality, that I believe haunted so many habitations of Renaissance thought.

The English government, like its citizens, was driven to give up on seeking essences and instead settled for phenomena. A key aspect of the Elizabethan theological compromise was that the state would not "make windows into men's hearts and secret thoughts" to see whether they believed the Protestant doctrine, so long as they complied with it outwardly.[22] This must have left some "Church papists" stewing in their own hypocrisies, and left some Protestants anxious—even more than Jesuit equivocation had already done—about lurking enemies to their beliefs and potentially to their government. The distinction between privacy and disguise dissolved in the corrosive paranoia. As Peter Lake has observed, the emphasis on conformity "opened up a gap between the inward and the outward, the real inner convictions of a person and his or her outward behavior, a space which, it seemed to many contemporaries, could be exploited for all sorts of dissimulation by the faithless and the unscrupulous."[23] These fears were distinctly homologous with the other anxieties this book traces: artistic, scientific, colonial, and sexual exploits in which the gap between the outward manifestation and the inward being could never quite be closed. Precisely because it was so supremely important, doctrinal affiliation became impossible to read. Persons on either side of the religious wars might have found it a delicious relief to slip into a theater where they could hear the soliloquies in which those windows to the private soul flew open and the secret thoughts turned into audible language. This brief reprieve from what philosophers discuss as the problem of other minds—their fundamental inaccessibility—would, moreover, only have emphasized the similar problems of represented reality, of the *theatrum mundi*. The link between a Pyrrhonist resignation to making the best of the appearance of things and the Elizabethan theological compromise becomes visible in a complaint against the Marprelate tracts: "I never entred into other mens hearts to see their consciences: I never looked into their Cofers to see their treasures: I never was desirous to be privie of their secret doings. I must therfore by that I see, heare, and know, judge the best."[24]

Representation

Around the beginning of the seventeenth century, people in England were hearing a crescendo of warnings about the failure of representation—long before it became an explicitly political issue and helped provoke the Civil War (and much earlier than Michel Foucault claims that any fundamental mistrust of resemblance, let alone of representation, could emerge).[25] Developments such as single-point perspective, empirical science, and improved maps and optical devices marked progress; but, as so often, progress brings with it a recognition of limitations. As the technologies get better at replicating reality, it becomes harder to blame them for the imperfection of our representations: it becomes clear that the problem is not one of method. Toward the end of his *History of the Royal Society*, Thomas Sprat warns that if this new collective empirical approach to science were to fail, "They will have reason in all times to conclude, That the long barreness of *Knowledge* was not caus'd by the corrupt method which was taken, but by the nature of the *Thing* itself."[26] Radically improved optics surely promised to make reality more visible; and yet that innovation finally drove reality further off in at least five ways, as it enabled the expanded voyages of discovery and colonization that brought home the dis-eases of multiculturalism, established the unfathomable depth of the physical universe, revealed that organisms were not merely themselves but also colonies of micro-organisms, contributed to the self-conscious fraudulence of perspective painting, and taught scientists lessons about the functioning of human perception that suggest our experience of reality is merely virtual, merely a highly contingent system of mental representation.

The back-to-nature movement of the late 1960s was echoed by a popular song whose refrain ended, "Get back to where you once belonged." By the early 1970s, a more abstract and dubious note had entered, with a chorus that ended instead, "The nearer your destination, the more you're slip slidin' away"[27]—at least, the more you find yourself living in Zeno's paradox instead of Adam's Paradise; Achilles decelerates near the tape, the arrow hovers just short of the bull's-eye. The fantasy of regression to an absolute truth decayed similarly from the mid-sixteenth to the mid-seventeenth century, though Francis Bacon kept bravely assuring his fellow investigators (as if to preclude Paul Simon's wistful warning) that "the nearer it [the investigation] approaches to simple natures, the easier and plainer everything will become."[28] As Pierre Gassendi would demonstrate in the mid-seventeenth century, however, language is a lens that makes close-ups blurry.[29] Leonardo da Vinci, though confident about visual science, characteristically anticipated the problem with scientific language: "the more minute your description the more you will confuse the mind of the reader and the more you will lead him away from the knowledge of the thing described."[30] Francis Quarles warned that "The road to resolution lies by doubt: / The next way home's the farthest way about."[31] There is no direct route to truth; inquiring minds must, as the circumlocuting Polonius advises, "by indirections, find directions out."[32] Sprat observed that "it frequently happens to *Philosophers*, as it did to *Columbus* . . . by prosecuting of *mistaken Causes*, with a resolution of not giving over the persute; they have been guided to the *truth* it self."[33]

Bacon's heirs in the Royal Society were eventually compelled to acknowledge that they could never quite bridge the gap between a highly probable belief about nature and direct knowledge of nature, nor the gap between the sensibly observed properties of an object and the essential identity of that object. When John Locke tries to identify a material essence, he seems to define it by its ability to withstand that endlessly divisive paradox: "Primary qualities . . . are utterly inseparable from the body, in what state soever it be; and such as . . . the mind finds inseparable from every particle of matter, though less than to make itself singly be perceived by our senses: v.g. Take a grain of wheat, divide it into two parts; each part has still solidity, extension, figure, and mobility: divide it again, and it retains still the same qualities; and so divide it on, till the parts become insensible; they must retain still each of them all those qualities."[34] Cream of wheat notwithstanding, this sets a daunting standard for the aspects of nature our senses can truly claim to savor. As Shakespeare's Touchstone reminds his companions (2.4.16–18), the pastoral escapist has to face the fact that he—usually he rather than she—will never really achieve an unselfconscious symbiosis with the fields (at least, not while alive, and especially not while speaking), a fact he could ignore while sitting in the court and the city, the currency exchange and the commodity markets, the scholar's library and the artist's studio, dreaming of escape from the artificial human world.

This version of Zeno's paradox afflicted theological entities as well. The more an image looked like God, the more it threatened to alienate God: Queen Elizabeth placated the Puritans, paradoxically, by replacing the West Cheap Cross with a pagan pyramid, and turning its Virgin Mary into a semi-nude Diana.[35] The zealous Protestant may feel at moments the presence of the divine spirit as intimately as the Catholic may feel the divine body in the Eucharist, but such Protestants were also tortured by the uncertainty and incompleteness of that divine presence: by the way sin, fallen reason, inscrutable predestination, and residual ceremonial structures still somehow remained between themselves and full knowledge of God. Furthermore, the very arguments Luther and his fellow reformers made for a purified text in vernacular tongues finally implied that there could be no meaning independent of context and hence no stable ultimate truth; in the cultural kitchen, philology proved to be less a dishwasher than a mixmaster blender.[36] To use language-study, as Valla did in the fifteenth century, as a tool for exposing the Donation of Constantine as a forgery—a foundational event in Renaissance humanism, and above all an effort to get back to original truth—is finally to expose the internal referentiality and historical instability of any verbal system, a recognition that refutes any lingering hope that words will directly reflect things, uninflected by local circumstances and evolving vocabularies.[37] While Valla's conclusions undermined the legal basis of papal empire, his method—especially in the *Dialectical Disputations*—undermined the Scriptural basis of Protestantism before it began.[38] Absolute truth and origins again recede together. Hence the period's nostalgia for Hebrew, as the true primeval language, rumored to have some pictographic and even magical connection with the things it described (it was speculated "if a child were taught no Language in his Infancy, but left to his own conduct, he would speak *Hebrew*").[39] Ancient Chinese and Egyptian hieroglyphics were attractive for similar reasons: alphabetic writing had some of the disenchanting implications of atomism.[40] To attempt (as Donne, Cudworth, and many others did) to resolve disputes within Christianity by studying its origins in Judaism, however, was to risk heresy and apostasy, to risk dissipating doctrine rather than providing it with stable foundations. Only the paradox by which Christian religion could claim chronological priority over Judaic religion, and the related hermeneutics by which it could convert the Pentateuch into a mere allegorical representation of the New Testament's absolute truth, could keep the hunger for original truth from driving late-Renaissance Christians back into the arms of the Judaic Yahweh.

The art of dialectic itself, which became central to the university curriculum in sixteenth-century England, is a search for truth that systematically defeats, by perpetually deferring, the effort to settle on a truth (even religious truth; no wonder there was a movement back toward Scholasticism in the early seventeenth century). Montaigne ends up arguing that "the opinion of knowledge" is the source of endless human suffering and folly, and that if it would "please nature some day to open her bosom to us . . . what mistakes we should find in our poor science! I am mistaken if it grasps one single thing straight as it is."[41] Along these many different paths, the quest kept turning Quixotic: Cervantes' work captures the paradox of an age that kept finding itself most laughably derivative, most caught up in imaginary sophistications, at the moments it tried hardest to return proudly to the authentic truth of a posited Golden Age.

Conjuring Quintessences

Don Quixote parodies the struggle to look past the immediately apparent physical reality to the more exalted, bookish truth behind it—a good joke for an era trying to laugh off a thousand years of Western European ontology that deemed the world a mere delusive figure of the Word. (Cervantes tactfully displaces the joke from the theological realm into a form of literary criticism; in 1637, the Little Gidding community, rather less prepared to see the humor in such things, actually arranged a bonfire fueled mostly with the kind of romantic tales that beguiled Don Quixote.) Don Quixote himself even anticipates Descartes in positing a malign enchanter who has made his senses unreliable, while Cervantes himself playfully claims authority from original sources that can never be found. When he provides a pastoral inset, Cervantes makes it evoke redundantly the mournful quest to return to bases and origins: Gristómo demands to be buried "at the foot of that rock where is the spring of the cork tree, because, the rumor goes—and they say they had it from his lips—that it was the spot he saw her for the first time."[42] Marvell's mower Damon will seek a similar fate for similar reasons.

Long before Descartes makes the problems explicit, the epistemological anxieties brought on by mediation were diseasing the Renaissance body-cultural all across Europe, which developed a kind of hydroptic appetite for things in and as themselves. Montaigne admires the cannibals for their lack of mediations (and, as Hamlet points out, when "a king may go a progress through the guts of a beggar" by passing through the bodies of other animals [4.3.31], mediations are all that differentiate carnivores from cannibals). Resistance gradually emerged to the "conservative formalism" of the Ciceronian style, which, in "Stressing words over matter," "offered nothing to an 'intellect intent upon the discovery of reality.' "[43] In the first half of the seventeenth century, John Amos Comenius developed an entire educational program based on the idea that "things are the kernel, words the shell and the husk."[44] But that nutritious core sits teasingly out of reach, like the apples of Tantalus. In the same period, Marin Mersenne and Gilles Personne de Roberval exemplify "the denial that human knowledge can ever encompass the essences of things,"[45] which obliges us to settle for their quantitative manifestations; others, such as Pierre Gassendi and Christiaan Huygens, decide that we can reach out toward essences, but only as hypotheses and probabilities. The reification of statistical observation would culminate in the nineteenth century; only in the twentieth century, thanks to quantum physics, would science be prepared to follow the implications toward the Copenhagen interpretation which suggests—with a loss of certainty and presence intolerable even to Einstein—that reality itself, not just our limited knowledge of it, consists of mere probabilities. The problems that would lead there were already troubling scientific minds, however. Gassendi's *Parhelia* (1629), seeking to replace scholastic categories with empirical observation, mocks the claims of the Peripatetics to "see things from the inside" when knowledge actually stops "at the bark of things." "You give me matter, form and privation as principles," Gassendi declares, "But I ask you to show me the essence of just one object, even the tiniest in nature."[46] Even quantity and probability were at risk: Wilkins and Glanvill (following Henry More) decide that not even math is certain.

Various proto- and pseudo-sciences would attempt to bridge the gap. Some were verbal. Erasmian humanism, David Quint has demonstrated, involves both "the destructive criticism of human idols and the critical reconstruction of God's Word. These two activities are mutually consistent in their common goal, the separation of the human counterfeit from the divine original."[47] Ramist logic, which promised to break through language, with all of its deceptions and approximations, gained unprecedented popularity; soon other, experimental sciences would attempt to polish language to a perfect transparency. This kind of purification was sought in the physical realm as well. Aided by the efforts of Ficino and his students, Hermeticism blossomed as a kind of dual fulfillment of the Renaissance quest to recover origins, since it involved the fantasy of recovering, philologically, a (supposedly) very ancient and divinely inspired text, which itself promises, philosophically, to redeliver to human consciousness a vision of pure forms. Alchemists believed "they were following the same kind of procedure employed by God in the creation of the world."[48] Robert Fludd "elevated his pictures beyond mere *representation* or description," following those Continental Hermeticists (such as Valentin Weigel) "who taught that man gained true knowledge of nature only when human *experientia* became the *scientia* innate in natural objects. . . . By the middle of the seventeenth century, Weigel, Croll, and Boehme were much in vogue in English translation."[49] If it is true that the Rosicrucian sect was inadvertently spawned or spread by a Lutheran theologian, John Valentin Andrea, who had intended to parody the appetite of late Renaissance culture for ancient texts purporting to reveal the inner secrets of nature, then both the aim and the backfire of that project reveal how strong that appetite—for natural essences spiced with antiquity—really was. Though the Renaissance swells with systems purporting to trace (as medieval systems had, in perhaps less multicultural circumstances) the analogous cosmic order, Ronald Levao shrewdly suggests that we "ask ourselves whether such texts certify a continuity of attitude or reveal a willed conservatism, a strenuous and self-conscious effort to shore up a profoundly unsettled edifice."[50]

Hermeticism had a technical as well as a theoretical aspect, and again it turned to ancient authorities to try to recover original purities. The most visible application of Hermetic doctrines—and one that remained quite active long after modern historians of science often assume it was discredited—was alchemy. As in bullionism, gold was thought of as an originary value, something that has a retrievable pure identity. Alchemical practice was therefore often described as a passage through various gates toward some central truth, and the knowledge was generally presented in the form of texts within texts: antique knowledge, presented by a mediator, which the reader could now summon into a material presence.[51] Alchemy offered a traditional way of searching for an absolute material, the quintessence, an unmoved mover in the world of metals; and it was commonly supposed to require, not just the techniques of the laboratory scientist, but also the spiritual purity of a saint (a claim Jonson parodies in *The Alchemist*).[52] So the material object was still not the absolute referent, at least not in any detached way; making the "philosopher's stone" still involved the inner moral condition of the philosopher, not just the outward physical condition of a stone.[53] Making that stone (as Jonson also shows) required a specialized language. Words and subjectivity were supposedly still of the essence. The anthropomorphic terms and the emphasis on sublimation identify alchemy as a transaction between the physical and spiritual realms, each still capable of influencing the other. In this laboratory, subjectivity was an indispensable tool and part of the ultimate substance. The alchemist's highest dream was the Baconian empiricist's worst nightmare.

Eventually the Baconians were able to awaken their society—that is, to convince it that empiricism *was* an awakening, that surrendering its grand visions was rising to a higher state of consciousness rather than sinking to a lower one. That claim was useful for competing against the "true alchemist" to whom "the real significance of gold was spiritual, and its physical properties were merely signs pointing the way to that significance." But the tide of intellectual history was also advancing empiricism: "it was impossible for alchemy long to survive the collapse of the analogical universe. Alchemy is the practical attempt to realize the spiritual essence, or *telos*, of matter. It assumes that the objective existence of a thing is only a representation of its ideal form."[54] Could Neoplatonism, or poetry as Sidney defended it, survive much longer? Sidney's assertion that poets "deliver a golden" world hovers revealingly between a boast that poets uncover deep truth and a confession that they cannot deliver the real world; "Nature never set forth the earth in so rich tapestry," but tapestries are only representations of reality woven by the human hand and mind.[55] Does the physical foundation have any connection to the spiritual and literary superstructures? Without the assumption that the material world participated in higher correspondences—the Renaissance shift toward literalist reading of the Bible emphasizes the question—could a predominant mode of literary depth and intricacy, a rich suggestiveness, survive in any recognizable form?

As things take dominion over thoughts (with the tag-team of Bacon and Hobbes leading the assault), even sexual love seems threatened by the dualism and reductivism this change invites. Indeed, Donne's "Love's Alchemy" suggests a comparable fear about both practices (or perhaps about all three, if we notice poetry itself implicated along with alchemy and eroticism): a fear of a bait-and-switch swindle that promised some glorious transformative absolute, but delivers only worldly by-products (coins, babies, medicinal salves) as consolation-prizes.[56] An early biography of William Perkins describes him, before he sought ultimate truth in the Protestant Word, as "much addicted to the study of naturall Magicke, digging so deepe, in natures mine, to know the hidden causes and sacred quallities of things."[57] In the opening line of Donne's poem, the disturbing proximity of that same familiar opening metaphor to the crude anatomy of sexual intercourse suggests the continuing futile struggle to pursue the physical with enough intensity to transcend it, or at least discover its essence:

> Some that have deeper digged love's mine than I,
> Say, where his centric happiness doth lie:
>   I have loved, and got, and told,
> But should I love, get, tell, till I were old,
> I should not find that hidden mystery;
>   Oh! 'tis imposture all:
> And as no chemic yet the elixir got,
>   But glorifies his pregnant pot,
>   If by the way to him befall
> Some odoriferous thing, or medicinal,
>   So, lovers dream a rich and long delight,
>   But get a winter-seeming summer's night.

Instead of becoming the affirmation of something permanent and primary, love becomes utterly transient and derivative, "this vain bubble's shadow," and all Donne is left with, at the end of "a bridegroom's play," is the bitterness of marriage to a body essentially devoid of consciousness (except perhaps that of a demonic intruder): "Hope not for mind in women; at their best / Sweetness and wit, they are but mummy, possessed." This is a horror-movie image and, like the most effective ones, it offers emptiness at its core. Versions of this specter undermined the confidence of an entire society that its people knew enough about God, the world, the self, or each other to make real contact or offer authentic love.

Skepticism and Empiricism

The works of the Greek Pyrrhonist known as Sextus Empiricus were rediscovered late in the fifteenth century and translated in the sixteenth. The overlap of names notwithstanding, Sextus Empiricus makes an odd ally for Baconian empiricists; like extreme left- and right-wing politics, however, these seeming opposites display some striking similarities. Though Pyrrhonist philosophy would seem to assert pervasive doubt about knowing the world, and Baconian science assumes that such knowledge is possible, they end up agreeing to replace questions about ultimate truth with questions about the world as practically manifest, to focus on the transactions one finds reliable (by experiment, which is to say, experience) with the externalities of that world. "For no man can rightly and successfully investigate the nature of anything in the thing itself," warns Bacon in the preface to his *Great Instauration*; "let him vary his experiments as laboriously as he will, he never comes to a resting place, but still finds something to work beyond."[58] This is the observational equivalent of Sextus Empiricus's warning that seeking to resolve disputes by criteria can only lead "to a regress *ad infinitum*."[59]

Was there any middle ground between infallible knowledge and absolute skepticism? Would either pure faith built on Scripture (from Luther and Erasmus) or purified reason built on observation (from Bacon) offer something more stable, even if only within its own special realm—the house of God or the halls of scholarship? Sir Thomas Browne would ask that question entrancingly (and would once observe that "the wisest heads prove at last, almost all Scepticks,"[60] though he sought to convert the dangerous energies of skepticism into an amplifier of faith); Descartes would ask it more influentially. Leading intellectuals at Great Tew tried to find a third way. But the coincidence of religious faction with the rediscovery of classical skepticism produced (as Richard Popkin has noted) a powerfully corrosive substance, and history has proven how easily efforts to dilute it could, like attacks on atheism and other heresies, end up spreading it instead.

The rediscovery of Sextus Empiricus would have tended to aggravate the pervasive yearning for original and foundational truth, a desire to renounce mediations and get back to sources, to find something that had at least a chronological claim to priority over other beliefs and modes of life—including or even especially the classical ones (hence the ready market for forgers of supposedly ancient Etruscan histories and prophecies such as Curzio Inghirami and Giovanni Nanni da Viterbo).[61] The search for the lost Eden took the form of a search for the source of rivers,[62] which became an obsession among explorers in the New World and also a popular trope for the way reality reaches the senses.[63] Nor was Eden itself still a safe origin, since alternative creation-myths were arriving from the classics (notably Hesiod, as well as better-established figures such as Aristotle, Virgil, and Ovid), and some were arriving from newly colonized societies that, well-educated scoffers such as Christopher Marlowe observed, had written records dating back past the generally accepted date of Adam's creation.[64] The place where innocent knowledge had once been, and had then been lost, was now itself being lost. Everything and nothingness seemed to stand between human beings and certain truths. In the mysterious middle ground between the thought and the object, where Galileo placed discourse, the Stoics (via Sextus) placed yet another mediation—the *lekton*, sense-experience—as an independent third entity.[65] As each attempt to establish a valid criterion crumbled, something other than logical deduction was needed to choose among beliefs; in a world that seemed to be spinning on an outward gyre, toward increasing confusion, the notion of a previous time (and hence natural place) where simple truths seemed manifest and self-evident must have had extraordinary appeal.

Nor was Sextus the only ancient ghost who returned to haunt the Renaissance with rumors of a death of meaning. Theologians and philosophers were perpetually shadow-boxing with Epicurus and Lucretius;[66] and in denouncing Heraclitus for his pre-Christian insistence that there was no stable truth to go back for, Renaissance moralists unwittingly affirmed his point. By dismissing Heraclitus's argument as a product of his cultural milieu—by historicizing the man who warned about the irresistible and irretrievable character of any historical moment—these Christians stumbled right into his flowing stream. The literature of the period seems divided on whether to treat this stumble into the flux as a comic pratfall or an Ophelia-like tragedy: in some cases (like Cervantes' Don Quixote and Marvell's Damon) it seems to be a wonderful mixture of the two. At the turn of the road from alchemy to science, where Roger Bacon hands over the driving to Francis Bacon, late-Renaissance artists such as Shakespeare and Marvell stand diverting traffic onto a detour—into a labyrinth—that this book will attempt to map.

The scouts sent back to look for the simple, redemptive, original truth were also questers like Lot or Jesus, Orpheus or Hercules, on a rescue mission through a ghastly infernal landscape with only their purity and determination (and a few slogans) to protect them. But that truth about the world wasn't where the Renaissance had last seen it: it had already departed on its amazing modern itinerary—I will argue—from meaning to matter. The search for what was behind—behind in time, but also behind the surface—was largely a search for an elusive essence. As so often, it is tricky to extricate cause from effect here, but the Renaissance intellectuals had neither an established scientific means for gaining access to essences, nor an agreement on what "essence" even meant. Were they still looking for some divine first principle, or were they ready to look into something like molecular structure? They found themselves pausing in a dark woodland path in the middle of the journey from a medieval reliance on God's intentions toward a modern notion of biochemical determinants. The common reflex was to look back to nature, but what would that mean? Was the fundamental truth in the forest rather than the distracting trees, in the wood behind the bark, the cellulose structure of that wood, the secret generative formula (like a compressed program file) within the seed that made that wood, the signature that God had coded into that formula, or in the use (whether cross or ark) to which the lumber would be put? What was sought could not be found partly because the voyagers had not chosen a destination and therefore could hardly ask directions.

For this uneasy trip, Francis Bacon was a principal navigator. His fictional voyage to the New Atlantis conflates the discoveries of the New World with the discovery of the scientific method: the truth is out there. We might also call him a principal interrogator, since the vocabulary of Bacon the prosecutor often slips into the language of Bacon the researcher.[67] He was thus never free from the cultural web that language weaves, even when complaining (in words) that Aristotelians were "always more solicitous to . . . affirm something positive in words than about the inner truth of things."[68] In fact, the will to domination which colors the rhetoric of colonizer, prosecutor, seducer, and scientist alike in this period recurs vividly in Thomas Sprat's praise of the Royal Society's determination "to overcome the mysteries of all the Works of Nature; and not onely to prosecute such as are confin'd to one Kingdom, or beat upon one shore."[69]

Bacon insists that "all trial should be made, whether that commerce between the mind of man and the nature of things, which is more precious than anything on earth, or at least anything that is of the earth, might by any means be restored to its perfect and original condition."[70] Notice that the book becomes a trial about the efficacy of trials; that Bacon values the human connection to nature above anything in nature (and avoids valuing it above God only by a tactful afterthought); and that he aims for a lost original of that connection, which he assumes is synonymous with a perfect connection. " 'Things are preserved from destruction by bringing them back to their first principles' is a rule in Physics; the same holds good in Politics (as Machiavelli rightly observed), for there is scarcely anything which preserves states from destruction more than the reformation and reduction of them to their ancient manners."[71] Another facet of the regressive character of Bacon's program emerges in the aphorisms of the *New Organon*: "the entrance into the kingdom of man, founded on the sciences, being not much other than the entrance into the kingdom of heaven, whereunto none may enter except as a little child."[72]

That the natural world is centered and focused on humanity, and that the world consists, first and last, of verbal meanings, are deeply connected assumptions in medieval and earlier Renaissance culture. Zoological texts were based on other texts instead of field observation: they collected old lore or listed Scriptural instances. As the culture surrendered its belief in signatures—for example, in pharmacopoeias, the way curative plants resembled the body part to be cured (walnuts for the brain)—human beings ceased to see themselves so clearly in nature, or to see nature in themselves. The science of botany exemplifies the growth of empiricism as part of an effort to remove the human prejudice and get back to things in themselves, particularly natural things. In the early sixteenth century, plants were generally described and categorized by their effect on the human body, yet "By the end of the century, attention focuses more on observing and describing the visual physical characteristics, particularly the structure."[73] On the path from anthropocentrism to abstract schematics, late-Renaissance botanists practice a kind of observational nominalism: like still-life painters, they focus on an individual plant in a specific place at a specific moment in its life span. The shift of emphasis from human legacies to direct observation is also demonstrated by the shift from increasingly degraded copies of old woodcuts to ones that "take plants themselves rather than pictures as their model and there is a remarkable increase in detail."[74] Here again, Protestantism assumes an alliance—or maybe a marriage of convenience—with empiricism. In opposing superstition, especially its tendency to locate saving powers in material objects, zealous Reformers tended to dismiss the symbolic and even homeopathic potential of plants, and to distrust their engagement with human needs and sentiments: "To put a garland of flowers on a hearse at a funeral was monstrous idolatry, urged an Essex lecturer in 1617. To hang up evergreens at Christmas was paganism, thought William Prynne; and in December 1647 the Lord Mayor of London went round the City pulling down the holly and ivy."[75]

Faced with a choice that had, long ago, troubled Pliny the Elder (whom a recent study has identified as a great early environmentalist),[76] late-Renaissance scientists thus increasingly resist founding natural history on tradition rather than observation. "It was only in Tudor times," Keith Thomas observes, "that there began an unbroken succession of active field naturalists."[77] But, as Marvell suggests at the end of "Damon the Mower," no amount of work in the field allows us to know nature more thoroughly than death does, in turning all flesh literally into grass above the grave. That Pliny the Elder was smothered when he sought a closer scientific look at the eruption of Vesuvius in the year 79 C.E. offers another poignant emblem of the same point: ashes to ashes.

Bacon turned to the ancient sources of knowledge for the sake of turning readers against them, or at least for turning them from mediators into cures for mediation. His *Wisdom of the Ancients* is an overdetermined quest for original truth, a voyage back in the earliest available cultural history for confirmation of scientific views that are themselves focused on origins. He seizes on the story of Cupid as if it were an exposition of atomist first causes: "This fable relates to the cradle and infancy of nature, and pierces deep. This Love I understand to be the appetite or instinct of primal matter, or to speak more plainly, *the natural motion of the atom*, which is indeed the original and unique force that constitutes and fashions all things out of matter. Now this is entirely without parent, that is, without cause."[78]

Purifying away the Christian residue of divine purpose and the Platonic residue of ideal forms may leave, not the sought-after object-in-itself, but instead an amalgamation of accidents (in the Scholastic sense), none of which is identical with that object, or even exclusively proprietary to it. It proved impossible to bracket teleology and simply proceed with science. What did it mean to read only the phenomena, if there was no agreement on whether words were a mere, or instead an ideal, expression of things; on whether we should push past words to get at things, or vice versa? How, in any case, could we trust our childlike selves to read correctly the message in the building blocks, whether of George Herbert's "JESU" puzzle[79] or (proleptically) Watson and Crick's DNA double helix? Could language be made so transparent or so connected to things that we read through it without even exactly reading it?[80] The Great Instauration was not a Tower of Babel: by no series of steps could one arrive at the absolute, the lexicon would always sow confusion, and a leap of faith would always still be necessary.

Bacon's invocation of idolatry in categorizing the obstacles to empirical science, in the *New Organon*, is therefore a bold stratagem. Despite some familiar defensive gestures toward piety, toward God as at once the goal of all science and beyond all science, Bacon is reversing the epistemological flow. Idols are no longer the physical objects that, by demanding attention for and as themselves, stand between the human mind and the divine Word, the ultimate reality. What he condemns as idols are instead the words (and other customary or instinctual human practices, including "tribal" prejudices, which would seem to include religion, especially Catholicism) that stand between the human mind and physical objects, which he deems (as they are in modern Western science) the ultimate reality—a reality so drained of will, divine or otherwise, that its key identifying marker is its inability to act differently under identical stimuli. An essential criterion of modern experimental science—that a result can be replicated—implies a loss of the voluntary and subjective character of the universe under both medieval and earlier Renaissance theology. The Rock is a rock. If it seems to move or morph, check the curvature of the lens or posit volcanic activity; if it emits a torrent of water, look beneath it for a rain-fed spring. "The final cause rather corrupts than advances the sciences," warns the *New Organon*.[81]

What the Reformers insisted would enable a recognition of firm truth—reading the Bible without prejudice—Bacon asserted about the reading of physical reality.[82] Sprat notes "the agreement that is between the present *Design* of the *Royal Society*, and that of our *Church* in its beginning," which is that "each of them passing by the *corrupt Copies*, and referring themselves to the *perfect Originals* for their instruction; the one to the *Scripture*, the other to the large volume of the *Creatures*."[83] But the alliance of Protestantism with empirical science was in important ways illusory, and some of the diseases of each of these new belief-systems proved contagious to the other. Luther believed that "what conscience is compelled to believe on reading Scripture is true";[84] the fears and enthusiasms of the individual interpreter, which for Bacon are the obstacles to truth, are for Luther their only valid criterion; divine prejudice was at the heart of predestination, and human prejudice was the form in which that predestination could become manifest. For Bacon, the whole inquiry into divine intention looks something like what New Criticism dismisses as the intentional fallacy.

Bacon talks about a perfect receptivity to a complete external reality: "the truth of being and the truth of knowing are one, differing no more than the direct beam and the beam reflected."[85] For those who suspected that Baconian taxonomy resided only in the eye and mind of the beholder, however, that hope for truth is haunted by the terror of a universe of indifferentiation in which the mind sits passive, the eye open but unfocused: in other words, an image of death, the great unspeakable back-to-nature movement and the great triumph of materialism. The problem with regression (as with skepticism) is knowing how and when to stop. Will pushing backward lead to the absolute truth of the observed being, or to the erasure of the observing one? The shift towards a deistic Christianity not only turns God into a metaphor rather than a person, but also threatens any conception of afterlife that sustains the individual consciousness essential to human personhood. Notice again the fixed eye, the passivity of the senses, the erasure of the imagination, and the apocalyptic treading under God's foot that signal a subliminal association between scientific method and mortal annihilation when the *Great Instauration* announces that "all depends on keeping the eye steadily fixed upon the facts of nature and so receiving their images simply as they are. For God forbid that we should give out a dream of our own imagination," rather than hoping for God to "graciously grant us to write an apocalypse or true vision of the footsteps of the Creator imprinted on his creatures."[86]

To track God devoutly is thus to ignore Him completely. After all, Bacon is only talking about tracking the footprints, not kissing the foot. Unlike the great scientific mystics of the Renaissance such as Bruno and Campanella, Bacon was not seeking any absolute encounter with the absolute, but (on behalf of humanity) a profitable trade-negotiation with the material universe, with phenomena as his translators and native guides: "For the testimony and information of the senses has reference always to man, not to the universe."[87] Like Galileo, who implies that, because of the way representations intervene in perception, "their 'truth' is merely their *utility* for the betterment of men's lives,"[88] Bacon antici- pated the central arguments of the American Pragmatist movement in philoso- phy (no wonder both Peirce and Popkin sometimes seem mesmerized by the legacy of the Renaissance). Despite some profound differences in the philoso- phies, Baconianism and modern pragmatism shared a functional view of epis- temology; so, I will claim now and argue later, did perspectival painting. All that mattered—all that could be called real—was what worked.

Carving Up the World

Like so many of the period's new and improved claims on nature, single-point perspective finally drove its practitioners back into their own humanity: they were addressing the peculiarities of human perceivers, not supplying anything inherently true about the bodies depicted. Neither could science, despite the often heroic campaigns of the empiricists, conquer epistemological ground high enough to assure perfect observation of the world; the late Renaissance sold only obstructed-view seating. Galileo ruefully discovered that the tele- scope offered no more complete an escape from culture than did the camera obscura. The philological recovery of the classics by Renaissance humanists may have encountered similar limits, while at the same time reminding the culture as a whole that an alternative, internally coherent view of the universe was possible—that they both could, and could not, gaze through the eyes of the human past. The common description of humanism as a return *ad fontes* revealingly defines the effort to recover cultural sources as an effort to unearth the primal sources in nature. Similar complications vexed a prime alternative avenue of research, as sea-voyagers strove to move across space in order to move back in time, toward exploratory contact and colonial consumption of "primitive" cultures in Africa and the Americas.[89] As Stephen Greenblatt re- minded my generation of cultural students, the result was more often a com- plication than a simplification of experience even for the colonizers, who found their own assumptions compromised by their efforts to mimic (for the sake of exploiting) the assumptions of the natives.[90] Renaissance travel and sci- ence showed that human beings adapt to different natural environments in different ways, including cultural as well as physiological divergences[91]—which implied that we do not have a shared and simple first nature, either environ- mental or human, to get back to. Donne depended on Christian origins to ori- ent and redeem him:

> We think that Paradise and Calvary,
> Christ's Cross, and Adam's tree, stood in one place;
> Look Lord, and find both Adams met in me

Otherwise, he could never have answered all his doubts about homecoming: "Is the Pacific Sea my home? Or are / The eastern riches? Is Jerusalem?"[92] Human minds are often profoundly agoraphobic (because the openness of thought that provides our evolutionary advantage has potentially dangerous side-effects), and this global marketplace was opening everywhere, encompassing everything.

One predictable response to this vast new culture-scape was to insist on the identity and materiality of things by shrinking them down or cutting them up (preferably into the neat forms offered by taxonomy). Sir Thomas Browne engages in an uneasy search, through autopsy, for the organic container of the human soul.[93] Less pious agents of seventeenth-century espial used both the anatomy theater and the genre of satire to undertake their own, arguably reductive, returns to the body (which itself, recent scholarship argues, is hardly an irreducible biological-material fact). Back to nature meant back to basics, and mystifications were supposed to melt away under the cold eyes of scientists and the warmer ones of seducers. The icy heat of the torturer's eye similarly promised insight, forcing the body to confess the secrets of the soul, forcing hidden truths to the surface[94]—unless equivocating language (notably, of Jesuits) somehow kept that secret masked, by subordinating ordinary truth to "the truth of Christ."[95] The horrible dramas of the autopsy and torture thus played out, in an intense localized form, the doomed struggle of the entire culture to replace a language-based epistemology with one based in tested material reality.

Yet again, though, Donne was watching dubiously, warning—not only in the winking songs and satires, but also in mock autopsies such as "The Damp" and "The Legacy"—that even after carving the body down to the heart or dragging the discourse down to the genitals, the mysteries of the love that makes us might remain unknown. That is the implication of George Herbert's "Love Unknown," which makes God a mysteriously benign amalgam of the torturer and the anatomist. When the collapse of his old world-order leaves King Lear with little but madness, he reduces generative love to a genital infection and proposes that they "anatomize" his ungrateful daughters to see whether there is "any cause in nature that makes these hard hearts" (3.6.77–78)—neglecting to inquire into the even greater mystery of his other daughter's tender and forgiving heart. This struggle extended beyond literature—the Duke of Lennox's promise to send James VI "his embalmed heart" was not enough to win back the king's trust[96]—but Shakespeare opens out the implications. As Othello learns, even a bosom friend cannot be known entirely and therefore cannot be trusted at all: "You cannot, if my heart were in your hand," Iago tells him (3.3.163; cf. Sonnet 24).

The absence of any fully reliable referent in the material world may be compensated (as at the end of Petrarch's *Rime Sparsi*) by an absolute referent beyond. In a Christian culture, one can at least defer to God the comprehension of things in themselves, in their perfect form, and (as Augustine, Petrarch's spiritual master, proposes) outside of the illusion of time and place. Faith in heaven can serve as a sublimation of damaged belief on earth. The knowledge is not missing, it is just in a blind trust. But if Stuart culture was besieged by the way (as Bacon warns) multiplication of religions leads to atheism, and thence to early intimations of mortality as annihilation, many would find this Christian solution no longer satisfactory. What if (as modern entropy theory suggests) the ultimate referent is not an eternal one but an approaching zero, what if the ultimate condition of our knowledge is its own erasure, and we will finally regain our unity with the natural world only by losing our ability to contemplate it or anything else? Perhaps the problem of the abyss at the center and the end of meaning described by post-Saussurian linguistics could become visible only once an abyss became visible at the center and end of the universe. The Scholastics certainly achieved glimpses of the problems of meaning, but these problems were safely delimited by the Word of God; however flawed our readings of that Word, it had been spoken, and the evidence was in and all around us. As that Word became less manifestly present, the questions—though already perceptible in the explorations of John Duns Scotus and Nicholas Cusanus—took on new urgency and darker tones. If self-consciousness is the only absolute (as Descartes suggests before ducking back behind an invisibly rewoven Christian tapestry), and as the divine consciousness becomes more remote or uncertain, what is left to verify fundamental truths about this world, or even that such truths exist?

In some form, this poverty of knowledge seems always to be with us. Augustine recalls wondering

in what way I was to find the truth, my sighs through love of which are known to no one better than to yourself. Often it seemed to me that it could not be found, and huge waves of my thoughts would roll toward deciding in favor of the Academics. Often again . . . I thought that the truth lay not hid, save that in it the way of search lay hid, and that this same way must be taken from some divine authority. It remained to enquire what was that authority, where in so great dissensions each promised that he would deliver it. Thus there met me a wood, out of which there was no way, which I was very loath to be involved in: and amid these things, without any rest, my mind was agitated through desire of finding the truth.[97]

Those who felt lost in these figurative woods (as Dante would be also) some-times found themselves in love with the actual woods; but well into the Renais-sance, turning to nature for redemption was uncommon, though the motif of testing oneself (like St. Jerome) alone in the wilderness might be mistaken for it. Another solution traditionally—perhaps instinctively—arises from the more conventional "sighs of love": the conjunction of the erotic and procreative im-pulses. As usual, Petrarch showed the way: not only in the flirtation with a reli-gion of nature on Mount Ventoux, but also in an obsessive version of what is now called romantic love, which seeks the essence of another—the heart, the center, and the troth—without quite acknowledging this desire as a displace-ment of broader yearnings. Certainly in modern Western European culture, with its presumptive secularism, the quest for erotic pair-bonding seems an al-most ubiquitous and reflexive way of defining both short- and long-term goals.

But (as in theatrical cross-dressing) where is the ultimate referent of that desire? As Petrarch already recognized, to see from afar was to crave seeing more nearly, to be near was to crave touching, touching provoked kissing, and so on. Nor does that last circumlocution elide an easy answer: does the epistemologi-cal solution—the prospect for real contact with otherness, and therefore per-haps between the mind and body—reside in genital glands now, as in pineal glands for Descartes? What is "love-making" made of? Does physical penetra-tion constitute "intimacy," as another popular euphemism presumes? A familiar question at the boundary between science and philosophy—at what level of magnification can an observer know the inner nature, the fundamental truth, of an object?—also troubles the pornographer, who needs to provide ever larger organs, ever more inward views and closer close-ups, as if somehow "more" can solve the problem of "other." Montaigne noticed the problem, basing part of his argument about the unreliability and incompatibility of senses on "Those persons who, to enhance their voluptuousness, in ancient times used mirrors made to en-large and magnify the object they reflect, so that the members which they were to put to work should please them the more by this ocular growth."[98] Grotesque as such voluptuousness may seem, it is also a logical extension of common notions of erotic desire.

How big does sexuality have to be to eclipse the darkness of mortality? Sexual intercourse may be wonderful, but is it ultimate? The premise (or some-times pretense) is that intercourse is the expression of something else, whether in a traditional Christian understanding or in the modern mystical sacraliza-tion of the love bond. Perhaps the goal is orgasmic pleasure, but that is finally an inward experience—and the evolutionary bait for something else. The ulti-mate goal of love-desire may thus be procreation—certainly Catholic moral the-ology has long insisted on that teleology, which promises to control the slippage

I have been describing—but (as Joyce wryly asks through Stephen Dedalus's musings about the Venus de Milo) to what end? To bequeath the question—of meaning, or mortality—down the generations seems to replicate the problem of infinite deferral, rather than to solve it. Getting there may be half the fun (as advertisements for trans-Atlantic sea voyages used to claim), but there may be no there there (as Gertrude Stein famously remarked about her home town). The final Books of *Paradise Lost* assure Adam and Eve that the generations will not be an endless road built by a chain-gang in order to move supplies so that the road can continue being built, but instead a bridge between their newly mortal selves and the Second Coming and its accompanying resurrections. God provides an end. If we have only means, however—if we are trapped in mediations indefinitely—someone had to begin breaking the news to us. As usual, that kind of unwelcome cultural work was left to creative artists, who were, yet again, arguably centuries ahead of the scientists. Evolutionary biology now suggests that procreative desire does not exactly belong to the self—is not, in fact, even exactly a desire, but instead a corollary function of genes, which act as if they had a will to reproduce themselves, and convince us that our chief goal is to serve their chief goal. So what looks to most modern readers like a rather quaint echo of morality-play *psychomachia*—that is, the description of lust as an entity external to the self that leads it astray—turns out to be the new scientific perspective as well.

Carving up love thus into its constituent motives may seem cruelly reductive, but late-Renaissance men were at once appetized and disgusted by the banquet thereby produced. As the tradition of the *blason* demonstrates, as countless moralistic and misogynistic tracts warned, as the Neoplatonists asserted more optimistically, the object of desire is never exactly the woman herself anyway. It is another zeroing in that ends up with a zero at its center: a no-thing, or at least a quality elusive enough to leave Donne wondering (in "Love's Alchemy") where love's "centric happiness doth lie," and wondering (wistfully in "Air and Angels," more harshly in "Love's Progress" and "The Comparison") whether love itself is inevitably lost when a love-object is found. Modern psychoanalysis warns of the same problem, though it places the problem more squarely in the lap of the desiring mind, which makes a montage of all its deprivations and then projects the negative onto a plausible candidate. Renaissance moralism pointed instead to the target of desire, who was herself an assemblage of parts, put together (Jonson quips) "like a great German clock."[99] Montaigne (citing Ovid) points out that it does not seem to matter to desire "if we are aware that these tresses are borrowed from a page or lackey, that this rosy complexion is a product of Spain, and that this whiteness and smoothness comes from the ocean sea . . . in this there is nothing of the lady's own: 'Jewels and gold hide flaws; we are tricked by art; / The girl is of herself the smallest part. / Oft in all this you ask where your love lies: / By this Gorgon shield rich love deceives the eyes.' " Perhaps this refers to the version of the myth in which Perseus can look at Medusa only in his reflecting shield, an indispensable mediation; but it also suggests the version in which Medusa is forced to see her own snaky image and is thus turned to stone. The fetishist loves only indirectly, perhaps only something that is really already his own. The phallic aggression arguably inherent in masculine desire is thrown back onto itself—and Montaigne immediately goes on to invoke the way Narcissus "Unwitting, loves himself."[100]

If fetishism is treason to any rational model of desire, many seventeenth-century Englishmen made the most of it—made, in fact, a narcissistic crisis that was itself a miniature of the conceptual struggles going on around it, a symptom of the search for a stable and tangible item in which to invest meaning and anchor desire. Unable (particularly in the absence of any articulate version of either Darwinian evolutionary theory or Freudian drive theory) to locate and isolate an essence of the sexual object, men seem often to have settled for the fascination with women's clothing characteristic of Cavalier erotic poetry.[101] As Restoration comedy makes clear, English culture was heading into a period in which desire became more openly focused on external signs such as clothing and money. Jonson offers a devastating analysis of this fascination in the class-resentful sexual practices of a tailor in *The New Inn* and links it convincingly back to the pathological worship of money for its own sake in Volpone, whose craving for otherwise unneeded wealth correlates with the endlessly multiplying mirrors and sensual scenarios he offers to Celia and with an overt idolatry of gold, which he puts in the place of God in the sky, and in place of the body in the Eucharistic ritual.[102] Markers take the places of essences, like a swarm of ants making a nutritive corpse disappear, and the effort to find a material basis for desire drives desire back into the artificial. The more Volpone tries to offer Celia the physical, the clearer it becomes that what he really has to offer is the verbal, acquired by reading and reproduced by rhetoric; it is like his money, which pretends to be the means to physical ends, but finally seems to be little more than a self-justifying end in itself, the flesh made word, another conveniently manipulable second-hand object in place of the thing itself. And such money is of course like language as now commonly understood by scholars: an internally justifying system, arguably correlating to some material universe of necessities, but finally (and dangerously) referrable only to itself. Gresham's law spills over from economics into sexuality: adulterated desire, a game of markers, drives out anything more pure and precious. In Jonson's *Epicoene* the central joke—one that sits in tension with the play's pervasive misogyny—is whether there is any central gender-determinative physical thing at the center of sexuality; the double joke in Jonson's chief classical source was that it didn't finally matter anyway, since desirability depended on the quirks of the one desiring, a kind of sexual Pyrrhonism enabled by ephebophilia.[103]

The emphasis on the *blason* and its gradual conversion into the fetish in this period similarly reflect a determination to convert a human being into a love object and thence into a depersonalized commodity, something that can be known, conquered because divided. The Augustan sneer at the way women composed their decorative public selves was just the flip side of the Petrarchan swoon. Like other commodities, women could be bought—and therefore proved all the more tormentingly impossible to know truly and completely. If matter and the female were conventionally associated in this period, the emphasis in English Renaissance tragedies on reaching and extracting women's buried truths seems all the more epistemologically significant. As Elizabeth Hanson suggests, "the problem of evidence appears for a time as a problem of how to read a woman."[104] In *Bussy D'Ambois*, Montsurry racks his adulterous wife Tamyra; in Webster, the Duchess of Malfi and Vittoria Corombona undergo special tortures for their secrets; Shakespeare shows women interrogated to death in various ways (and Lear would like to participate). Women have their secrets, even when (like Shakespeare's slandered Hero, Desdemona, Hermione, Imogen, even Mistress Ford) they don't. Actually Iago, Iachimo, Falstaff, along with the not-so-gallants of Jonson's *Epicoene*, are the ones with the dirtiest secret, which is the emptiness of their claims to knowledge of the women's inner secrets. The real scandal is not the truth, but the pretense of access to it.

None of this is meant to stake an "inventionist" claim: jealousy, fetishism, sexual slander, even phallocentrism are traceable across a very long history. All I am saying is that the problems of gender and eroticism seem to acquire a noticeably different focus in the context of the Renaissance crisis of origins— which must itself be put in a long history of crises of origins. There is, in any case, no reason to suppose that sexual notions arise independent of circumambient cultural notions; and the fear that there might be nothing left beyond the fetish was a prevalent one, connecting attacks on idolatry not only with attacks on cosmetics and elaborate dress, but also with the fear that language was coming unstuck from reality, and with the mistrust of the symbolic nature of value in currency. If "A fetish is an objective representation of something that is, in reality, subjective,"[105] then a culture living in constant fear of recognizing its own bad faith (in whichever sense), of finding out that all of its supposedly objective perceptions were actually subjective, would be extremely sensitive to the implication that its entire experience was fetishized.

The dominant theological premise had long been that the seeming individuality of physical entities is, in an important sense, illusory, since all are extensions of divine being; in a kind of Christian anticipation of the Big Bang theory, time would eventually reveal space as a transient phenomenon. Nominalism emerged to assert, on the contrary, that nothing could be said to exist *except* individuals. Then empirical science, dissolving the body into pieces, even inert matter into its component materials, attempted to break through the barriers that forestalled full knowledge, and hence full possession, of other minds and physical objects. Yet science had to establish some limit—some method of "chunking" reality—before reaching the level of Lucretian atomism, where all identity turns out to be an illusion because nothing individual belongs permanently and exclusively to any creature, and life turns out to be a mechanism because even mental experience is mechanical. Arguing that the self resided in the continuous consciousness rather than any physical part, John Locke would strive mightily to exempt humanity from Hobbes's mechanistic model, from the shift from meaning to matter as the essential truth of things. In the realm of identity and ontology, that materialist conclusion is the equivalent of the overeager (physical) colonizer finding himself (culturally) colonized: as comic depictions of misers have long implied, devote yourself to possessing objects, and you become one. The fetish-lover thus makes himself a comic object.

Modern nature-lovers had to find another approach, and I believe they find it in the model of collective identity and its providential character that was partially eclipsed by atomism, materialism, and mathematical physics, circling in each others' gravity. The pre-Enlightenment model re-emerges as the structure on which modern environmentalist consciousness would be built. Because they are largely homologous, our systematic ecological understanding could easily evolve from the systematic eschatological understanding of late-Renaissance physico-theology, which tried to explain all aspects of the natural world, especially the seemingly destructive and hence counter-providential ones, by giving them a role in a functionally and ethically balanced universe—in other words, by seeing what use they had in making the universe make sense. Providence was a kind of moral ecology, a network of connections and compensations. All modern science really had to do was change some moral explanations (flies exist to punish uncleanliness and enforce humility) to evolutionary ones (flies exist because decaying matter offers energy that competing creatures cannot reach or cannot digest). The tendency of deism toward nature-worship has developed into a sanctification of the ecosystem.

Chapter Summaries

Following these two chapters of introduction—this one exploring the relationship of "green" consciousness to the philosophical problems of other minds and objective reality, the next focused on the role of language and literature (especially Spenser and Shakespeare) in grasping God, nature, and truth—the book will turn to specific works of literary and visual art. "As You Liken It: Simile in the Forest" (Chapter 3) interprets the longing for reunion with the world of nature as a sentimental manifestation of a philosophical problem: the suspicion that our cognitive mechanisms allow us to know things only as we liken them.[106] *As You Like It* is packed with similes that straddle the boundary between human and other forms of life, reflecting the impulse of the human family to impose its familiarities. What kind of nature-lover is Jaques when he "moralizes" the wounded deer "into a thousand similes" (2.1.44–45)? Shakespeare adapts a Renaissance literary tradition—men who wander into the wilderness so obsessed with a seemingly unachievable beloved that they populate nature with thoughts of her—to indicate that the otherness of a woman in a man's hetero-eroticism reflects an unconquerable otherness already present in nature. An era that turned to nature for affirmation and wisdom encounters (in Touchstone) a dubious, even farcical demur: "You have said; but whether wisely or no, let the forest judge" (3.2.121–22).

"Shades of Green: Marvell's Garden and the Mowers" (Chapter 4) traces these themes in five lyrics, combining close reading and philosophical speculation to articulate their exploration of the paradoxes underlying—and undermining—the late-Renaissance eagerness to recover the simplicities of agrarian nature. Marvell's puns expose the tension between the professed innocence of his rustic speakers and the sophistication they cannot finally disavow. Marvell consistently depicts the Fall as an onset of self-consciousness, for which the Other—a field or a woman, almost indistinguishably—becomes the scapegoat. Death, the obvious consequence of that Fall, is also its radical cure: the last hope for participation in nature without the obstructions of language and consciousness.

The next three chapters—one on Metaphysical and Cavalier modes in seventeenth-century English poetry and politics, and two on Dutch painting—trace the implications of these ontological and epistemological paradoxes for the religious culture-wars of the period. Collectively they seek to explain why, although Protestant poetics predictably value words and personal subjectivity over physical objects and the world of nature, Protestant painting in the same period appears to do the opposite, while Catholic painters emphasize the paradoxes of reproducing natural reality.

"Metaphysical and Cavalier Styles of Consciousness" (Chapter 5) offers a first hypothesis toward a Unified Field Theory of seventeenth-century England by tracing the origins of the Civil War in the contrast between Metaphysical poetry, which expresses a radical Protestant faith in the revolutionary power of the intentions of self and word, and Cavalier poetry, the decorative, traditional, ritualized tendencies of which reflect royalist conservatism and High Church theology. The individual spontaneity and anti-materialist innovations of Puritanism which the established church especially mistrusted resemble Metaphysical conceits; conversely, the traditional formalism of both royalist poetry and royalist religion is precisely what the Metaphysicals and Puritans emphatically rejected. The underlying distinction—whether the manifest world is an arbitrary mental and verbal construction or a stable material hierarchy—is still generating major conflicts between radical and reactionary factions four hundred years later.

"The Retreat of God, the Passions of Nature, and the Objects of Dutch Painting" (Chapter 6) traces the consequences of the Protestant Reformation in the visual arts, particularly the way that the iconoclastic reluctance to make sacred objects inadvertently helped to make ordinary objects sacred. From Ruisdael's efforts to envision the human struggle in a universe of physics and biology, to Saenredam's depictions of cathedrals drained of conventional piety, northern European painting shows the way iconoclasm led toward something like atheism; and, in the substitution of creaturely death within the visual traditions of Christian martyrdom, it may have (no more intentionally) opened the door to modern concerns about the innocent suffering of animals. Ruisdael's oeuvre comprises a recantation of the belief that nature is merely a setting for the great spiritual adventure of humanity; and as he retracts the sentimental notion that nature sympathizes with human endeavors, his colleagues invent the means by which modern Western culture would begin instead to sympathize with nature as our collective victim.

"Nature in Two Dimensions: Perspective and Presence in Ryckaert, Vermeer, and Others" (Chapter 7) takes off from the history of single-point perspective and a little-known 1638 painting of an artist at work to demonstrate the engagement of the visual arts with the nexus of environmentalist nostalgia and epistemological skepticism I have been describing, and goes on to look briefly at the emerging genre of portraits set out in nature, as well as the ironies of this new form of reassurance and propaganda. Finally, it revisits the question at the core of these middle chapters, namely, what different beliefs about nature and about the nature of reality have to do with factional theology.

As the book's readings began by pairing Shakespeare with Marvell to show how troubling epistemological questions were raised through pastoral literature, its readings end by pairing Shakespeare with Traherne to show what consolations, conciliations, and cures were proposed for these cultural troubles. "Metal and Flesh in *The Merchant of Venice*: Shining Substitutes and Approximate Values" (Chapter 8) reads the play as replying to all these anxieties by suggesting that, however much mediation may feel like preterition, it remains (in the person of Christ the Mediator) our only hope for salvation; and that performance and approximation are necessary and sufficient replacements for identity. Partial resemblances, which *As You Like It* warns are untruths, here emerge as the only truths by which humanity can navigate the fallen world. Shakespeare uses his dramatic poetry and its fragmentary allegories to disguise the capitalist revolution (which looks so threatening in Venice, the archetypal marketplace of the Renaissance) as a reversion to antique values of truth and an analogy to Christian soteriology. Resemblances between the tolerant epistemologies of *Merchant* and of Hooker's *Laws of Ecclesiastical Polity* suggest that a particular kind of repair work was demanded by the English culture of the mid-1590s.

"Thomas Traherne: The World as Present" (Chapter 9) interprets this neglected writer's ostentatious regressiveness—which went not only back to nature, but to nature as viewed with the innocent eye of childhood as a kind of primitive religion—as an effort to spiritualize the Baconian process of observation. Traherne offers a model whereby the subjectivity of perception is compatible—in fact, is the only thing compatible—with perceiving the true essence of the objects, which can be truly seen only when God shimmers within them; and God is visible in his shimmering objects. Human perception is not a lost cause, but humanity's grateful present to God, who could not otherwise appreciate his own Creation. The defeat of Traherne's peculiar brand of mysticism by Enlightenment rationalism squandered a last chance to prevent the progress from a universe of meaning to a universe of matter from taking on the tone of a deadmarch, headed down a one-way street.

Chapter 2
Theology, Semiotics, and Literature

Transubstantiation

Though it was spoken in a different vocabulary from that of deism or atomism, let alone environmentalism or quantum physics, the question of whether matter could itself be God, or God could be matter, was not at all foreign to Renaissance culture. The clearest analogue to the problem I have been sketching—indeed, the form in which it is most openly and extensively discussed—is the bitter Renaissance controversy over transubstantiation. The difference between identifying things with an absolute material essence, or else believing them to achieve their identity only within the experiential scope of each individual, correlates with the difference between doctrines of Real Presence (as articulated by the Fourth Lateran Council in 1215) and doctrines (notably Protestant ones) that place the transformative miracle within the subjectivity of the recipient, however unworthy—a kind of host-reception theory articulated in various ways by leading Reformation theologians.

There are, of course, significant subdivisions within these positions; and describing them in semiotic terms is tempting but difficult, because the Eucharist presents a profoundly complex case. The chief divisive question is familiar, one scholars now tend to associate with post-structuralism but which was already active in Renaissance debates about natural language: how much connection is there between the signifier and the signified? The usual case now involves the function of words as signs for physical objects. But the case of the Eucharist works the other way around: the signs are the fully tangible material things—wine and bread—while the thing signified is less a physical object than a spiritual entity and spiritual force.

Fundamental to the agonized differences between Catholicism and Protestantism was the difference between the Old Religion's emphasis on sensual experience of material reality—including the eating and drinking of Christ's flesh and blood in Communion—and the Reformation emphasis on Holy Scripture as the Word that continually reveals God to humanity, but also stands necessarily between God and humanity. To northern radicals such as Karlstadt and

Zwingli, the answer to Catholicism's purportedly superstitious investment in the objects was to insist that it was valuing the wrong things, holding the instrument of salvation by the wrong end—that the outward sign was a completely separate and (therefore) inefficacious aspect of the Eucharist; the bread and wine were merely themselves, though they commemorated and stood in for a true value concealed spiritually in the believer's transaction with them. "This is my body" meant, to Oecolampadius, "this is the sign of my body"; Tyndale similarly thought "is" meant "signifieth."[1] Luther's position had been that of consubstantiation: Christ could "maintain His body within the substance of the bread as truly as within its accidents."[2] Luther did not object to the doctrine of Real Presence, but he did reject the Aristotelian basis for that doctrine, which located Christ in the substance of the Eucharist while leaving its accidents unchanged. This would have seemed to Protestants a piece of magic "effected by the ritualistic actions of the priest . . . a 'finished work,' or *opus operatum*. The consequence of this doctrine was that the priestly labor of the mass was rendered efficacious, and thus valuable, in itself. It became a *thing*, a commodity that could be bought and sold."[3] In other words, it took on the taint of factorial mediations—alienated signs paid for alienating work—associated with the money earned by hired labor. As David Hawkes observes, "What Luther found idolatrous was not the adoration of the sign but the belief that the sign was made sacred by the fetishized actions of the priest."[4]

Calvin would push instead to have the outward sign recognized as itself complete and efficacious, even if it appeared to us only as sign, only as wine and bread.[5] God being God, the promise is a reality. The presence may be purely nominal—or, better, spiritual—and nonetheless fully real. This piece of Calvinist theology—which relies on something like metonymy—seems to me to correlate to modern theories of metaphor (such as Paul Ricoeur's) in which the figure and the figured can be at once the same and not the same. Calvin himself argues that Christ's offer of his body is "a metonymy, a figure of speech. . . . For though the symbol differs in essence from the thing signified (in that the latter is spiritual and heavenly, while the former is still physical and visible), still, because it not only symbolizes the thing that it has been consecrated to represent as a bare and empty token, but also truly exhibits it, why may its name not rightly belong to the thing?"[6] He grants the sign itself (as all we are given here on earth) an immediacy and efficacy that other theologians believed awaited evocation *through* the sign, much as Pyrrhonism, pragmatism, and capitalism alike produced a need to believe by universal assent in the markers, whether or not there was any identifiable physicality or bullion to back them up. In this new religion of the cultural and economic marketplace, the word must either stand between us and the substantial thing, or else be itself deemed substantial.

Surely, though—unless we take the Gospel of John at its initial Word—something will be felt to have been lost in surrendering any hope of access to what lies behind the signifiers; that feeling of loss is a central topic of this book.

Each of these several ways of understanding transubstantiation implies a particular phenomenology. Is the reality fully present out there in the living material substances, does it acquire its full reality only in us, or are we always limited to signals from that reality that remind us of a lost presence that we can hope to regain only by miracle? Can we (like angels) hold the essence of a thing, vital or otherwise, without fully participating in its material substance? Whether the Communion can be good enough if Christ is not physically present in the Host is largely the same question as whether our communion with natural reality can be good enough if we cannot ever incorporate, encompass, comprehend the things in themselves, rather than just virtual representations of them in our sensory and cognitive arrays.

Idolatry

Idolatry—valuing the object rather than a transcendent value speaking through the object—was generally understood as both a moral and perceptual failure. The etymology from *eidola*—especially given how that term was used by Epicurus and Lucretius—confirms a connection between idols and the emanation or surface-impression of physical reality that reaches the eye. Protestants were, in this sense, amplifying rather than rejecting the long-standing Christian dedication to venerating things for some covert, essential, and transcendent entity they *represent*, rather than for what they are in themselves (though Augustine complicates the distinction, he still stresses the priority of the divine element). Thomas More insisted that a worshipper was not an idolater so as long as he was "not fixing his final intent in the image, but referring it further to the honor of the person that the image representeth."[7] From this perspective, the Reformation—often considered the engine of modernity—can be construed as traditional Christianity's desperate last stand against an emerging consensus that the fundamental reality is the material reality.

In the case of idolatry, it for once does not seem like hyperbole to talk about a cultural crisis. The record of fierce and widespread attacks on precious objects speaks for itself, and I think it says something about the conjunction of two recognitions this book has been describing: the belief of the more intense Protestants that false images formed in the mind were no less sinful and dangerous idols than those created outwardly by a painter or sculptor,[8] and the growing suspicion in the elite culture that our entire experience of the physical world consisted of false images, epiphenomena of our own creation that stood in for God's Creation. If (as William Perkins asserted) "A thing fained in the mind by imagination is an idol,"[9] and if all perception is really a form of imagination, then Protestants had to suppose they were damned from the word go, cut off from God and Creation alike in ways absolutely beyond their control. Images were an evil delusion, and images were all they had. Trying to make the best of this as an argument against the iconoclasts, Luther only raises the stakes, and his affirmation finally retreats uneasily to the level of a rhetorical question that begs the actual question: even in reading Scripture, "it is impossible for me not to make images of this within my heart, for whether I want to or not, when I hear the word Christ, there delineates itself the picture of a man who hangs on the cross. . . . If it is not a sin, but a good thing, that I have Christ's image in my heart, why then should it be sinful to have it before my eyes?"[10] The argument of Hobbes's *Leviathan* that mental images are merely decaying sense impressions would have aggravated the iconoclasts' epistemological pessimism: what the mind sees is even further from the absolute truth than what the eye sees.

Accusations of idolatry seem surprisingly ubiquitous in this period, applying to areas of thought and conduct far beyond the making and worshipping of divine images forbidden by the Old Testament. Protestants discerned idolatry in anything implying veneration of the created world (especially human creations within it) in place of the Creator. It is not hard to see the moral sense in condemning capitalistic practices for valuing money above things; or condemning lust for making erotic objects ends in themselves rather than means (as in Neoplatonism) toward something higher, more abstract, and predominantly spiritual; or condemning theater for the exploitative reproduction of reality—or, especially, theology—at yet another remove. In other cases, however, accusations of idolatry make sense only as expressions of a fear—almost Gnostic— that involving oneself in the physical universe, even believing in that universe, implies a neglect of God's ultimate and mysterious nature.

The inherent substance of a material thing is no more legible to human eyes than the true destiny of a soul in Calvinist theology; the waves and particles of the world—isn't this still dogma?—move in mysterious ways.[11] According to Maimonides, the great medieval Jewish philosopher, "Matter is a strong veil preventing the apprehension of that which is separate from matter as it truly is . . . whenever our intellect aspires to apprehend the Deity or one of the intellects, there subsists this great veil interposed between the two."[12] So while Protestantism may be historically associated with the birth of capitalism, it also partakes of a largely medieval set of attitudes toward the relation between words and things. Even in John Bunyan's writings, where the world has a history, that history is allegorical and eschatological at its core, not physical or chronological; time and space (as Augustine had insisted) are less real than divine consciousness. Nature is more severely fallen in most Reformation theologies than in most Catholic ones; and if the chief task of the human soul was no longer *contemptus mundi*, it still entailed contempt for the senses and cognitive faculties by which we reach conclusions within and about that nature. While Protestants clearly resented mediation (by priests, translators, and accretive institutions generally),[13] they also evidently hated the predominance of things—relics, Communion materials that claimed full presence of Christ's body and blood, decorations on cathedrals and on priests—which (while claiming to lure souls toward divine beauty and greatness) often led instead to an aesthetic focus in place of a pious one and consolidated the power of human authorities. These, the Reformers argued, had become spectacles to see rather than see through: sights rather than windows to something more righteous.

Nature may have retained some reserve of sanctity: the Scriptural warning against using tools to make the altar suggests a connection between anxieties about idolatry and anxieties about violating nature. George Herbert's admonition that "The Altar" should be shaped by "no workmans tool" shades into Anne Finch, Countess of Winchilsea's wish that "The Tree" would "stand / Untouch'd by the rash Workman's hand."[14] This would eventually produce deism and nature-worship—an ideal in which one can't see the adiaphorous for the trees—as a common-ground compromise between a Protestant mistrust of mediations and a Catholic attraction to bodies. But the quest often expressed by the revival of the pagan pastoral genre—the more so as it was supposed to involve direct unself-conscious contact with the material world—was for a place to "rest in Nature, not the God of Nature" (as George Herbert's God complains in "The Pulley"). In the absence of Christian allegory, nostalgic writing about pastoral *otium* suggested not only a regression toward classical paganism, but also a settling into Creation without regard for moral and even intellectual obligations toward a Creator. In recalling obligations to the Maker as well as the things made (a conventional admonition), and thereby climbing to heaven by a first sunbeam, Herbert's "Mattens" articulates a form of worship that resembles nature worship (on its way toward Natural Theology), yet also reminds the flock of the all-importance of *looking through*; Herbert is a pastor against pastoral. The Word was the window, made of unstained glass.

Obviously, this reversion to a pure intuition of Scripture did not dissolve all the irritants into a crystalline simplicity, as recusant polemicists were quick to point out: a sinner in possession of the Word still had to decide what that Word meant, and so would be driven back to the question of whether to believe accumulated tradition or individual revelation. This inspired some advocates of Catholicism to claim an otherwise unsuitable alliance with the ancient skeptics, who (in the Pyrrhonist mode) claimed that our incurable uncertainties left humanity no wise choice except to obey the traditional beliefs and behaviors the human community had developed, rather than innovating on the basis of personal conviction.

All the Reformers could insist in return was that at least they were not making the mistake of reifying the wrong words—those of the Vulgate, priest, and pope—as infallible absolutes. But the claims that inner certainty proved anything about universal reality were inevitably circular to some degree, and the variety of conflicting certainties (most visible, if not necessarily most pervasive, among the radical sects) took the wind out of Protestant sails by shredding the very fabric of mutual affirmation. Antinomian doctrines of personal conviction hardly escaped, but instead multiplied, the problems of a doctrine of papal infallibility; this may have driven the Church of England to reject both. In a sense, therefore, the secular scientific epistemology of the modern Western world constitutes a Counter-Reformation, reverting to an atomistic doctrine of works (or at least, things) as the ultimate referent, in place of any less stable doctrine of faith (and therefore, words).

Words and Things

Perhaps the broadest implication of my study is that the arts of the late Renaissance reveal a culture negotiating—necessarily by indirections—an absolutely fundamental change in its consensual interpretation of reality; and thus producing profoundly interesting works. As Western Europe moves toward Enlightenment science and philosophy, an assumption about the nature of reality is turned something like inside out. Instead of worrying about things getting in the way of the Word, truth-worshippers worry about words getting in the way of Things.[15]

For zealous Protestants such as Bucer and Karlstadt, Scripturalism combines synergistically with "the belief that all created things, all corporalities, stand between ourselves and God."[16] The threat (which Plato conceived one way, the Reformation another) had been that particular physical entities would occlude something pure which could be grasped only by the spirit; Bacon articulates an opposite danger, in which collective prejudices and passions obstruct pure perception of particular objects. Consider Augustine's pious view of perfect knowledge:

The human mind of man, therefore, knows all these things which it has acquired through itself, through the senses of its body, and through the testimonies of others, and keeps them in the treasure-house of its memory; and from them a true word is begotten when we say what we know, but the word that is anterior to every sound and to every thought of sound. For then the word is most like the thing that is known, and from which its image is also begotten . . . the word that belongs to no language, the true word about a true thing, having nothing from itself, but everything from that knowledge from which it is born.[17]

Then contrast Augustine's view with Thomas Sprat's description of the Royal Society's proposal to return the language of seventeenth-century science "back to the primitive purity, and shortness, when men deliver'd so many *things*, almost in an equal number of *words*. They have exacted from all their members, a close, naked, natural way of speaking; positive expressions; clear senses; a native easiness: bringing all things as near the Mathematical plainness as they can: and preferring the language of Artizans, Countrymen, and Merchants, before that of Wits, or Scholars."[18] These two views appear remarkably similar, both associating regression with purification, yet they are irresolvably opposed: for Augustinian Christianity the truth resides in a word (the Word before the word, an idea of a word of an idea, genetically kin to whatever it describes) that remains prior to anything expressed in the world, whereas for empirical science the truth resides in things (which for Augustine are a local stop between the sign and the ultimate meaning), for which words can provide only demarcation, and will more often impose distortion. Galileo, in so many ways a herald of the modern, advocates the change quite explicitly:

I think that in discussions of physical problems we ought to begin not from the authority of scriptural passages, but from sense-experiences and necessary demonstrations; for the holy Bible and the phenomena of nature proceed alike from the divine Word, the former as the dictate of the Holy Ghost and the latter as the observant executrix of God's commands. . . . nothing physical which sense-experience sets before our eyes, or which necessary demonstrations prove to us, ought to be called in question (much less condemned) upon the testimony of biblical passages which may have some different meaning beneath their words.[19]

Despite gestures of subservience to Scripture, Galileo (like many more recent intellectuals) blames language for indeterminacy, while granting material objects a necessary and discernible truth.

In the *Meditations*, Descartes struggles to establish the existence of such objects; and he was hardly alone. Language would make a natural scapegoat or archvillain for a culture increasingly anxious that our perception of objects might never be other than what Puttenham called *hypotyposis*, a trope which offers "things, in such sort as it should appear they were truly present before our eyes though they were not present."[20] Bacon declares it "the first distemper of learning, when men study words and not matter."[21] A. D. Nuttall has observed that "In seventeenth-century England the harder heads were all in favour of putting notions on one side and attending formally to *things* in themselves"; that, to do so, "we must, so to speak, allow ourselves to be imprinted once more, as we were in our first infancy, by reality"; and to do that, we must resist "metaphor which most relentlessly, most recklessly presupposes the relational character of reality."[22] But there were flaming swords blocking our return to that cognitive-linguistic Eden; as Locke might say, a "veil of perception" between us and reality. Emanuele Tesauro's *Il cannocchiale aristotelico* (1654) "emphasizes that what is called 'truth' is therefore in its essence a 'lie': for what is 'known' of any object is but the consequence of these activities of mind."[23] Ralph Cudworth's *True Intellectual System of the Universe* (1678) "questioned the whole myth of the mind's passivity in cognition," as would Vico's *New Science*; and before long, Swift's *Gulliver's Travels* would satirize the regressive aspect of scientific "progress" in the portrait of Laputa, where wise men can speak only with and therefore only about the physical objects they lug around—an " 'atomist-objectivist' orthodoxy" that literally makes a mockery of nominalist strictures. [24]

The suspicion that subject-position reigns absolutely over supposedly objective perception—so prominent a concern in sociology and "constructivist" cultural studies at the start of the twenty-first century—may thus have been another way in which the Renaissance could be called "early modern." In a world habitually struggling—in Christian modes from *contemptus mundi* to Neoplatonism and Protestantism—to look past the material object to its meaning for the human soul, Shakespeare and his fellow artists (no less than Bacon and his fellow scientists) begin to ask whether it isn't at least as hard to look truly at any object without that distorting imposition of human meaning.

The battle between words and things for ontological, epistemological, and teleological superiority was thus partly a surrogate for the emerging war between the needs of Reformed Christianity and the needs of reformed science, which usually seemed good neighbors. The idea that things were ultimately more real than words—the dominant idea in schools, derived from a standard Aristotelian position—threatened to carry a corollary valuation of temporal history as ultimately more real than religious intuitions (debates about the historical Jesus still reflect this tension). What Christian anti-Semitism liked to characterize as "the Jewish choice" of material over spiritual reality thus seemed poised to dominate Western ontology—another painful historical change, like capitalism, for which the Jews could be made the scapegoat. The great figural tradition traced so compellingly by Erich Auerbach's *Mimesis* was in retreat, even if it was still assumed that the material histories of the Old Testament were subordinate to their figural transformation by the Gospels. The lesson was supposed to be the one Christ taught Mary Magdalene, among others: that the persistence of the body mattered far less than the promise of the Word. As Auerbach puts it, "The world beyond . . . is God's design in active fulfillment. In relation to it, earthly phenomena are on the whole merely figural, potential, requiring fulfillment. This also applies to the souls of the dead: it is only here, in the beyond, that they attain fulfillment and the true reality of their being."[25] Therefore "in the Biblical stories [the] aim is not to bewitch the senses, and if nevertheless they produce lively sensory effects, it is only because the moral, religious, and psychological phenomena which are their sole concern are made concrete in the sensible matter of life. What [the Biblical narrator] produced, then, was not primarily oriented toward 'realism' (if he succeeded in being realistic, it was merely a means, not an end); it was oriented toward truth."[26] In prefigurations of the Passion, "the sensory occurrence pales before the power of the figurative meaning. What is perceived by the hearer or reader or even, in the plastic and graphic arts, by the spectator, is weak as a sensory impression, and all one's interest is directed toward the context of meanings. In comparison, the Greco-Roman specimens of realistic presentation are, though less serious and fraught with problems and far more limited in their conception of historical movement, nevertheless perfectly integrated in their sensory substance. They do not know the antagonism between sensory appearance and meaning, an antagonism which permeates the early, and indeed the whole, Christian view of reality."[27]

So, in re-encountering the classical past, as well as in developing the new sciences, the Renaissance may also have been turned back onto the road that Auerbach describes as Homeric, in which material things are allowed to be absolutely themselves, fully present, imbued with historicity but not entangled with psychology. Their meaning is their present being, and their being is accessible to an intense but detached application of sensory perception. This marked a critical move away from the exegetical model that dominated medieval Christianity (and reaches its artistic zenith in Dante), in which things mattered as transactions with the transcendent—their true meaning lurking in intention, waiting for interpretation to conjure it into presence—instead of in their own tangible aspects, as in the Homeric catalogues.[28] The functions of the medieval *figura*, which made narratives into codes for deeper Christian truths, shaped also the perception of objects. Whereas the model Auerbach describes is diachronic, about one figure prophesying the future one, my adaptation of it is more strictly perceptual, about each perceptible phenomenon—though manifestly real—surrendering its full presence as the divine intention behind it is recognized. What changed epistemologically in this period was that this progression no longer moved consistently toward a Christian enlightenment, but often instead toward the rationalist Enlightenment. What was sought was increasingly the inherent material essence of the object, of which its outward markers (including its noun) were at best figurations.

Words had been more than dispensable markers, more than media: the meaning did not hide behind them, but lived in them. As Foucault writes, "The Renaissance came to a halt before the brute fact that language existed: in the density of the world, a graphism mingling with things or flowing beneath them; marks made upon manuscripts or the pages of books . . . summoned up a secondary language—that of commentary, exegesis, erudition—in order to stir the language that lay dormant within them, and to make it speak at last."[29] Yet in this period words were themselves increasingly being perceived as things, and as having their meaning in relation to other words.[30] Sir Thomas Browne wants to keep words implicated in the essence of the things they define, but he knows that, in this, he is rowing against the tide:

in this Mass of Nature there is a set of things that carry in their Front (though not in Capital Letters, yet in Stenography and short Characters,) something of Divinity, which to wiser Reasons serve as Luminaries in the Abyss of Knowledge, and to judicious beliefs as Scales and Roundles to mount the Pinacles and highest pieces of Divinity. The severe Schools shall never laugh me out of the Philosophy of Hermes, that this visible World is but a Picture of the invisible wherein, as in a Pourtraict, things are not truely, but in equivocal shapes, and as they counterfeit some more real substance in that invisible fabrick.

As a scientist, Browne chooses to leave "Contemplations Metaphysicall" to theologians, himself "content to trace and discover those expressions hee hath left in his creatures, and the obvious effects of nature." This, however, is still a science dependent on what was already considered an old-fashioned attention to signatures; and as a Christian, Browne argues that while speculations about the movements of the sun and moon may be interesting, contemplating "why his providence hath so disposed and ordered their motions . . . is a sweeter piece of reason."[31] Meaning could still outrank matter.

But not for long. Words, fighting what may have seemed a doomed battle to sustain their ontological ascendancy over things, may have chosen a separatist policy instead—much as religion was obliged to do in relation to the rise of science, a similarity which is probably much more than mere coincidence. In impressively deep and learned presentations, Richard Waswo and Timothy Reiss assert that a new (or, at least, renewed) theory of autonomous language emerged in the Renaissance.[32] Major theorists from Auerbach to Foucault have also observed that the late Renaissance was marked by the collapse of a model of analogy, resemblance and interconnectedness. Both the rise of skepticism and the Cartesian efforts to suppress it questioned the connection of thoughts to things, and therefore also the connection of signs to the objects they were supposed to signify.[33]

Protestantism may thus be viewed as less a last flurry of the falling empire of the word than a prophecy of a future in which the word would declare itself independent and self-sufficient, pushing aside the material connections of the traditional Christian belief-system and eventually establishing its autonomous state. The familiar problems with the radical Protestant system—the discomforts of being connected only by the unstable and subjective workings of the human psyche to a distant God immune to material blandishments—resemble the discomforts still generated by radical skepticism, semiotics, and constructivism. The anxiety some see as structured into Reformation faith, in which only God's inscrutable and possibly arbitrary choice stood between the soul and its damnation, would have found a distinct parallel in the epistemology of Occasionalism, which tried to solve the seemingly absolute distinction between mental states and physical events (and hence presumably between ideas and objects, signs and signifieds) by concluding that God needed to intervene specially on every occasion to produce a connection.[34] Indeed, as Joseph Koerner's admirable study of Reformation iconophobia observes, "By Luther's definition, sacrament is precisely that which 'fastens' (*fasst*) words to things, supernature to nature, spirit to matter."[35] Some radical thinking was invested in what looks like a reactionary cause, an effort to save the adherences. Ficino and Pico claimed the authority of Plato's *Cratylus* for the idea that names are natural rather than merely conventional; Erasmus—in several ways an unlikely advocate—clung to the idea of a "likeness between the word and the object."[36] Yet the Reformation required the full liberation of the Word, which became part of the campaign against popular superstition (and thence against Catholicism).[37] Unsurprisingly, this is a change Western culture is still struggling to assimilate, despite our daily training in trusting a universe of mutually referring monetary markers; the notion of a language system with no actual reference to anything outside of itself remains an extremely uncomfortable one for most of the people (including me) who are even willing to consider it.[38]

Even if we believe that the influence of the word is, in these poststructuralist days, undiminished from its days as Scripture, there has nonetheless been an important change from the old world of the Word: modern thinkers tend to grant power to language, not because they feel (as Augustinian theology suggested) that is ultimately where truth resides, but instead because they know it may be as close as we can get to a truth that they suspect resides in the material universe, which language represents, whether by homology or mere metonymy. As Wittgenstein would argue in *Philosophical Investigations* (1953), language is less either true or false than it is a convention that has value to the extent that it achieves practical goals. Accepting an autonomous system of language is like accepting that the reality received by consciousness is virtual. We need not believe that words have any deep hold on reality, only that we are permanently trapped on the surface and must make the best of it. Perhaps we can convince ourselves that merely arbitrary signs are actually the best ones, because (like ideal scientific instruments, and like paper money) they point to an object without actually touching it and without prejudging (by any implied claim to resemblance) its characteristics; and because, lacking even partial involvement in material reality, the sign-system can easily sustain its own coherence (as consciousness, by accepting its map of the world as really and exclusively the world, can sustain its own sanity).

Unfortunately, the separatist view of semiotics implies a forfeiture of any authentic contact with the world of nature. The lyrics of Orpheus can no longer mesmerize the wilderness, which thus becomes both dangerous and endangered. The epistemological ironies Shakespeare and Marvell weave into their versions of pastoral can be taken as an acknowledgment of this forfeiture, which could only have aggravated the cultural anxieties I have been tracing about mediation and the lost objective universe. No wonder the Elizabethan charlatan John Dee could mesmerize his contemporaries with the claim to have rediscovered a divine language in which the letters actually reflect "the quiddity of the substance" and therefore generate "proper words . . . signifying substantially the thing that is spoken of in the center of his Creator."[39] A standard reading of Genesis was that Adam gave names so deeply linked to the essences of all the creatures that the names gave him a magical kind of command over those creatures. Perfect organic semiotics and an Edenic grasp of nature were virtually inseparable. Because people had lost touch with Creation, they no longer had true words to describe it; because they lacked such words, they could no longer really take hold of Creation. Even leading scientists such as Bacon, Browne, Fludd, and Boyle complained that the lost ancient books of Solomon had once provided full and perfect information about the natural world.[40] The inability to know that world completely is persistently associated with a dictionary mislaid long ago.

At least it seems important, especially for environmentalist advocacy, to assert that words have consequences in the material world; that our connection with the environment is essential even if philosophically elusive; that, whatever the extent of our entrapment in the prison-house of language, we cannot abjure our responsibilities in the killing-fields of nature; and that (for example) calling animals "venison" (as in *As You Like It*, 2.1) means something very different, consequentially so, from calling them "deer" or not presuming to know their identity. Language may be thought of as itself an ecology—an interdependent system of relations struggling to maintain dynamic equilibrium against entropy by accommodating historical change—but its arguable lack of connection to the biological ecology does not mean human beings are entirely unconnected to the natural world, or exempt from obligations to life as a collective abstraction that actually exists in beseeching particulars. To decide that the world outside us does not exist because we cannot know it absolutely or force it into our categories is only the last refuge of the anthropomorphic scoundrel; it is the sociopath's solution to the problem of other minds.

The more radical deep-ecology movement would warn that sentimental and even scientific environmentalism entail violations of their own. The more insistent the human embrace of nature—a nature defined as void of intention, resistant or at best unresponsive in this mode—the clearer the implication of seduction or even rape. This sexualized anxiety about the effort to isolate and observe nature's secrets is most vividly articulated in George Herbert's "Vanitie (I)":

> The fleet Astronomer can bore,
> And thred the spheres with his quick-piercing minde :
> He views their stations, walks from doore to doore,
>   Surveys, as if he had design'd
> To make a purchase there: he sees their dances,
>   And knoweth long before,
> Both their full-ey'd aspects, and secret glances.
>
> The nimble Diver with his side
> Cuts through the working waves, that he may fetch
> His dearely-earned pearl, which God did hide
>   On purpose from the ventrous wretch;
> That he might save his life, and also hers,
>   Who with excessive pride
> Her own destruction and his danger wears.
>
> The subtil Chymick can devest
> And strip the creature naked, till he finde
> The callow principles within their nest:
>   There he imparts to them his minde,
> Admitted to their bed-chamber, before
>   They appeare trim and drest
> To ordinarie suitours at the doore.
>
> What hath not man sought out and found,
> But his deare God? who yet his glorious law
> Embosomes in us, mellowing the ground

With showres and frosts, with love and aw,
So that we need not say, Where's this command?
    Poore man! thou searchest round
To finde out *death*, but missest *life* at hand.

My adoration for Herbert's poetry and even (usually) his piety does not preclude my wondering, here and elsewhere, whether it is ever really so easy. Marvell's Mower will take a similar position against gardens, and Wordsworth's affectionate primitivism will sometimes echo it. Sex and sophistication are conjunctive illnesses, they suggest, and the will to knowledge is generally fatal. One may go from the top of the skies to the bottom of the seas, and into the interior of the atom, and yet really know nothing of Creation but its mortal limits: this is knowledge only of good lost and evil got, as for Adam and Eve in Milton's Eden. Heaven (as Robert Browning's "Andrea del Sarto" would later imply, in the persona of a Renaissance painter almost too good at reproducing reality) tries to keep things out of our grasp that are within our reach.

Such naturally-pious arguments—though in the voice of angels—could not sate the century's appetite for scientific inquiry by feeding it generalities about God above and his law within us (though Kant's *Critique of Practical Reason* would eventually try to build systematically from these two wonders, "the starry sky above and the moral law within"). Isaac Newton sets about filling this vacuum in astonishing ways, but is driven back (like Charleton and Mersenne) to an epistemological modesty, conceding—in the *Optics*, for example—that he cannot claim to know essences; his theories of physics may be superb tools for handling the world, but they are still only conceptions and representations. So mysticism thrived, promising access to the oldest and most inward secrets—or justifying their inaccessibility. Renaissance Kabbalism bore some resemblance to environmentalism: it described fulfillment in terms of seeds, roots, and fruit (*spermata, rizai,* and *karpoi*), and its goal was the repair of the world, partly by the correction of human sins. In some ways the Gnostic view was more like a dyspeptic version of deep ecology, which rejects the ameliorative path as a dangerous deception, and instead calls for a kind of relinquishment that resembles Indian belief-systems in demonizing the imperial and empirical tendencies of the human ego. In their search for *sefirot* hidden (like the Word, for some Protestants) behind the demonic materiality of our universe, the Gnostics practically made Descartes' hypothesis of an evil deceiver controlling sense-experience into a religion. On the pilgrimage of the human spirit, the roadside scene was merely a Potemkin village, constructed by the Archonic tyrant. In an era struggling with the stubborn inaccessibility of the material universe, Gnosticism's attitude toward that universe looks a bit like the attitude of Aesop's fox toward the inaccessible grapes.

Many people, even or perhaps especially those who would declare it impossible, evidently hungered to know things in themselves; and even out in the wet and cold of that lovely, mellow English countryside, they felt that nature— always twisting away like Proteus, or maybe like Daphne—was tantalizingly just barely beyond their fingertips, or barely out of focus, or barely beyond the depth that our mortal bodies allow us to fathom. What begins to emerge is a homology in these many forms of desire: according to Timothy Reiss, "what we find in Galileo, in Descartes, and in the other writings of Bacon: the new scientist *imposes* the discursive / upon the world outside him. He is a conqueror enforcing his will, a man ravishing a woman: whether it be Galileo tearing the veils concealing the moon's nakedness in the *Sidereus nuncius*, diverse later grammarians disrobing a language they speak of as a woman, or Sir Walter Ralegh bluntly asserting the future rape of a relatively untouched part of South America."[41] How, then, to express love of nature properly? How can one get a grip on otherness, especially when that is precisely what the self destroys in the very act of acquiring it?

Arrogating reality to the a priori categories of the human mind resembles exploiting all nature for the immediate service of human selfishness, and while both have their conveniences, neither (as nominalists and environmentalists would remind us) seems satisfactory, any more than a tyranny of masculine will can resolve satisfactorily the complexities of human sexuality. Where, though, is the sustainable middle position between these subjectivist resolutions and the pure passivity toward external reality that is the death of mind and body alike— seeking a quiddity with a bare bodkin? If, in the classical formulation that Montaigne made famous, "to philosophize is to learn how to die,"[42] perhaps learning to love nature entails the same curriculum as learning to love wisdom. And if we accept Descartes' provisional formulation that "I exist thinking" is the only certain reality—all there may be to the universe—then to surrender consciousness seems as intolerable as it is inevitable.

To see without prejudice and subjectivity is to have no self; to look upon God is to die—"Thou canst not se my face, for there shal no man se me, and live"[43]—and there is no way to look on anything piously without seeing (through however dark a glass) the face of God. Can one push aside the prideful ego and still have a soul to offer? Can one recognize each irreducible bit of material reality, perhaps (as Hobbes would urge) recognize those bits as the only reality, without dazzling cognition into stupefaction and sinking the soul into despair by replacing (like Herbert's second "Employment" lyric) deity with entropy, the Ten Commandments with the Second Law of Thermodynamics? Though there may be some hint of a positive answer in Shakespearean "negative capability" and the hypothetical functions of theater, there is also, in Shakespeare's depictions of jealousy, a warning about the dangers of losing patience with partial knowledge: a warning about the way extreme doubt and extreme certainty, like the older sins called despair and pride, empower each other; and about the ways doubt and certainty conspire to drive us disastrously away from nature.

Shakespearean Drama and Cartesian Doubt

The inability of human consciousness and its linguistic markers to seize hold of reality was originally a comic topic for Shakespeare. *The Comedy of Errors* is largely a joke about the insufficiencies of markers—names and even appearances—with the consequences played out in bruised psyches and bruised bodies until origins can be verified, signatures read, true identities thereby conferred, and likeness elided with love. *The Taming of the Shrew* toys with the capacity of words to change realities. *Twelfth Night* is another long series of misread signifiers and illegible other minds, and the epistemological-ontological resolution (again, dependent on a fetishizing of the genitalia themselves) hardly surpasses Feste's "that that is, is . . . for what is that, but that? and is but is?" (4.2.14–16). The premise of *Love's Labor's Lost* is a retreat out into nature for the purpose of transcending nature. The young king, believing words to hold the highest truth, attempts to construct a world where nothing else matters. Even beyond death, the opening lines suggest, what they hope to make endure in the hard metals of the world are words about their dedication to words: "Let fame, that all hunt after in their lives, / Live regist'red upon our brazen tombs" (1.1.1–2). From there on, the play is a kind of semiotic demolition-derby.[44] Language and all other kinds of markers persistently fail to locate the essences they supposedly define; empty praises, delusive masks, bad translations, false etymologies, misdirected letters, and near synonyms expose the inadequacy of intellectual systems to overrule the demands of nature, especially the facts of bodily desire and death. At the end, as winter sets in, "coughing drowns the parson's saw" (5.2.922). In each of these comedies, the elusiveness of firm reality for the human mind, tangled as it is in language, elides into the elusiveness of women for the men seeking to grasp them.

In moving "from myth to history" (as Alvin Kernan has eloquently demonstrated),[45] the Henry IV tetralogy also traces English society's move from religion toward physics. The angels conjured by divine anointment prove no match for the soldiers gathered by Realpolitik, marking a shift of epistemology in the guise of a shift of dynasty: meaning yields to force, with materiel as a code for materiality. Henry IV says Richard's error was destroying his own mystique, making his physical person too available, to the extent that it eclipsed the shining symbol of his sovereign person. The divine designation of a king, though a necessary illusion, is an illusion nonetheless. By the time Henry "hath many marching in his coats" (*Henry IV, Part I*, 5.3.25) to divert potential assassins, the old armorial signifiers have become meaningless, even evasive. The body concealed at the core (botchy or otherwise) of those armors still matters, but as in capitalist economics, the alienated signifier learns to live on its own, its connection to ethical significance no more than a marriage of convenience. Does it matter who Prince Hal really is, in moral character, if he can master the dialects of majesty and of his people? Falstaff tries, and finally fails, to put his masterful words in front of his eminently material body. "Honor" may indeed be merely "a breath"—the nominalists would have agreed—but what more do we have than breath? What do we have (as Leontes and—finally, terribly—Lear are compelled to ask) without it?

In Shakespearean tragedy, fallen kings such as Lear and Richard II try to strip down to the essence, shedding their royalty as a dramatic instance of the more general problem of shedding culturally conferred identity and perception. This leads them to larger metaphysical questions—Lear in his rages, Richard in his melancholic dungeon. Among the many world-views *King Lear* undermines is that of pastoral, which is shattered and parodied; and every definition of nature produces an equal and opposite one, while human efforts to project our meanings onto the world melt away in indifferent rainstorms and bestial humanoids, as well as in age and death. By the time we arrive on the heath in *King Lear*, pastoral is already too hard, no retreat at all: the life in the straw hovel about as far from contentment as one can imagine. Lear tries to peel down to "the thing itself, unaccommodated man" (3.4.106–7), but it is the peeling of an onion—complete with tears. There is no thing, only change, which human consciousness reads as loss. What persists in nature is the fact of mortality, which Lear smells on his hand (4.6.133), and sees distilled into its spirit-poisoning essence in the corpse of his youngest daughter (though it was already lurking in the old men whose loss of mind and sight were preludes to imminent, more encompassing losses). The acceptance of death in Arcadia, the passivity that we will see in Marvell's Mower, emerges only in Gloucester's observation that "a man may rot even here" (5.2.8), which sits in the middle of a play of desperate material and even evolutionary striving, or in Kent's queasy pun equating long life with elongation on a torture rack (5.3.314–16). Morality is present as a palliative, not as any stable or essential truth (unless Cordelia is actually Christ)—flax and egg whites on Gloucester's eyes, but no vision.

From the perspective of my argument, Lear begins to look like a representative of England's entire senescent culture. He regresses toward infancy (as a crawling, weeping fool seeking a nurtured place in women's breasts, though susceptible to women's punishment) and tries to withdraw from court into an pastoral idyll troubled only by unrequited love (the crown of weeds, the fantasy of a retreat from which he and Cordelia can laugh at gilded butterflies), until the world begins to look like a film of human evolution run backwards and at very high speed (Edgar backpedals frantically to keep up with that retreat), so that soon "humanity must perforce prey on itself, / Like monsters of the deep" (4.2.49). Lear and his world seek a way back to what they understand as childhood and nature, and end up instead (with an ending devoid of teleology, a pietà without resurrection) darkening a path toward Hobbes and Darwin. When he cannot evoke from Cordelia the breath of her separate living which he once resented, when he says "She's dead as earth" (5.3.262), he shows only too keenly how it feels to inhabit a world where the willful mysteries of nature have been turned into a passive object, a mass of materiality.

The preceding chapter argued that the inscrutability of the female Other, and the impossibility of locating exactly the commodity desired from her, evidently troubled not only men's heterosexual pursuit in this period, but also their comfort in the possession of women. Men find they cannot know exactly what it is they want (leading, then as now, to smirking assent that it is self-evident), nor can they know when they have it, or whether they still have it—even if they hold the questionable heart literally in their hands, like Ford's Giovanni. In Middleton's *The Changeling*, Alsemero tries to turn the question of a woman's erotic loyalty into a laboratory project, using a volume called *The Book of Experiment, Call'd Secrets in Nature* which dictates neat measures from various letter-indexed vials (4.1.24–25), but all he ends up proving is that a woman can fake paroxysms much like orgasm; and he is tricked again in Act 5 when he believes he bursts his bride's maidenhead, which is a revealingly persistent synecdoche in this period for a woman's chastity. Other brides throughout late Renaissance drama prove to be one-woman bed-tricks, and even the innocent are dangerously unfathomable. In Shakespeare's *Cymbeline*, Imogen is much more truly represented by what she is reading—the tale of the rape of Lucrece—than she is by the intimate physical markers Iachimo steals a look at, which purport to define her instead as a willing adulteress; meanwhile the décor of her bedchamber sends intensely mixed signals. Locating a core truth, a definite essence, of a woman's sexual being is difficult if there is no physical place (nor in fact any legible mark) that can be fully equated with her chastity—especially in a Protestant culture that preferred married fidelity over absolute virginity.

The literature suggests a converse problem for women, of how to know themselves and how to be known by men. This arises most acutely in cases of rape, where women struggle to distinguish the body that has supposedly been polluted from the mind which has not—a problem that vexed Shakespeare and his contemporaries in their reconstructions of Lucrece's suicide. The dirty joke at the end of Jonson's "Celebration of Charis" insists that the lower-class woman knows exactly the "one good part" she wants from a man. But if, according to the jocular Renaissance parlance, the woman's part is "no-thing," where is the commodity, the *coign*, that men seek to acquire and accumulate? Little wonder that men are driven to fetishistic surrogates, nor that those surrogates—think of Desdemona's handkerchief, or Celia's in *Volpone*—gain prominence in cases of jealousy. Women's ultimate illegibility to men, which is a persistent comic theme in *Love's Labor's Lost*, becomes persistently tragic in Shakespeare's Jacobean plays.

The relationship between Cartesian skepticism and the psychodynamics of Shakespearean tragedy has been studied by Stanley Cavell; I will not duplicate his arguments here, nor attempt to match his oracular style. I do want to suggest, though, that the resemblances run in channels beyond those Cavell traced: they involve the problem of ungraspable reality as well as of unfathomable other minds, and they connect back to the search for lost natural origins I have been diagnosing in the culture as a whole. In *Othello*, Shakespeare uses anxieties surrounding race and sexuality to meld the unavailability of certainty (here instanced as marital fidelity) with "nature erring from itself " (3.3.227; here instanced as interracial marriage). In *The Winter's Tale*, Shakespeare will similarly associate Leontes' fall into radical subjectivity with his alienation from nature.

That Othello is bedeviled by the inherent problems of evidence, as much perhaps as by Iago, is a point suggested by forensic as well as philosophical contexts of the play.[46] The story seems to ask, as the lawyers and skeptics did, about criteria and the consequences of doubt—in principle and in practice. It also keeps hinting at the problem of infinite regress, the nagging desire (which I have been attributing to the culture as a whole) to move back to some originary moment where reality could be located absolutely and grasped reliably. The exact location, in time and space, of Othello's possession of Desdemona (and the counter-colonial acquisition she represents) proves elusive. Their love began only in words, which comprised stories of Othello's origins. The play then teases us, as it does Othello himself, with the repeated deferral of the sexual consummation of his marriage, from the initial arrest to the separate voyage toward Cyprus to the brawl that rouses them there (and perhaps reflects their own interrupted but potentially bloody encounter)—after which Othello goes off to tend to Montano's body rather than Desdemona's. Perhaps the consummation is achieved later; perhaps it fails; interesting psychological readings can be built on any of these speculations. But the moment itself is missing, as Iago keeps reminding Cassio and thereby reminding us early on that night in Cyprus. In the imperatives of theatrical decorum, Shakespeare found an opportunity to nurture doubt. By asking Emilia to put the wedding-night sheets on the bed, apparently to induce some reconciliation with the furiously jealous Othello, Desdemona tries to revisit that missing moment, whether by reminding him that she was obviously a virgin at the time, or by offering him a second chance at a consummation that became entangled in his own psychological conflicts as well as the conflict in the streets.

There is no going back, however: not for Brabantio, who wishes he could undo the marriage and even his conception of Desdemona, nor for Cassio or Emilia, who wish they could undo their negligent complicity in the destruction of the marriage and of Desdemona herself. Othello pushes even further back with the strawberry-spotted handkerchief which seems to be a displacement of those wedding sheets, and which he claims (by now we no longer even know whether his stories are true or manipulations of Desdemona) could provide some supernatural assurance through its connection to origins: the virgins who made it, the parents who exchanged it, the magical African world from which both he and it have come. Finally he can only erase himself by retreating back to his originary moment as the brave and loyal Moor of Venice.

Iago, the seeming origin of Othello's doubts, is notable for his own lack of origins—one aspect (I have argued elsewhere) of a self seemingly composed of absences.[47] At first he seems part of Brabantio's dream; later it becomes hard to tell whether he is part of Cassio's dream or that dream part of Iago's own fantasy (1.1.142; 3.3.413–27). He creates a similar ontological disturbance in all those around him: their sense of identity and relationship audibly collapses into chaos, partly because he effaces the boundary between truth and illusion. Shakespeare's scenario here is like Descartes' experimental case for skepticism: "suppose therefore that not God, who is supremely good and the source of truth, but rather some malicious demon of the utmost power and cunning has employed all his energies in order to deceive me."[48] This creature is all the more dangerous for having been assumed benign, and under his sway it becomes impossible to believe almost anything with confidence. In *Othello*, Shakespeare moves Descartes' unsettling hypothesis from the philosophical library to the marital bedroom.

To find his way out of this maze of unknowing, Descartes' first rule "was never to accept anything as true if I did not have evident knowledge of its truth: that is, carefully to avoid precipitate conclusions and preconceptions, and to include nothing more in my judgements than what presented itself to my mind so clearly and distinctly that I had no occasion to doubt it."[49] This seems a safe way to proceed philosophically (though Shakespeare suggests it underrates the power of the imagination to induce certainty); but psychologically it can be calamitous. Shakespeare energized this warning (I have argued elsewhere) by linking transhistorical aspects of male sexual possessiveness with religious anxieties specific to the new Reformation culture.[50] Of course Protestants denied that their experience of faith was any less certain or any more subjective than whatever assurance was provided by the more gradualist and materialist conception of salvation under Catholicism. Though individuals might experience it with different degrees of imperfection (which correlate with their reprobation), faith was inherently a conviction: something rawly felt. Nonetheless, a lack of complete and stable certainty, tied to tortuous self-examination, was the signature disease of Protestant soteriology as well as late-Renaissance epistemology. The idea that true faith was unshakeable set a high standard, the more because Protestants were being obliged to keep asking themselves whether their faith was indeed beyond doubt, which can hardly be asked without implying a negative answer.

This trap is mimicked by Iago on the topic of marital faith: once he can convince Othello to take a reasonable-sounding mixed view of Desdemona—"Wear your eyes thus, not jealous nor secure" (3.3.198)—the experience of doubt becomes both intolerable and incurable. With shocking yet only too plausible rapidity, Othello must retreat to a position which, for Descartes, was an essential answer to radical skepticism. The divine would not compromise itself in this way: "If she be false, [O then] heaven [mocks] itself! I'll not believe't" (3.3.278). But what if "the divine Desdemona" is (as her name could suggest) part of the demon rather than part of the divinity? The same cluster of questions arises in Beaumont and Fletcher's *Philaster*, which repeatedly asks how a woman who looks so innocent can be so guilty without proving "that womankind is false" (3.1.91) and, worse, that ultimate truth is generally indiscernible. "Every man . . . hath not a soule of Christall, for all men to reade their actions through: men's hearts and faces are so farre asunder, that they hold no intelligence" (1.1.248–52). Now even dramatists are reluctant to make windows into men's souls, and the resolution of *Philaster* depends instead on the revelation that Bellario has female rather than male genitalia.

The search for perfect erotic possession is one facet of the search for absolute knowledge of any entity outside the self. What Iago tells Othello—knowing it will be an endless torment rather than a satisfaction—is that

> If imputation and strong circumstances,
> Which lead directly to the door of truth,
> Will give you satisfaction, you might have't.
>   (3.3.406–8)

As the gatelike frontispieces of many learned tracts of the period suggest, late-Renaissance culture stood at that entryway dreaming up spells to open the door (while Mersenne and Gassendi, like implacable *maitres d'*, shook their heads discouragingly).

Stalled in that line, Shakespeare's Leontes loses his temper, and with it, almost everything else. *The Winter's Tale*, like *Othello*, entails an exploration of skeptical anxieties, partly hidden behind a parable of marital anxieties; or, looking at it the other way, the play uses Cartesian problems to lend power and currency to a story of domestic trauma. The chronology alone should make clear that I am not claiming any direct allusion to Descartes; but the striking similarities do suggest that there was a shared cultural source—a crisis of not quite knowing—for the philosophical inquiries into skepticism and the dramatic explorations of sexual jealousy that occupied Shakespeare and his fellow-playwrights so intensely in this period.

Leontes is haunted by four things that would soon become fundamental to Descartes' exploration of radical skepticism: the hypothesis of a demonic deceiver, a dreamer's belief that he is awake, the radical variations of opinion among people, and the unreliability and incommunicability of sense-evidence. Like *Othello*, *The Winter's Tale* appears to ask what it would mean to perform, in a home laboratory, Descartes' most famous thought-experiment: to doubt everything we have ever believed; to disallow even the most basic recognitions of our senses; to distrust affections and traditions, religious as well as familial; to suppose that the informants we trusted most were evil conspirators deceiving us[51]—all in hopes of reaching some basic irrefutable truth from which we could begin to rebuild a more dependable structure.

It would mean disaster, according to these plays, followed by a repentance in which the skeptic must (in the Pauline/Paulina solution) be prepared either to "awake your faith" (5.3.95) or rest forever in torment. Descartes' defensive position notwithstanding, no refuge can be reached by climbing the rungs of reason, or by clinging to sensation. Perhaps "the evidence of things which are not sene" (Hebrews 11:1; Geneva Bible) could compensate for the damage skepticism was doing to the evidentiary value of things seen, but that is theology and teleology; meanwhile, Leontes, like the rest of us, must decide how to navigate a mortal and physical world he knows he cannot know.

At first Leontes wrestles with the awkward conjunction of *res cogitans* and *res extensa*, mental and physical states, that would soon prove so central to Cartesian philosophy: "To mingle friendship far is mingling bloods. / I have *tremor cordis* on me; my heart dances, / But not for joy; not joy" (1.2.109–11; the same dualistic questions underlie Leontes' speculation at 2.1.41–42 about whether a man can be sickened by a spider-poisoned drink if "his knowledge / Is not infected").

Polixenes' immediate reply is "What means Sicilia?" and editors have agonized over that question ever since. In the absence of any better explanation of Leontes' rant, perhaps we should notice its anticipation of the Cartesian struggle to understand how the mind can possibly verify its beliefs about the physical universe:

> Affection! thy intention stabs the centre.
> Thou dost make possible things not so held,
> Communicat'st with dreams (how can this be?),
> With what's unreal thou co-active art,
> And fellow'st nothing. Then 'tis very credent
> Thou mayst co-join with something . . .
> (1.2.138–43)

This can play comically: Leontes as a Don Quixote who has gone mad reading too much skeptical philosophy rather than too many chivalric romances.[52]

If the Cartesian "I think, therefore I am" proves unsatisfactory, the Scriptural "I am that I am" may take its place. As King Lear discovers, royal power could seduce a man into thinking he possesses the divine *fiat* that turns thought into being. Leontes poses as the omniscient God judging the fall in Eden: when Hermione says that she and Polixenes "are yours i' th' garden," Leontes replies that they and their "bents" will "be found, / Be you beneath the sky" (1.2.178–80). But the diabolical voice of uncertainty and mistrust—the Iago of "I am not what I am" (*Othello*, 1.1.65)—speaks to Leontes from within; and in consequence, nothing is what it is. Leontes becomes the sinner, turning to Camillo, who has regularly "cleans'd my bosom" (1.2.238); and what Leontes seems to crave is as much the epistemological absolute as any theological absolution. He launches into a tirade—actually, a univocal dialogue of the kind commonly found in the period's philosophical tracts, but suggestive of his solipsistic isolation—about that favorite topic of seventeenth-century skeptics, the limitations of sense-evidence:[53]

> Ha' not you seen, Camillo
> (But that's past doubt; you have, or your eye-glass
> Is thicker than a cuckold's horn), or heard
> (For to a vision so apparent rumor
> Cannot be mute), or thought (for cogitation
> Resides not in that man that does not think)
> My wife is slippery?
> (1.2.268–73)

Despite the semi-comic drop from the philosophic mode to the emotive topic at the end, the skeptical point endures: perhaps his wife seems slippery because reality itself is. The adjective implies less that she has slipped than that she cannot be confidently held.

In a speech which seems to undo the Creation ex nihilo, Leontes then wonders how Camillo can negate what seems to Leontes himself overwhelming evidence:

> wishing clocks more swift?
> Hours, minutes? noon, midnight? and all eyes
> Blind with the pin and web but theirs, theirs only,
> That would unseen be wicked? Is this nothing?
> Why then the world and all that's in't is nothing,
> The covering sky is nothing, Bohemia nothing,
> My wife is nothing, nor nothing have these nothings,
> If this be nothing.
>
> (1.2.289–95)

Behind his overt syllogistic point—if his wife is not cheating, then everything he perceives about the world is unreliable—lurks the converse: if everything he perceives about the world is unreliable, how can he be sure his wife is not cheating? Descartes' thought-experiment at the end of the "First Meditation" requires not only imagining that the Being he had supposed "supremely good and the source of truth" is actually treacherous, but also that Descartes therefore "think that the sky, the air, the earth, colours, shapes, sounds and all external things are merely the delusions of dreams which he has devised to ensnare my judgement. I shall consider myself as not having hands or eyes, or flesh, or blood or senses, but as falsely believing that I have all these things. I shall stubbornly and firmly persist in this meditation; and, even if it is not in my power to know the truth, I shall at least do what is in my power, that is, resolutely guard against assenting to any falsehoods, so that the deceiver . . . will be unable to impose on me."[54]

Descartes' "Second Meditation" then begins with quite a plausible paraphrase of the stance Leontes takes in 2.3: "So serious are the doubts into which I have been thrown as a result of yesterday's meditation that I can neither put them out of my mind nor see any way of resolving them. It feels as if I have fallen unexpectedly into a deep whirlpool which tumbles me around so that I can neither stand on the bottom nor swim up to the top. Nevertheless I will . . . attempt the same path which I started on yesterday. Anything which admits of the slightest doubt I will set aside as if I had found it to be wholly false."[55] To this, Descartes should add the familiar warning: do not try this experiment at home. From this perspective, Leontes' behavior is less psychologically verisimilar than philosophically derived: a domestication of the problems of the revived skepticism of the early seventeenth century.[56]

Leontes tries to feel his way back to positive convictions, along the lines of conventional opinion and report, and sense-correlation and resemblance, as Descartes would predict: he tries to convince himself Mamillius is truly his son, twice with "They say" and twice with "like me." But Descartes would also predict the insufficiency of such evidence in the absence of divine assurance: hence the emissaries to the Oracle at Delphi, a primary source if there's ever been one. When the death of his son appears to confirm the Oracle's not-guilty verdict, Leontes says, "I have too much believ'd mine own suspicion" (3.2.151). This is supposed to signal a retreat from skepticism, but may instead reinforce skepticism by an iterated version of the Cretan liar's paradox (which was already lurking in Leontes' "All's true that is mistrusted" at 2.1.48, another self-consuming claim to certain proof). Do two skepticisms make a certainty?

Paulina attempts to introduce physical evidence of resemblance, as more convincing than language:

> We do not know
> How he may soften at the sight o' th' child:
> The silence often of pure innocence
> Persuades when speaking fails. (2.2.38)

But even this physical evidence turns metaphorically textual: "Although the print be little," this child is supposedly "the whole matter / And copy of the father—eye, nose, lip. . . ." (2.3.99). What anyway is the evidentiary power of either the human face or human language? In the initial banter about Polixenes' intended departure, Hermione insists that "a lady's 'verily' is as potent as a lord's" (1.2.45–51). If the only confirmation is "verily," how can one person's assertion be weighed against another's? This issue returns in graver costume in the trial scene, where Hermione complains that her testimony can carry no weight if her depravity is a premise of the trial (3.2.22–31).

Hermione remarks that Leontes' accusation will grieve him "When you shall come to clearer knowledge," and he replies, "No; if I mistake / In those foundations which I build upon, / The centre is not big enough to bear / A schoolboy's top" (2.1.100). In this Shakespeare anticipates the challenges to Descartes (and to Lord Herbert of Cherbury in England) by philosophers wondering whether truths can really be verified by the fact that they are perceived "clearly and distinctly," given how confidently people sometimes hold their transient illusions. Again a key instance of the problem—an obsessive one for Descartes[57]—is the blurry line separating reality from dreams that seem real to the dreamer:

> *Hermione:* You speak a language that I understand not.
> My life stands in the level of your dreams,
> Which I'll lay down.
> *Leontes:*   Your actions are my dreams.
> You had a bastard by Polixenes,
> And I but dream'd it. (3.2.80–84)

Absent a leap of faith, distinguishing the actions of others from the dreams of the self can be tricky. Hermione's body lingers in the dungeons of Sicilia because Leontes leaves her reality languishing in the House of Morpheus: she protests against being "condemn'd / Upon surmises (all proofs sleeping else / But what your jealousies awake)" (3.2.111–13). Even the noble Antigonus will convict her by the dream-standard—augmented, as in Descartes, by the questionable testimony of what seems to be a phantom.[58] Antigonus is then promptly dragged back to nature; the consumption of this protesting aristocrat by the bear serves as an overture to the symphonic ways in which Bohemia re-subjugates civilized figurations to their natural referents.[59]

Shakespeare embodies the nostalgia for a perfect criterion in the markedly anachronistic and supernatural oracle; but in more mundane territory, the exemplar of evidence is Autolycus's insistence that his obviously untrustworthy ballads about wildly unnatural events are validated by "five or six honest wives that were present" or by "Five justices' hands at it, and witnesses more than my pack will hold" (4.4.270–84). No wonder Leontes, for such a long time, won't listen to the exculpatory testimony of women and court authorities. What comes back toward the end of the play, what is implicitly even reborn, along with lost kin, is a confidence in evidence itself: Paulina's doctrine gradually retreats from the Pauline emphasis on things unseen. The Third Gentleman insists that the report of a recovered heir is "Most true, if ever truth were pregnant by circumstance. That which you hear you'll swear you see, there is such unity in the proofs . . . evidences proclaim her, with all certainty, to be the King's daughter" (5.2.30–39). This is still a plausibly Protestant idea of seeing by hearing, but soon we will see for ourselves.

How do we value a promise of "All certainty" about identity in a theatrical context of suspended disbelief? What finally is the difference—and this is especially true on stage, and even more so where this play offers interesting choices in doubling, for example, Hermione and Perdita—between Hermione and "another, / As like Hermione as is her picture" (5.1.74)? The work of Giulio Romano is said to put all but breath into a human likeness (5.2.98). Descartes asks how we would know the difference, "if any such machines bore a resemblance to our bodies and imitated our actions as closely as possible."[60] Leontes is not sure he does know the difference: "does not the stone rebuke me / For being more stone than it?" and perceives Perdita "standing like stone with thee" (5.3.37–42).

The only answer is a kind of Pyrrhonist decision to have faith, however absurdly, in a functional approximation of reality, and to posit the unfathomable presence of other minds—to take all that fully and pleasurably for life:

> *Paulina:* My lord's almost so far transported that
> He'll think anon it lives.
> *Leontes:*   O sweet Paulina,
> Make me to think so twenty years together!
> No settled senses of the world can match
> The pleasure of that madness. (5.3.69–73)

As Paulina goes on to explain, "It is requir'd / You do awake your faith" (5.3.95). By the end Leontes must learn to accept appearance as reality. At the same time he must accept representation and approximation: Florizel as a surrogate son, Perdita as a prospective replacement for Hermione; the statue, the perfect simulation (even to the point of aging), as a real living being.

That is finally what the statue becomes—what love becomes: belief in an other, however impossible absolute knowledge may be. A signature disease of English culture in the first half of the seventeenth century is the desire to have the fetish instead of the wife, to have the palpable and unchanging stone instead of the evanescent flesh and all its evanescent meanings. That desire and its dangers are manifest in Othello's description of Desdemona as "smooth as monumental alabaster" and exchangeable for "such another world of one all and perfect chrysolite" (5.2.5, 145), and Ovid's version of the Pygmalion story connects a mistrust of women's sexuality to the fantasy of an enlivened statue. Love must constantly find new ways to sustain the intuition of something precious infused, but not reified, into material bodies. The miracle of God—here, as in Descartes, and especially in his Occasionalist colleagues such as Malebranche— is that He bridges the difference, holds the ideas and imaginings together with the substance of the world. It was a miracle that Protestantism sought to highlight, and not only in its doctrines concerning the Incarnation and the Eucharist.[61] The shattering of the statue-form actually resurrects the blessed original and originary life it represented—a perfect fantasy-endorsement of the icono-clastic project.[62] Smash the image and you get the real.

What if it doesn't work, though—what if it produces only shards? Wipe away deceptions and illusions, and what is left? God, or maybe just Eden—or maybe nothing but an endless extension of the Hobbesian Leviathan where every kiss is finally just another kiss of atomistic billiard balls. Infinite love, or maybe just an infinite regress—and maybe an infinite abyss. Or, via Descartes, what is left is the thinking self, which is necessary but only dubiously sufficient to carry people back from those emptier possibilities to the divine plenitude. Perhaps people have marriages; certainly, the play suggests, they have bodies ag-ing toward death, which make the task of renewing life as Sisyphean as that of achieving conviction. Would it not at some point become more comfortable just to take the worst case (as Leontes does) as the truth: to believe that a spouse, a best friend, and all the trusted others are untrustworthy, and then to embrace guilt and mortality in seemingly unchanging, irredeemable forms, until there is nothing to do but slump weeping for years by the family tomb?

Drawing the Pygmalion myth into *The Winter's Tale* may be partly Shake-speare's ironic commentary on his own role in staging a reality at once markedly natural and markedly artificial. What such artists fall in love with may look re-markably like nature, but the passion is always at least partly narcissistic and possessive, a love for the art produced by their own consciousness and accultur-ation. The fantasy that it might prove to be nature after all—that a man can marry the simulacrum of life he has created, knowing it intimately and in-wardly—is a compelling one, one that again links a kind of controlling male hetero-eroticism with the cognitive aggression always implicated in human per-ception of reality. This is the dangerously insular territory Shakespeare would explore in his very next play through the figure of Prospero, who must finally relinquish the domination of the verbal mind and re-immerse himself in the fears and the flow of mortal nature.

What Leontes gets is finally not certainty—Hermione's apparent death brought much more stability than her recovery can promise—but another chance to endure uncertainty: to watch, for example, his wife embrace his friend. Nearby the uncanny likeness of that friend prepares to bed the uncanny likeness of that wife; if Leontes were simply to believe his eyes, his earlier jealousy would be affirmed rather than refuted. In this world, evidence is necessary but not suf-ficient, and something real—a spouse (like Paulina's), a child (like Hermione's), a certainty (like Leontes')—is lost forever in the temporal flux.

The play's final speech promises a voyage back in time and a filling-in of truth, both of them curative. But as a whole the play demonstrates that the desire to return to simple, healthy origins is almost as all-consuming as jealousy—which fits my suggestion that both are facets of late-Renaissance man's reaction against irreducible uncertainty. *The Winter's Tale* practically radiates the regressive impulse: while explaining his nostalgia for home, Polixenes offers protracted recollections of boyhood innocence, a timeless and sexless pastoral universe which Leontes desperately tries to import into the urbane present, despite a "fall" into heterosexual desire that, here as in Marvell's mower poems, provokes and symbolizes the loss of the solipsistic egomania of childhood (1.2.1–3, 1.2. 62–75). In the play's opening lines, Camillo seems to lament the way this simple and authentic early companionship has been smothered by culture (1.1.22–32); later he yearns audibly for a return to an idealized Sicilian homeland (4.4.510).

Paulina locates innocence back at the originary moment of life, the child freed from the womb-prison (2.2.57). Leontes has another formula, the purification by fire he proposes for both the babe and its defender; Polixenes also tries to go back to a primally cleansed moment, threatening to remove Florizel from his acknowledged kin "Farre than Deucalion off " (4.4.431). Bohemia seems to be offered as a test-case for primitivist fantasies,[63] and the Old Shepherd is not alone there in fixating on the good old days. Even that countrified world compulsively stages fake pastorals of Doricles and Flora. Still regressing in Act 5, Leontes fantasizes that Florizel is a new Polixenes (5.1.125; or a new Mamillius, 5.1.116) and Perdita a new Hermione (5.1.228); he says they are welcome "As is the spring to th' earth" (5.1.152), but he still will not let the years go around—will not, that is, let this spring run like the stream of Heraclitus.

Running against the grain of all this agrarian atavism are almost as many signals of capitalist alienation, with its uneasy markers of value. "In *The Winter's Tale*—beyond the terms tell and count themselves, and beyond account and loss and lost and gain and pay and owe and debt and repay—we have money, coin, treasure, purchase, cheat, custom, commodity, exchange, dole, wages, recompense, labor, affairs, traffic, tradesman, borrow, save, credit, redeem, and—perhaps the most frequently repeated economic term in the play—business."[64] Clearly this cluster of terms is invoked to signal a tension between pastoral and marketplace values, but also I think to signal a broader tension between past and present in the play, and thus between organic and artificial systems of meaning. All of these words were part of the old Scriptural and medieval economic discourses as well as the new capitalist one, and those old economic discourses had once been seamlessly compatible with religious values, but then became associated with the materialist facets of a fallen world. Capitalism drained its own vocabulary of any positive spiritual resonance (as evinced by the discomfort texts like Herbert's "Redemption" cause modern students, for whom money is a kind of guilty open secret). Like so many other things in *The Winter's Tale*, these words are finally summoned back toward their sacred origins, from their flirtation with a modern world of skeptically alienated signifiers. Money is in Bohemia just as surely as death is in Arcadia. Mamillius is still missing; and his name as well as Leontes' remarks about his upbringing make him a marker for the lost breast of nursing, the primal symbiosis of life lost back somewhere "in this wide gap of time, since first / we were dissevered" (5.3.154–55).

The Winter's Tale experiments explicitly with the retreat to pastoral simplicities before offering a more sophisticated and complicated solution. The play describes a perpetually incomplete journey back to nature, which is depicted as a real force that comes to us in allegorical guises. David Young observes that *The Winter's Tale* exemplifies two key characteristics of Shakespeare's romances: "In the late plays engagement and detachment in both structure and style are more pronounced, more taut and stretched," and "The primitivism of these plays," generally coded as pastoral, "seeks our attention and invites our participation."[65] I believe that these are deeply linked tendencies in a late-Renaissance culture that was constantly reaching back for original simplicity and seeking to participate in a natural world that seems to oscillate between engaging humanity automatically and alienating humanity completely.

Back from nature, back in time, Perdita is and is not the former Hermione, as metaphors are and are not the things they stand for. The promise of comedy (*As You Like It* will demonstrate) is that everything can be replaced, if we are willing to liken things. Among its various weighings of nature against art, *The Winter's Tale* weighs two versions of the quest for originary truth that were competing in Jacobean culture: a skeptical Cartesian struggle (resembling Baconian empiricism in character but finally pushing further) to wipe away all unfounded assumptions that the sophisticated culture had accumulated, and a pastoralist nostalgia which assumes that some regenerative truth resides back out in a natural setting and its rustic, unsophisticated forms of community.[66] But neither version proves reliable: as Leontes' intense skeptical inquiries lead him into obvious and destructive falsehoods, so "the sea mock'd" the sailors it drowned and "the bear mock'd" the nobleman it tore to pieces. So much for Touchstone's suggestion that we "let the forest judge." Those who go to nature hoping to escape doubts and mediations risk discovering that the only certainties nature can really offer are the unwelcome kind.

Yet within that mortal uncertainty and certain mortality await miracles of renewed innocence—miracles that take us back to nature, without necessarily going back in time, or even going out of the hyper-civilized setting of the art-gallery within Paulina's Sicilian chapel, all upon Shakespeare's stage. If Paulina's revelation of the statue offers a triumph of art, her revelations about that statue are a wonderfully defamiliarizing reminder that the surviving Hermione is surely no less a miracle than her animated statue would be: "So much the more our carver's excellence." (5.3.30). Hermione is herself, not a representation of herself forbidden to the touch (5.3.80–84); that distinction is glory enough that audiences sit rapt or even weeping to see something as ordinary as a middle-aged woman quietly embracing her husband and daughter. And that daughter—the third image of Hermione to populate this scene, the living image of the retrospective statue Leontes anticipated—is such a common kind of miracle that we needed to imagine her lost to be able rightly to value her presence. Leontes becomes a joyous version of the agonized Lear in learning to treasure the breath in his beloved. Though nature in *The Winter's Tale* gloriously renews, the great moral force of the play may be the way it renews our experience of nature.

Spenser, Pastoral, and the Lost World

Cultural history associates the yearning—not only for nature, but for wilderness, and not only for retreat from civilization, but for a metaphysical charge (whether childlike or sublime) derived from that wilderness—with the Romantic period of the early nineteenth century rather than the Renaissance of the early seventeenth. Though I believe that Philippe Ariès overstates the degree to which emotional attachment to children was an invention of the seventeenth century, there still remains some evidence that the sentimental exaltation of childhood innocence increased during the Renaissance.[67] What looks like a rehearsal for the Romantic revolution was held two centuries earlier, and the "nostalgia for the object" that Paul de Man perceives in Romanticism was no less active in this earlier generation of nature-lovers.[68] The conflicts that the Romantic theorist Schiller articulated so well in *On Naive and Sentimental Poetry* (1795)—between a consciousness that assumed it was directly absorbed in its milieu and one that mourned or jeered over the lost connection to nature—were clearly manifest and deeply troubling to Shakespeare, Marvell, and some of their fellow practitioners in the pastoral mode.

Pastoral is thus another cultural phenomenon explicable as a response—often simultaneously as an inscribed banner of protest and a blank flag of surrender—to the burdensome knowledge of mediation. Pastoral "had an enormous vogue in the Renaissance,"[69] and this book seeks to explain that vogue, which seems to me overdetermined in the collective dream-work of Elizabethan and Jacobean England. E. K., Spenser's mysterious first critic, claimed that pastoral sought "to unfold great matter of argument covertly";[70] although it can be (in the mode of Mantuan) matters of theological politics, it may be philosophical as well. W. W. Greg (among many others) sees pastoral as "the reaction against the world that is too much with us";[71] my point is that, in another sense, pastoral reacts against a suspicion that the world is no longer with us at all, and maybe never has been. Hallett Smith, claims that "The central meaning of pastoral is the rejection of the aspiring mind";[72] Smith is setting pastoral *otium* against the Elizabethan ambitions typified by Tamburlaine, but I would use the same terms to set it against the quasi-solipsistic epistemology confronted by Descartes. The question again is whether we can get the human mind out of the path between ourselves and the material world by retreating to some primal and simple version of that world.

The answer is generally discouraging. If knowledge in pastoral "is often a present-tense, physical experience of relief from the disappointingly incomplete world of abstractions,"[73] it would naturally have been deeply alluring and no less deeply disappointing. The ostensible quest for simplicity characteristic of pastoral is also a quest for truth—which several great Renaissance artists remind us is actually almost infinitely, almost unbearably complex. Whom the gods would drive mad, they first grant a wish to know the plain truth of things.

From its earliest days, pastoral has in fact been at war with its own claims to simplicity,[74] perhaps suggesting the way the human desire for simplicity is itself inauthentic—or at least a rash-wish motif that leads only toward death, as the surrender of individual cognition. When nature calls, it calls collect. Early in the history of the Renaissance pastoral, Jacopo Sannazaro's *Arcadia* opens its prologue with a preference for wild forests over cultivated orchards, but later "has his shepherd Sincero approach a mysterious temple where the pediment is *painted* like Vitruvius's exedra, with a landscape of 'woods and hills, very beautiful and rich in leafy trees and a thousand kinds of flowers' " so that Sincero can "know what this arcadia was actually supposed to look like."[75] We can push back much further and still see the same artfully engineered redundancies keeping nature at several removes. The prologue to Longus's *Daphnis and Chloe* claims as his inspiration nothing natural, but instead "a painting that told a love story," to which he felt compelled "to write a verbal equivalent . . . As a source of pleasure to the human race—something to heal the sick":[76] in other words, an experience multiply mediated through culture. The first line of Theocritus's first Idyll—generally recognized as the earliest extant pastoral—has a pine tree singing sweet, whispering music. Is this a first instance of sweet nothings whispered in the ear of a helplessly doting nature-lover? A symptom of the disease of anthropomorphism by which pastoral defeats its stated purpose of surrendering to nature and thereby escaping human complications? Is this the original sin, passed down to all its heirs, by which pastoral implicitly forbids itself the primal garden? Was there never a primary pastoral, as scholars speak of primary epic, unselfconscious of its own belated literary character?

As Raymond Williams points out, the pastoral idyll forever retreats with the horizon. Massinger's *A New Way to Pay Old Debts* and *The City Madam* (about 1622 and 1632) already complain of a "new commercialism . . . breaking the old landed settlement and its virtues"; and then one can look back and find similar urgent warnings in Bastard's *Chrestoleros* (1598), More's *Utopia* (1516), and so on.[77] Pastoralists must try to remember something they never really knew. Paul Alpers begins a book called *What Is Pastoral?* with Irving Howe misremembering Primo Levi not quite remembering a verse in which Dante's character tries to remember his humanity; Alpers notes the parallels with Virgil's Ninth Eclogue, where again the shepherds seem to recall only fragments of the beloved verses, at once quoting and imitating his original, Theocritus. It seems ironic that, when René Rapin writes his treatise on pastoral in the midseventeenth century, he says he is seeking "Things and solid truth" by trying to trace this literary mode back to its origins. And yet Rapin seems to sense the futility of this quest: "Pastorals were the invention of the simplicity and innocence of [the] Golden Age, if there was any such."[78]

Georgic does not really bloom until late in the seventeenth century;[79] perhaps its ethos of a diligently controlled nature could not thrive until its ambient culture gave up on the allure of a more leisurely pastoral premised on human passivity. With the acceptance of agrarian capitalism came a parallel emphasis on empire rather than exploration: imperialism is the georgic of the geopolitical earth, replacing the fantasy of a rediscovered Eden. It constitutes a concession that there is no easy road back, no second innocence: that there is always human work involved in any embrace of the land. Pastoral yearning—like the Renaissance arts and sciences—is haunted by Zeno's paradox, by the tantalizing approach that never quite becomes an encounter, eventually exhausting the hapless racer with a recognition that his task is impossible; a recognition that only becomes clear when the race seems nearly won. We know that Achilles will reach the finish line or the arrow reach the target, but—this is why it is a paradox—our rational intellects struggle to explain how, and struggle harder the closer we look.

Late-Renaissance culture zeroed in on its natural target with five senses, but (as Montaigne warns)[80] the distance and the distortion of parallax never quite reached zero. Asking how many approximations it takes to screw a bright shining truth into place, they surrounded the beloved foe with similes: a polygon of infinite sides that is nonetheless not quite a perfect circle.[81] Jaques's "*ducdame*" called fools into a circle around an empty word. "The world Cusanus presents, one where the search for empirical as well as theological precision would lead to endless approximation, might provoke a Neoplatonist to cry out for such transcendence"[82]—but it was a forlorn cry. The positivist project, which recent scholarship (mostly condemnatory) sees as founded on the Enlightenment and emergent only in the early nineteenth century, had already been given up for lost by Renaissance poets.

Despite his reputation for Elizabethan Protestant militancy, which *The Faerie Queene* would largely seem to justify, Spenser's emotional mode is largely elegiac: the systematically antiqued tone conveys the burdens of belatedness, and the madly populated world of the poem feels oddly empty, lacking any center or substance except perhaps Mutability itself. The "salvage knight" who seems to triumph on behalf of raw nature in 4.4 proves to be Arthegall in disguise; in 6.8, the Salvage Nation as a whole confronts Serena with pastoral gone to seed, and bad seed too. Pastoral unease characterized by belatedness was hardly new—even Hesiod wistfully commented that he had missed the Golden Age—but in Spenser it is especially plangent and pervasive. His "Ruins of Time" suggests that nothing can satisfy the soul tormented by the memory of a lost Eden: "Since that I sawe this gardine wasted quite, / That where it was scarce seemed anie sight"—nothing to see, but perhaps also no longer any vision (stanza 3). Similarly, his "Ruins of Rome" delves sadly for a past whose glories and self-assurance prove irretrievable. The only legacy is a sense of cultural disinheritance: "But that this nothing, which they have thee left, / Makes the world wonder, what they from thee reft" (stanza 13).

To begin filling these gaps, and thereby to envision any positive future, Spenser feels he must gain access to some posited originary, generative moment of the past. This surely anticipates Milton's quest at the start of *Paradise Lost* (and again at the start of Book 7) for identity with the shepherd who recorded the Holy Scripture—a stance itself reflected in the competition between Satan and Christ for the authority that would come from being prior, closest to God's beginning. Spenser's mission of retrieving the glory of a ruined world seems inseparable from the mission of recovering the voice of the ancient poet: "O that I had the *Thracian* poets harpe. . . . Or that I had *Amphions* instrument," or could write

By pattern of great Virgil's spirit divine!
I would assay with that which in me is,
To builde, with level of my loftie style,
That which no hands can evermore compyle.[83]

This dual redemptive mission—back to natural pastures and back to pastoral-poetic origins—recurs in the June eclogue of *The Shepheardes Calender* lamenting the death of Daphnis:

But if on me some little drops would flow
Of that the spring was in his learned head,
I soon would learn these woods to wail my woe,
And teach these trees their trickling tears to shed.

(stanza 12)

In lamenting another paradise lost (or at least an idealized shepherd lost), this speaker simultaneously seeks access to the original fountain of that prior shepherd's poetic voice, and, like Marvell's mower, threatens to enforce the pathetic fallacy on a nature that has not yet adequately responded to human loss.

The Vision of the Graces disappears when Spenser's Calidore tries to understand it too directly—a mild version of the emblematic fate of Actaeon—and what replaces that lost vision is Colin Clout's Petrarchan love song to Rosalind. What is left for Calidore, as for Marvell's mower, once the direct view is lost, is a kind of parable of that loss encoded in heterosexual desire—at least, in sexual desires that enforce the recognition that the world is hetero to the self. As Peter Harrison notes in his excellent work on science in the Reformation, "Several of the Fathers had taught that Adam originally enjoyed a sexless state, and that his Fall was occasioned by his division into two beings—male and female. The Fall was nothing else than the separation of Eve from Adam."[84] This perpetually incomplete yearning toward a source is partly Platonic (the hermaphroditic conception of recovered immortality in the *Symposium*), and partly Neoplatonic, most obviously so in the *Foure Hymnes*—"In Honour of Beautie," stanzas 5–13, for example, or "Of Heavenly Beauty," stanza 39, where again the pain of mediation and incompletion seems to outweigh even the bliss of anticipated reunion with the absolute:

Ne from thenceforth doth any fleshly sense,
Or idle thought of earthly things remaine:
But all that earst seemd sweet, seemes now offense,
And all that pleased earst, now seemes to paine.
Their joy, their comfort, their desire, their gaine,
Is fixed all on that which now they see,
All other sights but fayned shadows bee.

So we are dealing with shadows within shadows within shadows. The work of art is a copy of a thing—a presence—which itself copies imperfectly an idea of a thing. Moreover—here again the term "Early Modern" might again come in handy, though Thomas Greene's *The Light in Troy* shows these anxieties arising from Renaissance humanism and haunting its poetic responses to the classics— the elite culture was evidently beginning to notice an antechamber to the

Platonic cave, as nascent cognitive science suggested that, even in the presence of the thing, human perception of that object is itself a copy, a mental representation, created by a complex overlay of electrochemical systems (in some regards like the replication technology in a modern office), and sustained (research on memory suggests) as a schematic not unlike compressed data on a computer, with information stored in algorithms to exclude essentially redundant or irrelevant information. Readers are left, as at the provisional end of *The Faerie Queene*, with a rather forlorn yearning for a certain and stable "Sabaoths sight" that would lift them out of a shifting and shimmering universe ruled by "*Mutabilitie.*" The effort to channel (as if with lightning rods) the entire problem of representation, of the second-handedness of the object as image, into the figures of Archimago and Duessa, seems like whistling in an epistemological graveyard.

Furthermore, as Spenser's Garden of Adonis makes clear (3.6.29–50), nature is a literal graveyard for all who grow from mortal seed. Spenser's Fradubio, dubious about the choice between his true lady and the disguised Duessa, sees the essential difference only when he catches Duessa "Bathing herself in origane and thyme: / A filthy foule old woman I did vew" (1.2.40). The emphasis on age and (three lines earlier) on the corrective force of "Prime" days activates puns on "origin" and "time" in this herbal formula. Duessa then, in a twist on the Actaeon story, transforms Fradubio into a tree, a metamorphosis he reports in terms reiterating the late-Renaissance psychopathology (which we will see in Marvell's mower) that insistently links the allure of a woman's "neather partes," a man's uneasy re-absorption into nature, and the oblivion and confinement of mortalist death:

> The divelish hag by chaunges of my cheare
> Perceiv'd my thought, and drownd in sleepie night,
> With wicked herbes and ointments did besmeare
> My bodie all, through charmes and magicke might,
> That all my senses were bereaved quight:
> Then brought she me into this desert waste,
> And by my wretched lovers side me pight,
> Where now enclosed in wooden wals full faste,
> Banisht from living wights, our wearie dayes we waste.
>   (1.2.42)

The cure for flawed perception—with *eros* standing in for all such errors—is also the punishment: the deadly embrace of nature itself.

Though I cannot do him justice here, it is worth noting that Milton brings the self-refuting function of pastoral to its logical conclusion. He begins "Lycidas"—the suicide note of the pastoral elegy—by complaining that it is too soon to write the poem he intends, though the obvious point seems to be that it is too late. There may be more to this than anxiety over the arc of a literary career. If "Lycidas" can be aptly (if not encompassingly) defined as "apocalyptic pastoral,"[85] it may be partly because those in despair of recovering origins (in the face of death, loss, and ignorance) must settle for anticipating conclusions: teleology now expresses itself as a pastoral looking into a mirror set at the end of time, a true if transposed image of primal purity and direct knowledge, positing (as the means of simplification) an end-stopped future instead of an end-stopped past. What was lost with the world of lambs is restored by the Lamb of God, whose resurrection takes the place of cyclical rebirth, and who sees through to essences in a non-contingent act of judgment.

For the most part, the pastoral stayed past and (except when functioning as covert political critique) out of touch. The legacy of the Golden Age was essentially verbal; its imaginative landscape was strewn with lyrical dialogues, and in lyrical dialogues it kept almost coming to life. The nostalgia for a world of unmediated things manifested itself as a fabric of language. With the advent of colonial expeditions in the Renaissance, however, there was suddenly an objective correlative to these words, a real materiality to be found to verify those words, something for them to signify, something (as several scholars have observed) not "back then" but "out there."[86] As Harry Levin writes, "The Middle Ages had buried the golden age under the conception of Eden; the Renaissance not only revived the original conception, but ventured forth on a quest to objectify it. When its locus shifted from the temporal to the spatial, it became an attainable goal and a challenge to the explorers."[87] Thus "chronological primitivism" gave way to "cultural primitivism"; but the destination proved endlessly elusive, psychologically as well as geographically.[88] Ralegh thought himself close to the navel of the earth; Columbus spotted its nipple; Drayton placed the primal paradise in Virginia, while Hakluyt and Vespucci believed it farther south, and others proposed the North Pole or even out in space.[89] The idealist-primitivist vision of a trip to the Virginia colony is ridiculed, in *Eastward Ho*, when the bold adventurers wash up on a Thames garbage-dump before even reaching the open ocean—the objective correlative to a variety of Jonsonian disillusionments.

The cognitive discomforts of multiculturalism were an inevitable side-effect of imperial expansion; by a coincidence that may have felt like something more (because in both cases a native innocence associated with the homeland was lost), deforestation was another inevitable side effect.[90] Moreover, as in most multicultural crises, the dominant culture had to define the other in its own pre-existent vocabularies. Stephen Greenblatt has described the Native Americans striving to understand the "invisible bullets" with which the Spaniards were slaying them in such numbers; he has also suggested that some reciprocal problem would, though of course less brutally, trouble the Spaniards themselves. To describe what they were finding in the wilds of the New World, the Europeans often looked to their old poetry. Once "brought face to face with genuine primitives"—if that is really what they were—the colonizers resorted to a sophisticated literature of primitivism, as Harry Levin has observed. Again the drive toward unspoiled nature and the drive toward direct realism fail together. The late Renaissance could not look on "natural" men in any unmediated way: "Nothing like them had thus far been imprinted upon the European consciousness, which was therefore bound to eke out its first impressions by drawing upon its imagination—and, even more, upon the precarious analogy of a well remembered myth." This is why comparison was, according to some Renaissance rhetoricians, an inherently limited and prejudicial trope. "The discoverer who has looked upon *terra incognita* must explain it in terms which those who have never been there can readily comprehend."[91] The way these limiting attributes of simile entangle colonial, sexual, and natural appetites will be a principal focus of my reading of *As You Like It.*

PART II

Paradoxes
Alienation from Nature in
English Literature

Chapter 3
As You Liken It: Simile in the Forest

God said, Let us make man in our image according to our likenes, and let them rule over the fish of the sea, and over the foule of the heaven, and over the beastes, & over all the earth.
—Genesis 1:26, *Geneva Bible*

A Similitude is a likenesse when two thinges, or more then two, are so compared and resembled together, that they both in some one propertie seeme like. Oftentimes brute Beastes, and thinges that have no life, minister great matter in this behalfe. Therefore, those that delite to prove thinges by Similitudes, must learne to knowe the nature of divers beastes, of mettalles, of stones, and al such as have any vertue in them, and be applied to mans life.
—Thomas Wilson, *The Arte of Rhetorique*

For why should I presume to prefer my conceit and imagination, in affirming that a thing is thus or thus in its own nature, because it seemeth to me to be so; before the conceit of other living creatures, who may as well think it to be otherwise in its own nature, because it appeareth otherwise to them than it doth to me?
—Sir Walter Ralegh, "The Sceptic"

In the four syllables of its title, *As You Like It* contains both the words used to signal simile, and places "like" as a barrier between "you" and "it." From that title onward, this pastoral play is permeated with the idea of likeness, which is to say, imperfect identity—and the way that both "liking" and "likening," even in apparently benign forms, necessarily impose on their living objects. Shakespeare describes the chronic nostalgia for nature as a sentimental manifestation of Pyrrhonist anxieties, the suspicion that we can know things only as we liken them, never in or as themselves.

As You Like It emerged from a culture I have depicted as infatuated with hopes of recovering some original and authentic reality. Elizabethan theology was inquiring about the primitive church and shattering iconic representations.

Gardening manuals boasted of reproducing Eden: "Thus we approach the resemblance of Paradise."[1] Political pamphlets—including those of the great radical Gerrard Winstanley, who suggested that digging could extirpate Original Sin—contrasted recent enclosure controversies and urban dystopia with a lost organic community. The fact that the Royal Society, at the opposite end of the period's political spectrum, would offer a similarly regressive idealism suggests how pervasive this nostalgia became in seventeenth-century England.[2] As fears about the substitution of a primarily urban society for a primarily rural one blended into fears about the substitution of representations for reality—the enclosure-controversy of the self—pastoral drama was well situated to sample the blend. While philosophers wrestled with a resurgence of skepticism, philologists strove to recover urtexts, Baconian scientists sought a transparent descriptive rhetoric, and painters tested the limits of verisimilitude, poets were bemoaning their artistic belatedness, particularly in the rediscovered pastoral mode. If my argument conflates a variety of conflicting definitions of nature—as Eden, as fauna, as entropy, and as reality—my excuse is that Shakespeare's play does too, and, in doing so, echoes the characteristic cries of a culture in the agony of a major epistemological transformation. *King Lear* will demonstrate how agonizing the shifting definitions of nature could actually become.

The multiple and elaborate explorations of the polarity of art and nature in *As You Like It* are mapped analogically onto a polarity of the linguistically entangled human mind and the material objects which that mind can know only partially, only by the constraints of comparison—the vocabularies and categories of mind people use to carve the sensory feast into edible bites. As in *Richard II*, *Hamlet*, and *The Winter's Tale*, Shakespeare's story of the Fall is always partly a story about the irreversible human fall into the mediations of self-consciousness and language, whether in terms of ontogeny or phylogeny, childhood or evolution. The arc of the human experience of knowledge is, in this regard, the same as the Christian story of humanity's exile from the Garden. The pastoral genre is stubbornly artificial, as if to acknowledge that our hunger for simplicity is actually a symptom of sophistication, a self-conscious desire at once expressed and prevented by language.[3] We gaze lovingly at ponds, but so did Narcissus; and the gates of Eden are firmly closed. *As You Like It* begins with that originary exclusion: "As I remember, Adam, it was upon this fashion bequeath'd me . . ." (1.1.1). Efforts to bridge, through simile, the gap between ourselves and nature, and between our minds and reality, again only confirm that there is really no way back.

The world we compose in our consciousness is never the same as the world in itself—too obvious a point to seem worth making, and yet a mote to trouble the mind's eye.[4] Though it would not receive effective philosophical articulation until some forty years later, by Pierre Gassendi,[5] that mote seemed to be troubling Shakespeare's vision in 1599, as he moved into a theater called the Globe and wrote, not only *As You Like It*, but also *Henry V*, a history play obsessed with the difference between reality and its representations. *Hamlet*—arguably the most epistemologically skeptical play of all—was probably next: a universe of rumors, forgeries, mistrusted ghosts, unanswerable questions, provocative simulations, plays within plays within plays, a sky "like a weasel" to one and "like a whale" to another (3.2.379–81), but out there only a numinous cloud, a ghost reporting irrecoverable losses. According to the Platonic vocabulary, it was a time to acknowledge shadows; to recognize what it means to live—as Duke Senior does—in a cave.

And to die into a grave. Does it profit a man to lose consciousness and regain a simple relationship with the material universe? What death teaches is that conscious knowledge and complete symbiosis with nature are mutually exclusive. Little wonder the late-Renaissance quest to achieve them in parallel was so consistently baffled. Montaigne agrees that "if simplicity leads us on the way to having no pain, it leads us to a very happy state," but adds that the logical conclusion of the Epicurean program might thus be a collapse into "insensibility and nonexistence."[6] In *Paradise Lost* (7.775–78), Adam flirts with death as perfect return to Mother Nature's physical embrace, but then recognizes, not entirely happily, that humanity comprises something not so easily resolved. We may seek perfect knowledge of nature, but it knows us carnally; and (as Marvell's mower Damon discovers) throws shockingly unsympathetic welcome-home parties over our fallen bodies. When Rosalind observes that "Men have died from time to time, and worms have eaten them, but not for love" (4.1.106–8), the final clause may refer to the motives of the worms as well as of the men—especially in a play that often compares the love between men and women with the love between humanity and nature, and that asks how we reconcile that claim to love nature with our compulsion to consume it (in the form of venison, for example). Is vermiculation nature's way of loving us back—that is, pursuing an appetite for our bodies that constitutes a critique of men's claims to love women or nature in any more benign and sophisticated way?

Starving and freezing indeed bring us back to nature, as Duke Senior observes; so do snakes and lionesses. Death is in Arden, as in Arcadia; Touchstone's "now am I in Arden" (2.4.16), may recall the ominous associations of *et in Arcadia ego*.[7] "The general challenger" Charles echoes nature's general challenge to pastoral sentimentalists, the challenge of the play to its regressive audience: "Where is this young gallant that is so desirous to lie with his mother earth?" (1.2.200–201). Though this conflation of incest and suicide invites psychoanalytic reading, the philosophical implications are no less compelling. Charles's question applies both to wrestling him and to embracing nature, and young gallants are still on camping trips, nature trails, whitewater rafts, all for a closer walk with Mama Gaia. Touchstone's lament about being stuck in the forest could speak for anyone imagining a voluntary return to the Garden: "The more fool I. When I was at home, I was in a better place, but travelers must be content" (2.4.16–18). Mortals are always uneasily in transit, until they rest in peace, their most natural destination. As Rosalind warns Orlando about Charles, the "odds" and the ghoulish scorecard all suggest that nature is an insurmountable opponent, defying us all and defeating all comers. And even our rare, hard-won victories—like Orlando's over Charles, like those of many Shakespearean heroes over natural limitations—soon prove to be dangerous defeats. Even after imposing "a fall" on that powerful opponent, we ourselves remain fallen, condemned (like Orlando) simply, unfairly, because we are our parents' children. Individual existence and consciousness are uprisings against a biological nature that will outlast them, even though they are its offspring. Our little lives are rounded with a sleep—or something like it.

Act 2, Scene 1

Editors beginning with Theobald have often emended Duke Senior's "Here feel we not the penalty of Adam" (2.1.5, Folio) to "Here feel we *but* the penalty of Adam." On this textual crux rests the play's most persistent question: can we redeem ourselves by returning to nature, or are we cursed if we abide there? The emendation makes sense: Duke Senior clearly *does* feel the pain of nature's enmity. But other editors resist the change, for two structurally similar reasons: first, they believe that the Duke may be saying that the pain doesn't bother him because it is a good, honest, primal, outdoorsy pain, and, second, they believe that they should stick to the original reading unless the sense absolutely forbids it. The defenders of the Folio's "not" are thus like the Duke Senior they thereby preserve: they are willing to endure some discomfort for the sake of recovering what seems like the true, original, rough-hewn experience, whether of nature or of Shakespeare.

I favor the original "not," but principally for its ironic value: it signals how deeply this displaced court is in denial. What follows from Duke Senior and his lords proves that the penalty of Adam is fully in force; as the words suggest, Arden resembles Eden, but is not Eden, and the difference between likeness and identity will haunt all the play's similes, facsimiles included. The Duke here boasts how happily his displaced court has escaped "painted pomp" and given itself over completely to an authentic experience of nature. He then proves himself a liar at almost every word. The wind isn't "chiding," it has no "fang" to "bite" with, and it certainly isn't a "counsellor" seeking to "persuade" (2.1.6–11). By the time this ostentatiously alliterative speech ends six lines later, the anthropomorphizing—a pastoral symptom since the originary moment of the genre, the first line of Theocritus's first idyll—has become epidemic: the Duke is finding "tongues in trees, books in the running brooks, / Sermons in stones, and good in every thing" (2.1.16–17).[8]

Amiens, putting the most amiable face on this, praises the Duke's ability to "translate" his experience of untamed nature into "so sweet a style" (2.1.19–20). In classical and Renaissance rhetoric, *translatio* was the term for metaphor, as *similitudo* was for comparison; etymologically, "to translate" is "to carry across." Farmers regularly used "stiles" to cross into animal compounds, and the Duke's translation across the human-animal boundary threatens to produce an ass-headed monster, as it does when Bottom is "translated" in the forest of *A Midsummer Night's Dream* (3.1.119); Jaques will soon assert that to flee to nature, as Duke Senior has, is to "turn ass" (2.5.51). This, we shall see, is the pot's critique of the kettle. But what makes the Duke asinine is his assumption that he can cross this border, into the non-human, so easily. Toward Mother Nature as toward Lady Fortune, the Senecan stoicism the Duke praises is a kind of epistemological aggression, as the free mind subjects everything to itself, itself to nothing.

"Come, shall we go and kill us venison?" the Duke then asks, regretting this necessary violence against the "native burghers of this desert city" (2.1.21, 23). Again he is presuming, not only anthropomorphically, but (more subtly) anthropocentrically: "desert" defines the place by human abandonment, and the deer are not "venison"—animals hunted for game, or (more often) their edible flesh—until his need and aggression make them so.[9] Even before the hunt begins, they are already no longer their animal selves, already a product for consumption by the human mouth, through the presumption of the human mind. Things are named by our need for them. As Martin Heidegger observed, a threatened humanity "postures as lord of the earth. In this way the illusion comes to prevail that everything man encounters exists only insofar as it is his construct . . . it seems as though man everywhere and always encounters only himself."[10]

That this perceptual crime against nature is distinct from the more perceptible one becomes clear in Jaques's reaction. The lord who reports that reaction is himself incapable of turning off the anthropomorphic switch that generates antique peeping roots, brawling brooks, and a poor "sequestered" stag in a "leathern coat" (this resembles the Duke's slip: "leather" generally meant skin prepared for use by tanning rather than that on a living animal) who has been hurt by "the hunter's aim" (a revealingly solipsistic metonymy for an arrow). When Duke Senior asks, "But what said Jaques? / Did he not moralize this spectacle?" the lord replies, "O yes, into a thousand similes" (2.1.43–45). Capturing the deer is certainly more brutal, but captioning its picture may be no less appropriative. Which has done more insidious violence to pristine nature as a collectivity, during its long siege by humanity: shooting it with arrows or shattering it into similes? The answer may not be obvious, but the question brings Shakespearean drama into the active field of ecocriticism in a duly ambivalent way, without blunting the literary works into tools of facile social advocacy. Shakespeare sustains the moral tension by evoking at once the myth of the English greenwood, associated with the peaceful co-existence of the classes in local communities, and the myth of the hunt, which (though communal in German culture) was generally associated in England with abusive central authority.[11] The ethical quality of human relations thus implicates the human relationship to other animals.

But deep-ecology movements, which attempt to abjure the human perspective and expiate even seemingly benign human interventions, are very different from popular or reform environmentalism, which tends (like Jaques here) toward sentimental identification with particular lovely creatures rather than anything arduously philosophical (like Jaques later).[12] Though the deer-hunt scenes offer some emotional aid and comfort to the animal rights movement, the play as a whole undercuts that endorsement by demonstrating that such pervasive anthropomorphizing sentiments may invade and constrain the animal world more insidiously than sporadic open warfare—just as a Petrarchan worshipper can cause a woman more deep and protracted misery than a loudmouthed misogynist transient.

Jaques's projection of his own social complaints onto this animal (2.1.46–59) is interesting characterologically; what is interesting philosophically is the parallel suggestion that he could not cease to do so even if he were a sincere nature-lover—indeed, that he becomes all the more invasive the more he tries to be sympathetic.[13] The "bankrupt" but fashionably "velvet" deer, abandoned by companions "full of the pasture," does not need Jaques's tears, any more than the stream needs those of the deer (2.1.46–49). Jaques concludes (the lord reports) that Duke Senior's court

Are mere usurpers, tyrants, and what's worse,
To fright the animals and to kill them up
In their assigned and native dwelling place.

Duke Senior: And did you leave him in this contemplation?
Second Lord: We did, my lord, weeping and commenting
Upon the sobbing deer.

(2.1.61–66)

Jaques's position, leaning over the stream with this deer, signals the narcissistic self-involvement of his claim to care for an other (a signal confirmed by
the joke at 3.2.285–90 about Jaques seeing his own reflection in the stream as he
looks for a fool). He calls the hunters "usurpers," but comparisons between human beings and other creatures, and projections of qualities across that boundary, are themselves, according to George Puttenham, "common usurpations."[14]
Jaques has inserted himself in the place of the deer as assiduously, and arguably
as uselessly or even tyrannically, as the hunter who will later have the hide of the
deer placed over his skin and the horns of the deer placed on his head
(4.2.10–11).[15] We may indeed weep—I don't mean to belittle the empathetic impulse here—but we are always commenting as well. As his name may imply (a
"jakes" was a privy or outhouse), Jaques is, to put it politely, rather full of pasture himself.

Still, this empathetic impulse may help explain Jaques's eventual decision
to "put on a religious life" and to try to learn from "these convertites" such as
Duke Frederick who have left their former selves behind (5.4.181–85)—a decision that seems to shock Jaques's comrades and the play's editors alike. As others arrive from court into the forest and rediscover themselves, Jaques takes the
next step, toward rediscovering something beyond himself. The quest for transcendence, for sorrowful thought and absolute truth and self-overcoming, inevitably looks like folly in a comic context. Jaques's maunderings about the deer
may sound quite different, however, if one hears in them a new translation of
the exiled speaker of Psalm 42, who had once enjoyed singing and feasting with
his comrades, but for lack of divine certainty has fallen into a melancholy, like
that of a hart fleeing to the water. Jaques had been "a libertine / As sensual as the
brutish sting itself" (2.7.65–66);[16] and one analogue that may have been on
Shakespeare's mind here is the medieval figure of St. Hubert, who once held "a
prominent position among the gay courtiers . . . a worldling and a lover of pleasure." When "The tyrannical conduct of Ebroin caused a general emigration of
the nobles and others," Hubert joined it, until one day,

As he was pursuing a magnificent stag, the animal turned and, as the pious legend nar-
rates, he was astounded at perceiving a crucifix between its antlers, while he heard a
voice saying: "Hubert, unless thou turnest to the Lord, and leadest an holy life, thou shalt
quickly go down into hell." Hubert dismounted, prostrated himself and said, "Lord,

what wouldst Thou have me do?" He received the answer, "Go and seek Lambert, and he will instruct you." Accordingly, he . . . renounced all his honors and his military rank, and gave up his birthright to the Duchy of Aquitaine to his younger brother.

Eventually St. Hubert went seeking converts "in the fastnesses of the forest of Ardennes."[17]

Like so many before him, and like Duke Frederick shortly after, Jaques is inspired by the wilderness to seek more absolute truth, to leave behind his likes.[18] Like the speaker of the psalm, Jaques abandons his "sensual" self (2.7.66) and averts his eyes from the facile matchings by waiting them out in Duke Senior's "abandon'd cave" (5.4.196): "from the vulgar, civil and ordinary man he was, he becomes as free as a deer, and an inhabitant of the wilderness . . . in the unpretentious rooms of the cavernous mountains, where he contemplates . . . free of ordinary lusts, and converses mostly freely with the divinity."[19] This is not, however, a modern rhapsody on the conversion of Jaques, but instead Giordano Bruno's commentary on the transformation of Actaeon—the classical archetype of the man who saw too much, the hunter who forfeited language, and therefore community, and therefore life, because he gazed (rashly, desirously) on a divine form in a woodland stream.

Actaeon and Others

Dressing the victorious hunter in the coat and the horns of the stag he has killed is the logical culmination, but also a brutal parody, of this effort to enter into the unmediated experience of nature, to pluck out the mystery of the hart. That costume also evokes the claim of many humanist critiques of tyrannical hunters who "settinge all humanitie apart, become salvage beastes, and through monstrous naughtinesse of nature, are channged like *Acteon* into the nature of Beasts."[20] Ovid recounts that, as punishment for seeing Diana and her nymphs in their lovely nakedness, the hunter Actaeon is transformed into a hart: "by and by doth spread / A payre of lively olde Harts hornes upon his sprinckled head," according to Golding's translation, and Diana then "wrappes him in a hairie hyde."[21] Ashamed to return to the palace but afraid to remain in the woods—a plausible metaphor for the human dilemma, trapped between culture and nature—Actaeon is then fatally hunted by his own dogs. After citing Stesichorus's version, in which Diana sewed Actaeon "within the skin of a Stag," George Sandys then offers his own interpretation, whereby "Actaeon . . . puts off the minde of a man, and degenerates into a beast; while hee dayly frequents the wild woods to contend with such enimies."[22] Indeed, Duke Senior's entire court looks notably like the summer bachelor herd they describe,[23] and the horn-sprouting Actaeon is a demonic figure that threatens to possess not only Jaques and the lord who killed the deer, but also Orlando and perhaps Touchstone as well. Even old Adam becomes a fawn in this forest (2.7.128). By diligently blurring these boundaries, Shakespeare addresses the fear that we might (like colonizers who "go native") lose ourselves if we engage with wilderness too entirely.[24]

Dizzyingly alongside this suggestion, however—in Ovid as in Shakespeare—stands a contrary suggestion that these invaders are so absorbed in self that they can receive no true impression of an other. Ovid's description of the metamorphosing Actaeon foreshadows the story of Narcissus only a hundred lines later, but also anticipates Jaques's description of, and identification with, the weeping deer at the edge of the stream:

> But when he saw his face
> And horned temples in the brooke, he would haue cryde alas,
> But as for then no kinde of speach out of his lippes could passe.
> He sight and brayde: for that was then the speach that did remaine,
> And downe the eyes that were not his, his bitter teares did raine.
> No part remayned (saue his minde) of that he earst had beene. (lines 236–41)

And even that mind, now obliged to recognize its incongruity with the body, is transformed. Ovid implies that "the secret [Actaeon] witnessed when he saw Diana bathing is the secret of self-consciousness."[25]

For Actaeon as for Adam and Eve, the cost of knowledge—maybe the costly knowledge itself—is self-awareness, the enfoldings of reflexivity represented by the serpent. When they are expelled from Eden in Theodor Boeyermans' painting (Stuttgart), they flee, like Actaeon in contemporary depictions, into the uneasy greeting of a pack of hunting dogs. Henry More's *Conjectura Cabbalistica* (1653) speculated that God put the fallen Adam into "in the skins of wilde beasts" (Genesis 3:21) to signal he had fallen to the condition of other animals, but also refused to let Adam settle comfortably into that bestial identity.[26] Several Renaissance commentaries associate Actaeon with impudent inquiries into the secrets of nature, and Alexander Ross's version of the warning stresses that one never really escapes one's own mind anyway: "pry not too much into the secrets of heaven, least with Actaeon, your understanding be taken from you; & ye become a prey to the beastly imaginations of your owne brain."[27] Like Adam's, Actaeon's is a crime of presumptuous knowing; it recalls the Biblical warning that to look on God directly is to die. Luther calls nature "the mask of God," and both warnings suggest that perceiving the full reality of divine creation, unfiltered by dark glasses or cognitive categories, would consume soul and synapse alike.[28] The truth hurts. Pierre Bersuire's commentary on Actaeon in the Christianizing *Ovid moralisé* "revives an ancient divine interpretation of the story that will reappear as Renaissance Platonism, i.e., that the hero enters upon visionary experience and as a result must perish."[29]

Actaeon appears prominently in Giordano Bruno's *Degli eroici furori*, where (as in many other Neoplatonic texts) the erotic quest provides a model for the hermeneutic quest[30]—or at least provides a first stage of the upward journey, which (like the bulky first stage of a rocket) must be jettisoned if the journey is to continue beyond the earth's atmosphere. Actaeon is the hunter diverted from his pursuit of natural game to the pursuit of divine beauty—which turns him finally against himself, as the quest for epistemological perfection founders on the jagged rocks of psychological imperfection. Like Orlando, he must undergo an elaborate education before seeing the woodland beauty out of her forester clothing, and then he must recognize her by likeness.

According to the gloss on Bruno's initial Actaeon sonnet, the hunter discovering Diana in her bath indicates the way the quester seeks out "the intelligible modes of ideal concepts" by exploring nature, and may discover ultimate beauty and truth "in the mirror of similitudes."[31] Bruno deems it "impossible for anyone to see the sun, the universal Apollo and absolute light as the supreme and most excellent species; but very possible to see its shadow, its Diana, the world, the universe, the nature which is in things." His dogs must "devour this Actaeon, and make him dead to the vulgar" in order to "free him from the snares of the perturbing senses and the fleshly prison of matter, so that he no longer sees his Diana as through a glass or window."[32] You can know the essence of the inviolable goddess of the forest—provided you are willing to be eaten back up by the forces of nature you once seemed to rule. You can know nature from the inside—from the inside of its belly—but that is hardly knowing. This may be why the goddess taunts Actaeon (in Ovid's version), "Go, tell the world you have seen Diana unrobed, if you can," at the moment she has taken away his powers of speech.[33]

No wonder Actaeon, in Titian's painting *Diana Surprised* and again in Maratti and Dughet's version of the same scene, appears to be flinching away from the sight. The godhead, according to St. John of the Cross—a contemporary of Shakespeare's—is "like to the hart wounded by thy love," but the absolute that the soul seeks, "she cannot receive without its almost costing her her life."[34] Cavalcanti, characteristically haunted by the barrier between human perception and eternal truth, suggests something similar about the object of his desire:

O God, what she looks like when she turns her eyes
Let Love say, for I could not describe it. . . .

Our mind was never so lofty
And never was such salvation granted us
That we could really have knowledge of her.[35]

Idolatry is the shield of Perseus, in which we can stare at the face (of God as of Gorgon) that would otherwise turn us to stone. The radical Protestant iconoclast Andreas Karlstadt stressed that "When God rises up, all likenesses fall. Where images sit, God cannot be."[36] Even the prophetically skeptical Cusanus recognized the incompatibility of similitude with divine truth: "if anyone should set forth any likeness and say that Thou wert to be imagined as resembling it, I know in like manner that that is no likeness of Thee."[37] If you see it, it isn't really God; if you know it, it isn't exactly true.

If a little knowledge is indeed a dangerous thing, total knowledge seems much more so. Harry Berger argues that "A major theme of Renaissance literature centers on the techniques of controlled and experimental withdrawal into an artificial world—a 'second nature' created by the mind—where the elements of actuality are selectively admitted, simplified and explored."[38] But the most sophisticated Renaissance pastorals recognize the real or first world as no less selectively perceived, no less necessarily simplified. The mind is its own place, and necessarily makes a pastoral retreat of an infinite universe of bustling sense-perceptions. Know the world perfectly, and you will have no mind of your own; you become a mirror, incapable of the other kind of reflection. We cannot bear to leave nature, reality, or God unknown; nor can we bear to know them. Selfhood can best be defined and sustained (as in a Freudian model) by our individual blind-spots.

"What the Petrarchist use of the Actaeon myth shows," observes one comparatist scholar, is that there can be "No bliss of identity without the pain of alienation, and the bliss itself is taken up in the play of domination."[39] Shakespeare's use of simile in this play shows the same dangers of partial alienation and domination. That "moonish youth" Rosalind is "like Diana in the fountain" (3.2.410, 4.1.154). Orlando stumbling across her in the forest associates him with Actaeon,[40] and does so in a way that again links men's desire toward women with human impositions on nature. As in Nonnus' fifth-century *Dionysiaca*, where "Actaeon's hunting is made explicitly parallel to his voyeurism and to his lust for the goddess,"[41] as in Petrarch's *Rime* XXIII (lines 147–60) where the object of desire transforms the poet from hunter to wandering stag, Orlando's fantasies about the disguised Rosalind link two archetypal modes of male aggression, two meanings of "venery": hunting and lusting. A subsequent chapter will trace the same insistent association in seventeenth-century Dutch depictions of the hunt.

Orlando anthropomorphizes the moon as the "thrice-crowned queen of night," with Rosalind as a "huntress" in her service, but he immediately betrays himself as the aggressor, imposing literature on nature even more directly than Duke Senior does: "these trees shall be my books, / And in their barks my thoughts I'll character" (3.2.1–6).[42] Again the crimes evident to popular environmentalism stand distinct from those only ecological philosophy can detect. As Duke Senior's aggression against the deer is to the more subtle and sentimental aggression of Jaques, so is Orlando's vandalism to that of the nature-loving speaker of Marvell's "The Garden" who, in a revealingly misguided gesture of love (which my next chapter will explore), vows to carve into the bark of trees the human names for their species. "Adam in a state of nature had perfect knowledge of signatures and named everything aright";[43] the rest of us are imposers, and impostors. Nature's revenge is like Diana's: making masculine aggressors self-conscious, turning the linguistic tools by which we conquer reality against us, letting slip the dogs of word, sending us into a wilderness where (Shakespeare and Marvell warn) we may hunt ourselves to death. The shortfall of knowledge and the alienation from nature again appear indistinguishable in Margaret Cavendish's "Dialogue Betwixt Man and Nature," where Man describes the hunger of consciousness that threatens to make him an Actaeon:

> Nature gives no such Knowledge to Mankind,
> But strong Desires, which do torment his Mind;
> And Senses, which like Hounds do run about,
> Yet never can the perfect Truth find out.
>   (lines 13–16)

Nature replies by complaining about the way her trees are "Defac'd" and her animals hunted by Man (lines 21–32).[44] In a rhapsodic eclogue, Philip Sidney had asked, rhetorically, "What Man graftes in a Tree dissimulation?"[45] Shakespeare and Marvell reply that every man who applies a simile or a name to a tree does exactly that.

Where God had written signatures into trees, and the rest of nature, from the inside, Orlando imposes his writing from without. How appealing is any love letter or love lyric when it is obsessed with the lover (the human mind) and direly ignorant of the beloved (the world of nature)? For many years I found the archly fake rusticity of high pastoral, including *As You Like It*, off-putting for that reason. The pasture could justly accuse the pastoralist as Rosalind does Orlando: of a controlling narcissism, "as loving yourself [rather] than seeming the lover of any other" (3.2.383–84). When Touchstone responds to Orlando's verses hanging in the forest by observing that "the tree yields bad fruit" (3.2.116), we may suspect that Orlando's poetic fruits bear the knowledge of self and other. He lets a thousand comparisons bloom, praising Rosalind as

> Helen's cheek, but not [her] heart,
>   Cleopatra's majesty,
> Atalanta's better part,
>   Sad Lucretia's modesty.
> Thus Rosalind of many parts
>   By heavenly synod was devis'd
> Of many faces, eyes, and hearts,
>   To have the touches dearest priz'd.
>   (3.2.145–52)

Similarity has become anatomy, Professor Petrarch has become Doctor Frankenstein, and the temple devoted to the worship of Rosalind has exploded into a junkyard of others. The homology between the anthropomorphic invasion of nature and the misogynistic shadow of Petrarchism becomes unmistakable: the beloved is anatomized, even atomized, into the vocabulary of the desiring mind.

Petrarchan lovers were constantly shattering their lovers with balms of similitude: belying women (as Shakespeare's Sonnet 130 warns) by false compare, by a blast of *blason*. Love and violence thus seem almost inseparable; you always hunt the one you love. Alongside the humanist attacks on hunting were works such as *The Master of Game* and *The Noble Arte of Venerie*, which vividly evoke the nature-loving motives behind the chase in the wood.[46] When Rosalind hears that Orlando is "furnish'd like a hunter," she says it is "ominous! he comes to kill my heart" (3.2.245–46). And the play's references to the arrows of Cupid (1.3.1, 4.1.48, 213–15), as well as the inevitable jokes about the cuckold's horns (3.2.82, 3.3.51–63, 4.1.59–60) tie the story of hunting in the forest closely to the story of loving in the forest.

Deer-stalking provides modern law and psychology with their common term for the love that turns to possessiveness, then violence, and finally a ritual of sentimental regret. *As You Like It* has more than its share of relentless unrequited lovers: Silvius toward Phebe, Phebe toward "Ganymede," Orlando toward "Rosalind," William toward Audrey—and, I believe, most of the ardent nature lovers toward the Forest of Arden. The self-deluded, self-indulgent lovers who stalk nature produce the same dialogue that typifies erotic stalking between humans. The possessive voice says: I give you everything, you mean so much to me, you are beauty and truth, you are my soul and my destiny, I speak your name, acknowledge me. The unwilling beloveds reply, if only by a cool silence: this is merely your fantasy, you don't really know me, you have nothing I want or need.

Orlando thus resembles the namesake hero of Ariosto's *Orlando furioso*—who, finding Angelica's love for another attested by her name carved in a tree bark, destroys almost an entire forest—but he also resembles Petrarch's persona and Sannazaro's Sincero: men who wander off into rustic solitude so obsessed with a lost or unachievable beloved that they populate nature with thoughts of her, imposing her name and image on everything.[47] Shakespeare's twist on that tradition (though Sannazaro arguably anticipates this by providing an elaborate topography) is an emphasis on the way the otherness of a woman in a man's hetero-eroticism resembles and perhaps reflects an unconquerable otherness already present in nature, present in material reality itself; the pastoral retreat exposes another failed connection, this one more abstract but also more definite than unrequited human love, which is a social or psychological contingency, not a philosophical and cognitive-scientific necessity. What Petrarch's "Augustine" calls the "traveler who cannot escape from himself" is an instance of the human mind that cannot escape itself,[48] whatever the surrounding landscape. As George Wither puts it in captioning an emblem, "When *woe* is in our selves begun, / Then, whither from it, can wee run?" The accompanying engraving is an antlered deer with an arrow in its side, ignored by another deer drinking from the stream, gazed upon by a man in a cave.[49]

The Forest of Arden may be hard to read reliably—"the Duke sees good, Jaques evil, Touchstone both, Corin neither"[50]—but so is everyone and everything else. The difficulty of knowing nature objectively becomes part of the entire subject-object problem, as well as the problem of other minds and its subsidiary problem of erotic desire. When Phebe denies that her mere appearance can have done the material harm claimed by Silvius's Petrarchan complaints,[51] Ganymede insists there is "no more in you than in the ordinary / Of nature's sale-work," which materiality gives her no hold over Ganymede's inner nature:

'Tis not your inky brows, your black silk hair,
Your bugle eyeballs, nor your cheek of cream
That can entame my spirits to your worship.
(3.5.42–48)

Within a year, Shakespeare would give his most skeptical hero a strangely similar dissent:

Seems, madam? nay, it is, I know not "seems."
'Tis not alone my inky cloak, [good] mother,
Nor customary suits of solemn black,
. . . .
That can [denote] me truly.
                              (*Hamlet*, 1.2.76–83)

Representation is a symptom, not a cure, of otherness. Despite Ganymede's neat checklist of "marks" for true love (3.2.373–81), inner nature remains inaccessible; despite the hunters and lovers of deer, so does outer nature. Hamlet admonishes Ophelia, "I have heard of your paintings, well enough. God hath given you one face, and you make yourselves another," then adds that "you nickname God's creatures" (3.1.142–45); in other words, the crime of making a false second self to replace the divinely dictated reality is associated with the crime of giving affectionate new names to other animals.

By the time we see Orlando taking out his erotic obsession—his mourning for a lost object—on innocent natural entities, Touchstone has prepared us to ridicule that displacement:

I remember when I was in love, I broke my sword upon a stone, and bid him take that for coming a-night to Jane Smile; and I remember the kissing of her batler and the cow's dugs that her pretty chopp'd hands had milk'd; and I remember the wooing of a peascod instead of her . . . (2.4.46–52)

Indeed, less than twenty lines after Orlando announces his own program of pastoral displacement, the old shepherd Corin offers a flatter reflection of the natural world, an empiricism that stubbornly resists the imperialism of human ingenuity: he claims that "the property of rain is to wet and fire to burn; that good pasture makes fat sheep; and that a great cause of the night is lack of the sun; that he that hath learn'd no wit by nature, nor art, may complain of good breeding, or comes of a very dull kindred." Touchstone replies dismissively, "Such a one is a natural philosopher" (3.2.26–32). Certainly the words aren't doing much, and they are all that's doing anything: if we take "fire" and "burn" as mutually defining terms, Corin's speech is tautology. But isn't any more active, sophisticated, interventionist way of understanding and loving nature than the shepherd's a form of stalking? Doesn't pastoralism share the dangers of Petrarchism: not just disguising verbal convention as individual emotion, but disguising aggression as submission, appropriation as donation—in other words, war as love?

Love and War, Nature and Culture

As You Like It depicts love and war simultaneously as natural (the Darwinian reading of nature) and cultural: both "falling in love" and the "falls" of the wrestling are called "sports" in the play's second scene (1.2.26, 100), at once civilized ritual and mortal struggle, leaving their practitioners at once psychosocially and physiologically silenced and "overthrown" (1.2.254, 259). Orlando's Petrarchist lyrics and Touchstone's taxonomy of quarreling then offer more fully acculturated versions of desire and combat. The calibration provokes an audience to meditate on the paradoxes of civilization elaborately simulating the wild.

Touchstone himself patrols this boundary as a double agent, tending to drag the courtiers back to physical reality,[52] while posing as an agent of high culture for the country folk.[53] His puns repeatedly expose the resemblance between lustful animals and literary humans, as when he tells Audrey, "I am here with thee and thy goats as the most capricious poet, honest Ovid, was among the Goths" (3.3.7–9). The Ovid of the *Metamorphoses* is supremely relevant to this failure of boundaries—Touchstone himself is arguably the reincarnation of Battus, who, Ovid reports, was disincarnated into a touchstone by Mercury—but (like punning itself) the classical *topos* is also so ostentatiously cultural as to reaffirm human distinctness even while animalizing the rustics. In an instant parody of Orlando's poetic claim that "No jewel is like Rosalind" (3.2.89), Touchstone finds a different kind of similarity that renews her citizenship in the animal kingdom, beginning with a pair of puns that reduce romantic love to animal magnetism, beloveds to their bodies, and bodies to their sexual apertures:

> If a hart do lack a hind,
> Let him seek out Rosalind.
> If the cat will after kind,
> So be sure will Rosalind.
>   (3.2.101–4)

She is the material girl, however transcendentally Orlando may perceive her, or think he does. Touchstone's concluding pun about feeling "love's prick" (3.2.112) similarly teeters on the boundary between a biological base and a Petrarchan superstructure.

According to Montaigne, even the Pyrrhonists accept that reality exists, "and there is in us the means to seek it, but not to test it by a touchstone."[54] Shakespeare is able, by dramatic fiat, to overcome that lack—but only for the sake of suggesting it still hardly solves the problem. The impossibility of understanding one world from the perspective of another, and the differences that language makes, are the only points that come through decisively in Touchstone's analysis of "this shepherd's life" (3.2.11):

in respect of itself, it is a good life; but in respect that it is a shepherd's life, it is naught. In respect that it is solitary, I like it very well; but in respect that it is private, it is a very vild life. Now in respect it is in the fields, it pleaseth me well; but in respect it is not in the court, it is tedious. As it is a spare life (look you) it fits my humor well; but as there is no more plenty in it, it goes much against my stomach. (3.2.13–21)

Again here (and in the moralizing debate about court versus country manners thirty lines later) the alienation of the sophisticate from rusticity points to the deeper and no more resolvable alienation of the prejudicial mind from any absolute, pre-existing reality. Nature—as inscrutable in its judgments as the Calvinist God—has the last laugh on the quest for truth: "You have said," remarks Touchstone, "but whether wisely or no, let the forest judge" (3.2.121–22). As Bacon observed, "The subtlety of nature is greater many times over than the subtlety of the senses and understanding, so that all those specious meditations, speculations, and glosses in which men indulge are quite from the purpose, only there is no one by to observe it."[55] If humanity falls in the forest—falls short of truly knowing that forest—does the tree that hears it make a sound judgment, if only by paying no attention?

Rosalind says that Touchstone's first entrance "makes Nature's natural the cutter-off of Nature's wit" (1.2.49–50), but even this surrender of wit to nature is compromised—a white flag with lawyerly small print—since Touchstone is the kind of court fool who uses urbane wit under the guise of being merely what Renaissance England called a "natural," a born imbecile. Jaques observes that Touchstone "uses his folly like a stalking-horse, and under the presentation of that he shoots his wit" (5.4.106–7). The simile is not only apt, it is overdetermined in its evocation of the animal disguises we place on sophisticated human motives—and the dominion such disguises (and such similes) allow us to exercise over the animal universe.

What is left of the higher things—of a sacrament such as marriage—if Touchstone can find "no temple but the wood, no assembly but horn-beasts" (3.3.50–51)? All he can do (as we will see Marvell do in the willfully obtuse yet cleverly pun-laden reading of symbolic plants in the opening stanzas of "The Garden") is translate the likely result of marrying Audrey into a neutral fact of nature, the marks of the cuckold into the mere physical features from which cuckoldry derives its symbolism: "Horns? . . . the noblest deer hath them as huge as the rascal" (3.3.56–58). And when Jaques challenges this reductive view, Touchstone reasserts it in other words: "As the ox hath his bow, sir, the horse his curb, and the falcon her bells, so man hath his desires; and as pigeons bill, so wedlock would be nibbling" (3.3.79–82). This is sexist in more than the conventional sense: desire converts people into domestic livestock, at once enslaved by reproductive functions and constrained by human artifice.

The play divides each pair of brothers into one who inhabits a court and one who inhabits the forest. Oliver du Bois is repeatedly condemned as "unnatural" (4.3.122, 124), whatever that means for our anti-natural species; and his liminality as he arrives in the forest brings the uneasy boundary between humanity and wilderness again to our attention:

> *Oliver:* Good morrow, fair ones. Pray you (if you know)
> Where in the purlieus of this forest stands
> A sheep-cote fenc'd about with olive-trees?
> *Celia:* West of this place, down in the neighbor bottom,
> The rank of osiers by the murmuring stream
> Left on your right hand brings you to the place.
> But at this hour the house doth keep itself,
> There's none within.
>
> (4.3.75–82)

A purlieu was a concept so ambiguous that it makes the *Oxford English Dictionary* sound like Henry James: "A piece or tract of land on the fringe or border of a forest; originally one that, after having been (wrongly, as was thought) included within the bounds of the forest, was disafforested by a new perambulation, but still remained, in some respects, especially as to the hunting or killing of game, subject to provisions of the Forest Laws." There may be laws in the forest, but are there any of or by it?[56] Have the olive trees been cut into pieces for a fence, or do they merely serve as a fence in their living natural form? Is a sheep-cote a place of nature or of culture?

Celia's reply echoes the pastoral anthropomorphism of Duke Senior. Is the bottom a neighbor, do osiers form a rank, does a stream murmur? Directional words are essential to human navigation through the landscape, even if "west" is arbitrary—meaningless to the landscape itself—and "left on your right hand" furthermore depends on the position of the observer. The map, as Alfred Korzybski famously observed, is not the territory. A house does not and need not keep itself, and there is no hour there if no one is there to tell it. Time proves no more definite than space. When the disguised Rosalind asks Orlando, "what is't a' clock?" he admonishes her: "You should ask me what time o' day. There's no clock in the forest." Her reply exposes time as another supposed fact of nature that actually depends on human subjectivities—in this case, whether one is in a hurry (3.2.299–333). As Marvell asks teasingly in "The Garden," isn't all nature a sundial that "computes its time as well as we" (line 70)?[57]

Oliver's story about coming to know himself by pursuing his fraternal likeness into the woods is at once a narrative of natural predation and defense and a highly acculturated mythological displacement of his personal history. Food is for thought as well as for eating in this forest—no longer actually starving, Orlando was "Chewing the food of sweet and bitter fancy" (4.3.101)—and even the old oak is both a family tree and a human likeness, both of which Orlando encounters in the rusticated Oliver, who reports that

> Under an old oak, whose boughs were moss'd with age
> And high top bald with dry antiquity:
> A wretched, ragged man, o'ergrown with hair,
> Lay sleeping on his back; about his neck
> A green and gilded snake had wreath'd itself.
>
> (4.3.104–8)

Are these the tree and the serpent of Genesis, or only of evolution; are they (and the hungry lioness) allegory, or only naturalistic narrative? The boys of the family named de Boys play out their crucial scene in and under this *bois*, and even the geographically surprising appearance of a lion six lines later seems partly a weird play on the suggestion of Lodge's *Rosalynde* that the Oliver character was in the forest "thinking to get to Lions," meaning the city of Lyon. Textuality and reality sway in each other's gravity, and Duke Senior is hardly the only one who "translates" questionably across the gap between nature and the human lexicon. Jaques warns Orlando that he should "mar no more trees with writing love-songs in their barks," but in the very next scene warns Touchstone that he should not rely on marriage by a Mar-text in the woods (3.2.259–60, 3.3.84–89).

The oak tree which looms over both Jaques's meditations on the deer and Orlando's rescue of Oliver resembles the Tree of Knowledge that looms over the fallen Eden at the end of Dante's *Purgatorio*.[58] But Shakespeare's tree offers the knowledge of self and other, and both scenes beneath it are mortal combats between human and animal entities that had lived harmoniously in Eden. And sometimes the tree is just a tree—or a representation of one, anyway. When, at the end of a recent outdoor production of *As You Like It*, my young daughter was obsessed with whether the blades of grass climbing the facing of the low stage (having escaped the edging capacity of the mower) were real or part of the set, something beyond parental dotage allowed me to construe the question as perceptive rather than reductive: this play insistently tests the membrane separating the biological world from human artifice and illusion.

Isms

As You Like It organizes its discussions of the politics of race, class, and gender—the modern martyrological trinity—around this distinction between what is natural and absolute, and what is instead imposed by human preconceptions. Rosalind's complaint that "I was never so berhym'd since Pythagoras' time, that I was an Irish rat, which I can hardly remember" (3.2.176–78) reminds us that (as the nearly universal amnesia of infant experience indicates) a mind that has moved beyond sound into language has difficulty knowing the world outside language. Rosalind recurs, by simile, to the relationship between human speech and Ireland's wildlife when she complains (with puns that remind us of the difference between sounds and words) that the unrequited lovers sound "like the howling of Irish wolves against the moon" (5.2.109–10).[59] The accusation that Rosalind here participates, however obliquely and unthinkingly, in Elizabethan racism conceals a philosophical question behind a political one: isn't Rosalind here participating, however obliquely and unthinkingly, in anthropomorphism? Are either the rats or the wolves Irish, or do they merely reside in what she calls Ireland? The question is not purely rhetorical. Michael Drayton's relentlessly nationalist chorography *Poly-Olbion* (1612) is also relentlessly anthropomorphic, and Spenser's *View of the Present State of Ireland* (probably drawing on Camden) mentions a belief that Irishmen "were once every yeare turned into wolves":[60] the boundary between the human and animal worlds may yield to alternation (as in the Pythagorean metempsychosis Rosalind joked about), but not penetration or communication. That may be one reason Shakespeare has Rosalind and Celia banter about the inefficacy of throwing words at dogs (1.3.1–6). The only real contact is predatory, and the rediscovery of Pythagoras (and of other influential voices of vegetarianism such as Plutarch) offered a vocabulary for the nascent revulsion against the hunt, which can offer only a bad-faith illusion of capturing nature and a barely displaced cannibalism in which (as Hamlet's grim banter and Actaeon's grim fate imply) we finally consume ourselves. A later chapter will trace a similar revulsion in seventeenth-century Dutch painting.

The class issue, as in Touchstone's disdain for Corin, also turns quickly into a debate about what role nature plays in defining human virtue. Oliver will pull rank in order to purge Orlando's aspiring "rankness," a pun between organic odor and social status that Rosalind revives in the following scene (1.1.86,

1.2.107–8); Celia's reference to the "rank of osiers" then conflates nature and culture, with trees yet again as the test case (4.3.79). Orlando's paradoxically eloquent complaint that his brother has raised "a gentleman of my birth" (1.1.9–10)
like a farm animal recalls the standard pastoral motif whereby nobility shines
through the most insistently rustic upbringing.[61] Indeed, the complaints against
Oliver recall contemporary complaints that Scottish peasants were "little better
than the cattle of the nobility," as well as the complaints of the 1596 Oxfordshire
rioters that servants were "kept like dogs."[62] But behind the pastoral code this
time lurks a recognition that, as rusticity can never erase aristocracy, neither can
it ever erase humanity:

> His horses are bred better, for besides that they are fair with their feeding, they are taught
> their manage, and to that end riders dearly hir'd; but I (his brother) gain nothing under
> him but growth, for the which his animals on his dunghills are as much bound to him as
> I. . . . He lets me feed with his hinds, bars me the place of a brother, and as much as in
> him lies, mines my gentility with my education. This is it, Adam, that grieves me, and the
> spirit of my father, which I think is within me, begins to mutiny against this servitude.
> (1.1.11–24)

A person raised as mere domestic livestock is still not meet, not meat, for a
"butchery" (as if to cap the point, the argument then closes with a dispute about
Oliver calling Adam "old dog" at line 81). Orlando may be stalled like an ox, but
he is not an ox, any more than the hunter who is dressed like a deer becomes
one. That is not just because he is the son of a nobleman, but because he is a son
of Adam.

Rosalind, on the other hand, is a daughter of Eve; but gender distinction, too,
is complicated by the interplay of biological base and cultural superstructure—
and further complicated by hints that the model of base and superstructure
oversimplifies a problem implicated in the interplay of a posited reality and its
representations. Rosalind seeks refuge in a simile exploiting the external con-
structedness of the supposedly biological category of gender:

> Were it not better,
> Because that I am more than common tall,
> That I did suit me all points like a man?
> A gallant curtle-axe upon my thigh,
> A boar-spear in my hand, and—in my heart
> Lie there what hidden woman's fear there will—
> We'll have a swashing and a martial outside,
> As many other mannish cowards have
> That do outface it with their semblances.
> (1.3.114–22)

The handy-dandy game of cross-dressing—by which the audience knows that the person playing Ganymede is really female, even while knowing that the person playing Rosalind (who plays Ganymede) is really male—shows how difficult it is either to discover or to erase the facts of biology, to end the dialogue of artificial and natural. In swooning over the sight of Orlando's blood, Rosalind provides a moment of gender-essentialism: she proves herself to "lack a man's heart," and the "testimony in your complexion" proves that "This was not counterfeit" (4.3.164, 169–70). Shakespeare's audience, though, would have known that it was precisely so, as the work not only of an actor, but a boy actor. As "the truest poetry is the most feigning" (3.3.19–20), so the actor's best simulation of nature is the most deeply counterfeit. Getting down to "reality" is impossible, even regarding something as mundane as the qualities of pancakes and mustard, since the women (who are boys) may safely swear by their beards to the truth of something that would be a lie if they were men (1.2.63–80).

The breakdown of traditional family obligations causes a cascading failure of the referential utility of language. Old Adam therefore stumbles through a seemingly urgent report:

> Your brother—no, no brother, yet the son
> (Yet not the son, I will not call him son)
> Of him I was about to call his father.
> (2.3.19–21)

Duke Senior and Orlando both mistake identity for mere likeness in Rosalind:

> *Duke Senior:* I do remember in this shepherd boy
> Some lively touches of my daughter's favor.
> *Orlando:* My lord, the first time that I ever saw him
> Methought he was a brother to your daughter.
> But, my good lord, this boy is forest-born. . . .
> (5.4.26–30)

Their insight remains obstructed by the binaries of gender and class, and by the assumption that anything seen in the forest must be simply itself and manifestly true.

As You Like It is ostentatiously concerned with the narrowly failed effort to crush together polarities such as female and male, rich and poor, civilization and savagery. To that list I would add not only the binary of signified and signifier, but also the polarity of the existing material world and the conceiving human mind, which builds a likeness of the world and then inhabits it.[63]

Humanity grasps the world more as squatter than as owner, and the problems of simile therefore haunt even the play's odd excursion into economics. The shift toward the alienated labor of capitalism (which many scholars believe originated in fifteenth-century England) emerges out in the Forest of Arden—a little shockingly, though historically its problems were sharply felt there[64]—in the form of an invisible bourgeois investor. If it is true that most Renaissance poets (and painters) "manifested an extreme reluctance to mention the practical aspects of rural life" such as absentee landlords and hireling farmers,[65] that only indicates how striking Shakespeare's insistence on those things here must have been for his original audiences. The true rustics cannot feed these urban refugees because capitalist economics, in the archetypal guise of an absentee owner, controls the foison of the earth:

> I am shepherd to another man,
> And do not shear the fleeces that I graze.
> My master['s] . . . flocks, and bounds of feed
> Are now on sale, and at our sheep-cote now
> By reason of his absence there is nothing
> That you will feed on.
>   (2.4.78–86)

A "golden world" indeed: the laws of money, and what Marxism calls alienated labor, are already evident, already resident in this alien forest. Perhaps always-already: Virgil's first Eclogue thanks Octavius for preventing the confiscation of his farm.

Yet also never-completely: Arden's visitors must re-invest in the feudal economy rather than simply buy a meal. If the hungry Orlando is surprised to discover civility among the inhabitants of these woods, imagine how surprising it must be for these other hungry travelers to discover a proletariat there as well. The situation appears quite superfluous to the plot, but it does seem to fit the themes I have been sketching—especially because the loss of symbiotic contact with the land was inextricable from the loss of unmediated value. Between the bewildered city-folk and the countryside's food supply stand financial transactions for which they fortunately have the means; and for this, Celia's careless inheritance is just as good as old Adam's "thrifty hire" (2.3.39). The color and count of the specie matter more than the character of its acquisition; the coin of the realm is a tool of moral amnesia. Money launders itself.

Celia may "like this place," but she can obtain it only by offering for the soil comparable value, an equipoise of cash (2.4.75–100). According to Aristotle's *Nicomachean Ethics*, "Money, then, acting as a measure, makes goods commensurate and equates them."[66] Various seventeenth-century writers such as Rice

Vaughan began to recognize the implications of the fact that "money is used to create resemblances between things; it allows us to conceive of a figurative equivalence between objects that are essentially distinct."[67] Again the problem lies in likeness. Capitalism is to economics what atomism is to physics—a new mystery that erases the quiddity of things, disenchants them (as Donne recognized)[68] by radical fungibility:

> In order for two different things, say a chicken and a goat, to be exchanged for one another, it is necessary to conceive of an *equivalence* between them. These two things are not, of course, *identical*; if they were, there would be no point in exchanging them. A chicken and a goat are different from one another in nature, in essence. Nevertheless, they can be made equivalent by an act of human conception. Human beings have the ability to impose equivalence upon things that are essentially and naturally different. . . . The simplest act of barter thus assumes that an object has two distinct identities—a natural essence and a customary value. In Greek philosophy, this is expressed as the opposition between nature, or *phusis*, and custom, or *nomos*."[69]

So the problem of capitalist ownership that prevents the farmer from directly feeding the refugees becomes cognate with the problem of yearning for true natural perception that partly brought them there, and also cognate with the whole problem of simile as an imperfect representation imposed by the human system that haunts the play. No wonder *As You Like It* seems strangely obsessed with both cash and comparison.

Likening

Theater is likeness. Comedy (whether Bergsonian farce or Shakespearean romance) is about the transmission of likeness, about stock characters and breeding stock; the closing marriages stand for the likelihood of liking producing likenesses. *As You Like It* is a comedy that ostentatiously imitates two "nondramatic narratives, *Arcadia* and *Rosalynde*, which stress their status as imitations,"[70] and representational anxieties permeate the fabric of the play. It is a likeness full of likenesses. Shakespeare seems to be toying with his culture's lively conceptual and rhetorical struggle to sustain the distinction between humanity and other animals.[71] The astonishing array of similes in *As You Like It* that cross the boundary between humans and other creatures suggests the tenacity of the impulse they reflect: the impulse of the human family to impose its familiarities, even while recognizing they are not true identities. While there may be "much virtue in If " (5.4.103), in "Like" there lies the temptation to a great sin, an appropriative violence; "If " may be a "peacemaker," but "like" is a gesture of conquest—a kind of provisional occupation that stops just short of the totalitarian presumption of metaphor. The "remarkably extensive use of 'if' in *As You Like It*"[72] is another way Shakespeare signals that all the world's a hypothetical.

Similarity is the play's acknowledgment of the desire to connect, of the failure of that desire, and of the fears aroused by both the desire and the failure. The play clearly exploits anxieties (both psychoanalytic and theological) about the idea that women are almost men, but not quite; Arden is similarly similar to Eden (and seems to be at once the romantic fantasy of Lodge's Ardenne and the homely reality of Shakespeare's Warwickshire Arden). "Truth" is not quite "troth," and "feign" shadows "fain." The list of *dramatis personae* includes the distracting and seemingly superfluous overlap of two men named Jaques and two named Oliver, one of whom is desperate not to recognize his brother Orlando as kin, or as the likeness of their father, the "memory / Of old Sir Rowland" (2.3.3–4), whose name Orlando shares, but in translation. The doubling of roles in the original performance likely reinforced, and ironized, many of these imperfect overlaps. Not even "like," Shakespeare insists, is quite like itself:

> *Jaques:* Good my lord, like this fellow.
> *Duke Senior:* I like him very well.
> *Touchstone:* God 'ild you, sir, I desire you of the like.
> (5.4.51–54)

In other words, he desires a like liking; he would like him to do something like like him. Earlier Silvius had asked his father "If thy love were ever like to mine," and insisted that it must have been mere liking because it was unlike his own obsessive passion (2.4.28 ff.). In the Epilogue (line 19), "like" will become different yet again (completing a cluster of puns on likeness and liking that Ben Jonson used in his epitaph "On My First Son"), taking on its archaic transitive sense of "please." As Brutus warns in *Julius Caesar*, "Every like is not the same."[73]

When Orlando is condemned for being like his father, Rosalind replies by likening herself to her own father, who "lov'd Sir Rowland [Orlando's father] as his soul" (1.2.223–39). In the following scene, she again speaks of "liking" her father's friend's child, and when she is also accused of inherited disloyalty, she demands that Duke Frederick "Tell me whereon the [likelihood] depends" that physical likeness would dictate political likeness (1.3.28, 57)—a question linking resemblance and probability in way that Montaigne would have admired.[74] Celia insists she is identical to Rosalind—"thou and I am one. / Shall we be sund'red?"—but they must be sundered, because (as her father reminds her) she really isn't identical to Rosalind; neither is Ganymede; and they aren't exactly "like Juno's swans . . . coupled and inseparable" either (1.3.97–98, 75–76).

Women's faults are "like one another as halfpence are" only within the misogynist discourse Rosalind mimics as Ganymede (3.2.354). Rosalind—who claims to live "in the skirts of the forest, like fringe upon a petticoat" (3.2.336–37)—is, and is not, what her name and Celia designate her: "my sweet rose" (1.2.23).[75] Human life is, and is not, what the song's commonplace makes it: "but a flower" (5.3.28).

Shakespeare wrote *As You Like It* during the relatively brief period when a new genre, the reference-book of similes, proliferated. The play sometimes sounds like a parody of that genre. Jaques rejects courtly compliment as "like the encounter of two dog-apes" (2.5.27). Yet when Duke Senior seeks him out two scenes later, a lord suspects that Jaques has been "transform'd into a beast, / For I can no where find him like a man" (2.7.1–2). For Jaques to complain that human pride flows "as hugely as the sea" (2.7.72) is itself an act of human pride, an appropriation of great creating nature through the presumption of simile (Rosalind chooses a similar simile in describing her affection as "like the bay of Portugal" at 4.1.208). Through the conventional satiric ploy of making accusations conditional, Jaques (who repeatedly likens humans to animals in the "seven ages" speech) only replicates that presumption: "If he be free, / Why then my taxing like a wild goose flies" (2.7.85–86).

Duke Senior declares that human adversity is "like the toad" (2.1.13). Encountering the Duke's suave civility where he "thought that all things had been savage," Orlando announces, "like a doe, I go to find my fawn" (2.7.107, 128). Le Beau provides court news "as pigeons feed their young" (1.2.93–94). Touchstone derides Corin for being "like an ill-roasted egg" (3.2.37–38). He then chooses not to marry a chaste woman, who is "as your pearl in your foul oyster" (5.4.61), and therefore Jaques predicts that his marriage is doomed to warp "like green timber" (3.3.88). Only thirty-two lines after the hunter is given the deer's "leather skin," Ganymede dismisses Phebe as having "a leathern hand" (4.3.24), and adds that love has made Silvius "a tame snake" (4.3.70). The Second Page claims that he and his partner sing "like two gipsies on a horse"—a satyrical image reinforced (through homophonic likeness) by the First Page's claim in the previous line that "we are hoarse" (5.3.12–15).

When Celia first describes Orlando in the forest, her similes oscillate between simple botany and romantic literature: is he "like a dropp'd acorn," as she first claims, or "like a wounded knight" as she claims a moment later (3.2.235, 240–41)? He is "concave as a cover'd goblet or a worm-eaten nut" (3.4.24–25). When Orlando proves unreliable, Celia subordinates his chivalric side to his biological one, comparing him to a rider who "breaks his staff, like a noble goose" (3.4.44–45). Rosalind therefore says she "had as lief be woo'd of a snail" (4.1.52). But if Orlando is willing to question the romanticizing of his biological cravings, she (as Ganymede) will "wash your liver as clean as a sound sheep's heart" (3.2.422–23).

Pressing Orlando to recognize some hard realities behind the time-denying love-game he is playing, Ganymede brings the natural comparisons to a crescendo:

men are April when they woo, December when they wed; maids are May when they are maids, but the sky changes when they are wives. I will be more jealous of thee than a Barbary cock-pigeon over his hen, more clamorous than a parrot against rain, more new-fangled than an ape, more giddy in my desires than a monkey. I will weep for nothing, like Diana in the fountain, and I will do that when you are dispos'd to be merry. I will laugh like a hyen, and that when thou art inclin'd to sleep. (4.1.147–56)

No wonder Jaques compares all the closing marital pairs to "couples . . . coming to the ark" (5.4.36)—the primal scene of likeness on its way to breed more likeness, again bridging (or, I suppose, boating) the gap between human and other creatures. Across the boundary between animal vulgarity and human romanticism, as much as any boundary of gender, Rosalind and Orlando play their tug-of-love. When she says, "I thought thy heart had been wounded with the claws of a lion," he replies, "Wounded it is, but with the eyes of a lady" (5.2.22–24).

Similitudes tell us very little when they try to leap this disputed border between cultural and biological realities: Celia teases that Orlando's hair is "Something browner than Judas's," and Rosalind replies that "his kissing is as full of sanctity as the touch of holy bread" (3.4.8, 13–14). To adopt the model of transubstantiation this reply proposes: is the spiritual essence (good or bad) truly manifest in the physical realm? Is the world under a traditional Catholic dispensation whereby the similitude of red liquids (wine and blood) and of spongy solids (bread and body) reflects full presence, or a radical Protestant system of representation (and Derridean system of referentiality) whereby the name or the likeness provides only a commemoration or experiential presence of the thing (bread or otherwise) named or simulated?[76] And in which of these ways do people receive the substance of the world of God?

Philosophies

In a sense, Michel Foucault was impressively right about all this, except that he was also entirely wrong. His description of the tantalizing, self-referential circulation of likeness in Renaissance Europe nicely evokes the game I see *As You Like It* playing: "an endless zigzag course from resemblance to what resembles it . . . knowing that thing only at the unattainable end of an endless journey."[77]

Foucault's main point, however, is that no one could stand outside that episteme to examine it critically until well into the seventeenth century; and yet Shakespeare's play was written in the sixteenth. This chapter is partly a challenge to that bold chronology of knowledge's shift from a system of similarity to a system of tabular distinctions.

But it is not my intention to follow Kierkegaard in making literature merely an occasion for philosophy: I believe the skepticism I have been describing is a real, active, and pervasive presence in Shakespeare's text. Along with the more obvious functions of *As You Like It*—popular entertainment, literary competition, social commentary—is a substantial anticipation of John Locke's argument that we can know only word definitions of physical things, never the things completely, and Kant's even later argument that we cannot know things in themselves, apart from the modes of knowledge we bring to them. The irreducible distances between likeness and identity, and between the human and the natural, are (though the term has become anathema to Shakespeare scholars) themes of the play, recurring—often in parallel—with a remarkable frequency and intricacy quite apart from any necessities of plot or realistic characterization.

Nor is this insight anachronistically imposed. Descartes would recall that, in his youth, "I thought I perceived clearly, although I did not in fact do so . . . that there were things outside of me which were the sources of my ideas and which resembled them in all respects."[78] Montaigne, whose work we know Shakespeare read, warned in his early, skeptical "Apology for Raymond Sebond" that

Our conception is not itself applied to foreign objects, but is conceived through the mediation of the senses; and the senses do not comprehend the foreign object, but only their own impressions. And thus the conceptions and semblance we form is not of the object, but only of the impression. . . . And as for saying that the impressions of the senses convey to the soul the quality of the foreign objects by resemblance, how can the soul and understanding make sure of this resemblance, having of itself no communication with foreign objects? Just as a man who does not know Socrates, seeing his portrait, cannot say that it resembles him.[79]

Surely there is something impish about arbitrarily bringing in Socrates here, the master of the cave allegory. But the same lesson was being taught by the far-from-skeptical Francis Bacon, who argues that many of the "Idols of the Cave" arise "from an excessive tendency to compare or to distinguish,"[80] and by the mystical believer St. John of the Cross:

a man can know nothing by himself, save after a natural manner, which is only that which he attains by means of the senses. For this cause he must have the phantasms and the forms of objects present in themselves and in their likenesses. . . . Wherefore, if one should speak to a man of things . . . whose likeness he has never seen, he would have no more illumination from them whatever than if naught had been said of them to him. . . . If one should say to a man that on a certain island there is an animal which he has never seen, and give him no idea of the likeness of that animal, that he may compare it with others that he has seen, he will have no more knowledge of it . . . than he had before.[81]

The soul must therefore find faith, in this dark cave, by some device other than simile, by some higher or more absolute form of Word.

Indeed, the broadest historical implication of my argument may be that Shakespeare is heralding a huge inversion in his culture's quest for truth. For centuries—and with increasing fervor during the Reformation—that culture had prominently feared that material objects would stand between humanity and any pure encounter with the Word, the divine absolute and its intentions. *As You Like It* articulates a converse fear—increasingly visible through modern semiotics—that words stand between us and any pure encounter with absolute reality, which a secular-scientific culture assumes resides in material objects. These are diametrically opposed ways of looking at nature. As Peter Harrison's fine study of the relationship between the Reformation and science shows, there are conflicting ways of reading reality, the first typified by Hugh of St. Victor:

For the whole sensible world is like a kind of book written by the finger of God . . . and each particular creature is like a figure . . . instituted by the divine will to manifest the invisible things of God's wisdom. But in the same way that some illiterate, if he saw an open book, would notice the figures, but would not comprehend the letters, so also the stupid and "animal man" who "does not perceive the things of God" may see the outward appearance of these visible creatures, but does not understand the reason within.[82]

Galileo articulates the alternative: "Philosophy is written in this grand book, the universe, which stands continually open to our gaze. But the book cannot be understood unless one first learns to comprehend the language and read the letters in which it is composed. It is written in the language of mathematics, and its characters are triangles, circles, and other geometrical figures without which it is humanly impossible to understand a single word of it."[83] Looking backward over four centuries to Hugh, and forward over four centuries to us, it becomes possible to see what was at stake in the late Renaissance. Which should one try to decipher as the ultimate referent: the divine intention or the technical reality? The world may still be a book for Galileo, but where true learning once showed a way past mere things to reveal the Word, now true learning seeks to reveal things in their pure structural essence. What had been anathematized as idolatry—seeing objects as important, final, efficacious in themselves rather than as media toward a higher intelligence called God—is here giving way to a condemnation of idols as Francis Bacon defines them: as cultural traditions, individual subjectivities, and mental qualities of the species including language itself, that prevent or distort any true empirical view of the natural universe.

"It is incredible," Bacon comments ruefully in the *New Organon*, "what a number of idols have been introduced into philosophy by the reduction of natural operations to a correspondence with human actions, that is, by imagining that nature acts as man does . . . though there be many things in nature which are singular and unmatched, yet it [the human understanding] devises for them conjugates and parallels and relatives which do not exist."[84] Is it nature, or ourselves, or similitude, that we love too much to see the world clearly? Nicholas Cusanus suggests that God chose to take on a lowly human appearance so that our narcissism could be channeled into piety: "We embrace our likeness, because we are pictured in the image, and love ourselves therein."[85]

As You Like It depicts the folly called pastoral as merely one genre of the problem called solipsism, which revived in the same decades (anthropomorphism seems not of an age, but for all time). Simile is a symptom. Nearly a century later, John Locke would offer a comparable warning against "letting the mind, upon the suggestion of any new notion, run immediately after similes to make it the clearer to itself," which "is by no means a right method to settle true notions of any thing in ourselves, because similes always fail in some part, and come short of that exactness which our conceptions should have to things. . . . If all our search has yet reached no farther than simile and metaphor, we may assure ourselves we rather fancy than know, and have not yet penetrated into the inside and reality of the thing, be it what it will, but content ourselves with what our imaginations, not things themselves, furnish us with."[86] In another work, Locke would argue that the "power of comparing, which may be observed in men, belonging to general ideas, and useful only to abstract reasonings, we may probably conjecture beasts have not"—so comparison only distances us further from nature—and that "the understanding is not much unlike a closet wholly shut from light, with only some little opening left, to let in external visible resemblances, or ideas of things without."[87] Drawing on early modern anxieties about attempts to read the Word of God through the world of God, and St. Bonaventure's warning that the book of nature offers us only a "trace," even saints only a "likeness," of the divine absolute,[88] Shakespeare begins to explore some modern anxieties about our ability to know the world itself, to move beyond comparison into truth, to see the absolute face to face, as we feel we should and once did. Along with the other most brilliantly elusive writers of his time—Marvell and Montaigne—Shakespeare depicts as at once tragically and farcically futile our efforts to return to the primal feast: the symbiotic union of breast-feeding, the innocent nurturance of Eden, a renewed communion with Mother Nature.

When Celia needs a pseudonym for her sojourn in the forest, she chooses "something that hath a reference to my state: / No longer Celia, but Aliena" (1.3. 127–28). Human beings are all aliens in the woods—and maybe in the world as well, partly because we have reference to that world by words. Orlando brings the charade to an end by insisting that he "can no longer live by thinking" (5.2.50), but no one ever could; nor could they live unthinkingly. We are, as Sir Thomas Browne noted, painfully awkward amphibians, not really at home (like the transformed Actaeon) either in nature or in culture. And, like most amphibians, like Narcissus, we spend a lot of time staring at the surface of the water. Gazing on wilderness may get us no further than gazing with similar infatuation on a human beloved—no further out of the mirrored box of self, I mean. This may be why Shakespeare caps a joke rather heavy-handedly, so that we will not miss the warning that unconquerable narcissism makes our effort to embrace nature into a dangerous folly:

> *Jaques:* By my troth, I was seeking for a fool when I found you.
> *Orlando:* He is drown'd in the brook; look but in, and you shall see him.
> *Jaques:* There I shall see my own figure.
>
> (3.2.285–89)

If we were to go check this conclusion, we would surely see our own.

Reflecting on this chapter, I can see a self-interested, appropriative simulation of the play, instead of the play itself. Perhaps I have detected a sufficient clustering of themes and verbal tendencies to justify likening the play to a philosophical argument partaking of phenomenological skepticism; but evidently no one else has seen the same play I claim to see, the same original intent, the same organic form. I have queried and quarried the determination to recover the pure original textual identity of *As You Like It*, yet I have—like most Shakespeareans—been stalking the play, loving it for reflecting my own mind, and claiming to uncover its naked self, its true meaning. In these books our thoughts we character. Reading produces readings, not an unmediated conversation with the playwright. So the pathetic fallacy I am challenging permeates the intentional fallacy I am using to challenge it: finding sermons in stones and finding them in Shakespeare may be similar impositions. Rather than "let the forest judge," we turn trees into paper, on which professions of love for nature become confessions of crime against it.

Chapter 4
Shades of Green: Marvell's Garden and the Mowers

Green Thoughts in the Garden

Like many Renaissance dialogues, this chapter invites you to stroll through a garden and the fields around it, contemplating some lovely but nettlesome questions. Fortunately, we have Andrew Marvell along, opening "The Garden" with a praise of rustic simplicity and a corresponding renouncement of secondary or symbolic meanings:

> How vainly men themselves amaze
> To win the palm, the oak, or bays,
> And their uncessant labours see
> Crowned from some single herb or tree,
> Whose short and narrow vergèd shade
> Does prudently their toils upbraid,
> While all flow'rs and all trees do close
> To weave the garlands of repose.
> (lines 1–8)

Yet—like the irrepressible "serpent old" in "The Coronet"—puns have infiltrated, practically vermiculated, the stanza that defies them.[1] "Amaze" meant "stupefy," but also "put into a labyrinth," which the more ambitious Renaissance gardens often included. "Shade" means the literal shadow, but also a figurative one, the ghost who "upbraids" in the sense of "reproaches," even while the literal shade is provided by a literal upward braiding of the garlands, which toil (in the sense of "work") creates a toil (in the sense of "snare"). This is awfully urbane rusticity.

Only by willful ignorance could one mistake the arguments of language for Quiet, the wit of the artificer for Innocence, and the symbolic value of the plants for the plants themselves:[2]

> Fair Quiet, have I found thee here,
> And Innocence, thy sister dear!

Mistaken long, I sought you then
In busy companies of men.
Your sacred plants, if here below,
Only among the plants will grow.
Society is all but rude,
To this delicious solitude.
                              (lines 9–16)

Petrarchism thus must yield to pastoralism, but is the new love any less forced, appropriative, and discreditably trapped in verbal conventions?

No white nor red was ever seen
So am'rous as this lovely green.[3]
Fond lovers, cruel as their flame,
Cut in these trees their mistress' name.
Little, alas, they know, or heed,
How far these beauties hers exceed!
Fair trees! wheres'e'er your barks I wound,
No name shall but your own be found.
                              (lines 17–24)

The oak (or plane, cypress, poplar, elm) will give him little thanks for that.[4] In the sense that it can want anything, it wants an intact bark, and "oak" is our name for it—for its species, in fact—not in any way its name for itself.[5] Or its identity in itself: though usually misinterpreted, this ironic passage provides as emphatic an assertion of nominalism as we could expect from anyone, and miraculously clear in a thinker as elusive as Marvell. The word or idea of a thing misrepresents any real individual entity, and (in this fallen garden) the signifier is arbitrary.[6] Marvell may even be pushing the nominalist mistrust of the categorical functions of language toward post-structuralism, by suggesting that many words presumed to refer legitimately to things rather than delusively to abstractions are still false impositions of the human mind on the material universe. The garden begins to look like Lewis Carroll's "dark wood where things have no names"; Alice stammers, " 'I mean to get under the . . . under the . . . Well, *this*, you know!' putting her hand on the trunk of the tree. 'What does it call itself, I wonder?' "[7]

What else can one do to pay homage to nature, or—part of the same project, I am arguing—to recuperate referentiality itself? Some gestures were made in this direction in England in the 1580s: for example, "the use of real tree bark (at Theobalds) and real tree trunks (at Hardwick) in order to assure the representational accuracy of plaster friezes, in a mode of naive naturalism."[8]

The best hope, however, might be the German Enlightenment *xylothèque* which sought "to go one better than the botanical volumes that merely illustrated the taxonomy of trees. Instead the books themselves were to be fabricated from their subject matter, so that the volume on . . . the common European beech, would be bound in the bark of that tree. Its interior would contain samples of beech nuts and seeds; and its pages would literally be its leaves."[9] Short of this kind of fanatically literal-minded rejection of literacy, nature remains immune to the many loving transcriptions attempted in this period, which here stand condemned as forgeries. We are not Adam, naming the world with prelapsarian wisdom, authority, and kindness. Courtship has quickly transmuted into stalking, as we are left to protest on behalf of the victim: you did not really love her because you did not really know her; she did not ask for your attention or tell you her name; you do not even speak the same language; and now you have really harmed her.[10]

The next stanza emphasizes rape and the rationalization of rape—committed almost indistinguishably against women and trees. Sophisticates often make the most voluble tree-huggers, but the embrace is awkward. All of the supposedly simple-hearted speaker's first four rhyme words—"heat," "retreat," "chase," and "race"—are puns (as is "Still" and perhaps "run"), playing against the extended metaphor of an Olympic track meet, as the nature lover turns into a pagan fetishist:

> When we have run our passion's heat,
> Love hither makes his best retreat.
> The gods, that mortal beauty chase,
> Still in a tree did end their race.
> Apollo hunted Daphne so,
> Only that she might laurel grow.
> And Pan did after Syrinx speed,
> Not as a nymph, but for a reed.
> (lines 25–32)

Aspiring to higher values, people go out into nature; the gods go there seeking earthier ones. There they meet, in an act of love, or of violence—no easier to differentiate here than in *As You Like It*—but, in any case, a distinct act of objectification. Or, they almost meet, but the very act of turning the beloved into the object makes this race another instance of the paradoxical race Zeno imagined for Achilles which never quite reaches its finish: there is no real intercourse with nature.

The fifth stanza then transmutes this erotic fantasy of capturing nature into a fantasy of nature reciprocating our sensual appetite. Women loved as nature become (with no less obvious a distortion) nature loved as women. Direct contact with the garden resembles a sexual embrace (as people often seek in sexual embraces direct unselfconscious experience: pure involvement in an other, even pure acceptance of their own animal nature). Here there is no problem of doubleness, because Marvell tries (even knowing he must fail) to depict experience as if one had nothing but body. The depiction resembles the infantile supposition that the feeding breast is merely an extension of the primary-narcissistic self—as James Swan's often-brilliant readings propose[11]—except that here it is the self rather than the external world that seems deprived of intention, making this a version of the sanitized rape of the previous stanza with the roles reversed:

> What wondrous life in this I lead!
> Ripe apples drop about my head;
> The luscious clusters of the vine
> Upon my mouth do crush their wine;
> The nectarine, and curious peach,
> Into my hands themselves do reach;
> Stumbling on melons, as I pass,
> Ensnar'd with flowers, I fall on grass.
>   (lines 33–40)

There is no fall here, or no pain in the fall, and nowhere to fall that is outside the embrace of a benevolent nature. Apples, wine, and falling seem inconsequentially themselves, unfallen into meaning; innocent of their potential theological import (which Marvell tempts readers to pack back in), the speaker's mind becomes radically innocent, absent of thought and volition. But few of these fruits would grow in England without considerable human intervention. Anyway, one can feel trapped by the luxury, almost smothered by the relentlessness with which the world visits our appetitive senses; even the green world can be too much with us, until the good life starts looking a lot like death.[12] "All flesh is grass," yet the living embrace never quite achieves the union for which it hungers—except perhaps as the union it fears.

So much for the body: unhurt, but unfree. Trying to twist free, in the other direction, from the human dilemma, Marvell shifts from the condition of the body in mindlessness to the condition of the mind disembodied:[13]

> Meanwhile the mind, from pleasure less,
> Withdraws into its happiness:
> The mind, that ocean where each kind

Does straight its own resemblance find,
Yet it creates, transcending these,
Far other worlds, and other seas,
Annihilating all that's made
To a green thought in a green shade.
(lines 41–48)

What is the connection, what is the distinction, between these modes of green?[14] Is the mind gazing narcissistically on the reflecting surface of the water and imagining it sees depths that resemble its own world; or does the hidden world indeed correspond to the known one? Can we ever even know the difference?[15] The creation ex nihilo is undone—"annihilated"—so that the mind can re-do it.[16] The notion (which Sir Thomas Browne, among others, identifies as a Renaissance commonplace) that each creature on land has a counterpart in the ocean—porkers and porc-pisces, horses and sea-horses—establishes a metaphor for a nominalist model of valid cognition, in which each entity in the world has an equivalent marker in the mind, a one-to-one correspondence of thought and thing.

The fantasy of the universal-language projectors (contemporary with Marvell) of having only a single word for each entity, and none for non-entities, remains a temptress, alluring yet elusive and sinister, throughout this poem. The mind begins to run away with the game—and never had any meaningful way to keep score anyway. How can we ever make real contact with nature if we derive from classical and Renaissance skepticism alike an insurmountable dualism?[17] We may be seeing a green shade, and we may be having a green thought, but those are incommensurable entities. As Lord Herbert of Cherbury argued, "if the visual species are nothing but the Rays of Colours . . . the Memory to produce these species must have interior colours, and be truly colour'd as well as the objects that produce them. Since the images of objects which the senses have perceived are present in the Memory, they must be different from those which the objects sent thither"[18]—different, or at least "other."[19] Locke proposed a similar distinction, arguing that the coloration of porphyry, which disappears in darkness, must consist of "a configuration of particles, both night and day, as are apt, by the rays of light rebounding from some parts of that hard stone, to produce in us the idea of redness, and from others the idea of whiteness; but whiteness or redness are not in it at any time, but such a texture that hath the power to produce such a sensation in us."[20]

And perhaps not in all of us: the skepticism about perceiving essences blends into the skepticism about sense-perception generally, and thence into the skepticism concerning other minds. If earlier stanzas could remind modern readers of the vengeful apple trees in *The Wizard of Oz*, unwilling to have their

fruit picked for human satisfaction, this one plunges us into the solipsistic paradox of the Emerald City, which (in L. Frank Baum's book) appears so only because all visitors are required to wear green-tinted glasses, under pretense of
protecting their eyes from the overwhelmingly magnificent glow. As Sir Walter
Ralegh observed, "The very object which seemeth unto us white, unto them
which have the jaundice seemeth pale, and red unto those whose eyes are bloodshot. Forasmuch then as living creatures have some white, some pale, some red
eyes, why should not one and the same object seem to some white, to some red,
to some pale?"[21] We may note that bloodshot eyes actually replace white with
red for the person looking at them, not the person looking through them, but
that only proves Marvell's point: it is easy to entangle the problem of unreliable
perception with the problem of other minds; and certainly the question of how
objects produce our perception of color was a nagging one throughout the seventeenth century. In 1605, Sir Thomas Bright had specifically warned that the
imagination sometimes "putteth greene spectacles before the eyes of the witte,
to make it see nothing but greene."[22] Commentators on Marvell's verse all try to
lend a meaning to "green" here, but what if it is just a green to which we lend
meanings (as plants are described, with odd flatness, as only plants in the opening stanzas)?

The "ancient dilemma" explored by Wesley Trimpi was the inverse propor-
tion between the knowability and the excellence of any objects of human attention.[23] But late-Renaissance science was finding that even the seemingly meanest
material object was both wonderful and incurably mysterious. Shakespeare's
Sonnet 53 begins by asking his beloved the same question science was beginning
to ask natural entities:

What is your substance, whereof are you made,
That millions of strange shadows on you tend?

The reality is out there, instead, as an infinitely complex noumenal flow:[24] waves,
as Christiaan Huygens argued, in the unbroken range of frequencies that we
sort and name, but remain themselves; a flux of particles, according to Isaac
Newton (both these seventeenth-century geniuses seem to have been correct);
and we can never see them face-to-face until we somehow abandon the bodies
through which we see them. Donne experiments with a version of this amorous
transcendence in "Air and Angels"; Marvell's own "Dialogue Between the Soul
and Body" explores its difficulties, in which the hands are themselves the manacles of a soul that hangs "Here blinded with an eye; and there / Deaf with the
drumming of an ear" (lines 5–6). One critic justly warns that "it makes no sense
to talk about 'The Garden' as if its author were conversant with the works of

Freud or Sartre or Heidegger."[25] But the idea of mistrusting the senses as a means toward reality goes back to Parmenides, and the understanding of poetry as primarily a medium for philosophy was commonplace in the literary criticism of the late Renaissance—for example, in studies of Ovid by Sabinus and others. Anyway, these ideas were blossoming in cultures with which Marvell was quite probably familiar. In *De utilitate credendi*, Augustine had distanced himself "from the minds of vain men, who, having too far advanced and fallen into these corporeal things, think that there is nothing else than what they perceive by those five well-known reporters of the body; and what impressions and images they have received from these, they carry over with themselves, even when they essay to withdraw from the senses; and by the deadly and most deceitful rule of these think that they measure most rightly the unspeakable recesses of truth."[26] In 1648—about the time Marvell would likely have been composing "The Garden"—Descartes was speculating similarly about transcending the very limited ways normal human sensations and reason take hold of God: "Intuitive knowledge is an illumination of the mind, by which it sees in the light of God whatever it pleases him to show it by a direct impress of the divine clarity on our understanding, which in this is not considered as an agent but simply as a receiver of the rays of divinity. . . . Can you doubt that our mind, when it is detached from the body, or has a glorified body which will no longer hinder it, can receive such direct illumination and knowledge? Why, even in this body the senses give it such knowledge of corporeal and sensible things."[27] Dutch art, particularly as it abjures story and even single-point perspective, flirts (I will argue) with this possibility of seeing the object itself, without subjectivity; for the late Vermeer, "the conceptual world of names and knowledge is forgotten, nothing concerns him but what is visible, the tone, the wedge of light."[28] Marvell, like twenty-first century cognitive scientists, asks whether the human mind can ever function as such a perfectly passive receiver.

Donne's "Of the Progress of the Soul: The Second Anniversary" demonstrates that the issue was alive in early seventeenth-century England: "Thou shalt not peep through lattices of eyes, / Nor hear through labyrinths of ears. . . . In heaven thou straight know'st all" (lines 296–99). So, again, does Ralegh: "For suppose that some man is born blind and deaf, and yet can touch, smell, and taste: this man will not think that there is any thing which may be seen or heard . . . he will only think there are those qualities in the object, which by reason of his three senses he conceiveth."[29] Montaigne "doubts whether man is provided with all the senses of nature. I see many animals that live a complete and perfect life, some without sight, others without hearing; who knows whether we too do not still lack one, two, three, or many other senses";[30] Pierre Charron expresses similar doubts.[31] Blake's "Marriage of Heaven and Hell" would raise the same philosophical question in a poetic mode: "How do you know but ev'ry Bird that cuts the airy way / Is an immense world of delight, clos'd by your senses five?" When Marvell observes that an heir of Appleton House

> laid these gardens out in sport
> In the just figure of a fort;
> And with five bastions it did fence,
> As aiming one for every sense
> ("Upon Appleton House," lines 285–88)

he too seems aware that the self is a fortress as much as a garden, with the senses as its outer barriers.

But "The Garden" shows that Marvell can also dream of what it might mean to join Blake's visionary company:

> Here at the fountain's sliding foot,
> Or at some fruit-tree's mossy root,
> Casting the body's vest aside,
> My soul into the boughs does glide:
> There like a bird it sits, and sings,
> Then whets, and combs its silver wings;
> And, till prepar'd for longer flight,
> Waves in its plumes the various light.
> (lines 49–56)

The craving for the youthful beauty, or the classical godhead, that is now hidden in a tree (as in the Daphne and Syrinx stories of the fourth stanza)—the lingering sense modern nature lovers share with Renaissance culture that some lovely and ultimate truth awaits discovery in a leafy grove (and its fractals)—has migrated from the stem up into the branches; but it is still just out of reach.

As in the theology of Incarnation and transubstantiation, even the most sublime presence needs materiality to become manifest: an idea needs a host. Furthermore—as Kant would emphasize—the host needs an idea. In 1553 Philip Melanchthon remarked that "if living things took in a great number of objects without discernment or composition or any reason whatsoever, how little use would be the flow of objects to the inner senses! Thus in addition to the outer senses there is another superior faculty, more marvelous than the simple apprehension of the outer senses."[32] The effort either to enter the natural world completely or escape it completely therefore stalls exactly where it stalled in *As You Like It*, at the distance of simile: "like a bird." The "easie Philosopher" of "Upon

Appleton House" imagines taking on the identity "Or of the fowles, or of the plants" and conferring

> In their most learned original:
> And where I language want, my signs
> The bird upon the bough divines.
> (lines 564–72)

Other, harder philosophers take a different view, and (to adapt Blake's phrase about Milton) Marvell is of their party without quite saying it. Only at the level of pure light does the barrier dissolve; this time it is the mysticism rather than the science of the seventeenth century that anticipates Einstein. Ficino speaks of "a light diffused almost through the immense inane, which is made beautiful with innumerable colors, and turns in a circle; and by that revolution it sings in the sweetest modes, filling and softening our ears. . . . The phantasy, friend of the senses, creates nothing more sublime."[33] Hermes Trismegistus celebrates a moment when "forthwith all things changed in aspect before me, and were opened out in a moment. And I beheld a boundless view; all was changed into light."[34] The far less mystical Francis Bacon nonetheless seems ready to concede the point: "Truth may perhaps come to the price of a pearl . . . but it will not rise to the price of a diamond or carbuncle, that showeth best in varied lights."[35] The same point could be—and sometimes was—couched in a Platonic vocabulary: we see the shadows, not the forms. Bacon, adapting Democritus, even applies that principle implicitly to our understanding of nature itself, for all his empirical work with it: "the truth of nature lieth in certain deep mines and caves."[36]

Or perhaps in the dazzling air, where we can briefly imagine rising, where perhaps we will hover longer after earthly life (and then see God face-to-face; Donne argues that "Moses saw God . . . Removed from all benefit and assistance of bodily senses").[37] This full shimmering spectrum of the phenomenal world, or more precisely, the self that can accept that world in its full undefined presence, is what is lost in our fall into mortal bodies, categorical thinking, and the semantic staccato of words. Joseph Glanvill believed that, before the Fall, "even the sense, the Soul's windows, were without any spot or opacity."[38] Even in this scintillating bird, Marvell (or his speaker) is both the observer and the observed. It takes one to know one, and we aren't one anymore:

> Such was that happy garden-state,
> While man there walked without a mate:
> After a place so pure, and sweet,
> What other help could yet be meet!
> But 'twas beyond a mortal's share

To wander solitary there:
Two paradises 'twere in one
To live in paradise alone.
("The Garden," lines 57–64)

Marvell turns the identification of "*amoenus* and *amorem*, a lovely place and a place for loving," familiar from Servius,[39] into an opposition; here we are invited to mistake this attempt for conventional misogyny, but it is no more so than the rest of the poem is simple regressive pastoralism. The neurosensory processes of the body mean that all reality is virtual; the cultural conventions of society merely add another level of mediation to what is already second-hand, misrepresented because rendered representable.[40] The pun on "share" suggests that—even before it became various because vicarious—experience was never, could never be, privately owned: there is no title on this real estate, nor any deed that can confer one legitimately.

Shakespeare's experience as a "sharer" in his theater company must have alerted him to these complications in their socioeconomic and artistic manifestations, and in "The Phoenix and the Turtle" he explores what they mean to a lover:

Property was thus appalled,
That the self was not the same;
Single nature's double name
Neither two nor one was called.
(lines 37–40)

As Plato asked Cratylus, if a god were to provide a full copy of him, body and soul, "would you say that this was Cratylus and the image of Cratylus, or that there were two Cratyluses?"[41] Marvell suggests that perception narrowly fails as that god, creating a simulacrum of the world that does not erase the separate and perhaps superior existence of the world in itself. Indeed, that Platonic dialogue pulls together the ironies of the name carved on the tree in stanza 3 and the model of the parallel undersea worlds in stanza 6: "how ridiculous would be the effect of names on the thing named, if they were exactly the same with them! For they would be the doubles of them, and no one would be able to determine which were the names and which were the realities." Descartes' *Optics* makes almost exactly the same argument about visual perception that the *Cratylus* made about names: "in no case does an image have to resemble the object it represents in all respects, for otherwise there would be no distinction between the object and its image."[42]

While the aforementioned universal-language projectors sought a simple system of indicators—only one name for each object, only one object for each name—the poet saw that the beast of consciousness could not be tamed by merely tying up its tongue. Since our fall into cognition, and as long as that damns us to the uneasy coexistence of green thoughts and green shades, equal but separate, no one can be alone in paradise, it is always two in one—the one we can perceive and name and claim to love, and the one that is that it is, moving in mysterious ways:

> How well the skilful gard'ner drew
> Of flowers and herbs this dial new,
> Where from above the milder sun
> Does through a fragrant zodiac run;
> And, as it works, the industrious bee
> Computes its time as well as we.
> How could such sweet and wholesome hours
> Be reckoned but with herbs and flowers!
> ("The Garden," lines 65–72)

Is this an artificial, chronometric sundial ingeniously contrived by a gardener out of flowers, the imposition of our chronological grid on a spatial grid; or is the garden its own sundial, made by the maker of the first garden, whose seasonal order still looks to us, or now looks to us, like chaos? Can we understand this garden in its own terms—or except in its own terms? Even the sun and stars we may channel into our zodiacal grid of time and space and myth (perhaps by watching their shadows move on the earth—another green shade), but the seasonal heliotropic flowers track them in a different way.[43] To every thing, there is a season, but not the same season. We have time, and the bee (in a pun that persists in Marvell's Latin version of the poem) has its thyme. The garden is self-referential, and so are we. The garden is lovely, and our alienation from it is complete. It is in us, more than we are in it. The closer we come to embracing it, the more decisively we feel ourselves failing.

We withdraw from the world into the garden, and then from the garden into the mind; can we go any further, or even know where we have been? Marvell's "Garden" begins by rejecting the social-symbolic power of the leaves we wrap around our heads; in the middle, persons become trees; but by the end we wonder—as in *As You Like It*—whether we can ever get the leaves outside of our heads, whether we can ever let nature be itself.[44] The inverted tree of "Upon Appleton House" (line 568) becomes here an introjected tree. The epistemological work of the poem is as futile as the aesthetic work is superfluous. Nature measures time, manifests order, creates beauty—all the prime works of the lyric art—whether we attend to it or not.

Against Gardens

At least outside any severely Calvinist revulsion from nature, the green world often implied salvation. Henry Vaughan praises "St. Mary Magdalene" as "fresher than morning-flowers," an "innocent," "Native," "Bloomy and fresh" beauty who has left behind the meretricious sophistications, and now bends down to the earth because

> thou knew'st, flowers here on earth
> At their Lord's foot-stool have their birth;
> Therefore thy wither'd self in haste
> Beneath his blest feet thou didst cast,
> That at the root of this green tree
> Thy great decays restor'd might be.

Shakespeare—in more of a psychological, less of a theological vein—often suggests that the green world offers an escape from culture, back to basic in-stinctual truths of the self. Though it usually hedges its hedges, pastoral is always proposing itself as a cure: for love, courtly corruptions, the ills of modernity. Yet the hope of a redemptive return to the Garden fails in "The Garden" and the "Mower" poems—as in *Paradise Lost*—because the self-regarding reflex of the mind is always already bringing the fallen world back in.[45] Marvell's ecological pilgrims might echo Donne's lovelorn "Twickenham Garden": "And that this place may thoroughly be thought / True paradise, I have the serpent brought"—a picnicker carrying a basketful of ants, just in case.

People are also bound to fail as unprejudiced recipients of natural beauty because of how their minds work—and this is not only a theological judgment on their inner moral fiber, but also a psychological one about the way that fiber is woven. They fail because of the frailty, not just of their sanctity, but also of their sanity. The imposition of garden onto nature offers an apt metaphor for the imposition of cognitive process onto the raw data of the senses. As in Jacob van Ruisdael's landscapes (and later in Van Gogh), "the Abyss . . . Of that un-fathomable Grass" evokes the terrifying complexity of the information that we are constantly seeking to assimilate and that creative artists are dangerously obliged not to simplify prematurely into categories and conventions; "To see men through this meadow dive, / We wonder how they rise alive" ("Upon Ap-pleton House," lines 377–78). Yet that is the task of mowers: to cut nature down so it can be consumed.

"The Mower Against Gardens" makes the primitivist case most directly.[46]

The nature that people make is, more obviously than in the other "Mower" poems, a perversion of the nature that exists in itself, and our tendency to build ourselves a simulation of what is already there looks like a spiritual error (as a surface reading of "The Garden" would suggest) rather than a philosophical necessity (as "The Garden" implies more deeply):

> Luxurious man, to bring his vice in use,
>   Did after him the world seduce,
> And from the fields the flowers and plants allure,
>   Where nature was most plain and pure.
>
> (lines 1–4)

This version of the *hortus conclusus* keeps innocence out (and nature corrupted takes on the meretricious aspects of woman corrupted;[47] Adam has passed on to the earth the disease he caught from Eve, a transaction "The Mower's Song" will re-examine). Here we have not Annunciation but denunciation, as human solipsism and narcissism impose, by genetic engineering, their own in-carnation. The opening line's "use" (as in "usual") yields to "use" (as in "usury"), crushing with multiplicity the desire for simplicity:

> He first enclosed within the gardens square
>   A dead and standing pool of air,
> And a more luscious earth for them did knead,
>   Which stupefied them while it fed.
> The pink grew then as double as his mind;
>   The nutriment did change the kind.
>
> (lines 5–10)

The mower divided from his thoughts, and the green shade divided from the green thought, surely come to mind here; this plaintiff claims alienation of affection, as if real unity had ever been possible.

But the association between human estrangement from nature and human erotic frustrations seems conventionally satiric, rather than essentially tragic as in the other "Mower" poems:

> With strange perfumes he did the roses taint,
>   And flowers themselves were taught to paint.
> The tulip, white, did for complexion seek,
>   And learned to interline its cheek:
> Its onion root they then so high did hold,
>   That one was for a meadow sold.
>
> (lines 11–16)

The fall from simple nature manifests itself partly in complications (the pun on "complexion" associates man-made complexity with meretricious make-up), and then specifically in the fall into capitalism—of which Holland and its tulipomania were even then considered exemplary. The fear of nature corrupted expresses itself as a fear of the arbitrary way monetary signifiers and absurd exchange values can take the place of original objects—and indeed much of the inflationary bubble had to do less with the flowers than with paper transactions of commodity futures, which were bought and sold at several removes from the actual objects. Capitalism carried to its logical absurdity, where the things themselves became almost irrelevant to the speculative process, stands in here for the collapse of any comprehensible signifying order; and it rouses the simple man's notorious, instinctive, conjoined suspicions of novelty, abstraction, aesthetics, and women's sexuality.

The world has been turned upside down (and if the commentators who have plausibly viewed this poem as Marvell's political critique of a naive Leveller primitivism are correct,[48] it is nonetheless important to note that this critique is built on broader grounds: philosophical, psychological, economic). Now that world will also be turned inside out, and ransacked—and again, as in "The Garden," the trees themselves are threatened with something like rape, a human attempt to force the other into the self that repeatedly marks the Fall in Marvell's "Mower" poems:

> Another world was searched, through oceans new,
>   To find the *Marvel of Peru.*
> And yet these rarities might be allowed,
>   To man, that sovereign thing and proud,
> Had he not dealt between the bark and tree,
>   Forbidden mixtures there to see.
> No plant now knew the stock from which it came;
>   He grafts upon the wild the tame:
> That th' uncertain and adulterate fruit
>   Might put the palate in dispute.
> His green seraglio has its eunuchs too,
>   Lest any tyrant him outdo;
> And in the cherry he does nature vex,
>   To procreate without a sex.
> 'Tis all enforced, the fountain and the grot,
>   While the sweet fields do lie forgot:
> Where willing nature does to all dispense
>   A wild and fragrant innocence:
> And fauns and fairies do the meadows till,
>   More by their presence than their skill.
> Their statues, polish'd by some ancient hand,

May to adorn the gardens stand:
But howso'er the figures do excel,
The gods themselves with us do dwell.
                              (lines 17–40)

The struggle to weigh the value of artistic statues against living figures may remind us of Shakespeare's *Winter's Tale*. As in that play (as well as in "The Garden"), the mistrust of sexuality in this poem always seems like a subconscious displacement of larger epistemological questions that no one quite dares confront directly. A reader almost expects some Marvellian Polixenes to stand up and answer this Perdita voice, with its mixture of natural appetites and proud pieties. But Polixenes would argue—at least where gillyvors are concerned—that the natural and the artificial can and should be blended. Marvell's other "Mower" poems acknowledge that desire, but doubt the possibility: unadulterated nature and the human mind have irreconcilable differences. They stand divorced, not because a perversion made the marriage abusive (as the speaker of "Against Gardens" implies), but because (as Marvell here and elsewhere implies) the marriage is never really consummated. By a kind of flower-bed-trick, the nature we embrace never turns out to be the one we imagined ourselves in love with.

Glowworms and Lost Light

"The Mower to the Glowworms" introduces, in its single sentence, the problems of pastoral nostalgia that *As You Like It* explores in so many voices. The first three stanzas, separately and together, seem to comprise an apostrophe to benevolent natural forces; yet the very rhetoric that carries the praise also signals the estrangement, through the speaker's anthropomorphizing reflex and sophisticated punning. Sometimes a worm is just a worm, not a supernatural emissary to the human race; the pioneering field naturalist John Ray insisted that the mystically anthropomorphized "will-of-the-wisp" was really just a glowworm.[49] After all, these glowworms are not really lamps, nor are they "courteous" or "officious" to any human aim. The nightingale does not use them to study sheet music, nor does it sit meditating its songs.[50] "Matchless" puns on the fact that it sings to attract an avian mate (rather than to impress a human judge), and the humble disavowal of any "higher end" is belied by the means, by the puns on each word that carefully balance the measurably physical and the humanly figurative:

Ye living lamps, by whose dear light
The nightingale does sit so late,

And studying all the summer night,
Her matchless songs does meditate;

Ye country comets, that portend
No war, nor prince's funeral,
Shining unto no higher end
Than to presage the grass's fall;

Ye glowworms, whose officious flame
To wandering mowers shows the way,
That in the night have lost their aim,
And after foolish fires do stray. . . .

We are likely to lose our own way here, supposing we are being invited to join a collective loving embrace of nature, only to find that this is a profoundly solitary itinerary, one in which the speaker has lost contact with both the human community (that is why he is talking to glowworms) and nature (their response, if any, is meaningless to him). That disease of alienation, of which the anthropomorphism is an early symptom,[51] suddenly sets in. Plot and psychology enter, serpent-like, the garden of eulogy, producing a fall from the rising arc of the previous stanzas into the painful bewilderment of self-consciousness and (its usual Renaissance companion) separation from nature:

Your courteous lights in vain you waste,
Since Juliana here is come,
For she my mind hath so displaced
That I shall never find my home.

In the final stanza, while the syntax finds a suitable destination, the mower's story takes a dark turn indeed: this is a sentence of exile (as Gloucester says in *King Lear* [4.1.18], "I have no way, and therefore want no eyes"). The anthropomorphic rhetoric suggests that the speaker cannot quite recall, let alone reacquire, that lost symbiosis; again, as in the normal human amnesia about infant experience, it seems virtually impossible for adults to remember how the world seemed before the intervention of language.

This, then, is the complaint of the body confused by thought, the body that, in Marvell's dialogue, complains that it "could never rest, / Since this ill spirit it possessed" ("Dialogue Between the Soul and Body," lines 19–20). It is the same "never" as in the last line of "The Mower to the Glowworms." In the *Institutes*, Calvin warned that postlapsarian humanity can no longer discern the path God has lit for us, because something has come between us and any clear, direct reading of created nature:

But although the Lord represents both himself and his everlasting Kingdom in the mirror of his works with very great clarity, such is our stupidity that we grow increasingly dull toward so manifest testimonies, and they flow away without profiting us. . . . It is therefore in vain that so many burning lamps shine for us in the workmanship of the universe to show forth the glory of its Author. Although they bathe us wholly in their radiance, yet they can of themselves in no way lead us into the right path. Surely they strike some sparks, but before their fuller light shines forth these are smothered.[52]

My point is not to reduce Marvell's lyric to a theological allegory, but to suggest the way it draws and comments on epistemological pressures in the culture— "the sense of dislocation caused by the crumbling of familiar landmarks"[53]— which provoke a primitivist impulse manifest in pastoral nostalgia and Protestant theology alike.

"Song" and Separation

"The Mower to the Glowworms" is ostensibly a poem of frustrated love that never in fact mentions love at all. This certainly suggests that something else is at stake; Juliana has displaced his mind, not broken his heart. All the same can be said of "The Mower's Song." Again the woman is a marker of otherness, nothing in herself—notice the complete absence of her voice or her description in these poems—and the desire for her produces (or reflects) a recognition of a loss of symbiotic presence in the universe that is a perpetual fact for the human creature, despite the impulse to hide it behind a particular erotic betrayal. For Marvell's mower as for Spenser's Colin,[54] the warnings, so characteristic of Mantuan pastoral, that men should not fall in love with women come under an interrogation that reveals their misogyny as a displacement of problems of identity and knowledge. The conventional love complaint explodes into an epistemological bereavement.

"The Mower's Song" begins by proposing a radically transparent—or more precisely, reflective—theory of the mind, a theory the speaker is not quite prepared to surrender, even though he is by now out of that mind:

> My mind was once the true survey
> Of all these meadows fresh and gay,
> And in the greenness of the grass
> Did see its hopes as in a glass;
> When Juliana came, and she
> What I do to the grass, does to my thoughts and me.
>
> (lines 1–6)

The latent pun on "hopes" and "hops" (perhaps abetted by the association of green with hope in liturgical vestments) echoes the notion of the first two lines that mind is merely an echo of meadow. This notion was hardly the exclusive property of artless rustics. Leonardo da Vinci suggested that simile can be passive and therefore perfect: "The painter's mind should be as a mirror, which transforms itself into the color of the thing that it has as its object, and is filled with as many likenesses as there are things placed before it."[55] This again resembles the universal-language project, mapping the world onto words in a one-to-one correspondence. Sprat asserted that "the mind of Man is a Glass, which is able to represent to itself, all the Works of *Nature*" (p. 97).

But even a "true survey" is not the soil: Richard Carew's *Survey of Cornwall* (1602) apologizes that, rather than showing the full delights of a landscape, he must instead "do my best, to trace you a shaddow thereof, by which you shal (in part) give a gess at the substance."[56] As a later, more skeptical stage of Renaissance thought (best exemplified by Descartes) would predict,[57] this mower has now become not only divided from nature, but also divergent from it; or, more precisely, he perceives that nature has diverged from him, leaving him alienated from his own mind as well, now that he can no longer assume that it reflects the world by a simple system of reception or correspondence. His vision is doubly doubly troubled, and (as the speaker turns to evergreen-sick pine) the grass seems to wield a dangerous "blade" of its own:

> But these, while I with sorrow pine,
> Grew more luxuriant still and fine,
> That not one blade of grass you spied,
> But had a flower on either side;
> When Juliana came, and she
> What I do to the grass, does to my thoughts and me.
>
> Unthankful meadows, could you so
> A fellowship so true forgo?
> And in your gaudy May-games meet,
> While I lay trodden under feet?
> When Juliana came, and she
> What I do to the grass, does to my thoughts and me.
>   (lines 7–18)

He has ceased to intervene with his blade, but his mind is still subjugating the grasses to human purposes: they are mocking him only because he has ceased mowing them, but in another sense, they are mocking him only because he has made them volitional and conscious creatures. The play on the names of Juliana and July—which makes her represent a time in nature as the Silvias of other pastorals sometimes represent the places in nature called *silvae*—is pushed to the forefront by the reference to May. Is it the random advent of the woman, or simply the inevitable time of the season, that has driven this young man's heart to love? Is the force that drives the flowers to build their garnished poles in May so different from the force that drives country community to do the same? In other words (and the same cluster of issues arises in Petrarch's *Rime*),[58] is human subjectivity controlling the biological world around us, or controlled by it?

In Book 9 of Milton's *Paradise Lost*, a sympathetic groan of nature marks the Fall; in Marvell, what betokens the Fall is the observed absence of any such sympathy. The speaker's sense of betrayal derives as much from a lapse of pathetic fallacy in his beloved nature as from any failure of requital from his beloved Juliana. He does not even imagine doing anything about her, but—like the protagonist of Ariosto's *Orlando furioso*, who destroys the forest that records Angelica's love for another—toward nature his course is clear. Perhaps (as the shift to present tense implies) in a display of resentment designed to threaten and punish the approaching Juliana, he will forcibly renew that broken correspondence, save the appearances, make the meadow reflect his fallen mind, even though his divided self must now know that it is projective rather than perceptive, that (as the end of each stanza suggests) he is divided from himself, in bad faith to himself, when he compels the faithfulness of the natural world to his mind:

> But what you in compassion ought,
> Shall now by my revenge be wrought;
> And flow'rs, and grass, and I and all,
> Will in one common ruin fall.
> For Juliana comes, and she
> What I do to the grass, does to my thoughts and me.
>   (lines 19–24)

It's a compulsory round of ring-around-the-rosy, and the fall into ashes is the compulsory finish. Nature might aptly here complain as the Soul does in Marvell's "Dialogue Between the Soul and Body" (with the pun on "pine" this time recalling Ariel "Imprison'd" magically "Into a cloven pine" in *The Tempest*, 1.2.277): "What magic could me thus confine / Within another's grief to pine?" (lines 21–22). This "magic" is exactly the one that Descartes tried to locate (in the pineal gland, or perhaps the thalamus) and that Geulincx and Malebranche concluded required divine intervention on each occasion. Marvell reminds us that, as the soul protests the compulsion to share the body's suffering and degradation, so might nature easily protest (if this were not itself pathetic fallacy) against the pathetic fallacy, beloveds against their unrequited Petrarchan wooers, and objects generally against human subjectivity.

Marvell here re-enacts the collapse of denial in the late-Hellenistic *Lament for Bion* (often attributed to Moschus), which claims that Bion's death "The trees of all their fruitage strips; / And all the little flowers are stark and dead," yet then acknowledges that

> Another year revives them presently
> And they once more will be what they have been.
> But we, the wise, the great, the valiant men,
> When we once die, deaf in the hollow ground
> We sleep full well, never to wake again;
> Unending is our slumber deep and sound.[59]

The connection between the collective fall to the ground proposed by the mower and the ruinous universal Fall that alienated human beings from nature becomes unmistakable, and it can lead him nowhere but to death:

> And thus, ye meadows, which have been
> Companions of my thoughts more green,
> Shall now the heraldry become
> With which I shall adorn my tomb;
> For Juliana comes, and she
> What I do to the grass, does to my thoughts and me.
> (lines 25–30)

And what does this finally mean? Were his thoughts simply greener—more full of youthful hope—than they are now (even the left-margin typography suggests regression); or does he (as in the similar phrase in "The Garden") recognize that the meadow's greenness was more truly present in his mind (which reads as green a particular frequency of light-waves it seems to receive) than in the meadow itself? Or are these two meanings essentially the same, since his despair arises precisely from recognizing that his mind and his meadows are not the same thing, and indeed that (in a reversal of Descartes) the mortality of the former is marked most clearly by the immortality of the latter? The midsummer crisis is a midlife crisis, and the manifest world is the lover he has lost in his encounter with otherness, figured here (as so often in men's writing) as the female object of desire.[60] It may seem true that (as one Marvell scholar suggests) "the Mower group contains possibly his finest ironic commentary on the incompatibility between love of nature and love of woman":[61] the mower feels he has foolishly abandoned the love of a warm nature for the love of a cold woman.

On another level, however, these both represent the same doomed love, and both manifest the incompatibility of consciousness with total immersion in reality. As Carolyn Merchant has shown, the history of human aggression against the natural environment is deeply intertwined with the history of masculine aggression against the feminine.[62] As Janet Adelman has shown, however, a mother's over-eager embrace (at least in Shakespearean drama) can kill as effectively as rejection by a mistress;[63] the same may be true of Mother Earth. A study of contemporary environmentalism concludes by warning that the alliance of ecologism with primitivism is ultimately "a death-wish";[64] I believe that such an alliance was first forged in the late Renaissance and that some poets, painters, and playwrights already recognized that its logical conclusion was a very dark victory.

As "half adjuncts of the estate, half free agents" in the labor economy of the period,[65] mowers seem apt bearers of questions about (to adapt Wordsworth's formula) "what they half create / And what perceive" ("Lines . . . Tintern Abbey," lines 106–7). Moreover, even the hardest practices of pastoral imply acceptance of and nurturance toward nature that contrasts sharply with what now seems the appalling callousness of many hunting (and game-fighting) practices;[66] this mower's demise is only the natural conclusion of the element of passivity implicit in tending cultivated fields and domesticated livestock.[67] These other living things are his life's work; he is in their service, and gives his body that they may grow. In this sense, nature plays a slow-motion Diana to the agricultural Actaeon, turning him fatally into the foodstuff he intended to exploit.

The site of burial raises questions similar to those about the cause of death. Apparently the mower intends the fallen grass to mark his grave[68]—I suspect a latent pun on the background "field" of heraldry (as in the final line of Marvell's "Unfortunate Lover")—though we are doubtless invited to recognize that before long it will spring back up eagerly, will write his epitaph in its own language, just as the flowers of "The Garden" compose a sundial that outlasts the kind the "skillful gardener" might have imposed. The Biblical proverb that "all flesh is grass,"[69] which seems so much on Marvell's mind in these poems, is a metaphor that time will literalize. Can any verbal epitaph gain the last word against the whispering campaign of the grasses, or any eulogy (though many try) refute the biodegradation? Can the mower actually control nature by this dying representation of it, or is he merely trying to pre-empt its imminent defeat of him (and arrogation of his body to express itself), appropriate its inevitable action of growth as if it were his will (and testament), just as he had earlier cut the grass into that kind of conformity? Unable to answer these questions, I can only observe that it is characteristic of Marvell's lyrics that they drive us into fields of question marks, which replicate—like flower buds flanking blades of grass—the more we chop them down.

"Damon" and Death

The classic motto of the pastoral world during the Renaissance was spoken either by a dead man or by death itself. Erwin Panofsky argues that "I [am] in Arcadia too" (or, "Death is even in Arcadia" as Panofsky renders it) is "a grammatically correct, in fact, the only grammatically correct, interpretation of the Latin phrase *Et in Arcadia ego* . . . our modern reading of its message—'I, too, was born, or lived, in Arcady'—is in reality a mistranslation," because there is no justification for "supplying the missing verb in the form of a *vixi* or a *fui* instead of a *sum*."[70] But what if there is a third choice: what if, overcoming our natural reluctance to put the first translation in the corpse's mouth or the second translation in the present tense, we acknowledge that the dead man is now in Arcady—is no less truly in organic harmony with nature as a corpse than he was as a shepherd?[71] In the Guercino painting (Figure 1), just above the equivocal inscribed motto, mouse, worm, and fly are welcoming whatever is left of the brain back into nature. Poussin's meditative versions of *Et in Arcadia ego* would sustain the same reading. Death may be present even in Arcadia, but Arcadia may be truly present only in death, where the human ego is erased: Arcadia is also in me, says the Grim Reaper, encouragingly. Come die with me and be my love, says nature to the pastoral amorist. This is a voice that Tibullus heard,[72] as did Pseudo-Dionysius,[73] and perhaps Sidney;[74] my chapter 2 described the deathly seduction that turned Spenser's Fradubio into a tree. The mower Damon's intuitive response to the displacement of his mind—the alienation that Juliana has caused, the death of pathetic fallacy, or whatever mediations are encoded in those—is to mow his body, to take on suicidally the role of that Reaper. The moral is almost Zen: the enemy is selfhood and its desires, a corrupt consciousness that becomes manifest as ineradicable self-consciousness, which is coded as alienation from nature, which is blamed (passionately by the speaker, but only half-heartedly by the author) on unrequited love. Again, however, we do not have to look so far afield: Montaigne observes that the Pyrrhonist program of "taking all things in without adherence or consent, leads them to their Ataraxy, which is a peaceful and sedate condition of life, exempt from the agitations we receive through the impression of the opinion and knowledge we think we have of things."[75] This *ataraxia* seems disturbingly similar to the Arcadia found in death. Oblivion is a state of nature.

Figure 1.   Giovanni Francesco Barbieri Guercino (Il Guercino, 1591–1666), *Et in Arcadia ego*, 1618–22. Oil on canvas, 82 × 91 cm. Galleria Nazionale d'Arte Antica, Rome. Photo: Scala/Art Resource, NY.

The first stanza of "Damon the Mower" suggests that Damon's experience of nature has become infected with culture, including song-writing, painting, theater, and persistent Petrarchan similes:

> Hark how the Mower Damon sung,
> With love of Juliana stung!
> While everything did seem to paint
> The scene more fit for his complaint.
> Like her fair eyes the day was fair,
> But scorching like his am'rous care.
> Sharp like his scythe his sorrow was,
> And withered like his hopes the grass.
>   (lines 1–8)

The pun from "The Mower's Song" recurs: on a grain farm, hopes are, and are not, hops. One critic describes the mower as "a childlike figure, unable or unwilling to distinguish between his own desires and reality";[76] but the poems seem to me to suggest that such inability or unwillingness is not exclusively childlike, even if children help us recognize this universal human tendency by performing it unsubtly. As in *As You Like It*, the thrumming bass of "like" here suggests that the human mind cannot quite stay absorbed in nature, and therefore imposes its own identities on objects that previously simply were, imposes false equivalencies (and hence limitations) on the infinite variety and infinite power of nature. In this lyric as in that comedy, the conventionalized artistic markers sit uneasily in a supposedly back-to-nature setting.

The second stanza flirts with the anthropomorphic impositions that characterize Duke Senior's rhetoric in *As You Like It* (2.1), but the irony (typically for Marvell) is more delicate. The meadows could be scorched by the sun, the grasshopper has a relevant wind-pipe if no Pan-pipe, the frogs wade (if not exactly dance) on hamstring muscles:

> "Oh what unusual heats are here,
> Which thus our sunburned meadows sear!
> The grasshopper its pipe gives o'er;
> And hamstringed frogs can dance no more.
> But in the brook the green frog wades;
> And grasshoppers seek out the shades.
> Only the snake, that kept within,
> Now glitters in its second skin."
>
> (lines 9–16)

The interior snake that slides glittering into view—the inner secret of nature—is partly a low-lying version of the soul that has "cast its bodily vest aside" and become the molting bird whose essence shimmers over "The Garden." But the distinction between the frogs and grasshoppers who change their environment and the snake who changes himself is (as modern ecological theory would insist) a blurry one. Furthermore—as "The Mower's Song" has already suggested, and "Damon the Mower" finally will too—the only way to know the interior of nature may be to enter it through death. In the "Apology for Raymond Sebond," Montaigne quotes Lucretius's assertion that, if people believed in heaven,

> Then would the dying man not wail about his death,
> But gladly leave behind his body and his breath
> As the snake sheds his skin.[77]

Damon insists that personal desire rather than objective climate creates this extreme heat:

"Not July causeth these extremes,
But Juliana's scorching beams.

Tell me where I may pass the fires
Of the hot day, or hot desires."
                    (lines 23–26)

These are as hard to distinguish as green thoughts from green shades; and the perceptual situation is hardly simplified by the introduction of the "chameleons, changing hue" in the next stanza. There is a chameleon on Damon's mind, and it stands for all of nature.

If Damon cannot quite know nature, he insists (in that wonderful assertion and acceleration the poem offers in its middle stanza) that he can be known by it, known quite carnally as a lover:

"I am the Mower Damon, known
Through all the meadows I have mown.
On me the morn her dew distills
Before her darling daffodils.
And, if at noon my toil me heat,
The sun himself licks off my sweat.
While, going home, the evening sweet
In cowslip-water bathes my feet."
                    (lines 41–48)

But self-knowledge comes harder:

"Nor am I so deformed to sight,
If in my scythe I looked right;
In which I see my picture done,
As in a crescent moon the sun.
The deathless fairies take me oft
To lead them in their dances soft:
And, when I tune myself to sing,
About me they contract their ring."
                    (lines 57–64)

Now the egoism, literally the egocentrism, seems to have returned, not just in this circle (where the frog dances become fairy dances, and the grasshopper's singing throat becomes the mower's own), but also in the crescent vanity-mirror in which he can play the sun (an intensification of the earlier suggestion that his own desires were overheating the summer). Actual nature retreats to the level of a metaphor, and the scythe to a lisping pun:

> "How happy might I still have mowed,
> Had not Love here his thistles sowed!
> But now I all the day complain,
> Joyning my labour to my pain;
> And with my scythe cut down the grass,
> Yet still my grief is where it was:
> But, when the iron blunter grows,
> Sighing, I whet my scythe and woes."
>
> (lines 65–72)

Sighs and scythes never quite connect; elements of nature may not be moved emotionally just because they are moved physically, and his emotions cannot be shifted by an assault on the external universe. Damon is already fallen (from his Edenic symbiosis with nature) before he is felled, aptly by his own distracted, displaced stroke. That stroke fulfills yet another revealing piece of anthropomorphic diction, "depopulating all the ground" (line 74): all grass is flesh. It is the same physical action that seeks to enforce the pathetic fallacy in "The Mower's Song," but the inverse intention: Damon seeks forcibly to restore a non-humanized nature. But to attempt it, he has to turn nature into the human, the human into nature:

> While thus he threw his elbow round,
> Depopulating all the ground,
> And, with his whistling scythe, does cut
> Each stroke between the earth and root,
> The edgèd steel by careless chance
> Did into his own ankle glance;
> And there among the grass fell down,
> By his own scythe, the Mower mown.
>
> "Alas!" said he, "these hurts are slight
> To those that die by love's despite.
> With shepherd's-purse, and clown's-all-heal,
> The blood I stanch, and wound I seal.
> Only for him no cure is found,
> Whom Juliana's eyes do wound.
> 'Tis death alone that this must do:
> For Death thou art a Mower too."
>
> (lines 73–88)

He cannot cure his wound with "shepherd's-purse and clown's-all-heal" if the wound represents (and perhaps results from) his alienation from nature, which Renaissance literature most keenly signals by exactly the kind of anthropocentric presumption—nature in service to humanity, as in the opening lines of this lyric—that those names entail.

If Milton's fatal tree yields the "knowledge of Good and Evil" only as "Good lost and Evil got" (9.1072, 11.87), Marvell's landscape of the Fall shows the lovely other as perpetually lost, and the self found in all its temporal and conceptual limitations. In these little poems, Marvell seems already to be recognizing what the philosopher Richard Rorty would argue at length a quarter millennium later: that there is no way out of the epistemological maze, that the mind-body dualism is neither a truth nor a falsehood, but a dilemma faced by human beings irresolvably, to be toyed with, and enjoyed in its multiplicity, perhaps, but not to be treated as a scientific project, only as an aesthetic field of absorption. Quietism on the epistemological point might have served Marvell's compatriots well. Whether the true and essential world is the subjective or the objective one, though it may seem an idle and abstract question, helped to divide not only their *poesis* into Metaphysical and Cavalier modes, but also their *polis* into Puritan rebels and High Church Royalists, with devastating consequences.

PART III

Reformations
Protestant Politics, Poetics, and Paintings

Chapter 5

Metaphysical and Cavalier Styles of Consciousness

A Tale of Two Ontologies

The same Andrew Marvell who so mesmerizingly walked the tightrope between solipsist/subjectivist and materialist/objectivist views of the universe walked, with no less amazing skill, the tightrope between the Puritan revolutionaries and the Royalist forces. This may be more than a mere coincidence. The conflicting ontologies—one that deemed the essential reality the one created within the individual believer, especially through language, the other believing in an essential reality received through the senses as a shared legacy—correlate significantly with radical Protestantism and the High Church respectively. They also correlate with the old division between Metaphysical and Cavalier poetry.

Though I am omitting here most of my book-length draft on these correlations, for fear of trying readers' patience and blurring my ecological focus, this chapter offers a sketch of its search for a taxonomy of late Renaissance lyric motives and for correspondences between those motives and the religious beliefs and political affiliations that shaped the English Civil War. My compass for this race through the notoriously complicated and disputatious theological landscape puts at one pole the radical Protestantism (including that of John Milton) that attributes redemptive power to the Word as deeply understood by an individual subject. At the opposite pole I place the conservative English High Church and Catholic view that truth generally resides in tradition, that power resides in collective public rituals, which (rather than human thought) give language its power, and that this divine power is manifest in full material presence and transmitted through hierarchies homologous to those of the social order.

Protestant poetics involve the domination of material nature, a cross-examination of the evidence of things seen. The conceits of Metaphysical poetry (as its name would suggest) share the radical Reformation faith that unique thought can transform the universe through language; the more traditional aristocratic mode known as Cavalier poetry tends toward the other extreme, remaining (as its name would suggest) closely in touch with nature along established hierarchical lines. In this sense, John Donne's conceitedness in the old literary sense of the term elides into the modern sense of a character flaw. His vivid narcissism manifests itself partly as a belief that his poetic restructurings of the universe can alter its reality: mind over matter.

The other key attribute of the Metaphysical mode is something Francis Quarles abjures in his preface to a lengthy and popular 1629 pastoral poem: "I have not affected to set thy understanding on the Rack, by the tyranny of *strong lines*" which offer "non-sense . . . not unlike some painters, who first make the picture, then, from the opinion of better judgements, conclude, whom it resembles."[1] My point is that "strong lines" thus betray their kinship with startling conceits, because both permit the poet to invent reality rather than being enslaved from the start to predictable patterns and commonly perceptible resemblances—to either sense of "sense." Simile is a way of drawing the mind into a kind of congruence with the external world, a way of introjecting a likeness of things—though I have described *As You Like It* as warning that the mind still imposes itself in that process, always misrepresenting the object itself. This chapter contemplates the Metaphysical conceit as a simile that not only concedes but celebrates that act of cognitive aggression. Donne's lyrics are, in this regard, an amplification of the argument I heard in Shakespeare's comedy, as the unexpected comparison reconfigures the material universe to suit the poet's will and seduces the reader into adopting a new mental stance.

The link between Cavalier poetry and the Royalist cause—if not its epistemological basis—is obvious enough. More complex and speculative are the links between Metaphysical poetry and the new modes of thought accompanying the Protestant revolution. In that revolution, a theology that preferred words over things combined synergistically with the psychology of embattled outsiders to produce poetry fascinated with its own power to reshape reality. The Puritan movement produced forms of consciousness resembling those traced by John Dryden, Samuel Johnson, and the other early literary taxonomists who invented retrospectively the English Metaphysical mode. This bit of literary history has never been adequately connected to political history, though the influence is clear in at least one direction. As power shifted from the king's High Church faction to the Puritans, the Cavalier poets begin to take over the reality-defying function of inwardness, the transformative power of subjectivity, that had been a prime Metaphysical motive. Meanwhile the conceited Metaphysical style becomes—as the Cavalier style arguably had been earlier—merely decorative, complacent, stripped of compelling motives. One reason the great Metaphysical poems appear earlier than their Cavalier counterparts may be that the Puritans cried in the wilderness before the Anglicans were driven there.

In a subtler way, poetry may also have influenced politics. Though Metaphysical poets were hardly visible in the Parliamentary army (an absence that threatens to leave me rowing with one oar in this argument, and hence in circles), their work may represent an effort to incorporate and accommodate the revolutionary energies. Perhaps, in a malfunction of the subversion-containment model often described by New Historicist scholarship, the cultural disease these poems sought to absorb into the body of literature instead gestated there into an even more dangerous strain: inoculation produced contagion instead of control. George Herbert may not have been anything like a Puritan revolutionary, but for decades after his death he was still the main poet to whom the Dissenters turned for a prototype.[2] The others may not have been as close to General Fairfax's revolutionary New Model Army as Marvell was, but they may still have provided a voice—and, through that voice, a way of thinking—for new modes of consciousness that would overthrow the English state just a few decades later.

The cultural struggle this book has been describing—between a belief that truth resides primarily in spiritual conceptions and in words as expressive of intentions, and a belief that truth is instead primarily located in an objective material universe—makes this old-fashioned binary of literary history worth revisiting. The Metaphysical poets—particularly as defined by Johnson in the famous passage of his "Life of Cowley"—begin to look like part of the Reformation's fierce last stand against materialism, the death-flurry of a culture of the comprehended word and its subjective glories;[3] and the Cavaliers appear as the vanguard, not just of a political restoration of Stuart rule and the re-ascendancy of high classical attitudes, but also of the triumph of physics.

Stuart subjects were split subjects, factions in a kind of cognitive civil war—often against each other, sometimes within themselves. Metaphysical poetry expresses a Protestant faith in the revolutionary power of the self, intention, and word; Cavalier poetry expresses the deference to traditions, senses, and hierarchies that characterized both the Royalist party and its Catholic tendencies. The unconventionality and colloquialism of the Metaphysical style correspond, in important ways, with radical Protestant styles of worship. Metaphysical poetry therefore takes on political implications inseparable from its epistemological restlessness: as Mikhail Bakhtin has argued, "In familiar speech, since speech constraints and conventions have fallen away, one can take a special unofficial, volitional approach to reality."[4] If, as King James warned, "no bishop" meant "no king," perhaps "no Common Prayer" would mean "no thing"—at least, nothing held in common as objective. Though less directly, the second pairing was part of the same revolutionary threat as the first.

What I am reaching toward floats, I suspect, safely beyond anyone's grasp: a Unified Field Theory of seventeenth-century English culture. The differences between the two sides are often subtle. Archbishop Laud himself, constructing a neatly binary list, could not wedge a single letter of the alphabet between his allies and his enemies: "the Names of Ecclesiastical Persons were written under the letters O and P; O standing for Orthodox; and P for Puritan."[5] But aligning these polarized poetic styles with other polarities prominent in the culture-wars of the period—building outward from what I believe is clearly enough legible in the conception and texture of the poetry—reveals a meaningful division. To engage all the related historical arguments, acknowledge all the exceptions, and exemplify all the styles involved would certainly require not only several books rather than a single chapter, but also an interdisciplinary team of authors (who would surely end up strangling each other long before completing a first draft). This cannot claim to be more than a preliminary and impressionistic sketch. I ask my readers' indulgence in the hope this hypothesis may nonetheless offer some interesting ideas about the way large forces in the period might have affected each other—some unscientific cultural-poetic version of the study of plate tectonics.

In 1624, Richard Montagu still hoped some moderates would emerge "to stand in the gapp against Puritanisme and Popery, the Scilla and Charybdis of antient piety";[6] but his letters show that gap was widening, and abysmal. The two great cultural centers that emerged in this period outside of the royal court—Lucius Cary's group at Great Tew and Nicholas Ferrar's at Little Gidding—seem to be efforts to bridge this division, or at least to find some habitable third mode. Both (as Reid Barbour has recently shown)[7] sought to reconcile external and internal models of heroism—whether to battle physically within the terms of the given universe, or to transform it in mental experience. Great Tew leaned heavily on Grotius's probabilism, which entailed neither a High Church complacency about the manifest world nor the radical skepticism that authorized outlandish Metaphysical conceits and antinomian religion. George Herbert, a key figure in Ferrar's group, tries not only to split the difference but also to cross the wires by arguing (in "The British Church") that meretricious Catholicism has painted itself with its corrupt desires, while the extreme Reformers have wrongly equated stark nakedness with simple innocence. Although I will present Herbert as a compelling advocate for the interior mode of worship,[8] he also defends public prayer:

> Though private prayer be a brave designe,
> Yet publick hath more promises, more love:
> And love's a weight to hearts, to eies a signe.

We all are but cold suitours; let us move
Where it is warmest. Leave thy six and seven;
Pray with the most: for where most pray, is heaven.
("The Church-Porch," lines 397–402)

In another reversal of the familiar, theologically divisive binary in which the eye perceives material reality whereas the heart knows spiritual truths, Herbert describes the heart experiencing weight, while the eye comprehends the abstract signifier. The factional debate becomes merely a fractional split between six and seven. Herbert's willingness to resort to rhetorical and syllogistic sleight-of-hand to defend Laudian practice reveals his determination to find common ground: "more promises" does not necessarily mean "more promise," and "where most pray is heaven" blurs syntactically a distinction between understanding heaven as the place of most prayer and defining the place where the most people pray as heavenly. Barnabas Oley reported Ferrar himself complaining that "he was torn asunder as with mad horses or crushed betwixt the upper and under millstone of contrary reports; that he was a Papist and that he was a Puritan."[9] The Latitudinarians themselves were split along very much these ontological/epistemological lines: "Even the first descriptions of the 'Latitude Men' noted that some favored the 'Platonic Philosophy,' and others the 'Mechanick' Philosophy and the 'atomical Hypothesis.' "[10]

Is nature, as it seems in Metaphysical conceits, an object for mental work that challenges conventional world order, or instead an affirmation of such order, as Cavalier poetry often implies? A georgic of the mind or a pastoral pleasuredome? An unfathomable divine mystery, discernible by the light of individual conscience, or an occasion to trace, by proto-Enlightenment rationality, the manifest laws that govern even divinity? There are at least forty other binary oppositions I associate (at varying degrees of correlation) with the division between Metaphysical and Cavalier schools, but even these few that bear on ecological issues should make clear that I am not describing a neat division so much as a cultural bias, which Mary Douglas defines as "an array of beliefs locked together into relational patterns" (though I would prefer "drawn" to "locked": the metaphor of magnetism attracting small particles by degrees suits the situation better than that of manacles holding persons by force).[11] Doubtless such groupings (like other alliances) alter as historical circumstances do. But the main underlying question—whether the world is a contingent mental construction or a stable material hierarchy, whether it is best understood as a text controlled by will and interpretation, or instead as a physical entity with inherent and permanent properties—still roils the culture-wars of the twenty-first century.

Of course things have changed over four hundred years: even the wilder

Protestant sects assumed some ultimate reality in God, even if that reality was scarcely accessible to humanity, and Puritans were not shy in practice about imposing strictures on their communities. But even with God still absolutely in charge, there was room for debate over whether He ruled through the mysterious inward experience He evoked from individuals, or through the visible forms of state sovereignty. If the Puritan revolution was not purely a casting off of authority, it at least involved the casting off of traditional authorities mediating between the self and the truth. For Calvinists, the freedom of the individual soul to make such choices could co-exist with their doubt that it would make the choices virtuously. The individual mattered, not because it could be entirely free, nor because it was inherently virtuous, but simply because it was where the work of salvation was done.

This version of a Unified Field Theory does not claim to be able to locate every quark particle—every poetic quirk—in a single predictable position in its universe. But it does describe a field of forces dividing literary modes into oppositions that look suggestively like those of the English Civil War. Reading backwards may encourage fallacious readings (usually anathematized under the category of Whig history), and scholars such as Conrad Russell and Kevin Sharpe have offered shrewd reminders of the ways in which the Civil War was contingent, not the necessary result of pre-existing forces neatly massed in two opposed camps. But retrospect is also a privilege, an opportunity to see where things were leading, even if no one quite foresaw or intended the final outcome. While I am not going to participate in the literary-scholarly megalomania that claims that artistic forms dictate social reality, they may have offered a distant early warning.[12] A leading scholar of eighteenth-century culture looks back on the Civil War as "a war of *styles*," the patterns of Cavalier "lace" against the "dark clothes" of the Puritans;[13] I am suggesting that the contrast between the neat symmetries of Cavalier verse and the dark transitional conceits of the less obviously lovely Metaphysical verse evokes the same larger conflict.

Several important historians have sensed, in the political configurations of the period, some version of the cultural polarity I have sensed in the lyrics. Christopher Hill long ago made a disputable but still compelling case for the fissiparous nature of that society and its culture. Lawrence Stone asserts that "By the early seventeenth century England was experiencing all the tensions created by the development within a single society of two distinct cultures, cultures that were reflected in ideals, religion, art, literature, the theatre, dress, deportment and way of life."[14] More recently, David Underdown has argued intriguingly that

The division in the English body politic which erupted in civil war in 1642 can be traced in part to the earlier emergence of two quite different constellations of social, political, and cultural forces, involving diametrically opposite responses to the problems of the time. On the one side stood those who put their trust in the traditional conception of the harmonious, vertically-integrated society—a society in which the old bonds of paternalism, deference, and good neighborliness were expressed in familiar religious and communal rituals—and wished to strengthen and preserve it. On the other stood those—mostly among the gentry and middling sort of the new parish elites—who wished to emphasize the moral and cultural distinctions which marked them off from their poorer, less disciplined neighbors, and to use their power to reform society according to their own principles of order and godliness. . . . Two alternative societies existed side by side, both increasingly polarized between rich and poor, but one relatively stable and reciprocally paternalistic and deferential, the other more unstable, less harmonious, more individualistic.[15]

Given the distinction in the same decades between two dominant models of poetry—one typified by paternalistic visions of good fellowship, traditional hierarchy, and stable ritual forms, the other (no less elitist, but elitist by intellectual rather than aristocratic pretensions) caring less about harmony than about individualism—the correlation between politics and poetry seems worth exploring.[16]

The followers of Donne responded to notes of subversive individualism, a minor-key chord produced by the conjunction of his brilliant narcissism and Protestant theology, on which the Puritan revolution would play its long and loud variations. A few years before the Scripturalists overthrew a more conservative, materialist tradition, Metaphysical language had staged a parallel campaign—perhaps a preparatory campaign—against the arguably corrupt rituals of Italian poetic traditions. Poetic and Parliamentarian radicals shared an aggressive, interventionist model of representation that overrode the reality handed down by their fathers. Puritans convinced that the only meaningful reality was that generated (or discovered) by the soul of the believer in its conversation with the Word went to war against Royalists whose acquiescence to the established social order correlated with an obedience to the tangible and traditional ceremonies of the High Church.[17]

Another historian asks, "What do [the Ranter] Abiezer Coppe, the Blasphemy Ordinance of August 1650 and Oliver Cromwell have in common?" His answer is, "They are all made anxious by *formality*."[18] We could add the name of the Digger prophet Gerrard Winstanley, who condemns those who, encouraged by the priests, "rest upon the bare observation of Forms and Customs, and pretend to the Spirit."[19] In denying that God wants prayers "conceived always new, according to the exigence of present occasion,"[20] Richard Hooker could be attacking the characteristic Metaphysical devotion to novelty and pretence of spontaneous response to an immediate occasion, as well as attacking the enemies of the Book of Common Prayer. In condemning the "set forms" used by "prostrate worshippers of Custom," Milton could be condemning Cavalier poetry as well as Laudian religion; in fact, when attacking rhyme in his prefatory note to *Paradise Lost*, Milton attributes it to "Custom," a "modern bondage" which (like royalty in his earlier pamphlets) can be broken by appeal to ancient origins. In associating Formalist with Hypocrisie on the road of life, Bunyan could be attacking the elegies produced by patronage as well as the rituals produced by Catholicism.

This is not to deny that official Calvinism had its own formalism. Ramie Targoff has shown that the Protestantism of the established Church of England insisted, no less than Catholicism, on externalities and set forms of prayer. But the fact that the state officials running a nation's religious institutions preferred cultural stability managed by centralized authority is hardly surprising, and it does not change the fact that these authorized vernacular prayers were still new words intended to transform interiority. The fact that they were emphatically not free enough for the Puritan factions demonstrates my point: the power of spontaneous personal speech was as essential to the Protestant political revolution as it was to the Metaphysical poetic revolution.[21]

Like the category of Puritan, the category of Metaphysical poet originates as an accusation. John Dryden, who had been a Tory spokesman for many years and had become a Catholic, complains in his "Discourse Concerning the Original and Progress of Satire" (1693) that Donne "affects the metaphysics, not only in his satires, but in his amorous verses, where nature only should reign: and perplexes the minds of the fair sex with nice speculations of philosophy, when he should engage their hearts, and entertain them with the softnesses of love."[22] In chapter 16 of the *Eikon Basilike*, Charles I (or whoever wrote it for him) raises similar doubts about the ability of eccentric Puritan prayer and argumentative Puritan sermons to engage the souls of non-intellectual worshippers: "I ever thought that the proud ostentation of men's abilities for invention, and the vain affectations of variety for expressions in public prayer, or any sacred administrations, merits a greater brand of sin than that which they call coldness and barrenness . . . nor are constant forms of prayer more likely to flat and hinder the spirit of prayer and devotion, than unpremeditated and confused variety to distract and lose it."[23]

In defining "a race of writers that may be termed the metaphysical poets," Samuel Johnson echoes the *Eikon*'s warning against "the pride of those that study novelties," those who prefer individualist expression over shared reality and therefore promote spontaneity and intellectual perplexity over set forms and their emotional accessibility. The *Eikon* complains that "violence must needs bring in, and abett these innovations"; Johnson complains that, because Metaphysical poets are determined to innovate, "The most heterogeneous ideas are yoked by violence together." Discussing the prayer-book controversy, the *Eikon* condemns the Puritan preachers "who gloried in their extemporary vein and fluency . . . so impatient not to use in all their devotions their own invention . . . they are many times (even there, where they make a great noise and show) the affectations, emptinesse, impertinency, rudenesse, confusions, [flatnesse], levity, obscurity, vain, and ridiculous repetitions, the senselesse and ofttimes blasphemous expressions . . . they must every time affect new expressions when the subject is the same; which can hardly be presumed in any man's greatest sufficiencies, not to want (many times) much of that compleatnesse, order, and gravity becoming those duties." Johnson's critique so persistently recalls the debates over the Book of Common Prayer as to be worth quoting at length:

> The metaphysical poets were men of learning, and to shew their learning was their whole endeavour . . . they cannot be said to have imitated any thing: they neither copied nature nor life; neither painted the forms of matter nor represented the operations of intellect. . . . Their thoughts are often new, but seldom natural; they are not obvious, but neither are they just; and the reader, far from wondering that he missed them, wonders more frequently by what perverseness of industry they were ever found. . . .
>
> From this account of their compositions it will be readily inferred, that they were not successful in representing or moving the affections. As they were wholly employed on something unexpected and surprising, they had no regard to that uniformity of sentiment, which enables us to conceive and to excite the pains and the pleasure of other minds. . . . Their wish was only to say what they hoped had been never said before. . . .
>
> Sublimity is produced by aggregation, and littleness by dispersion. Great thoughts are always general, and consist in positions not limited by exceptions, and in descriptions not descending to minuteness. . . . Those writers who lay on the watch for novelty could have little hope of greatness; for great things cannot have escaped former observation. Their attempts were always analytick: they broke every image into fragments, and could no more represent by their slender conceits and laboured particularities the prospects of nature or the scenes of life, than he who dissects a sun-beam with a prism, can exhibit the wide effulgence of a summer noon. (pp. 19–21)

The lens of a particular consciousness actually conceals the integrated beauty—the ecology—of nature at its height. Even what Johnson concedes in favor of Metaphysical poetry resembles what the moderate enemies of Puritanism sometimes conceded as its virtues: "To write on their plan, it was at least necessary to read and think. No man could be born a metaphysical poet, nor assume the dignity of a writer, by descriptions copied from descriptions, by imitations borrowed from imitations, by traditional imagery, and hereditary similes, by readiness of rhyme and volubility of syllables"(p. 21). The same could be said of anyone trying to be a good Puritan (and especially of an Anabaptist), poring over Scripture and composing individual prayers in the quest to be born again.

Sanctuaries

Let me bring this argument back to nature, which is the first refuge of the re-treating Cavalier: a place where commonsensical affirmations await him, as in Herrick's earliest datable poem, "The Country Life." The refuge of a true Meta-physical is his own mind, which has the opposite qualities—not common sense dictated by a stable external universe, but unique conceptions that subject the world to personal volition. The Cavalier affinity for the *carpe diem* and Great House sub-genres reflected, not only the obvious desires for sexual and patronly favors, but also a submission to convention, to physical objects, to classical as opposed to Biblical learning, and to the exaltation of ancient privilege. To clar-ify the difference, set these *carpe diem* poems against Herbert's insistence in "The Forerunners" that the "bleak palenesse" of wintry age deprives him of nothing if he retains the holy words (*"Thou art still my God"*), if "all within be livelier than before." Set the Great House motif (which Jonson derives from Martial) against Herbert's assertion in "Sion" that "All Solomons sea of brasse and world of stone / Is not so deare to thee as one good grone," or against his reconception of "The Altar" and *The Temple* as processes of the individual soul and constructions of words, rather than stone artifacts of a collective institu-tion; in fact, zealous Protestants sometimes turned their homes and churches alike into texts, covering the walls with pious writing. Donne's "Twickenham Garden" also subordinates the country-estate garden to a state of mind. Set the suave repartee of the Cavaliers against Herbert's "Quip," where God's assertion of love erases all human insults; the fetishism of Julia's clothes in Herrick against the figurative dressing of "Aaron" in Herbert; the appetites for food and wine and collective festive experience in Jonson's "Inviting a Friend to Supper" with Herbert's "Love (III)," where (with only a trace of the notorious Puritan abstemiousness)[24] even the heartiest kind of feast becomes a metaphor for an intimate spiritual transformation. No wonder Herbert emphasizes finding "Re-demption" amid "a ragged noise and mirth / Of theeves and murderers," rather than "in great resorts; / In cities, theatres, gardens, parks and courts"; and find-ing "Love" in an intimate dialogue with Christ rather than in a worship of His artifacts. Herbert's "Mattens" also looks at "mans whole estate," including "Sil-ver, or gold, or precious stone," for the sake of recalling that it is finally mean-ingful only as an expression of God's benevolent intentions; the world is not

contemptible (as in the darker medieval traditions), only ontologically derivative.[25]

Jonson's "My Picture Left in Scotland" scoffs at the hope that language can
alter the imperatives of the bodily landscape: "My mountain belly, and my
rocky face" have reached the eyes of the woman he hoped to seduce through poetry, and "stopped her ears." In contrast, Donne's "Valediction: Of My Name in
the Window"—in what seems to me a striking echo of "the Puritans' insistence
in their funebral oratory that the subject's name somehow anagrammatically
embraces his essential qualities"[26]—credits the engraving of those letters with
the ability to replace his actual body and command his mistress's continuing
devotion. The Cavalier willingness to trace a pre-existing physical world and
imitate classical texts—the world as inherited, not reborn—contrasts with Herbert's determination, in "Jordan" (II), to "Copie out onely" the "sweetnesse
readie penn'd" in divine "love," and—as in Protestantism generally—to recognize words not as ends in themselves (which would be idolatrous, a form of superstitious magic) but instead as the means to a conversation with God that will
transcend them. That the great love of the Word might decay into an infatuation
with words (as transubstantiation into the materialist idolatry of Mass) was a
problem that haunted English Protestant poetry from Spenser to Milton.[27] Indeed, Hieronymus Emser deployed a kind of *tu quoque* defense against the
iconoclasts, whom a naive observer might think "worship the paper or material
on which the holy Gospels are written"; and the Lutheran tendency merely to
replace pictorial altarpieces with gilt-text altarpieces risked confirming that impression.[28] The efficacy of the human will, which Protestants were obliged to
deny so generally, expressed itself with great force in the one channel open to it:
the experience of language transcending the hierarchies and overriding the
judgments of the ordinary world (the notoriously lengthy Puritan sermons may
reflect another facet of this phenomenon).

In an era painfully conscious of the division between language and nature,
the revolutionaries thus primarily chose one side, the Royalists the other. Aristocratic withdrawal to country estates and their gardens, both geographically
and poetically, was a familiar theme even before the Civil War;[29] John Donne
adapted this motif only to turn it into a metaphor of reformed interiority:

We are but farmers of ourselves . . .
.   .   .   .
Manure thyself then, to thyself be approved,
And with vain outward things be no more moved.
        ("To Mr. Rowland Woodward," lines 31–35)

Donne's references to pastoral and georgic are persistently negative, and he never practices the nature-loving genres himself; socially and financially embarrassed by his lack of land, he strives to subordinate landscape to mindscape.[30] Even in his love poetry, Donne is visibly pushing away from Catholic and royal monumentalism, shattering the association of benevolence with grandeur. "The Canonization" not only devalues "the Kings real, or his stamped face," but also associates that rejection with a rejection of the public valuations of the Catholic tradition:

> As well a well wrought urn becomes
> The greatest ashes, as half-acre tombs,
> And by these hymns, all shall approve
> Us canonized for love.
>
> (lines 33–36)

Donne's closing replacement of a high papal decree with a Protestant hymnal defines his love poetry as a rejection of the materialist claims of high society and High Church alike (he and his lover seize and redefine the "hermitage" as imperiously as Henry VIII did England's monasteries). In the *Institutes* (3.20.32), Calvin warned against being more attentive to the melody than the meaning in singing hymns; in Donne's versions of the genre there is little danger of that. The essence of the zealous argument of both the "Hymn to God My God, in My Sickness" and "Goodfriday, 1613, Riding Westward" is that the mental state must eventually override the demands, the momentum, even the definition of the material world. As the "most Puritan of literary forms" was "the diary of spiritual life,"[31] so the most Metaphysical of poems posed as half-secret explorations of a mysterious inward transformation; and both were often figured as journeys. Donne's "Valediction: Forbidding Mourning"—for many commentators, the archetypal Metaphysical poem—resembles Puritan efforts to reconceive difficult passages in life allegorically, as a divinely sanctioned pilgrimage: to seek consolation during oppressive moments by discerning a test of the sufferers' ability to see through to the higher connection that gives worldly events their true and positive meaning.

The Cavaliers often depicted conventional transactions between the sexes and classes: men as swooning or snickering wooers of reluctant or clueless beautiful women, aristocrats as indulgent parents to quaintly oafish if well-meaning peasants (as in Jonson's "Penshurst" and other paeans to rustic retreat such as Herrick's "The Country Life"). The eroticism that the Metaphysicals and radical Reformers alike tried to convert into transcendent meaning—the Dissenters were great devotees of the Song of Songs[32]—becomes a comfortable ritual in which nothing but passing pleasure and familiar sentiment was at risk. Though the distinction between liberation and libertinism can be a tricky one, the fetishistic aspect of much Cavalier sexuality befits an effort to deal with stable exterior objects rather than dangerous subjectivities; even parts of the woman's body can become fetishized, as in the *blason* tradition generally, and in Carew's "Upon a Mole in Celia's Bosom," which ponders "the mistress's birthmark in a way that removes any sense of the woman or the relationship."[33] The aestheticizing of the female body also correlates with the High Church susceptibility to sensual allurements in worship; the Puritans repeatedly condemn such allurements as carnal snares, seductions leading to "spirituall whoredom."[34] Idolatry was fetishism displaced into the sacred forms of desire.

If (as the feminist slogan puts it) "the personal is political," so is the impersonal. Cavaliers believed in the possibility of an easy consent of parts, in politics as in poetry; and "the frequently expressed Cavalier *esprit* of fellowship between like-minded individuals"[35] contrasts with the solitude (or duality) of Metaphysical meditation. In defining that world, as in justifying royalty and High Church practices, Cavaliers equate long-standing common consent with manifest and unalterable reality. The familiar modern critical vocabulary about Metaphysical poetry was already audible in seventeenth-century criticism of Puritan theology: "In the 1620s and 30s, the negative associations of Puritanism with fancy are commonplace. In his apologia for the rituals, ornaments, music, and liturgy of the English Church, Ambrose Fisher protests against the 'windie fancies' of his opponents; so too Peter Heylyn protects the king's temple from any basis in 'the particular fancie of one private man.' Time and again, Heylyn decries what he takes as heretical thought in terms of 'dreames,' 'wits and fancies,' or 'conceits and fancies.' "[36] Conversely, the traits the Reformation primarily condemned in the Roman version of Christianity find sanctuary in Cavalier poetry during the Metaphysical revolution. The fact that Donne had a "school" (in Alexander Pope's taxonomy) while Jonson had self-proclaimed "sons" reflects the difference between a movement that gave priority to mental construction and one that gave priority to material inheritance.[37]

A major premise of much Laudian practice was that the spirit must work through the body, whereas the Puritan position largely sought to suppress the body in a dualistic construal of purification; this resembles my distinction between a Cavalier mode premised on physical realities, and a Metaphysical mode in which the mind must overcome such realities. Donne's "The Ecstasy" might seem to fall on the Laudian side of that distinction, but there Donne is actually seeking to impose his will on another's flesh, and he insists on the body only inasmuch as the body is a book. If Laud's goal in the theological-political conflict can be described as, above all, "ceremonial, externalized . . . worship" and its opponent as the "anti-ceremonial, internalised and spontaneous gathering of sectarians,"[38] then the parallels to Cavalier and Metaphysical poetic practice respectively do not seem so far-fetched. The Metaphysicals, like the Reformers, placed their faith in intense dramatic dialogue—whether with God as in Herbert's catechistic verse, or with the beloved as in Donne's obsessive quest for romantic mutuality (and at times with the self, as a result of either of these love-crises). They worshipped the vindicated abstraction, rather than communal and tangible events such as Masses in cathedrals and banquets in great houses. The High Church devotee Herrick's insistence that "A prayer, that is said alone / Starves, having no companion" stands in stark contrast to these solitary poetic-meditative sessions; and elsewhere Herrick expresses a terror of the way "by night, w'are hurl'd / By dreames, each one, into a sev'rall world,"[39] seemingly amalgamating psychological anxieties about unregulated individual experience with political and theological ones. The Calvinist Eucharist was more a metaphysical than a physical presence, more a transformation inside the believer than a direct material inheritance from the ultimate Lord. Though the differences on this point were often subtler than that phrasing or their polemical exchanges might suggest, they ran along the spectrum between those poles, with Protestants drawn toward the subjective definition and Catholics toward the objective. Moreover, the Civil War itself was partly a battle between Royalists who understood England as the king's material inheritance and Puritans who cared less about what England had actually been than what the King of Heaven intended it to be.

The radical George Wither attacks simultaneously King Charles's grand reconstruction of St. Paul's and Edmund Waller's grand praise of that project, and "contrasts the open, experimental architecture of his own poem with Caroline monumentalism."[40] When the Royalist poet John Taylor strikes back, he does so by parodying Wither's radical poetic style: as one critic observes, "The enjambement that violently breaks the heroic couplet's bounds is linked here with Wither's support for Parliament."[41] Against the monarchical values of "elegance, lucidity, and propriety," Attic rhetoric emphasized "heroic selfhood and contemplative inwardness—styles characterized by brevity, wit, archaism, innuendo, paradox, and suggestive density":[42] all part of the curriculum of the School of Donne. The writing of Matthias Flacius Illyricus, one of Luther's strictest disciples, "is explicitly anti-Ciceronian, stressing brevity over *copia*, difficult suggestiveness over harmonious lucidity, asymmetry over periodicity, the numinous over the natural."[43] Marc Fumaroli recognized that "these stylistic alternatives articulate the fundamental socio-political divisions within French elite culture,"[44] and I believe they do so—though with significant exceptions[45]—in English theological politics as well. In fact, European manifestations of the Metaphysical style confirm my sense that it tends to accompany Protestantism.[46]

The finest Cavalier lyrics display a suave mixture of flowing ease and precise control, which seems to correspond to the ideological function of conservative (in this case, monarchical) literature in naturalizing power, glossing over the distinction between what comes naturally (and hence comfortably) in the human social order and what is enforced by the mechanisms of hierarchy. The best Metaphysical lyrics, in contrast, suggest the hard-won achievement of new vistas revealing alternative forms of order—a triumph gained and sustained by the unprejudiced mind of the reader in intimate dialogue with the unique perceptions of the poet. Nature need not apply.

So it may not be mere coincidence that the great trio of Metaphysical poets—Donne, Herbert, and Marvell—seem to have been socio-economically frustrated, sexually conflicted men,[47] and intense thinkers about truth and religion (with Milton again as a culminating case), while the Cavalier poets typically (if temporarily) enjoyed greater access to ordinary comforts and greater affiliation to the hierarchical status quo. Maybe social preterition encouraged a Calvinist perspective—it seems to have happened that way in France[48]—while accession to privilege, portrayed as the reward of merit through elaborate cultural rituals, encouraged a more Roman, if not Pelagian, view of the prospects for salvation and the value of currying favor in order to achieve it. Maybe the Metaphysical aggression of the will against common sense created a zone that compensated psychologically, not only for worldly deprivations, but also for the Calvinist sense of the irrelevance of will and effort to otherworldly destiny. The language of a hidden truth and a hidden power is the rightful property of the culturally, politically, and/or economically marginalized; that is presumably why it passes to the Royalist side around mid-century, with the mysticism and Hermeticism of poets such as Traherne and Vaughan.[49] Both Donne and Herbert, with high court prestige almost within their grasp, slid to the social margins while developing their Metaphysical poetics; and the most socially radical wing of the Protestant rebellion emerged from "a literate and skilled urban group, the most socially mobile part of the early modern population."[50] What crept into the Calvinist theology of Puritanism in the form of Arminianism, and had its worldly manifestation in the Weberian model of Puritan discipline leading to a middle class distinguishing itself from the undeserving poor and competing with hereditary wealth, may also be traceable in Metaphysical assumptions about the power of figurative language and creative thought—the almost transcendent efficacy of mental as well as physical work. These poets appropriated some version of the "voluntarism" that Puritans tended to attribute to

God[51]—not just the freedom but even the obligation constantly to re-invent the laws of reality.

As zealous Protestants invited Scripture to transform them, to overcome their will with its own (as in Donne's "Batter My Heart"), they also sought a fresh grasp of the natural world; perhaps this is why they are over-represented among the early empirical scientists. More particularly, the Calvinist belief that God's role in the world is both active and beyond human understanding tended to reinforce a notion that the world was to be understood, not by any process of deduction from presumed analogies or symmetries, but rather by a direct test of an individual instance. Theological voluntarism meant that the laws of nature rested "upon divine will rather than divine reason,"[52] as Metaphysical poetry was a poetry of discovery and transformative will rather than predictable symmetrical structure.

From Reformation to Restoration

Neither of the great English Protestant poets of the later sixteenth century— Sidney and Spenser—employed a Metaphysical style to complement their theology, but Sidney's defense of poetry is fully compatible with his strong advocacy of the Reformation: the poet makes a world that is not only purer in its internal order, but actually closer to divine truth, than any he can copy from the historical world; it is a form of resistance as well as of transcendence, a rejection of the role of mere historical transcriber, "captived to the truth of a foolish world," but instead proud to provide "forms such as never were in nature." Spenser's verse "always rejected facile harmonies for an emphasis on difficulty and struggle," anticipating the way Milton "designedly disrupts the closed couplet that is the favorite form of Jonson and the Cavaliers,"[53] and isolates the smooth allurements of Cavalier verse—and of forest life—in his Comus and his serpent. The Metaphysical conceit takes the emphasis on labor that characterizes Protestant nature-poetry from Spenser to Milton,[54] and turns it into purely mental work: Clerk Maxwell's demon is John Donne's muse. However elitist their intellectualism may seem to us, the Metaphysical poets are thus revolutionaries, and not only on the level of poetic style; the peculiarities and extremities of their conceits bespeak a determination to reshape an unsatisfactory universe that had accreted around their spirits—a twelve-tone riposte to the music of the spheres. "Protestant devotion to the word created a subculture . . . it amounted to cultural nonconformity and thus met rejection, incomprehension, and hostility in the wider society"[55]—much the fate contemporary commentators predicted for Donne's lyrics, the fate of experimental artists throughout history, who have always been linked (fairly or otherwise) to social revolution. As David Norbrook has observed, "the Puritan emphasis on spiritual experiment, on pushing beyond traditional forms, was a powerful reinforcement for political change."[56]

That change did not last—or, more precisely, it kept on changing. Perhaps neither the Puritan nor the Metaphysical modes, like other radical perspectives, could endure the achievement of dominance; this is not to say that they are invalid, only that they are oppositional, and therefore viable only in oppressed individuals. Metaphysical conceits have to hone their edges against patterns of common reality, as revolutionaries against established tyrants.[57] In other words, Metaphysicality could no better survive in a popular mode than a Puritanism tinged with antinomian radicalism could survive as a national government. Though some Metaphysical attributes survive in the satirical writing of the late Marvell or in Dryden, they are transfigured by participation in "communal activity"; the mode could not "go out into the world in this manner without losing its purity. In some sense, it ceased to be itself."[58] I believe this is because its identity—like that of Protestantism—is so deeply bound up with individual subjectivity, a subjectivity that can only fully assert itself by turning the world upside down (and insisting on what has thereby been set right).[59]

The Restoration, from this perspective, entailed the predictable renewed dominion of the ordinary qualities of bodies natural and politic.[60] Denham's "Coopers Hill" (which equates the balances of neoclassical poetry with the benign ebb and flow of the Thames)[61] ends by equating that political reversion with the inevitable restoration of natural order, as the waters of England seek their own level. In retrospect, the road toward deism was being paved with nonintentions: the assumption that divine providence could and would express itself only through the laws of nature marks the ultimate triumph of mechanism, of the forces of order. Going where Bacon feared to tread, [62] Hobbes places subjectivity back under the control of material objects: "the imagination of men proceedeth from the action of external objects upon the brain."[63] The characteristic Metaphysical "conception of a natural order in which spiritual and material natures continually interwork"[64] yielded at once to what Eliot famously describes (in his 1921 review-essay "The Metaphysical Poets") as a "dissociation of sensibility," to the material victories of Restoration forces (as the revolutionary coalition melted away), and to the materialism of physics as a triumphant discipline. The compromise known as constitutional monarchy was a logical development, in ways that extended beyond national politics: it suited a universe whose God was constrained by some basic physical laws, and it reflected a balance between subjectivity (now forbidden to be entirely arbitrary) and objectivity (which now had to tolerate human variety). A middle category known as "common sense" was invented and nearly deified (while metaphor itself, if a Restoration bishop had his way, would have been banned).[65] The refutation of the Calvinist God—no longer permitted to be a Metaphysical Creator himself, no longer authorized to include and exclude with a seemingly unreasonable Word, no longer exempt from the orders of the visible universe—was thus overdetermined.

The return of Protestant rule in 1688 would be celebrated above all as the triumph of mind over matter (though it doubtless did matter that William of Orange had an army at hand). The so-called Bloodless or Glorious Revolution was a moment when politics took on some basic attributes of Metaphysical poetics, a moment when mental powers defeated lineal inheritance, and divine intention overrode the ordinary orders of power:

> No dull Succession sanctifies his Right,
>   Nor Conquest gain'd in Fight,
>   But o'er the Peoples minds, and there
> Does Right Divine Triumphantly appear.
>   The mind, impassible and free,
> No Pow'r can Govern, but the Deity;
> Hower'e o're Persons, and o're Fortunes, may
>   A bold Intruder sway;
> The Right Divine is by the People giv'n,
> And 'tis their Suffrage speaks the mind of Heav'n.[66]

Vox populi, vox Dei implies, among other things, the supreme efficacy of speech. This early panegyric to William demonstrates the internal coherence and political-theological valence of the seventeenth-century epistemological struggle.

Arguably the costliest strategic mistake made by the Metaphysical revolutionaries in that struggle was ceding the baseline authority of nature to the opposition. They may have had little choice: that concession is an almost inevitable consequence of an epistemology that privileges interior subjectivity over exterior realities, and values uniqueness more than common sense. But—like the New Left in the 1960s ceding the American flag and the Christian God to their conservative opponents—they doomed themselves to isolation among a reactionary populace once the initial reformist enthusiasms began to wane. Indeed, all through the English Civil War, Royalist poets such as John Taylor depicted the rebels as pests on the farmland and enemies of farm animals.[67] The repudiation of nature's endorsement was a mistake that the visual revolutionaries of Dutch Protestantism would emphatically avoid. The next chapter will show them forming a passionate alliance with nature, and thereby striking a

populist note (against the elitist grandeurs of Counter-Reformation art) by offering a seeming transparency to what is commonly sensed.

Listening to the voices of radical Protestant dissent under the restored
monarchy reveals not only efforts to use literary back-channels to make political arguments that were impossible in any more direct form; this literature also
reveals deep kinship with its Metaphysical ancestors. The standard attack on Dis-
senting consciousness looks remarkably similar to standard critiques of Metaphysical poetry:

> The conservative Anglican apologist Samuel Parker called Dissenters "Brain-sick Peo-
> ple," "morose," repeatedly contrasting their irrational or "fanatique tempers" to his own
> "sober," "rational," and "civil" approach to religion. Nonconformists' irrationality ex-
> tended to their writing style, as Parker accused them of "hiding themselves in a maze of
> Words . . . rowling up and down in canting and ambiguous Expressions." Parker linked
> these communicative failures with unstable politics. . . . Thomas Hobbes, writing in *Be-
> hemoth* in 1668 of the causes and consequences of the civil wars, faulted crafty preachers:
> the people "admire nothing but what they understand not"; and were "cozened" with
> "words not intelligible."[68]

This is the flip-side of Ben Jonson's remark (in his 1618 "Conversations" with
William Drummond) that "Donne, for not being understood, would perish."

Thomas Sprat's argument in favor of Royal Society science could easily be
interpolated into both Ben Jonson's warning about Donne and Samuel Johnson's argument in favor of neoclassical poetry: "Spiritual Frensies, can never
stand long, before a clear and deep skill in Nature."[69] The purpose of the Society
was to grant "Mankind . . . a Dominion over *Things*, and not onely over one an-
others *Judgements*"—objective rather than subjective power. It sought "to bring
Knowledg back again to our very senses," opposing those who stand "in open defiance against *Reason*; professing, not to hold much correspondence with that;
but with its Slaves, *the Passions*. . . . Who can behold, without indignation, how
many mists and uncertainties, these specious *Tropes* and *Figures* have brought
on our *Knowledg*" through "this trick of *Metaphors*." Sprat then wonders "What
depth of *Nature*, could by this time have been hid from our view," if only earlier
generations had "communicated to us, more of their *Works*, and less of their
Wit"—"if they had only set things in a way of propagating Experiences down to
us; and not impos'd their *imaginations* on us, as the only *Truths*."[70]

T. S. Eliot observed that "Wit is not a quality that we are accustomed to associate with 'Puritan' literature, with Milton or with Marvell. But if so," he added,
"we are at fault partly in our conception of wit and partly in our generalizations about the Puritans."[71] Though these revolutionaries seem anti-artistic, the

characteristic Metaphysical wit—bringing opposites together in startling ways—was also characteristic of Puritan theology and conversion-narratives: a more rarified God and a more corrupt humanity yoked by violence together, the sinner and the saint within each believer yoked together too, in whiplash shifts of perspective.

That the Cavalier poets were virtually all Royalists may seem too circular an argument to be probative, since the Cavaliers were partly identified by their political affiliations (as in Johnson's definition of the term). Still, those most identified with the poetic mode were also those most active in the royal military cause: Lovelace (twice imprisoned by the Parliamentarians), Suckling ("a royalist martyr"),[72] Denham (affiliated with the kings' parties at every stage), Waller (whose costly if quirky role in the king's cause is reflected in his verse by a "subordination of independent thought and fancy to the severest artificial laws of style"),[73] and Herrick (whose 1648 *Hesperides* repeatedly echoes and evokes high Laudian formulas and rituals, with a touch of classical paganism).[74] Other markedly Cavalier-style lyricists such as Richard Corbett clearly would have followed the same warpaths had they lived into the 1640s.[75]

By the late 1640s, however, the downward path of their army led the Cavaliers into new poetic territory. As George Sandys notes in his translation of the *Metamorphoses*, "The wit that misery begets is great:/Great sorrow addes a quicknesse to conceit" (6.617–18). When Richard Lovelace's Royalist position started bringing him serious trouble instead of casual pleasure, he does, in a Cavalier way, something very Metaphysical: suggesting that the literary imagination can reconceive a miserable reality as a kind of happiness. This is most obvious in the prison poems. The conversion of a sense of boundedness into a sense of protected private space for pleasure, so persistent in Donne, becomes the Royalist theme throughout the 1640s, where the tavern, the country retreat, the garden, the secret, even the cell become havens—associated, for some, with the place where a priest would be harbored and administer the wine for blood. Assertions of simple nature become acts of fantastic defiance, or at least denial.[76] If Marvell conceived of the garden of nature as secretly a prison, the Cavaliers conceived of their prison cells as secretly a garden of nature. In this, they were adopting an old radical tactic: the imprisoned Puritan poet George Wither has his imprisoned hero Roget hear the grim sounds of his dungeon as the merry music of pastoral.[77]

According to a plausible contemporary report, "after the murder of K. Ch. I, Lovelace was set at liberty, and having by this time consumed all his Estate, grew very melancholy (which brought him at length into a Consumption) became very poor in body and purse . . . went in ragged Cloaths (whereas when he was in his glory he wore Cloth of gold and silver)."[78] Like Shakespeare's

Richard II, who (from Act 1 to Act 5) moves from the Ciceronian formalities of power to the Metaphysical conceits of despair, Lovelace's poetry deepens as his troubles do, because he has to transform his prison verbally into the place of power and space of liberty he formerly enjoyed. This would explain why Lovelace's final volume of verse seems both "an account of Cavalier destitution *and* a confirmation of the demise of a literary mode, even as it poetically excels itself."[79] In Lovelace's "The Grasshopper," the old *carpe diem* motif takes on a melancholic and elegiac flavor; instead of recommending a careless seizure of the pleasure of the moment, these poems argue that pleasure is still possible, even if only by retreating from the world and accepting that, outside of the brief intimate moment, there is only despair. Lovelace's compensatory plea in "The Grasshopper" for "A Genuine Summer in each others breast" (line 22), or in "To Althea from Prison" for the "freedome in my Love" (line 29), curls back around to meet Donne's insular "The Sun Rising" and "The Good Morrow," which seek the consolation of a single intense relationship in a world that otherwise so frustrated his ambitions for social affirmation.[80] Shakespeare understands that impulse thoroughly, too, but—whether for King Richard and his wife, King Lear and his daughter, or Prince Hamlet and his girlfriend—seems to doubt that the world will ever let it survive.

The bonds with non-human creatures are no less significant. Like the Herrick of "Farewell Frost," who depicts the revolutionaries as enemies of fruitful nature, and therefore doomed to fail eventually, Lovelace implies that Restoration is as natural an inevitability as the coming spring when the defrosted grasshopper "hath his Crowne againe." For the interim, however, Lovelace must rely on Stoic inwardness: "Though Lord of all what Seas imbrace; yet he / That wants himselfe, is poore indeed" (lines 32, 39–40). The unusual and increasingly pessimistic focus on insects and animals in Lovelace's *Lucasta: Posthume Poems* collection may be (like the politicized beast-fables and, I will argue, Dutch still-life paintings of the period) a preconscious glimpse ahead to the recognition of non-human beings as an oppressed class: claiming kinship with their suffering innocence requires registering their innocent suffering. What begins as a rhetorical stance for a poet deprived of status becomes psychological identification with creatures (a snail besieged by ants, for example) who never had status to begin with; and dismissing political defeat as a seasonal inevitability rather than an ideological failure requires some acknowledgment that the forces of nature outweigh those of society.

Lovelace's late poems often intend to make an insect stand in for a human type in a parable, but they come to life as the poet finds himself imagining the vivid strangeness of the insect's experience as itself. "The Ant" starts off in the *carpe diem* mode, with the pathologically diligent insect as a character in a fable, but ends up as (in both senses) demoralized biology:

> Thus we unthrifty thrive within Earth's Tomb,
> For some more rav'nous and ambitious jaw:
> The *Grain* in th' *Ants*, the *Ants* in the *Pies* womb,
> The *Pie* in th' *Hawks*, the *Hawks* i' th' *Eagles* maw:
> So scattering to hord 'gainst a long Day,
> Thinking to save all, we cast all away.

It is hard to imagine a more discouraging, dispiriting argument for libertinism. Instead of viewing the food chain as endorsing (by naturalizing) the moral authority of human social hierarchy, as Cavalier poets had so often done, Lovelace now depicts that ecological network as rendering absurd both prudence and ambition. The materialist acceptance of natural reality that was so convenient for the Cavalier when he was on horseback now gives him a foresight of Darwinian competition that leaves him a sadder but wiser man.

Counter-Reformation literature thus takes on many of the attributes of the Reformation in its nascent phase—a tendency augmented in Henry Vaughan by his wonderful mimicry of George Herbert—though often with a supplement of mysticism or stoicism. Vaughan's "The Night" undertakes the classic Reformation quest for original purity, trying like Milton to claim access to more of the original Scriptural story; and, in doing so, Vaughan reaches back to primal nature and rejects something that looks very much like the High Church:

> No mercy-seat of gold,
> No dead and dusty *Cherub*, nor carv'd stone,
> But his own living works did my Lord hold
> And lodge alone;
> Where *trees* and *herbs* did watch and peep
> And wonder, while the *Jews* did sleep.
> (lines 19–24)

Vaughan is both a Royalist and a Metaphysical poet; it is therefore predictable that he worships but also deeply transforms the world of nature, enjoys gazing calmly on landscapes but also transforming them startlingly into metaphor. So his "Praise of a Religious Life" (in *Olor Iscanus*, 1651) begins by insisting that any

> worldly *He*
> Whom in the Countreys *shade* we see
> Ploughing his own *fields*, seldome can

Be justly stil'd, *The Blessed man*.
That title only fits a *Saint*,
Whose free thoughts far above restraint
And weighty Cares, can gladly part
With *house* and *lands*.

(lines 1–8)

Vaughan's insistence that happiness awaits in Christian-Stoic acceptance rather than aristocratic luxury marks simultaneously an adaptation to the straitened circumstances of the Caroline courtiers and a shift toward a Metaphysical-poetic way of ruling the world. Happiness belongs only to the man who "Sits in some fair *shade*, and doth give / To his *wild thoughts* rules how to live."

The shift of some Cavaliers after 1640 from a public ethos of common sense to a private ethos of paradox, under the pressure of collective defeats and consequent personal deprivation, seems only too predictable by my hypothesis, and indeed is replicated on the other side when Milton finds himself obliged to move after 1660 from writing pamphlets about re-organizing the government to shrinking the epic project of nation-building into the "Paradise within," the only garden still accessible. A scholar has observed that "The Civil War 'internalised' the epic, be it as royalist retreat or as fallen Miltonic individualism . . . heroic language was made to refer to inward states of human constitution and consciousness";[81] I would add that both Royalist retreat and *Paradise Lost* respond especially to defeats in the Civil War—defeats that were both cause and effect of epistemological shifts.

In the second half of the seventeenth century, Royalists attempted to recapture control of a number of the new cultural principles—including scientific innovation—that had unsettled the old structures of authority. They also reclaimed the values of the "country" faction that had (in one simplifying interpretation of the Civil War) risen up against them: they moved into the "Happy Man" mode derived from Horace's second Epode by claiming to be—to have been all along—the party of quiet agricultural life, sensibly in touch with their native land (and Horace's poem perfectly demonstrates that one can take this position very earnestly without being capable of actually living it for more than a few days).

Laudian late-Metaphysicals such as Cleveland, Crashaw, and Cowley represent an appropriation of the Metaphysical mode. In abjuring its earlier scholastic tenor, Metaphysical poetry seems to have broken free from its revolutionary and Protestant tendencies as well; the dominant theme becomes wit for wit's sake. By the time of the Restoration, the revolutionary energies have been co-opted to a conservative ethic, like the Beatles' song "Revolution" resurfacing twenty years later as an ad campaign for high-priced footwear. Counterculture becomes a cute and comfortable hook, sparing the audience even the minimal displeasure of noticing that they have ceased to rethink for themselves. Cleveland (enough of a Royalist to be an early public enemy of Cromwell, dispossessed by Parliament in 1644–45, and part of the king's besieged garrison at Newark) was among the most beloved poets of the seventeenth century—perhaps because, in popularizing the Metaphysical mode, he disarmed it; it became just another decorative ritual, *concetti* as confetti, a display of homespun miracles and homely wit, with no more than a tourist's sense of the potential foreignness of the world he encounters.[82] As Dryden observed, where Donne "gives us deep thoughts in common language, though rough cadence," Cleveland "gives us common thoughts in abstruse words"; the private, intentional core of Metaphysicality has been emptied out. Only in the famous eight lines protesting the regicide (assuming they are by Cleveland rather than Montrose) does the Metaphysical imagery seem fully committed.[83]

Abraham Cowley's formula of "one sentence per rhyming couplet . . . signified the respect for hierarchy in *The Civil War*."[84] His "Ode: Of Wit" makes clear that he refuses to let Metaphysical ontology overrule commonsensical definitions of reality. The second stanza uses the classic instance of delusive art overriding natural reality—"*Zeuxes Birds* fly to the painted *Grape*"—to warn against the London wits and warns that "if the *Object* be too far, / We take a *Falling Meteor* for a *Star*" (lines 12, 15–16), which implies not only that there exists a real object with fixed properties out there somewhere, but also that the ultimate superlunar referents may indeed be stable, despite what the New Science (with its unreliable "Multiplying Glass") had been suggesting.[85]

So Cowley's definition of wit is as opposed to what I have been calling Metaphysical wit as his politics were to the Puritan revolutionaries. The poetic mind is here forbidden "upon all things to obtrude, / And force some odd *Similitude*" (lines 53–54) and should instead provide the kind of public agreement, and the kind of obsessive pairing, that will characterize Augustan culture:

> In a true piece of *Wit* all things must be,
> > Yet all things there *agree*.
> As in the *Ark*, joyn'd without force or strife,
> All *Creatures* dwelt; all *Creatures* that had *Life*.
> > Or as the *Primitive Forms* of all . . .
> > > (lines 57–61)

The primitivist argument of the radical Reformers is safely recuperated to the Restoration model, and "joyn'd without force or strife" is the distinct opposite of Metaphysical witticisms where (according to the disapproving Samuel Johnson) heterogeneities are "yoked by violence together." The poem then ends with the same maneuver Jonson uses in praising Lucy of Bedford: not with the poet's

definitions (here, of wit) in control, but with the poet removing himself and offering instead a supposed transparency to an ideal material reality already fully
present: "I'll only shew your Lines, and say, 'Tis this."[86]

Cowley's ode "To the Royal Society" might include Donne and his poetic
schoolmates among those who corrupted natural Philosophy:

> They amus'd him with the sports of wanton Wit,
> With the Desserts of Poetry they fed him,
> . . . .
>   . . . they led him
> Into the pleasant Labyrinths of ever-fresh Discours:
>   In stead of carrying him to see
> The Riches which doe hoorded for him lie
>   In Natures endless Treasurie,
>   They chose his Eye to entertain
> . . . .
> With painted Scenes, and Pageants of the Brain.
>   (lines 20–30)

Cowley then praises Bacon for moving English science

> From Words, which are but Pictures of the Thought,
> Though we our Thoughts from them perversely drew
> To things, the Mind's right Object . . .
>   (lines 69–71)

Cowley's conceitedness thus has nothing to do with the revolutionary alliance of
word and individual intention by which I have been linking Metaphysical verse
to Protestant rebellion; in fact, Bacon had openly disapproved of those who
would, to resist plain reality, "have tumbled up and down in their own reason
and conceits."[87] Instead Cowley allies himself with Bacon's critique of the way we
"create worlds, we direct and domineer over nature, we will have it that all things
are as in our folly we think they should be . . . I know not whether we more distort the facts of nature or our own wits" with "these volatile and preposterous
philosophies, which have . . . led experience captive."[88]

Method and Madness

Cowley's critique may have the last laugh on this chapter, which is obviously
more prescriptive than human complexity can really tolerate, whether in the

mode of judgment that divides too neatly (Metaphysical versus Cavalier) or in the ingenious combinative mode of wit (radical Protestant equals Metaphysical poet). Are "Metaphysical" and "Cavalier" merely words—merely a binary ripe for deconstruction—or do they reflect something fundamental on which a large theory can be built? Fulke Greville can be summoned to defend my argument both specifically and generally. Greville was himself a Calvinist, scientific, ironic plain-stylist who valued inward experience and practiced "metaphysical 'wit'."[89] Though he acknowledged that only God can make a recursive tree, while fools like me instead build "Formes of Opinion, Wit, and Vanity," which are "with many exceptions overthrowne," Greville also insisted that scholars should still sometimes attempt general theories.[90] Outlying instances don't preclude meaningful concentrations; imagine them as scattered dots produced by a database that nonetheless condenses its instances around diagonally opposite points on a Cartesian graph, or clusters produced by recursive-partitioning, discriminant-function, and factor analyses.[91] And if the value of any argument is a multiple of its probability and its scale of significance, then (to switch the terms from mathematics to gymnastics) I hope some of this chapter's awkward twists and wrong-footed landings may be compensated by a high degree-of-difficulty score.

For all the overreaching and special pleading it may seem to entail, my argument leaves room for poets to have both temperaments and politics,[92] for literary modes to have their own ideological tendencies, and for each of these factors to sway in the others' gravity. It protects the realm of personal psychology from total eclipse by the claims of social constructivism, while recognizing the power of a political or economic group to shape even the aesthetic preferences of its members, and for material conditions to alter the position of an author, not just on a political spectrum from left to right, but also on an epistemological spectrum from subjective to objective. A child with a strong appetite for authority and order may be especially susceptible to intellectual endorsement of fascism later in life, but the reflex and the idea are not quite the same thing, and in the gap between the two lies almost all the hope for culture and education to shape the character of society.

How do the relationships among psychological, political, theological, and scientific orders evolve? It may seem nothing more than an amusing parlor trick that market-research demographers can predict simultaneously (by a zip code) not only a person's political and religious beliefs, but also which style of the aforementioned high-priced footwear that person will buy. But if we are old-fashioned enough to imagine that humanist pedagogy can produce social reform, or new-fangled enough to explore the limits of individual autonomy, then we need to understand how the cognitive style of human communities shapes individual behavior.

If we could track such patterns among the Stuart poets, we might gain leverage (which is always better at a distance) on questions about cultural construction, pluralism, and personal agency that seem so urgent in our own culture wars. In a world where (as also in the Renaissance) the battles among Christianity, Islam, and secularism—and among the various forms of each— promise only to escalate, we desperately need to understand what leads people to choose their ideological frames, cling to them so absolutely, and deduce from them so broadly. Indeed, the solution of party politics by which Restoration England eventually reconciled the need to avoid outright warfare with the need to acknowledge competing interests and perspectives seems to be regressing in the twenty-first-century United States toward wars of good against evil that set us bitterly apart by region and religion.

Beliefs tend to cluster: the politics of an English department are generally to the left of the politics of an engineering department, the politics at a dance rave to the left of those at a country-and-western concert, those of the soccer and Ultimate Frisbee teams to the left of the baseball and golf teams. Even in explicitly political settings, the correlations among attitudes about war, race, internationalism, environmentalism, civil liberties, and economic inequality in the crowd at a rally far exceed any demonstrable interdependency of the causes; and the styles of dress correlate markedly as well. Long-dead poets may serve as surrogates, and indeed as visionaries, as we try to see the inner workings of our prejudices, and thereby to see beyond them.

Donne and Jonson historically mark the sealed boxes in the opposite corners, and (though I have omitted my explications here) both the style and content of the elegies their deaths provoked—those by the notably uncommitted Carew provide a particularly neat contrast—confirm that configuration: the tributes to Jonson loaded with good fellowship, couplets of good sense, and winking references to Catholicism, where the tributes to Donne harp on individualism and interiority in transformative metaphors and asymmetrical verses. But artistically these two poets offer something more complex; the starting places of these categories are a good place to start taking them apart. The fact that their followers created a dogmatic schism may support my claim (no less so because of all they had to ignore in order to sustain the schism) that a battle line was being drawn along this axis, between those whose stance—toward reality as well as toward monarchy—was either rebellious or else courtly and courteous.

The supposed Jonsonian position would much better describe, say, Richard Corbett, in whose poetry the signature of his Royalist and anti-Puritan affiliations (and their accompanying psychological tendencies) is only too easy to read. Very few English poets were so polemically anti-Puritan so early in the seventeenth century, and very few so perfectly anticipate the conservative stylistic formula that would dominate English poetry by the end of that century. Corbett articulates memories of his father Vincent and hopes for his son Vincent (the patrilineal emphasis is itself tendentious), all in a mode that is recognizably Augustan, not just in form and rhythm, but in its emphasis on moral distinctions conveyed by modulations of diction, and in its use of nature and the noble gardener as affirmations of true, basic, lasting values overlooked by the crude and feverish revolutionary forces. The main theme is that his father was a gardener:

> Simple he was, and wise withall;
> His purse nor base, nor prodigall;
> Poorer in substance, then in friends;
> Future and publicke were his endes;
> His conscience, like his dyett, such
> As neither tooke, nor left too much:
> Soe that made Lawes were uselesse growne
> To him, he needed but his owne.
> Did he his Neighbours bid, like those
> That feast them only to enclose?
> Or with their rost meate racke their rents,
> And cozen them with their consents?
> Noe; the free meetings at his boord
> Did but one litterall sence afforde.[93]

The old-fashioned worship of nature, as a touchstone of personal morality and benevolent social order, was associated with the embattled Cavalier, Catholic, and Royalist camps; when Jonson himself writes an epitaph on the elder Vincent Corbett, it strikes many of the same mutually confirming ethical and stylistic notes. How did good sense, generosity, and backyard gardening ever become coded into values divisive enough to fight a war over?

At the very least, it is worth looking back at the disastrous and successful ways Western societies have dealt with the pressures of cultural conflict, which this book has been suggesting were so multiple and intense in early seventeenth-century England that people looked yearningly backward toward some imagined moment of unity and simplicity, back to a time when God spoke to us directly as we sat in a garden perfectly attuned to our needs and names for it. The quest for essences encouraged what cultural studies now call "essentialism," which is understandably mistrusted for its politically regressive character: its pressure toward a conformity imposed from the outside in, under pretense of the opposite. The twenty-first century needs a safely distant model of multicultural explosion—and the Renaissance was such an explosion—to open out our assumptions and test our solutions.

So while I may be barking up the wrong recursive tree for sinking my teeth into Shakespeare,[94] or for catching the complex consciences of his greatest poetic contemporaries, I suspect there is nonetheless something up there worth hunting, if literary scholars hope to justify their privileged place in the social workforce. As the arts provide a place where cognitive dissonance and cultural change can be negotiated, because reality and material interests are not obviously at stake, so universities provide a place where these fundamental psychological and ontological differences can be diagnosed and analyzed prior to their manifestations in political and theological conflict, where popular passions are still as tragically intractable as they were during the Stuart monarchies.

Chapter 6

The Retreat of God, the Passions of Nature, and the Objects of Dutch Painting

Who to the life an exact Piece would make,
Must not from others Work a Copy take;
No, not from Rubens or Vandike;
Much less content himself to make it like
Th'Ideas and the Images which ly
In his own Fancy, or his Memory.
No, he before his sight must place
The Natural and Living Face;
The real Object must command
Each Judgment of his Eye, and Motion of his Hand.
—Abraham Cowley, "To the Royal Society"

In religion the Dutch were Protestants, an important matter, and to
Protestantism alone the important thing is to get a sure footing in the prose of
life, to make it absolutely valid in itself independent of religious associations.
—G. W. F. Hegel, *Aesthetics*

The conclusion is that one should paint or represent nothing except what is
visibly apparent, and that the majesty of God, which cannot be seen by the
eye, should not be polluted by perverted and indecent effigies. As for the things
that one may lawfully represent, there are two types. In the first are included
histories, in the second, trees, mountains, rivers, and persons that one paints
without any meaning.
—Jean Calvin, *Institutes of the Christian Religion*

Anyone eager to see ordinary objects depicted in Renaissance painting must aim for the northern European section of museums. Though real
household items and naturalistic scenery populate some fifteenth-century religious paintings, they become much more common and prominent in the later
sixteenth century. At first glance, this seems odd, given the mistrust of materialism fundamental to Protestant religion and the Reformers' penchant for turning

whatever physical objects they did not destroy into metaphors of human subjectivity. As seventeenth-century English poetry has shown, it was Catholic religious culture that had a structural and traditional affinity for objects as they present themselves outwardly to common perception.

But the Christian schism breaks down the old Horatian *ut pictura poesis* formula: what happens in the visual field is very different from what happens in the verbal field. The enthusiastic subjectivity of Reformation radicals exercised its power in the realm of words. Marvell works amazing conceptual transformations on Oliver Cromwell in the "Horatian Ode," but (according to Horace Walpole's *Anecdotes of Painting*) when Sir Peter Lely was to paint a portrait, Cromwell insisted it be "truly like me . . . warts and everything." The zeal that infused and transmuted ordinary physical reality was largely drained from the world of pictorial representations by Protestant iconophobia, and filled instead the verbal universe. Altarpieces that once displayed gilded saints were now often covered with scriptural language instead. The painting of officially Protestant societies allowed the given physical universe to be simply itself; art submitted to the manifest natural order that Metaphysical poetics, Puritan rhetoric, and even the Netherlanders' own markedly artificial pastoral literature so vigorously subverted. In the visual field (as Chapter 7 will show), it is instead Counter-Reformation artists who try to disrupt all assumptions about reality. The way these art-based chapters of my book reverse the pattern of the previous literary one (Chapter 5) is an index of the disagreement about where the transformative power of holy consciousness and divine intention is to be found: in the mental engagement with language, as Protestants believed, or instead in images and other physicalities that carry metaphysical implications, as Catholics believed.

Reformation iconophobia clearly liberated—or others might say, prevented—painters from striving to make the divine visible, and from focusing repeatedly on scenes from the Christian mythos where saints, angels, and the Virgin Mary watch the sacred story with us. Though Old Testament topics remain active in the first half of the seventeenth century, the loss of commissions from church and state for traditional devotional images necessarily pushed painters toward new markets, those of an increasingly materialist and consumerist society.[1] In Utrecht, for example, as the power of patronage shifted from the clergy to the aristocracy, the topics shifted from religion to nature—especially because that aristocracy sought to mimic the better-established courts elsewhere in Europe, where pastoral had a distinct *haut-chic* status.[2] In the new Protestant universe, objects can finally be present for their own sake. The natural is no longer obliged—in fact, no longer permitted—to manifest the supernatural. This correlates to the overall figural change during the late Renaissance, as traced by scholars as different as Erich Auerbach and Michel Foucault, in which things ceased to be essentially part of a constellation of signs of some larger meaning and could speak for themselves[3]—or could at least have their quiddities ventriloquized by the painters. Reformation iconoclasm may have been caught in a vicious cycle, whereby Calvinist theology compelled artists to depict things without attempting to show their mystical aspects; and yet the more their illusionist naturalism blurred the distinction between a picture of a thing and the thing itself, the more intensely the depiction of anything sacred raised the threat of idolatry.

In 1628, Pieter Saenredam made a series of prints parodying Catholic claims to discern the image of a priest in the ring patterns of a felled tree and suggesting instead (in a step toward the pattern-passionate decorations of iconoclastic Islam) that the stump should be viewed—and admired—as itself; aesthetically, not for any allegorical presence one might inject into it (Figure 2).[4] The text accompanying these prints entails an attack on the Catholic claim—audible also in Cavalier poetics—to provide a transparent view of pre-existing realities.[5] Again there is a competitive primitivism built into the factional debate: "Protestant reformers held up for scorn the naked facts they claimed to uncover behind the fictions: the wood and stone that idols really are."[6] But what if wood and stone themselves become idolized?

Archibald MacLeish's "Ars Poetica" begins by declaring that "A poem should be palpable and mute / As a globed fruit," and ends with an assertion that "A poem should not mean / But be"; many painters of the late Renaissance, especially in northern Europe, seem to have believed the same about their art.[7] According to Francis Bacon's dicta, nature demands a kind of flat, respectful reading; so do these paintings of nature. Human tendencies are not so easily silenced, however: one of the "Idols of the Tribe" is its appetite for idols, and the effort to look at nature instead of its holy symbols—to see the rings of a tree instead of tracing the profile of a priest—eventually conferred on nature itself the attributes of traditional holiness. This chapter traces (if that delicate verb will serve for my headlong pursuit of a thesis) that subtle yet tremendously consequential process.

The works of Jacob van Ruisdael comprise a recantation of the belief that nature is merely a setting for the great spiritual adventure of humanity. And, as Ruisdael retracts this early Christian version of the sentimental notion that nature sympathizes with human endeavors, his colleagues invent the means by which modern Western culture would begin instead to sympathize with nature as our collective victim. Reformation art obliged flora and fauna to take the place of the visible Christian godhead. The great upward void was hard for the Low Countries to fill, and one major (if presumably inadvertent) consequence was the substitution of ecological for theological consciousness. I therefore hope—though

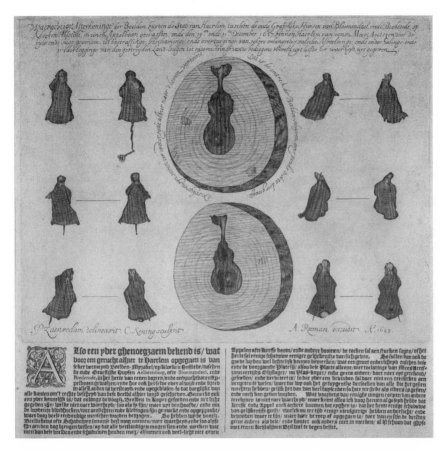

Figure 2. Cornelis Korning, after Pieter Saenredam (1597–1665), *Print to Belie Rumors About the Images Found in an Apple Tree*, 1628. Etching. Noord-Holland Archive, Netherlands.

art historians will understandably judge me a reckless driver through their field— that this excursion may get the book a little further toward its goals.

Jacob van Ruisdael and the New Landscape

When Dutch painters deliberately stopped making sacred images, I believe they inadvertently started making images sacred. To say that "Dutch painters approached reality with a naïveté and purity of sense, and even an awe and devotion, that were almost religious, and cannot be called devoid of any ideal or spiritual value,"[8] is to defend the works on the very grounds that might, in their own time, have condemned them. The suppression of divine images (at least, certain kinds of images in divine spaces) may have been a Pyrrhic victory for the Protestant iconoclasts, because the human response to images may be inherently sacral, attaching reverence to the things depicted. As Catholic apologists sometimes wondered aloud, is it really less pious to venerate a divine object than a secular one? Iconophiles such as Martinus Duncanus tried to push the high-and-mighty iconoclasts down a slippery slope, arguing that if these Reformers really wanted to follow the Commandments so literally, they should smash all images, attacking secular paintings and stamped coinage more eagerly than pious depictions.[9] Even Luther, in his critiques of iconoclastic Reformers such as Karlstadt and Zwilling, acknowledged that it was "better to paint pictures on walls of how God created the world, how Noah built the ark, and whatever other good stories there may be, than to paint shamelessly worldly things."[10] Were Catholic aesthetics creating a corrupt desire, or instead steering a pre-existing desire back into Christian channels, by giving God the best glories human art could offer? In the absence of a sacred narrative implicitly behind the painting (what Alberti's seminal 1435 study *De pictura* called the *istoria*),[11] even seeming transparency can produce idols. Otherwise, why would people bother with these recreations? Do images that are studiously not of God nonetheless (or all the more) threaten to take the place of God?

Presumably replacing God was never the intention. Instead, the burgeoning of Dutch landscape painting must be understood in (at least) three related ways: as a predictable careerist response to the lost prestige and sponsorship of religious imagery in what was a predominantly Protestant society,[12] as a corollary to the Protestant task of cleansing away human-institutional mediations between human consciousness and God's Creation, and as the pastoral fantasy life of the most urbanized society in Europe.[13] The Catholic advocacy of presence rather than mere reference (as in the Eucharistic controversies) reappears—the repressed returns—in the artistic valuation of the realistic rather than allegorical object.[14] It may recall the movement from a Homeric to a Hellenistic nature: from one constantly asserting itself as a story of divine intentions to one in which "realistic and vivid nature description is distinct from religious themes."[15] Reformation iconoclasm gave new presence, inadvertently, to the secular objects that would become the deity of the age of physics. That new deity (like Milton's in the "Nativity" ode) was born quietly, but not without some grievous throes in the universe and some desperate questions about the transfigured culture. How can that culture get from "I am that I am" to "What is, is"? What does the journey cost; what are the sights along the way; and what is life like at the destination?

These aspects of Dutch painting are all the more interesting because, geographically, Holland is itself a living example of land created by the human imagination.[16] No population in Europe could less afford simply to let nature be itself. What draining and poldering gave, peat-cutting largely took away. And in a society accustomed to investing in the craftsmanly creation of land, why not invest in landscapes as well?[17] Purchasing this kind of art and maintaining Holland's dikes were, in this sense, cognate activities. Was the painting of natural objects and the buying of those paintings some kind of collective totemic strategy for worshipping, but also recapturing, a material universe that was threatening to claim independence, perhaps even dominion? Putting a threateningly fluid world into static form had always been part of the appeal of painting, and (given the perpetual threat of flooding) the Dutch must have felt that appeal in pragmatic as well as aesthetic terms.

These issues become most interesting, therefore, in landscape painting, which (as largely an innovation of that time and place) not only connects directly to the constructed Dutch territory (and both are arguably linked to Protestant zeal),[18] but more broadly renews the link I have been suggesting between a search for unambiguous epistemology and a search for uncorrupted nature; between the effort to see things as they really are and the retreat to a world resistant to human markings. The early seventeenth-century trend toward paintings of nature and rustic life reflects, not merely visually, a nation that was producing both poems of pastoral retreat and country houses at a remarkable rate.

In these paintings, there is much more hard pastoral than soft, and certainly nothing traditionally literary. Looking at a landscape by Jacob van Ruisdael (especially early in his career) or by many of his compatriots, it is hard to believe that anything humanly conceived, including language, has a more dominant or lasting reality than this huge, heavy world through which people drag their bodies. Cut away from its religious markers, the obvious power of that physical universe had to be expressed otherwise, and these paintings—greatly beautiful, and no less dispiriting—do so with remarkable conviction. They present a world in which the effects of human intention are, in every regard, minuscule. The trails look as lengthy as those trudged by Bunyan's Pilgrim, but—again, at least in Ruisdael's earlier works—emptied of allegorical abstractions; indeed, Bunyan's landscapes are so ostentatiously unrealistic that the Dutch painters hardly seem to be part of the same Reformation culture-work.[19] There are things being done in the paintings, and things to be done, but we are systematically deprived of anything—even facial expressions—that might encourage us to project a particular narrative onto the scene or even to project emotion onto the people so obliquely and obscurely depicted. Life is just life,

Figure 3. Jacob van Ruisdael (1628/29–82), *The Jewish Cemetery*, 1655–60. Oil on canvas, 142.2 × 189.2 cm. Detroit Institute of Arts. Gift of Julius H. Haass in memory of his brother Dr. Ernest W. Haass. Photograph © 2004, Detroit Institute of Arts.

and the ordinary remains itself, not obviously the clue or window to a deeper meaning available only in words.

Granted, sometimes there are hints of something deeper, of some divine intention—heavy-handed, as in the rainbow over Ruisdael's *Jewish Cemetery* (Figure 3),[20] or more elusive and evanescent, as in the occasional strong rays of light through the storm clouds. In both the Detroit and the Dresden versions of *The Jewish Cemetery*—the Dresden version, along with many other images helpful for this chapter, is visible in sequence at www.humnet.ucla.edu/ backtonature—a tomb receives the front-central white-lit prominence that Ruisdael denies his living figures. Yet the birch steals much of even that posthumous glory, and the mourners at the rear set of tombs—though in the middle of the Detroit picture—are rendered practically invisible. There is, for once, writing here, but it is not seemingly meant to be legible; instead—all the more so since these are presumably Hebrew characters, the form of writing most often thought to have magical power in its material presence—the characters become just another form of decorative texture, like the leaves on the branches that cast their shadow across this writing.[21] So even in becoming allegorical, both *Jewish Cemetery* paintings suggest the erasure of words and thought, rather than their preservative function. The painting joins time and death in defeating the pride of human expression.

Often in Dutch still lifes, the light seems to come from the object itself; perhaps the surface is not the only truth of the thing, but the deepest truth of the thing may nonetheless be its own—a resident quiddity, rather than any residue of a divine other. As Karel van Mander, the senior theorist of the Haarlem Mannerists, argued, the artist "must combine observation and understanding in order to be true to the essence and not just the appearance of things."[22] Around the end of the seventeenth century, Arnold Houbraken claimed that "ordinary people look at things only to delight their eyes: but the wise look beyond the same, in order to know what is concealed behind."[23] Certainly the evidence shows that Ruisdael was not a proto-photographer; he freely recomposed scenes, rather than merely replicating them, mixing and transforming the natural elements of a setting "to create an image of its essence."[24]

The glow may suggest some kind of divine presence. But if we do not know—and by some Protestant criteria, must never presume to inquire—what that inscrutable supplement is, then can it ever be liberated from its concealment? And, if not, doesn't it remain part of the object—both the depicted object and its depiction on canvas—rather than leading us anywhere beyond? Does it profit us to gain a whole world and lose a teleology? There is rarely any obvious higher referent for Ruisdael's earthy depictions, any more than there is a goal beyond survival, with an occasional sprinkling of transient pleasures, for his human figures. So the paintings are realistic in a modern colloquial sense, but not in the philosophical sense that refers to the argument that concepts are no less real than physical entities: these paintings emphasize material experience in a way that—like nominalism and, later, William Carlos Williams's Imagist precept, "no ideas except in things"—devalues ideas apart from manifest entities.

The history of the reception of and responses to these Dutch paintings centers on this issue, from the early disdain of those who saw a degrading submission to the merely physical, to the modern dispute between admiring materialist readings such as Svetlana Alpers' on one side, and on the other side those who detect pilgrimage motifs or Baroque allegorical allusions to poems and emblem books.[25] Recently, a prominent critic from my own field has enlisted Dutch art in the New Historicist campaign, seeking out the sexual and national politics behind what may look like ordinary domestic settings.[26] Seymour Slive and David Freedberg try to balance those extremes of pure description or pure allegory,[27] but the dispute seems far from resolved. Perhaps this irresolution is a symptom of the ambivalent cultural function of these paintings, by which the sacred power of images and the intuition of hidden value slide across into depictions that are ostensibly striving to exclude such iconic energies. Sometimes these are deliberate encodings. Other times the painters are of the iconophilic party without knowing it—or at least, without quite being able to say it, for lack of a deistic spiritual vocabulary that was only beginning to emerge.

Technique provides some useful clues to the ontological implications of Ruisdael's paintings. Especially early in his career, Ruisdael's paint is itself material, real: a thick impasto that demands a place beyond two dimensions. Furthermore, these landscapes (like the camera obscura that was emerging as an artistic tool) offer an abstractly optical as opposed to perspectival image—there is often no single place recommended for the viewing eye, but rather a full unprejudiced presence of objects as if there were no viewer. Mural-like, they refuse to orient themselves to us, as if human consciousness had no particular role in this transaction. "You have painted," Touchstone might have commented, "but whether rightly or no, let the forest judge."[28] This abdication of a single subjective viewpoint in these paintings—like the same quality of "negative capability" that John Keats recognized in Shakespearean drama—becomes manifest in Ruisdael's biography, or rather lack of one, even more definitively than in Shakespeare's: "Not a single line written by him survives. None of his immediate contemporaries has left us a word about him or about their reactions to his art. No portrait of the artist has ever been identified."[29] This is not so unusual for Dutch painters of the period, and may only prove that Ruisdael was a nobody—but being a nobody seems itself a significant culmination of a career that shrank humanity into anonymous figures almost too small to notice.

It is tempting to speak of a decentering of the human in these pictures, except that there is so often a person near the center of the canvas. When viewers find that human figure, and then notice that they have sought it, they have been tricked into recognizing (by something like the "affective stylistics" that Stanley Fish's *Surprised by Sin* explicates in *Paradise Lost*) their anthropocentrism, their disproportionate investment in the human figure. That investment is promptly punished by the exhausting prospect of the depicted figure's journey into civilization, into the town that takes the form of a daguerreotype of steeples in the distance, flat behind the blooming presence of a huge and heavy nature in the foreground—clouds of bushes, blossoms of clouds, muddy paths and riverbanks, winding sandy tracks over dunes. I rarely see a Ruisdael landscape without suddenly recognizing the gallery-fatigue in my legs, even if I have newly arrived at the museum. Civilization awaits off in the distance, but sustained effort will be involved in getting there, the reward for which (in the universe of the picture) will be merely to disappear, the culmination of becoming smaller and ever more absorbed in darkness—a compelling if not exactly inviting parable of annihilationism.[30] Do these struggling figures, with night closing in on them in their paths and their tasks, really luxuriate in the "peaceful harmony between man and his environment" that some critics see in Ruisdael's landscapes?[31] That might be a fair description of Herman van Swanevelt's *Italian Sunset* (where the end of the day implies at worst a pleasant melancholy), Aelbert Cuyp's travel scenes, or several of the younger Teniers's genre pieces where talk and leisure are part of the work; but it ignores Ruisdael's stubborn refusal to present such idylls, despite their suitability to the urban market that provided his living. The light, centrality, size, and conventionalized beauty lent to the human figure at the center of Nicolaes Berchem's *Pastoral Landscape with Bentheim Castle*—its healthy, happy livestock offering a kind of soft-core soft-pastoral idyll—contrasts sharply with his friend and colleague Ruisdael's treatments of the same site.

For all its own complexity, Ruisdael's nature simply dominates. The warped, crumbling planks set up as a fence in *Windmill by a Country Road* or as a shed in *Landscape with a Cottage* suggest the transience of human works: our labors of protection have neither the durable power nor the colorful glory of the wood that remains in the blossoming trees, which human uses can only diminish. The people in these scenes are small, dark figures, lacking texture or facial expression, often crouched, and rarely facing the viewer.[32] It will hardly do to suppose that Ruisdael was too cheap to pay for decent staffage. Indeed, the odd tendency of some Dutch artists to hire each other to insert the human figures in their landscapes suggests a taboo guarding the barrier between the human and the natural. Gerard and Gesina Terborch's *Commemorative Portrait of Moses Terborch* (Figure 4) illustrates the effect vividly. No less striking is Ruisdael's collaboration with Thomas de Keyser on *The Arrival of Cornelius de Graeff and Members of His Family at Soestdijk, His Country Estate*, in which the family hovers eerily atop the rustic landscape to which they have supposedly returned. Bad technique, or simply bad news for the back-to-nature crowd? Hardly better than the miserly-painter explanation is the warning that "it would be a fallacy to equate size with significance, for it is not uncommon in Northern art for small, rudimentarily sketched shapes, glimpsed on the horizon, to set tone to the whole composition."[33] In Ruisdael's landscapes, what the composition implies is the belittlement of a humanity whose weary tone contrasts with the tonic energies of the landscape engulfing it, while the contrasting size evokes the brevity of individual human life in geological time.

I am not rejecting the conventional art-historical wisdom that suggests these tiny anonymous figures serve to establish a scale for the massive wonders of the nature engulfing them. I am only suggesting that there is a reciprocal effect, whereby painters and viewers alike would become increasingly aware of the near irrelevance of the human project to the material universe. Perhaps Ruisdael seized upon an expressive opportunity he recognized in the nearly-as-overshadowed

Figure 4. Gerard II Terborch (1617–81) and Gesina Terborch (1631–90), *Commemorative Portrait of Moses Terborch*, ca. 1668. Oil on canvas, 76.2 × 56.5 cm. Rijksmuseum, Amsterdam. © Rijksmuseum Foundation.

Figure 5. Jacob van Ruisdael (1628/29–82), *A Bleaching Ground in a Hollow by a Cottage*, 1645–50. Oil on oak, 52.5 × 67.8 cm. National Gallery, London. © National Gallery, London.

human figures in his uncle Salomon van Ruysdael's landscapes, and perhaps in Rembrandt's *The Stone Bridge*, which sharply lights the intricate branches at the center while sinking the slouched and faceless human beings into the dark red-brown palette of the earth around them. In the nephew's work, their faceless-ness seems more than casual—especially when the trees are each so beautifully individual. Indeed, Ruisdael is justly famous for his botanically precise trees,[34] and for seeking "heroic effects without sacrificing the individuality of each oak, coppice, and clod of earth."[35] So why are the human figures so systematically de-prived of precision and personality? Why, in *A Bleaching Ground in a Hollow by a Cottage* (Figure 5), are the people faceless, while the tree on the upper left has all the articulated character—indeed, has a more intimate and lively relation-ship with another tree than the people do with each other? Does Ruisdael, Moses-like, see God in these radiant bushes—and nowhere else? Is he, like his countryman Spinoza—who, suggestively, spent years as a grinder of high-quality lenses—inventing a kind of clear-eyed pantheism that resists the anthropomor-phic conception of the Christian deity?

Ruisdael's people are found, almost by accident it seems, on some sandy track that, rather than straight, lies wearyingly subservient to the topography.[36] While the trees often dance with the clouds, as in *The Bush*, the people are mice on the floor of the ballroom. If this is secularism, it isn't humanism. Even in Ruisdael's bright and linear moments—his *View of Haarlem with Bleaching Grounds* paintings are good examples—the little human figure on the muddy path still sets out under a dizzyingly vast sky. These canvases are more than two-thirds sky (as Van Goyen's often were),[37] the workers only a quarter-inch high. Though John Walford argues that "small scale does not necessarily imply insignificance,"[38] it does seem remarkable just how consistently negligible Ruisdael's human figures are. One could play an extended "Where's Waldo?" (or *"quo homo"* anyway) search-game with Ruisdael's *Grainfields* or *Oaks Beside a Pool*: the people are hardly more evident on the canvases than in the paintings' titles. In *Landscape with Waterfall*, there are human figures near the middle, but so small and dark as almost to disappear. Even when they occupy the foreground, in *Landscape with a Ruined Castle and a Church*, they remain peripheral, and come late to the eye. The catalogue commentary on *A Village in Winter* (Figure 6), which depicts a man and a boy moving away from us down an icy path into further darkness under a stormy sky, rightly comments that the human figures are "unapologetically anonymous."[39] I defy the art historians who posit a Christian optimist in Ruisdael to find any escape from mortal misery (aside from handing it off to the next generation) in this scene; winter may not even be a symbol of death, simply its most natural and usual context.

Just because "Dutch landscapes consistently identified the world as the scene of man's activity" does not mean that activity is viewed as pleasurable, glorious, or more than very marginally efficacious. There is certainly an adaptation of the medieval *vanitas* admonitions here, but is the point exactly the "impermanence of the physical world,"[40] or instead the superhuman durability of that world? The dominant trees may be read allegorically as "a symbol of the transience of earthly life,"[41] but they may just be realistic evidence of it; by the same token, sometimes "the image of a transient world"[42] is just an image—not a symbol—of that transient world, a reflection whose lesson lies in its material reality rather than in allegorical precedents. If there were a text behind these paintings, it might be Job: "Man that is borne of woman, is of short continuance, and ful of trouble. He shooteth forthe as a flowre, and is cut downe: he vanisheth also as a shadow, & continueth not. . . . For there is hope of a tre, if it be cut downe, that it wil yet sproute, and the branches therof wil not cease. . . . But man is sicke, and dyeth, & man perisheth, and where is he?" (Job 14:1–10, Geneva Bible).

Prints of Dutch garden scenes in the earlier seventeenth century may carry distinct prudential and political allegories,[43] and some Dutch landscapes resembling Ruisdael's doubtless carry allegorical freight as well. In Simon de Vlieger's

Figure 6. Jacob van Ruisdael (1628/29–82), *A Village in Winter*, date unknown. Oil on canvas, 36 × 32 cm. Alte Pinakothek, Munich, Germany (Staatsgalerie, Schleissheim). © Bayerische Staatsgemäldesammlungen (Bavarian state painting collections).

Wooded Landscape with Sleeping Peasants / Parable of the Tares of the Field, for example, the small figures and the roadside fatigue in marginal light take on distinct scriptural associations and a didactic moral thrust (of a familiar Dutch kind: idleness breeds sinfulness).[44] Ruisdael, however, usually shows the direct consequences of emptying out the Christian core of Renaissance painting; if he was, as the evidence suggests, raised as a Mennonite, then his systematic elimination of the supernatural from the canvases, and its replacement by simple, dutiful human work, makes sense. If the Christian story behind the path up Calvary

Figure 7. Joachim Patinir (ca. 1485–1524), *St. Jerome in the Desert*, ca. 1515. Oil on wood, 78 × 137 cm. Musée du Louvre, Paris. Photo: Erich Lessing/Art Resource, NY.

(or, more accurately, in front of it) were erased, leaving only ragged men miserably hauling wood, some depictions of that scene could pass for a weary Ruisdael trek. Joachim Patinir's *St. Jerome in the Desert* (Figure 7) offers plausible proto-Ruisdaels as its left and right sections, where tiny anonymous figures trudge away on sandy paths; all Ruisdael had to do was remove the heroic saint and his extraordinary setting from the middle.[45] The resulting *paysages* are less *moralisés* than demoralizing; to call Ruisdael a deist is to overlook this pessimism.

Some interpreters see Ruisdael's works offering "an archetype of the loneliness and grandeur of nature."[46] It is not nature that appears to be lonely, however, but rather humanity, which crawls on the back of the earth like scattered fleas on a dog. Even an art historian who believes that Ruisdael presents a largely happy and arguably Christian view of the world also notices that Ruisdael (compared even to his Dutch contemporaries) "gives less prominence to figures and buildings, and pays more scrupulous attention to the particulars of the indigenous vegetation, their growth and leaf patterns, their individual branch forms and barks." Yet this scholar still suggests that "By contrast to the landscapes of his predecessors, Ruisdael presents . . . a more peaceful environment for a quiet country stroll and a time for reflection."[47] At the risk of striking the facile and academically fashionable pose of more-wholly-sympathetic-to-the-proletariat-than-thou, I would suggest that, while Ruisdael may indeed allow the viewer to tour the country in a peaceful faded light and reflect upon it, for the figures in the paintings there is little sign of reflection, and usually less a stroll than a trudge or a slog, leading toward a rest in peace only in the euphemistic sense of the phrase. The melancholy sunsets are sweeter for those who have to get only as far as the clean, well-lighted museum café.

In fact, as so often in Renaissance and Baroque painting, a crucial clue is who or what gets the light. The middle foreground of Ruisdael landscapes often provides a zone of strong whiteness, but it does not belong to humanity. In *Banks of a River*, what stands front and center, exclusively spotlighted, is the rear end of a horse, matched with a considerable sand trap for the light-hungry eye in the distance. The white foreground in *Spruce Trees at a Waterfall* is foaming water; there are people at the center of the canvas, but they are hardly the center of attention. In *Country Road with Cornfield* it is the white dog who stands out, and seems alive and alert, with the man an extension of the dark, low-slung, passive brush around him. Similarly, in *A Pool Surrounded by Trees and Two Sportsmen Coursing a Hare*, the white central figure is a dog, while the sportsmen, though relatively large and central, each systematically take on (chameleon-like) the palette of the nature behind them, and so disappear; contrast this with Gillis van Coninxloo's *Forest Landscape*, where the central human figure is tiny but so brightly colored against the earth-tones that his importance is unmistakable. Occasionally human works—the bleaching fields, as in the *View of Haarlem*—begin to claim that center of light, but the people themselves are still shadowed and minuscule figures. The *View of Alkmaar* is mostly a view of sand, pale stalks, and clouds, and those are certainly the best-lit as well as the largest parts of the composition. Foaming water, eroded bedrock, dried grasses, and swarming clouds each have shape, striking detail, and the power of light in Ruisdael's *Bleaching Ground in a Hollow by a Cottage* (see Figure 5), while the human works are smeared into shadow. In *Landscape with Blasted Tree by a Cottage*, the human contributions are dim and slumped, but the tree stumps still seem to be radiating back, by their own edges of white reflection, the wiry forks of lightning that must have blasted them.

Often in Ruisdael's middle period, the white foam of turbulent waters or weirdly lit dune grass seizes the low-middle foreground block of light that so casually ignores humanity. Though aggressively present and presented, the focal object remains elusive: the unreadable inscription, peeling bark, faceless animal, churned sea or stream, eroding dune or wind-buffeted foliage in all their shifting multiplicities—like the silver bird of Marvell's "Garden" waving in its plumes the various light—stand for the full presence of perceptible reality that overwhelms the human ability to absorb it.[48] Calvin warned that if messages had arrived from God unmediated by words, "our senses would have been stunned in looking at the bare sign,"[49] and the same may apply to any full perception—reception, really—of the material universe. Indeed, Calvin points out that even God's visual manifestations within Scripture, as a pillar of cloud or a burning bush, "clearly told men of his incomprehensible essence."[50]

If God is here at all, He is beyond the grasp of the human perception and comprehension, imperiously distant from His tiny, transient creatures. The presence of *vanitas* symbols does not restore these paintings to the religious tradition unless there is some divine immanence implied. The very text that Josua Bruyn cites as evidence that Ruisdael's waterfalls were Christian emblems seems (despite its source in Augustine) to express existential despondency better than it does any providential reassurance: "As the river swells from rainwater, overflows, rages, flows and in flowing slides down—so is the course of mortality: Humans are born, they die, and while some die others are born and supersede them, step forth, but do not long remain. What remains in place here? What does not vanish in the abyss as if it were swollen from rain?"[51]

Later in Ruisdael's career—as he becomes increasingly dependent on the patrons of urban Amsterdam—the paint thins out, the world and its mood lighten up. Thus, in the second half of the seventeenth century, in keeping with the more figurative Enlightenment, the weight of the physical yields more and more to human intention. "Around the middle of the seventies Ruisdael's forms become thinner, his touch acquires a miniature-like meticulousness, composition loosens, and the mood turns idyllic."[52] This development may not be as welcome as it sounds. One can see that Meindert Hobbema was a student of Ruisdael, but in adding prettier light and decorative precision, Hobbema often merely explicates Ruisdael's decline in this regard, forfeiting whatever was left of Ruisdael's burdensome point, his implication of a messy and weary world. To deal with revived classicism and a diminishing commercial market (which tended now to value romanticized outdoor scenes and cosmopolitan interiors), Ruisdael, I believe, yielded some of the uniqueness of his vision—which is to say, in a way, his abjuration of anything beyond common vision.[53]

Many of the Dutch painters and their early advocates stressed their efforts to mirror nature, approaching what modern technologies of virtual reality call WYSIWYG: what met the eye would be matched in the print.[54] This was a boast easily converted into an insult, especially given the low social status associated with landscape painting. Sir Joshua Reynolds dismissed hyper-naturalistic landscapes as "mechanical drudgery," though he acknowledged "some pleasure in the contemplation of the truth of the imitation" (and he bought and kept some Ruisdael works).[55] Horace Walpole called such painters "drudging mimics of nature's most uncomely coarseness"; and a century later, John Ruskin would be similarly disdainful, at one point urging a bonfire of the whole genre.

But halfway between Walpole and Ruskin, something changed. Though Ruisdael's paintings had already earned some acceptance in the artistic mainstream

(Gainsborough admired them), they predictably came into their own in the company of Romanticism—another cultural revolution in northern Europe attempting two tasks that are sometimes in concert, sometimes in conflict. The first was to depict ordinary people in ordinary struggles; Romanticism, like Dutch Protestantism, hence took on associations with democratic revolution.[56] The second, broader task was to worship nature as itself, to find the sublime in the way nature overwhelmed human bodily and imaginative strength with a mute spiritualized power that seems to be co-extensive with the ecosystem.

Ruisdael's great heir may therefore be John Constable, rather than the more obviously proximate Hobbema. Goethe's 1813 essay "Ruisdael as Poet" describes the tombstones in *The Jewish Cemetery* as "tombstones to themselves"— a pattern of deferred meaning, as if the erosive *longue durée* were a metaphor for the meditative peeling back of semiotic layers in any present expressive moment; what physicists call entropy thus stands in for the very different kind of entropy described in communications theory. In fact, after Goethe, responses to Ruisdael's painting begin to refer to him as a poet with striking regularity. This seems apt: his works share the Romantic lyric's compact, concrete, agonized expression of what is at once plain and unspeakable in an ordinary moment, and abjure the long and high narrative arc of the Bildungsroman or other literary forms built on plot and character.[57] But the full message—the empty message—I read in Ruisdael does not find expression in literature. He is a poet, paradoxically, because he evokes so well a universe apart from language—a poet unmaking the Western human mythos.

Sacred Spaces and Secular Sacrifice

The Reformation was largely a program for unmaking a prominent piece of that human mythos, without anything nearly so familiar or vivid to put in its place: hence the turn back to nature. This chapter uses Dutch nature-painting to extend the work of the book as a whole: tracing a cluster of major shifts in humanity's relationship to the rest of Creation (along with its supposed Creator). Ruisdael's paintings suggest an effort to confront the natural universe's vast superiority over, and indifference toward, humanity. The human figures, negligible for all their striving, seem to endorse Rick's conclusion in *Casablanca*: it doesn't take much to see that the emotional problems of a few little people don't amount to a hill of beans in this crazy world.

The implied argument of Pieter Saenredam's paintings is not entirely different: like the vast skies in Dutch panoramas—and using the same extremely low vantage point to do so—Saenredam's church interiors suggest the insuperable distance and irreducible difference between minute, messy, earthbound humanity and the high, expansive beauty of God. There is surely piety in the contrast, but (especially under Protestantism) there is also a potentially threatening recognition of how little God understandably has to do with us; nor is there a Really Present Christ to make the connection and to be magnified by its improbability. Saenredam shows—perhaps inadvertently, perhaps argumentatively—the problem with wiping the church clean of idolatrous images and placing God's qualities high above human perception. Scholars generally describe the soaring white vacancies of Saenredam's church interiors as warm and worshipful, but they strike me as often chilly and blank instead, and they reduce humanity to a temporal incursion—dark, lowly, creaturely—on the sacred space. Religiosity loves a vacuum no better than nature does, and so (in response to the Reformation) believers had to fill that sacred space back up with life, re-invest it with affect. One result is that humanity, having been pushed down toward the merely animal, down into the world, turns its attention to that world in landscapes; and in game pieces, pushes non-human creatures into the sacred role of martyr, thus applying to prey animals the pity that had for centuries been focused on the crucified Christ.

Churches depicted in seventeenth-century Dutch art often seem disengaged from traditional religion. In Ruisdael, the steeple remains a distant shadow, and divine Providence seems even less immediately relevant. Even when a cathedral is closely examined in paintings from this culture, it generally manifests its own architectural character much more insistently than any divine presence. Often the churches have (to my modern eyes) a weirdly belated feeling to them: unlike the vast majority of churches in Italian paintings, these appear already old and marginal, the stone already cracked, and the whitewash chipped and discolored; this fascination with detailed flaws may be characteristic of northern art over many decades and genres, but it becomes especially uneasy when the domestic space examined is the house of God. While there may have been an implicit critique of decadent Catholic institutions in some of these suggestions of physical decay, that critique usually seems incidental to the culture's uneasy new intimacy with physical reality.

Not all are as degradingly physical as the bleak interior of Jacob Duck's *The Deposit of the Spoils*, where gambling, whoring, and smoking proceed against the decaying gray-green walls and on the trash-strewn floors of an old Roman church. But—from the child care and child's play in the foreground of Gerard Houckgeest's *The New Church at Delft* to the burials (and the dog) that dominate Hendrick Van Vliet's depictions of *The Old Church at Delft (with the Tomb of Admiral Maerten Tromp)*, where gravity not only holds people to the earth but seems to be pressing them down into it—the business of the body seems to seize the floor from the concerns of the soul. Even the relatively ceremonious

Interior of the Grote Kerk at Haarlem by Gerrit Berckheyde places foremost a dog being petted, and to its left and right children being admonished by adults whose backs are to the preacher. All this may indeed celebrate the opening of church spaces to community life by the Reformation, and the rejection of the Catholic view that the physical church commanded reverence as inherently sacred; but the distance between the earthbound visitors (who often behave more like tourists than like worshippers) and the immense void above them (as in Emanuel de Witte's *Choir of the New Church, Amsterdam*) suggests a dangerous disconnection between humanity and God—a disconnection stressed by Catholic polemics against Protestantism. Furthermore, when these church paintings do provide light and purity, they project it into empty architectural spaces with only the most conjectural spiritual content. These are too obviously buildings.[58]

Pieter Saenredam lived under a Protestant regime in the nationalist stronghold of Haarlem, and "the banishment of all fancies and superfluities"[59] that marks his artistic method arguably corresponds to Protestant efforts to ban what they deemed Catholic superstition and irrelevant ritual. That method also reveals the risk Dutch painting in general reveals: that the curatorial cleansing away of idolatry may inadvertently remove God as well as his image, leaving only the physical and the unknown. Saenredam's "first picture representing a church interior . . . differed from earlier ones in every respect. . . . It showed nothing more nor less than what he (himself) beheld, what anybody else might behold."[60] If things are so purely what they are, if anything subjective or metaphysical is relegated to the category of the errant or imaginary, what room is there for divine presence? Saenredam has been called "The first artist to abandon the fanciful tradition. . . . When he appears on the scene, true realism enters Dutch architectural painting."[61] It enters, furthermore, through markedly mechanical techniques for reproducing (with occasional improvements) the interior appearance of churches; he offers "an image of a space already formed."[62]

Along with that naturalism comes an implied revocation of the anthropocentric values supposedly reified and purified in these buildings. And to the extent that Saenredam goes beyond simple transparency, he employs "minor spatial reorganisations" of the actual churches to force us to see "like a one-eyed person looking into an ordered depth . . . there is a focal narrowing into the architectural infinity."[63] The space between God and humanity is vast in Protestantism, as vast and uninhabited as these unadorned high vaultings imply; and the space between the human and the animal worlds shrinks correspondingly (as it often does for small children). What I have said about the diminished human role amid the less tidy expanse of nature in Ruisdael could as easily apply to these churches, and to their doctrine.[64] There are a few scattered human figures, but the dogs are more central, and the upward space oppressively hollow, in Saenredam's *Interior of the Mariakerk in Utrecht* (chancel from the west). What has been called the "silence and serenity"[65] of Saenredam's church interiors may be read instead as an emptiness. As Blaise Pascal wrote at about the same time Saenredam was painting, "The eternal silence of these infinite spaces fills me with dread."[66] Even in Saenredam's *Interior of the St. Laurens Church at Alkmaar,* the human figures are small, distant, partly concealed (unless we count the decorative ones above, the ones made into objects), while a series of huge open doors lead only into more immense unpopulated space. In a rare case such as *The Transept and Part of the Choir of the St. Bavokerk in Haarlem* (from north to south) where a Saenredam church has fairly large and dignified persons in the foreground, research has shown them to be eighteenth- and nineteenth-century additions.[67] The fact that such figures were presumably added in order to make the scenes more salable supports my sense that Saenredam's original depictions were disturbing in their diminishment of humanity.

When Saenredam does populate the floor, those populations hardly seem to "add to the spirituality and stillness," as more enchanted interpretations of these paintings have asserted.[68] In *Interior of the Buur Church, Utrecht* (interior through the nave from the north), there are grave markers, at least one dog, and perhaps some graffiti in the foreground, but no sign of piety among the small scattered human figures, overwhelmed by the vertiginously high white arches that hold only each other.[69] In his *Choir of the Church of St. Bavo at Haarlem with an Imaginary Tomb of a Bishop* (Figure 8), Saenredam omits the top vaulting, but the persons remain small, and only a statue (which has no choice) is praying—a legacy from some lost era of the history of a church already given over to light tourism; the fact that this praying statue was Saenredam's imaginary addition to the scene suggests that the irony is deliberate. Even when—as in Saenredam's *Interior of the Church of St. Odulphus in Assendelft* (interior from the choir to the west) (Figure 9)—the church does not appear worn and dirty, the vertical space is again immensely vacant, the churchgoers merely like crows or pigeons irreverently hunched on the floor in the distance.[70] Contrasting these pictures with something like *Church Sermon* (Figure 10) shows that, at least before the Reformation took hold, the worshippers could appear as prominent, dignified, individualized human presences, and the church could appear as a warmly colored space that displays the full height and depth of its vaulting without dwarfing those worshippers (indeed, the heights hold a variety of human forms at various levels of presence). So, though one may disagree with my interpretation of the eccentricities of Saenredam's church interiors (as, to describe the extreme cases most extremely, vast ice caves visited by small, primitive, seemingly soulless creatures), one cannot dismiss those eccentricities as the inevitable result of an effort to present a contemporary-looking scene that captures the magnificent architecture of a preaching-based church.

Figure 8. Pieter Jansz Saenredam (1597–1665), *Choir of the Church of St. Bavo at Haarlem, with an Imaginary Tomb of a Bishop*, 1630. Oil on wood, 41 × 37 cm. Musée du Louvre, Paris. Photo: Erich Lessing/Art Resource, NY.

In all probability, Saenredam and his patrons or purchasers were pious men: church wardens or others recording reverence for Dutch religious institutions and their wonders. Yet it is still worth recognizing the potential of such paintings to provoke and perhaps to express—to create an opportunity for registering—the emptiness that is the chillier side of Protestant purity. Perhaps this is why comparable subjects painted in the Catholic regions of the southern Netherlands "never developed a feeling for the suggestion of true-to-life reality and atmosphere on which the innovative church interior style of Saenredam, Houckgeest or De Witte was based."[71] The blankness of the churches matches the blankness of the inscrutable Calvinist deity's visage; the smallness and anonymity of the human figures within the vast, abstractly geometrical churches, with their dizzying bright upper spaces, matches the smallness and anonymity of the human figures within the vast Dutch landscapes, with their own dizzying skyscapes. Again there is a beauty here, but one no longer answerable to human

Figure 9. Pieter Jansz Saenredam (1597–1665), *Interior of the Church of St. Odulphus, Assendelft*, 1649. Oil on panel, 50 × 76 cm. Rijksmuseum, Amsterdam. © Rijksmuseum Foundation.

needs—as, comparably, botanical science shifted (my Chapter 1 has suggested) from a study of human uses toward a more abstract and objective taxonomy. As impressive new research uncovers evidence that Saenredam not only had close Catholic associates, but actually went out of his way to Catholicize many of his depictions,[72] it becomes plausible that the warning signals I detect in these images—warnings about the vulgar degradations at the base of the sacred space and, above, chilly alienations from any perceptible divine presence—were less an accidental by-product and more an argumentative intention of these drawings and paintings.

Saenredam certainly finds ways to smuggle avatars of the Holy Virgin back into these Reformation churches. In several of Saenredam's paintings, a mother uses the church as casual shelter while she nurses a baby, as if (in a Christianized version of the Pygmalion story) the figures of Madonna and Child had been dragged down from the (formerly Catholic) church's walls and windows and placed back into normal, natural, secular life.[73] At times this process appears benign enough. As the painters' formula of Venus and Cupid turned into Virgin and Christ-child, so it can turn again into simply mother and child; if the Holy Family formula is jovially retouched as Jan Steen's *The Happy Family*, the echo

Figure 10. Anonymous (perhaps by Aertgen van Leyden), *Church Sermon or, The Calling of St. Anthony or, The Reading of the Lord's Prayer*, ca. 1535. Oil on panel, 132.7 × 96.3 cm. Rijksmuseum, Amsterdam. © Rijksmuseum Foundation.

Figure 11. Gabriel Metsu (1629–67), *The Sick Child*, ca. 1660–65. Oil on canvas, 33.2 × 27.2 cm. Rijksmuseum, Amsterdam. © Rijksmuseum Foundation.

seems at worst innocuous. In England, the transference of worshipful obedience from the Virgin Mother Mary to the Virgin Queen Elizabeth became a fundamental piece of Protestant statecraft.

The placid, generous-breasted mother who holds her child in front of ancient Roman ruins in Jan Baptist Weenix's *Italian Landscape with Mother and Child* is surely the Madonna who finds herself still with an infant but without any *istoria*, arriving many centuries too late for her very natural activity to hold any supernatural implications. Mary's flight into Egypt, subject of so many Renaissance and Baroque paintings, yields to notably similar images of ordinary women caring for a baby in a landscape.[74] Gabriel Metsu's *The Sick Child* (Figure 11) would strongly suggest a secularized conflation of Madonna-and-Child and pietà motifs even without the faint picture of the Crucifixion occupying the back wall. Though Seymour Slive is an evocative describer of pictures, his remark that any such association "seems far-fetched"[75] strikes me as perverse, considering how often he rightly takes inset paintings as codes for interpretation; it isn't as if Metsu had been taking a photograph and therefore included the background inadvertently. These are the opposite of the *portraits historiés* which cast the person commissioning the painting as a holy figure in some Scriptural scene: now the holy figures are themselves recast as ordinary persons.

In late 1620s, Abraham Bloemaert and a colleague painted "the earliest of the multi-figured shepherd scenes."[76] How did Bloemaert decide to compose the relationship between those figures? Alison Kettering describes Bloemaert's *Shepherd and Shepherdess* (Figure 12) as "modeled directly on . . . the eighth print of the *Otia delectant* series," but changing the virtuously industrious peasant girl into something "more graceful and refined," and taking out the third figure—an older man—altogether. This is certainly true, but the resulting dynamic design, including the relative postures and gestures and the diagonal thrust, echoes Bloemaert's altarpiece from a few years earlier depicting the Wise Men offering gifts to the infant Jesus (Figure 13). The older men from both precedents have been condensed into this young wooer, the Lamb of God diminished to some sheep on the left, and the clouds of angels on the upper right have become a tree. Comparing traditional Catholic scenes such as Cornelis Bloemaert's engraving of *The Vision of Saint Ignatius* (Figure 14) with Jacob van Ruisdael's *Windmill at Wijk bij Duurstede* (Figure 15) shows how angelic clouds could be replaced by meteorological ones, as God retreats behind natural phenomena, which Luther called "the masks of God" (*larvae Dei*) and which thus acquire their own upward magnificence. There is still a visible reciprocity between the earth and the heavens in Ruisdael's painting, but both are conceived as primarily physical; Ruisdael even replaces the usual trio of holy women below the hill-mounted cross mourning Jesus's departure from the earth with three ordinary women below the cross-like, hill-mounted windmill, apparently watching their men float away to sea.

Dutch painting in this period reconstitutes the supernatural scenes and figures of Christianity as exclusively natural. The paintings of Jan Weenix (son of Jan Baptist), Metsu, and others suggest that the principal Dutch response to Creation's diminished sympathy with humanity after the Reformation was to increase human sympathy with nature; and that if God could no longer be made physically visible, the heartfelt pity formerly invested in images of Christian martyrdom would instead be invested in the creatures one could actually see suffering: the prey animals of the hunt. So the templates of certain kinds of religious painting persist, whether for philosophical or craftsmanly reasons, and

Figure 12. Abraham Bloemaert (1564–1651), *Shepherd and Shepherdess*, 1627. Oil on canvas, 60 × 74.5 cm. Niedersächsisches Landesmuseum, Hanover, Germany. Photo: Niedersächsisches Landesmuseum, Landesgalerie, Hanover.

they result in the emergence of something like modern ecological conscious-ness, a humane attitude toward non-human life.

Let me begin defending this ambitious claim by inviting attention to a rather uninviting seventeenth-century painting—Jan Weenix's *Birds of Prey Around a Dead Lamb* (Figure 16)—and proposing three questions. Why would anyone have chosen to paint such a scene and imagined it would find a buyer? What became of all the bloody scenes of holy martyrdom Dutch artists would have produced if Reformation iconoclasm had not largely divided their profes-sion from that of their southern colleagues? And what produced the sympa-thetic identification with the suffering of non-human creatures that led toward today's animal-rights and ecology movements? This portion of the chapter will argue that the questions essentially answer each other. This is, and is not, the martyred Lamb of God; the things that Christ represented are emptied out into nature, toward which the viewer must begin constructing a new, more direct, affective relationship.

Figure 13. Abraham Bloemaert (1564–1651), *The Adoration of the Magi*, 1623. Oil on canvas, 420 × 290 cm. Musée de Grenoble, Grenoble, France. © Musée de Grenoble, Grenoble, France.

Figure 14. Cornelis Bloemaert (1603–84), *The Vision of St. Ignatius*, 1622–25. Engraving after a work by Abraham Bloemaert (1564–1651), 17.4 × 13.4 cm. Rijksprentenkabinet, Rijksmuseum, Amsterdam. © Rijksmuseum Foundation.

Figure 15. Jacob van Ruisdael (1628/29–82), *Windmill at Wijk bij Duurstede*, 1670. Oil on canvas, 83 × 101 cm. Rijksmuseum, Amsterdam. © Rijksmuseum Foundation.

Another depiction of a kneeling swain courting a reluctant shepherdess— usually called *Pastoral Scene* and probably painted by Gerard Seghers, whose work often reflects devout Catholicism[77]—gives the gesturing wooer a cloak that billows out behind him like the wings of the archangel in similarly con- structed Annunciation pictures. At times it is tempting to read some of these echoes, these quotations of sacred art in a secular tenor, as parody rather than mere displacement. Though he was also evidently Catholic, Jan Steen was al- ways ready for a tasteless joke, and he appears, in *Sick Woman* (Figure 17), to be creating a secular burlesque of the Annunciation scene: the doctor may be treat- ing the woman's virginal green-sickness, or instead her morning-sickness (as the putative or prospective mate hovers in the background), and he stoops to deliver the results of the urine test with a balletic reciprocity of gestures that typifies the archangel's message to the Virgin Mary in earlier Renaissance Annunciation paintings such as Botticelli's (Figure 18).[78] The Cupid statue point- ing a dart from high above neatly takes the place of the impregnating dove and

Figure 16. Jan Weenix (1642–1719), *Birds of Prey Around a Dead Lamb*. Photo: Christie's, Long Island, New York.

the shafts of light it commonly darts at Mary's body. Incursions on the imagery of Catholicism (and hence of medieval and Renaissance European painting) flirt—whether willingly or not—with mockery of Christianity itself, which is brought not only back to nature, but down to biology.

Alternatively, the mimicry of Christian images could lend gravity to the *natures mortes*—the stilled lives—of the myriad Dutch game pieces. In translating conventional depictions of the Slaughter of the Innocents into his *Eagles Attacking Waterfowl*, Jan Fijt simply redirects the pathos. In many other paintings, Christ, traditionally symbolized as a captive lamb, is often not so much figured as replaced by a dead bird or rabbit who has died for our supper, often suspended and stretched to a human phenotype, piteously gazing at us from the foreground. So many versions of this queasy pattern emerge in seventeenth-century Netherlandish painting that one must suspect either that the idolatrous function overrides the variation of subject-matter (the painters cannot erase the residue of the pious traditions), or that these works represent less an avoidance of traditional Christian imagery than a fairly savage attack on it (the painters are taking some kind of revenge on the pious traditions). As

Basil Willey noted unadmiringly over seventy years ago, "It was, of course, one of the advantages enjoyed by seventeenth-century 'Protestant' writers, that under cover of the usual attack on 'Popery' they could, with every appearance of religious zeal, demolish the very foundations of religion itself."[79] As in writing, so perhaps in painting.

Mostly, however, the process seems to me more decorous; it reassigns rather than mocks the emotional valence of the Christian scenes. My point is not to insist on a cruel symbolic in-joke among these painters, but rather to suggest that a space of a certain shape and attributes had been hollowed out on the traditional European canvas, and nature (as it is known to do) rushed to fill the void. Ordinary lives certainly gain attention. The ascendancy of the secular—itself a clear if unforeseen corollary of the Reformation[80]—is visible in sixteenth-century works by Pieter Aertsen and his close associate Joachim Beuckelaer that show Scriptural scenes in the background of a busy ordinary marketplace; it continued in the way the baptism of Christ recedes discreetly into the darkness at the center of Abraham Bloemaert's *Preaching of John the Baptist*, with few paying any attention; and extends into the religious painting of Cornelis van Haarlem, Bartholomeus Spranger, and Claude Lorrain. This is a theological use of an inversion technique that goes back at least to Lucas van Leyden, and a version of the decentering that W. H. Auden's "Musée des Beaux Arts" noted in Pieter Brueghel the Elder's *Icarus*. David III Ryckaert's *The Yard of the Inn at Emmaus* is based on his *Kitchen Still Life with Peasant Family*, and "In this instance Ryckaert altered the meaning of the work by padding the background with the apparently inconspicuous detail of three talking figures . . . one of them is decidedly identifiable as Christ wearing the crown of thorns."[81]

The Flemish refugee Coninxloo—"the most important landscapist who worked in Holland during the first decade of the century"—moved (as he moved from Catholic Antwerp to Protestant Amsterdam) from early works where "Nature is a stage for biblical or mythological scenes" to "the late Coninxloo who broke with the anthropocentric tradition of Netherlandish landscape," leaving men "completely dwarfed by primeval trees."[82] What began as a modest eclipse of the holy figures eventually becomes the return of such figures transformed into mere nature—the Incarnation in overdrive. As early as Aertsen (who put a haunch of meat spectacularly in the foreground of his 1552 *Christ with Maria and Martha*), one can trace the residue of Crucifixion and Deposition paintings in the domestic slaughterhouse; and Beuckelaer's three versions of *Plentiful Kitchen with Christ in the House of Martha and Mary* actually put an abundance of food—featuring birds stripped and hung up, spikes driven into the sides of meat—in the foreground, while Jesus speaks in the background: the viewer is in the position of Martha, and Jesus is, on multiple levels, the victim of her worldly priorities.[83] (Readers who suspected this book

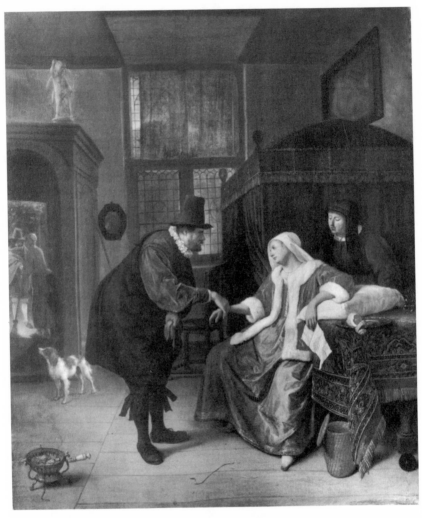

Figure 17. Jan Steen (ca. 1625–79), *Sick Woman,* ca. 1660. Oil on canvas, 61 × 52 cm. Alte Pinakothek, Munich, Germany. © Bayerische Staatsgemäldesammlungen (Bavarian state painting collections).

of tossing in everything but the kitchen sink may now deem the set complete.) Lest we think such depictions must have been innocent in their time, it is worth noting that the Inquisition forced Veronese to change the name his of huge 1573 *Last Supper* painting to *Feast in the House of Levi* because the inquisitors deemed it intolerable to surround Christ with so much mundane and hedonistic de- tail.[84] Another of Christ's meals, this one at Emmaus, received notably similar

Figure 18. Sandro Botticelli (Alessandro di Mariano Filipepi, ca. 1445–1510), *Annunciation*, 1489. Tempera on wood, 150 × 156 cm. Uffizi, Florence, Italy. Photo: Erich Lessing/Art Resource, NY.

treatment in other northern paintings of the period: small and faint, tucked behind a vivid set of dead and strung up game animals or fish.

Abraham Bloemaert's 1612 *Adoration of the Shepherds* provides a bridge between the visions of food preparation and of Christ's preparation, by placing in the very foreground of his Nativity scene a sprawled lamb with its limbs tied together, just below a Christ child (his ankles similarly crossed) of the same size and at the same angle—a familiar emblematic adumbration of the sacrifice for which this Lamb of God was born,[85] but still oddly similar to both the form and the content of many ostensibly secular pictures to follow. Aertsen places a live bovine head in the forefront of his *Christ with the Four Evangelists, Virgin and Child*, and *Adoration of the Shepherds* paintings; he also establishes a reciprocity

Figure 19. Pieter Aertsen (1508/9–75), middle panel of a triptych, *The Adoration of the Magi*, 1560. Oil on panel, 167.5 × 179 cm. Rijksmuseum, Amsterdam. © Rijksmuseum Foundation.

between the Holy Infant and the hairy bovine at the lower right of the middle panel of his 1560 triptych (Figure 19), and again in the *Shepherds* scene where Christ's little raised arms match the horns. The bull may be associated with Luke, but it is also traditionally associated with the sacrifice of Christ. Aertsen then places a similar head at the front of his *nature morte*, which breaks the animal up so decisively into its anatomical bits that it feels like a sixteenth-century blend of Dali and Cubism, and has a background scene often identified as the flight of Mary and the Christ-child into Egypt. Something extra is at stake in the livestock. In Beuckelaer's *Market Scene with Ecce Homo*, Jesus in the background is clearly doomed to look very soon like the animal carcasses hung up in the foreground.

From there, and from the many depictions of the martyrdom of saints, it is a short leap—though over a rather scary abyss—to a series of still lifes that make a gored and suspended animal their centerpiece. Jan Baptist Weenix offers a *Dead Partridge Hanging from a Nail* and a *Dead Deer*, also splayed, suspended, and bleeding from a wound in its side. In several such paintings a monkey is poised to raid the carnage—a residue perhaps of Deposition scenes (such as the one by the Master of the Virgin among Virgins) where a diabolic monkey reaches for a skull in the foreground. So the still life, which had generally been a vehicle of moral admonition in the *vanitas* mode (especially among the Leiden painters), starts taking on more of the functions of the theological narrative. The "associative habit of Dutch thought" in the seventeenth century—including that culture's "delight in exegesis and multiple meanings"[86] and its fondness for puzzles—make such interpretations more plausible. As a viewer must look sideways to discern the admonitory skull in some anamorphic paintings (Holbein's so-called *Ambassadors* is a famous example), or (a more typically Dutch device) gaze into a mirror to gain true perspective, viewers must blur the eyes and rouse the memory to read the palimpsest of the Christian story in much of this Reformation art—to see pushed back in the other direction the process by which St. Ambrose theologized Virgil's nature. There is finally a significant congruence between the way Christians were supposed to identify piteously with the Christ who at once does and does not share their nature as mortal animals, and the way they began to identify piteously with prey animals on the same basis. The sympathetic imagination seized on a shared mortality—its struggles and its sufferings.[87] A quick juxtaposition of Jan Weenix's *Dead Hare with Partridges* (Figure 20) and the elder David Teniers's *Calvary* (Figure 21) suggests how marked these unacknowledged correlations could be. In Pieter van Boucle's *Meat from the Butcher with Dog and Cat* (Figure 22), the eviscerated figure sprawled at the center is actually a lamb, with its placid gaze weirdly sustained; it appears benignly conscious of the sacrifice it is making for humanity. Seldom has the distinction between living animals and meat for food—between deer and venison, in *As You Like It*—been more disturbingly blurred.

None of this is to deny that these game paintings were generally objects of pride, both for the painter (who rendered magnificently the complexities of fur and structural anatomy) and for the patron (for whom hunting was a declaration of both social and species privilege). My interest here, as with Saenredam's churches, is in giving voice to the sentiment that may have been a secondary, probably preconscious cause or effect of the new type of image: the kind of collective Freudian slip whereby a proud assertion comes so close to a guilty fear that the charge leaps the gap, the tongue leaks the secret, and the image becomes the occasion for a culture to contemplate the darker implications of its practices.

Often the Crucifixion is translated in less gory and more intellectually

Figure 20. Jan Weenix (1642–1719), *Dead Hare with Partridges,* ca. 1690. Oil on canvas, 91 × 74 cm. Wallace Collection, London. Reproduced by kind permission of the Trustees of the Wallace Collection, London.

Figure 21. David Teniers the Elder (1582–1649), *Calvary* (also *The Crucifixion, Le Calvaire*), ca. 1625–40. 86 × 69 cm. Musée du Louvre, Paris. Photo: Herve Lewandowski/Réunion des Musées Nationaux/Art Resource, NY.

Figure 22. Pieter van Boucle (1610–73), *Meat from the Butcher with Dog and Cat*, 1651. Oil-base paint on fabric, 1.13 × 1.49 m. Musée du Louvre, Paris. Photo: Jean-Gilles Berizzi/Réunion des Musées Nationaux/Art Resource, NY.

subtle ways. In many pre-Reformation paintings—Jacob Cornelisz van Oostsanen's 1510 *Calvary*, for example, or a number of fourteenth-century Sienese paintings—wine goblets or chalices catch the blood from each of Christ's wounds. Quite a few seventeenth-century Dutch still lifes feature wine that suggests the Eucharistic blood more subtly: for example, Willem Claesz Heda's and Gottfried Von Wedig's depictions of partly consumed wine and bread, and Dou's 1650 *Housewife*, who holds up a dead bird—*sans pitié, sans piété*—alongside a spilled beaker. Wine is spilled in Harmen Steenwijck's *Vanitas Still Life*, drained in Jan Davidsz de Heem's *The Dessert*.[88] Whose cordial essence is flowing here? Steen's *Meal at Emmaus* (Figure 23) displays some partly consumed wine and bread as Christ fades away, as if the former were taking the place of the latter, as indeed they did; the eggshells on the ground (though commonplace in Steen) here suggest the Easter Resurrection so closely associated with this story, and the lemon peel, here as in several other seventeenth-century Dutch still lifes, looks like an ominously diamond-headed serpent poised to strike. What has generally been taken as a craftsmanly flourish, or some kind of symbol about the sour accenting the sweet, may thus sometimes have a theological thrust.

Figure 23. Jan Steen (ca. 1625–79), *Meal at Emmaus* (*Christ at Emmaus*), 1665–68. Oil on canvas, 134 × 104 cm. Rijksmuseum, Amsterdam. © Rijksmuseum Foundation.

Floris van Dijck's 1613 *Breakfast Piece* places the half-full glass just above the oval of bread, and just to its left, in the center foreground, a lemon-peel snake that seems ready to attack through the plane of the picture, as if to refuse the viewer any exemption from Original Sin. Pieter Claesz's 1636 *Still Life* places a fish (an ancient symbol of Christ) between a roll of bread and the familiar roemer wineglass, with the lemon peel snaking into the lower foreground.

Figure 24. Jan Davidsz de Heem, (1606–83/84), *Still Life (Stilleben mit Blumen und Steingutkanne)*, 1650. Oil on canvas, 47 × 61 cm. Kunstmuseum St. Gallen. © Schweizerisches Institut für Kunstwissenschaft, Zurich.

In de Heem's *Still Life* (Figure 24), the rind again twists into the foreground looking uncannily like an exotic venomous snake about to strike; around it lie a hunk of bread, a spilled wineglass, and symbols of sweet, transient life.[89] In Heda's 1630s *Still Life with Pewter and Silver Vessels and a Crab*, the serpentine peel beside the spilled wine even somehow acquires a beady little eye. The knowledge, not of good and evil, but of natural and artificial—especially as that uneasily correlated with interior and exterior—brings something dangerous into the world; viewers are seduced, not only by the beauty, but also by a tantalizing first glimpse of the inside of the skin—by the drive to penetrate nature that Herbert's "Vanitie (I)" warns is rape under the guise of science. That moral will become quite clear in paintings of Doubting Thomas, such as Caravaggio's and Terbrugghen's versions (Figure 25), where it is Christ's body that has been peeled open, and the scene becomes an occasion for critiquing the modern desire to look (through spectacles, in Terbrugghen's case) for the thing itself, for material proof of even the highest spiritual truths, to test God's love

Figure 25. Hendrik Terbrugghen (1588–1629), *Doubting Thomas*, 1622. Oil on canvas, 108.8 × 136.5 cm. Rijksmuseum, Amsterdam. © Rijksmuseum Foundation.

with our senses and technologies so aggressively that the insertion of a finger in Christ's wound begins to look like a sexual violation.

That Christ could be implied behind some of the objects in a still-life painting is proven by the Munich collaboration of de Heem and Nicolaes van Veerendael, which includes a crucifix and an inscription reading, "But one does not turn to look at the most beautiful flower of all"; the painters are pushing directly back against the conversion of religious figures into flora and fauna, insisting that the sacrificed Christ be recognized as the ultimate still life. De Heem's *Eucharist in a Fruit Wreath* features a wine goblet like those in supposedly secular still lifes, but hangs an almost invisible crucifix, white on off-white, just above the cup. The painting recalls the many flower wreaths into which the Jesuit painter Daniel Seghers smuggled images (such as that of the Virgin Mary) even less welcome under Protestant authority. Claes Jansz Visscher's engraving *Grace Before the Meal* has a Last Supper picture on the wall, and the depiction of *Grace* on which Visscher collaborated with Pieter Feddes shows the Holy Spirit overseeing what otherwise looks like a standard Dutch breakfast piece. Heda's *Banquet Piece with Mince Pie* takes out the explicitly supernatural entity, but sets, just below the wine cup and bread roll, a depiction of Abraham preparing to sacrifice Isaac, which was the chief Old Testament type of God's sacrifice of His son; this juxtaposition provokes, in an unpublished dissertation,[90] the only Eucharistic reading of such still lifes I have found in the art-historical literature.

While these works seem intended partly as reminders of the omnipresence of Christ's sacrifice, and possibly as safe displacements of Crucifixion images for Catholic painters such as Heda (and their clients) in a largely Protestant society, others seem to appropriate the Crucifixion on behalf of the stilled lives they primarily depict. Many depictions of the carnage *après la chasse* recall the carnage after the Cross; these are Deposition scenes, inviting us to mourn the spirits here made flesh, the life made meat. The Last Supper shrinks into the breakfast leftovers. In Jacob Fopsen van Es's *Preparations for a Meal*, a disturbingly ambiguous and gory hunk of abandoned meat is surrounded by theologically suggestive items, including bread, red wine, an apple, and three pieces carved from the sacrificed lamb. Rembrandt's *Slaughtered Ox* is spread vertically on the canvas, as a flesh thoroughly anonymous but too close to the human configuration for comfort.[91] It is therefore disturbing to recall that the Rembrandt painting now generally called *Saint Bartholomew*, on the supposition that the pensive figure holding a knife was destined to be flayed, was once known as *Rembrandt's Cook*.

A more obscure but perhaps more significant example is David III Ryckaert's version, *Kitchen with a Flayed Ox*, which presents a huge, feverishly lit carcass in the foreground looking like a brawny crucified and eviscerated human form; on the wall hangs a sieve, the ancient Roman symbol of the Vestal Virgins, which was adopted for the Virgin Mary. It may thus be not merely coincidental that " 'slaughtered oxen and other animals appear with some frequency in sixteenth- and seventeenth-century Northern painting,' " and that (via the forgiveness motif of the Prodigal Son in Luke) "many commentaries equate the ox with the crucified Christ."[92] In Isaac van Ostade's pig-slaughter images, the carcass is splayed upon what is distinctly a standing cross of wood; in Beuckalaer's version (Figure 26), the pig bears an even more distinct resemblance to a crucified person, and the background figure bringing in wine adds Eucharistic reference to the physical resemblance.[93]

The pattern linking the sacrificed Christ to lamb-as-mutton (or bull-as-beef or pig-as-pork) would have been provided by radical Calvinist polemics concerning the Eucharist, which sought to associate Catholicism (in its doctrine of full literal presence) with cannibalism; but the Protestant radicals may thereby have created, however unintentionally, a cultural vocabulary for the modern

Figure 26. Joachim Beuckelaer (1530–74), *Slaughtered Pig*, 1563. Oil on oak, 114 × 83 cm. Wallraf-Richartz Museum, Cologne, Germany.

vegetarian aversion to meat. To celebrate the Incarnation but remain a carnivore could have been awkward. The pattern would also have had some bitter ironic background in Protestant memories of the massacre of imprisoned Huguenots in Lyon, which was performed by the local butchers with their tools after the official executioner and soldiers refused to do it. The sensibility from which cross-species sympathy arose seems to have been linked in several ways with the emergent sensibility of Reformation zeal. Even before he began publishing his famous chronicles of Protestant martyrdom, John Foxe wrote that he could "scarce pass the shambles where beasts are slaughtered, but that my mind recoils with a feeling of pain."[94] Puritans such as Stubbes were prominent condemners of bear-baiting. "Familist Giles Randall, Ranter Giles Robins, and Roger Crab, the mad hatter of Chesham, all advocated the vegetarian regimen," mostly on the grounds that animals were our fleshly kin and deserved more kindness.[95] Evidently animals become, for radical Reformers, the locus of the garish pity that had formerly been captured in bloody crucifixes and in pictures of tortured saints. Like St. Hubert and St. Eustace, they began to envision a crucifix in the antlers of the deer.

Unwittingly pointing the way toward utopian vegetarianism, Richard Baxter argued (in the 1680s) that God enabled fallen human beings "to take away the lives of our fellow creatures and to eat their flesh to show what sin hath brought on the world."[96] This connection uncovers a potential meaning of Metsu's *Woman Peeling Apples*, which juxtaposes a slaughtered hare with a woman preparing apples to be eaten. She may represent (as generally supposed) an archetype of the good housewife, but a woman offering an apple to her mate seems archetypally ominous. Like the still lifes that juxtapose herpetological citrus-rinds with bread and wine, and like Cornelis van Haarlem's *Baptism of Christ*, which puts Adam and Eve in the foreground, Metsu may be placing a domestic version of Christ's sacrifice alongside a domestic reminder of the forbidden fruit that obliged that sacrifice. This may also help explain why so many Dutch kitchen scenes featuring pinioned animals in the foreground place a seduction scene in the background. Along the same lines, Gerrit Dou's *Girl Chopping Onions* offers multiple suggestions that the kitchen-maid is a fallen woman,[97] while a dead fowl hangs from the wall in the spot where, in a Catholic household, one might expect a crucifix; the little boy holds up a globe as the infant Christ does in so many Renaissance paintings, while the golden ring of a candle-holder mounted on the mantelpiece behind him floats conveniently over his head like a halo. Frans Snyders's *Merchant of Game* (Figure 27) features a large animal at the center, bleeding from the trunk, with lesser corpses strung up around it, while the young woman smiles much too blithely on the scene of carnage, and seductively offers a man a piece of fruit; the foreground is the gory world to which the background has doomed us.

Later in the seventeenth century, the pattern seems to circle back to its origins in the anonymous *Mutilated Corpses of the De Witt Brothers* (Figure 28),[98] with the two men disemboweled and hanging from their crossed feet (with hungry little animals nosing around beneath) like the hares of the *natures mortes*—for example, Jan Weenix's *Deerhound with Dead Game and Implements of the Hunt*. The connection may be more than accidental, because the brothers were flayed and killed to save the skins (by absorbing the sins) of their fellow-citizens: a propitiatory sacrifice to Amsterdam's French conquerors. In seventeenth-century Dutch history, "the atrocious murder of the de Witts might be seen as a catharsis. . . . The blood guilt, remorselessly invoked by preachers as the price for profane living, was thus displaced onto the heads of scapegoats."[99] So as the human bodies become the slaughtered beef, they also come to retake the function of sacrificial Christ that the culture had been uneasily displacing onto its butchered game and livestock.

Figure 27. Frans Snyders (1579–1657), *Merchant of Game*, 1630. 2.21 × 1.87 m. Musée du Louvre, Paris. Photo: Giraudon/Art Resource, NY.

The Isaac story (and paintings of it) generally offer an apt emblem for the shift I am describing, by which an executed animal takes the place of the sanctified human body. If we are willing to add a twist to the stretch, Metsu's *The Sacrifice of Isaac* (Figure 30) has echoes in his *Dead Rooster* (Figure 31). It may seem a silly comparison, yet Metsu is distinctly registering similarities in the bodies presented for sacrifice, and perhaps also recording the fact that (though they are bathed in similar patterns of light) no pitying force is coming to save the bird. Guercino and Titian offer images of *Apollo and Marsyas* that show the pinioned figure about to be flayed as half man, half goat—a condensation of the

Figure 28. Anonymous, *Mutilated Corpses of the De Witt Brothers* (*Hanged at Groene Zoodje on Vijverberg in The Hague*), 1672 or after. Oil on canvas, 69.5 × 56 cm. Rijksmuseum, Amsterdam. © Rijksmuseum Foundation.

Figure 29. Jan Weenix (1642–1719), *Deerhound with Dead Game and Implements of the Hunt*, 1708. Oil on canvas, 173.5 × 157 cm. National Gallery, London. © National Gallery, London.

Abraham-and-Isaac pictures that show the alternative animal sacrifice off to the side. The agonizing exposure of the body again offers an occasion for looking into the moral functions of the deity.

As artists developed sympathy for the mangled animal bodies, they seemed to develop a reciprocal detachment from human corpses. Palimpsests of both game carcasses in the kitchen and Isaac under the knife are visible in

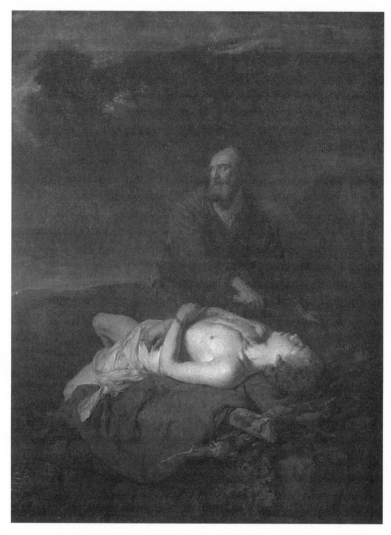

Figure 30. Gabriel Metsu (1629–67), *Abraham and Isaac* (*The Sacrifice of Isaac*), mid-seventeenth century. Israel Museum, Jerusalem.

anatomy-theater depictions such as Rembrandt's *Anatomy Lesson of Dr. Nicolaes Tulp*; but the emotional atmosphere has cooled considerably. We gain something like an objective grasp on biology, but only at the cost of recognizing that we ourselves are biological objects. Nature reclaims us just when we start claiming the power to name it objectively and view its essences. Thus, in Nicolaes Pickenoy's *Anatomy Lesson of Dr. Sebastien Egbertsz de Vrij*, a skeleton seems

Figure 31. Gabriel Metsu (1629–67), *Dead Rooster*, 1650. Oil on panel, 57 × 40 cm. Museo Nacional del Prado, Madrid. Though properly shown with the rooster head-down, the image is here turned sideways to facilitate comparison.

to be sharing a chummy greeting with the students of bone-nomenclature. A depiction of the *Anatomy Theater at Leiden* by Willem van Swanenburgh (Figure 32) shows a human autopsy, with a man lifting a sheet off the hollowed trunk of the corpse. The spectators arrayed around the theater include not only a number of marginally attentive persons, but a number of human skeletons holding flags, and quite a few animal forms in various stages of skeletonization, which seem to be paying better attention. In the foremost central position stands a tree from which one human skeleton has picked a piece of fruit and prepares to hand it to another skeleton (who holds a delving-tool), as if this were an X-ray or time-lapse picture of Adam and Eve. The human effort to objectify the natural world is here reversed; our ancient victims look back at our defeat with the unmistakable if inscrutable grins of the skull: the silent last laugh. We have said, but whether wisely or not, let the fossil record judge. A visual culture that diligently depicted surfaces on the supposition it was thereby capturing truth had to recognize that the complete flayed human skin (held

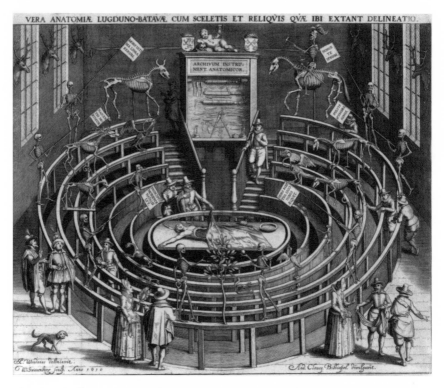

Figure 32. Willem van Swanenburgh (1581–1612), *Anatomy Theater at Leiden*, 1610.
Engraving, based on a woodcut by J. C. Woudanus. Rijksprentenkabinet, Rijksmuseum,
Amsterdam. © Rijksmuseum Foundation.

draped by a man at the lower right) was missing something essential. In fact, the
anatomy lesson faces the problems attributed to pornography in Chapter 1, at
least in terms of spiritual and epistemological limits. Autopsy offers itself as
technologically objectifying observation, as an acceptance of natural truth, and
as an opening out of the inmost secrets of human being. But the suspicion remains that something has escaped in the process and mocks our claims to a
grasp on truth, a dominion over nature, and a meaningful end.

In the seventeenth-century Netherlands, the effort to paint mere physical
reality fails—to some extent it was booby-trapped by Counter-Reformation
painting, Chapter 7 will argue—and I think both the fact and the side-effects of
that failure are worth contemplating. The persistence of moral implication and
allegory demonstrates (as does much of the drama and poetry I have been ex-
amining) that the task of removing human motives from representations of nature is a Sisyphean one; and when that consciousness re-imposes itself on
representations of natural rather than supernatural situations, the consequence

is a moral identification with nature and the investment of nature with its own will and sanctity—crucial elements in modern environmentalism. While "the great Catholic subjects of death and martyrdom are imbued with a new pathos" in Baroque painting,[100] that pathos is distributed to new objects—really, new subjects—in northern nature painting.

Arguably this eco-sentient innovation is actually a reversion, if we look back from the Eucharist, through the Jewish Pesach feast understood as an oblation, toward some version of the totemic traditions in which the communal feast is accompanied by reverence toward the prey animals eaten there—accompanied, that is, by some amalgam of gratitude and penitence intended to rebalance the universe from which we take life to live. But that must, of course, remain speculation.

At a minimum, one can say that the compositional principles of the sacred gatherings are legible as palimpsest in the still lifes and that the affective tricks and signals of the scenes of martyrdom similarly invest the scenes of slain animals. To say this was done unthinkingly produces a situation hardly less consequential (for the reading of the culture-work) than if it had been done with great deliberation. It may be laziness or habit rather than anything more actively subversive; a traditional reflex within the craft rather than a blasphemy within the broader culture; but whatever the intentions, these paintings are persistent signals of a process whereby the sympathetic love of Christ became channeled partly into a sympathetic love of nature.

The wonderful engravings by Hendrick Goltzius of his beloved dog and of the poor monkey chained to a chair—even his intricate studies of trees—strike me as clear evidence that this relationship was developing in late-Renaissance Holland; in the "Taste" engraving in Goltzius's "Five Senses" series, the chained monkey distinctly mirrors the human figure. The late-Renaissance English writer Margaret Cavendish compares human slaughter in battle to the ordinary work of a kitchen,[101] and her poem "The Hunting of the Hare" (like her 1653 "Dialogue of Birds") puts explicitly into words the agonizing sympathy for the prey animal that the paintings imply. Her works consistently imply an association between sexism and speciesism, between male and human arrogance. The fact that it was another of the period's scarce female poets—Katherine Philips—who praised the vegetarianism of the Golden Age would seem to confirm the thesis (of Carolyn Merchant and others) that women are especially attuned to advanced environmentalist consciousness. Discernible in the arts of seventeenth-century Europe are early steps on a journey toward twenty-first-century animal-rights advocacy, in which People for the Ethical Treatment of Animals recently "ran ads comparing the deaths of women murdered and dismembered by a serial killer to those of animals killed for meat."[102] A new moral foundation was being built, necessarily from the bottom of the "chain of being" upward.[103]

Figure 33. Jan Weenix (1642–1719), *Still Life with Peacock and Dog (Trophies of the Hunt)*, 1696. Oil on canvas, 144 × 187 cm. Musée du Louvre, Paris. Photo: Gérard Blot/Réunion des Musées Nationaux/Art Resource, NY.

At whatever level of deliberation, Dutch artists authorized their viewers to transfer the compassion traditionally bestowed on Christ to other creatures who died that we might live. Christian sentiment thus begins to manifest itself as an ethical concern for all bodies being consumed by human appetite. As the Reformation abstracted this concern, it rendered it applicable to new objects: the objects of the hunt, but also (by the later seventeenth century) the objects of seduction. Jan Weenix's *Still Life with Peacock and Dog* (Figure 33) depicts vividly a variety of dead prey—a glassy-eyed rabbit in the foreground, a peacock with its feathers filling the center and its head twisted below, and several smaller birds of varying plumage; it also shows a gun and an alert hunting dog in the lower right, with a seemingly angry bird swooping open-beaked toward the dog, and in the upper left, as if to balance and judge these weapons, a large cylindrical cistern decorated with bas-reliefs of soldiers attacking women, presumably some version of the rape of the Sabines. In other words—as in Shakespeare's *As You Like It*—the predations of the hunt elide with those of Petrarchan

Figure 34. Jan Weenix (1642–1719), *Port with a Vendor of Baubles* (*Seaport with Trinket-Seller*), 1704. Oil on canvas, 1.39 × 1.17 m. Musée du Louvre, Paris. Photo: Hervé Lewandowski/Réunion des Musées Nationaux/Art Resource, NY.

desire.[104] The alternate title of this picture, *Trophies of the Hunt*, sounds disturbingly underspecified. A similar juxtaposition appears in Weenix's *Seaport with Trinket-Seller* (Figure 34). Playful courtly seduction replaces violent rape, but the symmetry between the white décolletage of the lady on the right and the white underbelly of the dead hare splayed on the left is ominous; the trinkets are a lure, and the boy reaching for the bird on the far right extends the association between erotic and predatory pursuits, especially since both he and the gentleman reach from behind toward the throats of their objects. Wouwerman's mid-seventeenth-century *Departure for the Hunt* paintings in the Louvre both emphasize (by the allocation of light) a man seducing a woman as the (other kind of) chase commences. Metsu's *Lady and the Hunter* again equates human courtship with hunting. The two forms of venery are balanced in the background of Robert Peake's *Elizabeth of Bohemia*—it is worth recalling how Florizel meets Perdita in Shakespeare's Bohemia—and another version of this association appears in Jacob Jordaens's strangely bacchanalian depiction of *The Rest of the Huntress Diana*. Snyders's *Merchant of Game* (see Figure 27) seems on the brink of becoming instead one of the "daughters of the game" (*Troilus and Cressida*, 4.5.63)—a prostitute—and thence (like the carcasses strung up along-side her) just another tasty piece of game that the leering male customer has come to acquire and consume.

In some cases there may be nothing much deeper or more sympathetic here than the vulgar Dutch pun associating bird-hunting with copulation,[105] but I believe there is often something more, something that points toward a la-tent recognition of women as well as animals as the victims of imperious mas-culinity. Svetlana Alpers suggests that some of the greatest Dutch paintings represent "the world as ungraspable. Vermeer repeatedly thematized this truth in his works as the ungraspable presence a woman offers a man."[106] The aggres-sion toward nature finds an analogue in erotic aggression, and I believe that the analogy (here as elsewhere in Renaissance culture, notably through the Actaeon myth) points toward anxieties about the aggressive quest for knowledge gener-ally, for the precious secrets within. No wonder open doors in seventeenth-century Dutch paintings seem so often "to suggest the sexual availability of women,"[107] as open gates often suggest access to truth in the frontispieces of seventeenth-century scientific and Hermetic treatises. Karel van Mander re-ported that Vredeman de Vries painted so convincing a trompe l'oeil portal in a wall mural that people tried to enter it, and that Pieter Brueghel the Elder capped the joke by painting a pair of lovers as if seen through it. This may be one more piece of evidence that late-Renaissance culture in northern Europe increasingly recognized the desire to see past the artificial mediator as funda-mentally an erotic drive—or perhaps recognized the erotic drive as partly aimed at overcoming artificiality and mediation.[108]

Returning to Jan Weenix's *Birds of Prey Around a Dead Lamb* (Figure 16), we may now recognize that, while the topic is markedly novel, the painting is actually based on a familiar compositional and emotional template. It translates a long and prominent tradition of paintings of the tormented Christ: the dark, jeering brutes around the sweet white delicate victim evoke the same old re-sponses—pity, outrage, and some vicarious guilt—applied now to a crime that is truly (as was argued theologically about the Crucifixion) repeated every day in a fallen world. For how many creatures—including Ruisdael's human figures—is that world a *via dolorosa*? And how could the culture, after centuries of cele-brating hard-won dominion over various natural forces, accommodate that recognition? Stoic endurance, with its erasure of personal emotion, was not entirely satisfactory. Instead of taking the subjectivity out of the human, Ruis-dael's compatriots go the other direction, ascribing to nature some accessible

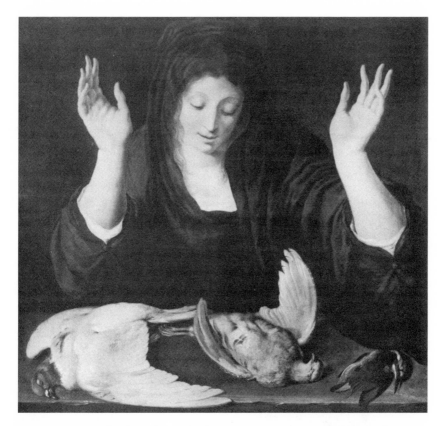

Figure 35. Jacques de Gheyn (ca. 1532–82), *Woman Mourning Dead Birds*. Sweden, private collection.

version of human emotions. Where Ruisdael begins to attribute personality to the inanimate nature that dominates us, another strain of Dutch painting decides to attribute subjectivity to the animate nature we (as predators) dominate.

Let me close this piece of the argument by inviting attention to another seventeenth-century Dutch painting that has attracted very little interest: Jacques de Gheyn's *Woman Mourning Dead Birds* (Figure 35). In several regards, but especially in the anguished gesture of the upward-spread hands, this woman gazing at the three dead birds (the central one wounded in the side) is distinctly reminiscent of the women mourning over Christ in Renaissance paintings of the Deposition and Entombment; I will provide famous versions by Perugino (Figure 36), Caravaggio (Figure 37), and Dürer (Figure 38), but similar poses abound.[109] Furthermore, De Gheyn seems to have used the same

Figure 36. Il Perugino (Pietro Vannucci, ca. 1448–1523), *Deposition of Christ*, 1495. Oil on wood, 214 × 195 cm. Galleria Palatina, Palazzo Pitti, Florence, Italy. Photo: Scala/Art Resource, NY.

model as a *Half-length Figure of the Virgin Mary*, with an almost identical costume and facial expression; and De Gheyn's early sketch for a Deposition painting shows a woman, similarly hooded, making the same gesture over the dead Christ (Figure 39).[110]

The learned catalogue commentary on *Woman Mourning Dead Birds* expresses bafflement about "how it should be interpreted," wondering whether perhaps "the picture refers to a particular event or a classical text." While concluding that "the true meaning of the subject still eludes me," the commentator is

Figure 37. Michelangelo Merisi da Caravaggio (1573–1610), *Deposition (The Entombment)*, 1604. Oil on canvas, 300 × 203 cm. Pinacoteca, Vatican Museums, Vatican State. Photo: Scala/Art Resource, NY.

Figure 38. Albrecht Dürer (1471–1528), *Deposition*. Germanisches Nationalmuseum, Nuremberg, Germany. Photo: Scala/Art Resource, NY.

nonetheless firm on one point: "The birds cannot be interpreted as symbols of ideas."[111] Perhaps not; but I believe they can be interpreted as symbols of the crucified Christ—especially in a group of three[112]—and as displacements of Catholic ideas (De Gheyn was probably Catholic) in a society suspicious of Mariolatry. In De Gheyn's as in the previous cases, the painter may simply have been reflecting his apprenticeship in the works of past masters, but most viewers would have had residual affective associations from the Catholic traditions.

Figure 39. Jacques de Gheyn (ca. 1532–82), *Deposition* (preliminary sketch).
Rijksprentenkabinet, Rijksmuseum, Amsterdam. © Rijksmuseum Foundation.

Even when the intent was to preserve those traditions surreptitiously, one effect
would have been the transfer of the emotions they carried onto the creatures
they depicted. At whatever level of intention, the Reformation thus transformed
Cross-specific images into cross-species sympathies, preparing the way for a
great shift in Western culture from a primarily theological to a primarily ecological world-view.

Nature in Two Dimensions: Perspective and Presence in Ryckaert, Vermeer, and Others

Perspective

The suggestion that "It was Kepler who for the first time turned away from the world to a representation of it, to the picture of it on the retina"[1] should remind us that technical developments could unsettle both individual subjectivity and universal beliefs. Understanding the perceiver was essential to understanding external reality, but it also marked the barriers between them. If the mind receives an ellipse and infers a tilted circle, which one is the truth? The development of linear or single-point perspective in Renaissance painting seems to be a movement toward nature, or at least toward naturalism: the paintings look more like reality to modern eyes, encouraging us (in a self-affirming cycle) to mark them as progress in a positivist march toward absolute representation, perhaps even (to evoke the Eucharistic model) toward the impression of Real Presence. But the technical mastery of this type of painterly effect brings with it a recognition of its own limitations—perhaps failures, certainly deceits.[2] Even the earliest experts in England recognized the problem: Nicholas Hilliard saw single-point perspective as a way "by falsehood to express truth," Richard Haydocke accused it of "shewing False and deceitful sights insteede of the true," and Edward Norgate called the paintings using this technique "nothing but Deceptive visions, a kind of cousning or cheating your owne Eyes, by [y]our owne consent and assistance."[3] Earlier systems of representation suggested a belief that the object can be made sufficiently present, like the Aztec sculptures Tzvetan Todorov describes, which (by being equally "worked on all sides, including the base") assumed that art "gives us essence and is not concerned with the impressions of any one man."[4]

In single-point perspective, however, what allows the prized illusion of real depth is precisely the surrender of any illusion that reality can be known, stably identified, beyond a single point of view. Hence the perspectival effects of the court masque, aimed at the royal seat.[5] King Claudius has the privileged place at the "Mousetrap" play, but the elusive truth thereby revealed is personal and interior, if not necessarily subjective. The only validation of the historical facts of Old Hamlet's murder lies in Claudius's psychological response to them. By situating Claudius in the audience of a play that somehow puts him (in several senses) on the stage, Hamlet seems, almost and momentarily, to solve the problem of other minds.

Another angle, and the viewer perceives something quite different—as the anamorphic paintings that quickly became popular emphasized. These paintings raise the question (as does perspective in more moderate forms) of which is more real, the tangible physical surface of the painting (where objects are measurably distorted and disproportionate), or the more real-looking three-dimensional impression that the conscious technique of the painter has contrived to convey to the unconscious technique of our cognitive faculties. The same questions arise from projective mapping techniques—"As west and east / In all flat maps (and I am one) are one," writes Donne in the "Hymn to God My God, in My Sickness." It is a lie that arrives bearing gifts of truth.

Furthermore, such illusionistic painting becomes an extreme instance of *sprezzatura*, in that the artist exercises elaborate craft in order to give the appearance of merely allowing natural reality to manifest itself; if "the truest poetry is the most feigning" (*As You Like It*, 3.3.20), then *ut pictura poesis* (or vice versa). "Indeed the perfection of an image often depends on its not resembling its object as much as it might," observes Descartes; "in accordance with the rules of perspective they often represent circles by ovals better than by other circles, squares by rhombuses better than by other squares."[6] The world looks like itself because of the way we look at it. To practice single-point perspective painting effectively, one must (paradoxically) deal, more consciously and obediently than ever before, with the recognition that one is not so much opening a window onto the world itself as simulating a distortive process of optics and subjectivity.

No wonder Renaissance artists clung to Pliny the Elder's claim (in book 35 of the *Natural History*) that Zeuxis fooled birds into trying to eat the grapes he painted, but also to the claim that Parrhasius outdid Zeuxis by fooling him into trying to pull back a painted curtain that appeared to cover Parrhasius's painting. The method of making something appear the way it actually appears involves recognizing, so they can be built in, the way eye and mind construct, rather than passively and objectively receive, the material universe. The triumph over the flat "artificiality" of medieval painting was, epistemologically, a Pyrrhic (because Pyrrhonian) victory.

Alberti's seminal *De pictura* suggests "that a painting in single-point perspective is a representation of a representation."[7] He also joked that Narcissus was the inventor of painting, because he practiced "a similar embracing with art of what is presented on the surface of the water in the fountain";[8] but the narcissism is no joke to Echo, or whatever else might have wished to be the real object of desire. Leonardo da Vinci wrote that "perspective is nothing else than seeing a place behind a pane of glass, quite transparent, on the surface of which the objects behind the glass are to be drawn."[9] But there is no way around the window-frame or through the looking-glass, to the object itself. The artist, in a sense, does not so much present the object as compete with it for the space of the real: Erwin Panofsky suggests that "the 'claim' of the object (to use a modern term) confronts the ambition of the subject. The object intends to remain distanced from the spectator (precisely as something 'objective'); it wants to bring to bear, unimpeded, its own formal lawfulness (its symmetry, for example, or its frontality). It does not want to be referred to an eccentric vanishing point, nor certainly, as in the oblique view, governed by a coordinate system whose axes no longer even appear objectively in the work, but rather exist only in the imagination of the beholder."[10] The intense and protracted debate about whether paintings should specify a position for the viewer and a track for the viewer's eye—in Albertian perspective, the viewer stands in front of the vanishing point—is partly an outgrowth of the debate about whether reality exists fundamentally in an objective material universe, or instead in the perception of each individual.

There is certainly a case to be made for the more conventional notion that perspective affirms the primacy of matter over meaning, and hence of science over subjectivity. During the Renaissance, "The medieval 'active' theory of vision (whereby the eye bounces rays off the object) was being replaced by the modern theory (whereby light reflected from the object is received passively by the eye)."[11] Medieval depictions that sized objects according to their importance in the culture gave way to perspectival rules that sized objects by observed mathematical proportions—it would seem apt to say, "objectively." Again the ultimate measure of things became, not their meaning to humanity, but their physical attributes to a neutral and even passive observer.

Yet perspectival painting also tends to imply that the organizing principle is in the perception of any single viewer, which is only formally predictable. Nothing retains its own dimensions. The dominant medieval model had conceded a veil between humanity and the reality of the universe, or the meaning of a text; but once that veil is lifted, the truth would be there to be seen equally and similarly by any person. The newer model—which Thomas Greene attributes largely to Petrarch and his reshaping of metaphor,[12] and which I have linked to the Metaphysical conceit—suggests that the coherence resides only in the subjectivity of the poet, and that reality may look very different among persons or across historical time. So again, even within the models of mediation, Renaissance culture slips from an assumption that reality can eventually be seen face-to-face, toward an insistence that reality will vary from mind to mind—or at least will lose its identity on the way to those minds. The truth somewhere *out there* yields to a more evanescent one *in here.*

Ryckaert Paints Nature in the Studio

In his 1661 poem *Het Gulden Cabinet,* Cornelis de Bie praises a Flemish painter, David III Ryckaert (1612–61), who commanded little other attention even in his own time:

> See how he adapts his brush to the nature of all sorts of vegetables
> And all kitchen utensils
> And in their quiet secret display[s] the quality of life
> In such a way that the mind is worthy of a laurel-leaf.[13]

On the very rare occasions when Ryckaert has been mentioned by art historians at all, it has been as a moderately successful but uninteresting craftsman in the family business. Yet there does seem to be an intellectual theme to much of his work that has eluded attention even in the one full-length study that finally appeared.[14] Though the surviving evidence is scant, the preponderance of it points to a man fascinated by the epistemological ironies of his role in representing nature, ironies that (I have been suggesting) fascinated seventeenth-century northern European culture. Puzzles, paradoxes, and trompe l'oeil tricks are common in Baroque painting, but in Ryckaert's work they consistently challenge the complacent epistemology of pastoral nostalgia. The "quiet secret" of Ryckaert's representations of nature is the presence of the laurel crown, not as nature encompassing his head (as the speaker of Marvell's "Garden" recommends), but insistently assimilated into his poetic mind (as Marvell implies must always happen) as the marker of poetic vision. His talent for letting each thing have its own "nature" and "quality" apparently obliged him (as single-point perspective obliged Italian Renaissance painters) to confront the impossibility of truly passive and hence perfect representation, the impossibility of investing art with the truth-value of nature.

The ironies of a back-to-nature movement—and specifically the links between a new nostalgia for wilderness and a new set of epistemological anxieties—are neatly displayed in Ryckaert's three little-known depictions of the painter's studio, particularly the last (Figure 40). In that 1642 version (now on display in Dijon), a pipe-smoking peasant model sits in the crowded workroom of an

Figure 40. David III Ryckaert (1612–61), *Painter in His Studio*, 1642. Musée des Beaux-Arts de Dijon, Dijon, France. © Musée des Beaux-Arts de Dijon.

urban artist while being painted into an archetypal rustic landscape, his back to some trees, though his back is actually to the blank wall of the studio, which thus functions like a blue screen in special-effects film-making. (Vermeer's *Lady with a Guitar* gestures quietly toward this motif, since her head sticks up halfway into a landscape painting on the back wall.) Ryckaert's artist himself sits with his back to two pastoral paintings and a "real" dog (a cat takes the same spot in the 1638 Louvre version; Figure 41). The upper right is occupied by three related ovals of similar sizes: the face of an assistant grinding the colors, a drawing of a face hanging from a scroll on a shelf directly above the assistant's face and turning the same way (except that it is not turning but drawn as if it were, though of course the assistant himself is merely painted as if he were turning), and (a mediating instance) an artist's palette hanging from the wall, with hints of a face in it, but really only the grasping-holes and some drips of paint.

The center background is occupied by a rectangle in which we see a landscape and sky, and might possibly mistake it for a window to an actual exterior, except that the top left corner of the canvas has pulled loose and curls forward. In the small actual window sits a vase of flowers, overlapping out of the frame of the window just barely enough (as in a Magritte) to remind us it is not a

Figure 41. David III Ryckaert (1612–61), *Painters in Their Studio*, 1638. Oil on wood, 59 × 95 cm. Musée du Louvre, Paris. Photo: Erich Lessing / Art Resource, NY.

two-dimensional still-life painting (except that of course it is). In the Louvre version (Figure 41), the blank stretched canvas behind the subject curls away like the painted canvas on the back wall.[15] In Dijon, the painter himself is the one perfectly framed in the blank canvas—blank, because its back is to us (not that it has a back—or, if it does, it is probably a blank canvas). Ryckaert, producing for an increasingly urbanized market doubtless nostalgic for pastoral scenes, gives his customers what they want on the inset canvas, but the Dijon canvas as a whole constitutes a rug pulled out from under the whole northern industry of landscape and genre painting.[16] As a French study of pictures-within-pictures observes, "the figure in the outdoors whom the artist is in the process of painting indisputably resembles the model, but this model is found in the interior of the studio and not out in nature, and he has struck, under the directives of the master, a stereotypical pose, that of the 'Flemish smoker.'"[17] So is this a representation of nature, or of its inextricable entanglement in culture?

In Ryckaert's first painting of the studio (1636; location unknown), "The still-life arrangement on the panel presented within the painting is not actually set up in the studio itself, indicating that the artist is not working from nature or even a sketch but simply from memory. . . . Another interesting detail is the inclusion of a still life of another kind consisting of the tools of the artist."[18] This somewhat understates the interplay of nature and art here. The painter is shown painting a still life of his own paint brushes (rather than flower stalks) in bowls: again Ryckaert seems to be anticipating Magritte—or Escher's famous hands sketching each other into existence—with this *mise en abyme* of his creativity. Looking back from the Dijon version (see Figure 40), we may also notice that what here looks like a passage out into nature, rich in light, is on closer view given away by shadows as a picture frame rather than a door frame. In other words, Ryckaert was already (in what may be his earliest known work) redundantly insisting on reminding his viewer that the painting of nature is really a reflection of the mind and craft of the painter. To use the terms offered by Karel van Mander, the leading art theorist within Ryckaert's own culture, what looks like a *doorsien* offering a view through the depicted space is merely another *insien*, a view into that space; and our view is refused passage to any place beyond a painted canvas.

In the Louvre version (Figure 41), the sitting peasant is also being set into a countryside scene (presumably painted earlier) that is utterly absent from the studio, and again a rectangle of outdoor scenery, in the place and shape that one might anticipate for a window, is revealed to be a canvas (as in comic-strip drawings) by a curled-over top corner. The canvas currently being painted appears to melt into the table it rests on; and among the pewter cup on that table, the silver jug in the sitter's hand, and the redepiction of that jug just above, it is hard to say which ones resemble each other most. The paired colors of the cat have been distinctly adopted in the painter's clothes—whether by the painter in life, or in the act of depicting himself, we cannot tell—and then the same palette is applied in the ongoing painting of the sitter, whose clothes in life are depicted as quite other hues.

Is the cat curled up on the floor finally any more real than the goats on the inset painting next to it? In both the Dijon and Louvre versions, propped on the floor behind the artist are panels of more facile and conventionally idyllic Italianate pastorals; perhaps those represent the illusory nature Ryckaert is figuratively, as well as literally, turning his back on, putting behind him in the studio. Zirka Filipczak argues that, by emphasizing the contrast between the elegant painter (in the Louvre version) and his peasant subject, "Ryckaert is reminding the viewer that although a painter may depict low life scenes, he shares neither the outward appearance nor the locale of his subjects."[19] That contrast between the artist and his subjects may, however, be a statement about the alienation-effect of art, as much as a boast about the class-status of the painter himself. After all, as David Evett deduces from late Tudor art, the Renaissance "involves not only a developing consciousness of the world, but also and in consequence a developing awareness of the difference and distance between artist and subject. This distance, even as it afflicts the artist with certain kinds of uncertainty, also enhances the degree to which the data of experience can be brought under control."[20]

Literary critics may have squandered, through overuse, their license to convert obvious artistic flaws ingeniously into brilliant secret meanings. I will therefore not make too much of Jean Baptiste Descamps's 1764 observation that Ryckaert is good at heads but careless with hands because he did not generally paint from life, though he does strike me as a painter who believes that we hold the world only with our minds—as opposed to the typical northern landscape painter, who Lampsonius said kept his "brains in his hands."[21] What Touchstone describes as the chronic condition of wastrel Renaissance travelers—"to have seen much, and to have nothing, is to have rich eyes and poor hands" (*As You Like It*, 4.1.23–24)—was also the condition of epistemological exiles in the same period, unable to get from perception to a real grasp. Yet I cannot resist proposing a coherent theme in the lapses and peculiarities that the sole substantial commentator finds in Ryckaert's oeuvre. Bernadette van Haute complains that, "In his 1640 *The Warm Hand*, to an even greater extent than in *The Children's Procession*, Ryckaert has failed to adapt the scene to its exterior setting. The view of the landscape on the left, though better integrated, seems to have been added as an afterthought, as if the artist made an effort to conform to the public taste."[22] But if Ryckaert's lesson was about the failure of human integration into nature, then this discrepancy (like the alienated staffage Chapter 6 described in Ruisdael and Terborch) may have been strategic: perhaps the landscape seems an afterthought because Ryckaert wanted to provoke afterthought, primarily about our inability ever to enter either nature or reality completely.

If Ryckaert's two versions of *Social Gathering in the Country* are remarkable for being "representations of musical companies played out *en plein air*,"[23] they provide suggestive inversions of what we saw in the representations of the painter's studio: now high culture tries somewhat incongruously to play itself out within wild nature, perhaps (like Orpheus) to hold nature in its aesthetic spell. The 1641 *Guitar Player* is generally thought to be an allegory of the senses set in a prostitution scene (Ryckaert elsewhere seems to paint allegories of one sense or another), but the absence of an item representing sight has led to speculation that the canvas may have been cut at some point. My suggestion is that—as prostitution is an encompassing archetype of sensual corruption—this is an allegory of the deceptions of the senses, and the crowning instance is sight, represented by our experience of the painting itself: the long-craved physicality, or maybe its fraudulent simulation, that Ryckaert uneasily puts up for sale.

Nature-Lovers

Renaissance painters, as a general rule, did not work outdoors, except to prepare the preliminary sketches they would use to reconstitute landscape scenes (often with radical changes) back in the studio. But aspects of these paintings make them a complicated commentary on that process, not merely a product of it. The irony underscored (I believe) by Ryckaert resides also in the many portraits that begin to appear in this period whose commission must have stipulated that they be set out in nature. My preceding chapter traced the evolution of religious scenes into pastoral ones; at the same time, patrons who had formerly asked to appear as witnesses to the Nativity scene now asked to be painted into realistic modern mangers as shepherds and shepherdesses.[24] Slive mentions "a vogue that begins about the middle of the century for portraits of the sitters in the guise of hunters, a type traditionally reserved for royalty and nobility."[25] Though landowners no longer commonly seek paintings to confer their legal domain, the supplementary motives may not be entirely unfamiliar to us: not only vacationers, but many other people now crave photographs of themselves in wilderness or at least garden settings—a legacy of Romanticism, designed to show vitality, authenticity, courage, and fundamentally sound values. The associations are used to sell SUVs and celebrities: whatever their actual feelings about actual nature, people like the idea of themselves liking the country life.

What interests me about many of these portraits is that the sitters are generally portrayed, only too aptly, with their backs to nature. Even the top celebrity of high culture, the smooth Mona Lisa, is depicted with her back to a jagged wilderness (from which, some argue, she seems to have just turned away). Van Dyck's portrait of Charles I—which hedges a bit, a kind of side-to-nature experiment—may be the king's way of staking some claim to his land, but he is not much interested in getting dirty; the land is his before he is the land's. The implied assertion of property, which partakes at once of an exalted royal progress and an animal marking territory with its urine, is a prelude to the assertions by which twenty-first-century advertisers disguise material possessiveness and even conspicuous consumption as something deemed far more attractive: an ability to retain simultaneously dignity and naturalness, as the twin marks of true nobility. The leverage gained by showing wealthy, business-friendly politicians such as Ronald Reagan and George W. Bush clearing brush on ranches may help us recognize these portraits as media spin in an older medium: "At the very same time that Charles I had van Dyck depict him as the new St. George, mounted beneath a great umbrageous oak of the realm, he was busy selling off vast tracts of the royal forests to noble entrepreneurs like the earls of Pembroke and Warwick, who then cut them down."[26] Georgic poses, then as now, take the place of environmentalist policies. This compensatory function is verified by Van Dyck's depiction of other court luminaries in natural light; Philip, Lord Wharton, even holds a shepherd's crook against his fine silks. Gerrit van Honthorst's depiction of the first Earl of Craven in armor looks rather like

Figure 42. Marcus Gheeraerts the Younger (1561/62–1636), *Portrait of Captain Thomas Lee*, 1594. Oil on canvas, 230.5 × 150.8 cm. Tate Britain, London.

an advertisement for a gleaming black SUV set against the usual rugged backdrop.

Isaac Oliver's *Edward Herbert of Cherbury* actually has the subject resting sidelong on the ground among the bushes and trees; the leaf pattern suggested on his outfit, though, is nothing compared to the interweaving of the subject with the surroundings in Marcus Gheeraerts the Younger's *Captain Thomas Lee* (Figure 42), where the subject is not only barefoot on the soil, but appears to be wearing a design integrated with the tree branches just behind his arm. In Nicholas Hilliard's miniature *Young Man Leaning Against a Tree Among Roses* (Figure 43), the leaf patterns on the subject's garments are supposedly real plants between him and the painter; but in two dimensions the distinction

Figure 43. Nicholas Hilliard (1547–1619), *Young Man Leaning Against a Tree Among Roses*, 1585–95. Oil on parchment, 13.7 × 7 cm. Victoria & Albert Museum, London. Photo: Victoria & Albert Museum, London/Art Resource, NY.

between artifice and nature is illusory. In Rubens's *Self-Portrait with Isabella Brant* (Figure 44), the floral patterns and color tones of their needle-lace and the brocade on her stomacher weave the human subjects into their natural setting.[27] The happy couple seems on its way into arboreal metamorphoses like those Marvell's "Garden" proposes for the nature-loving figures of ancient myth, who "Still in a tree did end their race."

But the point is usually that the race continues, lap after lap. Adriaen van de Velde's *Portrait of a Couple with Two Children and a Nursemaid in a Landscape* (Figure 45) is markedly a back-to-nature portrait celebrating the promise of generations (which disarm mortality) and the glories of social class (which

Figure 44. Peter Paul Rubens (1577–1640), *Self-Portrait with Isabella Brant*, 1609–10. Oil on canvas, 178 × 136.5 cm. Alte Pinakothek, Munich, Germany. From the Düsseldorf Gallery.

Figure 45. Adriaen van de Velde (1636–72), *Portrait of a Couple with Two Children and a Nursemaid in a Landscape*, 1667. Oil on canvas, 148 × 178 cm. Rijksmuseum, Amsterdam. © Rijksmuseum Foundation.

provide the barrier between people and other animals with a second line of defense). The highlighting of the human above the natural makes this almost the opposite of a Ruisdael, with only the lowly goatherd on the right sinking and blending into the earth among his livestock, and the tree-remains on the left utterly devoid of energy or individual identity. Jan Lievens's *Self-Portrait*, though with the concession of a framing porch, sets the human at ease amid nature. In the 1570s, Giuseppe Arcimboldo rendered the faces of the four seasons out of what appear to be pieces of each season's foison—a portrait of the reassimilation by death reframed as life, shifted from the tragic mode to the comic (*Vertumnus*, Figure 46).

Marvell's "Mower" poems suggest, however, that re-absorption by nature can be at least as threatening as alienation from it. When nature frames us, do we become the exalted subject of time-defying portraiture, or the condemned

Figure 46. Giuseppe Arcimboldo (1527–93), *Vertumnus (Emperor Rudolf II)*, 1590. Oil on panel, 70.5 × 57.5 cm. Slott, Skokloster, Sweden. Photo: Erich Lessing/Art Resource, NY.

convict of mortal time? Gerard and Gesina Terborch's 1668 *Commemorative Portrait of Moses Terborch* (Figure 4) sets its ill-fated subject with his back to nature, and it seems to be obsessed with the ways nature recaptures him (by snake and clocks, as in *As You Like It*, though he was actually killed in a sea battle). Ultimately, the whole point of the picture, as of other tomb markers, is to keep the subject from being completely consumed; and Moses does seem oddly set off from the dark natural forces that so obviously threaten him. The impression that he stands uncannily apart from the wild landscape and lifescape around him is presumably the result of collaborative painting, but perhaps not an accidental result. Moses' half-brother Gerard evidently painted what we can see of the body—the captivating face, hair, and hands—while Moses' sister Gesina likely painted almost everything else.[28] Perhaps the contrast between Moses' presence and the seeming flatness of the natural background merely reflects the superiority of Gerard's verisimilar technique, but there are two conflicting ideas of nature at work here that match the two painters: Gerard was notable for favoring realism over symbolism, whereas Gesina had a lifelong fascination with pastoral literature and produced a heavily iconographic watercolor on which this painting is based. Gerard's other work shows a remarkable sensitivity to the relationship between human and animal life (horses and riders, a boy grooming a dog, a woman milking a cow), an interest in imperfect erotic communication between men and women (in intriguing but finally indecipherable encounters or letters), and a determination to signal the inscrutability of his human subjects (to the extent of repeatedly setting their backs to us instead of to nature). Along with the astonishing shimmering light of the satins in which he loved to dress his women, these themes align Gerard quite well with the Marvell described in my Chapter 4, meditating in overlapping ways on the different barriers raised by skepticism: between humanity and the material-natural world (both light and life so vivid as to demand our attention even while forbidding our superior comprehension), between the sexes in love (under the assumptions of a heterosexualist Petrarchan tradition), and between any observer and the inner consciousness of the person outwardly observed.

Thoughtful painters in this period thus found themselves fighting back a tireless incursion by the botanical environment, like Milton's Adam and Eve trying to keep Eden in trim around their own spheres of discipline. Jan de Bray's 1663 *Abraham Casteleyn and Margarieta van Bancken* (Figure 47) splits the background between high artificial culture (books, statues, a globe—all representations) and the wild leafy beauty of the world itself. The image is conventionally gendered: Abraham's side (suitably for a printer) is the bookish one, and his free hand hovers open over a globe, while Margarieta is in touch with nature, her free hand hovering open over the greenery. In fact, a preparatory drawing suggests that the wall of greenery, which already seems poised to creep around the neat gray edge of the porch, was originally envisioned as a fully equal portion of the canvas before De Bray trimmed it. Nature is not something you can afford to turn your back on; but perhaps you can marry it. Under the influence of Romanticism, the painter will instead sit in front of the landscape attending to it, with his back to us (like a Renaissance Catholic priest facing the altar rather than the worshippers), as in Anthony Oberman's *Painter in His Studio* (1820); Hendrikus van de Sande Bakhuyzen's *The Artist Painting a Cow in a Meadow Landscape* (1850) suggests the same intriguing insult. This is not Vermeer sustaining his mystery by painting only the artist's back; in an implicit critique of previous landscapists, these artists remind us how a true nature-lover's portrait would look.

What this regressive move in the history of civilization—the move back to

Figure 47. Jan de Bray (ca. 1627–97), *Abraham Casteleyn and Margarieta van Bancken,* 1663. Oil on canvas, 84 × 108 cm. Rijksmuseum. © Rijksmuseum Foundation.

nature—has to do with questions of ontology and mediation is evident from the difficulty Ryckaert creates in knowing which rectangles on the walls are paintings of the world outside and which are actually windows to it. The same issues persist throughout Vermeer's and Rembrandt's depictions of geographers, astronomers, and other philosopher/scholars poised between the light of a window and the representation of the world in their maps, instruments, and books. Ryckaert takes a first step toward (and lands not so far from) Magritte's 1933 *La condition humaine* (Figure 48), which superimposes a canvas on a tripod easel over some portion of a landscape and sky, seen through a window, from which it is apparently indistinguishable. Green thought and/or green shade? If not for the tiny offsets of the edges Magritte provides, would we have known the different versions (painting, window, reality) we were seeing—which is to say (on closer consideration), would we have thought we were seeing differences of being that are in fact not there? Amid all this representative summer greenery, we may again feel the chill of Wallace Stevens's "The Snow Man," gazing blankly at "Nothing that is not there, and the nothing that is."

Figure 48. René Magritte (1898–1967), *La condition humaine (The Human Condition)*, 1933. Oil on canvas, 100 × 81 cm. National Gallery of Art, Washington, D.C. Gift of the Collectors Committee, 1987.55.1. Image © 2004 Board of Trustees, National Gallery of Art, Washington, D.C.

Jan Soens's *Rinaldo and Armida* (Figure 49), which is based on some dizzying stanzas from book XVI of Tasso's *Jerusalem Liberated*, offers an extraordinarily lively precedent for this representational play. This poetic moment was therefore almost irresistible to Renaissance painters—along with Soens, Van Dyck, Poussin, Tiepolo, Pittoni, Domenichino, and others depicted the affair. Armida is a temptress from whom two fellow crusaders must rescue Rinaldo:

> XIX
> His hungrie eies upon her face he fed,
> And feeding them so, pinde himselfe away;
> And she, declining often downe her hed,

Figure 49. Jan Soens (1547–1611), *Rinaldo and Armida*, ca. 1581. Oil on panel, 46.9 × 36.8 cm. Walters Art Museum, Baltimore.

His lippes, his cheekes, his eies kist, as he lay,
Wherewith he sigh'd, as if his soule had fled
From his fraile breast to hers, and there would stay
With her beloved sprite: the armed pare
These follies all beheld and this hot fare.

XX
Down by the lovers side there pendant was
A Christall mirrour, bright, pure, smooth and neat,
He rose, and to his mistresse held the glas,
(A noble Page, grac'd with that service great)

She, with glad lookes, he with inflam'd (alas)
Beautie and love beheld, both in one seat;
Yet them in sundrie objects each espies,
She, in the glasse; he saw them in her eies:

XXI
Her, to command; to serve, it pleas'd the knight;
He proud of bondage; of her Empire, shee;
My deare (she said) that blessest with thy sight
Even blessed Angels, turne thine eies to me,
For painted in my hart and purtrai'd right
Thy woorth, thy beauties, and perfections bee,
Of which the forme, the shape, and fashion best,
Not in this glas is seene, but in my brest."[29]

The printer's failure to notice that "(she said)" should be "(he said)" in stanza XXI suggests how thoroughly the poem has tangled the identities of the two lovers here, as the ambiguity of "sight" blurs subject into object; and the metaphor of the "Page" in stanza XX not only displaces them both into some third person, but may even offer a pun that ensnares immediate vision in literary mediation.

This description allowed Soens to depict the couple in a wilderness suggesting uncontrolled passions, but it is really a maze, with Armida, the archetypal object of view and desire, at its center; and civilization pushes through to reclaim them from any simple experience of desire. The lovers are echoed in a lovebird pair kissing nearby, but the pair of soldiers spying behind them—doubtless, in the narrative, the figures of Carlo and Ubaldo arriving to reclaim their comrade—seem to represent also the lovers' alienated watchful selves. Humanity will be chased out of the garden by complications the avian couple need never fear. Meanwhile, as if to insist on the problem of mediation (as opposed to naturalness), Soens shows the lovers looking together, perhaps at each other, in a mirror—with just enough offset to suggest (as in Tasso) that Armida is regarding herself in the mirror he provides (" 'Tis not her glass," Rosalind tells the lovelorn Silvius at 3.5.54 of *As You Like It*, "but you that flatters her"). Rinaldo is instead looking at her eyes as they look at herself, but thereby seeing what she sees, which is itself an amalgam of "Beautie and love"—that is, a physical fact and the subjective response to that fact. He then asks her to "turne thine eies to me" to see the version of her that is "painted in my hart," which he judges truer than any of these reproductions. But it is still not quite enough to make the "babies" that Renaissance lovers were often said to put into each other's eyes. The discrepancy between the male and female viewpoints here, augmented by the fact that he is Christian and she a pagan, makes their encounter an overdetermined emblem of the impossibility of ever quite sharing a reality: these two may desire, they may even reconcile at the end of the poem, but they will never really unite. Rinaldo is rescued from this enchantment by fellow soldiers who force him to look in both a figurative and literal mirror to recognize that he has been effeminized by love—by the same love that absorbed him into a pastoral idyll (stanzas 29–30). The commonplace of the man called back from such an idyll offered a parable for the way those who try to retreat to natural simplicity and the maternal embrace find themselves perpetually drawn back into the epistemological struggle.

Vermeer and the Faith of Things Seen

When we attend to objects, what happens to our souls? Do we take, or endure, possession? Can desire, wit, or even bloodshed liberate us from the epistemological version of Zeno's paradox that precludes our ever quite reaching the goal of knowledge—carnal or otherwise? As in the problems of modern quantum physics, the instrumentalities we employ to approach knowledge finally stand between us and our goal, reminding us of the gap between what is observed and what simply is. One of David III Ryckaert's versions of *The Alchemist* (in San Diego) shows the practitioner too lost in the mess of his equipment and readings even to look at the dull radiance of his window, while another (echoing a trick of Vermeer's) puts an almost illegible map on the alchemist's back wall (Budapest), and a third has his wife showing him a page in a book that matches their unregarded window (Brussels). In his tireless exploration of this figure (Madrid, Vienna, Milan, and others) Ryckaert always seems to be observing (at once wryly and dolefully) the hopeless quest to find, know, isolate, and capture the thing itself, the essence of the material universe. Both Vermeer's astronomer and his geographer try to grasp external reality with their right hands, but all they hold are tools of representation; and they rest their left hands unthinkingly for support on more solid pieces of reality. Vermeer's *Astronomer* puts a book, a geometric abstract, a mythologized model on a globe, and a merely translucent window between the scientist and the sky he is trying to know; much the same pattern appears in Jacob van Spreeuwen's *Scholar in His Chamber*, where books and globes stand ironically juxtaposed with a clouded window. Vermeer's *Geographer* is similar; there the book is open, but the writing washed out, so flooded with light from outside that it seems unreadable; these are what Marlowe's Tamburlaine dismisses as "blind geographers" (Part I, 4.4.81) who mistake their arbitrary maps for an absolute reality. In contrast, Rembrandt's figure of the meditating philosopher (like Salomon Koninck's version) suggests an open window onto the actual world, though the higher truths require negotiating what George Herbert mistrusts on the path to truth, "a winding stair" ("Jordan").

Vermeer's evident interest in maps and mapmakers (as in *The Art of Painting*) might suggest an effort to connect to history and its material realities; but it might, at least as easily, signal that no one can expect to make any such real contact, trapped as we all are together in the web of representations. No matter how skillful the cartographer, the map is never the same as the territory it depicts, any more than a green thought is a green shade. At times Vermeer spreads his paint so thin that the weave of the canvas can suggest the weave of a tablecloth:[30] another way in which we are being challenged to identify any boundary between what is real and what is represented. Svetlana Alpers argues that "the lozenge-like brushstrokes that patch together [Vermeer's] last works signal the rift between the image and the world it describes that Dutch art had almost managed to hide."[31] The technique is just as masterful, but now it announces rather than disguises the presence of the representational media: we see that it looks like the world, but we can also see that it addresses the peculiarities of our vision rather than the particularities of reality in itself. To say that Vermeer displays a determination "to transform the setting of his daily life into a dream palace of light and color"[32] may overlook the strong possibility that Vermeer is simply undoing the cognitive work by which the human mind habitually transforms a dream palace of light and color into the settings of our daily life.

Vermeer's *Allegory of Faith* (Figure 50) asks elaborately—as this book has been asking—how seventeenth-century culture should recalibrate ontological scales. The only "natural" items here—the once-bitten apple and the serpent—are also the mostly obviously symbolic (and the only distinct moral dangers in an otherwise sanctified and aestheticized atmosphere). They are unpleasantly realistic, though the picture somehow contrives to make them also seem displeasingly fake. What crushes the serpent seems merely a rough-hewn slab, perhaps symbolizing Christ as the cornerstone of the church, but it is also the size and shape of a folio volume like the Bible on the right, as if the Word had been sent in this form to bruise the tempter's head—and some kind of face is just discernible enough on the edge of the stone above the serpent's head that the viewer is left wondering whether it is "really there" at all. The woman does not regard these poisonous discards on her floor, though she is supposedly regarding what they represent. The apple sits like an escapee from a still life, whereas the newly crushed serpent is (not only in the theological sense) the compensatory opposite, a creature propelled kinetically toward death while attempting to flee outside the frame. The chivalric tapestry on the left is pulled back, so that it no longer looks much like a representation, only a blind; the medieval media and topic indicate an archaic ontology now being peeled back to reveal fundamental

Figure 50. Johannes Vermeer (1632–75), *Allegory of Faith* (*Allegory of the New Testament*), ca. 1671–74. Oil on canvas, 114.3 × 88.9 cm. Metropolitan Museum of Art, New York. The Friedsam Collection, Bequest of Michael Friedsam, 1931 (32.100.18).

beliefs. If the object of faith is, as Paul insisted, things unseen, the painter's task becomes a tricky one. Is Christ most real in this female Faith's experience? Or as realistically crucified in what is clearly a painting in the back? Or as more symbolically condensed in the little figure on the crucifix, which she regards and toward which she seems perhaps to be striking a pose imitative of the woman's pose toward Christ in the background painting? Or in her heart, which she clutches with passion? Or in the chalice before her, which might actually be (a vehemently disputed point in this era's theology) Christ's redemptive blood? Or in the Bible open before her, where Protestants would feel the Word was superlatively present?

Above her hangs a crystal bubble upon which Vermeer has simulated a three-dimensional reflection of the room that is provided on a two-dimensional surface by the painting. How does this compare, ontologically and epistemologically, to the globe that is under rather than over the woman: a more standard geographical (and thus theoretically more mediated) representation of the world, though it is turned so that the forms visible on it are Hondius's geometric and perhaps politically expedient decorations rather than real land-masses? Hamlet's remark about his "distracted globe" (1.5.97) should remind us that it can represent at once the world, and the mind that reflects the world, and the artistic medium. And how real is the actual planet on which that representation of itself implicitly sits, when the entire depicted world comes to the viewer in two dimensions disguised as three? Is the crystal bubble (like the similarly shaped and suspended egg in Piero della Francesca's Brera altarpiece) "a symbol of eternity,"[33] or merely a reflection of the intensely transient present and what is present in it? On the checkerboard floor, the viewers may find themselves stalled, amazed and stalemated, asked to decide how much faith they will have, how they will reconcile (as Christians so often must) a desire to believe and a recognition of all the dubieties, all the things that stand between them and absolute knowledge, even though those mediators may also be their only sources of knowledge.

This may all seem a rather strenuously overdetermined version of a familiar artistic game that plays illusion off against reality. Yet the fact that Vermeer could invest so much, at so many levels, in his exploration of the practices of faith as at once a (necessary?) theological and (nonetheless questionable?) epistemological stance, suggests that these questions—about mediation and its relation to truth—were crucial to Western culture in this period. If Vermeer did indeed use the camera obscura device, and considerable evidence has accumulated suggesting that he did, the implications are not merely technical. It allowed him a kind of detachment in the establishment of his line, an automatic corrective to the tendency to indulge the peculiarities of human perception; and it would have brought him very close to the epistemological version of Zeno's paradox, in recognizing that the most accurate two-dimensional depiction of the physical world was also a multiply mediated projection.

Whether or not abetted by such technology, Vermeer's extraordinary verisimilar skills would have driven him toward recognitions very much like those imposed by twenty-first-century digital imaging, which again promises the ultimate approach to presence, the most distortion-resistant form of reproduction, yet therefore permits us the uneasy knowledge that the more we zoom in on detail, the more we will recognize that we have been pixelated, producing vision out of quantitative equivalents, out of juxtaposed small blocks of solid color. Vermeer thus provides a foretaste of pointillism,[34] and moves atomism from its ancient realm in the material object to the process of the perceiving subject. Perhaps this is one reason Renaissance artists (like modern aesthetes who cling nostalgically to analog rather than digital music or images) largely abandoned mosaics, which did not trouble the medieval or classical vision; indeed, probably the greatest "Renaissance man" of them all, Leonardo da Vinci, developed his sfumato technique to blur over this problem entirely. A medieval culture that assumed a perfect reality, present in the mind of the one God if only partially present in the temporary human representations of it, would feel far less compelled to perfect its illusions than a culture afraid that reality might be endlessly multiple and permanently inaccessible.

It may seem surprising that the masterpieces of epistemological play in the seventeenth century—not only Ryckaert's (and Michael Sweerts's) underrated depictions of the artist in his studio, and Soens's of Rinaldo and Armida, but also famous works such as Vermeer's *Allegory of Faith*, Jan Brueghel the Elder's *Allegory of Sight*, and Velázquez's revered *Las Meninas* and *Fable of Arachne*—tend to be the work of Catholic painters. After all, Catholicism seems to offer more stable earthly knowledge of ultimate truths, and seems to be a far more materialized religion than Protestantism, not only in its sensuality and soteriology, but specifically in its Eucharistic doctrine, which insists on the Real Presence of Christ in the bread and wine. Moreover, my study of seventeenth-century English poetry has suggested a correlation between the quasi-Catholic beliefs of the High Church and the belief that objects are self-evidently—objectively—present. Metaphysical poetry bespeaks a belief that the process of language can reconstitute the universe, thereby pointing out the contingent and paradoxical nature of perceived physical reality. This belief put makers of poetic conceits in league (in a cognitive if not a direct political mode) with the Puritan tendency to take the world as an allegory, a universe ruled by story rather than sight.

In the visual arts, however, the opposite happens: when Protestants discourage the depiction of the supernatural, they encourage the natural to appear as itself. The painters who insist on their command of the universe by emphasizing the contingent and paradoxical nature of perceived physical reality tend instead to be Catholics. This is not finally so surprising. The theological controversies of the late Renaissance show Catholicism obliged to play a complex defensive game on the topic of idolatry, obliged to meditate on the way images both are and are not a reality, the way icons have a presence of their own and yet also offer a kind of transparency to something beyond the visual field. Those debates also suggest that the High Church position on transubstantiation lent itself to playfulness and paradox on questions of ontology, perhaps because it demanded an ability to believe that Christ's physical body simultaneously was and was not really present in the Host. Without a real appetite for ontological paradox, a believer would lose any real appetite for the Host—that is, would be driven either to accept the radical Protestant doctrine of merely memorial presence, or else to take on (as Puritans liked to insist, and as we have seen Dutch Protestant painters imply) the character of a cannibal. Interpreting Christ's "This is my body," Lancelot Andrewes was therefore extraordinarily agile— more so even than President Clinton—on the meanings of "is." Joan Webber rightly discerned heightened playfulness and self-consciousness as characteristic of High Anglican prose style, as opposed to the blunt literalist tendencies of the Puritans;[35] and vandalizing the wall between what goes on in the world and what goes on in the mind is a prime amusement of Counter-Reformation literature (including Spanish Golden Age classics such as Calderón's *Life Is a Dream* and Cervantes' *Don Quixote*). In this limited regard, the Horatian formula is vindicated: what was true in rhetoric and literature can also be applied to pictures. If Protestantism allied itself (as I suggested at the beginning of Chapter 6) with a search for an unambiguous epistemology and unmediated nature, the Catholic reply would be that these destinations were unreachable, and that wayfaring sinners had better therefore seek refuge in the institutions that organized Christianity had built over time to house its beliefs. That is presumably why Catholicism found skepticism a useful ally—and in fact the great practitioners of late-Renaissance skepticism tended to be professed Catholics such as Montaigne and Descartes.

The Painted Word

With its stories erased and its love of images shamed, the art of painting made a kind of suicide attempt in the Reformation culture of the seventeenth-century Netherlands. It tried to reduce itself to a transparency, to wipe out the experiential self, cease its transformative work on the world, and resign its duties to

power. It was a half-hearted attempt that mercifully failed. Sight could not finally bring itself (as Protestant iconoclasm urged) to surrender unconditionally
to words or to abdicate its role in the making of meaning. But meanwhile its subjects had gained their freedom. With divinity and language preoccupied by their
mutual embrace, Reformation culture evidently liberated things to be seen as
themselves, and those things threatened not only to reclaim their outward properties, freed from the colonial control of their iconic functions under Catholicism, but even to reclaim some of their pre-linguistic priority over creaturely
consciousness. Dutch painters provided a representation of experience before
words, perhaps even (in Jacob van Ruisdael's case) prior to anything one might
call individual experience.

   "The Netherlands Confession states that God may be known first through
the creation, sustenance, and government of the whole world; secondly and
more completely through His Holy Word"; but painters in the north at that
time—"raised to believe that the world around them was worthy of scrutiny
and description"—seldom take that second step.[36] When Dutch paintings carry
a paraphrasable meaning embodied in an implied story, it very often proves to
be the illustration of a proverb.[37] This is yet another way in which Reformation
art establishes the word as prior to the image, establishes moral language rather
than sensual vision as fundamental. But otherwise, northern art seems oddly
wordless: women (in Vermeer and Leyster) reading correspondence whose words
(the letters within the letters) are as impossible to read as in a dream; all those
scenes of work and play in which language (either directly, or as the histories so
much southern European painting draws on) is absent and/or irrelevant. Svetlana Alpers claims that "texts are given what could be called separate but equal
place in Dutch pictorial representations. Rather than supplying underlying
meanings, they give us more to look at. . . . Again and again, the words stand
for, or to put it precisely, represent what would in another art and another culture be pictured as dramatic enactments of self or society."[38]

   There are clearly tales that could be told about these scenes, but they are
not told. Except in distinctly allegorical endorsements of the scriptural Word
such as Gerrit Dou's *Reading of the Bible*, where redemptive light makes an ostentatious entrance,[39] the words seem disabled. Perhaps not as consistently as
Alpers suggests, but still in many cases, "These inscribed texts, rather than
existing prior to the work as motives for picturing—a story to be evoked, a
theme to be presented—are themselves made part of the picture."[40] Since it
seems clear enough that Protestant theology prefers words to things, why would
Dutch (rather than, say, Spanish or Italian) painting be the place where things
become so prominent, where indeed (if Alpers is correct) words become mere
things? Did the Protestant assault on the visible world backfire? Certainly the

paradoxes of Max Weber's thesis about Protestant super-capitalists present one version of this malfunction (extreme otherworldliness producing extreme worldliness, a rejection of works producing a worship of work); and I suspect that northern painting presents another. This most vivid instance of this irony may be the way the great iconoclastic religions—Judaism and Islam as well as Reformation Christianity—insisted on reverence for the divine message rather than any representative physical object, only to find their own fundamentalists treating the books or scrolls containing that message as themselves taboo and magically efficacious: ritualized handling of a Torah, death-sentences elicited by the wrong hands on a Qur'an, true testimony elicited by the right hand on a Bible. One can easily imagine the founding prophets, who had demanded that contemplation of the Word replace the worship of idols, staring down in astonishment at some of their supposed disciples.

With so many sacred scenes disqualified from representation, the human appetite for presence was no longer disguised as a nostalgia for the divine figures of the past: saints and angels, Mary at the Annunciation, Christ at the Crucifixion, the two together in nativity and nursing (as summoned also in meditation). Instead this yearning fixed itself (as in the middle stage of Donne's "Air and Angels") on a nature unsubordinated to a divine organizing consciousness (and therefore sometimes unmanageable), and on human constructions (domestic as well as pious), on quotidian work and play. What had been essentially signifiers of God's Creation and monarchical authority now stood for themselves. As these ordinary folk and their domesticities would recover status as the subjects of the modern "history of everyday life," so the ordinary scenery of nature would emerge as the deity regarded by scientific materialism.

For realistic painters as for Baconian empiricists, all that matters—all that can be allowed to matter—is what the eye can witness. As Alpers observes, "northern images do not disguise meaning or hide it beneath the surface but rather show that meaning by its very nature is lodged in what the eye can take in—however deceptive that might be."[41] This blend of Pyrrhonism and utilitarianism may not get anyone either to the *Ding an sich* or the Father in heaven, despite some optimistic hints and conciliatory pious gestures in Bacon's rhetoric or Ruisdael's rainbows. Humanity is left to wrestle firewood in against the cold and dark. Ruisdael shows us a creature in transit, not a pilgrim in progress: a painfully compelling instance, but not an articulated allegory, of life's travails. No story leaps to mind; nobody is even speaking.

Only in Rembrandt—raised as a Protestant and possibly a Mennonite—do words retain a special presence and magic. His *Belshazzar's Feast* (Figure 51) rounds out my race through the galleries of seventeenth-century Dutch art, because it shows the way holy language can retake the canvas from a table of

Figure 51. Rembrandt van Rijn (1606–69), *Belshazzar's Feast*, ca. 1635. Oil on canvas, 167.6 × 209.2 cm. National Gallery, London. Bought with a contribution from the National Art Collections Fund, 1964. © National Gallery, London.

pewter, grapes, paring knives, bread rolls, and spilled wineglasses. It also rounds out, emblematically, this middle phase of my book, because it suggests—like my argument about the Metaphysicals and Cavaliers—that the divine force of the Word behind the word could overwhelm royal power, that the writing hand could overthrow a king who reveled in the stolen and inherited material opulence that violated the sacred covenant of the church. As the king drinks and debauches, revolutionary graffiti spring up, startling and angular, demanding and compelling his downfall: for Belshazzar as for Charles I, the writing was on the wall. The poet John Cleveland condemned the Puritan rebel as one who "with his peremptory scales can doom his prince with a Mene Tekel."[42] When Rembrandt illuminates this *Mene, Mene, Tekel, Upharsin* in the 1630s, he is partly endorsing that revolutionary power, and perhaps also warning about a world that "has been counted and counted, weighed and divided" without yielding its essential truths, which art can suggest better than science and which God's Word will reveal best of all when the material universe is swept away.

In Rembrandt's 1650–52 *Faust* etching, the spirit comes to visit the doomed scholar as a glowing circular chart of legible letters. The danger of language presumes its power. Though scarce—or maybe because so[43]—Rembrandt's words emanate divine power and glory, the sense that they are not merely things, but partake of the secret behind things, beyond the picture. In his 1661 self-portrait as Paul, as well as in the Belshazzar painting, Rembrandt uses Hebrew characters, traditionally considered the alphabet of inherent hieroglyphic power from the tetragrammaton on down. Like medieval illuminated manuscripts, they are not really there to be read, but to stand for the Word whose full meaning the viewer can only begin to intuit. It is this same Rembrandt who brings full psychological depth into his portraiture, so that humanity itself both achieves and escapes the status of thing.[44] The tension between Rembrandt's forward-looking artistic psychology and his backward-looking religious ontology lends his works much of their greatness, their promise of a discovery of something real and important, something that retains individuality without losing universal significance. The miraculous evocation of human values, presence, and spirit by daubed approximation rather than by more literal-minded, proto-photographic forms of realism, was—as we are about to see in Shakespeare's *Merchant of Venice*—part of a late-Renaissance artistic effort to prove that imperfect representations are not a loss of reality, but instead the best means toward redemptive truths amid the moral and intellectual complications of the modern world.

PART IV

Solutions

The Consolations of Mediation

Metal and Flesh in The Merchant of Venice: Shining Substitutes and Approximate Values

Economics

By taking the supernatural out of the perceptible world, Dutch art paradoxically sanctified that world. When iconoclasm forced artistic energies into new channels, the Christian culture's piteous response to its martyrs was redirected or re-cathected onto humanity's victims throughout the ecosystem—much as (according to Max Weber's controversial theory) the penitential exertions formerly offered by Catholicism for self-improvement, rendered inefficacious by Reformation theology, were channeled into profitable hard work in the ordinary world.[1] Karl Marx claimed that capital undermined "the deification of nature,"[2] because nature became an object for humanity to use rather than worship; the Reds were seldom Greens. But capital also introduced yet another set of mediations that fueled the late-Renaissance hunger for things in and as themselves, and made nature a kind of *deus absconditus*, inaccessible (like Luther's God) by direct perception. Socio-economic trends (away from subsistence farming and daily hunting, for example) provoked a yearning for return to some primal relation to the world. By eliding capitalism with Protestantism, Shakespeare (among others) helped reconcile his society to its continuing and deepening alienation from absolute presence. *The Merchant of Venice* reminded audiences that God was still accessible by revelation and intuition, that Christ was Himself a mediator who had once participated in physical nature, and that Reformation theology therefore offered something analogous to capital: a sign with an inscrutable good somehow behind it.

Protestantism was not automatically at ease in the emerging capitalist economy. The post-bullionist belief in the representing object (money) instead of the original treasure (gold) is idolatrous in form and function, and the notion that these representations were efficacious in themselves would have recalled the superstitious aspects of Catholicism. Furthermore, to rely on something because it has become customary, rather than because it is true to the nature of the original source of its value, was exactly the error the Reformers saw in Catholic ceremonialism;[3] and the use of the imprinted image of the sovereign to locate and affirm value in the currency made the idolatrous functions (and its affiliation to England's Arminian rulers) even more prominent. It is hard to know whether Donne is ultimately criticizing coinage or a more directly theological error when his "Litany" cautions that

> plenty, God's image, and seal
> Makes us idolatrous,
> And love it, not him, whom it should reveal.[4]
>
> (lines 185–87)

A version of what numismatists call the "seigniorage gap"—the degree to which the face value of a coin exceeds the value of its constituent metal—became extreme under the Calvinist God. Grace became more like "fiat money," which bases its value almost entirely on an assertion from above. Granting credit is (as the word suggests) a leap of faith, and Protestant theology declined to offer collateral. Especially when these systems were new, people must have inhabited them uneasily. Capitalism, like human sexuality, runs on an essentially irrational system of valuation, in which the markers can seem almost infinitely precious, but exactly what the underlying commodity is, and where it resides, remains almost impossibly obscure, hidden behind layers of mediation: objects that refer to other objects in an almost endless regression. It seems practically good enough—but not philosophically so—merely to trade the markers day after day, to keep the circulation going, to invest in projections as if they were manifest goods. Anthropologists, evolutionary biologists, economists, or theologians may suggest sources of these valuations, but we need not be conscious of those sources for the markers to work on us. Sometimes, in fact, they will work much better if we take the values on faith.

They only work, however, as long as the brethren all agree to believe in them and to believe that each piece will mean something equivalent to each of them. Therefore these capitalist beliefs, like Calvinist ones, often looked more like suspension of disbelief, and remained continually under threat: doubt is contagious, a self-fulfilling prophecy that sets off a run on the banks, a Counter-Reformation craving for something more tangible. The notorious Dutch tulip bubble consisted largely of contracts upon contracts, for which no bulb was actually ever touched. In the sixteenth century, "the meteoric and relentless inflation, unlike any that Europe had ever experienced,"[5] must certainly have threatened to break down people's trust in any stable relationship between these monetary signifiers and the value, the material equivalents, they were supposed to signify. In other words, in the economy as in the many other cultural arenas I have described, the material world kept threatening to become alienated and unreal in the late Renaissance. Policies such as the severe penalties against coin-clipping, and Elizabeth's 1561 re-coinage that sought to bring the nominal value of money back down to that of its constituent metal, may thus have served pressing psycho-social needs as well as more obvious economic ones. If economy and epistemology tried to lean on each other for support, they risked dragging each other into the void.[6]

Capitalism, as the economic version of this entrapment into an economy of signs, emerged (beginning prominently in fifteenth-century England) with peasants deprived of land becoming proletarian workers, exchanging labor for goods.[7] It was a loss of contact with the land that was also, simultaneously, the onset of economic mediations. David Hawkes makes the intriguing suggestion that "The Reformation began as a protest against the fetishization of alienated labor. A papal 'indulgence' was a sign that represented a particular quantity of human penitential labor, or 'works' . . . a fetishized sign, representing in a falsely objective form a determinate amount of subjective activity, and it was believed to be valuable and efficacious in itself. It was, that is to say, a form of *paper money*."[8] Reformation zealots were not shy about condemning trade and usury on religious grounds; the Protestants' drive toward original simplicities and authenticities made them natural enemies of an emerging financial marketplace that nonetheless represented the logical economic extension of their sign-and-faith-based theology—a conflict, I suspect, between the emotional reflex underlying the movement and its theoretical superstructure.

The capitalist model of ownership made at once for alienated labor and alienated nature. *As You Like It* demonstrates that the practical socio-economic and broad philosophical changes were inextricable on this point. Cash crops such as woad and tobacco became increasingly important, and the real-estate market became "a vehicle through which individuals could legitimize their success by transforming capital into landed property."[9] Enclosures cut people off from natural life and from their livings simultaneously, producing both practical outrage and fantastic nostalgia.[10] According to William Harrison's 1580 report on the English forests, "Whole populations were transformed from habitual users and gatherers of the woods into dispossessed consumers, required to purchase firewood at market prices."[11] Nature itself began to function as a commodity, made valuable by its scarcity rather than its bounty[12]—an economic shift that the climatic shift known as the "Little Ice Age" could only have aggravated. Though motives of survival and justice were certainly primary, the rhetoric of anti-enclosure campaigners suggests that they also felt, or sought to enlist, a broader sense of being excluded from an ancestral place in nature from which their lives derived.

More broadly, by a kind of reification that medieval nominalists and Frankfurt School modernists would equally mistrust, some concepts began to be treated as realities. Ideas of value and possession became the unanswerable master of the material world, and made human masters into owners in simple of the land itself, rather than proprietors of certain transactions between the land and its users: "In precapitalist English society," Don Wayne argues, "property was understood as a *right*, that is, a right to revenue (in service, produce, or money) based on title to land. With the ascendancy of a market economy and its accompanying ideology, the distinction between the right and the thing became blurred: property became the thing itself."[13] For nature itself, to be conceived was to be colonized and commodified; and the consequences of that philosophical point bombard us with mutagens every day. Simon Schama's wide-ranging study notes that "For some historians it was the Renaissance and the scientific revolutions of the sixteenth and seventeenth centuries that doomed the earth to be treated by the West as a machine."[14] And not only the earth: as Theodor Adorno and Max Horkheimer observed, "Animism spiritualized the object, whereas industrialism objectifies the spirits of men."[15] On the other hand, Raymond Williams would warn us not to let urban industrialism be conveniently framed for the crimes of capitalism, which has become so pervasive that (with a little discouragement from the privileged class) people are generally unable to recognize the capitalist system as an agent at all.[16]

In any case, it is not hard to imagine a vicious cycle in which the growing capitalist marketplace would both intensify, and be intensified by, a culture desperate to get control of things, to know them physically and absolutely: since the objects themselves would themselves seem increasingly inaccessible—mediated and alienated—the appetite for ownership would be constantly piqued but never satisfied. Marlowe's *Doctor Faustus* is the great early exemplar and parable of this fear, adjoined to the fear that the soul itself might be turned into a commodity and exchanged for other commodities. What the Reformation began by attacking (in the form of indulgences) eventually seeped back into Protestant culture in the form of capitalist acquisitiveness.

At stake simultaneously were the nature of value and the nature of reality: economics and semiotics were deeply linked by the epistemological controversies arising from theology, and mercantilism was a doctrine of material presence. Though remarkable, these correlations were not entirely new. Heraclitus himself (in Fragment 90) suggests that money and exchange value epitomize the elusive universe he is describing; and Shakespeare is not, I think, entirely anachronistic in allowing Troilus to ask provocatively, "What's aught but as 'tis valued?"; nor in having Hector reply that value is limited to the degree an object is "precious of itself"; nor in leaving the dispute unresolved (*Troilus and Cressida*, 2.2.51–96).

Thomas More's Utopia mistrusts the modern functions of money and imposes an arguably parallel regression on language.[17] Marc Shell argues that "Since the ancients, theorists of money and language have considered money to be a combination of inscription (sign) with the inscribed thing," but that both money and language have evolved from inherent material force toward attributed symbolic force.[18] Capitalist monetary ideas and post-structuralist linguistic ideas have steadily increased the self-sufficiency of the signifiers, the sense that they participate in their own legitimate marketplace, and can function autonomously apart from whatever their originary objects may have been. According to Jean-Joseph Goux, "Just as in the economic sphere there arises the question of *convertibility*, that is, the existence or not of a deposit serving to back the tokens in circulation, likewise in the domain of signification the truth value of language will become a crucial concern. Language will no longer be conceived as fully expressing (or as being *capable* of adequately expressing) reality or being; it will necessarily be conceived as a means, a relatively autonomous instrument, by which it is possible to represent reality to varying degrees of exactitude."[19] Looking over this and the preceding three paragraphs, I see that (doubting the validity or salability of my amateur speculations about economics) I have repeatedly stamped distinguished names on the top of my sentences—a formal tic that reflects the sense in which such words can be, like coinages, mediators to whom a community attributes transferable value, designations of seigniorage or surplus value superimposed on material of otherwise questionable worth. But let me leave that meta-scholarly issue aside, in favor of a larger ethical and intellectual question. Does granting these formerly dependent signifiers their sovereignty really produce (as complacently implied by some deconstructionist writing)[20] any analogous liberation for the human underclasses, or instead an ingenious new form of enslavement (to fetishized representations and to a global economy) that sacrifices the economic and spiritual freedom of human individuals to the autonomy of that voracious and amoral marketplace?

With the Soviet Union now many years in its grave, one may hope that criticism of capitalism will no longer be mistaken for a treasonous affiliation with Communist tyrants threatening our lives and liberties. As Cold War politics cease to dictate the categories, it becomes easier to excavate late-Renaissance complaints about wage labor, complaints that articulate the links between mistrust of capitalism and the other mistrusts of mediation this book explores. Hawkes suggests that we can now "acknowledge what was obvious to most people in the sixteenth and seventeenth centuries: that the conquest of the world by capital was an unmitigated disaster, an irremediable injustice, and an unadulterated tragedy."[21] Certainly he is right to ask whether our modern assumption that these objections correlate with a class struggle is anachronistic: a vestige of a contingent and temporary situation of the (roughly) Victorian world and Karl Marx's responses to it.[22]

Some scholars blur late-Renaissance economic critiques into modern leftist politics, perhaps for fear that registering the differences will make it harder to play the heroic role of defending, in the classroom, the oppressed social classes. Yet the broadest and liveliest student activism at the start of the twenty-first century—against globalization, which smothers diversity, exposes wages to the downward forces of an open market regardless of place, and proposes that everyone worship the alluring commodities that monopolies offer as the essential goods of life—is more compatible with late-Renaissance critiques of capital than with classic Marxist ones. In a formative document of 1960s counterculture, Herbert Marcuse lamented the conversion of humanity into "one-dimensional man," devoid of self-awareness or spiritual amplitude, trapped in an empty cycle of desires for simulacra of life for which industrial capitalism provides both the need and the product.[23] This dimensional shrinkage was already under way and under challenge in Elizabethan England. What does Jonson's *Volpone* really want, other than to keep others wanting what he has, and to keep himself wanting? Capitalism is now so triumphant in contemporary geopolitics, and consumerism so fundamental to contemporary life, that we cannot quite see the strangeness and contingency of a system in which "Every day, virtually everyone in a capitalist society exchanges a portion of their lives for an objectified representation of life."[24] Twenty-first-century workers sell their time and effort for the potential latent in a paycheck; they obtain objects only by surrendering, to some equivalent degree, the self; and they often unthinkingly seek to buy selfhood back, at a mark-up, in the form of branded goods. But early modern laborers might well have felt something wrong with the new structure of their lives. Thus Gerrard Winstanley's economic radicalism and his radical Protestantism were intertwined, and he explicitly condemned wage labor as an offense against Creation itself.[25]

The frenzy of exchanges of flesh for gold in *The Merchant of Venice* mark the play as a deep, early meditation on the wage-labor society we inherit. Shakespeare uses the moral complexity of those overlapping exchanges to suggest a Pyrrhonist epistemology and even a Latitudinarian theology. In the economic realm as in the others this book has been describing, epistemology takes on the deep imprint of teleology: what people see, and whether people are deemed to be seeing truly, depend on what a culture designates as the ultimate reality. For those who suppose that the world is (merely) an accommodative translation of the Word to which they must finally return and by which they will rest eternally judged, the quest for the real will not stop at the object; *contemptus mundi* entails a contempt for materiality, and they will demand to know what a thing means in order to know what it is. This is the archaic, redemptive world Shakespeare locates in Belmont, with the casket test as its archetype, finding ways to evoke the inward signatures that alone differentiate virtue from evil in the Protestant universe.

If, on the other hand, the word is merely a human tool for holding an inevitably imprecise and culturally contingent perception of an eternal physical universe bound only by its own internal (and essentially mechanical) rules, then the quest for the real will not stop at the word, but will attempt to find the nature of the *Ding an sich*, with a disdain for subjectivity and value-judgment as well as for the reliability of signifiers such as language. The material world gets to repay, in kind, Christianity's contempt. This is Shylock, standing in for Venice as a whole, which in turn stands in for despiritualized capitalism, which may stand in for materialism in the broadest sense. The goal of the word is the contract, with its absolute meaning, and the goal of the contract is the actual body. *The Merchant of Venice* shows these goals never quite reached, and induces its audience to recognize that shortfall as very good news for fallen beings like themselves.

Flesh and Gold

The Merchant of Venice is not a green play. Even without counting the variant forms and compounds, the word "green" appears well over a hundred times in Shakespeare's works, but this play manages only a single glancing reference to "green-eyed jealousy" (3.2.110). The setting helps to explain this: Venice is hardly rich in arable land (and U.S. dollars were not yet in circulation). Even in Belmont, however—the "green world" in Northrop Frye's and C. L. Barber's formulations of Shakespearean comedy, and a place editors have been revealingly eager to characterize with Lewis Theobald's unfounded 1726 stage direction, "A Grove or Green Place before Portia's House"—the implied light is distinctly silver. In both settings, metal and flesh tones dominate the palette, along with the red of blood that threatens to surface in blushes and wounds. Given the association between "green thoughts" and nostalgia for simplicity, I suspect that this spectrographic gap is an index of the play's cancellation of such nostalgia: Shakespeare refuses to lure us back to nature. The rejection of pastoral is one facet of a rejection of any absolute epistemology. Shakespeare welcomes us instead to the Exchange—the opposite of a pastoral retreat, not just in being city rather than country and a place of work rather than *otium*, but also in proposing a model of relative rather than absolute values. On the Rialto, things are fungible markers, never entirely themselves. At moments Shakespeare almost seems to be taunting us with the economic eclipse of pastoral, since he brings in a story of shepherding—the Biblical narrative of Jacob accumulating his flock—only to turn it into a metaphor of usury (1.3.76–96).

Developing the ability to accept what things stand for, what they resemble, and how they function, rather than insisting on knowing what they absolutely are in either material or divine terms, is the fundamental task of late-Renaissance epistemology. *The Merchant of Venice* is—among other things—an instruction manual for that task. In an era that was taking flight from a mob of mediations, along comes a play to praise mediation; in an age increasingly haunted by the merely approximate character of knowledge, the play reconciles us to approximation. It ensnares and abjures the hope that the object can be either entirely identical to, or entirely independent of, its signifier. The audience must learn to accommodate a universe of imperfect readings, trusting intuitions whose foundations remain mysterious. Characters keep straying from the essences that the religious allegory demands of them, and failure of allegory serves to punish the audience's desire to find such absolute identities. A central question for capitalism—how much dependency on trust, mediation, figuration, and approximation the system can tolerate—is also a central question for both the inhabitants and the interpreters of *The Merchant of Venice*. So this is a course in hermeneutic arbitrage, a morality play for a new era: it teaches, not what to do about pure good and evil—known entities saturated with a particular quality—but rather what to do without them. "Whether we speak in terms of family of ideas, or climate of opinion, or dominant intellectual movement, what is distinctive about seventeenth-century English intellectuals is that they were prepared to face the imperfections of all human knowledge and, nevertheless, to seek that intermediate goal which they called moral certainty."[26] But something in the late sixteenth century must have prepared them. *The Merchant of Venice* not only explored the new moral and epistemological landscape, but also helped make it comfortably habitable.

From its very first lines, *The Merchant of Venice* richly earns its reputation for depriving audiences of any simple and stable truths. "It" is a nagging unknown:

> In sooth, I know not why I am so sad;
> It wearies me, you say it wearies you;
> But how I caught it, found it, or came by it,
> What stuff 'tis made of, whereof it is born,
> I am to learn.

The verse line then stops prematurely, and the failure of knowledge lingers in the silent theatrical air for an implicit six syllables before Antonio produces yet more mental negations and renunciations: "And such a want-wit sadness makes of me, / That I have much ado to know myself " (1.1.1–7).

Salerio, intending to offer the most practical and quantifiable kind of explanations for the shipping merchant's inward distress, answers, "Your mind is tossing on the ocean." Yet the vivid description of the rise and fall of waves, and the addendum that "I should not see the sandy hour-glass run / But I should think of shallows and of flats" (1.1.25–26), evoke the archetypes of elusive definition invoked by ancient atomism, seventeenth-century Dutch nature painting, and modern chaos theory alike: the way weather, fluid dynamics, and infinite tiny grains shift over time in ways too complex and subtle for the human mind to predict by calculation. Consider, for example, Richard Lovelace's "Advice to My Best Brother":

> Nor be too confident, fix'd on the shore,
> For even that too borrows from the store
> Of her rich Neighbour, since now wisest know,
> (And this to *Galileo's* judgement ow)
> The palsie Earth itself is every jot
> As frail, inconstant, waveing as that blot
> We lay upon the Deep; That sometimes lies
> Chang'd, you would think, with's bottom's properties.
>   (lines 17–24)

The failure of absolute knowledge is again coded as a failure to plumb the depths of nature.

Solanio's explanation offers no better escape from empirical indirections and imperfect representations:

>   I should be still
> Plucking the grass to know where sits the wind,
> [Peering] in maps for ports and piers and roads.
>   (1.1.17–19)

These are secondary modes of perception. Antonio's reply, though it claims to offer reassurance, only multiplies the uncertainties of space and time:

> My ventures are not in one bottom trusted,
> Nor to one place; nor is my whole estate
> Upon the fortune of this present year.
>   (1.1.42–44)

Antonio's economic worries about the ships of merchandise thus echo epistemological worries in the era's wars of truth, as a practical subset of a technical and philosophical problem. In place of certainty, he can claim only a diversified portfolio of uncertainties. His material possessions, we are repeatedly reminded, are neither here nor there; like phenomenological reality, they are his but not in his hands, away but not in any specifiable location, always in transit and therefore uncertain, at risk. Shylock's showy dithering about whether Antonio is actually wealthy, because of all his ships in transit, or actually bankrupt, because all of his ships are in transit, re-emphasizes the point. As complexity theory would eventually point out, even the seemingly quantifiable may be incalculable. Even the mechanistic universe of Hobbes moves in mysterious ways. Salerio wonders whether Antonio is upset because those uncertain shipments are "in a word, but even now worth this, / And now worth nothing?" (1.1.35–36). The instability of worth, its arbitrary assignment, becomes a motif of this scene and the play it introduces, as it does of capitalism and the world of imputed values it typifies.

The second scene opens with Portia complaining, in terms that closely echo the complaint of weariness with which Antonio opened the first scene, about "the will of a living daughter curb'd by the will of a dead father" (1.2.24). A few decades later, Edward Stillingfleet's *Origines Sacrae* would use merchants who (like Antonio) send ships to unseen destinations and children who (like Portia) obey the questionable claims of paternal authority as prime instances of the kind of leap to moral certainty that Christians must practice in a skeptical age.[27] My point is not to convert this entire play into an allegory of radical skepticism, or of radical economics. In fact, I will argue that the play resists allegory, and I favor a verisimilar psychological reading of Antonio's sorrows as homoerotic, implicitly the consequence of his uneasy mixture of emotional and financial stake in Bassanio's semi-passionate pilgrimage to Portia. The interplay between the two proposed motives—money and love—seems to me a dominant theme of the play, which thus anticipates and interrogates the marriage theme that will dominate novels for centuries thereafter. Though dowries had long offered a version of the same transaction, bodies exchanged for money remain the troublesome emblems of capitalism (and its attendant ills) up to the present day.

These themes collide when the main plot and subplots collide at the close of the fourth and fifth acts. The "merry bond" in which Antonio offers his body in return for Shylock's gold, and the wedding bond in which several characters offer their bodies in exchange for the golden rings, culminate, on the level of plot, a mingling of flesh and gold that permeates the play at a micro-level as well, shaping its diction and imagery, and lending a kind of queasy flavor to all of its gestures toward romantic comedy. The play can plausibly be described as obsessed with how to attach financial values to human ones, how to weigh precious metal against living bodies. This was hardly a new problem in personal and political ethics in Shakespeare's world, nor is it an outdated one now, but the late-Renaissance anxiety about how to know and value both persons and substances placed special emphases on that problem.

Solanio and Salerio depart to make room for what they call "worthier friends," and Antonio's reply—"Your worth is very dear in my regard" (1.1.62)—redoubles the confusion of personal affection with monetary value. He then proposes that his "credit . . . be rack'd, even to the uttermost" (1.1.180–81), a test of his financial standing that is nearly applied to his body instead. Through the remainder of the play, characters continue to mix "goods" with "goodness," "purse" with "person," "ewes" with "usury," living "life" with making a "living," the "getting" of wealth with the "getting" of children, the contractual "will" left by a dead man with the erotic "will" of his living daughter, taking an "interest" in someone with taking "interest" from them, emotional "bonds" and "engagement" with financial ones, and so on. As in *The Winter's Tale*, this deluge of financial language obliges audiences to ask whether these are signals of a world falling into modern economics, or instead a world striving to infuse the new system with some version of the old values.

Shakespeare must have known that playing simultaneously in these two discordant keys, one plucked on the heart-strings and the other on the purse-strings, would produce some odd notes. That charivari-style cacophony suits the satiric treatments of widow-hunting and other greedy courtships familiar on other Renaissance stages; but Shakespeare seems to be demanding romantic admiration for Bassanio and Portia, and the results are rather like trying to cast the Senate Banking Committee in a teen television love story—or teen heart-throbs in a script based on Senate Banking Committee hearings. If this is a "problem comedy," money is its most obvious problem, one that (here as elsewhere) points toward broader problems of representation and ethics. Virtually every action seems compromised by the marketplace through which it has to pass, tainted by its transmission through the money that is all things to all people: an ethical Typhoid Mary, carrying the disease of moral equivocation to everyone who uses it and everything they use it for. But is mediation—is the emergent modern money system, including loans whose interest is paid in other commodities—really the source of the trouble? Or is Shylock merely a provisional demonization of a medium—a mediating function—that finally proves capable of carrying benign as well as malign influences, the pejorative stereotype of the Jew standing in for the pejorative stereotype of money itself, and similarly proven simplistic?

Consider, for example, Bassanio's courtship of Portia and the friendship of Antonio that finances it. Bassanio speaks of sustaining the "rate" of his wooing without becoming too much further "gag'd" to creditors: "To you, Antonio, / I owe the most in money and in love," and he finds in that mixed commitment a "warranty" to seek further financial help by emotional appeal (1.1.130–34). Antonio answers with a similar pun of his own, offering "my purse, my person, and my extremest means" (1.1.138) to serve in Bassanio's quest. That, too, is appropriate, because Bassanio describes his goal in terms that meld human and economic quantities:

> In Belmont is a lady richly left,
> And she is fair . . .
>
> .   .   .   .
> Her name is Portia, nothing undervalu'd
> To Cato's daughter, Brutus' Portia.
> Nor is the wide world ignorant of her worth,
> For the four winds blow in from every coast
> Renowned suitors, and her sunny locks
> Hang on her temples like a golden fleece,
>
> .   .   .   .
> O my Antonio, had I but the means
> To hold a rival place with one of them,
> I have a mind presages me such thrift
> That I should questionless be fortunate!
>   (1.1.161–176)

The word "undervalued"—a Shakespearean neologism still rare outside of stockbroker recommendations—will soon appear again; and the reiteration of "means" as a desirable mediator between the self and its goals will echo throughout a play that presents meaning as itself transitional and transactional rather than teleological.

Antonio answers by turning the idea of "fortune" from this primarily personal meaning to one primarily economic: "Thou know'st that all my fortunes are at sea" (1.1.177). The setting then shifts to Belmont, haunted by that same tricky word: Portia answers Nerissa's insistence on her "good fortunes" by arguing that, though she has a monetary fortune, she must nonetheless depend on the other kind of fortune to select her husband. When Shylock muses that Antonio is "a good man," Bassanio misunderstands it as a judgment on Antonio as a person rather than a purse. Shylock then tries to justify his loan-sharking by comparing his skillful breeding of money out of money to Jacob's skillful breeding of sheep out of ewes, deliberately confusing fleshly procreation with financial multiplication. Antonio asks the natural question, "Is your gold and silver ewes and rams?" and Shylock answers, "I cannot tell; I make it breed as fast" (1.3.95–96). Like Gobbo's later complaint that the conversion of the Jews "will raise the price of hogs," Shylock's Biblical allusion demonstrates quite strikingly the replacement of absolute religious values and individual living creatures by the perpetual transactional adjustments of the marketplace.[28] It also effectively disguises as supernatural Providence the unique and benevolent way that natural providence distorts the capitalist model of exchange.[29] Shylock's equation holds up so well in Venice that Antonio ends up signing a bond offering his flesh for Shylock's gold. After briefly complaining that Antonio had "rated"— that is, berated—him, Shylock offers the money at no "rate" in order to "buy your friendship."

While Shylock is busy gloating over this financial bond that Antonio is tardy in repaying, Salerio talks about "love's bonds" that Lorenzo is tardy in repaying Shylock's daughter Jessica. When Lorenzo finally does arrive to elope with her, he follows Shylock's own method, making off not only with person but also with purse, not only what Shylock's flesh bred from himself, but also what Shylock's money bred from itself. Jessica counts on "fortune" to help her elope, and vows to "gild myself / With some moe ducats" (2.6.49–50) just before departing, as if she like Portia were a golden fleece, half physical beauty and half financial bounty.

Shylock's reaction fits the pattern perfectly: he cries alternately for "My daughter! O my ducats!" and "my ducats, and my daughter!" (2.8.15, 17), even going so far as to call the stolen money "my Christian ducats" as if they could undergo the same religious conversion that Jessica underwent. This could be just a standard anti-Semitic parody, except that the slippage crosses all lines of race and religion. No sooner has the golden fleecer Jessica gone in search of her fortune than the scene switches to Morocco pondering the caskets, seeking his "fortune" through the cogitations of his "golden mind":

"Who chooseth me shall get as much as he deserves."
As much as he deserves! pause there, Morocco,
And weigh thy value with an even hand.
If thou beest rated by thy estimation,
Thou dost deserve enough.

$$(2.7.23–27)$$

He cannot stop "rating" himself and weighing his value, as if he were a piece of precious metal, and as if he could know—or is it only, estimate?—his own inner worth by seeing himself vicariously from the outside.

When Arragon undertakes the same test, he too talks repeatedly about his "fortune," and lest we think only unworthy suitors use this word, it turns up seven times during Bassanio's choice. Upon choosing correctly, Bassanio immediately starts talking about his victory as a negotiated contract instead of as a miracle of love, unsure of his success in the precious-metals market "until confirm'd, sign'd, ratified by you" (3.2.148). Portia answers in a similar tenor:

> I would be trebled twenty times myself,
> A thousand times more fair, ten thousand times more rich,
> That only to stand high in your account,
> I might in virtues, beauties, livings, friends,
> Exceed account. But the full sum of me
> Is sum of something; which, to term in gross,
> Is an unlesson'd girl . . .
>
> (3.2.153–59)

Bassanio's response to this accounting course is to make the golden wedding ring indistinguishable from his flesh, its value conjoined with the value of life itself:

> But when this ring
> Parts from this finger, then parts life from hence;
> O then be bold to say Bassanio's dead!
> (3.2.183–85)

Gratiano then vows that he and Nerissa will compete with Portia and Bassanio for "the first boy for a thousand ducats." When Nerissa asks about making it a monetary bet—"What, and stake down?"—Gratiano answers with a characteristically crude pun that further links the monetary substance with the fleshly one: "No; we shall ne'er win at that sport, and stake down" (3.2.213–16).

On that instant, as if to punish complacency about the equation of money and human flesh, news arrives of Antonio's predicament, and that broken contract forestalls physical fulfillment of the marriage contract, Bassanio uses words like "dear" and "engag'd" and "rating" to try to explain the situation to Portia, and ends up making a muddle of all distinctions between his wealth and his blood, between Antonio's wealth and Antonio's blood, and between documents and bodies:

> When I did first impart my love to you,
> I freely told you all the wealth I had
> Ran in my veins: I was a gentleman;
> And then I told you true. And yet, dear lady,

Rating myself at nothing, you shall see
How much I was a braggart. . . .

. . . .

I have engag'd myself to a dear friend,
Engag'd my friend to his mere enemy,
To feed my means. Here is a letter, lady,
The paper as the body of my friend,
And every word in it a gaping wound
Issuing life-blood.

(3.2.253–66)

"Since you are dear bought, I will love you dear," Portia replies, and promptly packs Bassanio off to Venice, where Shylock will similarly describe the pound of flesh as "dearly bought" (3.2.313; 4.1.100).

Bassanio's attempt to use the word romantically in Venice rings predictably hollow: though his wife "is dear to me as life itself," he would "sacrifice them all / Here to this devil, to deliver" Antonio (4.1.283–87). When the disguised Portia does save Antonio, he offers to reward her with "the dearest ring in Venice," the most expensive. But she demands and finally receives the emotionally dearest ring when Antonio asks that his cause "be valu'd 'gainst your wife's commandment" (4.1.435, 451). As the money Shylock lent does not finally give him any claim on Antonio's flesh—or at least not to the mysterious possession for which the flesh serves as a frame—neither does the money Antonio lent give any claim on Bassanio's flesh. The assumption that love can be financially valued, which kept Morocco and Arragon from wedding Portia, now nearly causes Bassanio to be divorced from her. The marketplace of exchange appears to be the enemy of troth as well as truth.

The final act focuses on the failure of Bassanio and Gratiano to value their wedding rings properly: the authority of gold and contract over flesh, which looked so wrong in Venice, looks considerably more admirable in the love pacts of Belmont. The men's willingness to separate the rings from their fingers demonstrates a facile willingness to separate the symbol from what it symbolizes;[30] for the women, the band is not just "a hoop of gold, a paltry ring," as Gratiano calls his, but a powerful acknowledgment of union and fidelity, and even a cause rather than just a commemoration of those ideals. As in the *figura* discussed by Erich Auerbach, and as in the Eucharist described by most mainstream (or at least midstream) Renaissance theologians, the thing can remain both truly itself and a symbol of something else; these are instruments that give what they signify. The rings are therefore not fetishes, even though they can stand in for the women's erotic bodies; again mediation is a part of truth, a representative holding its place while the original entity seems absent, rather than an obstacle between the self and truth.

As the women's threat of sexual vengeance suggests, the rings are bonded to the various things they represent, including the women's sexual organs and the marriage oaths that were supposed to devote them to a single man. Portia says a wedding band is "a thing stuck with oaths upon your finger, / And so riveted with faith unto your flesh" (5.1.168–69). Bassanio seems to acknowledge this riveting: "I were best to cut my left hand off / And swear I lost the ring defending it" (5.1.177–78). Are the rings the genitals? Are the genitals the marriage? Do we ever (as Donne's "Love's Alchemy" wonders, as the Cavalier fetish-poems ask less directly) escape the symbols and get to love itself? *Merchant* offers the same three-part answer to each of these three questions: in effect, but not quite, and we should not wish it were any other way.

If not for the implicit Social Darwinism of a plot in which fine persons and full purses always end up together, Belmont might offer a nice proto-Marxist critique of the modern capitalistic world epitomized by Venice, a reverse gear for the vehicle of historical dialectic. In Belmont, gold can still dictate the ownership of human bodies, but only in the special case of the wedding ring, not where the gold is a fungible commodity. Words (such as those on the caskets) find ways to connect people, and Portia finds ways to subvert words that separate people from their bodies—Shylock's bond, but also her own vows of vengeful infidelity. Like Bohemia in *The Winter's Tale*, like the so-called Green Worlds in many Shakespearean comedies, Belmont is an imaginary place where reality seems nonetheless to regain its grounding: precisely what Bassanio gains from Portia, what the play itself gains from Belmont, is a piece of solid land, distinct from the status of Venice as essentially a membrane of transfer. The late-Renaissance world was also a place that had found itself imaginary and sought to ground itself somehow in reality nonetheless.

Shylock represents money as a distancing form of mediation. He courts business, but rejects community: "I will not eat with you, drink with you, nor pray with you" (1.3.36–38). He gloats over the breaking of Antonio's bond and—in an act of vandalism on the broader social contract—rejects all efforts to repair it. His determination to cut apart Antonio's body draws Bassanio back apart from Portia before they can be fully joined in marriage. But alongside the Shylock functions of money—unproductive fretting, a constant fear of being cheated and temptation to cheat others, an impaired sense of charity, and a miserly withdrawal from the qualities of communal life—the play recalls alternative, connective functions of the monetary mediator: a means for giving to friends, for furthering love, for repaying debts, for daring voyages that bring rich spices and bright silks to the human senses.[31] So an ambivalent play about a dreary subject like money becomes a lesson about maintaining humaneness in the commercial world Shakespeare saw emerging from feudal Europe. The secret is not avoiding mediating symbols such as money and language; nor is it getting back to nature, or (I will argue) achieving perfect identity. The secret is an inner miracle to which the exterior offers only approximate and, at times, paradoxical clues. If the mediator is somehow an embodiment of love—that is to say, of a desire for connection—then there are still grounds for hope, on earth as in heaven.

Words and Things

Flesh and gold are thus unmistakably but incalculably linked—as are human perception and the material universe, as are words and things. Shylock's supposedly Jewish literalism in reading his bond not only corresponds to a Judaic reading of the Book, but also reflects a compulsive linking of language and object: he will have his oath, and so he will have that pound of flesh, that core sample of his enemy as a material being. What is offered him instead in the Venetian courtroom is more money, the mediator *as* mediator—and Christ, as mediator, ventriloquized by the disguised Portia and then imposed judicially as the only means by which Shylock can recover any of his investment (4.1.380–87). Coin and Word prove no easier to distinguish from each other than Antonio's flesh and Antonio's blood, or Antonio's blood and Antonio's life.

By enforcing his bond, Shylock would not only be fighting free of his role as a subservient victim of Christian society, but more specifically he would be escaping a role that countless other Jews in Western Europe could not escape: the discreditable dealing in credit, rising queasily on the endless sea of means, where money can breed money but cannot buy solid land or full citizenship—cannot make him a man of substance. His landlessness echoes that of Venice itself and evokes the situation of human consciousness in the material world. Shylock uses this bond to try to invade the world of the real, to move (like so many philosophical minds in the decades ahead) across that mysterious gap between *res cogitans* and *res extensa*. He fails because he failed to reckon with the problem of ultimate referents, with the sense that this entity called Antonio is not any single substance that can be separated cleanly from the others in the courtroom—or in a Mass, or in an autopsy—no matter how finely Shylock whets his knife on his soul or sole (4.1.123). Even if Antonio could be so identified, even if the flesh could be extricated from the blood and quantified, it contains another, more remote essence—"the life of any citizen" (4.1.355)—to which Shylock is emphatically denied access. The interaction between words and the material world is far beyond his grasp—far beyond his effort to grasp either one as sufficient.

The futility of Shylock's effort to seize possession of the entity called Antonio recalls the futile efforts (described in introductory chapters) to seize erotic possession of women[32]—and perhaps of some of the discomforts of Eucharistic theology as well. In fact, several of Shakespeare's absolutists begin trying to win love but end up, like Shylock, trying to take life: men's hunger for certainty leads them to destroy the women they wanted to possess. As Blaise Pascal would ask a few decades later, "what about a person who loves someone for the sake of her beauty; does he love *her*? No, for smallpox, which will destroy her beauty without destroying the person, will put an end to his love for her. And if someone loves me for my judgement or my memory, do they love me? *me*, myself? No, for I could lose these qualities without losing my self. Where then is this self?"[33] In the homoerotic sonnets such as number 20 ("A woman's face with Nature's own hand painted"), Shakespeare describes a problem much like Antonio's toward Bassanio: by what fleshly consummation could he claim ownership of another man's love? The efforts of critics to interpret the pound of flesh "nearest [Antonio's] heart" as displaced circumcision may inadvertently prove the point. There is no there there to be owned, no deed that is the property, no one piece of the flesh (not heart, not genitals) that can be neatly isolated as exactly what was sought or promised. The new anatomical biology provides no firm answer to the complications of identity and no real end of desire. If Shylock slinks off pathetically dragging the little scale he had brandished triumphantly, as directors have often and reasonably deduced from the text, empirical science is visibly implicated (as is erotic possessiveness, less visibly) in his defeat. Something important has proven immune to measure. As Shylock prepares to slice into Antonio's chest, both the image and the implication evoke those Caravaggio and Terbrugghen paintings of Doubting Thomas digging into the chest-wound under the illusion that the essence of the martyred Christ-figure will be accessible in the realm of the flesh (see Figure 25).

The Merchant of Venice challenges the assumptions behind the culture's emerging binarism of human consciousness and the material world. Both flesh and gold prove to be inextricable mixtures of meaning and matter. In the casket test as in the trial scene, the essence of a human being is treated as a quantifiable commodity, to be won or lost by gamblers, whereas metal—generally the epitome of the stubbornly physical thing to be known as mere structured substance—becomes the residence of intention, love, and mysterious values. The scientific and economic revolutions are apparently thrown into reverse: hidden meanings finally prove more important than material facts, and the human is measured and evaluated by the metal, not vice versa. A suitor who can see into the metallic blocks and find Portia's picture will obtain her body.

The set for the casket experiments is a storehouse of medieval figuralism, one the lesser suitors—like Shylock at the trial—mistake for a countinghouse or a laboratory of the material sciences.[34] Morocco, who makes the first attempt, seems well prepared to focus on interior values, since he immediately urges Portia, "Mislike me not for my complexion, / The shadowed livery of the burnish'd sun," because in competition with a fairer-skinned suitor she should "make incision for your love, / To prove whose blood is reddest, his or mine" (2.1.1–2, 6–7). He falters in this empiricist commitment, however, by asking her to accept, through the mediation of the women who have desired him, that his surface is actually desirable; and he mediates his own desire by identifying it with "what many men desire," which means the gold casket, which means Portia. Though he compares Portia favorably to the English "coin that bears the figure of an angel" (2.7.56), his meditations show him failing to register the incarnated Word:

> 'Twere damnation
> To think so base a thought; it were too gross
> To rib her cerecloth in the obscure grave.
> (2.7.49–51)

If there were any doubt that Morocco has placed too much faith in visual perception and too little in language—some might say, too little in Reformation principles—it should be stilled by his discovery of "A carrion Death, within whose empty eye / There is a written scroll" (2.7.63–64) inside the casket; reading it is practically redundant to that emblematic message. The eye holds nothing except the word, which holds the truth that can bless or damn.[35] Arragon also fails to sort out the nexus of words and things, which leaves him standing stranded in the worthless middle ground—trapped perhaps in his own name, and the "stamp of merit" he assumes it provides.[36]

Will the third suitor be different? This failure to pry to the interior, to look past monetary value and lovely initial appearances, immediately recurs in a servant's praise of Bassanio's messenger. That messenger, however, scrupulously brings both words and things, and signals by prophecy rather than analogy:

> he bringeth sensible regreets:
> To wit (besides commends and courteous breath),
> Gifts of rich value. Yet I have not seen
> So likely an embassador of love.
> A day in April never came so sweet,

To show how costly summer was at hand,
As this fore-spurrer comes before his lord.
                    (2.9.89–95)

As many critics have noted, Portia's filial righteousness is soon compromised by hints she appears to offer Bassanio as he chooses among the caskets.[37] It remains unclear whether his meditations follow (as they plausibly would) from the song she provides, the first three lines of which end with words that rhyme with "lead," and which warns against the "fancy bred . . . in the eyes" (3.2.63–70). But his remarks, which I think are worth quoting in full here (Shakespeare arranged that everyone would be hanging on every word for clues of his likely decision), certainly resemble the period's standard arguments for skeptical epistemology more than they do the period's standard musings of erotic curiosity. Bassanio seems to be channeling Montaigne's "Apology for Raymond Sebond" rather than Petrarch's rhapsody for Laura:

So may the outward shows be least themselves—
The world is still deceiv'd with ornament.
In law, what plea so tainted and corrupt
But, being season'd with a gracious voice,
Obscures the show of evil? In religion,
What damned error but some sober brow
Will bless it, and approve it with a text,
Hiding the grossness with fair ornament?
There is no [vice] so simple but assumes
Some mark of virtue on his outward parts.
How many cowards, whose hearts are all as false
As stairs of sand, wear yet upon their chins
The beards of Hercules and frowning Mars,
Who inward search'd, have livers white as milk,
And these assume but valor's excrement
To render them redoubted! Look on beauty,
And you shall see 'tis purchas'd by the weight,
Which therein works a miracle in nature,
Making them lightest that wear most of it.
So are those crisped snaky golden locks,
Which [make] such wanton gambols with the wind
Upon supposed fairness, often known
To be the dowry of a second head,
The skull that bred them in the sepulchre.
Thus ornament is but the guiled shore
To a most dangerous sea; the beauteous scarf
Veiling an Indian beauty; in a word,

The seeming truth which cunning times put on
To entrap the wisest.

(3.2.73–101)

The profound suspicion of substitution and mistrust of perceptible value throughout this passage means that Bassanio can find little guidance in the material surface, and he has little access beyond it (he even echoes Portia's prejudice against dark complexions). What Bassanio has to abjure is not so much greed as a miserly philosophy: a belief in the visible presence of value, as opposed to an acceptance of the mysterious productivity of exchange.

When he finds the enclosed "counterfeit" of Portia that signals his triumph, Bassanio's celebration is weirdly clouded by the failure of representation, by the uneasy borders between self and other and between human and non-human, by separation and enmeshment, by shadows (again) falling short of the reality that entangles us, and by the blindness in sight, leaving him no recourse but back to the written word:

Fair Portia's counterfeit! What demigod
Hath come so near creation? Move these eyes?
Or whether, riding on the balls of mine,
Seem they in motion? Here are sever'd lips,
Parted with sugar breath; so sweet a bar
Should sunder such sweet friends. Here in her hairs
The painter plays the spider, and hath woven
A golden mesh t' entrap the hearts of men
Faster than gnats in cobwebs, But her eyes—
How could he see to do them? Having made one,
Methinks it should have power to steal both his
And leave itself unfurnish'd. Yet look how far
The substance of my praise doth wrong this shadow
In underprizing it, so far this shadow
Doth limp behind the substance. Here's the scroll,
The continent and summary of my fortune.

(3.2.115–30)

Bassanio wins Portia by an act of reading that acknowledges its own limitations and accommodations—an important hint about how the audience should read the play. He has gazed into the caskets as if he were gazing out of the Platonic cave. Those metal caskets somehow hold Portia's body, but only by the magic of a verbal bond, and by whatever deep inarticulable qualities the words reflect and evoke. That those are enough to get the right things done, for body and soul, would have been heartening for a deeply dubious culture.

Still, the problem of doubt remains, notably (my Chapter 2 has argued) for husbands in Shakespearean drama: they cannot quite trust the verbal bond to sustain its magical hold over their wives' bodies. Perhaps that is another reason the color in which the Elizabethans sought reassurance appears only as "green-eyed jealousy" in *The Merchant of Venice* (3.2.110). The entire final act is focused on the threat of marital infidelity; Gratiano's closing vow that he will forestall cuckoldry by wearing his wife's vagina like a ring suggests that absolute assurance on this topic requires a grotesque and unsustainable stance. In the plays that follow, such as *Much Ado About Nothing*, mediators resume their character as sinister go-betweens, and Shakespeare acknowledges that a jolly Pyrrhonist acceptance of perceptual uncertainty is sometimes less viable psychologically than it is intellectually.

Morality, Identity, and Representation

The play—itself a reality that is not quite there, as Shakespeare liked to remind his audiences in the later 1590s, but an evanescent representation that may nonetheless offer superior truth—is full of realities that are not quite there. This includes Venice itself, the Renaissance archetype of the contingent place, a land that is not a land, a physical manifestation of a mercantile abstraction, its towers stalagmites of surplus value precipitated from the water over centuries. No wonder dramatists were so drawn to it as a setting. In Venice especially, where fortunes may sink and worth is susceptible to revaluation in each day's exchange, there is no way of knowing ethics any more certainly than we can know physics. *The Merchant of Venice* appears to be offering a solution to moral ambiguity analogous to the Pyrrhonist solution to epistemological doubt: because we can prove we know nothing, but we know we know something, we must trust to some combination of collective tradition, sense experience, instinct, personal intuition, and interpreted language. (In its early years, the dispute between Catholics and Protestants was largely over whether to favor the earlier or the later items on that list, and a coda to this chapter will argue that *The Merchant of Venice* notably resembles Richard Hooker's efforts to mediate that dispute in the 1590s).

Like Launcelot Gobbo hearing an angel urging him to remain with Shylock (because of his indenture, another flesh-for-gold bond) and the devil telling him to flee to Bassanio, we may in fact get everything completely turned around when we try to analyze ethics systematically. But Gobbo still senses the situation well enough to flee from a villain to a hero after all. Gobbo's father may be "sand-blind" and perhaps a bit deaf and senile as well, and the directions his son offers him are a maddening confusion (2.2.33–46, 74); but somehow they find each other and Bassanio, and somehow the father helps lead the son into a better life. The essential human action is less an intelligent certainty than a moral-instinctual guess, based partly on St. Paul's "evidence of things not seen" (Hebrews 11:1). Almost every step a person takes on earth implies a version of Bassanio's imperfectly achieved conclusion: "Here choose I; joy be the consequence!" (3.2.107).

Absolute truths resemble the "infinite deal of nothing" that Bassanio says Gratiano speaks: "His reasons are as two grains of wheat hid in two bushels of chaff; you shall seek all day ere you find them, and when you have them, they are not worth the search" (1.1.114–18). Instead Bassanio argues for practical empiricist tactics during journeys into the unseen, seeking repeatable results rather than theorizing causes:

> In my school-days, when I had lost one shaft,
> I shot his fellow of the self-same flight
> The self-same way with more advised watch
> To find the other forth, and by adventuring both
> I oft found both. I urge this childhood proof,
> Because what follows is pure innocence.
>
> (1.1.140–45)

As a lead-in to a plea for a loan, this is more tendentious than innocent, but it fits with the Pyrrhonist sense that will later shape Bassanio's meditation on the caskets. Given what we cannot know, all the ethical complications we cannot assort, how do we start reading the world and thus choosing a flight-path through it?

The Merchant of Venice encourages us to read figuratively. But the play is a labyrinth, strewn with the expired theories and mutilated conclusions of countless scholars. Some starve in the endless maze of seemingly parallel passages; others are gored when they confront this labyrinth's deadly Minotaur, which is morality. All the delusive echoes and dead ends might suggest that Shakespeare was discouraging ethical analysis of his play, but one can hardly ignore the moral questioning any more than one could ignore the Minotaur: it is constantly seeking us out, even if we cannot quite locate it until we are painfully on the horns of its dilemmas. Rarely in Shakespeare are the Biblical allusions more frequent or the allegorical signals more heavy-handed;[38] but if the ethics are etched in stone, like the Ten Commandments, the people who enact them have all the frailties of flesh and blood. With Christianity shaping the moral vocabulary of the Elizabethans, it seems natural to try to evaluate the play's characters by how well they adhere to the Bible's instructions, as if we were a fundamentalist group rating politicians. Yet the villain Shylock leans on the Bible frequently and comfortably, justifying his usury by the story of Jacob grazing Laban's sheep from Genesis, and basing his idea of contract and revenge on the ways of God in Exodus.

Clearly central to the deep structure of *The Merchant of Venice* is the transition from that Old Testament idea of law to the New Testament's introduction of Christ as a mediator—a locus of mercy, which is inherently inexact—standing between that vengeful God and the inevitable failings of the fallen human race. Like many earlier Christian apologetics, Portia's ingenious reading makes the literal level of the old law endorse rather than contradict the merciful new dispensation. Like the Critical Legal Theorists of recent years, she suggests that statutory language can and should be made to serve whatever outcome is self-evidently ethical; she finds a way to make the contract serve a prior moral truth. Following another Pauline formula—"The letter killeth, but the spirit giveth life" (2 Corinthians 3:6)—she makes the deadly letter of Shylock's strict contract work on behalf of a New Testament spirit that forgives those who act out of generosity and condemns those who act out of malice.

The dispute between the Jew and the Christians in *The Merchant of Venice* keeps pointing through to the dispute between Judaism and Christianity about the canon and functions of the Holy Book. Did the Pentateuch simply relate history and dictate laws, or should it be read anagogically as prophesying a Savior who would fulfill metaphors that had not been understood as such? In the Sermon on the Mount, Christ admonishes,

> Thinke not that I am come to destroye the law, or the Prophetes; I am not come to destroye them, but to fulfil them. . . .
> Ye have heard that it was said unto them of olde time, Thou shalt not kil: for whosoever killeth, shal be culpable of judgement.
> But I say to you, whosoever is angrie with his brother unadvisedly, shal be culpable of judgement. . . .
> After this maner therefore pray ye . . . forgive us our dettes, as we also forgive our detters. . . .
> Judge not, that ye be not judged.
> For with what judgement ye judge, ye shall be judged, and with what measure ye mette, it shal be measured to you againe.
> And why seest thou the mote that is in thy brothers eye, and perceivest not the beame that is in thine owne eye? (Matthew 5:17–7:3, Geneva Bible)

This text is more explicitly present in *Measure for Measure* a few years later, but the applications to Shylock's righteous, malicious, and literal-minded enforcement of Antonio's civil bond are obvious enough; add on the admonition, from the version in Luke (6:35), to "lend, loking for nothing againe, and your rewarde shal be great" and it becomes clear that the Sermon ties the casket scenes to the courtroom scenes.[39] Portia is the judge undoing a judgment with a "quality of mercy" that holds a mirror up to Shylock's quantitative claims and their merciless precision. When Shakespeare has Shylock answer the Duke's "How shalt thou hope for mercy, rendr'ing none?" with "What judgment shall I dread, doing no wrong?" (4.1.88–89), the exchange seems carefully crafted to distinguish invidiously between closed Judaic and more open Christian notions of justification. Shylock is a creature of the word—his contract and his vow about its enforcement—but it is very different from the Word that Jesus represents to Christians, which offers leeway for benevolent interpretation.[40]

Efforts to absolve the play of anti-Semitism by citing Shylock's impressive "Hath not a Jew eyes" speech and the Christians' distinct flaws seem to miss this point. The very fact that Shylock shows human potential (in that speech, and perhaps in lamentations for his lost family) actually deepens the accusation against the Judaic literalism that corrupts him. Conversely, the personality defects of the Christians emphasize the redemptive power of the religion that finally guides them nonetheless toward community, charity, love, and happiness. If Shylock is more appealing than Gratiano by the end of the trial scene, the reversal only emphasizes that their religious affiliations are more important than their interiorities: even a bad Christian is carried along to his group's good fortune. Thomas Coryat had a similar reaction to meeting actual Jews, whom he expected to be obviously repulsive: "I noted some of them to be most elegant and sweete featured persons, which gave me occasion the more to lament their religion."[41] In the victory over Shylock there is some room for pathos and regret; but the crushing of the Jew and the theft of his heritage command nothing but celebration. It hardly erases the discomforts of *The Merchant of Venice* to notice that, while its characters scorn the Jewish race, the play as a whole teaches scorn only for the Jewish religion.

All of the issues this chapter has been describing coalesce around Jessica's conversion. Can the theological Word (and the stolen metals she commits to it) alter the racial character of her flesh and blood?[42] Does a person have an essence if the body can keep insisting "Jew" after the soul has declared "Christian"? Can Jessica claim the identity of Christian within these limitations, or is it merely a role she assumes? The other characters repeatedly struggle with the uneasy choice between the conceptual word and the physical thing; struggle, that is, to resolve the indeterminacy of the entity called Jessica, who is playing a role that can never quite become completely her reality. She herself tries to divide her "blood" neatly from her "manners" (2.3.18–19), but that is no easier than for Shylock to divide Antonio's blood from his flesh and from "the life of any citizen." Even her lover Lorenzo, after punning on the difference between her hand and her handwritten words, can wish her well only with the proviso that she still might merit punishment for her heritage (2.4.12–14, 33–37). Gratiano swears she is now "a gentle, and no Jew" (2.6.51)—another pun blurring conduct into identity—but he is swearing by his masking hood, his artificial face; and Launcelot, who made the same move as a different race, suggests Jessica can be saved only if her father was not actually Shylock the Jew (3.5.4–12).

The hints of religious allegory that pervade *The Merchant of Venice* comprise a sophistication of earlier Renaissance traditions such as morality and mystery plays, but they exploit the same fusing of aesthetic allurement and spiritual education. Some critics identify Jessica as the New Testament: she is the offspring of the Old Testament figure Shylock, and her love moves her from the Judaic to the Christian world as a precious pearl.[43] The disguised Portia may be a figured Mary: a married virgin who, when a diabolical figure demands mankind as forfeit to him on the basis of legal judgment, casts the spirit of love into the shape of a man who will win mankind's salvation on the basis of a merciful reinterpretation of the law, a sermon from the Bel-mount. Some readers identify Antonio not as Mankind but as the true Christ-figure here, sacrificing himself to physical torment and death at the hands of infidels for unaccountable love of the Everyman Bassanio—to "pay his debt" (3.3.36). In any case, the play's villain is Shylock, who is certainly anti-Christian if not exactly the Antichrist, and is repeatedly called a devil (by Bassanio, Antonio, and Salerio).

Only the clown Launcelot Gobbo, however, translates his life explicitly into a morality play, and the fact that he ends up making a total botch of it by casting angelic conscience as the devil's advocate (2.2.1–32) seems like a warning to take the Christians' convenient moral formulas with a pound of salt.[44] For a psychologically verisimilar playwright such as Shakespeare, allegory is an awkward tool, because the greater the characterological credibility of an action, the less its allegorical force. To whatever extent we perceive Antonio sacrificing himself to gratify a death wish or to extort Bassanio's continued affection, to that same extent we lose the Antonio who is sacrificing himself because he represents Christ. The problem is worse than usual in *The Merchant of Venice*, because character not only distracts from the allegory but often seems to contradict it. In the trial scene, when Shylock is being the most diabolical in the plot, insisting on the pound of flesh, he becomes suddenly (in most modern productions, anyway) the most sympathetic as a character, creeping offstage sick with loss, humiliation, and helpless suppressed anger. When the Christian forces seem most Christ-like thematically, in their emphasis on sacrifice and mercy in that same scene, they are least Christ-like characterologically, hooting and mocking and piling punishment on the defeated old man.

This kind of surface noise interferes with the deep allegorical melody at other crucial points. If the casket test is (as some have understandably wanted to see it) a lesson in the medieval doctrine of *contemptus mundi*, why does the correct choice win Bassanio an attractive bed-partner and a pile of money—"the joys of heaven here on earth" (3.5.76)? If Jessica is the New Testament, how can we explain the New Testament making its glorious break from the Old by stealing its old father's life savings and selling the engagement ring he treasures as a memento of his late wife, so that she can have a monkey to play with? Commentators sometimes try to hide these incongruities behind attitudes-of-the-time scholarship—modern assumptions about Renaissance assumptions—but Antonio kicking, cursing, and spitting on an old man is hardly Christ, even the Christ who chased the moneylenders out of the temple. Gratiano shows his coarseness and cruelty—despite his name, he is unlikely to be hailed as full of grace—most clearly at the moments when he claims to be defending Christian values. The Christians are sadistic to Shylock because his religion is not gentle enough, and they condemn his buying of the pound of flesh while keeping slaves of their own. Shylock may not have earned any forgiveness from Antonio, but what had Antonio ever done to earn forgiveness from Shylock? From the Sermon on the Mount itself, one could mount a sermon thoroughly condemning the play's Christians.[45]

Shakespeare thus constructs a neat but flimsy partition between good and evil, and invites us to witness its collapse. He goes out of his way to offer parallels between Portia and Shylock, for example.[46] What, then, does the playwright teach (admittedly, an unfashionable kind of question) by withdrawing the morality-play comforts of cheering angels and jeering Satan? He certainly provokes audiences to consider what functions angelically and what satanically in the modern human universe. Although Portia may not be a perfect embodiment of New Testament values, and Shylock may not exactly embody the Old Testament ones, Portia still plays the role of bringing that saving message of mutual mercy to a world and a man suffering under the harsh letter of the law, which Shylock plays the role of enforcing (right down to the demand for a piece of that man's flesh—a literalist misreading of the Bible's persistent advocacy of a "circumcision of the heart" to fulfill the covenant).[47] All the world's a stage. These actions are not merely signals toward some more meaningful allegorical level: like Auerbach's (and Augustine's) premodern *figurae*, they are real and important in themselves, as well as in what they imply. In a world of only approximate virtues, it matters what one represents as well as what one does. In fact, as Walter Benjamin writes, "In the ruins of great buildings the idea of the plan speaks more impressively than in lesser buildings, however well preserved they are"; and Benjamin's association of such ruins with the melancholic quest, under early capitalism, for a posited lost language—originary and without mediation—and for compensatory allegory corresponds suggestively with what I hear in this play and throughout the late Renaissance.[48]

A distinguished scholar's recent conclusion about *The Merchant of Venice* typifies the modern critical tradition: "Of course, no allegorical interpretation can in itself encompass Shakespeare's complex treatment of the ethics of lending, venture capital, and contracts."[49] But the failure of one kind of positive reading may be the basis of another, more durable kind. The imposition of allegorical meaning on realistic narrative resembles the imposition of human consciousness on the flow of nature: a misrepresentation, but useful and maybe inevitable. Total truthfulness is a much less important obligation in this play than fundamental trust and generosity. Lacking a better way, Bassanio wins Portia through a speculative loan (gained by rhetorical trickery) and an irrational guess (perhaps aided by impermissible hints). Pretending to be absent on a pilgrimage to pray for his success in Venice, Portia actually helps her husband within the modes of the fallen world instead, taking the practical role of a judge interpreting human law instead of a guardian angel enforcing God's law. In return for their limited earthly versions of merciful virtue, Bassanio and Portia are fittingly rewarded with a limited earthly version of Christian heaven. Conversely, Shylock is not dragged down to hell at the end like Marlowe's Faustus, but he does discover that his attitude can make a hell on earth.

So the play becomes a course in translation, teaching its audiences how to decipher familiar moral lessons in the intricate language of the modern marketplace. If this is a play about the right way to read the Bible, it is also a play that uses the Bible to talk about the right way to read the play itself, and uses both to talk about how to navigate the mortal world with only indirect contact and imperfect evidence. No wonder Norman Rabkin found *The Merchant of Venice* an inviting "test case" for his theories of indeterminacy in Shakespearean drama. What this admirable modern critic says about the play is what a seventeenth-century Pyrrhonist would have said about human life generally:

> Yet by the end we have been through a constantly turbulent experience which demands an incessant giving and taking back of allegiance, a counterpoint of ever-shifting response. . . . The attempt to state the meaning of the play is not much more likely to produce an accurate account than an attempt to state the meaning of life. But to say that we cannot profitably talk about the meaning of life is not to say that life is meaningless. In the understanding of art as of life the decision no longer to be tied up in fruitless attempts to reduce significant process and teeming multiplicity to prosaic meaning is a liberating beginning, an invitation to examine the thing itself.[50]

My only objection is to the closing note, which makes the goal an examination of the *Ding an sich*. When amelioration thus supplants law and allegory, it surely represents a renunciation of truth-value.

Act 5 harmonizes the realistic and allegorical levels that conflicted so violently in Venice. The couples are married and the villain defeated by the end of Act 4; nothing remains but some lightweight wit about the rings and a foregone conclusion of the transvestite disguise. Shakespeare tacks on this epilogue to resolve the theme, not the plot. It resembles what post-structuralist theory calls an index or inset code, to guide our interpretation of the story he has told; and it warns that to condemn either the play or its heroes for so imperfectly fulfilling the allegorical model would be to replicate Shylock's error, a punitive literal reading with no allowances for our common frailties.[51] As with Spenser's Mammon,[52] the systematic frustration of allegory implies a condemnation of miserly grasping: direct figuration is the gold standard of the mind.

Act 5 opens with Lorenzo and Jessica sitting in the silvery Belmont moonlight, awaiting Portia's return. Meanwhile they are masters of the house, and they pass the time teasingly slipping their own names in among some notoriously unsuccessful couples: Troilus and Cressida, Pyramus and Thisbe, Dido and Aeneas. Though they are playing and exaggerating, they use these grand romantic tales to converse about intimate fears they could not express civilly otherwise, to sort through the ethical ambivalence of their own affairs. Shakespeare similarly uses Christian allusion to reveal the inner potentialities of the play's ethically complex characters, and throughout his career uses dramatically heightened or historically based events partly as amplifications and parables of the ordinary struggles of the human psyche. If Lorenzo's tardiness proved less costly than that of Pyramus, if the surrender of one ring doth not a Cressid make, these allusions still work as the Christian ones did earlier, pointing toward a kind of grand moral constellation by which people can navigate their own travels on the shifting seas below. Mediation, representation, and approximation again provide access to what are, for mortals, essential truths.

The sublunar world proves mutable, as the skeptics warned, and human perception of it remains imperfect; but Shakespeare's universe here is not Galileo's. The constellations are more real than the chaotic distribution of stars, and there are heavenly intentions behind the heavenly bodies. The music of the spheres is played and heard by angels somewhere above, but as Lorenzo tells Jessica in the play's loveliest speech—presumably delivered with gestures toward the inlaid gold patterns on the stage's canopy "heavens" that stood in for the actual stars—mortals must be content with the more limited (but still lovely) music being played simultaneously by Portia's (and Shakespeare's) human servants:

> Sit, Jessica. Look how the floor of heaven
> Is thick inlaid with patens of bright gold.
> There's not the smallest orb which thou behold'st
> But in his motion like an angel sings,
> Still quiring to the young-ey'd cherubins;

Such harmony is in immortal souls,
But whilst this muddy vesture of decay
Doth grossly close it in, we cannot hear it.
                    (5.1.58–65)

The soul is partly obscured while in the body, like the image of Portia trapped inside the lead casket, or the generosity of Antonio trapped in a world of money—or even (the Eucharistic allusion of "patens" suggests) the immortal Son of God encased in a mortal body. As the lesser music imitates the greater, so the play itself is a lesser imitation of the greatest possible acts of love and hate. When Portia declares that "I stand for sacrifice," and Shylock that "I stand here for law," they mean that they stand waiting, but Shakespeare also suggests that they represent those opposed criteria for salvation.[53] In a small yet meaningful way, the characters actually play the grand archetypal roles; but only if the audience suspends its disbelief, only if they become merciful critics of the inevitable flaws in the performance, hoping (like Prospero) for merciful reviews of their own performances on the great stage of the world. Shakespeare makes spiritual and ethical Christianity emerge almost exactly where capitalism would seem to have erased them, circulating imperfect markers of relative value. Karl Marx, in turn, depicts the modern marketplace as a theater: "persons exist for one another merely as representatives of, and, therefore, as owners of, commodities . . . the characters who appear on the economic stage are but the personifications of the economical relations that exist between them."[54] By eliciting the Good News latent in this situation, Shakespeare helps reconcile Elizabethan culture to its internal contradictions, which I believe is a fundamental role of the creative artist, particularly in comic modes. Another role of the artist, which in this case combines with the first, is making reality appear less opaque. Even scientists would have found these artistic functions worthwhile: "Johannes Kepler, the great astronomer whose three planetary laws provided essential corrections to the Copernican hypothesis, was nevertheless capable of seeing in the relation between the planetary periods and distances an illustration of the music of the spheres; and it was this same allegorico-naturalistic approach that led him to interpret the sun, the fixed stars and the planets as symbols of God the Father, the Son, and the Holy Spirit."[55]

In the conversation that follows Lorenzo's speech, Portia's comparison of a candle to a good deed reformulates this same idea, suggesting that small but virtuous acts like the one she has just performed in the courtroom will suffice as virtue until the Son (with the familiar pun on "sun") returns. The Sermon on the Mount reminds Christians, "Nether do men light a candel, and put it under a bushel, but on a candelsticke, & it giveth light unto all that are in the house. Let your light so shine before men, that they may se your good workes, & glorifie your Father which is in heaven" (Matthew 5:15–16, Geneva Bible). In *Merchant* as in *Macbeth*, the brief candle is the equivalent of the poor player, a pale substitute for the real thing.[56] But the *imitatio Christi* was not conceived as a hollow bit of theater, and Shakespeare suggests ways that divine enlightenment can enter earthly reality:

> *Portia:* That light we see is burning in my hall.
> How far that little candle throws his beams!
> So shines a good deed in a naughty world.
> *Nerissa:* When the moon shone, we did not see the candle.
> *Portia:* So doth the greater glory dim the less:
> A substitute shines brightly as a king
> Until a king be by, and then his state
> Empties itself, as doth an inland brook
> Into the main of waters. Music, hark!
> *Nerissa:* It is your music, madam, of the house.
> *Portia:* Nothing is good, I see, without respect;
> Methinks it sounds much sweeter than by day.
> *Nerissa:* Silence bestows that virtue on it, madam.
> *Portia:* The crow doth sing as sweetly as the lark
> When neither is attended; and I think
> The nightingale, if she should sing by day
> When every goose is cackling, would be thought
> No better a musician than the wren.
> How many things by season season'd are
> To their right praise and true perfection!
>
> (5.1.89–108)

Partial and approximate virtue redeems a world that seems wicked, much as partial and approximate reality redeems a world that seems—in the other sense of "naughty"—a nothingness, void of presence. The relativity of perception (and consequent instability of value) that Shakespeare's contemporaries felt threatening their connection both with God and with nature here becomes instead a blessing: a way to hear, through nature, strains of a higher harmony. As with Caliban's rhapsody about his dreams inspired by heavenly music (*The Tempest*, 3.2.135–43), Shakespeare evokes the privilege rather than the torment of sensing that, just beyond the reach of human hands and minds, there is something more to the universe.

As the plot of *Merchant* subsides into a nighttime quiet, its audiences are encouraged to listen for the grace notes that filter through to the uncorrupted corners of their souls. The sense of fleeting premonitory access to some deep ordering consciousness—a sense that is, I believe, near the core of the appeal of Shakespearean drama—becomes here also a license for belief in the intuitions and analogies by which human minds endure their imperfect contact with the universe. In any sophisticated perspective on cognition—and I have been arguing that the Elizabethans were struggling with one sophisticated by resurgent skepticism and nascent empiricism—a person cannot function without a belief in imperfect yet still meaningful correspondences, even if they fall short of the grand hermeneutic symmetries of Gothic architecture and Biblical exegesis in the preceding centuries. There is no "face to face" in earthly experience, and Shakespeare was no more willing than William Blake (challenging Wordsworth's version of pastoral) to have the human imagination of the physical universe dragged down to a model of "fitting & fitted."[57] Portia's suggestion that the crow's song is sweet as the lark's when no one is listening momentarily anticipates the absurdism of Touchstone's "You have said; but whether wisely or no, let the forest judge" (*As You Like It*, 3.2.121–22).[58] But only momentarily: judgment returns, even though it is—but also only because it is—provisional, relative, contingent on the prejudicial circumstances of the judge. That does not make it wrong. As Portia looks back to nature here for perspective on her experience, she discovers that her experience is perspective.

Inconclusion: Truth, Light, and Likeness

The Merchant of Venice works hard to reconcile its audiences to a world of likelihoods, representations, and imperfect approximations, recuperating these tendencies of the epistemological revolution on behalf of (what looks like) a traditional Christian moral order. It encourages us to recognize that a mediating Christ assigned humanity to represent ultimate virtues imperfectly (in anticipation of a perfecting end-time) and to read, through faith and love, the interior realities concealed by the fallen world and its marketplaces. The dialectical movement between the capitalist world of Venice and the fairy-tale world of Belmont encourages a reconciliation—however provisional and perhaps illusory—between modern circumstances and old values. In economic as in cognitive terms, the new dispensation requires a perpetual letting go (of specie, of reality-paradigms) in order to hold and to thrive. One must be prepared to "give and hazard all he hath" (2.9.21)—capital or cognition—in order to win the elusive daughter of time, whether we call her Truth or Portia. But Shakespeare does not insist on this almost unbearable recognition, retreating again to a sentimental domesticity, structured by class and gender, which again provides stable ground to inherit and pass on to a next generation. He also elides that recognition with the soteriology that requires faith and self-relinquishment in order to win Christ's saving embrace.

Like a Zen koan, *The Merchant of Venice* lures its audiences so far into the paradoxes of rationality, identity, and morality that they are almost forced to relinquish absolute values in favor of some amalgam of intuition and tradition. The play demands, but refuses to reward consistently, our attention to traditional ethical criteria; and, as in Renaissance skepticism generally, a disease of the criterion proves contagious to the entire epistemological realm. Instead of attempting to shore up the old order, Shakespeare implies that the new one may be more familiar and habitable than his contemporaries imagined, if they learn to embrace the mediated and approximate representations of truth that fallen experience permits.

Certainly the play provokes a range of anxieties about verbal and monetary systems, with puns functioning as an analogue of usury (as Marc Shell and others have noticed). But Shakespeare seems to expose this wound in the epistemological fabric in order to repair it, or at least anesthetize it, and maybe even hallow it. Words and coins produce redemption on earth, as Christ's mediation does in heaven. The adaptability of language can be used to correct, or render innocuous, the sinister functions of a contract; the mental universe (as the cognitive advantages of "fuzzy logic" confirm) is a court of equity, not law. The queasiness of puns yields to the beauties of metaphor. Christ brings the quality of mercy between the sinner and the punitive God—the New Testament comes between that sinner and damnation—by a creative act of reading. In the trial scene the disguised Portia remarks that "earthly power doth then show likest God's / When mercy seasons justice" (4.1.196–97); people are especially God's likeness when they accept liking and likening in place of more rigid judgments. The Creator overseeing *The Merchant of Venice* resembles the God that Donne addresses in the *Devotions Upon Emergent Occasions*: "Thou art a *direct* God, may I not say a *literall God*, a *God* that wouldest be understood *literally* and according to the *plaine sense* of all that thou saiest? But thou art also . . . a *figurative*, a *metaphorical God* too: a *God* in whose words there is such a height of *figures*, such *voyages*, such *peregrinations* to fetch remote and precious *metaphors*, such *extensions*, such *spreadings*, such *Curtaines of Allegories*."[59] It is the lesson that capitalism would teach bullionism in the seventeenth century, transposed to the moral and epistemological categories: value is not gold in a vault, but precious goods on a remote peregrination. Perception—and perhaps salvation—is a perpetually interactive process that floats free from any single place or absolute object. The premise of so many Renaissance pilgrimages toward truth—even toward nature, as Petrarch learned from Augustine on

Mount Ventoux, as Herbert complains in "Vanitie (I)"—is both presumptuous and simplistic.

By conflating the demands of high justice with the demands of the diabolical figure, the trial scene in *The Merchant of Venice* conflates Anselm's model, in which Christ stands (as defense lawyer) between man and the judging Father, with the model Calvin revived, in which Christ stands (as debt payer) between man and the soul-collecting Satan. What makes that holy intercessor necessary is the inability of human beings to become, rather than imitate, Christ; the inability (articulated in the Sermon on the Mount)—even of those able to obey the Ten Commandments literally—to embody inwardly and entirely the Christian virtues. "Let me give light," says Portia finally, "but let me not be light" (5.1.129)—a joke about sexual frivolity (as in Bassanio's casket ruminations) that nonetheless points to the deepest function of the human soul as a carrier of ideals that never fully belong to it. The characters, major and minor, stubbornly refuse to be purely virtuous or purely demonic, which suggests the importance of working within the imperfections—hardly a novel moral insight, but one that (here as in the Epilogue to *The Tempest*) obtains special articulation from its metadramatic treatment, and one that bears special weight in an era haunted by the shortcomings of representations and the shortfalls of belief, with new cargoes of uncertainty arriving regularly from the classical past, from overseas, and from scientific innovations.

Was the culture really better off if—puritanical on the road to rationalist—it forbade any gilded anthropomorphic figures to shimmer between heaven and earth? Would it prefer a radically Calvinist dispensation in which (at least as Catholic polemics reduce it) there is no ground for human attempts at goodness, because such attempts are all secondhand (on forced loan from God) or second-rate (directed by a reason that is unlikely to be right)? Why go back, the play as a whole also asks, to a purportedly primeval Judaic literalism that looks crude and dangerous in these circumstances, if one can instead stumble ahead to a soft landing in the new Christian dispensation, as Jessica and Launcelot do?

Partial resemblances, which *As You Like It* warns are untruths, serve in *The Merchant of Venice* as the only truths people have; and useful ones too, as Pyrrhonism looks ahead to pragmatism.[60] An indispensable if implicit clause in the social contract is a kind of cognitive contract, by which we agree to designate things no two of us ever quite hold or see in the same way as if we knew what they were and held them—things that function much as words do, or contractual pledges, in place of a commodity we may never actually possess but need nonetheless to keep in shared circulation. Representations—

metaphors or money—can provide the means to other redemptions: temporal and temporary ones, perhaps, but nonetheless obviously worth having. The words of a contract, whether with man or with God, are subject to revisionist reading, and it's a good thing they are.[61] The fact that everything is referred and deferred—even Shylock apparently borrows to lend—answers a true complexity in human experience, from which the fairy-tale world of Belmont offers at first an illusory escape, but with which it finally achieves a durable accommodation.

Or so it seems. Shakespeare—whom politically minded critics have often detected smoothing over the rough edges of his society—uses Belmont, and even uses Christianity, to disguise the capitalist revolution as a reversion to antique values of truth and an analogy to Christian soteriology. Silver and gold have moral meaning designated by a Father in heaven, and the mediator called money blends into the mediator called Christ.[62] In a similar way, Shakespeare blurs the distinction between anagogic exegesis, which assumes that a deep truth can be excavated from the literal surface, and skeptical semiotics, which conclude that there is no traceable connection between things and the words that denote them. More precisely, he seems to be providing these new semiotics with a providential aura—perhaps illusionistically, manipulatively, to prevent his audience from associating the new problematics of meaning with meaninglessness (and therefore fleeing horrified into denial).

Shakespeare is unmistakably alert to the problem of a capitalist system that pretends to be fair because maximally efficient, and efficient because open, whereas it is actually rigged to give the insiders a perpetual edge. Despite all the posturing about Venice's neutrality, the trial as well as the casket test show how foreigners can be put at a fatal disadvantage in what purports to be a fair game. But, by the end, the Ponzi scheme of capitalist circulation (if such it is) is blurred into the cornucopia of wealth production associated with Portia's married fertility.

So Shakespeare could be accused of selling a reassurance he doesn't quite believe in; but of course, not quite believing is essentially what he is selling. Like Portia in the trial scene, Shakespeare seems willing to promote an ameliorative reading in place of any absolute truth. Several years passed before Shakespeare, in *Hamlet*, conceded that imperfect knowledge and the substitution of representation for identity are felt as painful losses in the human family. Another decade had to pass before Shakespeare, in *The Winter's Tale*, combined the insights of these two riddling earlier plays, acknowledging without despair that these incompletions of truth and presence are both agonizing and necessary for that human family.

Coda: Shakespeare's *Merchant* and Hooker's *Laws*

The emergence of a cultural strategy for tolerating indeterminacy and indirect or imperfect knowledge in an era struggling toward religious and social toleration is more than a mere coincidence of words. The two projects can be connected (anachronistically) through the concept of tolerances in engineering: a degree of variation that can be accommodated, imprecisions that do not compromise function. In an era of burgeoning multiculturalism, there was predictably a resistance, but obviously a value, to accepting that various kinds of people were still people, and might be Elect or Chosen or Brethren in any of a variety of ways, including by imitation and analogy. Late-Renaissance culture amplified the tendency of the human mind to crave a single and simple truth, and overcoming that craving was a rehearsal for overcoming all the social intolerances produced by the same reactionary tendency. The fact that this effort failed to prevent religious persecution and civil war in this period, where the tyranny of metal over flesh became awfully direct, only affirms how important the project was. It dug the conceptual and emotional foundations for the programs of tolerance that arrived across much of Europe later in the seventeenth century.

The unmistakable power of *The Merchant of Venice* in the theater and in history arises partly from an intense internal contradiction: the play is a document of religious bigotry, doubtless at times even an amplifier of such bigotry, that is nonetheless close kin to what was (along with the imported work of Erasmus) the most important document of religious toleration in Shakespeare's culture. Shortly after drafting this chapter, I read books 2 and 5 of Richard Hooker's *Of the Laws of Ecclesiastical Polity*—the former published two or three years before *The Merchant of Venice* appeared, the latter a year or two after. The correlations struck me as remarkable—at least, more significant, because less predictable, than the opposite sequence in which one reads a philosophy and then discovers it informing a Shakespeare play. Though I see no evidence of direct connection, these correlations certainly seem to be something more than mere coincidence.[63] Shakespeare and Hooker are both seeking to bridge the same conceptual division, trying to insist that one can surrender the goal of an absolute legible or tangible truth without falling into radical subjectivity or nihilistic despair. They assuage doubt by tolerating doubt, recognizing it as integral to perception and faith.

If sensory perception usually seems to get us where we want to go—and moral intuition where we ought to go—then it seems clear we have some grasp of the world, and exactly how that world manages to reproduce itself inside our consciousness may not much matter. Hooker's discussion of the quest for truth seems more pertinent to Descartes' quest for "clear and distinct ideas" that cannot be doubted than to any Puritan's quest for cleansing away church rituals:

> The truth is, that the mind of man desireth evermore to know the truth according to the most infallible certainty which the nature of things can yield. The greatest assurance generally with all men is that which we have by plain aspect and intuitive beholding. Where we cannot attain unto this, there what appeareth to be true by strong and invincible demonstration, such as wherein it is by any way not possible to be deceived, thereunto the mind doth necessarily assent, neither is it in the choice thereof to do otherwise. And in case these both do fail, then what way greatest probability leadeth, thither the mind doth evermore incline.[64]

And though the Word of God or the proof of reason should outweigh countless opinions, in the absence of such Word or proof, a general predominance of established opinion should predominate, "although it did not appear what reason or what Scripture led them to be of that judgment, yet to their very bare judgment somewhat a reasonable man would attribute, notwithstanding the common imbecilities which are incident to our nature . . . the most which can be inferred upon such plenty of divine testimonies is only this, That *some things* which they maintain, as far as *some men* can *probably conjecture,* do *seem* to have been out of Scripture *not absurdly* gathered" (*Laws* 2.7.5, 2.7.9; emphases in original). Hooker seems hardly more certain here than Lorenzo—sounding more like a nervous lawyer than a passionate bridegroom—in judging Jessica:[65]

> Beshrow me but I love her heartily,
> For she is wise, if I can judge of her,
> And fair she is, if that mine eyes be true,
> And true she is, as she hath prov'd herself.
>   (2.6.52–55)

The Merchant of Venice creates a world in which almost every kind of certainty is exposed to qualification and potential refutation—"negative capability" in overdrive, with only love, and the necessity of action, to brake it. Indeed, the need of mortals to procreate is, for Hooker in the *Laws* as for Shakespeare in act 5 of *Merchant* and in the comedies generally, a crucial incentive for letting love reconcile people to imperfections and substitutions, as they strive to imitate God.[66]

Both Hooker and Shakespeare suggest that reading for good intentions, rather than demanding any strict correlation with Scripture,[67] allows a moral navigation through the earthly life. As allegory does not necessarily fail when some details fail to fit, so "it doth not therefore follow that of necessity we shall sin, unless we expressly intend this in every such particular." Instead, it "requireth no more than only our general presupposed willingness to please God . . . although no special clause or sentence of Scripture be in every such action set before men's eyes to warrant it" (*Laws* 2.2.1–2).[68] This kind of latitude is essential, cognitively as much as theologically, for a society to function: "For in every action of common life to find out some sentence clearly and infallibly setting before our eyes what we ought to do (seem we in Scripture never so expert) would trouble us more than we are aware. In weak and tender minds we little know what misery this strict opinion would breed, besides the stops it would make in the whole course of all men's lives and actions" (*Laws* 2.7.7).[69] One can, like the Gentiles, be ignorant of Scripture and still "notwithstanding judge rightly of the qualities of Christian men's actions" (*Laws* 2.3.1). What matters about earthly creatures is not perfection, but rather "an appetite or desire, whereby they incline to something which they may be."[70] As Portia points out, it is a mistake to assume that "to do were as easy as to know what were good to do" (1.2.12); but dance to her domestic music with enough lowercase grace, and the uppercase Grace may take care of itself.

In these passages Hooker is primarily attacking the Puritan rejection of any ceremonies not specified by Scripture. Defending an episcopalian mode of church discipline at that cultural moment, however, required defending an epistemology neither realist nor solipsist, but more like what is sometimes called constructive skepticism. What people do with the universe is *participate* in it; our view is partial, our role too multiple to define, and yet here we are, finding our ways, to some extent collectively.[71] So we need not follow radical skepticism in deeming that universe utterly lost to us. Hooker warns that the Zwinglian view of Eucharist would lead people to understand it "only as of a shadow, destitute, empty and void of Christ" but there is now "a general agreement concerning . . . the *real participation* of Christ and of life in his body *by means of this sacrament*" (*Laws* 5.67.2). "The bread and cup are his body and blood because they are causes instrumental upon the receipt whereof the *participation* of his body and blood ensueth. For that which produceth any certain effect is not vainly nor improperly said to be that very effect whereunto it tendeth. Every cause is the effect which groweth from it" (5.67.5). Thus, to know things by their fruits is appropriate; to know them by what blossoms in our consciousness as a result of them is sufficient knowledge. As long as Christ's body and blood become manifest "in the very heart and soul of him which receiveth them" (5.67.6), the notion of exactly where and when his substance is located in the sacrament seems unimportant.

Early in the 1590s, Richard Hooker recognized that finding a peaceful middle road between the Catholic and Puritan factions required finding an ontology that reconciled objective and subjective readings of the material world, with the Lord's Supper as the test case. The effort to establish a *via media* between the "papist" insistence that Christ's body and blood were truly, fully, and materially present in the Eucharistic bread and wine, and the Swiss Reformation's insistence that the body and blood were only figuratively or memorially present, necessarily entailed the same argument I have shown dividing Cavalier from Metaphysical poetics: the difference between a belief that humanity's task is to serve, observe, and take into ourselves an external physical reality, which carries within it a morally intelligent hierarchical order; and on the other hand a belief that humanity's task is to create within our own psyches a transcendent reality, to convert a corrupt material tyranny, by will and word and intuition, into a divinity that is always radical and always on the verge of either slipping away or being crushed by an institutional order.

The Catholic and Puritan factions each build from a claim to antiquity and fundamental truth. To resist and reconcile those claims, Hooker must insist that those need not always be the criteria—that human experience consists of progressive accommodations, improvisations, and approximations. Against the atavistic absolutism that underlies pastoral epistemology and religious extremism alike, Hooker adapts the legacies of Heraclitus and Pyrrho. Along with Shakespeare, Hooker was already visibly responding to renascent skepticism (Bacon was drawing on Montaigne in these same years) and seeking a resolution to the problems of sustaining morality in a world that would never quite match the Scriptural absolutes and of finding truth about that earthly world that people never quite hold except secondhand and by analogy.

The point is not that *The Merchant of Venice* was secretly conceived as a displaced *amicus curiae* brief for the compromises Hooker was articulating at about the same time in the same city. The point instead is that both authors proposed similar solutions to the loss of nature as a self-sufficient point of reference and to the awkward shift in the relationship between words and things—between mental states and material reality—that this book has been describing. An epistemological middle ground was needed to reconcile the soon-to-be-warring religious factions (as described in my chapter 5) and to move beyond "a mercantilist conception of value wherein money functions either as an objective measure or transparent medium of exchange" to the acceptance of "relative and fluctuating value."[72] Both Shakespeare and Hooker appear to be building on the Erasmian tradition (which set skepticism against dogmatism) and anticipating, by a century, the tolerant philosophy of John Locke:

Lack of certitude did not drive Locke, however, to scepticism, despair or a reactive rationalism. The experience of the senses led to the accumulation and consolidation of probable truths sufficient for God's purposes for man. Similarly, although no moral absolutes were graven upon the heart or head, the psychological mechanisms of pleasure and pain, desire and aversion, did in fact bring about a sound-enough practical grasp of good and bad, vice and virtue . . . his legacy to the eighteenth century was a cautious confidence in the educability of man as a progressive creature.[73]

Still, one could wish for something more positive than philosophical consolation and the evasion of political conflict. To see this *via media* as a shimmering highway to heaven—to change from these infinite half-tones of earth-tones and metallic gray-scale to the vivid green of nature's living presence—we must turn to Thomas Traherne.

Chapter 9
Thomas Traherne: The World as Present

The Sun in your Ey, is as much to you as the Sun in the Heavens. for by this, the other is Enjoyed. It would shine on all Rivers Trees and Beasts, in vain to you, could you not think upon it. . . . The World within you is an offering returned. . . . For GOD hath made you able to Creat Worlds in your own mind, which are more Precious unto Him then those which He Created. . . . a Thought of the World, or the World in a Thought is more Excellent then the World, becaus it is Spiritual and Nearer unto GOD. The Material World is Dead and feeleth Nothing.

—Thomas Traherne, *Centuries*, 2.90

. . . all our Thoughts must be Infant-like and Clear: the Powers of our Soul free from the Leven of this World, and disentangled from mens conceits and customs. Grit in the Ey or the yellow Jandice will not let a Man see those Objects truly that are before it. And therefore it is requisit that we should be as very Strangers to the Thoughts Customs and Opinions of men in this World as if we were but little Children. So those Things would appear to us only which do to Children when they are first Born. Ambitions, Trades, Luxuries, inordinat Affections, Casual and Accidental Riches invented since the fall would be gone, and only those Things appear, which did to Adam in Paradice, in the same Light, and in the same Colors.

—*Centuries*, 3.5

"Ecstatic" is the adjective many readers would reflexively apply to Thomas Traherne's rapturous writings,[1] but for the purposes of my argument it is important to note that he is almost the opposite—instatic, re-instating objects with identity by taking them into himself, rather than being lifted out of himself. It is a distinction almost without a difference, because the relationship is purely amorous and never adversarial: things are present essentially within him, but this renders them so vivid that the ego nearly dissolves into the given universe. Because the very purpose of that universe is to serve and delight the individual soul, Traherne's religious psychology ultimately rejects any version of

the Eastern apophatic theologies that describe God by negations of human categories, by blankings out of what the human mind can hold. He inverts (but
does not need to reject) the assertion of George Herbert's "Mattens" that humanity's role amounts, "and richly, to serve Thee." The dilemma that so haunts
Traherne's ambient culture—that to see God only indirectly is idolatry, but to
see Him directly is death—disappears in Traherne's childlike vision of nature,
which is open, full, intense, and unthreatened. There is life in Arcadia yet.

Objects thus have a glorious plenitude and presence for Traherne, in a way
that challenges the system I have been describing—at least by complicating it,
and perhaps by offering an alternative path that now looks merely like a quaint
dead-end country lane only because Western intellectuals have driven so far on
the other, materialist-pessimist freeway. Traherne swerves off of any straight
road that drives people either toward objects and away from God, or toward
God and away from objects; away from or toward subjectivism. The fact that
Bertram Dobell's hagiographic introduction to his 1906 edition (which helped
lift Traherne from oblivion) speaks of Traherne as "a Berkeleian before Berkeley
was born"[2] only reveals the limited choices offered by a retrospective vision. If
Traherne "avoided the spirit-matter duality,"[3] it is largely because he avoided the
subject-object duality. "Whereas Herbert locates his Davidic temple in the heart,
and Vaughan in the created world, Traherne locates it in the mind of the regen-
erate man who possesses true thoughts and conceptions of God, the self, the
world, and of felicity"[4]—which four are all pretty much one and the same.

Where Marvell offers an antagonistic "Dialogue Between the Soul and
Body," Traherne offers celebratory "Thanksgivings" for each that imply their syn-
ergy.[5] In Traherne's universe, the soul itself cannot function without objects to
give it occasion and dimension; nor do objects have any meaningful reality without producing a pious joy in the soul. The problem of knowing the essence of an
object is no problem at all, if its essence, its very being, is (as God intends) inseparable from that knowledge: it takes on the form of our knowing of it, and we
take on the form of the thing known: "The Rays of the Sun carry Light in them as
they Pass through the Air, but go on in vain till they meet an Object: and there
they are Expresst. They Illuminat a Mirror, and are Illuminated by it . . . represent the Effigies from whence they came. . . . Even so your Soul in its Rays and
Powers is unknown . . . But by their Objects are discerned to be present: being illuminated by them. . . . For as Light varieth upon all objects whither it cometh,
and returneth with the Form and figure of them: so is the Soul Transformed into
the Being of its Object" (*Centuries*, 2.78). If he had not dismissed Traherne as
"more a mystic than a poet,"[6] T. S. Eliot might have been obliged to acknowledge
at least one flourish of "unified sensibility" in later seventeenth-century verse.
When, at the beginning of his "First Century" (1.3), Traherne promises to "utter

Things that have been Kept Secret from the foundation of the World. Things Strange yet Common, Incredible, yet Known; Most High, yet Plain," he seems to be seeking (via Matthew 13:35) an originary point that would repair the rift that I have suggested between Metaphysical and Cavalier styles of consciousness.

The material objects of the world, especially natural ones, are the ultimate in revelation, pleasure, and purpose for the human creature. But they are so because that is how God intended them—a God conceived a bit like Santa Claus in his workshop, creating toys for the joy of the human child and taking his pleasure in the way the children enjoy them, not playing with the toys (or even the children, really) himself. God, Traherne points out (in a refraction of Augustinian theology that finally resembles Jacob Boehme's), not only does not need objects, He cannot have them. Knowing all, He cannot know any one thing, nor does He have our pleasurable division and limitation of senses by which to enjoy them. To love God requires an openness to something that transcends the senses—"We see the Heavens with our Eys, and Know the World with our Sences. But had we no Eys, nor Sences, we should see Infinitie like the H. Angels" (*Centuries*, 5.3)—but it does not contradict them. Traherne leads into his discussion of the value of wanting with the observations that "Pictures are made Curious by Lights and Shades, which without Shades, could not be."[7] The problem with divine perception is the lack of contrast produced by absolute light—a kind of aesthetic theodicy: "Suppose therfore that the most Beautifull that is Possible were created. What would follow? Being a silent and Quiet Object of the Ey, it would be no more noted, then if it had not a Being" (*Centuries*, 2.20). To see God is death; to see like God is to see like the dead: with a blinding lack of differentiation. So people are driven from the pure, direct love of God to something like the fetishism of the *blason*; but, to Traherne, this tactic of divide-and-cognize is a healthy perversion (*Centuries*, 2.68; cf. 1.23). It is a gleaming version of the dark insight underlying Renaissance Gnosticism, which warned that wherever a person has experience is necessarily a place the true God has partially abandoned. The Kabbala of Isaac Luria described a God obliged to contract his absolute presence in order to allow Creation, to create a space in which difference, autonomy, and all their dynamics could function.

Human consciousness thus does, in Traherne's worldview, something like what language does in Valla's: creates, by embodying, a reality which would not have definable being without it. The speaker of Herbert's "The Collar" can find only a satanic temptation to physical enjoyment:

> All wasted?
> Not so, my heart: but there is fruit,
>   And thou hast hands.
>   (lines 16–18)

Traherne's "The Estate" distinctly echoes this passage, for the sake of insisting that, on the contrary, physical enjoyment of the world is what the body is made for, and thus to be enjoyed is what the world is made for:

> Shall there no outward objects be,
>   For these to see and taste?
> Not so, my God, for outward joys and pleasures
> Are even the things for which my limbs are treasures.
>   My palate is a touch-stone fit
>   To taste how good Thou art.
>   (lines 11–16)

Again humanity seems to be a tool by which God can more fully (because more partially) appreciate his own Creation. "Had He not made an eye to be the Sphere / Of all things, none of these would e'er appear" ("The Improvement," lines 23–24). Divine intention is still the ultimate, but things in themselves are the only embodiment of divine intention people have, and we should indeed be absorbed and dazzled by them, not needing to look past them to have an intuition of the divine benevolence manifest in their very existence. If there is mediation, it is humanity as a medium between God and objects, rather than objects between humanity and God or God between humanity and objects; the emphatic complaints of iconoclasm and the euphemistic ones of empiricism both disappear into a vision of the human race as God's vision.

Neither the exterior of objects nor the interior of the human mind deceives.[8] In a visionary mode Traherne thus asserts what Descartes asserts philosophically: that the benevolence of God dissipates these skeptical threats, that it makes no sense to suppose that God makes no sense. Not that any of this would impose on the Pyrrhonists very much: they easily brushed off many challenges from those who tried to establish as a ground the divine intention of making objects sensible (in both meanings of the word), the idea that God tuned our sensors ideally to the objects He provided, thus authorizing us to trust sense-data. Even before Descartes raised the devastating demon-hypothesis—what if some superior power were deliberately misleading our senses or misaligning our reason?—skeptics were already able to point out that people often differ or fail in perceiving because of factors such as age, illness, or cultural difference. So perhaps Traherne can only evade the problem, not really refute the argument, by situating himself in a perfect original body of childhood wonder, with childhood being (as George Herbert asserted) health—health of the senses and thereby the spirit. Traherne posits a perfect clarity of perception in a universal spokeslad of the self. In a less systematic and less minimalist way than Descartes, Traherne plants his epistemological flag—his foundation for interpreting reality—in radical egoism; there is no doubt that, for Traherne, "I" is a capital letter. He treats this egoism as a worshipful acceptance of God, who has decreed it for soul-making and His vicarious pleasure, rather than a Promethean defiance. The difficulty of knowing whether there is anything beyond one's thoughts, Traherne and Descartes finally agree, is no reason to underestimate the way those thoughts reflect, manifest, and enjoy divinity. Precisely the solipsistic illusions that so trouble Shakespeare and Marvell—the fear of narcissistically mistaking the water's reflecting surface for a real exterior universe—become, in Traherne's "Shadows in the Water," a child's insights into the deepest truths:[9]

> In unexperienc'd Infancy
> Many a sweet Mistake doth ly:
> Mistake tho false, intending tru;
> A *Seeming* somewhat more than *View*;
>   That doth instruct the Mind
>   In Things that ly behind,
> And many Secrets to us show
> Which afterwards we com to know.
>
> Thus did I by the Water's brink
> Another world beneath me think.
>   (lines 1–10)

Otherness need never be more absolute than that.

Traherne thus brings together two of the chief themes this book has been tracing: his writing suggests that, if one regresses to a childlike innocence, then the dualism that such regressions were persistently trying to mend in this period simply melts into a glowing universe of mutual affirmations. Like so many mystical solutions, this can sometimes look facile: brute force applied to a problem under the claim of innocent acceptance, rationalization covered by a loud abjuration of rationality. Traherne's vision of childhood as itself visionary is surrounded by other gestures of primitivism: a worship of nature as Eden, a search for origins, and a mistrust of cultural artifacts and mediations—including, prominently, those of money (in its capitalist function as exchange value) and institutional Catholicism (in its impositions on the original Scripture and its impositions of priests between the soul and its recognitions of God).[10] He seeks to relume "The first Light which shined in my Infancy in its Primitive and Innocent Clarity" (*Centuries*, 3.7), and insists that God

> made the truth,
> In infancy and tender youth,
> So obvious to
> Our easy view
> That it doth prepossess our Soul. . . .
>   ("The Choice," lines 22–26)

Dobell cites "absolute spontaneity" as the one quality in which Traherne excels all other poets,[11] and Traherne's own prefatory "The Author to the Critical Peruser" claims to show

> The naked Truth . . .
> Whose inward Beauties very few hav known,
> A Simple Light, transparent Words.
> . . . .
>   An easy Stile drawn from a native vein,
> A clearer Stream than that which Poets feign.
>   (lines 1–3, 17–18)

Traherne's own "Advertisement to the Reader" of his *Roman Forgeries* accuses the papists of trying to "disguise and cover the face of *Primitive Antiquities*, which ought to be preserved most sacred and pure"—a crime Traherne claims to prevent by "Searching the most Old and Authentick Records."[12] Traherne's devotion to recovering true origins obviously went beyond an intense nostalgia for childhood and its enchanted view of nature. It reached directly into theology and, for that purpose, into philology.

Furthermore, Traherne's persistent declamations against gold and the material fripperies of market value reflect a parallel devotion to the direct and original value of things:[13] their use value, distinguishable in Marxist and other ways from their function as indirect value, as objects of what René Girard would call "triangulated desire," which values something because someone else values it. "The Apostacy" occurred

>   when I once with blemisht Eys
> Began their Pence and Toys to view,
> Drown'd in their Customs, I became
> A Stranger to the Shining Skies.
>   (lines 58–61)

The "Infant-Ey" sees reality and hence knows truth and hence assigns value perfectly, until monetary values distort it and his vision decays:

A simple Light from all Contagion free,
A Beam that's purely Spiritual, an Ey
That's altogether Virgin, Things doth see
   Ev'n like unto the Deity:
That is, it shineth in an hevenly Sence,
And round about (unmov'd) its Light dispence.
. . . .
O that my Sight had ever simple been!
And never faln into a grosser state!
Then might I evry Object still have seen
   (As now I see a golden Plate)
In such an hev'nly Light, as to descry
In it, or by it, my Felicity.
           (lines 1–6, 19–24)

In a condition of "Wonder," the mediated symbols of worth melt back into original beauty: "Rich diamond and pearl and gold / In every place was seen," so that everyone's "wealth was everywhere." In "Eden," Traherne inhabits a world where the Great Mediators, "Hard silver and dry gold / As yet lay under ground," and so he can share Adam's "original simplicity"; in other words, the absence of monetary exchange value is again equated with some primal condition of innocence in which the beauty of nature is its own. "The Vision" similarly laments the danger that "Ten thousand heaps of vain confused treasure / Will but oppress the land" if his countrymen lose sight of the divine beauty all around them. Warnings that "Riches are but Tarnish and Gilded Vanities . . . till you prize one Vertu, abov a Trunk of Mony, you can never be Happy" (*Centuries*, 4.89) may sound like banal moralism to modern ears, but for Traherne the distinction between meretricious exterior values and simple interior ones runs very deep and permeates his epistemology. The mistrust of monetary value appears again in "The Apostacy":

A juicy Herb, or Spire of Grass,
In useful Virtu, native Green,
   An Em'rald doth surpass;
Hath in't more Valu, tho less seen.
           (lines 6–9)

For Traherne, religious "Apostacy" is not merely a metaphor for this failure to value ordinary organic natural life: they are both facets of the same fall into a distortion of vision produced by mediations.

Traherne persistently contrasts the great value of sunlight to the empty value of gold—exactly the values that Jonson's Volpone equates in his cynically worshipful opening lines. For Traherne, the sun is worth more than "all the

Gold and Silver in all Worlds ... it was the Gift of GOD and could not be bought with Mony." Three paragraphs later, Traherne is again belittling the value of "A Purs of Gold ... Nature is still nearest to Natural Things ... Nature Knows no such Riches, but Art and Error makes them. Not the God of Nature, but Sin only was the Parent of Them" (*Centuries*, 3.6, 3.9). Though "poor" and "naked," Adam in Eden had full riches (*Centuries*, 4.36), precisely because there was "No Gold, nor Trade, nor Silver there" ("Adam," line 13). Alienation from natural function and (hence) original value, entanglement in the world of exchange where trade entails knowledge of otherness—these are both cause and effect of the Fall that (Traherne suggests) is replicated in each modern social being.

The Retreat from Civilization

Traherne's pattern of enthusiasms and dislikes certainly suggests a kinship to the deism of the eighteenth century, and to the Romanticism of the end of that century too—alternative solutions that Traherne apparently foresaw and attempted to fuse. Focusing on the wonders of nature, he argued systematically for transcendent bliss, elaborately for simplicity. He shares the foresight that weighs on Jacob Ruisdael's landscapes—the artistic recognition of what it would mean to live in a nature unmediated by culture, a nature whose meaning is identical to its presence—but Traherne sees it through rose-colored glasses, brightly. He may lack Wordsworth's sustained naturalness, and Blake's ability to surprise by condensation, but Traherne anticipates them both astonishingly—the first three sections of the "Third Century" alone would make the case—and he speaks in a voice of timeless joy that also answered some of his own time's anguish. The celebration of childhood vision, and its relation to the moral truths and dazzling joyfulness of nature, emerges in the poetry of two eras (we are probably now in another such) especially anxious about the incursions of rational philosophy, trade, and urbanization. Traherne's incompatibility with a modernist aesthetic for poetry—which built the Metaphysical canon on "such criteria as logic, paradox, drama, and irony, all criteria that in one way or another suggest a unified, fixed poetic effort"[14]—only partly explains the neglect of his literary achievements. That his work—spiritually beautiful if not always poetically subtle—has seemed sufficiently irrelevant as to disappear from the canon suggests that critics have forgotten how pressing the *crise Pyrrhoniste* became, and have perhaps forgotten also that the modern resolution of that crisis was not a foregone conclusion, in the mid-seventeenth century.

In his study of idolatry and capitalism, David Hawkes emphasizes "the economic dimension of Traherne's thought," as opposed to his echoes of Neoplatonism[15] or anticipations of Romanticism: "Traherne identifies this erroneous and alienated mode of perception as the epistemological effect of the market economy, and his general philosophical conclusions follow from his economic premises. The oft-remarked singularity of his thought stems from its unique historical location: It is a critique of political economy that postdates the era when such a critique could be mounted using purely religious criteria, but that antedates the time when it could be advanced on materialist grounds."[16]

Though finally applicable to only a respectable fraction of Traherne's works, Hawkes's thesis provides a useful corrective to purely sentimental responses (which Traherne provokes often enough to be well worth correcting).[17] Traherne seldom writes directly about economics; and even the persistent disdain for gold (on which Hawkes puts great weight) is not consistent, since at times the word appears in paeans to God's manifest glories on earth, and in any case often looks more like a facile legacy of the commonest medieval *contemptus mundi* themes than a deep analysis of market finance. But it is certainly worth recognizing that Traherne was not opposing some random set of worldly-wise attitudes and attributes such as greed, group thinking, urban settings, a preference for artificial frippery over simple nature, and bureaucratized religion. He was, I think, disturbed by nascent capitalism for the same reason he (like the other writers and painters this book has been discussing) was disturbed by a range of cultural developments in the preceding decades, which have in common the onslaught of mediations, a loss of the simplicity and directness that had supposedly once been present in childhood, in Jesus Christ, in production for use, in country villages, in Eden. Traherne sensed what might be wrong with capitalism because what was wrong with capitalism was something he was already sensing impinging on his world.

It even drove him into a seemingly faux-naive psychological posture, and into relatively crude literary forms (childishly forced rhyme and meter, and the merely numerical formalizing of the *Centuries* prose poems), in what seems a desperate if joyous effort (like a person loudly singing away his terrors) to spare his consciousness the costs of the sophistications that mid-seventeenth-century London was offering him on every side. As Marjorie Hope Nicolson observes, there has been a notable accumulation of evidence "that Traherne was deeply affected by the discoveries of the new science and the implications of the new philosophy."[18] So we must study the oddities of Traherne not on the basis of what he did not know, but rather on the basis of what he was determined to stop knowing and what manner of knowing he rejected.

These poems are therefore not (as they often pretend and have often been taken) the blinking genius of innocence; the poet is not a child, but an adult using childhood rhetorically and tendentiously. Though "no modern scholar has ever considered Traherne a serious or original thinker,"[19] and even an outstanding scholar of Renaissance prose remarks that "Traherne is better described as overflowing than as meditating,"[20] the preface to Traherne's *Christian Ethicks* refers intelligently to Pierre Charron's influentially skeptical *De la sagesse*. It seems wrong, in crucial ways, to view Traherne as the kind of simplistically idealizing "Christian Neoplatonist" who "viewed the corporeal world as a less perfect (because material) manifestation of the pure intelligibility of God's mind."[21] Traherne shows no signs of thinking this, and indeed implies there would be no way to know it; the interpretive error suggests the largely unpredictable turn in Traherne's thought away from dualisms, towards an embrace of physical reality as man's gift to God as well as God's gift to man. As Hawkes shrewdly observes, "The problem, as Traherne presents it, is emphatically not with matter per se; it is rather with a systematically mistaken tendency of human perception."[22] Again, I would amend Hawkes's identification of that mistaken system as capitalism, to include the many systems of mediation that roused anxiety and nostalgia in seventeenth-century England. Just because critics have been wrong to assume "that Traherne views this false consciousness as part of the eternal human condition"[23] does not oblige us to explain Traherne's view entirely in terms of economic history.

Certainly by looking at the alienated markers of things rather than at the things themselves, the Renaissance quest for absolutes dooms itself to perpetual incompletion, to unfulfillment. So monetary greed becomes a prominent version and symptom of the broader misdirected yearning: "men get one Hundred Pound a year that they may get another; and having two covet Eight, and there is no End of all their Labor; becaus the Desire of their Soul is Insatiable" (*Centuries*, 1.22). This is not a fault of the soul: its transitive verbs would be healthy, if it weren't for their indirect objects.

Traherne dreams of a time when words were not such alienated markers, when Adamic language (like Adamic sexuality in *Paradise Lost*) was both potent and innocent. At moments Traherne's willingness merely to name and list things recalls the old joke about the comedians' convention where a speaker can rouse laughter merely by shouting the number of any joke in their standard collection.[24] If the words are identical to the things, then poetic saying does not require any arduous making. But fallen language is at least under suspicion of conspiring with money to come between us and things; sometimes it is tempting to make this mistrust an excuse for the awkwardness of Traherne's prosody, as if he were forbidding readers to mistake his description for the actual spiritual experience in all its loveliness and grandeur. In "Dumbness," Traherne clearly suggests the way the acquisition of language replicates the Fall from the Garden in each human life, casting an abysmal shadow—the rectilinear shadow of the dictionary—between that life and Creation in its primal innocence. Man[kind] was "therefore speechless made at first" (line 5);

> Wise Nature made him deaf, too, that He might
> Not be disturbed, while he doth take delight
> In inward things, nor be depraved with tongues,
> Nor injured by the errors and the wrongs
> That mortal words convey.
> . . . .
> I then my Bliss did, when my silence, break.
> My non-intelligence of human words
> Ten thousand pleasures unto me affords.
>   (lines 9–13, 20–22)

Here, as earlier, words are depicted as a contagious disease, the corruption of a Passover cleanliness:

> Before my thoughts were leaven'd with theirs, before
> There any mixture was . . .
> . . . .
> There I was in the world myself alone

where his delightful duty was

>   . . . with clearer eyes
> To see all creatures full of Deities;
> Especially one's self.
>   (lines 27–41)

In this mode of divine synesthesia, his unconstrained sight allowed

> every stone, and every star a tongue,
> And every gale of wind a curious song.
> . . . .
>   . . . all things did come
> With voices and instructions; but when I
> Had gained a tongue, their power began to die.
>   (lines 61–68)

But they have not died, and in the emphatic moralizing line of the poem, Traherne attributes that survival to an initial originary innocence: "*The first*

Impressions are Immortal all" (line 85). The possibility of experience undistorted by language, which Marvell and others locate only in an impossible sophistication or in death itself, Traherne characteristically finds easily accessible in the native joys of life.

In "News" it is the fresh and innocent eye that makes the universe valuable, perhaps even makes it possible:

> Yet thus it was: The gem,
> The diadem,
> The ring enclosing all
> That stood upon this earthly ball;
> The Heavenly Eye,
> Much wider than the sky,
> Wherein they all included were;
> The glorious Soul that was the King
> Made to possess them, did appear
> A small and little thing!
> (lines 47–56)

This recalls some themes of Milton's "Nativity Ode"—especially the triumph of small holy things over grand material ones (and, to adapt Dr. Johnson's sour quip about second marriage, the triumph of hope over experience). In "Innocence," Traherne speculates that "Nature is so pure, / And custom only vicious" (lines 37–38), which means that he can become an Adam again if he follows the poem's closing imperative, much the same imperative that echoes through many forms (even Bacon's) of Renaissance primitivism: "I must become a child again" (line 60). Amid a Reformation culture that, despite its own regressive ideals, resisted the association of childhood with innocence—rejecting, for example, the visual tradition that had so decisively associated Jesus with infancy and the theological tradition of a limbo to protect those who died early from hell—Traherne shares with more political visionaries such as the Ranters a determination to defend the purity of early perceptions.

Indeed, in "The Preparative," Traherne feels obliged to push back even further, toward the oblivion before his birth, perhaps even before his conception, so that his participation in nature can stand uncorrupted:[25]

> My body being dead, my limbs unknown;
> Before I skill'd to prize
> Those living stars mine eyes,
> Before my tongue or cheeks were to me shown.
> Before I knew my hands were mine,

Or that my sinews did my members join,
    When neither nostril, foot nor ear,
    As yet was seen, or felt, or did appear:
        I was within
A house I knew not, newly cloth'd with skin.
                    (lines 1–10)

In that condition prior to cognition, the universe can become fully present:

Then was my soul my only all to me,
    A living endless eye,
    Just bounded with the sky
. . . .
A naked simple pure Intelligence.
                    (lines 11–20)

There are seemingly receptors in each human being for each reality of the world—Traherne describes the tongue in terms that anticipate Immanuel Kant and even Noam Chomsky—but Traherne remembers something before such categories, and the reflexive, inter-reflective complexities that come (as skeptics have always argued) with multiple senses:

For sight inherits beauty, hearing sounds,
    The nostril sweet perfumes,
    All tastes have hidden rooms
Within the tongue; and feeling feeling wounds
    With pleasure and delight; but I
Forgot the rest, and was all sight or eye.
    Unbodied and devoid of care,
Just as in Heaven the holy Angels are,
        For simple sense
Is Lord of all created excellence.
                    (lines 31–40)

Ideally, human experience is a pure reflection of reality, but that reality itself reflects divine energies:

Pure empty powers that did nothing loath,
    Did like the fairest glass,
    Or spotless polished brass,
Themselves soon in their object's image clothe.
    Divine impressions when they came,

Did quickly enter and my soul inflame.
 'Tis not the object, but the light
That maketh Heaven: 'tis a purer sight.
(lines 51–58)

Traherne thus appears to exemplify what Montaigne could only imagine: "If this ray of divinity touched us at all, it would appear all over: not only our words, but also our works would bear its light and luster. Everything that came from us would be seen to be illuminated by this noble brightness."[26]

In lamenting the impositions of "custom" on this pure vision. Traherne is partly manifesting his psychology (asserting a healthy narcissism) and partly manifesting his theology (attacking Catholicism as the most prominent institution imposing mediations between the devotional instinct and the Christian God). Yet Traherne's otherworldly worldliness makes him as much opposed to a Calvinist view of human alienation from God and nature as to the Catholic institutions of alienation: "our Misery proceedeth ten thousand times more from the outward Bondage of Opinion and Custom, then from any inward corruption or Depravation of Nature . . . it is not our Parents Loyns, so much as our Parents lives, that Enthrals and Blinds us . . . in my Pure Primitive Virgin Light, while my Apprehensions were natural, and unmixed, I can not remember, but that I was ten thousand times more prone to Good and Excellent Things, then evil" (*Centuries*, 3.8).

His quest for a purity that takes in rather than pushes away the physical universe aligns Traherne also (though both would be surprised to hear it) with Francis Bacon's program to purge science of traditions received as wisdom but obstructing the practice of empirical research.[27] Traherne might well have written, as Bacon wrote, that "God hath framed the mind of man as a mirror or glass capable of the image of the universal world, and joyful to receive the impression thereof."[28] The New Adam and the New Organon are achievable by the same process of clarification and receptivity to the manifest truth. Juxtapose Bacon's warnings, in the *New Organon*, against the four "Idols" distorting objectivity with Traherne's complaints about the idolatry distorting worship—for example, my epigraph from Traherne's "Third Century":

we must disrobe our selvs of all fals Colors, and unclothe our Souls of evil Habits; all our Thoughts must be Infant-like and Clear: the Powers of our Soul free from the Leven of this World, and disentangled from mens conceits and customs. Grit in the Ey or the yellow Jandice will not let a Man see those Objects truly that are before it. And therfore it is requisit that we should be as very Strangers to the Thoughts Customs and Opinions of men in this World.

What Traherne promises in order to glorify "The Person" applies also to the way he wants to read the material universe:

> Mistake me not, I do not mean to bring
> > New robes, but to display the thing:
> Nor paint, nor clothe, nor crown, nor add a ray,
> But glorify by taking all away.
> > > > (lines 13–16)

Things are thus best known

> When we all metaphors remove,
> > For metaphors conceal,
> > And only vapours prove.
> > > (lines 24–26)

This removal he compares to the glories of anatomical autopsy.

In other words, Traherne's "Preparative" for ideal experience becomes, by the final stanza, a Zen version of Bacon's preparations for ideal science:

> A disentangled and a naked sense,
> > A mind that's unpossest,
> > A disengaged breast,
> An empty and a quick Intelligence
> > Acquainted with the golden mean.
> > > (lines 61–65)

This sounds less like a religious poem than like a résumé submitted for employment in the laboratories of the Royal Society. When he asks, "Can you then be Righteous, unless you be Just in rendering to Things their Due Esteem?" (*Centuries*, 1.12), Traherne seems to be transposing into the realm of spiritual virtues Bacon's insistence that one cannot be right without provisionally emptying out the self and evaluating things simply as they are. Like Bacon's research assistants, Traherne's God-seekers "need nothing but open Eys" (*Centuries*, 1.37). Ideally, they should be nothing else.

Thoughts and Things

In "The Vision," Traherne seems neither daunted by the prospect of finding the absolute source of the flow of impressions nor particularly desperate to find it:[29]

> To see the fountain is a blessed thing,
> > It is to see the King
> Of Glory face to face: but yet the end,
> > The glorious, wondrous end is more;
> And yet the fountain there we comprehend,
> > The spring we there adore:
> For in the end the fountain best is shewn,
> > As by effects the cause is known.
> > > ("The Vision," lines 41–48)

As Traherne explains in "The Anticipation," "both are the very same,/ The End and Fountain differ but in Name" (lines 35–36). Here Traherne is happy to acknowledge the blessing of direct contact with God, because it does not lessen the value of sensing his presence more tangibly downstream, in nature (the same metaphor Donne uses in the Holy Sonnet "Since She Whom I Loved"). Things and God's intention for them, things and human impressions of them, differ but in name.

Traherne offers a visionary theory that seems prior to vision, because vision implies a distinction between the viewer and the viewed object, and also a differentiation among the senses. Instead of choosing between proto-Kantian models in which the brain imposes its categories and capacities on the universe and commonsensical realist models in which the brain receives valid views (however partial or approximate) of the ultimate physical reality, Traherne claims to have both at once, to have his material cake and eat it too. Surrendering the ego-barrier and participating in the full, blessed, organically whole creation, makes reality both completely real and completely interior, both physically established and spiritually determined, at the same time. Solipsism is—at least in the childlike unfallen soul—identical to open acceptance and full reception of the universe. Primary narcissism is not a psychopathology but a true theology: "You never Enjoy the World aright, till the Sea it self floweth in your Veins, till you are Clothed with the Heavens, and Crowned with the Stars: and Perceiv your self to be the Sole Heir of the whole World" (*Centuries*, 1.29). Neither the self nor the universe surrenders its integrity or sovereignty in this immensely hopeful epistemology.

Traherne's "My Spirit" begins in the celebratory primitivist register:

> My naked simple Life was I;
> > That Act so strongly shin'd
> Upon the earth, the sea, the sky,
> It was the substance of my mind;
> > The sense it self was I.
> > > (lines 1–5)

The second section clarifies this radical theory of perception, or something prior to perception:

> It acts not from a centre to
>   Its object as remote,
> But present is when it doth view,
>   Being with the Being it doth note.
> . . . .
>   . . . 'tis all eye, all act, all sight,
>   And what it please can be,
>   Not only see,
> Or do; for 'tis more voluble than light:
>   Which can put on ten thousand forms,
>   Being cloth'd with what it self adorns.
>   (lines 18–34)

Traherne has moved one step beyond Marvell's fantasy of watching the "various light" play off the plumes of the mysterious bird in the garden; Traherne, too, is enraptured, but not baffled or even exactly dazzled by the sight, because he is present to the full being of the object radiating that light.[30]

> This made me present evermore
>   With whatsoe'er I saw.
> An object, if it were before
> My eye, was by Dame Nature's law,
>   Within my soul . . .
> . . . .
> And every object in my heart a thought
>   Begot, or was; I could not tell,
>   Whether the things did there
>   Themselves appear,
> Which in my Spirit truly seem'd to dwell;
>   Or whether my conforming mind
>   Were not even all that therein shin'd.
>   (lines 35–51)

This recalls Marvell sweeping "all flow'rs and all trees" into the enclosures of garden and mind—"the mind, that ocean where each kind / Doth straight its own resemblance find";[31] Traherne's "Silence" describes the same transaction, this time with the Creator rather than merely the Creation:

> He mine, and I the ocean of His pleasures.
> He was an ocean of delights from Whom

The living springs and golden streams did come:
My bosom was an ocean into which
They all did run. And me they did enrich.
A vast and infinite capacity,
Did make my bosom like the Deity,
In whose mysterious and celestial mind
All ages and all worlds together shin'd,
Who tho' He nothing said did always reign,
And in Himself Eternity contain.
The world was more in me, than I in it.
(lines 70–81)

Humankind stands between God and the physical universe, not only in a hierarchy of importance, but also as a kind of interpreter.

According to "The Improvement," beauty is in the eye of the beholder, and nowhere else:

neither goodness, wisdom, power, nor love,
Nor happiness it self in things could be,
Did not they all in one fair order move,
And jointly by their service end in me:
Had he not made an eye to be the Sphere
Of all things, none of these would e'er appear.
(lines 19–24)

All such good things,

which now our care and sin destroys,
By instinct virtually were well discern'd,
And by their representatives were learn'd.
(lines 76–78)

But this is neither merely a symbolic presence, nor essentially a cognitive production: these virtues are

near and true:
Not by reflexion, and distinctly known,
But, by their efficacy, all mine own.
(lines 82–84)

Thus Traherne sets about reconciling his compatriots to the world of likeness, reflection, and representation that seventeenth-century minds so often felt to be their long-unrecognized prison. Instead of running away from these forms of mediation, he embraces them. He grants that some forms of likeness can stand between people and transcendent vision (as they do in *As You Like It*), between people and true valuation: people "get a few little Glittering Stones and call them Jewels. And Admire them becaus they be Resplendent like the stars, and Transparent like the Air, and Pellucid like the sea. But the stars them selvs which are ten thousand Times more usefull Great and Glorious, they Disregard" (*Centuries*, 1.34).

Yet Traherne attempts to rehabilitate similitudes, as finally not an obstacle to absolute knowledge, but the way to such knowledge. Nature's aggressive embrace of humanity in the middle stanza of Marvell's "The Garden" achieves full penetration in Traherne's "The Odour":

> Like Amber fair thy Fingers grow;
> With fragrant Hony-sucks thy Head is crown'd;
> Like Stars, thine Eys; thy Cheeks like Roses shew:
>   All are Delights profound.
> Talk with thy self; thy self enjoy and see:
> At once the Mirror and the Object be.
>   (lines 49–54)

This is not merely a triumph of the back-to-nature impulse; it is a con-frontation with nature as well, one that passes through the looking glass, passes through likeness past likeness. It recalls, not the hunter costumed in the skin and antlers of the deer he has slain, but the Arcimboldo portraits that designed a human face out of each season's vegetation.[32] Full knowledge of God, Traherne suggests, comes in much the same way as full knowledge of nature: "For then we Pleas God when we are most like Him. we are like Him when our Minds are in Frame. our Minds are in Frame when our Thoughts are like his. And our Thoughts are then like his when we hav such Conceptions of all objects as God hath, and Prize all Things according to their value. . . . It seemeth Arrogance to pretend to the Knowledg of his Secret Thoughts. But . . . he hath revealed unto us Hidden Things of Darkness. By his Works and his Attributs we know His Thoughts" (*Centuries* 1.13).

Divine intentions and objects actually validate each other, as God and our world validate each other, and have from the beginning: "The Choice" recalls "When first Eternity stoop'd down to nought / And in the Earth its likeness sought." Instead of taking us away from origin and authenticity, likeness— which may actually predate presence—thus takes us back toward them. "Sences cannot resemble that which they cannot apprehend; nor express that which they cannot resemble, but in a shady maner. But Man is made in the Image of GOD, and therfore is a Mirror and Representativ of Him. And therfore in Himself He may see GOD" (*Centuries*, 2.23).

We can hardly disdain reflections, images, likenesses for their failure to be true originals, if we recognize that we ourselves are nothing more (and especially if we realize this makes us nothing less than an aspect of God). That is where *The Merchant of Venice* finally took us, and it is where "The Circulation" begins:

> As fair ideas from the sky,
> Or images of things,
> Unto a spotless mirror fly,
> On unperceived wings;
> And lodging there affect the sense,
> As if at first they came from thence;
> While being there, they richly beautify
> The place they fill, and yet communicate
> Themselves, reflecting to the seer's eye;
> Just such is our estate.
> (lines 1–10)

That partial echo—though less seductive, hardly less complex—of Donne's "Air and Angels" and "The Ecstasy" (and of Nicholas Cusanus's *De conjecturis* as well)[33] implies that the condition of inert matter is a necessary medium for various physical and spiritual manifestations, but not their essence:

> All things to Circulations owe
> Themselves; by which alone
> They do exist; they cannot shew
> A sigh, a word, a groan,
> A colour or a glimpse of light,
> The sparkle of a precious stone,
> A virtue, or a smell, a lovely sight,
> A fruit, a beam, an influence, a tear,
> But they another's livery must wear:
> And borrow matter first,
> Before they can communicate.
> (lines 29–39)

Traherne articulates this phenomenological theory most forcefully in "The Demonstration," which takes us back to the paradoxical idea that the divine vision of reality must be mediated through the human, because God's absolute knowledge precludes the pleasures of sensual apprehension, which must therefore have been invented for human enjoyment. This poem initially emphasizes some ominous limitations of human perception, as in the skeptical fideism that becomes prominent in the seventeenth century, which argues that precisely because sense-data are unreliable, people must rely on intuitions (as Catholics on traditions) of divine truth:

> The highest things are easiest to be shewn,
> And only capable of being known.
> > A mist involves the eye
> > While in the middle it doth live;
> > And till the ends of things are seen,
> The way's uncertain that doth stand between.
> > As in the air we see the clouds
> > Like winding sheets or shrouds;
> > Which, though they nearer are, obscure
> The sun, which, higher far, is far more pure.
> > > > (lines 1–10)

There is "No certainty, where no perfection's shewn," because God's "works must needs exceed all sense."

William Blake's "Auguries of Innocence" aspires

> To see a World in a Grain of Sand
> And Heaven in a Wild Flower,
> Hold Infinity in the palm of your hand
> And Eternity in an hour.
> > > (lines 1–4)

Here as elsewhere, Blake is closely echoing Traherne:

> Be it a sand, an acorn, or a bean,
> > It must be cloth'd with endless glory,
> > > Before its perfect story
> > (Be the spirit ne'er so clear)
> Can in its causes and its ends appear.
> > > (lines 26–30)[34]

To know a thing, according to Traherne, we need to know (as Augustine's God does) its past and future too. But this intermediary state of imperfect knowledge is less a punishment of human weakness than a gift we can return to God, because of those limitations, with due gratitude:

And what than this can be more plain and clear?
What truth than this more evident appear?
    The Godhead cannot prize
    The sun at all, nor yet the skies,
    Or air, or earth, or trees, or seas,
Or stars, unless the soul of man they please.
    He neither sees with human eyes,
      Nor needs Himself seas, skies,
    Or earth, or any thing: He draws
No breath, nor eats or drinks by Nature's laws.

The joy and pleasure which His soul doth take
In all His works, is for His creatures' sake.
    So great a certainty
    We in this holy doctrine see
    That there could be no worth at all
In any thing material, great, or small,
    Were not some creature more alive,
      Whence it might worth derive.
    God is the spring whence things come forth,
Souls are the fountains of their real worth.
                  (lines 41–60)

In other words, they also serve who only stand and look:

In them He sees, and feels, and smells, and lives,
In them affected is to whom He gives:
    In them ten thousand ways,
    He all His work again enjoys.
              (lines 71–74)

As "The Anticipation" will put it, thus "may He benefit receive from things."[35] "The Recovery" even goes so far as to suggest that God is "Undeified almost if once denied," and that

    If we despise his glorious works,
      That they are all made vain;
      And this is even endless pain
    To Him that sees it.
          (lines 25–29)

So, instead of dismissing human reception of sense phenomena as mere thought, Traherne undertakes to exalt thoughts as things at least as valid and valuable as the material objects those thoughts purport to represent.[36] Instead of propping up thoughts by their exchange value, their equivalency, he gives them (in "Thoughts [I]") a use and reality of their own, apostrophizing them as "divine and living things," then showing that they allow us—as Juan Luis Vives had argued words do[37]—to hold realities beyond their local places and times:

> As in a mirror clear,
>   Old objects I
> Far distant do even now descry
> Which by your help are present here.
>   (lines 15–18)

This offers a pun on the present tense and Real Presence, and the controversy about full or transformative presence in the Eucharist seems to be on Traherne's mind here. He praises thoughts as actually the "most substantial treasures . . . living things within," which feed the soul:

>   And better meat
> Ye daily yield my soul to eat,
> Than even the objects I esteem
> Without my soul. What were the sky,
> What were the sun, or stars, did ye not lie
> In me, and represent them there
> Where else they never could appear!
>   (lines 40–46)

As Christ becomes present, according to most mainstream modes of Protestant doctrine, only in the person piously receiving the Eucharist, so Creation becomes present only in those who contemplate it piously. As sensuous objects would be worthless without humanity to offer God vicarious pleasure by enjoying them, so they would necessarily be useless in that process if humanity could not truly think of those objects. This nicely evades the epistemological question, restoring God as the ultimate referent in a way that precludes the scientific-materialist move that was threatening to unseat Him. In small and large ways, Traherne is opposing Hobbes's understanding of memory as decaying sense-impressions. "Thought . . . is the very substance of my mind," and while it may seem "strange that things unseen should be supreme," remember that "The eye's confined, the body's pent / In narrow room" (lines 55–62). Everything that limits sensual perception, thereby endorsing skepticism, falls away before a mind endowed (by God) with immortal thoughts that

can come to things, and view
What bodies can't approach unto:
They know no bar, denial, limit, wall,
But have a liberty to look on all.

(lines 69–72)

Where the meditating Descartes (needing to prove that "clear and distinct" impressions indicate reality) is obliged to insist that waking perception can be differentiated from dreams, Traherne's "Dreams" rapturously overrides the distinction:

Can all the Sky,
Can all the World, within my Brain-pan ly?
· · · · · · · · · · · · ·
May all that I can see
Awake, by Night within me be?
My Childhood knew
No Difference, but all was Tru,
As Reall all as what I view
· · · · · · · · · · · · ·
Till *that* which vulgar Sense
Doth falsly call Experience,
Distinguisht things . . .
· · · · · · · · · · · · ·
The Apparitions seem'd as near
As Things could be, and Things they were
· · · · · · · · · · · · ·
Sure Men are blind,
And can't the forcible Reality
Of things that Secret are within them see.

Thought! Surely *Thoughts* art tru;
They pleas as much as *Things* can do:
Nay Things are dead,
And in themselvs are severed
From Souls; nor can they fill the Head
Without our Thoughts. Thoughts are the Reall things
From whence all Joy, from whence all Sorrow springs.

(lines 13–56)

This edges quite close to radical skepticism, or at least the Stoic version of it echoed in Hamlet's "there is nothing either good or bad, but thinking makes it so" (2.2.250)—except that it is also perfect faith, and nothing is bad at all if experienced this way, and nothing experienced lacks absolute reality. The "Paradise within thee" that Milton offers as a moral redemption here offers an ontological cure as well.

"Thoughts (II)" asserts further that a thought is not a misrepresentation of Creation from the outside, but instead "The quintessence . . . of all He wrought . . . the fruit of all his works." Where Marvell points to the flowers flourishing over the fallen mower, Traherne claims that Eden itself could be lost simply by lacking an Adam or Eve to admire it:

> So tender is our Paradise
>> That in a trice
> It withers strait, and fades away,
> If we but cease its beauty to display.
>> (lines 9–12)

"For that all objects might be seen / He made the orient azure and the green"— and so that these works might remind us to love God, which means loving Him in the material world, not in opposition to it. Thoughts and things are both collaborations between God and humanity.

This, of course, is poetic theology, not philosophical exegesis; and consistency, that "hobgoblin of little minds," seldom haunts Traherne's epistemology. At times his writings seem less like pieces of an argument than like symptoms of extraordinarily benign brain-chemistry. Traherne is presumably, like Herbert, functioning at least partly as a professional religious adviser and comforter even in his lyrics, and he relies upon the opposite of Descartes's demonic hypothesis: Traherne's God is unmistakably benevolent, and remarkably direct. In fact, what may seem strangest about this God is that the deity of such a seemingly committed Protestant as Traherne should work so much more through the love of objects than through the love of words.[38] But if neither physical objects nor abstract representations are secondary, then loving them is not mediation and hence not idolatry:

> In giving me, beside thy self,
>> Those thine Images.
>> In every one of those,
> As the Sun shineth both naked to mine eye
>>> Again in a mirror
>> Hast thou given me thy self
>> A second time.[39]

Traherne thus makes his chapel out of the hall of mirrors that terrified skeptics with the prospect of solipsism and horrified Protestants with the prospect of iconophilia.

The World in the Self in the World

Traherne sets out, in effect, to join Duke Senior in the woods, Marvell in the garden; but he refuses to inflect the pastoral retreat with irony:

When I came into the Country, and being seated among silent Trees, had all my Time in mine own Hands, I resolved to Spend it all, whatever it cost me, in Search of Happiness, and to Satiat that burning Thirst which Nature had Enkindled, in me from my Youth. In which I was so resolut, that I chose rather to liv upon 10 pounds a yeer, and to go in Lether Clothes, and feed upon Bread and Water, so that I might hav all my time clearly to my self. . . . my very Study of Felicity making me more to Prosper, then all the Care in the Whole World. So that through His Blessing I liv a free and a Kingly Life, as if the World were turned again into Eden, or much more, as it is at this Day. (*Centuries,* 3.46)

Where other artists and moralists were trying to find ways past the subject-object schism in order to recover the virtues of childhood (including harmony with nature and with each other), Traherne was trying to awake the virtues of childhood to get past the subject-object schism. Marvell's mower seems to assume that the mind is produced by the world, which imprints that mind with its real forms. The dangerous knowledge that then impinges—the fatal fruit of a knowledge of self and other—is that consciousness flows in the opposite direction, that the mind must create the world it knows in the process of construing it. This is the dilemma that Traherne resists, the Fall beyond which he seeks to regress, in conceding that (in one important sense) the universe does exist only in the human consciousness conceiving it. The mind can nonetheless be (at least in childhood) a transparency,[40] or in Traherne's preferred metaphor a mirror: something that perceives the universe perfectly by conceiving it without the burdens of custom, which Traherne's most direct heirs, Blake and Wordsworth, define as "Experience" or "the light of common day" respectively. The world in here is, for Traherne, also the world out there; God dwells in us, and all the wonders of the universe are made to make us wonder, to serve us by helping us serve God with praise. We do not, or at least we need not, misconstrue this universe, because it does not meaningfully exist outside our nearly divine consciousness of it. Our world is ours, thanks to God; we and God give it to each other as presents, as presence.

Other minds—their words, their values—remain dangerous, a perpetual temptation to fall: "Nothing began to be present to me, but what was present in their Thoughts. Nor was any thing present to me any other way, then it was so to them. The Glass of Imagination was the only Mirror, wherin any thing was represented or appeared to me. All Things were Absent which they talkt not of " (*Centuries* 3. 10). The problem is not with the human conception of the world, however, so long as that remains individual and hence authentic. The Platonic darkness falls only on secondhand acquisitions, thoughts that cease to be a conversation with Creation and become commodities in the marketplace: "Being Swallowed up therfore in the Miserable Gulph of idle talk and worthless vanities, thenceforth I lived among Shadows" (*Centuries*, 3. 14).

If, on the other hand,

> Thoughts are the Things wherwith even God is crown'd,
> And as the soul without them's useless found,
> So are all other creatures too
> ("Thoughts [III]," lines 15–17),

then thinking of the world is the necessary step to its completion, not (as in *As You Like It* and the "Mower" poems) necessarily a violation of its integrity. For Traherne, the world is so provided for human thought, so accommodating and companionable to human thought, that we fulfill its nature only in conceiving it. This dispels the philosophical objection of deep-ecologists to sympathetic environmentalism. In an era confronting subjectivism, Traherne showed that the focus could shift from humanity's place in the universe to the universe's place in humanity without a dispiriting—and ecologically disastrous—diversion into addictive technologies and conformist consumerism that try to make the self a sufficient deity. The modern hope that human dominion over the rest of nature could be primarily affectionate rather than exploitative receives at once a spiritual boost and a philosophical premise in Traherne's vision.[41] To the extent that this poetic vision overthrows Cartesian dualism, the reconciliation of thought and thing promises a marriage of humanity and nature as well—a renewal of the bonds of Eden.

Conclusion

—*When I die, I will see the lining of the world.*
The other side, beyond bird, mountain, sunset.
The true meaning, ready to be decoded.
What never added up will add up,
What was incomprehensible will be comprehended.

—*And if there is no lining to the world?*
If a thrush on a branch is not a sign,
But just a thrush on a branch? If night and day
Make no sense following each other?
And on this earth there is nothing except this earth?

—*Even if that is so, there will remain*
A word wakened by lips that perish,
A tireless messenger who runs and runs
Through interstellar fields, through the revolving galaxies,
And calls out, protests, screams.
—Czeslaw Milosz, "*Meaning*"

Ted Hughes has asserted that "The story of the mind exiled from Nature is the story of Western Man."[1] This book has been describing the late Renaissance as a particularly tense chapter in those paired stories: a cliff-hanger in which the terrified collective mind of Western Europe clings tighter than ever to the outer face of the natural world, knowing that the surface is slippery and crumbling, and knowing that a fall may do irreparable damage. In several categories, the elite intellectual culture appeared obsessed with getting back to nature, hoping there and thereby to regain unmediated contact with simple reality—which that culture could no longer comfortably identify, because a supposition that reality ultimately resides in material objects was gradually eclipsing the supposition that it resides in divine intention. In an often-reprinted 1587 Latin-English dictionary, Thomas Thomas (citing Seneca) defines *Natura* as "nothing but God, or reason divine, sowne in all the world, and all the partes thereof: *also* the privie member of man or beast: that whereby a thing is properly in that kinde that it is: manners, conditions, facions, propertie, strength, virtue: natural inclination, or motion."[2] This multiple definition, which made nature both the world God first created and a code-word for the elusive essences of things, and hedged on whether nature is a manifestation of divine consciousness or a collection of entities with their own inherent properties, reflects the awkward conjunctions this book has highlighted. The association in Western culture between the essential substance of a thing and the primal universe of nature—which is very old and deep[3]—took on special value in the late Renaissance.

Pastoral nostalgia offered an invitingly indirect way of expressing the resulting epistemological anxieties; primitivism was an anti-intellectual response to problems European intellectuals were posing in increasingly explicit terms. Thomas Jackson's *Treatise Containing the Originall of Unbeliefe* (1625) identifies misprision of nature as the source of many spiritual diseases, then leaps to a long abstract meditation on sensation and cognition, before approaching his conclusion with a section headed, *"The beginning and increase of true knowledge resembleth the beginning and growth of vegetables, specially of man."*[4] The temple and the forest become almost indistinguishable, as do the two senses of pastoral. Despite a long legacy of mistrusting untamed, unframed nature, a legacy that had only recently begun to relinquish its grip,[5] and despite a nascent Calvinist view of nature as even more deeply corrupt, even more distant from the benevolence God originally invested in Creation than under medieval Christianity, English culture in the seventeenth century manifests a yearning for something primal that it suspected had been lost in the earlier Renaissance. But when these descendants of St. Jerome returned to the wilderness, the truth they sought had shed its capital T: in the old haunts of their deities, they found disenchanted verities. The idea that mathematics is the language of nature, which gained great strength during the seventeenth century, has the force of atomism in emptying the world of character. It defines quantitative phenomena instead of reading the qualitative signatures that gave each different piece of Creation a certain essence and a certain name.

What remained was uncertainty—about human subjects as well as inanimate objects: "in late sixteenth- and early seventeenth-century England the sense of discrepancy between 'inward disposition' and 'outward appearance' seems unusually urgent and consequential for a very large number of people, who occupy virtually every position on the ideological spectrum."[6] Richard Rorty argues that "To understand why the seventeenth century became intrigued with the relation between theory and evidence, we need to ask why Descartes' fantasies captured Europe's imagination. As Quine says: 'Epistemologists dreamed of a first philosophy, firmer than science and serving to justify our knowledge of the external world.' But why did everybody suddenly start dreaming the same dream? Why did the theory of knowledge become something more than the languid academic exercise of composing a reply to Sextus Empiricus?"[7]

This book has been proposing some answers to that question—answers suggesting that the dream (though it offered glory) could be a nightmare, and that the essence of the nightmare was that one might never awaken from a mere dream of the world. Using literature and visual arts as my clues, I have detected parallels and even synergies among (1) Protestantism, which struggled to restore a direct link between the Savior and the sinner through direct reading of the Bible, as opposed to the complicated institutional mediations associated with the Catholic version of Christianity; (2) emergent capitalism, which not only (like Protestant soteriology) destabilized personal identity, but also allowed money to alienate work from product and ownership from object, introducing an abstract mediator into the process of valuation and alienating the field-hand from the field; (3) urbanization, which promoted not only a new kind of anonymity, but also a sense that a past more directly linked to the land that provided life had been forfeited; (4) technological innovations, which, in providing better approximations of the world, obliged people to face the fact that approximate reproduction of the outside world was all their mortal consciousness could ever hope to achieve; and (5) multiculturalism, imposed by voyages of discovery across the seas and into the classical past, which proved that looking backward did not erase the fog of civilization, but only thickened it in ways that made realities (including "nature") appear all the more contingent.

The late Renaissance is characterized by increasing pressure toward representative government (the empowerment of Parliament), the burgeoning of empirical science (abandoning Aristotle's magisterial dicta for Bacon's experimental data), obsessive mapping, radically improved optics, controlled currencies, the suppression of slander,[8] the quest for true chronicle histories and accurate classical texts, and the fervent efforts to improve translations of the Bible. All these cultural projects seek to control the kinds of slippage I have been describing, to find representations that are true and just: if not to see things as they absolutely are, at least (like the improving mirror technologies) to reflect accurately, and deem that reflection all we can know on earth and all we need to know. This same tendency must underlie the explosion in the powers and diligence of artists to represent naturalistically, especially through linear perspective, which is simultaneously a diligent pursuit of truth and a diligent practice of fraud—ostentatiously the latter in anamorphic painting. Though England was quite a late starter in perspective painting, Tudor artists nonetheless "tended to shift away from the idealistic toward the ikastic pole, at a pace that accelerated rapidly in the last two decades. . . . We can trace through the sixteenth century a process whereby English writers and artists become increasingly attentive to the particularities of the physical landscape in which they live."[9] In the Netherlands, the process was even more aggressive.

Centuries before Heisenberg described his uncertainty principle, early modern scientists began to recognize that their data would always be both imperfect and merely a representation of the object, because of the way perception and its categories interact with phenomena—because, ultimately, of the extremely complex ecology of reality as we know it. Seeing the object in all its aspects and without any controlling preconceptions proved an impossible ideal.[10] The fact that Bacon himself felt compelled to deny that simultaneously deferring theory and abjuring assumptions inevitably brings judgment "to what the Greeks call *Acatalepsia*, a denial of the capacity of the mind to comprehend truth"[11] suggests that the accusation was threateningly active.

Marlowe's Faustus, whose magical powers sometimes seem to stand in for empirical science's conquest of the world, can never quite capture and hold any ultimate object of desire: Helen of Troy is a phantom, and death will too soon make everyone else into phantoms also. The appetite (expressed by Marlowe's *Jew of Malta*, 1.1.36) for "infinite riches in a little room" is sometimes taken as the perfect epithet for the Renaissance, especially its theater; but the experience may have felt like something more paradoxical: infinite riches in an empty room—that is what Saenredam's churches often look like—or perhaps, empty riches in an infinite room. The Protestant search for intimacy with God would have escalated this ambivalence to the highest levels, as God became at once more personally present than ever and more distantly inscrutable. Reformation theologians were not wrong to fear that, if ultimate referents were declared unreachable and unreadable, people would take fierce hold of the things they could see and touch and smell and hear and taste and re-invest those things with sacred value.

Many of these issues thus coalesce around the divisive (and recently well-worked) category of idolatry, which seems generally to refer to the problem of respecting a representative rather than a thing in itself. The traditional Christian perspective viewed the sign as material, whereas the referent should always be spiritual; and the danger (as in idolatry) was that people might fail to read past the sign. By the late twentieth century a new form of skepticism (notably in post-structuralist semiotics) led scholars to expect the elusiveness in the other direction, whereby cultural signs fail to establish full identity with the material objects they are supposed to stand for; and people can never read past the sign, though they may be trapped in (and manipulated by) the illusion that they have done so.

The Protestant revolution was both the final flurry of the traditional notion that the Word (intention, language, meaning) comprises the deepest truth, which material things tend to obscure, and also the birth-labor of the postmodern reign of the signifier. The recognition—nascent among Renaissance intellectuals, and dominant among today's—of the signifier's fallibility (not tied to the thing signified, different in different cultures, misleading in scientific evaluation, and so on) eventually leads to a recognition that the signifier is no longer so much erroneous as, for similar reasons, autonomous. As Richard Waswo suggests Renaissance scholars already intuited, as post-structuralist semioticians propose, as language-poetry celebrates, the word may be all there is for us. Seeing the world through the filter of language is not a distortion if there is no stable truth for it to distort.

Yet common sense and science both warn that language is an accommodative invention, and hence illusion or at best approximation, while reality sits (or dances) just beyond the reach of our means of describing it. To touch our world, the Word must take on substance by miracle; the Incarnation offered a squandered opportunity to return to Eden, and (though Communion may offer a fleeting taste of a restored perfect connection between Word and world) humanity will never again know God's primary reality face-to-face this side of the grave. Skepticism thus sounded like a funeral elegy for a world forever lost, a world that people discovered had kept its secrets even during the closest embraces.

Advanced thought in the late Renaissance had a depth-of-focus problem, striving to become a perfect transparent eyeball for scrutinizing the physical universe, while also striving to treat that universe as transparent, a dark glass through which to discern the divine intentions behind the things. What sees what? To look for something other than the object is to surrender to what Bacon called idols (or at least *idola*); but no one living can receive an object in a perfectly neutral way. To lose the translucency through to the ultimate is the pre-eminent sin Protestants especially called idolatry—a failure to look past the material object to the spiritual essence of Creation—but no one looks on God and lives. Neither transparency *to* things nor transparency *of* things was viable.

The Cartesian revolution, casually associated with modern thought, should not be confused with modern thoughts about objects and their objectivity. For Descartes, the realm of the physical is precisely that about which we must remain at least temporarily dubious; we may know beyond question that we have pain or thought, but we cannot say anything comparably certain about objects—unless we believe in a trustworthy God behind them. Thus, the idea of materiality as the grounding reality of the world is directly contrary to the Cartesian idea which made intention not the sand and slop to be avoided, but instead the only bedrock on which to build.

Descartes was already interested in the philosophical problems posed by the mechanical simulations of life called automata, which became a French specialty over the next century. Like single-point perspective, this technology may reflect a culture that, despairing of entering nature, instead moves nature into human artifice and imagination, sculpting (like Pygmalion) a nature that does belong to us, one we can own and know from the inside; it is fetishism carried toward its logical conclusion. Another strategy for coping with this despair is to reconceive ourselves as automata, as the atomists (and other Hobbesian materialists) did in subjugating free will to the playing out of physical potential; the world-view of the autopsy theater. The premise and the practice of science, which sought to take away the mysteries of nature, tended to erode the human mystery; interrogate thyself, says the scientific oracle.[12]

And then confess your sins against truth and nature. During the late nineteenth and early twentieth centuries, "scientists approached the problem of the pictorial representation of the facts of nature with increasing anxiety about their own agency in the production of images."[13] So the problems of idolatry did not just fade away: they returned to haunt the religion of physics as much as they had the religion of Jehovah, with the fear that the human contaminates the ultimate in the very effort of worshipping it, that simulation of the world is not enough.

Late twentieth-century critical theory found itself, for the most part unwittingly, back in the embrace of its Renaissance ancestors, back in a place where there is finally no reality, no more material-objective world; instead people somehow walk on the Word, eat and drink it, share not just a web of vocabulary but a collective hallucination, a dream made of language rather than images. *Il n'y a pas de hors-texte.*[14] It must sometimes have felt that way when "in many Protestant homes, hostels and inns, pious sayings covered every available support: walls, ceilings, furniture, pillows, towels, curtains and tapestries; New Year's greetings, postcards and Christmas-tree decorations; the blank spots on books, on picture frames, and on pictures themselves . . . at Charenton, Huguenots covered the walls with Bible verses, the ceiling with a biblical table of contents, and the vaulting with the Ten Commandments, the Twelve Articles of Faith and the Lord's Prayer."[15] The great post-structuralist move—which seems to have stalled in recent years—begins to look like a regression, whereby (even in the works of those theorists willing to make commonsensical concessions) things become merely cues that get us to language.[16] In insisting that "It is the world of words which creates the world of things," Jacques Lacan sounds remarkably like a Puritan reading Genesis.[17]

But there is a vertiginous falling-off in the shift to the lower case, from Word to word. A system of purely relative meanings and values supposititiously mapped onto the universe, with no Occasionalist miracles to hold it there like thumbtacks, feels very different from a universe written and signed by God. The late Renaissance was the moment when many intellectuals felt that ground—which was also the literal earth on which they thought themselves firmly planted—slipping away from under them. All the king's horses and all the king's men—all the nature painting and Royal Society experiments—could not put that world back together again. One scholar has noticed that "In several versions of twentieth-century interpretive theory the descriptive and methodological advantage of a standard of contextual fitness as a replacement for a standard of truth has been argued."[18] This would seem to fit an evolutionist model of nature as well as a semiotic model of language; yet it is an idea few can swallow whole even now. Imagine how hard it must have been for Renaissance minds to assimilate such a replacement.

Twenty-first-century Western culture often seems to be so resigned instead to a universe of mere substance outlasting us that we cling to the sign, paradoxically, as if it were a fetish: we reify, because the markers and descriptors can belong to us in ways the natural referent cannot. People still cling to unneeded money or trade it for brand names and their associated charisma, despite knowing on some level that the magic remains at a total remove from the product, which in turn is powerless to deliver the associated qualities. Many of us think that we believe in things, and certainly we steer around physical obstacles and in varying degrees resign ourselves to entropy in its various forms. Yet, like Milosz, we are still in quest of values, still in love with words, and still imagining that we can find some redemptive authenticity in nature—without asking, authentic to what?

George Herbert's "Vanitie" (discussed in my Chapter 2) may sound like creaky old moralism, echoing medieval Christian anxieties about science; but the warnings about the aggressions and truth-claims of research and technology remain quite pertinent. The sentimental environmentalism of the twenty-first century—especially as manifest in advertising, green tourism, and children's literature—suggests that the Renaissance association between the natural and the authentic has become an assumption, maybe even an obsession. While there is political leverage to be gained, on behalf of planetary life, from that association, there is also a danger that love will be equated with perfect knowledge, and truth equated with simplification.

Clutched less tightly and possessively, nature can instead be grasped as an affirmation of the promises of resurrection, as long as we are willing (in the regenerative spirit of comedy and the evolutionary method of biological life) to accept near likeness in place of identity—and to see the forest without naming or numbering the trees. The purgatorial burning down to a pure essence, which a more punitive version of Christianity demands (and the physical sciences seem to dictate), is a loss of life in its diverse possibilities; heaven then becomes as inhospitably cold as outer space. To choose zero over Zeno, to reach the completion that the ancient paradox denies us, is to achieve an elimination of difference. But difference is heat, attraction, and information; difference is what entropy attacks on our universal path toward absolute zero. The post-Renaissance world is only beginning to learn the immeasurable value of multiple variance, in both biodiversity and its sociocultural equivalents (even in textual editing). The search for a simple truth from an earlier time can become a betrayal of the magnificent variety that is our ecosystem's great achievement, and likely its best hope.

Life resembles Zeno's paradox, but with the contradictory aspects of calculation and experience reversed: by calculation, a human life quickly becomes so minute as to seem negligible, but in experience is capable of such multiple and intricate infoldings that it seems almost to contain (as Traherne's vision suggests) the infinity that surrounds it. The seemingly endless, seemingly instantaneous interval between the flying arrow and the target is the moment of possibility, the moment of volition, of dramatic tension. Irresolution has its discomforts, but living in nature requires learning to cherish the partial participation, the open possibilities, between the moment of origins and the final resolution. Absolutism is costly for environmental politics, at least in the United States. The standard of certainty is being systematically exploited by industrial interests to neglect the implications of global warming and to block litigation for pollution-induced illnesses,[19] while the vision of uncompromised wilderness diverts funding from urban parks. Fundamentalist Christianity—clinging with one hand to a founding moment and reaching with the other toward an eschatological resolution—now associates truth with a disciplinary purification. Rationalizing a desire not to be bothered with limiting consumerist consumption and repairing environmental damage, some evangelicals deem the destruction of the earth to be part of God's program: a way of punishing the infidels after lifting the faithful clear by Rapture, as if wiping the hard-drive clean of viruses after saving a few valuable documents. This modern reading of the Book of Revelation may prove as costly to life on earth as the medieval European reading of the Book of Genesis.[20] Connecting the green to the real, and then the real to the absolute, tends to char the green into blackness.

What makes Herbert, I think, such an appealing Christian poet is his quiet but forceful rejection of the millenarian and apocalyptic view that the world is not real, is certainly not worthy of loving care, if it is not the ultimate truth. Herbert does not belittle the beauties of this living world in human experience, even while making them secondary to the joys of heaven. Even Herbert's "Vertue"—which finally takes an uncharacteristically hard line—shows that he can treasure the sweetness of day, rose, and spring, while recognizing that eternal life will thrive chiefly amid their cinders. "The Pilgrimage" eventually makes earthly landscapes into metaphors, but everything from the delightful flowers to the noisome insects also retain their enchanting presence as natural reality in the reader's experience; so do the flowers in "The Flower." He forbids religion, as his "Vanitie" forbids science, to reduce nature to mere ashes for analysis and imperious judgment.

As there is more to the real than can be found in even a wonderfully educational nature-preserve, so is there more to the green than a way to resolve the epistemological diseases of human consciousness. Nature, modern science increasingly suggests, is not finally a simple truth, but is instead chaos: gorgeous, deeply patterned, but far too intricate to be parceled out or predicted. Accepting indeterminacy is key to coexisting in an intricate ecology, and the late-Renaissance association between finding certainty and loving nature is scar tissue from an old wound, an adhesion that needs to be broken, which can be done if we recognize it as a contingency of cultural history.

The Elizabethan elite found themselves in a paradoxical world in which language was expanding thrillingly (London's theaters were surely a market for this burgeoning commodity), and—despite royal admonitions that they should return to their country estates—the urban life seemed irresistible. At the same time (like Freud's primal horde building a totem to appease the ancestral god they had killed) they found themselves constructing beautiful little shrines to lost nature, in the form of faux-naive pastoral literature, in the gardens and summer houses that became so popular on the fringes of late-Renaissance London, and in the combination of nostalgia and pantheism implied in May Day and midsummer rituals. As we have seen also in the market for Dutch painting, "Those who were most entranced by rural scenes were sophisticated city-dwellers like Queen Henrietta Maria, who dallied at Wellingborough in 1628 because she liked the countryside and was amused by the dances of the peasantry."[21] As architecture moved from a Gothic into a Neoclassical mode, nature would be increasingly cultivated into rectilinear forms.[22] Given the paradoxes that baffled all Renaissance efforts to recover natural authenticity, one can hardly blame the subsequent era for choosing to make nature imitate art instead.

As culture advanced (if that is what culture does), the English wilderness and its ancestral open green-spaces were in significant retreat during the Renaissance:

In Tudor and Stuart times woodlands continued to give way, primarily to grazing and cultivation, but also to meet the expanding demand for building materials and industrial fuel, whether for iron manufacture or salt-boiling or the production of glass and pottery. Disparking, enclosure of chases, encroachment on the commons, the lax administration of the royal forests and the steady reduction in their extent: all meant the clearing of woodland and the felling of trees. It was not on Tower Hill that the axe made its most important contribution to English history.[23]

This move from conventional political history into ecological (and perhaps *annales*) history is enlightening, but I have tried to suggest that the distinction may not be so clear, since the stroke that beheaded King Charles may have been partly an extension of all the other axe blows by which England gradually moved from a feudal-agrarian society toward an urban-industrial one. Royal prerogatives that had long been associated with nature and with traditional rustic rituals fell to forces associated both with mercantile London and with its favored (iconoclastic and Parliamentarian) modes of representation. Coinage featuring a laurel-wreathed profile of Oliver Cromwell was poor recompense for all these losses. Although Christianity offered a positive teleology for the shift from country to city—humanity had come from the Garden of Eden, but was destined for the New Jerusalem—the widely noted stench and air-pollution of London precluded anyone mistaking that earthly city for a heavenly one.[24]

All the forms of nostalgia I have mentioned—for womb and mother-care, for Golden and classical ages, for green-space and Eden—are partly symptoms of a terrifying recognition of differentiation from the universe, often marked by recognition of sexual difference, inflected as desire, and thereby marking (or perhaps making) a lack in the individual or collective self. People often felt they had—feel they have—slipped from a simplicity that would permit a plenitude of perception without any collapse into schizoid madness, slipped into a distanced and diminished world, its otherness controlled as museum or boutique, as aesthetic, sexual or colonial object. "Love thy nature as thyself" is the modern ecological version of Christ's admonition; but it is not really easier than loving one's neighbor so selflessly. Indeed, the problem of whether one can know other minds becomes almost inextricable from the problem of whether one can know things—know them in some absolute way, as themselves, such that we can have them in common, not as private property.

Otherwise the self remains in command, and its victory may be Pyrrhic. Anxieties about being dominated by nature, or being too deeply implicated in it, gave way to anxieties about being alienated from it.[25] As the wilderness became more decisively conquered, it could not so easily be demonized as an enemy force; the victory conferred some glory, but the occupation could be miserable. The triumph could never be quite completed, nor could the human ego quite surrender; people never quite get hold of the world, but cannot accept that they must let it go. *Back to Nature* thus revisits the perception underlying my first book, *Shakespeare and the Hazards of Ambition*, that Renaissance culture wrestled with a double bind, haunted by the impossibility of either accepting and returning to our posited original (biological) nature, or leaving that nature safely and comfortably behind in pursuit of transcendent (cultural) values. It also extends the perception of my third book, *The Rest Is Silence*, that Renaissance culture was haunted by a sense of irretrievable loss and by a sense of the ultimate irrelevance of the human mind to the natural order. The latter book argued that the collision of modern Western narcissism with modern Western skepticism created a mortality crisis in the Renaissance. The same collision posed—poses—terrible problems for any reconciliation with the natural universe.

In what way did these struggles produce and shape a regressive impulse in the culture—not entirely unlike current reactions against multiculturalism, deconstruction, and moral relativism? What was implied and produced by all the good-old-days yearnings that England's Catholics and Diggers alike tried to commandeer? What did various modalities of aggression—Petrarchan love-desire, game-hunting, colonialism, and experimental science—have to do with each other? Was language their best tool or their wiliest foe? What were the unconscious motives behind the collective mission, and how does a society organize a collective mission beyond the consciousness of any of its individuals? And where should our own societies—which seem more consciously yet no more effectively ecological—be headed? The climb (beginning in the seventeenth century) toward scientific rationalism, also known as the fall into materialism, produces its own contradictions, ones that keep us alien to nature, even mark us as its enemies—and not only in our consumerist consumption of industrial products (most eagerly, those labeled "Natural"). Can the Christian presumption of a stewardship over nature actually be converted—even if some kind of democratic power-sharing is out of the question—from a tyranny to a benevolent dictatorship?[26] To none of these questions, I fear, have I offered anything like a final or fully satisfactory answer; but I hope I have illuminated some of their intricate, passionate, and mutually enriching engagement with the arts of the late Renaissance.

Even a scholar inclined to celebrate Renaissance skepticism believes that "Most people did not worry and do not worry that apparently neither eye actually gives the 'correct' view";[27] but I believe I did in childhood, when my persistent nightmare was an apparently stuffed tiger that seemed to shift position slightly when I closed alternate eyes, then leaped on me when I shrugged off the impression. Eventually my weary father advised me to shoot the tiger. "But I don't have a gun in the dream," I protested. "Next time have one," he replied. So I did; shot the tiger; and never had the dream again—as efficient a piece of psychotherapy as I've ever heard of. Only now have I started to think about what I was killing, and what empowering, in order to restore sleep to our household.

Convinced that we will look back on our willingness to manufacture massive suffering in other animals as a terrible moral blind spot, and our disruption of ecological networks as a terrible failure of prudence and reverence, I set out here to write a piece of ecocriticism; at least, to use scholarship to use literature to assess what in our cultures makes us at once so sentimental toward nature and so careless of it. Much against my conscious will, I found the project drifting into more philosophical questions for which my mind is neither well-stocked nor well-suited. Heidegger might have predicted this drift from the environmental to the teleological for me (had I been able to understand Heidegger): "The threat to man does not come in the first instance from the potentially lethal machines and apparatus of technology. The actual threat has already afflicted man in his essence. The rule of enframing threatens man with the possibility that it could be denied to him to enter into a more original revealing and hence to experience the call of a more final truth."[28] This idea—that our struggles with ecology are, in an important sense, an extension of struggles with epistemology, that we will not be free to choose a living future until we recognize that our minds are mourning a lost present, and that art may be the last best hope for that recognition—has taken center stage, however dimly I may have managed to light it. Nonetheless, a few ideas have arisen that may do service to my original intention.

Traherne's writings may serve to remind us that the conception of nature as something made for humanity, something whose meaning lies in the pleasure and profit we derive from it, could have led to a happy mystical symbiosis, rather than to the premise of exploitation that Heidegger articulates—a premise that connects Renaissance readings of Genesis, Baconian science, and Cartesian philosophy to twenty-first-century industrial depredations. Other contingencies have broken more auspiciously. The sympathetic love of animals resembles the evolutionary developments Stephen Jay Gould calls "spandrels": not perfectly efficient, coherent, predictable products of progress, but instead the incidental and accidental result of local innovations that end up making new uses of a fundamentally conservative collective legacy. The several congruent (and maybe concentric) kinds of searches I have been describing in the late Renaissance—the search for origins and truths prior to human corruption, a search provoked by an urbanized society and Reformed theology; the search, provoked by resurgent skepticism, for new ways into the problem of other minds and sensory subjectivity; and the search for objects of martyrdom to replace the crucified Christ in an iconoclastic Protestant visual culture—all these quests produced an unprecedented human willingness to identify with other animals and their innocent suffering. The detection of analogies between hunting and other presumptuous forms of inquiry and pursuit, and the Cavaliers' poetic efforts to claim alliance with nature itself in the English Civil War, helped articulate that willingness, which is still struggling to find an adequate voice in the battle for the moral and practical future of our species and our world.

After thirty years of alternately riding on and diving under various waves of critical-theoretical enthusiasm, I find myself floating back to an idea of the function of literature and the humanities not so different from the idea that predominated during the late Renaissance itself: commentary on literature allows us (I have been deliberately courting trouble by using that pronoun)[29] to learn from the immense wisdom of the ancients and to pass judgment on the areas where their sensibility seems to us still unenlightened (undeveloped and hence unjust), using that combination of praise and censure to try to improve our own culture. Interpretations of the arts also still allow us to revel in the magnificent capacities of the human mind (especially through language) for grasping the world and sustaining complexity; but an ecologically minded, twenty-first-century commentary must also acknowledge the conflict between those two values (even in its own work): the ways the human hold on the world tends to destroy its intricate and essential beauty, like a rainbow-sheen butterfly wing crumbled into smog-colored dust. Even in the very early Renaissance, Pico della Mirandola spoke for a recognition that humanity was structurally opposed to nature, though he read the resulting struggle more as epic than as tragedy. What I especially treasure about the artworks discussed in this book is that (long before the Industrial Age) they seem already deeply alert to that conflict, struggling to reconcile love for human mastery with love for the natural world thereby enslaved.

Notes

Chapter 1. Ecology, Epistemology, and Empiricism

1. The first Earth Day was held on April 22, 1970. Less than two weeks later National Guard troops killed four Kent State University students during a war protest; ten days after that, police shot students to death during war protests at Jackson State University. It is not hard to understand why environmentalism, with its far more soothing images and its promise of common ground, became the retreat (in either sense) of many young reformers.

2. McColley, "Milton and Nature," p. 424: "I hope it will become a maxim of literary study and teaching, especially in this age of ecological crisis, that attention to the relations between human beings and the natural world should be included among the principal approaches to literature." Boehrer's *Shakespeare Among the Animals* and his *Parrot Culture* show that such approaches are beginning to reach studies of Renaissance culture. Nonetheless, Estok, "Teaching the Environment," complains that "there has been almost no work done that looks seriously at how representations of the early modern natural environment fit into" other literary-critical discourses, including politicized ones.

3. E.g., Bate's *The Song of the Earth*, p. 267, which also briefly explores the depredations of Social Darwinism. Soper's *What Is Nature?* pursues this anxiety in a more elaborate philosophical vein, while seeking to integrate realist and constructivist assumptions concerning nature.

4. Several different approaches to this question appear in the *Environmental Justice Reader*, ed. Adamson, Evans, and Stein.

5. According to the OED, the use of "representative" in the political sense is a Caroline innovation. Manley, *Convention*, pp. 259–62, offers an admirable discussion of the emerging emphasis on consensus in both politics and natural philosophy. More generally, Manley proposes "Convention" as a third term complicating the nature-art dyad. I believe that—though subsumed by Protestants and empirical scientists into the largely pejorative category of art (whereas it was once synonymous with one sense of "nature")— "convention" recovered its connection to nature as people began to recognize that the physical reality they perceived was partly constructed and fundamentally probabilistic.

6. E.g., Guarini's *Il pastor fido*, Act 4, and Tasso's *Aminta*, 1.2.320; Samuel Daniel's *Pastoral* begins, "Oh, happy golden age / Not for that rivers ran / With streams of milk"; cf. McFarland, *Shakespeare's Pastoral Comedy*, pp. 46–47. In Jonson's masque *The Golden Age Restored*, Pallas promises fountains of milk.

7. John Parkinson's 1629 *Paradisi in Sole* is merely one example of the then-widespread notion that humanity could build its own new Edenic gardens; Keith

Thomas, *Man and the Natural World*, p. 236, explores the associations between gardens and the lost paradise. Peter Harrison, *The Bible, Protestantism and the Rise of Natural Science*, pp. 237 and 243, offers further examples.

8. Cf. Roberts, *The Shakespearean Wild*, and Ortner, "Is Female to Male as Nature Is to Culture?"

9. John Milton, *Paradise Lost*, 12.58; all citations of Milton's works in this book will be based on *Complete Poems and Major Prose*, ed. Hughes.

10. Though the topic is different, this book may therefore be considered a methodological companion-piece to my study of mortality-anxiety, *The Rest Is Silence*. Having upset some (Foucauldian) readers of that book by discussing the continuities of human experience and other (more traditionalist) readers by discussing the differences in human experience at different cultural moments, I wanted to state explicitly here the kind of argument I will be offering. Again I am trying to highlight a largely transhistorical problem that local circumstances amplified into a crisis, and to encourage close readings and large cultural changes to illuminate each other.

11. Walker, *The History of the Creation* (1641), p. 193; quoted by Harrison, *Rise of Natural Science*, p. 211. My defense thus resembles John Lyly's defense of mixed genre in the prologue to *Mydas*: "If we present a mingle-mangle, our fault is to be excused, because the whole world is become an hodge-podge"; quoted by Manley, *Convention*, p. 199.

12. See, for example, Tayler, *Nature and Art in Renaissance Literature*, and the sophistication of that model by a third term in Manley, *Convention, 1500–1700*.

13. Sterry, *A Discourse of the Freedom of the Will*, p. 99; quoted by Martz, *The Paradise Within*, pp. 35–36. Another intriguing instance is Cotton Mather's assertion that "the first *Age* was the golden *Age*: to return unto *that*, will make a man a Protestant, and, I may add, a Puritan"; quoted by Levin, *The Myth of the Golden Age in the Renaissance*, p. 67.

14. Harrison, *Rise of Natural Science*, p. 233.

15. Clarkson, *Look About You* (1659), p. 98; quoted by Thomas, p. 138. Even if this characterization of Ranter beliefs is unfair, it reflects plausible anxieties about where their beliefs could lead. Thomas Edwards's *Gangraena* (1646), 1:20, suggests that "there is no difference between the flesh of a man and the flesh of a toad"; cited by Thomas, *Man and the Natural World*, p. 166; see also his p. 180.

16. Thomas, *Man and the Natural World*, pp. 156–58, cites these and other strongly Protestant figures strongly protesting cruelty to animals. My chapter 6 below will add several other prominent radical Reformers to the list. Boehrer, *Shakespeare Among the Animals*, p. 192 n. 3, notes that Puritans were prominent opponents of bear-baiting.

17. Along with legislation assorting clothing colors by social rank, and the complaints about gender-bending garb in pamphlets such as *Hic Mulier* and *Haec Vir* (both London, 1620), consider the various costume markers legally imposed on Jews (apparently for fear of mixed marriages), such as the ones described by Janet Adelman, "Her Father's Blood," p. 11: "every Jew shall wear on the front of his dress tablets or patches of cloth four inches long by two wide, of some colour other than that of the rest of his garment."

18. Pascal, *Pensées*, sect. 1, no. 44, p. 40; see similarly sect. 5, no. 87, p. 53.

19. Hanson, *Discovering the Subject in Renaissance England*, p. 2, traces an Elizabethan/Jacobean "tendency to construe other people in terms of secrets awaiting discovery." Jonson and his Cavalier followers joke repeatedly about people, especially women,

disassembling at home their public selves until nothing remains but a wardrobe and a cosmetic table.

20. For the application of this anti-theatrical rhetoric back to the social practices of gender, see Philip Stubbes's *Anatomie of Abuses* (1583).

21. Sedinger, "'If Sight and Shape Be True,'" p. 64. The maze is certainly an intricate one, with many entrances and perhaps no exit. Sedinger, p. 69, quotes Thomas Randolph's epigram "*In Lesbiam, & Histrionem*," which speculates why a lesbian would keep a young male actor as a lover. Does theatrical cross-dressing provoke male homoeroticism (as John Rainolds argued in 1599) because the women's clothing allows the men to attach their heterosexual desires to these young male objects, or instead (or also) because that clothing provides repressed homosexual desires with an adequate cover story? In plays such as *The Roaring Girl* and *As You Like It*, the gender-blender is run at high speed, and the results are predictably fluid.

22. Bacon, *Works*, 8:98, attributing this deference to Queen Elizabeth. This remark is often quoted but seldom cited. For confirmation that it reflects Elizabeth's explicit position, see her "Declaration of the Queen's Proceedings" and "Declaration in the Star Chamber," in *Queen Elizabeth's Defence*, pp. 47 and 61. For an indication that Elizabeth did say something of the sort, see Richard Cosin's 1593 defense of church courts, which reports that the queen "*oftentimes caused to bee openly notified in the Starre-Chamber that her gracious meaning is not, to search into mens consciences*" (*Apology*, part 3, chap. 5; 3:50).

23. Lake, "Religious Identities in Shakespeare's England," p. 64.

24. Cooper, *An Admonition to the People of England* (1589), p. 113.

25. Foucault, *The Order of Things*.

26. Sprat, *History*, p. 437.

27. "Get Back," Lennon/McCartney, 1969; "Slip Slidin' Away," Paul Simon, 1977.

28. Francis Bacon, *New Organon*, bk. 2, aphorism 8, in Warhaft, p. 384; most of my citations of Bacon will be based on this widely available edition, though I will use the Spedding et al. *Works of Francis Bacon* (despite the frustrations of dealing with the different organization of volumes in its many editions) for some works that are either not included or not as satisfactorily translated in Warhaft.

29. Kroll, *The Material Word*, p. 119, nicely summarizes Gassendi's point: "Predictably, the moment the world is represented by those mental images is the very moment at which it begins to elude our grasp. The incursion of discrete images—as in Epicurus reflecting the mechanical effects of irreducible and indivisible material atoms—catalyzes the activity of judgment by which we abstract ordinary knowledge in the form of propositions. Thus as knowing creatures, we inescapably operate at an epistemological and perceptual remove from unfiltered sensation."

30. Quoted in Heydenreich, *Leonardo da Vinci*, p. 123.

31. Francis Quarles, *Emblemes* (1635), 4.2.2. John Donne says something similar about religious truth: "on a huge hill, / Cragged and steep, Truth stands, and he that will / Reach her, about must, and about must go" (Satire 3, lines 79–81); all Donne quotations in this chapter and elsewhere in the book, except where noted, are based on *John Donne*, ed. John Carey.

32. *Hamlet*, 2.1.63; all citations of Shakespeare's work in this book are based on *The Riverside Shakespeare*.

33. Sprat, *History of the Royal Society*, p. 109.

34. John Locke, *Essay Concerning Human Understanding* (1690), bk. 2, chap. 8, sec. 9.

35. Phillips, *Reformation of Images*, p. 144; his p. 164 notes that Archbishop Laud allowed some images, but not "the picture of Christ as God the Son . . . for the Deity cannot be portrayed or pictured, though the humanity may." This partly resembles the epistemological limits that prevent human sensation from directly registering the inmost identity of objects in their divine truth, though the objects themselves are visible.

36. See, for example the studies by Kristin Zapalac (1990) and Richard Waswo (1987), as cited by Spolsky, pp. 187–88.

37. Cf. Agrippa, *Of the Vanitie and Uncertaintie of Artes and Sciences* (1530), ed. Dunn, chap. 2, p. 21: "this is the alteration of times, that there are no Letters, no Tongues, the whiche at this day doo acknowledge, or understande the forme or manner of their Antiquitee." Greene, *The Light in Troy*, demonstrates the importance of such anxieties for Renaissance poets.

38. Valla can be seen as the first modern critic of the Greek New Testament. Cf. Waswo, *Language and Meaning in the Renaissance*, p. 208: "To open the divine text to the newly historical modes of interrogation was to perceive a temporal semantic fluidity that offered ample scope for competing attempts at determination." The Word could hardly serve as the ultimate stable referent if it proved unstable. No wonder Catholics clung to things commonly accessible to the senses (including the "thingness" of the Vulgate, present for those to whom it made no sense) all the more intensely as Protestants wrestled with the Word.

39. Sibscota, *The Deaf and Dumb Man's Discourse*, p. 24; he evinces the popularity of this theory by striving to refute it scientifically; so does Sprat, p. 96.

40. The dedicatory epistle of John Webb's *Historical Essay* calls Chinese characters a "GOLDEN-MINE of Learning, which from all ANTIQUITY hath lain concealed in the PRIMITIVE TONGUE"; quoted in Harrison, *Rise of Natural Science*, p. 251. Sir Thomas Browne preferred the Egyptian option.

41. Montaigne, "Apology for Raymond Sebond," in *Complete Essays*, pp. 359–60 and 400.

42. Miguel de Cervantes, *Don Quixote*, bk. 1, chap. 10; trans. Cohen. Foucault, *The Order of Things*, pp. 48–49, sees this book as "the first modern work of literature, because in it we see the cruel reason of identities and differences make endless sport of signs and similitudes; because in it language breaks off its old kinship with things."

43. Shuger, "Conceptions of Style," p. 177. The quotation is from Morris W. Croll's great "*Attic*" *and Baroque Prose Style*, pp. 59–60. Shuger reports that "Politian and Erasmus inaugurated the anti-Ciceronian reaction, but a fully developed alternative stylistic model only emerged in the last quarter of the sixteenth century" via Muret and Lipsius, "aimed at expressivity rather than formal beauty," in order to penetrate the secrets of individual thought and experience.

44. Slaughter, *Universal Languages and Scientific Taxonomy*, p. 99, citing Comenius's *The Great Didactic*; see similarly Slaughter's p. 88, and Comenius's *Janua linguarum reserata* (1631).

45. Dear, "Method and the Study of Nature," 1:161.

46. Quoted by Copenhaver, "A Tale of Two Fishes," pp. 374–75; citing Gassendi, *Opera omnia* (1658), 3:653; and *Dissertations en forme de paradoxes contre les aristotéliciens, Livres I et II*, ed. and trans. Bernard Rochot (Paris, 1959), p. 489.

47. David Quint, *Origin and Originality in Renaissance Literature*, p. 9; see also his p. 205 on the way Rabelais suggests that "no spiritual meaning exists that is not mediated through human interpretation subject to the contingency of history and to the imperfect, confusing processes of language and communication that have been mankind's lot since Babel."

48. Harrison, *Rise of Natural Science*, p. 228.

49. Copenhaver, "Natural Magic, Hermetism, and Occultism," p. 284.

50. Levao, *Renaissance Minds and Their Fictions*, p. xviii.

51. Myers, "The Man in the London Street," cites (among other instances) George Ripley's *The Compound of Alchymy* (1591).

52. At 2.3.129–32 of *The Alchemist*, Subtle defends the plausibility of his attempts by noting that a chick emerging from its shell, as opposed to gold from common metal, is "the greater miracle. / No egg, but differs from a chicken more, / Than metals in themselves." It is also interesting that Jonson depicts Puritans as hypocritically susceptible to the allure of alchemical enrichment. Chaucer, of course, anticipates some of these critiques; and in cases such as Newton, there is little doubt that a desire for golden wealth remained alongside any philosophical idealism. But Sprat, p. 34, notes similarities between the "innocent, and virtuous" qualities supposedly indispensable for alchemy and those valuable in the new empirical sciences.

53. Cf. Hawkes, *Idols of the Marketplace*, p. 151: "For a bullionist like [Rice] Vaughan, financial value is identified with the material body of gold. For an alchemist, however, the value of gold is not financial at all but moral and ontological."

54. Hawkes, pp. 155 and 152; alchemy does however remain an active practice for a long time; perhaps Hawkes's "merely" and his equation of essence with *telos* oversimplify the cultural transactions involved.

55. Sidney, *Defense of Poesy*, p. 9.

56. Cf. Donne's "The Cross." lines 37–38: "But, as oft alchemists do coiners prove, / So may a self-despising get self-love." Francis Bacon, "The Clue to the Maze," in *Selected Writings*, p. 394, says that the alchemist "lighteth upon some mean experiments and conclusions by the way, feedeth upon them, and magnifieth them to the most, and supplieth the rest in hopes"; see similarly Bacon's *The Advancement of Learning*, in Warhaft, p. 229, on Aesop's fable about men tricked into improving their vineyard by digging for the gold they were told was buried there.

57. Thomas Fuller, *Abel Redevivus* (1651), p. 432.

58. Preface to the *Instauration*, in Warhaft, p. 306. On this as so many things, Bacon hedges his bets a little. *The Advancement of Learning*, in Warhaft, p. 242, says we should not "rest only in the contemplation of the exterior" of God's Creation, because it would limit our worship of His wonders, as would judging a jeweler's treasures only by what is in the window. But what Bacon concedes to religion, he is often seeking to exclude from science. See also *Wisdom of the Ancients*, in Warhaft, p. 283: "particular objects are generally variegated on the surface, which is as it were their mantle or scarf."

59. Sextus Empiricus, *Outlines of Pyrrhonism*, trans. R. G. Bury, bk. 2, chap. 4, p. 101.

60. Browne, *Religio Medici*, part 2, chap. 8, in *The Major Works*, ed. Patrides, p. 148.

61. Grafton, *The Transmission of Culture in Early Modern Europe*, pp. 8–38, discusses Nanni's late-fifteenth-century forgeries of ancient history.

62. Quint, *Origin and Originality*, pp. 133–37; also Schama, *Landscape and Memory*, pp. 310–19, on Ralegh's fantasies about the Orinoco, which had allured Columbus as well.

63. Tasso, *Mondo creato*, 7.772–91, describes the unitary primal rivers migrating underground before they become "fountainheads in the steep cliffs of high mountains where they can be observed by the human senses"; see Quint, p. 152, who then cites the similar *Paradise Lost*, 4.223–33. Waswo, *Language and Meaning*, p. 284, notes the Renaissance "fascination with the idea of origins and hence with the biblical account of creation."

64. Richard Baines's official testimony in 1592 accuses Marlowe of claiming that "the Indians and many authors of Antiquitei have assuredly written of above 16 thowsande years agone, where Adam is proved to have leyved within 6 thowsande years." Thomas Hariot, *Briefe and True Report of the New Found Land of Virginia* (1590), recounts the natives' belief that God first created a woman.

65. On the *lekton*, see Elam, *Shakespeare's Universe of Discourse*, p. 162; on Galileo's third term within Cartesian dualism, see Reiss, *The Discourse of Modernism*, p. 36.

66. Dillenberger, *Protestant Thought and Natural Science*, p. 87, argues that "The atomist position was already widely held at the turn of the seventeenth century, though it did not come to full bloom until after the middle of the century," and that "when atomism was joined to a mechanical conception of the universe, serious philosophical and theological problems followed."

67. Hanson, *Discovering the Subject*, p. 123, discusses the rhetoric of "interrogation" in Bacon. She also observes (p. 129) how the word "secret" in *The New Atlantis* implies something owned and deliberately withheld—I would say, the tantalizing universe of nature itself.

68. Bacon, *New Organon*, bk. 1, aphorism 58, in Warhaft ed., p. 345.

69. Sprat, *History of the Royal Society*, p. 64.

70. *Proemium* to Bacon's *Instauratio Magna* (1620); in Warhaft, p. 298.

71. Bacon, *De dignitate*, bk. 3, chap. 1, in Warhaft, p. 413.

72. Bacon, *New Organon*, bk. 1, aphorism 68, in Warhaft, p. 348.

73. Slaughter, *Universal Languages*, p. 52. Cf. the anthropocentrism of Edward Topsell's *Historie of Foure-Footed Beasts* (1607). Copenhaver, "A Tale of Two Fishes," achieves something similar with the history of ichthyology.

74. Slaughter, *Universal Languages*, p. 54. Pyle, "The Art and Science of Renaissance Natural History," traces, by a detailed reading of the illustrations in some Vatican library texts, a similar pattern of development from authority to observation.

75. Thomas, *Man and the Natural World*, p. 78.

76. Healy, *Pliny the Elder on Science and Technology*.

77. Thomas, *Man and the Natural World*, p. 52. It is worth noting, however, that there was a significant movement around fourteenth-century Avignon toward observation-based depictions of plants.

78. Bacon, *Wisdom of the Ancients*, chap. 17 ("Cupid"), in Warhaft, p. 293. On p. 295, Bacon stresses the nakedness of this Cupid.

79. All George Herbert quotations that appear in this chapter and elsewhere in the text are taken from *The English Poems of George Herbert*, ed. Patrides.

80. Aughterson, "Redefining the Plain Style," p. 101, concludes that Bacon's style evolves toward a substantial, non-metaphorical language. Even the essays systematically shed neologisms as Bacon revises them. Aughterson insists, however, that "it is a fundamental misunderstanding of his writing and thinking to claim that he aimed at a trope-free language in which words and things matched isomorphically" (p. 117). Slaughter,

Universal Languages, p. 90, notes that Bacon (among others) took an interest in Chinese characters as more fully representative, less local, abstract, and arbitrary than English or Latin words.

81. Bacon, bk. 2, aphorism 2; in Warhaft, p. 377.

82. Webster, *The Great Instauration*, interprets Puritanism as a key element in the emergence and rapid dominance of empirical science, as the moral pessimism of Calvinism encouraged a laborious reconstruction of controls over nature.

83. Quoted by Harrison, *Rise of Natural Science*, p. 64; cf. Sprat, *History of the Royal Society*, p. 22, on empiricism emerging partly from "the *Reformation*, which put men upon a stricter inquiry into the Truth of things."

84. Popkin, *The History of Scepticism from Erasmus to Spinoza*, p. 3.

85. Bacon, *The Advancement of Learning*, bk. 1, in Warhaft, p. 227.

86. Bacon, in Warhaft, pp. 323–24.

87. Bacon, *The Great Instauration*, "The Plan of the Work," in Warhaft, p. 316.

88. Reiss, *Discourse of Modernism*, p. 34; his chap. 5 explores the difference between Bacon and more transcendental thinkers.

89. For an interesting example of the European ambivalence toward these savage innocents, see Richard Eden, *The Decades of the New World . . . Written in . . . Latin . . . by Peter Martyr* (London, 1555).

90. Greenblatt, *Shakespearean Negotiations*, especially pp. 21–65.

91. This is a fundamental recognition of Clarence J. Glacken's fine book *Traces on the Rhodian Shore*.

92. John Donne, "Hymn to God My God, in My Sickness."

93. Cf. Barbour, *Literature and Religious Culture*, p. 193; Barbour suggests that William Harvey "is confident about epigenesis—his anatomies showcase embryonic or fetal development from stage to stage—but he comes up empty on the trace of beginnings . . . the 'endless revolutions' so important to Harvey ironically exaggerate the difficulty of reaching 'the inmost secrets of generation and its hidden beginnings,' not least because no conceptual material is ever clearly in evidence during Harvey's inspections. The anatomist is left to ponder whether the divinity of nature creates now, as in the beginning, *ex nihilo*" (p. 205).

94. Hanson, *Discovering the Subject*, p. 25, suggests that official English torture was "conceptually allied to other knowledge-producing practices of the period, such as the anatomy lesson or the voyage of discovery, which locate truth in the material world but beyond the limits of common perception." See also Sawday, *The Body Emblazoned*, which I would seek to qualify only by questioning how decisively this culture of anatomy can be attributed to a withdrawal into human interiors, when much of the same divide-and-conquer fervor was being applied to inanimate external nature as well.

95. Robert Southwell, *Epistle of Comfort* (1587–88), p. 357; thus the Word would triumph after all, against its supposed Protestant allies.

96. Normand, " 'What Passions Call You These?' " tells the story of this failed propitiary tactic by an early favorite fallen from James's favor (pp. 183–86).

97. Augustine, "On the Profit of Believing," chap. 20.

98. Montaigne, "Apology," p. 453. Agrippa, *Of the Vanitie*, chap. 26, p. 84, uses the unreliability of mirrors as an argument for skepticism.

99. Otter complains about this trait of his wife in Jonson's *Epicoene* (1609), 4.2.84–94.

100. Montaigne, "Apology," p. 449.

101. In "Elegy: To his Mistress Going to Bed," Donne—the prototypical opposite of the Cavaliers—mocks men for letting women's gems, "like Atalanta's balls," distract them from the real prize; see similarly sonnet 56 of the *Caelica* sequence by the Calvinist plain-stylist Fulke Greville.

102. Watson, Introduction to *Volpone*, p. xxx. Jonsonian city-comedy is tirelessly interested in the new power of mediated desire—in money, sexuality, and language. Jonson's *The Staple of News* blends bad journalism into those other unreliable intermediaries.

103. Somewhat less prominent but still notable was a male fascination with genital erections, presented with all the hyperbole and decontextualization the model of pornography would predict: the boasts of Carew's "The Rapture" look ahead to those of the Earl of Rochester, but also to Aphra Behn's "The Disappointment."

104. Hanson, *Discovering the Subject*, p. 76.

105. Hawkes, *Idols of the Marketplace*, p. 58.

106. Most of the *As You Like It* chapter was given as a lecture at the Folger Library in the summer of 1996, then as a seminar paper at the Shakespeare Association convention in the Spring of 1998; a shortened version appeared in *Shakespeare Survey* 56 (2003), pp. 79–92.

Chapter 2. Theology, Semiotics, and Literature

1. Waswo, *Language and Meaning*, p. 240, explores the implications of these Eucharistic disputes for language theory.

2. Martin Luther, "Commentary on Galatians," in *Luther's Works*, ed. Pelikan, 27:267–68.

3. Hawkes, *Idols of the Marketplace*, pp. 68–69. Catholic theologians might object that Hawkes underestimates the aspect of sustained action in their dogma, more properly *ex opere operato*.

4. Ibid., p. 71. For further proof that Luther was not against signs as such, see his "The Babylonian Captivity of the Church" (1520).

5. In other words, one may provisionally divide interpretations of the Eucharist into two semiotic groups which do not follow any neat division between Protestant and Catholic. One group sought, either by Catholic nostalgia to cling to some sense of deep attachment between the sign and the object, or by Lutheran nostalgia to insist that the spiritual intention was always more real and present than the physical object. The other, Calvinist group rode the wave of the future, which was to attribute a certain kind of autonomy to the manifest signifier.

6. Calvin, *Institutes of the Christian Religion*, 4.17.21. One possible answer to Calvin's rhetorical question emerges in the case of Shakespeare's Angelo, whose recognition of his own hypocrisy in prayer leaves "heaven in my mouth, / As if I did but only chew his name" (*Measure for Measure*, 2.4.4–5).

7. Thomas More, *Dialogue Concerning Tyndale*, p. 20; quoted in Phillips, *Reformation of Images*, p. 44; Phillips, p. 104, records similar arguments by Bonner; Nicolas Sanders, *A Treatise of the Images of Christ*, evokes the struggle between material and idea

in arguing that Catholic practice is legitimate because "if we see the Image of Christ cru-cified, we straight lay aside the brass, iron, or wood where upon that Image was drawn or made, and we apprehend Christ Himself, to whose person that Image doth lead us" (quoted by Phillips, p. 124). So worshippers look through the material object to get to the Word, which is to say Christ in his necessary essence, not his contingent substance.

8. Gilman, *Iconoclasm and Poetry in the English Reformation*, pp. 41–42, describes this tendency.

9. William Perkins, *The Workes of That Famous and Worthy Minister of Christ in the Universitie of Cambridge*, 1:695. Only slightly less forbidding—not less at all for writers—was the opinion of John Smyth, a Leiden Brownist, who insisted that "bookes or writings are in the nature of pictures or Images & therefore in the nature of ceremonies," and that reading a book was therefore offensive (*The Differences of the Churches of the Separation*, 1608); quoted by Madsen, *From Shadowy Types to Truth*, p. 174.

10. Martin Luther, in *Luther's Works*, 11:99–100; quoted by Koerner, *Reformation of the Image*, p. 160. Indeed, Luther goes on from there to worry, half-jokingly, that his ar-gument might "give occasion to the image-breakers never to read the Bible or to burn it"; quoted by Koerner, p. 164. Koerner, p. 163, shows (using works such as Johann Arndt's 1596 *Ikonographia*) that "In the late sixteenth century, during Lutheranism's struggle against Calvinists" there were intense arguments about whether the "family of images . . . consisted only of graphic representations, or whether it also included mental and verbal imagery . . . more was at stake than church pictures."

11. According to Tasso's 1594 *Discorsi*—perhaps written under the stress of his late madness, and certainly after conversations with Montaigne—"matter is a source of un-certainty and obscurity, so that ancient philosophers compared it to the dark unfath-omed deep"; p. 171, quoted by Levao, *Renaissance Minds*, p. 132. Augustine makes a comparable suggestion late in the *Confessions*, but the reference there is clearly to un-formed matter, not material reality as a whole. Sprat, *History of the Royal Society*, p. 79, complains that "Men commonly think, that the *pit*, in which (according to *Democritus*) Truth lyes hid, is bottomless: and that it will devour, whatever is thrown into it, without being the fuller"—Zeno's paradox moved from two dimensions to three.

12. Maimonides, *Guide of the Perplexed*, 3.9.436–37.

13. Koerner, *Reformation of the Image*, p. 85, comments that "The fiction which iconoclasm chiefly unveiled was that of mediation, of a middle ground of acts, objects, institutions and persons that spoke on a person's behalf."

14. Anne Finch, Countess of Winchilsea, *Poems*, p. 267.

15. Words could even get in the way of thoughts; see Descartes, *Philosophical Writ-ings*, 2:21: "For although I am thinking about these matters within myself, silently and without speaking, nonetheless the actual words bring me up short, and I am almost tricked by ordinary ways of talking."

16. Koerner, *Reformation of the Image*, p. 93.

17. Augustine, *The Trinity*, 15:22; see similarly 15:25; trans. McKenna, p. 483.

18. Sprat, *History of the Royal Society*, p. 113.

19. Galileo, letter to the Grand Duchess Christina of Tuscany, 1615; quoted by Dil-lenberger, *Protestant Thought*, p. 88.

20. Puttenham, *The Arte of English Poesie*, p. 238.

21. Bacon, *The Advancement of Learning*, in Warhaft, p. 223.

22. Nuttall, *A New Mimesis*, pp. 1–2.

23. Reiss, *Discourse of Modernism*, p. 27. Crane, *Shakespeare's Brain*, provides some interesting examples of the insight cognitive science offers into Renaissance literature.

24. Nuttall, *New Mimesis*, pp. 2–3.

25. Auerbach, *Mimesis*, p. 196.

26. Ibid., p. 14.

27. Ibid., p. 49.

28. Richard Jenkyns, in his remarkable *Virgil's Experience*, pp. 21–36, observes the same characteristic of Homer's descriptions, enabled partly by locating the seeming personalities of natural phenomena in the gods who inhabit and instruct them.

29. Foucault, *Order of Things*, p. 79.

30. Anderson, *Words that Matter*, is especially illuminating in tracing this effect of printed bilingual dictionaries.

31. Browne, *Religio Medici*, Part 1, chap. 12–14, pp. 74–77.

32. Aristotle's *De interpretatione* had long since argued for the conventional nature of the sign: the word as attached to a mental experience and only thence to any real object, not by any organic or causative link. Reiss, *Discourse of Modernism*, p. 10, citing Wittgenstein, Peirce, and Bakhtin, discusses the emergence of the idea that "all human action, all human mental life, and indeed the universe as a whole, insofar as it relates to things human, are a matter of the production, interpretation, and interrelating of signs." This "emergence and growth to dominance of analytico-referential discourse," which is "a conscious process viewed as promising a 'truly objective' knowledge of the 'real order' of things" is in Reiss's view "largely the creation of the European sixteenth century" (pp. 12, 23, 31).

33. Thus, Montaigne's "Of Glory" begins with the assertion that "There is the name and the thing. The name is a sound which designates and signifies the thing; the name is not a part of the thing or of the substance, it is an extraneous piece attached to the thing, and outside of it" (*Complete Essays*, p. 468). In *The Advancement of Learning*, Bacon says words have "force only by Contract or Acceptation"; quoted by Donawerth, *Shakespeare and the Sixteenth-Century Study of Language*, p. 27. For Foucault, language was still (in 1966) on its way toward this autonomy.

34. For a prominent advocacy of this notion, see the writings of Arnold Geulincx (1625–69), who suggested that the mental and physical experience correlate only in parallel, that is, only because God set them like synchronized clocks. Some trace of this idea may be visible in the God-forsaken Macbeth's struggles—as his identity disintegrates, his grip on time loosens, and he cannot grasp in hand the dagger his mind perceives—to make "the firstlings of my heart" to be "the firstlings of my hand," to get things "thought and done" simultaneously (4.1.147–49).

35. Koerner, *Reformation of the Image*, p. 311.

36. Elam, *Shakespeare's Universe of Discourse*, pp. 123–24, quoting Erasmus and citing, for example, the fifty-third of Pico della Mirandola's "Platonic conclusions."

37. Ibid., p. 168, quotes Reginald Scot's 1584 claim that "no new substance can be made or created by man. . . . For by the sound of words nothing cometh, nothing goeth, otherwise than God in nature hath ordained." On p. 168–69, Elam quotes Perkins (1600): "That which is in nature but a bare signification, cannot serve to worke a wonder, and this is the nature of all words; for as they be framed of mans breath they are naturall, but yet in regard of frame and articulation they are artificiall and significant." Elam then cites similar arguments from Catholics trying to ward off charges that their rituals

constituted occult practices, which shows how damaging the association had become in the religious wars of the time.

38. Instead of turning to the authority of Plato, perceptive modern literary scholars now look for reassurance on this point from Shakespeare, as Elam reports (ibid., pp. 116–17): Mahood, *Shakespeare's Wordplay* (1957), asserts that Elizabethans thought of names as "at least the shadows of things, and where there was a shadow there must be a body to cast it"; Calderwood, *Forms of Drama*, p. 167, describes "the inherent rightness of words"; and Carroll, *The Great Feast of Language in "Love's Labour's Lost,"* p. 12, observes "that names are not arbitrary signs, but are in some sense the essence of what is named."

39. Quoted by Donawerth, *Study of Language*, p. 26.

40. Harrison, *Rise of Natural Science*, p. 137.

41. Reiss, *Discourse of Modernism*, p. 189; the relevant Ralegh passage, which speaks about the country still having its maidenhead and hence being ripe for invasion, is in the *Discoverie . . . of Guiana*, p. 96. While Reiss's argument may be a little overheated here—Descartes was hardly so domineering a personality as Galileo—the discomforts it raises were certainly being felt, as my study of *As You Like It* will suggest.

42. This serves as the title of an essay from the early 1570s; see Montaigne, *Complete Essays*, p. 56.

43. Exodus 33:20, Geneva Bible.

44. Elam, *Shakespeare's Universe of Discourse*, and Carroll, *The Great Feast of Language*, offer excellent full-length explications of this aspect of the play, so I will not duplicate their efforts here.

45. Kernan, "The Shakespearean Conception of History."

46. Cf. Maus, *Inwardness and Theater*, pp. 104–27.

47. Watson, "Tragedy," pp. 337–42.

48. Descartes, *Philosophical Writings*, 2:15.

49. Descartes, *Discourse on the Method*, Second Part, in *Philosophical Writings*, 1:120. Cf. Iago's claim that "I told him what I thought, and told no more / Than what he found himself was apt and true" (5.2.176–77).

50. Watson, "*Othello* as Reformation Tragedy."

51. Margaret Maurer, in a lecture at the 2002 Teaching Shakespeare Institute, Folger Library, Washington D.C., made the provocative argument that Shakespeare prevents even the audience from feeling completely sure of Hermione's innocence, from the opening emphasis on the nine-month interval between Polixenes' arrival and the birth of the child, to the final panorama that demands Leontes' blessing on a couple who have been said to resemble almost exactly Polixenes and Hermione respectively. The point is not that Hermione may be guilty, so much as that audiences must at moments feel uneasy about the one assurance that gives the play all of its usual meanings. Cf. Howard Felperin, " 'Tongue-tied Our Queen?' "

52. Descartes himself observes that "those who regulate their conduct by examples drawn from these works are liable to fall into the excesses of the knights-errant in our tales of chivalry, and conceive plans beyond their powers"; *Discourse*, in *Philosophical Writings*, 1:114.

53. Accusing Antigonus (as he had Camillo) of faulty senses, Leontes insists that his own knowledge is as certain as direct sensation (the experiential baseline that some philosophers refer to as "raw feels"): "You smell this business with a sense as cold / As is a

dead man's nose; but I do see't, and feel't, / As you feel doing thus—and see withal / The instruments that feel" (2.1.151–54).

54. Descartes, *Discourse*, "First Meditation," 2:15.

55. Descartes, *Discourse*, "Second Meditation," 2:16.

56. Here I am at once contradicting my claim, long ago, that Leontes' jealousy was psychologically explicable, and yet reinforcing my argument that it results from cultural symbols breaking too completely free from the natural reality they claim to oversee, because Leontes refuses to recognize his exile from the Garden; *Shakespeare and the Hazards of Ambition*, pp. 222–79.

57. Descartes, *Philosophical Writings*, 1:127, 130–31; 2:13, 15, 19, 61, 121, 137, 183, 231, 239, 244, 248–49, 279, 288, 315–16, 334–35, and 408. Cavell, *Disowning Knowledge*, p. 203, notes the epistemological collapse implied in Leontes' reliance on dreams, and his mistrust of both sense-evidence and report concerning the paternity of Mamillius.

58. Compare 3.3.16–46 with the end of Descartes' "Sixth Meditation," in *Philosophical Writings*, 2:61–62: "If, while I am awake, anyone were suddenly to appear to me and then disappear immediately, as happens in sleep, so that I could not see where he had come from or where he had gone to, it would not be unreasonable for me to judge that he was a ghost, or a vision created in my brain, rather than a real man."

59. Watson, *Hazards*, pp. 254–55, describes the way some Sicilian metaphors (lambs, for example) become literal and biological facts of Bohemia. The play's warp and woof is an elaborate dialectic of artifice and nature, though it produces a narrative tapestry on the surface; time enforces nature's claim, but culture provides nature's meaning.

60. Descartes, *Discourse*, Fifth Part, in *Philosophical Writings*, 1:139–40; his answer is that, even if the machine could somehow be made to speak, it could neither reason nor discourse with us—much the same tests Paulina then encourages.

61. The Zwinglian position—shared by the early Bullinger of the Zurich confession—is that the Eucharistic materials and rituals give rise to the spiritual purification of the believer, but they do not exactly create it (which would be Catholic superstition). Instead, God has willed a correlation that is not really a causation. In this sense, the Swiss theology is very much like Mersenne's Occasionalist philosophy of the following century, in which God must deliberately make every connection between a word and a thing, between mental experience and physical reality. Though Mersenne's position was a bit eccentric, the more mainstream Christian voluntarism also insisted on God's continuing participation in the perceptible world.

62. Cf. Siemon's admirable *Shakespearean Iconoclasm*, p. 278, on the conversion of the statue from likeness to life. In Ovid, Pygmalion prays for a wife like his statue—a likeness of his likeness—which Venus understands as a coy request for life in his statue. For a broader meditation on this motif, see Gross, *Dream of the Moving Statue*.

63. Studing, "Shakespeare's Bohemia Revisited," pp. 217–26, explores some of the limitations Shakespeare recognizes in this retreat.

64. Cavell, *Disowning Knowledge*, p. 200.

65. Young, in his illuminating *The Heart's Forest*, pp. 106 and 109.

66. I am thus considerably more skeptical than Estok, "Teaching the Environment," about the suitability of *The Winter's Tale* as a tool for advocating environmentalism in the classroom.

67. Ariès, *L'enfant et la vie familiale sous l'Ancien Régime*; his view, and the often-similar view of Lawrence Stone in *The Family, Sex, and Marriage, 1500–1800*, have been

effectively challenged, for example by Ozment, *Ancestors*, and Orme, *Medieval Children*, but even Orme notes a late medieval theological shift that seems to presume fundamental innocence in children; see Duffy, "The Cradle Will Rock." I will argue that Thomas Traherne creates an extreme version of the worship of childhood.

68. De Man, "Intentional Structure of the Romantic Image," p. 70.

69. Alpers, *What Is Pastoral?* p. 8.

70. Spenser, *Poetical Works*, p. 418; all references to Spenser's poetry will be based on this edition.

71. Greg, "Pastoral: A Literary Inquiry," p. 10.

72. Smith, "Elizabethan Pastoral," p. 19.

73. Spolsky, *Satisfying Skepticism*, p. 5.

74. Empson, *Some Versions of Pastoral*, identifies the putting of the complex into the simple as the chief identifying function of the pastoral mode. Rousseau observed, in *Le siècle pastoral*, that those who actually lived in pastoral contentment would never have troubled themselves to write it down. According to Spolsky, *Satisfying Skepticism*, p. 17, "early modern pastoral is an unrelentingly sophisticated attempt to leave behind (temporarily) just that sophistication that the high culture valued, and to abandon abstract knowledge in search of the satisfaction of learning what feels good, like a sunny day, good food, and sex without guilt."

75. Schama, *Landscape and Memory*, p. 531. On other ways Sannazaro builds mediations between his pastoral and nature, see Lerner's fine "Essay on Pastoral."

76. Quoted by Spolsky, *Satisfying Skepticism*, pp. 100–101.

77. Williams, *The Country and the City*, p. 11.

78. From the 1684 translation, pp. 11 and 14; quoted by Alpers, *What Is Pastoral?* pp. 16–17.

79. Low, *The Georgic Revolution*, p. 4, notes that "few georgics were apparently written in England between 1500 and 1700." See also Bending and McRae, *The Writing of Rural England*, p. 122.

80. Montaigne, "Apology," p. 446: "We have formed a truth by the consultation and concurrence of our five senses; but perhaps we needed the agreement of eight or ten senses, and their contribution, to perceive it certainly and in its essence. . . . From this extreme difficulty have arisen all these fancies: that each object hath in itself all that we find in it; that it has nothing of what we find in it; and this of the Epicureans, that the sun is no bigger than it looks to us: 'Whate'er it is, it has no greater size / Than what it seems to be, seen by our eyes' (Lucretius)."

81. Cusanus argued that "the intellect is to truth as [an inscribed] polygon is to [the inscribing] circle. The more angles the inscribed polygon has the more similar it is to the circle. However, even if the number of its angles is increased *ad infinitum*, the polygon never becomes equal" to the circle; quoted by Levao, *Renaissance Minds*, p. 21. Descartes observes at the start of the "Sixth Meditation," that he cannot imagine the thousand sides of a chiliagon the way he can a pentagon, even though intellectually he can know what a chiliagon is (2:50–51).

82. Levao, *Renaissance Minds*, pp. 25–26.

83. "Ruines of Rome," stanza 25; see also stanza 28 for an anticipation of the ancient oak tree that oversees the familial and moral renewals in *As You Like It*.

84. Harrison, *Rise of Natural Science*, p. 215.

85. Barbour, *Literature and Religious Culture*, p. 232.

86. E.g. Snyder, *Pastoral Process*, p. 3.

87. Levin, *Myth of the Golden Age*, p. 59.

88. Cf. the Gidding dialogue on Charles V, 70: "The Remembrance of Eden, wherein our First Parents were sett . . . hath in all Ages brought forth a strong & ravishing conceit; That there was yet remaining in the world a place of Perfect Hapines. Which because it appeared evidently false by the discoverie of that Portion, which wee inhabite, The Maintainers of this Fancie have alwaies cunningly described it to ly hid in farre removed Coasts . . . which some of them have pointed out to be under the Poles, other farre in the West in certain Ilands of the Atlantique"; quoted by Barbour, *Literature and Religious Culture*, p. 44. See also Harrison, *Rise of Natural Science*, p. 127: "In the seventeenth century, a steady stream of books . . . situated the original home of Adam and Eve variously in Mesopotamia, Ethiopia, Palestine, beneath the tropics, 'near the mountains of America', and at the South Pole."

89. For a still-useful survey of many such instances, see Levin, *Myth of the Golden Age*, pp. 175–84.

90. Robert Pogue Harrison's wonderful *Forests: The Shadow of Civilization* traces a strong transhistorical correlation between empire and deforestation.

91. Levin, *Myth of the Golden Age*, p. 59.

Chapter 3. As You Liken It

Notes to epigraphs: Wilson, *The Arte of Rhetorique*, pp. 188–89. See similarly Cawdray, *A Treasurie or Storehouse of Similes*, sig. A4, which believes they should be "fetched-off, and from the secrets and bowels of nature: as namely, from wilde and tame beasts, foules, wormes." Quintilian's principal example is "like a lion" (*Institutio oratoria*, 8:6); see similarly Aristotle, *The Art of Rhetoric*, chap. 3.4, p. 224.

The Works of Sir Walter Ralegh, ed. Oldys and Birch, 8:551; though often attributed to Ralegh since its publication in 1651, "The Sceptic" is largely a translation of Sextus Empiricus.

1. John Beale, *Herefordshire Orchards* (1657), pp. 48–49; quoted by Thomas, *Man and the Natural World*, p. 216.

2. Low, *The Georgic Revolution*, p. 218, notes similarities between the rhetoric of Winstanley and that of Hartlib: "One man was a half-crazed visionary, the other a New Scientist, but both thought that poverty and hunger could be averted and a new Golden Age brought in if only people could start to farm the common land and to make proper use of it."

3. As in Sidney's versions of Arcadia, there seems to be no interest in making the happy ending look "natural": it is improbable and seems forcibly imposed.

4. And the eye's mind; cf. Ralegh, "The Sceptic," in *Works*, 8:549: "If a man rub his eye, the figure of that which he beholdeth seemeth long or narrow; is it then not likely, that those creatures which have a long and slanting pupil of the eye, as goats, foxes, cats, &c. do convey the fashion of that which they behold under another form to the imagination than those that have round pupils do?" Baldwin's *Beware the Cat* also uses these creatures to express the possibility of a competing form of consciousness.

5. Kroll, *The Material World*, pp. 118–19, sees in Gassendi an insistence that "Contrary to what Descartes appears to claim, we cannot know what things *are*; we can only know what they are *like*, because objects appear to us only sporadically and merely phenomenally, resulting in a profusion of signs we must catalogue and compare."

6. Montaigne, "Apology," pp. 364, 366.

7. See Chapter 4 below; also Morris, "*As You Like It: Et in Arcadia Ego.*"

8. George Gascoigne offered Queen Elizabeth a similar kind of dominion in his pageant for her visit to Kenilworth: "The winds resound your worth,/the rockes record your name:/These hills, these dales, these woods, these waves,/these fields pronounce your fame." Comito, *The Idea of the Garden in the Renaissance*, p. 18, quoting *The Works of George Gascoigne.*

9. Saussure's *Course in General Linguistics*, p. 114, uses quite a similar example to demonstrate the problems of verbal designation generally: "The French word *mouton* may have the same meaning as the English word *sheep*; but it does not have the same value. There are various reasons for this, but in part the fact that the English word for the meat of this animal, as prepared and served for a meal, is not sheep but *mutton*." On the similarly revealing (though more consciously ironic) characterization of the deer as "burghers" (or, according to Jaques at line 55, "citizens"), cf. William Browne, *Britannia's Pastorals* (1613–16) on "forest citizens" (1.1.510); on the notion of wilderness as "desert," cf. J. N[orden], *The Surveyors Dialogue* (1607); cited by Thomas, *Man and the Natural World*, p. 194. The anthropocentric aspect of "desert" has a Latin parallel in the proximity of *nemus* (grove) and *nemo* (no one).

10. Heidegger, "The Question Concerning Technology"; quoted by Bate, *The Song of the Earth*, p. 68.

11. Schama, *Landscape and Memory*, p. 140, discusses the conflicting ethical valences of greenwood and hunt in English culture.

12. Compare Montaigne's "Of Cruelty," in *Complete Works*, trans. Frame, p. 316, which reports that the tears of the despairing hunted stag "always seemed to me a very unpleasant spectacle," but then pushes the question from this emotional swamp into broader philosophical territory. The introduction to Dobson's *Green Political Thought*, uses the term "ecologism" (itself divisible into maximalist and minimalist approaches) for something like the deep-ecology alternative to mere reformist environmentalism.

13. Cf. Williams's distinction, in *The Country and the City*, p. 134, between Gilbert White's technical observation of nature and Romantic observation: White's "close observation and description is of a separated object, another creature. It is at the opposite pole from the human separation of Wordsworth and Clare: a separation that is mediated by a projection of personal feeling into a subjectively particularised and objectively generalised Nature." Jaques is clearly drawn to the Romantic pole.

14. Puttenham, *The Arte of English Poesie*, p. 243.

15. For the feasting Jaques to acquire a "fair round belly with good capon lin'd" (2.7.154) is a subtler version of the same transaction—one that hunting-averse carnivores must contrive to overlook.

16. When Francis Quarles responds to Psalm 42 in his 1635 *Emblemes*, he stresses that lust is the force hunting and threatening to destroy this hart.

17. *The Catholic Encyclopedia*, 7:507.

18. Cf. Schama, *Landscape and Memory*, p. 152: "Obliged by Robin to spend the night in the forest, the sheriff is stripped of his clothes like St. Francis at the moment of his

spiritual rebirth, and garbed instead in Lincoln green, the cloth of the arboreal cloister, as if he were a novice preparing for his vows." See also Schama, p. 551: "Pursuing a stag, St. Louis had been thrown and was only rescued from certain death at the hands of robbers by a timely call on a hunting horn. . . . A more emphatically correctional apparition suddenly loomed up in front of Henry IV in the huge, black, and forbidding form of the phantom 'Grand Veneur' . . . bellowing to the startled king, Amendez-vous [Reform yourself]."

19. Giordano Bruno, *The Heroic Frenzies*, pp. 224–25; quoted by Barkan in his excellent "Diana and Actaeon," p. 344.

20. Agrippa, *Of the Vanitie and Uncertaintie of Artes and Sciences*, chap. 27, pp. 260–63. For an earlier version of this warning, see John of Salisbury, *Policraticus* (1159), book 1, chap. 4; cited by Uhlig, "The Sobbing Deer," pp. 90–91.

21. Ovid, *Metamorphoses*, book 3, lines 219–23.

22. Sandys, *Ovid's Metamorphosis Englished* (1632), p. 100; see similarly Geffrey Whitney, *Choice of Emblemes* (1586), p. 15, following Sambucus, *Emblemata* (1564), p. 128.

23. Daley, "The Midsummer Deer of *As You Like It*, II.i."

24. Yet at the moment humanity takes on its most animalistic form, the simile pushes in the opposite direction: the hunter is so costumed in order that he may appear before the Duke "like a Roman conqueror" (4.2.3–4). Rosalind reports that "There was never any thing so sudden [as the wooing of Oliver and Celia] but the fight of two rams, and Caesar's thrasonical brag of, 'I came, saw, and [overcame]'" (5.2.30–32). As in the sciences at the same time, the big question is whether wild nature, or instead classical culture, is really in charge.

25. Barkan, "Diana and Actaeon," p. 322. The French Renaissance poet Maurice Scève similarly makes the Actaeon myth serve to describe "the male poet's confrontation with himself," according to Kirk D. Read, "Poolside Transformations," p. 48, citing Scève's *dizain* 168 of *Délie*. The glorious other met out in nature proves again to be a mirror, an occasion for an unsettling encounter with the self.

26. More, *Conjectura Cabbalistica*, pp. 76–77.

27. Alexander Ross, *Mel heliconium* (1642), chap. 1, pp. 2–3, which then warns that "he that takes delight in murthering of beasts; proves somtime with Nimrod a murtherer of men; and such for want of humanitie may be said to be turned unto beasts, and tortured with their owne dogs, that is, by an evill conscience" (Ross's 1672 *Mystagogus Poeticus*, p. 73). Cf. Alexander Neckam, *De Naturis Rerum*, 2:137.

28. Luther, *Werke*, Weimar Ausgabe, 10:43, on Hebrews 1:3; quoted by Willis, "'Tongues in Trees,'" p. 67; the simultaneously thrilling and destructive effects of LSD and other psychedelic drugs may offer a modern analogue.

29. Barkan, "Diana and Actaeon," p. 329.

30. Murphy, "The Death of Actaeon as Petrarchist Topos," p. 147, discusses Bruno's assimilation of what Ernst Cassirer describes as a characteristic Renaissance conflation of "The act of knowledge and the act of love"; see Cassirer, *The Individual and the Cosmos in Renaissance Philosophy*, p. 169.

31. Bruno, *The Heroic Frenzies*, p. 124.

32. Ibid., pp. 225–26. Cf. the twenty-sixth entry in François de La Rochefoucauld's *Maximes* (1665): "Neither the sun nor death can be looked at fixedly" (my translation).

33. Pentheus learns something similar from his espial of the Bacchae, and consequent dismemberment, which Euripides locates in the same spot where Actaeon was torn apart by his dogs.

34. *Spiritual Canticle* (ca. 1578–88), stanza 13 in *The Complete Works of Saint John of the Cross*, 2:241; he is meditating on the same psalm (42) discussed earlier in this chapter.

35. Quoted by Gregory B. Stone, "The Philosophical Beast," p. 29; adaptation of the translation in *The Poetry of Guido Cavalcanti*, p. 7.

36. Karlstadt, *On the Removal of Images* (1522), in Mangrum and Scavizzi, *A Reformation Debate*, p. 26; quoted by Hawkes, *Idols of the Marketplace*, p. 72.

37. Cusanus, *De visione Dei* (1453); quoted by Levao, *Renaissance Minds*, p. 81.

38. Berger, "The Ecology of the Mind," p. 425.

39. Murphy, "Death of Actaeon," p. 153.

40. Two years later, another of Shakespeare's frustrated wooers uses a more explicit allusion to Actaeon to introduce himself (*Twelfth Night*, 1.1.20–22); in *The Merry Wives of Windsor*, Falstaff goes hunting for seduction and undergoes a version of Actaeon's punishment.

41. Barkan, "Diana and Actaeon," p. 326, citing 5.287–551 of the *Dionysiaca* of Nonnus.

42. For a much more recent and self-conscious extension of this aggression, see Innes, "Students to Preserve Human DNA in Trees": "The idea is to replace the unused 'junk' DNA in trees with entire human genomes. The 'humanised' trees would be unaffected by the change, but still carry the biological essence of the DNA donors. . . . 'We are interested in the moral, ethical and social issues this new kind of tree will raise. . . . How will a person's approach to a tree change, if the tree carries human DNA? Will it still be just a tree, or will it be more?' . . . Inserted into seeds, the human DNA would enter every cell of the growing tree, but would not influence it."

43. Oswald Croll, *Basilica chymica* (1609); quoted by Haydn, *The Counter-Renaissance*, p. 514; the notion, out of Genesis, became thoroughly conventional. Cf. Ovid's *Metamorphosis*, trans. Golding, 1.103–4: "Then sprang up first the golden age, which of it selfe maintainde, / The truth and right of every thing unforst and unconstrainde." Now, in the iron age, not only is "the loftie Pynetree . . . hewen from mountaines where it stood," but "The shipman" can thereby "hoyst his sailes to wind, whose names he did not knowe" (lines 109, 149).

44. Cavendish, *Poems, and Phancies*, 1664.

45. Sidney, "O Sweete Woodes," *Countesse of Pembroke's Arcadia*, Book 2 (p. 158).

46. Cited by Berry, *Shakespeare and the Hunt*, p. 162.

47. Kronenfeld, "Shakespeare's Jaques and the Pastoral Cult of Solitude," discusses these precedents. Orlando would presumably concede that his relation to nature is exploitative, and his relation to Rosalind erotic, when he "abuses our young plants with carving 'Rosalind' on their barks" (3.2.360–61). But Shakespeare muddles the distinction, implying an erotic element in Orlando's attachments to nature, and an exploitative one in his attachment to Rosalind.

48. Quoted by Kronenfeld, "Shakespeare's Jaques," p. 461.

49. Wither, *A Collection of Emblemes* (1635), p. 214.

50. Willis, " 'Tongues in Trees,' " p. 65.

51. "Now show the wound mine eye hath made in thee; / Scratch thee but with a pin, and there remains / Some scar of it; lean upon a rush, / The cicatrice and capable impressure / Thy palm some moment keeps; but now mine eyes, / Which I have darted at thee, hurt thee not" (3.5.20–25). This is a revealing reciprocal of the violence that the humans dart at the deer; "aim" is no longer identical with "arrow."

52. The aristocrats talk about Touchstone as "this natural" (1.2.54), and with them he plays the reductive materialist, but again and again he serves to remind them and us that the human universe is an utter mangle of irreconcilable opposites, of basic natural needs and higher cultural projects, of the material and the spiritual:

> *Rosalind:* O Jupiter, how weary [merry; F1] are my spirits!
> *Touchstone:* I care not for my spirits, if my legs were not weary.
> *Rosalind:* I could find in my heart to disgrace my man's apparel and to cry like a woman; but I must comfort the weaker vessel, as doublet and hose ought to show itself courageous to petticoat; therefore courage, good Aliena.
> *Celia:* I pray you bear with me, I cannot go no further.
> *Touchstone:* For my part, I had rather bear with you than bear you.
>
> (2.4.1–12)

There is no way home, even though we moderns, early and late, may feel we are (at least figuratively) commuting every day between a place in nature where we rest and a place in civilization where we work.

53. Touchstone's argument with William proves only that human language and wisdom may amount to nothing more than mystified manifestations of simple appetite: "The heathen philosopher, when he had a desire to eat a grape, would open his lips when he put it into his mouth, meaning thereby that grapes were made to eat and lips to open." Then, in a variant on the hollow legalistic maneuvers in *Love's Labor's Lost*, Touchstone continues to show how little the variations of language change the facts of life (5.1.40–54). For all its heady flourishes, this is really just (to borrow a term from Oliver's wooing of Celia) "the fight of two rams" (5.2.30–31).

54. Montaigne, "Apology," p. 375; for more on touchstones, see his p. 405.

55. Bacon, *New Organon*, bk. 1, aphorism 10, in Warhaft, *Francis Bacon*, p. 333.

56. The great Elizabethan source on this topic of John Manwood, *A Brefe Collection of the Lawes of the Forest* (1592). Schama, *Landscape and Memory*, p. 144, argues that "[t]he nomenclature 'forest' that now replaced the older Latin terms of *saltus* or *silva* was in all probability derived from foris, or 'outside.' It signified not a particular kind of topography but a particular kind of administration, cut off from the regular codes of Roman and common law." Schama, pp. 148–49, reports that "by the time of the Plantagenet Edwards, in the fourteenth century, the forest, legal and topographical, had come to mean two glaringly contradictory things in English culture. As royal greenwood it was governed sternly but impartially for the hunt. . . . But the legal forest was also a place of profit for noble entrepreneurs" and their "hard economic calculation."

57. All Marvell quotations in this chapter and elsewhere in the book are based on *Andrew Marvell: The Complete Poems*, ed. Donno.

58. Scoufos, "The *Paradiso Terrestre* and the Testing of Love in *As You Like It*," p. 216.

59. When Rosalind asks, "Why do you speak too, 'Why blame you me to love you?'" Orlando answers, "To her that is not here nor doth not hear" (5.2.106–8), which provokes Rosalind's remark about the Irish wolves—who would not hear the difference here between "hear" and "here" (and maybe "her"). Her complaint now seems to be either that words become merely sounds when they have lost individual meaning (in the echoes and the punning), or that plaintive lovers all sound alike—all sound like festered Lylys— at the very moment they are supposedly asserting their deepest subjectivity to their unique irreplaceable object of desire. The young swain Silvius feels himself to be deeply,

spontaneously, and unprecedentedly in love, but to his father Corin and the audience, it appears merely "a pageant truly play'd" (3.4.53). The fiction that seeks to disguise the biological basis of these courtships instead exposes it all too clearly. Is love poetry more than a mating call? Language sets us apart from the biological universe when we least want it to and then fails to distinguish us when we most eagerly seek distinction.

60. Quoted by Schleiner, " '"Tis Like the Howling of Irish Wolves,' " pp. 5–6. Sandys's *Ovid's Metamorphoses Englished*, p. 29, interprets Lycaon's transformation into a wolf as merely a metaphor for a man who had been driven "out of the Citty" and was therefore "living like an out-law in the woods"; cf. the description of Duke Senior and his men as having been driven from the court and living "like the old Robin Hood of England" (1.1.116).

61. The politically regressive character of this motif is here reinforced by Shakespeare's characterization of the exiled authorities, which closely follows the standard evasion analyzed by Williams, *Country and the City*, p. 83: "The real ruling class could not be put in question, so they were seen as temporarily absent, or as the good old people succeeded by the bad new people—themselves succeeding themselves." Schama, *Landscape and Memory*, p. 150, suggests that Robin Hood himself was a "nostalgic conservative who yearns for the restoration of a just, personal monarchy and who wants a social order dislocated by rogues and parvenues to be set right in its proper ranks, stations, and portions." But Shakespeare draws in the animal-rights issues to remind us that even supposedly rightful and benevolent authorities could easily be redefined as tyrants.

62. Quoted (along with similar examples) by Thomas, *Man and the Natural World*, p. 48.

63. Hymen seems to report cosmic harmony and affirmation—"Then is there mirth in heaven, / When earthly things made even / Atone together" (5.4.108–110)—but we may also hear (as in *Macbeth* and *Coriolanus*) a more sinister, less sympathetic kind of laughter from above, mocking the failure of humanity and nature to atone on earth, the incongruity of the marriage of human minds to a natural environment: a charivari deriding the mismatch lurking in any simile (even the classical "like himself "). Certainly Hymen's promise to complete the marriages "If truth holds true contents" leaves several questions open—including the question of whether these "contents" refer to liking or real interiors.

64. Berry, *Shakespeare and the Hunt*, p. 170, suggests that "the Forest of Arden was one of the most disaffected agrarian regions in the Midlands" during the enclosure battles of the 1580s and 1590s. Agrippa's criticism of hunting, *Of the Vanitie*, p. 262, builds on a criticism of aristocratic enclosures.

65. Thomas, *Man and the Natural World*, p. 251.

66. Aristotle, *The Nicomachean Ethics*, 5.5.1133b1, trans. Ross, p. 120.

67. Hawkes, *Idols of the Marketplace*, p. 150.

68. E.g., Satire 5, lines 9–12, where, with Donne's typically ostentatious wit, form replicates content: "If all things be in all, / As I think, since all, which were, are, and shall / Be, be made of the same elements: / Each thing, each thing implies or represents." This is a form of atomistic deism, and as such it virtually precludes the drive to see the inner essence of individual things, since they do not have such an essence, at least not beyond (as in modern molecular theory) the structures in which they array their common material.

69. Hawkes, *Idols of the Marketplace*, p. 30. None of this is to say that a Marxist view would be any friendlier, any more authentically accepting of nature as itself. Simmons,

Environmental History, p. 184, describes the view (notable in Marxism) that "In non-human nature, all value is an instrumental value which depends upon its contribution to human value, preferably as measured in monetary terms. So nature becomes either resources or non-resources without value."

70. Gibbons, "Amorous Fictions and *As You Like It*," p. 57; Gibbons notes that the pastoral genre typically "laments the gap between representation and its imagined subject" (p. 56). See also Ronk, "Locating the Visual in *As You Like It*," which argues that—by carefully layering the verbal and the visual, and balancing "seeing and *seeing as*" (p. 256)—Shakespeare "underscores the artificial and unrepresentable nature of what is being represented" (p. 255).

71. On this struggle, see Fudge, *Perceiving Animals*.

72. David Young, *The Heart's Forest*, p. 46.

73. *Julius Caesar*, 2.2.128. For a nicely ironic instance of the way this word runs away with its users, see William Tyndale, *Obedience*, pp. 25–28, warning against "false similitudes and likenesses" that enslave us to what he lists as clothing, rituals, and "an hundred thousand like things" (the lapse into "like" is apparently unwitting). For a somewhat feverish exploration of this word, see Malcolm Evans, *Signifying Nothing*, p. 161, which claims to have found 168 different meanings of the word in *As You Like It* (p. 161).

74. Montaigne, "Apology," p. 422, insists that non-Pyrrhonists are obliged to lean on "likelihood" of truth, which is never (however multiplied) other than likelihood; and "how can they let themselves be inclined toward the likeness of truth, if they know not the truth? How do they know the semblance of that whose essence they do not know?"

75. In a sonnet omitted from his early published works, George Herbert tells God, "Roses and Lillies speak thee; and to make / A pair of cheeks of them, is thy abuse." But isn't it also an abuse—partly for the same reason—of the roses and lilies?

76. Stephen Gardiner, *An explication and assertion of the true catholique faith* (Rouen: 1551), sig. B1r–v, rejects "resemblaunce" in favor of "beynge" Christ's body.

77. Foucault, *The Order of Things*, p. 30.

78. Descartes, *Philosophical Writings*, Third Meditation, 2:25.

79. Montaigne, "Apology," p. 454.

80. Bacon, *The New Organon*, bk. 1, aphorism 58, in Warhaft, *Francis Bacon*, p. 341.

81. *Ascent of Mount Carmel* (ca. 1578–88), bk. 2, chap. 3, in *The Complete Works of Saint John of the Cross*, 1:67–68.

82. Hugh of St. Victor, *De tribus diebus* 4 (*PL* 122, 176.814 B–C); quoted by Harrison, *Rise of Natural Science*, p. 1.

83. Galileo Galilei, *The Assayer*, in *Discoveries and Opinions of Galileo*, trans. Drake, p. 237; quoted by Harrison, *Rise of Natural Science*, p. 1.

84. Bacon, *New Organon*, bk. 1, aphorism 45, in Warhaft, pp. 337–38. This represents a strong objection to the Paracelsian legacy, among others. To some extent, *The Great Instauration* blames nature itself for "such deceitful resemblances of objects and signs, winding and intricate folds and knots" (*Works of Francis Bacon*, 4:18). Furthermore, Bacon's *Advancement of Learning* suggests that "whatsoever science is not consonant to presuppositions, must pray in aid of similitudes" (*Works*, 3:407).

85. Nicholas Cusanus, *De visione Dei* (1453), p. 15. On p. 11 of the same tract, Cusanus exclaims, "Blessed be Thou, o lord my God, who dost feed and nourish me with the milk of comparisons"; quoted by Levao, *Renaissance Minds*, pp. 79–80. Even such intense

Protestants as William Perkins defend rhetoric and its figures as part of Biblical hermeneutics: "An Anthropopathia is a sacred Metaphor, whereby those things that are properly spoken of a man, are by a similitude attributed to God"; quoted by Elam, *Shakespeare's Universe of Discourse*, p. 305.

86. Locke, *Of the Conduct of the Understanding*, in *The Works of John Locke in Nine Volumes*, vol. 2, sec. 32.

87. Locke, *An Essay Concerning Human Understanding* (1690), chap. 11, secs. 5 and 17. The same anxiety about failed likeness appears in chap. 8, sec. 15: "the ideas of primary qualities of bodies are resemblances of them, and their patterns do really exist in the bodies themselves, but the ideas produced in us by these secondary qualities have no resemblance of them at all. There is nothing like our ideas, existing in the bodies themselves."

88. Bonaventure, *The Breviloquium*, p. 12; quoted by Willis, " 'Tongues in Trees,' " p. 66.

Chapter 4. Shades of Green

1. Marvell is, of course, not alone in setting this noble-primitivist pose up for a fall. In *Love's Labor's Lost*, Maria makes fun of the poets who seek "To prove, by wit, worth in simplicity" (5.2.78). Levin, *Myth of the Golden Age*, p. 44, derides the Arcadian Academy established in Rome late in the seventeenth century, where "the academicians masqueraded as shepherds. In the name of a return to pristine simplicity, they imposed a rococo taste for an overrefined neoclassicism."

2. Cf. Edwards, *Milton and the Natural World*, pp. 161–62: "Plants are not represented as commodities" in *Paradise Lost*, and Eden is essentially "an enriched version of what we have all around us."

3. Ficino, *Opera omnia* (1576), 1:520, identifies green as the proprietary color of Venus.

4. Montaigne's "Of Cruelty," in *The Complete Works of Montaigne*, p. 318, argues that "there is still a certain respect, and a general duty of humanity, that attached us not only to animals, who have life and feeling, but even to trees and plants."

5. Andrew Willet, *Hexapla in Genesin* (1608), p. 37, echoes Luther's position about Adam naming animals according to their real inner attributes: "names were given at the first according to the severall properties and nature of creatures" (cf. *Paradise Lost*, 7. 352–54). But Genesis 2:19 (Geneva) seems to say that God brought the animals to Adam "to se how he wolde call them: for howsoever the man named the living creature, so was the name thereof." This makes language much more contingent, the realm of arbitrary and subjective human response to phenomena, not the necessary embodiment of their divine truth—less Platonic than post-structuralist. Already (if exceptionally) in 1533, Charles de Bovelles acknowledged this, linking language to human free will; see Waswo, *Language and Meaning in the Renaissance*, p. 286.

6. Toliver, *Marvell's Ironic Vision*, p. 143, sees this move from carving the lover's name to carving the tree's name as "common-sensical"—which I think shows the limitations of common sense. I prefer Frank Kermode's characterization ("The Argument of Marvell's *Garden*," p. 258): "farcically logical."

7. Carroll, *Alice's Adventures . . . through the Looking-Glass*, chap. 3, p. 151.

8. Evett, *Literature and the Visual Arts in Tudor England*, p. 160.

9. Schama, *Landscape and Memory*, p. 19. Cf. the entrancing natural-supernatural books in Peter Greenaway's 1991 film *Prospero's Books*.

10. Cf. Abraham Cowley's "The Tree" (from *The Mistress*, in *Works*, 1905–6), which begins: "I chose the flouri'shingest *Tree* in all the Park, / With freshest Boughs, and fairest head; / I cut my Love into his gentle Bark, / And in three days, behold, 'tis *dead*; / My very *written flames* so vi'olent be / They'have burnt and wither'd up the Tree." In contrast, to the extent the lover's consciousness and the nature he encounters are indistinguishable, the imperious claim of writing may appear valid, as it does in Marvell's "Upon the Hill and Grave at Bilbrough," where Fairfax loves his Vera, "And on these oaks ingraved her name; / Such wounds alone these woods became: / But ere he well the barks could part / 'Twas writ already in their heart" (lines 45–48). There may be a little strategic ambiguity of reference in the final "their," but in any case the claim is that he was fulfilling the symbiosis between a family's land and its heir; that, even if the name does not quite belong to the tree, the tree certainly belongs to the name. See Cunnar, "Names on Trees, the Hermaphrodite, and 'The Garden' "—though Cunnar believes that, via a full referential theory of language provided by God (through Adam), Marvell's tree-carving lover really would be worshipping that tree (p. 133). The lover may be "attempting to reunite *res* and *verba*, nature and art, male and female," but to me that only means three swings, three misses, and he is out.

11. Swan, "History, Pastoral and Desire." The beloved woman mutates from the unattainable adult object of desire (Daphne) to the mother of an infant not yet conscious of its differentiation from the provident breast.

12. Cf. Henry More, "Cupids Conflict," in his *Philosophical Poems* (1647): "But senses objects soon do glut the soul, / Or rather weary with their emptinesse; / So I, all heedlesse how the waters roll / And mindlesse of the mirth the birds expresse, / Into my self 'gin softly to retire / After hid heavenly pleasures to enquire" (37–42).

13. E.g., Berger, *Second World and Green World*, p. 286: "if at first [the mind] seemed to give play to the voice and tendency of the Body, it now becomes clear that its real aim was to put the Body to sleep so that the disencumbered Soul could sing."

14. The lovelorn king in *Edward III* (in what seems the most Shakespearean part of that disputed text) asks scribe Lodowick to write love poems for him in a "summer arbor": "Since green our thoughts, green be the conventicle / Where we will ease us by disburd'ning them"; cited by Toliver, *Marvell's Ironic Vision*, 143n. Empson's thought about this stanza (in "Marvell's Garden" in *Some Versions of Pastoral*; repr. in Carey, *Andrew Marvell*, p. 235) is to find a second thought, an "ambiguity . . . as to whether the *all* considered was *made* in the mind of the author or the Creator; to so peculiarly 'creative' a knower there is little difference between the two." But to a meditative thinker, it does not *feel* like a little difference. Marvell seems already to be recognizing what Richard Rorty would argue several hundred years later, namely, that there is no way out of the epistemological maze, that the mind-body dualism is neither a truth nor a falsehood, but a puzzle faced by human beings irresolvably, more to be toyed with, and enjoyed in its multiplicity, perhaps, but not to be treated as a scientific project, only as an aesthetic field of absorption. If, as Jonathan Crewe suggests ("The Garden State," p. 280), this garden is "a curious open-closed inside-outside space" so is the mower himself—humanity itself—epistemologically. Simmons, *Environmental History*, provides a very scholarly yet

clear overview of the way in which "Humans live in two worlds: an ecological world in which we have basic metabolic requirements analogous to any other form of life; and a psychological world in which our cognitive faculties have enabled us to construct complex cultures" (p. 48). Even the metabolic differences between human beings and plants seem to come into play here: animal cells never contain the chloroplasts that make plant cells green and let them live (in this regard, all flesh is emphatically *not* grass).

15. We will see Traherne wrestling with very much the same questions through a similar image in "Shadows on the Water." Compare also, not only lines 481–84 and 637–68 of Marvell's own "Upon Appleton House," but also Robert Southwell's "Looke home" (in *Complete Poems*, p. 65): "Retyrèd thoughtes enjoy their owne delightes, / As beauty doth in selfe-behoulding eye; / Man's mynde a mirrhour is of heavenly sightes, / A breife wherein all marveylls summèd lye, / Of fayrest formes and sweetest shapes the store, / Most gracefull all, yet thought may grace them more. / The mynde a creature is, yet can create, / To Nature's paterns adding higher skill; / Of fynest workes witt better could the state / If force of witt had equall poure of will: / Devise of man in working hath no ende; / What thought can thinke an other thought can mende" (lines 1–12). This is a familiar move from meditative practices, which Anthony Raspa links to Crashaw's Metaphysical poetry: "In the second step, the exercitant 'evacuated' his senses . . . The eye still could see but . . . The senses were made subservient to the intentions of the mind instead of being allowed to react spontaneously to whatever things they made contact with" ("Crashaw and the Jesuit Poetic," 39). Something similar happens in philosophy. Descartes too tries to permit the mind to withdraw into its happiness, denying even that passive contact. The Third Meditation begins, "I will now shut my eyes, stop my ears, and withdraw all my senses. I will eliminate from my thoughts all images of bodily things, or rather, since this is impossible, I will . . . converse with myself and scrutinize myself more deeply; and in this way I will attempt to achieve, little by little, a more intimate knowledge of myself. I am a thing that thinks . . ."; in *Philosophical Writings*, 2:24. And so he can move on to the mind as productive in the Sixth Meditation: "Now there is in me a passive faculty of sensory perception, that is, a faculty for receiving and recognizing the ideas of sensible objects; but I could not make use of it unless there was also an active faculty, either in me or in something else, which produced or brought about these ideas" (2:55).

16. The hint of (in both senses of this phrase) drawing in the mind is validated by the coded ideology and epistemology of Marvell's "Last Instructions to a Painter," as well as by the obvious ironies of the lovelorn mower's conventionalized world where "everything did seem to paint / The scene more fit for his complaint," ("Damon the Mower," lines 3–4).

17. Baker, *The Wars of Truth*, pp. 137–38, summarizes Ockham's nominalism as proving that "The mind has great power in juggling, assorting, and drawing inferences from the individual presentations of sense, and the resulting concepts and propositions make rational thought possible; but such concepts . . . have no universal (or Platonic) reality; consequently there is no necessary relation between them as the data of sensation from which we abstract them." Marvell seems to take it a step further: even when the mind lets go of its more transitive and abstractive powers, its experience is still, in an important sense, a contingency and therefore an illusion. This is the extreme of the Ockhamite position: "There is no relation between the thing and our conception of it, and therefore no basis for absolute truth" (Baker, p. 140). Clearly this position was accessible in the English

Renaissance: Sir Walter Ralegh "reaches the virtually solipsistic conclusion that since man's sensory knowledge of external nature is probably no more accurate than animals', and since he can never know whether the data of sensation correspond accurately to the objects of sensation, each man lives in a private world of his own imagining" (Baker, p. 152). This may help to explain T. S. Eliot's perception that Marvell's wit suggests "a constant inspection and criticism of experience . . . a recognition, implicit in the expression of every experience, of other kinds of experience which are possible" ("Andrew Marvell" [1921], repr. in Carey, *Andrew Marvell*, p. 57). The most we can safely say, with Descartes, is that objects "transmitted something which gave the mind occasion to form these ideas, by means of an innate faculty" ("Notes Directed Against a Certain Programme," quoted by Stempel in "Marvell's Cartesian Ecstasy," p. 108). I believe that the Platonic echoes (e.g., *Symposium* 210) are demonstrably active here as well, leaving us in a typical Marvellian equipoise between skepticism and idealism—between discomfort or celebration that the mind has an experience of reality separate from the reality itself.

18. Herbert of Cherbury, *De Veritate* (1624), trans. Carré, p. 40. In his *New Theory of Vision* (1709) Bishop Berkeley would later observe that the perception of color arises from particular stimulations on the retina and has no absolute correlation with anything outside the mind.

19. Notice that this stanza of "The Garden" hints at a celebration of the human imagination like that in Sidney's "Defense," but does not actually deliver any congratulation: the imagined world is insistently "other," not "better," and "transcending" did not necessarily denote an ascent, just a crossing over into independence.

20. Locke, *Essay Concerning Human Understanding*, bk. 2, chap. 8, sec. 19. Sec. 13 makes the consistent association of each texture with a particular color another occasionalist connection, requiring God to "annex such ideas to such motions, with which they have no similitude."

21. Ralegh, "The Sceptic," in *Works*, 8:548–49. The observation seems to have fascinated many of the deepest thinkers of the period. Flamineo in Webster's *The White Devil* (1.2.109)—echoing a speech by Euarchus near the end of Sidney's *New Arcadia* (line 797)—remarks that "they that have the yellow jaundice, think all objects they look on to be yellow"; Montaigne ("They who have jaundice see all things as yellowish," citing a similar observation by Lucretius; "Apology," p. 451); Francis Lenton, *Characterismi* (1631), chap. 39; and Descartes suggests that "someone with jaundice sees snow as yellow" ("Objections and Replies," in *Philosophical Writings*, 2:104); see also his Sixth Meditation (2:56–57): "it is therefore quite possible that these are false [judgments] . . . that when a body is white or green, the selfsame whiteness or greenness which I perceive through my senses is present in the body."

22. Quoted by Levao, *Renaissance Minds*, p. 146.

23. Trimpi, *Muses*, pp. 87–195.

24. Herbert of Cherbury, *De Veritate*, observed that "the visible spectre . . . had no permanent being, being in a continual flux" (p. 39).

25. Stewart, *The Enclosed Garden*, p. 182; Stewart here offers a valuable survey of Marvell's likely knowledge of these philosophical traditions.

26. Augustine, *De utilitate credendi*, sec. 1, in *Seventeen Short Treatises of St. Augustine*, trans. Cornish.

27. Descartes, *Philosophical Writings*, 3:331.

28. Gowing, *Vermeer* (London: Faber and Faber, 1952); quoted by Alpers, *The Art of Describing*, p. 37.

29. Ralegh, "The Sceptic," in *Works* 8:555.

30. Montaigne, "Apology," p. 444.

31. Charron, *De la sagesse* (1601/1604), p. 109, resists the Scholastic position that all knowledge comes through the senses; but more emphatically, refutes the assumption that our five senses register all that can be registered, since we would not know what we are missing, and since other animals seem to use fewer.

32. Melanchthon, "On the Soul," in *A Melanchthon Reader*, p. 239.

33. Ficino, *Theologia Platonica* 9.3; quoted by Toliver, *Marvell's Ironic Vision*, p. 149 n. 60. This is hardly the nature that Whitehead felt must come from a non-teleological reading of the universe: "a dull affair, soundless, scentless, colourless; merely the hurrying of material"; quoted by Willey, *Seventeenth-Century Background*, p. 11.

34. Comito, *Idea of the Garden*, p. 122, quoting Hermes Trismegistus, in Scott, *Hermetica*, 1:115.

35. Bacon, "Of Truth" (1625) in Warhaft, *Francis Bacon*, p. 47.

36. Quoted by Haydn, *Counter-Renaissance*, p. 535.

37. Donne, *Sermons of John Donne*, 8:226.

38. Glanvill, *Vanity of Dogmatizing* (1661), quoted by Harrison, *Rise of Natural Science*, p. 212.

39. See Servius's commentary on the *Aeneid*, 5.734, 6.638; cited by Comito, *Idea of the Garden*, p. 89.

40. Thus, at the next remove, "Thrice happy he who, not mistook, / Hath read in Nature's mystic book" ("Upon Appleton House," lines 583–84).

41. Plato, *Cratylus*, 1:221.

42. Descartes, *Philosophical Writings*, 1:165.

43. Compare William Habington's "To my noblest Friend, J. C. Esquire," which proposes a retreat "To the pure innocence oth' Country ayre" (line 22), away from (with the same pun Marvell uses) "forraigne plots" (31), and from ludicrously misguided "labors to inthrall / The world" (34–35), which finally prove "Th' unbusied onely wise" (41). Habington too rhymes "rude" with "solitude" (49–50), and concludes with the equivalent of Marvell's unattended sundial: "Time nere forgot / His journey, though his steps we numbred not."

44. I believe that the persistence, in the history of readings of this poem, of the view that it replicates and advocates a simple escape into pure nature reflects the system of denial that the poem critiques. Even when it is recognized that Marvell is doing something rather new, the newness is often mistaken for a prophecy of Romanticism rather than (as I see it) a reflection of skepticism. Sir Edmund Gosse in 1885 finds in "The Garden" "a personal sympathy with nature, and particularly with vegetation, which was quite a novel thing, and which found no second exponent until Wordsworth came forward"; in Donno, *Andrew Marvell: The Critical Heritage*, p. 245; A. Clutton-Brock in 1918 asserts that "Marvell believed in the natural man and in a simple, easy way of life. If only men would cultivate their gardens, they might enjoy the happiness which life offers them with both hands"; in Donno, *Critical Heritage*, p. 338. More recently, even David Kalstone, while recognizing that Marvell generally "sees the pastoral speaker as by nature an intruder,"

concludes that, in "The Garden," Marvell is "fully at rest with pastoral's recuperative powers" ("Marvell and the Fictions of Pastoral," p. 187). Lisa Low, "Ending in Eden," p. 77, sees "The subject of 'The Garden' " as "the recovery from the fall by a loving, amorous return to a nature which, in response to the narrator's empathy, humanizes itself." From my point of view, this reading is a predictable but finally unjustified bit of ecological Arminianism. It is natural to expect the deity to respond to loving human initiatives, but the evidence is not always reassuring. Low concludes that "By pursuing nature instead of self, the poet metamorphoses into post-lapsarian Adam in intimate conversation with a nature from which he is no longer alienated." My reading of "The Garden" suggests instead that one can never pursue nature *instead* of self, only through the self in ways as inextricable as pride and piety in Marvell's "The Coronet," and that the two paradises persist in a kind of epistemological alienation even (or especially) while celebrated as sensual experience.

45. This aspect of Milton's epic was most prominently illuminated by Fish, *Surprised by Sin*.

46. That Marvell retains even more distance from this speaker than from his other, more delicate ones, seems clear; after all, a mower can hardly be devoted in principle to non-interference in the life of nature (though, like Damon, he can imagine himself part of it), and he is self-interested in opposing gardens, since they put him out of work. On the primitivism of this poem, see Cook, *Seeing Through Words*, p. 156: "Right art, the implication is, consists in a return to and a restoration of the source, rather than in a divisive departure from it." Indeed, Marvell's poetry generally reflects an "urge to return to, to re-collect, an original integrity" (Cook, p. 158).

47. Malcolmson, "The Garden Enclosed / The Woman Enclosed," p. 252, observes whereas "the Cavaliers conceitedly and pornographically describe women in terms of the land and its fruits; in 'The Mower against Gardens,' Marvell reverses this process and describes the land and its fruits in terms of women." I will argue that the same thing happens more broadly in the other "Mower" poems, where Juliana is largely an extension or expression of the role the ongoing seasonal life of the fields plays in the mower's (narcissistic) psychology.

48. Malcolmson, p. 251, cites Bruce King's argument to this effect, and (on p. 262) makes a similar case herself, suggesting that the poem accuses the Levellers of failing to understand what structures society must impose under the authority of sophisticated men (such as Fairfax).

49. Ray, *Observations topographical, moral, & physiological*, p. 410; cf. Keith Thomas, *Man and the Natural World*, p. 79.

50. In an 1892 review, Sir E. K. Chambers remarks that Marvell here "makes of the nightingale a conscious artist, a winged *diva*"; in Donno, *Critical Heritage*, p. 269. The persistence of these anthropomorphisms is, alone, enough to refute Lawrence Hyman's claim that this is "one of Marvell's simplest poems" (*Andrew Marvell*, p. 15).

51. It may also be an incurable disease: that strange and remarkable Renaissance man Sir Kenelm Digby (in *Two Treatises*, 1645; 1.419) observed that "This is a general and main error, running through all the conceptions of mankind, unless great heed be taken to prevent it, that what subject soever they speculate upon . . . they are still apt to bring them to their own standard, to frame such conceptions of them as they would do of themselves"; quoted by Thomas, *Man and the Natural World*, p. 51.

52. Calvin, *Institutes of the Christian Religion*, 1.5.11 (p. 63); 1.5.14 (p. 68).

53. Rabb, *The Struggle for Stability in Early Modern Europe*, p. 90. In a sense, the "Mower" poems describe the obverse: a crumbling of familiar landmarks caused by a sense of dislocation.

54. Snyder, *Pastoral Process*, p. 28, observes—with characteristic profundity and lucidity—the transaction whereby Colin "blames his response on Rosalind's lack of response, but his words suggest that simply becoming aware of her has shattered his peace. A few lines later, he separates the experience of desire from the fact of being rejected and finds the first as much a cause for despair as the second." So Colin prefers Hobbinol, not out of pederastic drives, but because "the sameness of male and male implies . . . the safe, self-mirroring attachment that precedes the heterosexual encounter with difference. Rosalind is not simply an alternative love object but alterity itself."

55. Leonardo da Vinci, *Treatise on Painting*, 1:23, par. 34; quoted by Alpers, *The Art of Describing*, p. 46. Later in life Leonardo seems to turn against this model (as Marvell does later in the poem), insisting on the artist becoming some kind of reasonable mirror— reflecting, but selecting what to reflect.

56. Carew, *Survey of Cornwall* (London, 1602), p. 132v.

57. In the course of analyzing "The Garden," Stempel observes that "Descartes explicitly denies the truth of the scholastic axiom that nothing is in the mind which was not first in the senses" ("Marvell's Cartesian Ecstasy," p. 108). Sessions, "Marvell's Mower," p. 192, observes that, in "The Mower's Song," "the dichotomizing terms appear Cartesian, probably the first such inscription in any significant English literary text."

58. Comito, *Idea of the Garden*, p. 60, observes that "Laura is the *object* of Petrarch's concern only so far as she eludes his grasp. Experienced, she is not only *lauro* but also *l'aura, l'aere, l'aurora*—breeze, air, dawn—the whole vivifying milieu of the natural paradise. . . . Word and reality lose their hard, merely public outlines at the same time, and the scene becomes a possession of the self."

59. *Last Flowers*, pp. 68, 71.

60. Marvell does offer a gender-reversed instance of this phenomenon in "The Nymph Complaining for the Death of Her Fawn," where the treacherous Sylvio may be no more personally to blame than the mower's Juliana. The problem is structural, a problem of otherness, of which unrequited love is only an especially heartfelt symptom; the known other, the perfect beloved, is always false, or at least a falsehood, even when trying to be true. For the nymph to speak of a time "when yet / I had not found him counterfeit" (lines 25–26) implies that perhaps he always was.

61. Rees, *Judgment of Marvell*, p. 164.

62. Merchant, *Death of Nature* and *Earthcare: Women and the Environment*; see also Plumwood, *Feminism and the Mastery of Nature*. Again I would note that the late-Renaissance literary works this book studies seem aware of problems that the intellectual historians (in this case, ecofeminists) tend to date from the Enlightenment.

63. Adelman, *Suffocating Mothers*.

64. Bramwell, *Ecology in the Twentieth Century*, p. 248.

65. James Turner, *The Politics of Landscape* (Oxford: Blackwell, 1979), p. 222, n118.

66. Thomas, *Man and the Natural World*, pp. 143–50, offers more numerous and vivid examples of such cruelty being unreservedly enjoyed by the cultivated elites than many modern readers can probably bear to read. Thomas Tryon was an important voice of protest against these practices, especially important because he linked them compellingly

to the cruelties of human slavery and its foundational racism. His *The Good House-Wife* (1657), pp. 217–18, proposes vegetarianism as a cure for "a tumultuous, envious spirit"; quoted by Thomas, p. 292.

67. It is important to acknowledge a contrary viewpoint, however, which describes agriculture and domestication as ongoing assaults on the natural order, whereas hunting traditionally involved a more symbiotic relationship with the maternal earth and its ecological balances; see Oelschlager's shrewd, clear-headed, and wide-ranging *The Idea of Wilderness*, p. 28 and passim. Even from a more traditional perspective, the element of passivity is far less clear in the georgic than in the pastoral literary mode.

68. If he intends instead to carve a tombstone with images of grass, then we are back in the Chinese box/Russian doll paradoxes of nature and art that characterize the ending of Marvell's "The Nymph Complaining for the Death of Her Fawn." Marvell here also looks ahead to the implication of Thomas Hardy's "Drummer Hodge" that, in the counter-imperial flow, Hodge losing himself or adjusting his consciousness to an alien landscape and its flora seems indistinguishable from surrendering will, consciousness, and body altogether to that landscape in death, to re-assimilation by nature, passivity, and otherness.

69. Isaiah 40:6; Hartman, *Beyond Formalism*, pp. 151–72, suggests the prominence of this phrase in Marvell's mind.

70. Panofsky, *Meaning in the Visual Arts*, pp. 296, 316.

71. Panofsky's closing remark about Fragonard's Arcadia drawing, ibid., p. 320, may imply something similar.

72. Comito, *Idea of the Garden*, pp. 119–20, detects a comparable attitude in Albius Tibullus's *Rapax Mors* (1.3.65): "the Roman lover's paradise, unlike that of Phillis and Flora or of Guillaume's hero, is entered only after death. . . . In Tibullus, it is not, despite the claim of *ducet*, a movement toward a pregnant futurity, as death might be (for example) in an atmosphere of Christian doctrine. It is, rather, a drift toward non-being, a drift backward in time to a place in which the confusions of time and the self have not yet arisen . . . a daydream of Peace with her fruitful breast. . . . where what is opposed seems to be the very condition of life itself, he reaches back before agriculture and even before animal husbandry to a bliss all but explicitly infantile, in which full-uddered ewes come unbidden to the happy swain: 'The very oaks gave honey, and with milky udders came the ewes unbidden to meet the careless swain'" (lines 45–46). In other words, we have moved close to the "Penshurst" and "Garden" visions of a nature so *sponte sua* benevolent it threatens to swallow (or suffocate) us in feeding us.

73. Cf. Levao, *Renaissance Minds*, p. 11: "The mind does not create its symbols, but finds them in the nature of things themselves. Even so, these symbols are radically inadequate. In its search for God, the mind must transcend them, and it is here that the emphasis of Dionysius's *Mystical Theology* lies. The goal is one of total silence, the annihilation of all intellectual activity . . . 'absolute dumbness of both speech and thought'"; in Dionysius the Areopagite, *On the Divine Names and the Mystical Theology*, p. 198.

74. Lines 16–28 of the lyric beginning "O sweete woodes" near the end of the second Book of Sidney's *Countesse of Pembroke's Arcadia* (pp. 157–58), function by negation; again this is a clearing away more than a creation.

75. Montaigne, "Apology," p. 372.

76. Anderson, "The Nature of Marvell's Mower," p. 131.

77. Montaigne, "Apology," p. 324.

Chapter 5. Metaphysical and Cavalier Styles of Consciousness

1. Francis Quarles, *Argalus and Parthenia* (London, 1629), sig. A3r; Gardner's introduction to her collection *The Metaphysical Poets*, p. 16, quotes this passage (with a few slight differences in transcription).

2. Achinstein, *Literature and Dissent*, pp. 200–209, shows convincingly that, although Herbert was later recuperated as a voice of Anglican stability, he was a long-standing source and hero for Protestant dissent.

3. Lewalski, *Protestant Poetics*, p. 6, associates such poetics (including those of Donne) with an Augustinian position on language and meaning: "though words are important as signs, truth is conveyed not by words but by revelation and intuition." Perhaps the rediscovery of the Metaphysicals by Eliot and his followers reflects Modernism's interest in the autonomy of words and individual consciousness—though arguably Metaphysical poetry has even more in common with postmodern semiotics, which emphasize the inevitably subjective and arbitrary character of reading, even while granting epistemic vocabularies enormous determinative power over individual experience.

4. Bakhtin goes on to suggest that "This is why during the Renaissance familiar genres and styles could play such a large and positive role in destroying the official medieval picture of the world"; quoted by Nigel Smith, *Literature and Revolution in England*, p. 4. Smith also acknowledges that " 'conservative' or royalist journalists" resorted to "popular, carnivalesque" modes as weapons against "the serious and biblical language" of the Puritan resistance, though he insists that such modes remained more native in the Leveller writings.

5. Edmund Hickeringill, *The History of Whiggism* (1682), p. 8; quoted in Sharpe and Zwicker, *Politics of Discourse*, p. 233.

6. Richard Montagu [Mountague], in *The Correspondence of John Cosin*, p. 21.

7. Barbour, *Literature and Religious Culture*.

8. Strier, *Love Known*, discerns strong Lutheran tendencies in Herbert.

9. Maycock, *Nicholas Ferrar of Little Gidding*, p. 308; quoted by Barbour, *Literature and Religious Culture*, p. 37.

10. Barbara J. Shapiro, *Probability and Certainty in Seventeenth-Century England*, p. 107.

11. Douglas, *Cultural Bias*, p. 14. Douglas grants the status of cultural matrix to such patterns if they are integrated, as I believe this one is, with the larger actions of the society. Cf. Rogers, *The Matter of Revolution*, p. 2: "There was in seventeenth-century England, as, indeed in other cultures at other times, a large semantic field that contained and combined the language of the otherwise distinct intellectual practices of political and scientific speculation."

12. Though identifying the divisions somewhat differently, Guibbory, *Ceremony and Community*, asserts that "For all the shared Christian (and specifically Protestant) faith of those either defending or attacking ceremony, the controversy over worship shows the existence of two ideologies at odds on so many issues that there seems little meeting ground . . . each consisted of a constellation of interrelated beliefs . . ." (p. 14).

13. Doody, *The Daring Muse*, p. 45.

14. Stone, *Causes of the English Revolution*, pp. 105–6; he divides these cultures in terms that generally resemble mine (including, I should acknowledge, in their rhetorical bias against the Royalist side): country versus court, thrifty versus extravagant, chaste

versus promiscuous, sober versus drunken, nationalist versus xenophile, outspoken versus sycophantic, "solidly Protestant, even Puritan" versus "deeply tainted by Popish leanings." However, Stone associates "old ways" with the country faction, versus the "new tyrannical practices" of the court, which in some ways reverses my location of radicalism and conservatism in literary style.

15. Underdown, *Revel, Riot, and Rebellion*, pp. 40–41. Underdown sorts this division primarily by region, with the arable lands of "chalk" as inherently more stable, with divided fields under the purview of a traditional and resident manorial lord. Woodland and pasture "cheese" areas were more open to immigration and (therefore) innovation, leading to more radical change and also repressive mechanisms to control that change, each of which conduced to inroads by Puritanism. John Aubrey's *Natural History of Wiltshire* characterizes the cheese people as "melancholy, contemplative" Puritans (Underdown, p. 73)—neither cavalier nor Cavalier. Certainly there were lines of political causation more direct than anything we might call temperamental or stylistic. For example, the burden of new enclosures would be felt more severely in the woodland-pasture areas, and were more often on behalf of royal favorites from distant places, rather than negotiated with a resident lord. But the correlations still strike me as more than merely coincidental. For further if anecdotal corroboration on this, cf. Simmons, *Environmental History*, p. 21, citing a speculation "that the Scottish Highland region was so conservative because there were no trees: any form of innovative activity was reported to the neighbors in minutes."

16. The great contemporary provocateur of debates about the Civil War, Christopher Hill, senses a parallel between politics and poetry, because in both realms there is a discernible struggle to fit new ideas into an old world-order, "first by the violent and forced juxtaposition of Donne, then by the unresolved conflict of the later metaphysicals; until finally, after the victory of the new political and intellectual forces, we get a new type of poetry drawing on new philosophical assumptions, and disturbed by none of the doubts which have tormented the sensitive since the days of Shakespeare. The tortured conceit gives way to the neatly balanced rhymed couplet"; Hill, *Puritanism and Revolution*; repr. in Carey, *Andrew Marvell*, p. 76.

17. On the consensus that identifies "the royalists as the party of order," see Hughes, *The Causes of the English Civil War*, p. 145. Lake, "Puritan Identities," p. 112, describes the opposing sides, from a historical perspective, in terms that resemble those I derive from the literary-critical discipline: "On the one hand, we are presented with a conservative popular religious culture rooted in the traditional festivals of the liturgical year . . . centred on the capacity of the Church through certain ritual observances to impose order and meaning. . . . On the other hand, we have an aggressive Protestantism centred on a highly rationalised and articulated body of doctrine . . . which defined religion in terms of the effective internalization of those doctrines . . . by the individual believer." On the links between Protestantism and individualism, see also Sommerville, *The Secularization of Early Modern England*, pp. 165–66, and Loewenstein, "Politics and Religion," p. 15, which contrasts Laud's emphasis on "the formal and outward aspects of worship" (including the rectilinear boundaries of the altar railing) with "the Protestant belief that the supremacy of the individual conscience and the individual response to the holy scriptures are much more important than the correct performance of church ceremonies."

18. Davis, "Religion and the Struggle for Freedom in the English Revolution," p. 530.

19. Winstanley, "The True Levellers Standard Advanced" (1649).

20. Hooker, *Of the Laws of Ecclesiastical Polity*, bk. 5, chap. 26, sec. 2, in *Works*, 1:517.

21. Targoff, *Common Prayer*, passim.

22. Dryden, "Discourse," 2:76.

23. *Eikon Basilike*, pp. 113–19. If "the book's imagery too is conventional" (Potter, *Secret Rites*, p. 179), that may reveal the implicit ideological argument of conventional, as opposed to Metaphysical, imagery. On the other hand, Edward Stillingfleet's *Origines Sacrae* seems pointed mainly against Catholicism, but it employs a Royal Society argument about rhetoric, urging imitation of the apostles who eschewed "all affected obscurity, ambiguous expressions, and Philosophical terms"; quoted by Barbara J. Shapiro, *A Culture of Fact*, p. 172.

24. Herbert is certainly offering a Protestant reading of the Eucharist, but also a step toward the mentality that the Royalist "Water Poet" John Taylor, in his 1652 "Christmas In and Out," mocks as the belief "that Plum-pottage was mere Popery, that a collet of brawn was an abomination, that roast beef was anti-christian, that mince pies were relics of the Whore of Babylon, and a goose or a turkey or a capon were marks of the Beast"; quoted by Underdown, *Rebel, Riot, and Rebellion*, p. 258. Jonson—Royalist and (mostly) Catholic in his affiliations—mocks this same kind of Puritan censoriousness toward feasting in *Bartholomew Fair*.

25. Even apparent transactions with God himself prove, in Herbert's "Deniall," to be far more interior to the speaker than they at first appear. There were certainly Laudians expressing similar preferences for divine meaning over superficial materialism, and though such statements were partly a predictable defensive effort to claim the middle ground, I do not mean to adopt uncritically the Puritan caricature of Laud.

26. Cope and Jones, introduction to Sprat, *History of the Royal Society*, p. xxxi.

27. See Gregerson's deeply thoughtful *Reformation of the Subject*.

28. Mangrum and Scavizzi, *A Reformation Debate*, p. 62. Koerner p. 98, notes that this danger was projected out onto the Native Americans. Thomas Hariot, *A Briefe and True Report of the New Found Land of Virginia* (1590), p. 27, reports that when he provided a Bible, "I thought they did conceive, but onely the doctrine therein contained; yet would many be glad to touch it, to embrace it, to kisse it, to hold it to their brests and heades, and stroke over all their bodie with it; to shewe their hungrie desire of that knowledge which was spoken of." What Hariot cannot acknowledge—because of what it reveals about both his colonial role and about Protestant innovation—is that the natives were surely desiring material power rather than mere doctrine.

29. Fowler, "Genre and Tradition," p. 87, for example, finds that even the more strenuous mode of rustic withdrawal expressed by georgics "has found more practitioners . . . among royalists such as Robert Herrick and Sir John Denham than among the Commonwealth men." Though I believe that the georgic mode finds more explicit rejections than endorsements among the Cavaliers through most of the seventeenth century, and that the Puritan side at least prefers georgic to pastoral in that same period, it is interesting that the great early Protestant poet Sidney "in his *Defense of Poesy* despises georgic as merely imitative [because] the georgic poet 'takes not the course of his own invention'" (p. 87). What Protestant poetics especially value is the way verbal work transforms the world.

30. Low, *The Georgic Revolution*, pp. 74–79, offers a vivid survey of Donne's resistance to nature poetry.

31. Zwicker, "Lines of Authority," in Sharpe and Zwicker, *Politics of Discourse*, p. 232.

32. See Achinstein, *Literature and Dissent*, pp. 191–200, on the role of Canticles in the resistance to Restoration libertinism. Theorists of the second half of the twentieth century often shared the Metaphysical notion that sexuality could instead be the energy of revolutionary liberation.

33. Corns, "Thomas Carew," p. 210.

34. Guibbory, *Ceremony and Community*, p. 24, notes a few such examples and cites Cornelius Burges urging the Long Parliament to "cast aside (as *a Menstruous cloth*) all Idols and Idolatry."

35. Hannaford, " 'Express'd by Mee': Carew on Donne and Jonson," p. 64.

36. Barbour, *Literature and Religious Culture*, p. 98.

37. Ricks, "Allusion: The Poet as Heir," argues that Augustan poetry, Jonson's true heir, is itself characterized by filial allusions. It should be noted, however, that this kind of "son" is itself a figural transformation of biology.

38. Smith, *Literature and Revolution*, p. 260; it is tempting to compare "the spontaneous gathering of sectarians" in violent rebellion with "the most heterogeneous ideas yoked by violence together."

39. Herrick, *The Complete Poetry of Robert Herrick*, ed. Patrick, H-57 ("Dreames," p. 31) and N-158 ("Prayer," p. 503). Barbour, *Literature and Religious Culture*, p. 93, notes that Herrick also urges Corinna to abandon her "sev'rall world" so that she can instead "obay / The Proclamation made for May"—a half-metaphorical reference to the Book of Sports and other official-traditional observances that became surrogates for the collective mandates of Arminianism. The fear of the weird transformative power of individual consciousness is what Herrick mistrusts in Puritan theology and Metaphysical poetics alike.

40. Norbrook, *Writing the English Republic*, p. 144.

41. Ibid., p. 145, quoting Taylor's *Aqua-Musae* (1645), p. 12.

42. Shuger, "Conceptions of Style," p. 179.

43. Ibid., p. 182.

44. Ibid., p. 179.

45. The correlations are certainly not perfect or all-encompassing. What Shuger (ibid., p. 180) calls "Melanchthon's Protestant Ciceronianism" makes an awkward fit on one side, and on the other we face not only the ambiguous cases of relatively high-religious anti-Ciceronians such as Andrewes, Browne, and perhaps Donne, but also Catholics such as More, Lipsius, and Muret. Furthermore, although "In Catholic Europe, Ciceronianism implied absolutist ideology and religious orthodoxy . . . the 'English Seneca,' Joseph Hall, was a royalist bishop; and Milton, England's Virgil, a republican Independent" (Shuger, p. 185).

46. The fact that recognizable analogues of the Metaphysical mode appeared prominently in Dutch and German poetry, but much less so in the poetry of southern Europe, reinforces the impression of a genetic link between lyric styles and theological preferences. Cf. Frank Warnke's introduction to *European Metaphysical Poetry*, e.g., p. 19, though he believes "there is no validity in positing an association between specific religious faith and this sort of poetry" (pp. 79–80), preferring to associate the Metaphysical mode with countries tolerating doctrinal diversity. Nonetheless, I believe Warnke's own anthology supports some doctrinal links. In addition to being arguably Metaphysicals, these leading northern poets were explicitly and sometimes radically Protestant: Huygens (though Royalist in his English affiliations), Revius, and Dullaert were Calvinists,

Fleming a Lutheran, and Luyken an Anabaptist (Kuhlmann seems to have been something even further out). The versions of the passionate and paradoxical Metaphysical modes that appeared in France present a tricky exception—especially Sponde—though Warnke (p. 21) notes that poets such as de Viau and St.-Amant "show an enthusiasm for nature which contrasts with Donne's poetic world" and places them closer to the independent figure of Marvell (I would add that their libertine attitude places them close to Lovelace, Carew and Suckling), while d'Aubigné was actually a staunch Protestant, and Drelincourt a Huguenot pastor. In any case Malherbe's Jonsonian/neoclassical mode triumphed much more quickly in the French culture wars, "partly because the authoritarian ideals of the French court found in his principles a more complete embodiment" (p. 38): *ut politica poesis.* Warnke himself associates the death of the French Metaphysical mode with Richelieu's assumption of power (p. 82). Metaphysical poetry remains almost invisible in the cultural centers of Catholicism such as Italy and Spain (Sora Juana de la Cruz writes with some Metaphysical attributes in Spain, but here I would invoke again the overriding force of social preterition, which in her case would have been overdetermined).

47. In Donne the sexual instincts are almost overpowering, though tangled in narcissism; they become the objects of fierce displacement and repression, notably in the Holy Sonnet "Batter My Heart." On tendencies resembling what modern Western culture describes as repressed homosexuality in Marvell, see *The Transproser Rehears'd* from Marvell's own time and, more recently, Hammond, "Marvell's Sexuality," pp. 87–123; in Herbert, see Watson, *The Rest Is Silence,* pp. 258–59, and Pearlman, "George Herbert's God."

48. Cf. Goldmann, *The Hidden God,* p. 120: "I do not need to insist at any great length on the link between the economic and social position of the *officiers* of the *ancien régime* and the ideology of Jansenism. The *officiers* were dependent upon an absolute monarchy which they disliked intensely, but which had no means of satisfying their demands by any reforms conceivable at that time. The tragic teaching of Jansenism insisted upon the essential vanity of the world and upon the fact that salvation could be found only in solitude and withdrawal."

49. Potter, *Secret Rites,* p. 209, argues that "Royalist style, as it formed itself under pressure, was marked by a taste for obscurity, mystery, and playfulness"—in other words, it starts looking oddly Metaphysical. Hermeticism evidently became a language for the culture of retirement among the disenfranchised Royalists—especially the mystic-minded ones such as Vaughan—which lent their verse a strangeness that resembles Metaphysicality. However, it was arguably a new tactic in defense of a jeopardized authoritarian impulse, with the thrice-masterful Hermes holding a place for the second Charles.

50. Smith, *Literature and Revolution,* p. 144.

51. Rogers, *Matter of Revolution,* p. 4, describes "a tendency among Puritans to view all historical progress as the manifestation of God's arbitrary manipulation of forces on earth, a belief in direct divine determinism—a theological position often called 'voluntarism'—which the influence of Calvinism supported and strengthened."

52. Harrison, *Rise of Natural Science,* p. 7.

53. Fitter, *Poetry, Space, Landscape,* p. 300.

54. See, for example, Low, *Georgic Revolution,* pp. 152–53.

55. Sommerville, *Secularization,* p. 169.

56. Norbrook, *Writing the English Republic*, p. 143.

57. Hirst, "The Failure of Godly Rule in the English Republic," p. 66 concedes the likelihood "that the waning of anti-Catholicism, as the spectre of Antichrist dwindled in the years of godly rule, helped sap reformist zeal." Guibbory, *Ceremony and Community*, p. 9, suggests that "in rejecting ritual, which anthropologists believe is essential to social relations, puritan theology inevitably (if unwittingly) weakened the social fabric." Cruttwell, *The Shakespearean Moment*, argues that Puritanism killed Renaissance poetry, but it seems more helpful to say that the triumph of Puritanism exposed the contradictions in the cultural mode Puritanism represented, and released many of the tensions between Puritan and Royalist-Anglican perspectives that produced poetry on both sides of the debate.

58. Doody, *Daring Muse*, p. 42.

59. Underdown, *Rebel, Riot, and Rebellion*, p. 111, notes that "although inversion rituals were known in other parts of England, nowhere were they as prominent a feature of the local culture as in these western wood-pasture"—and hence Puritan-revolutionary—regions, which reflect these tendencies even in their sports: "The greater sense of individual identity expressed in the 'domestic' skimmington ritual, the tension between individual and community reflected in stool-ball." On many levels, then, a correlation persists between the poetic and socio-political forms of the consciousness that turns the world upside down.

60. It is worth being quite careful here, while associating the Puritan/Parliamentary position with revolutionary interiority, not to assume that position was one of liberation, as if it anticipated the French Revolution by 150 years. The battle against what was viewed as a corrupt tradition did not mean a battle against authority per se, let alone a battle against discipline. There were things the individual was to be freed from, but that individual was hardly intended to be free, or understood as such, in any mainstream Calvinist view. "Whatever the gathered churches may have demanded by way of corporate autonomy, internally they were about discipline, orthodoxy, conformity," reports Davis, "Religion and the Struggle for Freedom," p. 512. Even Winstanley subjugated most of what we now understand as civil freedoms to a socialistic program. If (as Christopher Hill has famously argued) forces of more modern and radical liberation found inspiration and opportunity in the revolutionary events, they were decisively repressed.

But that authority was handed down in more intense and jagged forms, and it was addressed toward the salvation of subjectively involved individuals who would have to stand up alone in God's judging presence. None of the pleasures or glories of the court, not the good sense or good fellowship, certainly not its claims to antiquity, stood up against that ultimate value; and to the extent that Cavalier poetry celebrated such pleasure and glory, tried to make sense and signal community, and claimed the authority of a classical past, its claims were the same appealing but vulnerable ones made by its political affiliate.

61. Cf. lines 157–92, ending with Denham's hope that his own poetry will be like the river, "Though deep, yet clear, though gentle, yet not dull, / Strong without rage, without ore-flowing full." Similarly, Michael Drayton, whose entire career was devoted to upper-class patrons, implies that poetry can be at once, without conflict, a work of pure nature and a work of high statesmanship: "Give me those Lines (whose touch the skillful eare to please) / That gliding flow in state, like swelling *Euphrates*, / In which things naturall be, and not in falsely wrong: / The Sounds are fine and smooth, the Sense is full and

strong, / Not bumbasted with words, vaine ticklish eares to feed; / But such as may content the perfect man to read" (*Poly-Olbion*, in *Works of Michael Drayton*, 4:422). Thus by 1622 the path was already blazed to a style and its accompanying ethos, with nature endorsing the political order, and an ideal man of letters sitting contentedly, in perfect balance, in its upper regions.

62. Bacon's essay "Of Atheism" (1625; in Warhaft, *Francis Bacon*, p. 86) begins, "I had rather believe all the fables in the Legend, and the Talmud, and the Alcoran than that this universal frame is without a mind."

63. Hobbes, *The Elements of Law, Natural and Politic*, part 1, chap. 10, p. 48. Rogers, *Matter of Revolution*, p. 7, rightly discerns a fundamental absolutism of power in "the mechanist movement in midcentury England, a movement demonstrably Anglican and Royalist in the political convictions of many of its practitioners. For all their attempts to establish a disinterested realm of objective knowledge, the members of the Royal Society tended more often than not to envision a corpuscular universe, governed arbitrarily by an absolutist power, that was peculiarly monarchic in design." My only disagreement would be with "arbitrarily": increasingly, and especially for High Church Royalists, the emphasis surely fell on a fundamental rational predictability underlying that power, even if the patterns were not always easy to recognize from the outside.

64. A. J. Smith, "Sacred Earth," p. 260.

65. Sommerville, *Secularization*, p. 168.

66. John Guy, "On the Happy Accession" (1699); quoted by Zwicker, *Lines of Authority*, p. 179.

67. Low, *Georgic Revolution*, pp. 247–50, provides several instances of this argument.

68. Achinstein, *Literature and Dissent*, pp. 11–12.

69. Quoted by Shapiro, *Probability*, p. 114.

70. Sprat, *History of the Royal Society*, pp. 62, 112, 116–17.

71. Eliot, "Andrew Marvell" in Carey, *Andrew Marvell*, p. 48.

72. Corns, "Thomas Carew," p. 211.

73. S. R. Gardiner (1897) on Waller; quoted by Potter, *Secret Rites*, p. xii. Waller does write an eager little Augustan poem praising Cromwell in power.

74. Smith, *Literature and Revolution*, p. 262, mentions this strong correlation; Post, *English Lyric Poetry*, p. 120, acknowledges it, but also recognizes the risks of oversimplifying it.

75. Alfred Harbage (among others) characterizes Fletcher as a distinctly "cavalier" kind of playwright, like those who went on to support the royal cause in the war Fletcher never lived to see. A good recent study of Corbett confirms my sense that his royalism is bound up with literary modes and tendentious reference to nature; see McRae, "Satire and Sycophancy."

76. Patterson, *Pastoral and Ideology*, pp. 151–52, comments insightfully on the way the Cavaliers' Virgilian reference becomes an implicit complaint instead of an implicit boast as they become dispossessed of their estates.

77. Wither, *The Shepheards Hunting* (London, 1615).

78. Anthony Wood, *Athenae Oxonienses* (1691–92); quoted by Post, *English Lyric Poetry*, p. 131.

79. Smith, *Literature and Revolution*, p. 255. Mackenzie, *The Metaphysical Poets*, p. 11, suggests that Carew and Lovelace "belong at least as much with the Metaphysicals" as with Jonson.

80. Lovelace, *Poems*, ed. Wilkinson. Lovelace even pushes into the realm of Donne's "The Dream" and other narcissistic fantasies, the inwardness reaching its natural conclusion in the melding of masturbation with wet dream that culminates "Love Made in the First Age: To Chloris." For a Counter-Reformation adaptation of "The Sun Rising" and "The Good Morrow," see Crashaw's "A Hymne for the Epiphanie," lines 1–14.

81. Smith, *Literature and Revolution*, p. 203. The case for a fully Royalist individualism is most passionately and extensively asserted in Anselment, *Loyalist Resolve*. On how Milton works from the inside out, see Fish, *How Milton Works*.

82. Where one might expect a more favorable description, Morris and Withington, in the introduction to *The Poems of John Cleveland* (Oxford: Clarendon Press, 1967), p. lxxv, concede that "What was in Donne a technique for the analysis of significant experience becomes in Cleveland's poems no more than a propulsive agent." Cf. Selden, "Hobbes and Late Metaphysical Poetry," p. 209: "in Donne's poetry scholastic 'terms' still possess the ambiance of their original 'meanings,' whereas, in Cleveland, that ambiance has been scoured of its deposits: scholasticism has become mock-scholasticism." T. S. Eliot comments that wit—"structural decoration of a serious idea" in poets like Marvell—is sometimes indulged "by Cowley or Cleveland, for its own sake"; in "Andrew Marvell," in Carey, *Andrew Marvell*, p. 50.

83. Wedgwood, *Poetry and Politics Under the Stuarts*, p. 98.

84. Smith, *Literature and Revolution*, p. 217.

85. Cowley, *English Writings*, ed. Waller. That this is not a random association becomes clear when Cowley repeats it in his ode "To the Royal Society," where the discovery of a star "Does to the Wise a Star, to Fools a Meteor show" (line 165).

86. See similarly Cowley's assertion, in his "To Sir William Davenant, Upon His Two First Books of *Gondibert*," that "*God-like Poets* do past things reherse, / Not *change*, but *Heighten* Nature by their Verse" (lines 21–22). In "The Dissembler," Cowley plays with the opposite notion—that his verse has poetically feigned love so well that it has risen "To this sad fame of *Prophesie*, / *Truth* gives a *dull propriety* to my stile, / And all the *Metaphors* does spoil" (lines 16–18).

87. Bacon, *The Advancement of Learning*, in Warhaft, *Francis Bacon*, p. 233.

88. Bacon, "The Natural and Experimental History," in the *Instauratio Magna*, in *The Works of Francis Bacon*, ed. Spedding, Ellis, and Heath, 5:132. It thus seems ironic (though the publication plan left him few alternatives) that Samuel Johnson would choose his "Life of Cowley" as the occasion to lodge similar charges against Metaphysical poetry generally.

89. Waswo, *Language and Meaning*, lists "metaphysical 'wit'" among Greville's chief styles (p. 80), with *Caelica* as the "chief exemplar" of the metaphysical—not necessarily in the modern critical associations of the term, but at least in focusing on transcendent reality "in terms of its emotional consequences for the subject" (p. 133).

90. Fulke Greville, *Treatie of Humane Learning*, lines 148 and 158.

91. Underdown's *Rebel, Riot, and Rebellion*, chap. 7, is largely dedicated to describing the overwhelming obstacles to his efforts to confirm his binary geographical model by mapping military recruitment statistics and the like—items considerably less slippery than some my division would propose.

92. Madsen, *From Shadowy Types*, p. 170, observes that "the controversy between St. Bernard and Abbot Suger regarding the use of the senses in worship, or on the style of Thomas Aquinas, or on St. John of the Cross' depreciatory view of images and

ceremonies might suggest that what we have to deal with is not an essential difference between Catholics and Protestants but rather a difference in psychological types."

93. Corbett, "An Elegie Upon the Death of his Owne Father," lines 29–42.

94. Extending his "negative capability" to yet another binary division in his culture, Shakespeare places himself systematically on both sides of the Metaphysical/Cavalier split. There are surely Metaphysical signals. Richard II imagines the flora and fauna of England rising up to protect his anointed kingship, but events then suggest that this naturalizing of power is delusory, and the grandly rhetorical Richard is driven back into his private imagination, with twin buckets in the place of Donne's twin compasses. In his dungeon, Richard announces that he will subjugate his intellect (which knows the comparison is wildly flawed) to the aggression of his desiring spirit, and thereby—that is, by an extended conceit—force the oppressive world into a more satisfactory shape: "I have been studying how I may compare / This prison where I live unto the world; / And for because the world is populous, / And here is not a creature but myself, / I cannot do it; yet I'll hammer it out. / My brain I'll prove the female to my soul, / My soul the father, and these two beget / A generation of still-breeding thoughts" (*Richard II*, 5.5.1–8). When Orlando says of the trees, "In their barks my thoughts I'll character" (*As You Like It*, 3.2.6), he is announcing a profoundly Metaphysical project, overriding and overwriting the prior character of nature with his own aggressive verbal consciousness; but he is also mocked for that project. If the voices of the plays' heroes seem generally more Metaphysical than Cavalier, that may be simply because Donne and his followers modeled their informal poetic personae after dramatic ones. Cruttwell, *The Shakespearean Moment*, p. 39, equates the "mature Shakespearean" style with the "Metaphysical," but Shakespeare himself, in Sonnet 76, seems to deny it fairly directly: "Why is my verse so barren of new pride? / So far from variation or quick change? / Why with the time do I not glance aside / To new-found methods and to compounds strange?" He replies that, because he writes of a stable object outside of himself, he cannot write with the conceitedness of a Donne, always creating and pursuing novelties.

The emergence of Shakespeare as a figure of cultural consensus in the Augustan period may partly be explained by the way he bridges this cultural gap, commanding assent as at once Metaphysical—a figure of native English culture, producing the colloquial vernacular in situations of dramatic immediacy, inventing language to match and manufacture his vision, registering but never merely submitting to classical and Continental influences—and Cavalier, an embodiment of high culture whose writing suggests a transparency to wondrous concentric orders of meaning and power already present in the universe, and (thereby) to universals in human experience, through characters who were at once unique individuals and perfectly recognizable types. In collectively worshipping him, Augustan English culture—generally eager to renounce the culture wars of the previous century—could bury and praise its Metaphysical and Cavalier fathers alike.

Chapter 6. The Retreat of God, the Passions of Nature, and the Objects of Dutch Painting

Though I have tried to include here the pictures most essential to my argument, it is not feasible to reproduce in print all the images useful for this chapter and the next one (let alone to offer them in color). So I urge readers to go to www.humnet.ucla.edu/ backtonature, where they will find, along with citations of printed sources, clickable URLs of the images currently available on the Internet, arranged in the same sequence as in the chapters, to make following along easy. Because museum websites evolve and links (which I will do my best to keep current) mutate, readers may sometimes wish to search directly through Google Images, or through the regular Google search, which often finds reproductions the Images database does not. To avoid breaking up sentences so frequently with information extraneous to the argument, I have identified the dates and current location of cited pictures in the Index and on the website, rather than parenthetically in the text, except where immediately relevant to the argument or necessary to distinguish different works.

Notes to epigraphs: G. W. F. Hegel, *Aesthetics*, 1:598. Hegel is, of course, overgeneralizing, but the observation is still applicable widely enough to be valuable.

Jean Calvin, *Institution de la Religion Chrestienne* (1545), 1.11.12, 1:135, my translation of variant "a."

1. "In the Reformation period, artists faced a crisis with respect to their livelihood. The church, once the chief patron of the arts, now played a minor role, except for the Catholic baroque period. This meant that artists had to find subjects sought by more secular patrons. Sometimes they could eke out an existence, but frequently they had to abandon their professions. Other artists continued to create works with religious subject matter but had no commissions for such works. Rembrandt, who did so many religious subjects, had only one minor commission for a private chapel"; Dillenberger, *Images and Relics*, p. 190.

2. Kettering, *The Dutch Arcadia*, p. 15.

3. Auerbach makes this argument in various forms, notably in the opening chapters of *Mimesis*; Foucault, in *The Order of Things*, comments that "Resemblance, which had for long been the fundamental category of knowledge—both the form and content of what we know—became disassociated in an analysis based on terms of identity and difference. . . . The activity of the mind . . . will no longer consist in *drawing things together* . . . but, on the contrary, in *discriminating*, that is, in establishing their identities" (chap. 3, sec. 2, p. 54).

4. Svetlana Alpers, *The Art of Describing*, pp. 80–82, makes these prints exemplary of her title.

5. Schwartz and Bok, *Pieter Saenredam*, p. 7, notes that this text (perhaps by Samuel Ampzing), in insisting no priest is visible in these cross-sections "even if you look at them closely through crystal spectacles [*Kristalijnen Bril*]," is likely parodying a notorious Remonstrant pamphlet—that is, one resisting the Dutch Calvinist Reformation— entitled *Christalijnen Bril*.

6. Koerner, *Reformation of the Image*, p. 85.

7. MacLeish, *Collected Poems*, pp. 106–7. For these painters, I am avoiding the term "Baroque," which encourages a confusion between the seventeenth century as a period and elements of style by no means proprietary or universal to that period.

8. Slive, *Dutch Painting*, p. 177.

9. Quoted by Moxey, *Pieter Aertsen, Joachim Beuckelaer, and the Rise of Secular Painting*, p. 200.

10. Luther, *Luther's Works*, 40:99 ("Against the Heavenly Prophets").

11. Svetlana Alpers's controversial claim is that seventeenth century Dutch painting is primarily intent on description, as distinct from the narrative goals implicit in Italian work of the same period.

12. One of the first learned commentaries on painting in English, Edward Norgate's *Miniatura; or, The Art of Limning* (1627–28), describes landscapes as "of all kinds of painting the most innocent, and which the Divill him selfe could never accuse of Idolatry."

13. Kettering, *Dutch Arcadia*, p. 30, observes that "The dream of an ideal environment, rooted in simplicity and tied to the land, was common to all European Renaissance societies. . . . Nearly all of the writers were residents either of Amsterdam, the city which provided the focus of Dutch cultural life, or of the Hague, the administrative capital."

14. It is also worth noting that the professional structure of Dutch painting in this period, with its lengthy apprenticeships, would have nurtured a technical meticulousness that abetted the cause of naturalistic representation.

15. Glacken, *Traces on the Rhodian Shore*, p. 25.

16. Hegel takes passing notice of the possible significance of this for artistic production; *Aesthetics*, 1:168–70, 597–98.

17. Chong, "Market for Landscape Painting," demonstrates that a wide range of the Dutch population purchased landscapes.

18. Underdown, *Revel, Riot, and Rebellion*, associates Puritan revolution in England with areas of land reclaimed by fen drainage; perhaps a related kind of revolutionary Puritanism was promoted by Dutch geology.

19. Bruyn, "Toward a Scriptural Reading of Seventeenth-Century Dutch Landscape Paintings," p. 88, argues that "Luyken actually provided a frontispiece for a Dutch translation of Bunyan's *Pilgrim's Progress* in 1682," but Luyken was often an emblematic moralizer; Ruisdael's early pictures are stubbornly antitextual.

20. Ruisdael's works will be listed here according to Slive, *Jacob van Ruisdael: A Complete Catalogue*. It is noteworthy that, although Christianity has long used the rainbow as a symbol of divine providence (notably through the story of Noah), it was also a symbol of the transience of earthly beauties in the Renaissance; cf. Bruyn, "Toward a Scriptural Reading," p. 100.

21. Alpers, *Art of Describing*, argues that writing in Dutch painting tends to be a thing to see rather than a text to read.

22. Walford, *Jacob van Ruisdael and the Perception of Landscape*, p. 18, quoting van Mander's 1604 *Het Schilderboek*.

23. Houbraken, quoted by Walford, *Ruisdael*, p. 29.

24. See for example Fuchs, *Dutch Painting*, quoted by Walford, *Ruisdael*, p. 198.

25. Bruyn argues for pilgrimage motifs; Wiegand's dissertation "Ruisdael-Studien" tracks Baroque allegorical allusions to literature—a view modified but fundamentally supported by Kousnetsov's "Sur le symbolisme dans les paysages de Jacob van Ruisdael." *Bulletin du Musée National de Varsovie* 14 (1973): 31–41.

26. Helgerson, "Soldiers and Enigmatic Girls."

27. Walford, *Ruisdael*, pp. 196–99, offers a brief summary of these disputes; Slive, *Dutch Painting*, p. 203, takes notice of such allegorical readings, but also asserts that "not a single contemporary source indicates that landscape paintings were viewed this way." Fuchs's *Dutch Painting*, pp. 134–35, argues for a strong element of *vanitas* moralization in Ruisdael's landscapes; I would suggest that this is not quite the same as the Christian *contemptus mundi* tradition, because the fact that life is difficult and transient does not here seem to be serving any idea that God offers a better alternative.

28. Shakespeare, *As You Like It* (3.2.122); Ruisdael (like Van Goyen, who shares Ruisdael's reluctance to dictate our focus) also rarely employs anything like the foreground framings of Hercules Seghers's *Landscape with a Lake and a Round Building* or *Houses near Steep Cliffs* from the 1620s, or Joos de Momper the Younger's *River Landscape with a Hunt* (Rijksmuseum, Amsterdam) or *Landscape* (Museo Nacional del Prado, Madrid), which provide a compositional perspective for the viewer.

29. Slive, introduction to *Jacob van Ruisdael* (1981), p. 16.

30. In Jacob van Ruisdael's *Egmond aan Zee* (Eindhoven), the town is far more central than usual, but the houses look ominously like the weathered tombs of his *Jewish Cemetery* paintings.

31. Walford, *Ruisdael*, p. 20; more moderately, Slive, *Dutch Painting*, p. 199, sees the people in Jacob van Ruisdael's early paintings as more leisurely than those in Salomon van Ruysdael's. Spolsky, *Satisfying Skepticism*, p. 137, sees "often a happy response to the human condition" in Dutch landscapes.

32. The figures in Vermeer's otherwise exquisitely detailed 1658 *View of Houses in Delft* are similarly crouched and faceless, seemingly almost irrelevant even to the cityscape their kind has built.

33. Schama, "Culture as Foreground," p. 71.

34. See Ashton, Davies, and Slive, "Jacob van Ruisdael's Trees"; Slive, *Dutch Painting*, p. 199, observes that "From the moment he picked up his brushes, Ruisdael saw trees as personalities"; Martin, *Basoque*, p. 71, comments that "in the works of Jacob van Ruisdael . . . trees, not men, play a heroic role."

35. Sutton, Introduction, *Masters*, p. 50.

36. Ruisdael's figures often appear to be slumping into what the grape-juice ads of my youth called the "Valley of Fatigue": a busy housewife's kitchen would distort optically to trap her in a slough of despair (or, we would now say, of hypoglycemia), which only the right fruit juice could boost back to a happy horizontal.

37. Spolsky, *Satisfying Skepticism*, p. 139.

38. Walford, *Ruisdael*, p. 68.

39. Sutton, *Masters*, p. 448.

40. Walford, *Ruisdael*, p. 82; Walford derives a message that people should "put their trust in God alone," because (here as in Isaiah 40:6–8) "All flesh is like grass and all its glory like the flower of grass. The grass withers, and the flower falls, but the word of the Lord abides for ever" (p. 100). But Ruisdael's fleshly figures cannot match the foliage around them in power and glory.

41. Bruyn, "Toward a Scriptural Reading," p. 90.

42. Ibid., p. 100.

43. Levesque, *Journey Through Landscape in Seventeenth-Century Holland*, pp. 75–81.

44. Abraham Bloemaert's similarly titled and composed 1624 painting (Walters Gallery, Baltimore), where the background figure is more clearly diabolical, affirms the validity of the allegorical subtitle.

45. Comparably, Lucas van Valckenbourg's 1581 *Mountain Landscape*, an early example of the genre, looks somewhat like Henri Met de Bles's earlier *Paradise* with the scenes of Adam and Eve erased.

46. Quoted by Walford, *Ruisdael*, p. 196.

47. Ibid., p. 72.

48. Hegel, *Aesthetics*, 1:162–63, praises the way Dutch painting delicately recreates the "fleeting appearance of nature as something generated afresh by man. Velvet, metallic luster, light . . . what at once claims our attention in matters of this kind, when art displays it to us, is precisely this pure shining and appearing of objects as something produced by the *spirit.*" Cf. Demetz, "Defenses of Dutch Painting and the Theory of Realism," p. 108.

49. Calvin, *Institutes of the Christian Religion*, 4.14.4 (p. 1279).

50. Calvin, *Institutes*, 1.11; quoted by Gilman, *Iconoclasm and Poetry*, p. 39.

51. Bruyn, "Toward a Scriptural Reading," p. 99, citing Augustine's commentary on Psalm 109 as quoted by Picinelli's late seventeenth-century emblem book.

52. Slive, *Dutch Painting*, p. 205.

53. Even Walford, whose optimistic reading of man as a "peaceful traveler" through these landscapes where "nature's noble forms echo man's dignified yet mortal existence" (*Ruisdael*, p. 205) fits these later works better than the early ones, acknowledges that the late works reflect an economically constrained compromise with the prevailing tastes of upper-class Amsterdam as the forces of Enlightenment advanced. On the changes in the Dutch art market at this time, see Montias, *Art at Auction in Seventeenth Century Amsterdam*—though he suggests that at least some forms of landscape remain popular, while historical painting declines.

54. Walford, *Ruisdael*, p. 17, cites and quotes various such claims. The acronym stands for "What You See Is What You Get" in computer graphics.

55. Ibid., p. 188.

56. Ibid., p. 193, notes the association between "republican views" and "the Dutch school." Demetz, "Defenses," observes that "later French disciples of Diderot do not hesitate to speak of the Democratic achievements of Dutch art" (p. 102), and Taine, in his *Philosophie de l'art des Pays-Bas*, perceived, in the words of Demetz, that "There now inevitably corresponds to the Dutch *republican* institutions a *realist* imagination" (p. 113).

57. Alpers, *Art of Describing*, p. 109, observes that Bacon's natural history "is, like the Dutch art with which we have linked it, description, not narration." When Romantic-era painters sought to convey a similar sense of nature's overwhelming power, the melodramatic note often forfeits Ruisdael's sense that human futility is ordinary; crossing the Alps conveys something different from crossing a scruffy Dutch dune. In Wijnand Nuyen's 1837 *Shipwreck on a Rocky Coast*, the *istoria* slips back in, not only in the implied grand narrative of maritime disaster, but also in the form of a sailor who appears crucified on the mast with which he has been beached.

58. Koerner, *Reformation of the Image*, p. 62, notes that effects of these kinds are sometimes interpreted as a Reformation tactic, "efforts to appropriate church space by displaying its mundane condition. Depicted empty of magical presence, church becomes a morally indifferent arena" where "the local congregation" lives out "its mix of sin and grace." As Koerner goes on to observe, "This model does little, though, to account for the ambivalence of that disenchanted display." My intention here is to explore that ambivalent potential.

59. Swillens, "The Paintings," p. 13.

60. Ibid., p. 12.

61. Rosenberg and Slive, *Dutch Art and Architecture*, p. 189.

62. Fuchs, *Dutch Painting*, p. 126.

63. Sjarel Ex, foreword to Helmut, *Pieter Saenredam*, p. 4.

64. For example, Fuchs, *Dutch Painting*, p. 127, notes Saenredam's "insistence on absolute clarity, on order totally visible, on order, one is tempted to say, outside human life. For even where human beings occur in Saenredam's paintings, they are small and not at all eloquent; they are just there to measure the spatial dimensions of the building." Fuchs therefore finds Saenredam's painting "so enigmatic . . . does its meaning lie elsewhere?" My suspicion is that the lack of accessible meaning may sometimes itself be the meaning.

65. Swillens, "Paintings," p. 12.

66. Pascal, *Pensées*, no. 206, p. 66.

67. Plomp, "Pieter Saenredam as a Draughtsman," pp. 62–66.

68. Van Heemstra, "Space, Light and Stillness," p. 73.

69. The boys in the foreground—one training a dog, the other completing some graffiti—could carry some old-fashioned didactic freight, but again these elements were apparently added by someone other than Saenredam; see Helmus, *Pieter Saenredam*, pp. 201–3.

70. Spolsky, *Satisfying Skepticism*, p. 149, observes that Saenredam's church space seems "washed clean not only of its icons but also of its transcendence." Still, in this instance, words do survive as a prime vehicle of piety: the foreground is filled with some surprisingly legibly detailed inscriptions on the floor, tombs, and tomb-tablets (one apparently of the artist's father); similar effects appear in Neef's depiction of the church at Anvers in about the same year.

71. Vlieghe, *Flemish Art and Architecture*, p. 201.

72. This is a key revisionist element throughout Schwartz and Bok's excellent study (*Pieter Saenredam*), which builds on much earlier speculation by P. T. A. Swillens. I believe that Saenredam's *Interior of the Church of St. Bavo in Haarlem* (1636; Rijksmuseum) provides an intriguing instance, since it brings golden warmth and cleverly accented crosses into the usually smooth, pale, blank heights of his church images—and does so by bringing back two other things the Calvinists sought to banish: images of the deity in its supernatural mode (the Resurrected Christ on the shutter panel of the organ) and sacred instrumental music (the organ itself, which parishioners had been campaigning to defend from the Calvinist authorities; Alpers, *Art of Describing*, p. 175, notes that the organ itself is inscribed with a recommendation of teaching by hymns). *Istoria* and *harmonia* return together—and together they remind us of what is insistently and perhaps plaintively missing from so many of Saenredam's other churches.

73. Schama, *The Embarrassment of Riches*, p. 540: "In one of the most telling inversions of icons and objects in all of European religious art, the Dutch abolished images of the Madonna and Child from their churches, only to reinstate them surreptitiously as simple nursing mothers in paintings of church interiors. In many examples of the genre by Emmanuel de Witte and Gerard Houckgeest, Mariolatry has collapsed into mother-love. Even when nursing scenes are purely domestic, as in the great series by Pieter de Hooch, it should not surprise us to find them often placed immediately below sacred images . . . if the domestic setting was, for the Dutch, a personal church, the nursing mother was its primal communion." But as Schama also notes, "the removal of the Blessed Virgin Mary icons from images of the nursing mother did not betoken a purely secularized, dispassionately observed naturalism" (p. 483).

74. Ross, "Gerard David's Models for Motherhood," looks at David's *Rest on the Flight into Egypt* and *The Madonna of the Milk Soup* to explore the way he (and his imitators)

secularized the notion of motherhood in response to the changing northern Renaissance art market. See also McDermott, "Eternal Triangles," on the transfer of religious schema into secular paintings.

75. Slive, *Dutch Painting*, p. 165.

76. Kettering, *Dutch Arcadia*, p. 2. She notes that *Shepherd and Shepherdess* "is the first dated shepherd piece by an Utrecht artist with figures shown full length against a natural setting" (p. 85).

77. The whereabouts of this painting are unknown, but a reproduction is visible in Kettering, *Dutch Arcadia*, fig. 119; on the attribution, see Vlieghe, "Een pastorale door Gerard Seghers," which suggests that the topic is a courting shepherd, but finds the painting otherwise unfathomable. Seghers's work, his itinerary, and his personal and professional associations all point toward active Catholicism.

78. On indicators that the doctor is performing a pregnancy test, see Arthur K. Wheelock and Beverly Louise Brown, *Masterworks from Munich: Sixteenth- to Eighteenth-century Paintings from the Alte Pinakothek* (Washington, D.C.: National Gallery of Art, 1988), p. 165. See similarly Steen's *The Doctor's Visit* (1658–62; Apsley House, London). That such satiric blasphemy was possible during the Renaissance is evident from Richard Baines's report that his Elizabethan associate Christopher Marlowe claimed "That Christ was a Bastard and his mother dishonest" (BL Harley MS 6853 ff. 307–8). But of course the allusion, if it is one, could also be read as a parodic comment on the way the modern woman falls short of the Virgin Mary, rather than on the Virgin Mary herself.

79. Willey, *The Seventeenth-Century Background*, p. 116.

80. Sinfield, *Literature in Protestant England*, pp. 129–52, develops Weber's suggestion that Protestantism leads to secularism.

81. Van Haute, *David III Ryckaert*, pp. 62–63. Liedtke says this backgrounding of the holy scene became common, though as Van Haute notes (p. 240), he does not give examples. For another possible (if more tenuous) instance of the transfer of religious motifs into the ordinary drama of secular life, notice the ways that the face watching Adam and Eve from on high during their Fall becomes merely a judgmental old person spying from a window in Ryckaert's *Old Man Courting a Young Woman in an Interior, Barn Interior with Amorous Couple, The Pipe Smoker, In a Tavern* (Bratislava version), and *The Seduction*. The same motif appears in several other works such as Adriaen Brouwer's *Tavern Scene*.

82. Rosenberg and Slive, *Dutch Art and Architecture*, pp. 141–42.

83. Wolters, *Still Lifes*, p. 41, notes that "The religious theme in Beuckelaer's painting is given even less prominence in relation to the cooks and the food" than in Aertsen's 1552–53 *Kitchen Scene with Christ in the House of Martha and Mary*. Now "the tangible plasticity . . . of the meat, vegetables and poultry in the foreground reflects a love of material things that contrasts with the less colourful manner of representation of the spiritual narrative." But this can hardly have been an unselfconscious expression of the painter's appetites: by making the foreground scene so aggressive, and the Christian background story so small and colorless, Beuckelaer is shouting his message, whether we take it to be his admiration for material reality or his mistrust of our admiration for it. Commentators have been similarly defensive about the oddity of Aertsen's depiction: "The fact that both artists depict the religious event as a small vignette at the back in no way implies that they wished to subordinate it to the still life or market scene. The biblical

story is the key, as it were, to understanding the picture." Van Os et al., *Netherlandish Art in the Rijksmuseum*, 1400–1600, p. 195. But that key, if such it is, may open up a door that had arbitrarily separated the incarnated Christ from these (other) hung up and skewered victims of worldliness.

84. Moxey, *Rise of Secular Painting*, p. 266, may therefore be overstating the degree to which "The 'problem' of the secular/religious scene" is only a retrospective "twentieth century phenomenon" that never would have disturbed the original viewers of these images.

85. Amico Aspertini's 1520 *Adoration of the Bergers* shows a pinioned lamb, the same size and color as the child and in the same supine pose; Giovanni Battista Caracciolo's *The Rest Before the Flight into Egypt* and David III Ryckaert's Budapest *Adoration of the Shepherds* again set the lamb in the foreground to echo the Christ-child above; Zurbarán's *Agnus Dei* is a picture only of a pinioned lamb. On the Catholic associations of "adoration of the shepherds" scenes, see Johns, "The Jesuits, the Crèche and Hans von Aachen." The strongly Catholic Bloemaert family created several of the shepherd scenes I have mentioned, including the arguably coy emptying of an adoration scene into a supposedly secular pastoral of shepherd courtship. I will argue that the Catholic Gerard Seghers does the same with an Annunciation scene.

86. Hollander, *An Entrance for the Eyes*, p. 3. The use of proverbs and emblems provides further evidence of the ways Dutch art invites decoding.

87. Kunzle, *From Criminal to Courtier*, p. 410, suggests that some animal carcasses "may have evoked, in the more sensitive, a sympathy akin to that engendered by the dead peasants lying naked, belly up, in the plundering pictures."

88. Torrentius's 1614 *Still Life, Allegory of Temperance* is a prominent instance of a wineglass as a moralizing symbol in this genre. Torrentius may have had some forbidden beliefs to encode, or at least lessons to learn about temperance: he was "tortured and sentenced to twenty years imprisonment by Haarlem's municipal authorities for immorality, blasphemy, and probably for membership in the outlawed Rosicrucian sect." Slive, *Dutch Painting*, p. 278.

89. That this effect is deliberate is confirmed by its recurrence in works such as Pieter de Ring's *Still Life with a Golden Goblet*. A trace of that poisonous-yellow snake lurks in Van Dijck's 1615 *Still Life* as well as in Steen's explicitly Christian *Meal at Emmaus* (see Figure 23).

90. Gregory, "Tabletop Still Lifes in Haarlem, c. 1610–1660," pp. 8–11, 14, 215, 225–28, 246–47. Gregory's survey of the literature seems to indicate that art historians, put off by some forced theological-allegorical readings of Dutch paintings (e.g., cheese must stand for Christ because Tertullian once called Christ "the Milk of God," cited by Gregory, p. 220), have prematurely ruled out the possibility that these works carry religious significance in another way. Lloyd, *Enchanting the Eye*, p. 71, is typical in suggesting that (apart from the familiar *vanitas* themes) these Dutch breakfast pieces "are generally free from moralizing or allegory."

91. Marc Chagall's 1947 *Boeuf Ecorchée* clearly recalls Rembrandt's painting of the same name, which was already hanging in the Louvre when Chagall devoted himself to studying that museum's paintings, and the latter version makes explicit the bridge between this corpse hung for koshering and the crucified Christ. Chagall would later relate a childhood incident in which, horrified by the prospective slaughter of a cow he loved, he promised the creature that he would never eat its body. See Chagall, *My Life*.

92. Van Haute, *David III Ryckaert*, p. 62, quoting Sutton, *The Age of Rubens*, pp. 423–24, who in turn cites C. Campbell and K. Craig.

93. See, for example, Ostade's *The Cut Pig* and *Pig-Killing* at the Museum of Fine Arts, Budapest. Spreading the limbs on a wooden cross was presumably a common practice, but it remains interesting that it was so commonly depicted.

94. Haller, *Foxe's Book of Martyrs*, p. 56; quoted by Thomas, *Man and the Natural World*, p. 293.

95. Harrison, *Rise of Natural Science*, pp. 232–33. This was again plausibly part of an effort to regress—in this case, to regress past the carnivorous legacy that was commonly thought to have begun with Noah.

96. Powicke, "The Reverend Richard Baxter's Last Treatise," p. 197; quoted by Thomas, *Man and the Natural World*, p. 289. Fudge, "Saying Nothing," p. 74, suggests that Reformation theologians resisted vegetarianism because they valued the reminder of shared mortality implicit in a serving of meat. Fudge's p. 77 discusses the Protestant tendency to associate the Catholic Eucharist with cannibalism.

97. Lloyd, *Enchanting the Eye*, pp. 61–62.

98. The painting of the De Witt brothers may be by Jan de Baen, and may be from the date of the event in 1672, but could have been done in the three decades that followed.

99. Schama, *The Embarrassment of Riches*, p. 276.

100. Martin, *Baroque*, p. 13.

101. See Cavendish, *Poems and Fancies*: (1653) "Here *beasts* and *men*, both in their *bloud* lay *masht*,/As if that a *French Cook* had them minc'd, *so hasht*,/Or with their *bloud* a *gelly* boyll/To make a *Bouillon* of the *spoyle*."

102. Specter, "The Extremist."

103. Lest we overrate the creature-sympathies of the Protestant movement, we should remember the practice of burning effigies of the pope with cats inside to provide exciting sound-effects; cf. Sommerville, *Secularization*, p. 40.

104. Cf. Cartmill, *A View to a Death in the Morning*, pp. 80–81: "By the mid-seventeenth century, hunting had ceased to furnish a vital and popular metaphor for honorable love. When later writers compare love to hunting, they either follow Shakespeare in making hunting a metaphor for rape, or use the comparison satirically to ridicule hunters and their machismo." Already in the early 1530s, the "May" panel of Van Orley's *Hunts of Maximilian* tapestry series sets aggressive seduction alongside arming for the hunt.

105. De Jongh, *Questions of Meaning*, pp. 21–58.

106. Alpers, *Art of Describing*, p. 188.

107. Hollander, *Entrance*, p. 163.

108. Ibid. pp. 8 and 42, recognizes the erotic aspect of the desire for *doorsien*—Van Mander's term for seeing through the depicted space in a painting.

109. See, for example, Hugo van der Goes's *Lamentation*, right wing of the diptych *The Fall and the Redemption* (ca. 1470; Kunsthistorisches Museum, Vienna), Donatello's Deposition relief sculpture (1448; Basilica of St. Anthony, Padua); Fra Angelico's *Lamentation* (1436–41; Museo di San Marco, Florence); Gaspar Isenmann's *Lamentation and Entombment of Christ* (1465; Musée d'Unterlinden, Colmar); Benvenuto di Giovanni's *Crucifixion* (1490; National Gallery, Washington); Lorenzo Lotto's 1512 version (Pinacoteca Civica, Iesi) and his 1516 San Bartolomeo altarpiece (Accademia Carrara, Bergamo); and

Bartolomeo Schedoni's *Deposition of Christ* (1613; Galleria Nazionale, Parma). It is also visible in some old illuminated manuscript illustrations. Sometimes the gesture belongs to the Virgin Mary or Mary Magdalene, but I believe it is often given to the relatively minor figure sometimes called Mary of Cleophas.

110. The initial sketch appears to be undecided about whether to give the mourning Mary this exact gesture, with the hands raised on either side of the face with palms forward and fingers spread, or instead to give her clasped hands. It appears as no. 487 (cat. 57 verso) in Van Regteren Altena, *Jacques de Gheyn*, 3:228. The *Half-length Figure of the Virgin Mary* is no. 16 (cat. II P2), 3:25, in the same collection.

111. Van Regteren Altena, *Jacques de Gheyn*, 3:12.

112. Van Regteren Altena speculates that the painting may be "a disguised political outcry. . . . But so far I have been unable to identify the three persons referred to here" (ibid., 1:136). Whether there is any Trinitarian correspondence to what are apparently a partridge, a dove, and a kingfisher, I do not know—though I have seen readings of "The Twelve Days of Christmas" as a secret catechism, with Christ as the partridge on a tree and the dove as (a standard association) the Holy Ghost, which would leave the suggestively-named kingfisher; and in De Gheyn's French the puns on *perdre/perdreau* and *pécheur/pêcheur* would have been vivid. The fact that De Gheyn made engravings of Christ between the two thieves may also be worth remembering here.

Chapter 7. Nature in Two Dimensions

1. Alpers, *Art of Describing*, p. 36. As usual with such assertions, there is room for dispute—what about Leonardo da Vinci, or even Robert Grosseteste?—but there seems little question that this change has implications that dug deep into the meaning of individual consciousness and also spread wide into readings of the physical universe.

2. Berger, *Second World*, p. 18, lists a number of Renaissance paintings that seem to invite interpretation by stretching the techniques of perspective to their breaking points.

3. Quoted by Gilman, *The Curious Perspective*, pp. 129 and 133.

4. Todorov, *The Conquest of America*, p. 121; quoted in Johnston's insightful "Heavenly Perspectives," p. 385.

5. Cf. Orgel, *The Illusion of Power*, as well as Orgel's other excellent work, with and without Roy Strong, on the masque.

6. Descartes, "Optics," in *Philosophical Writings*, 1:165.

7. Johnston, " 'Heavenly Perspective': Thomas Traherne and Seventeenth Century Visual Traditions," p. 51; Johnston adds that "From its inception, single-point perspective was a rhetorical strategy designed to convince viewers of a totality of vision" (p. 54).

8. Quoted by Gilman, *Curious Perspective*, p. 25.

9. Leonardo da Vinci, "Linear Perspective," p. 53 n. 83.

10. Panofsky, *Perspective as Symbolic Form*, p. 68.

11. Fowler, *Renaissance Realism*, p. 13; it is worth noting here that cognitive science has begun swinging back in the other direction, understanding the process of vision as significantly constructive and interactive.

12. Greene, *The Light in Troy.*

13. Trans. van Haute, *David III Ryckaert*, p. 221. Cf. Michael Sweerts's *Painter's Studio* (1648–50), in which the master paints a live nude, while the pupil reaches life only through the mediation of a reconstituted classical statue; this is the painting of a painting of a sculpture of a sculpture.

14. Van Haute, *David III Ryckaert*.

15. Cf. Jan Gossaert's *A Little Girl* (1520; National Gallery, London), where the subject is painted protruding just past the edges of the blank framed canvas, indicating that she is in front of it rather than painted in it, perhaps giving the impression that she is actually in the room with us rather than in a painting.

16. Van Haute, *David III Ryckaert*, p. 34, suggests that the painter depicted here may be not Ryckaert himself but David II Teniers, of whom Ryckaert was evidently an ambivalent follower; since there is no evidence of Teniers visiting Ryckaert, this scene "is simply a product of Ryckaert's lively imagination"—possibly another reminder that the painter makes the reality he imagines, and another layer of ironies that adds the substitution of painters-within-painters to the substitutions of paintings-within-paintings.

17. Georgel and Lecoq, *La peinture dans la peinture*, p. 165; my translation. For quite a similar depiction, but without the ironizing frame, see Roeland Savery, *The Bohemian Husbandman*, ca. 1616 (in Schama, *Landscape and Memory*, color illus. 12).

18. Van Haute *David III Ryckaert*, p. 22.

19. Filipczak, quoted by Van Haute, *David III Ryckaert*, p. 27.

20. Evett, *Literature and the Visual Arts*, p. 157.

21. Descamps, *Vie des peintres flamands et hollandais*; cited by Van Haute, *David III Ryckaert*, p. 1. Lampsonius, 1572; quoted by Sutton, introduction, in *Masters*, p. 8.

22. Van Haute, *David III Ryckaert*, p. 32.

23. Ibid., p. 48.

24. Kettering, *The Dutch Arcadia*, p. 64 ff.

25. Slive, *Dutch Painting*, p. 289.

26. Schama, *Landscape and Memory*, p. 156.

27. For an interesting reading of the meaning of floral nature in another Rubens family portrait, see Goldberg, "Fatherly Authority."

28. Wheelock et al., *Gerard ter Borch*, p. 168, discusses this division in its excellent catalog entry on the painting.

29. Tasso, *Jerusalem Liberated* [*Godfrey of Bulloigne*], p. 284.

30. Berger, *Second World*, p. 473, remarks on this effect.

31. Alpers, *Art of Describing*, p. 224.

32. Descargues, *Vermeer*, quoted by Berger, *Second World*, p. 458.

33. Berger, *Second World*, p. 448.

34. Cf. Mayor, "The Photographic Eye," p. 20: in Vermeer "the highlights on the objects in the immediate foreground—the carved lion-head of a chair or the bright threads of a tapestry—break up into dots like globules of halation swimming on ground glass." Quoted by Berger, *Second World*, p. 471.

35. Webber, *The Eloquent "I."*

36. Walford, *Ruisdael*, pp. 20, 45.

37. E.g., Aertsen, *The Egg Dance*, Jacob Cats ("Lovers feed on smoke"), Hieronymus Janssens ("The whore's lap is the devil's boat"), David Teniers the Younger (in his *Flemish Tavern*), various David III Ryckaert works ("As the old ones sing, so the young ones

pipe," "The cat and the chandelier," and so on), as well as several by Roemer Visscher and earlier works by Hieronymus Bosch and Pieter Brueghel the Elder.

38. Alpers, *Art of Describing*, p. 187.

39. In Quentin Metsys's *The Weigher of Gold and His Wife*, the moral argument is evident—though even here it is complicated by the implication of a parallel between the man's absorption in money and the mediation introduced into the artistic process by a mirror on the table showing the artist, with the wife distracted from her Bible that might have offered the Word as a healthier mediator.

40. Alpers, *Art of Describing*, p. 169.

41. Ibid., p. xxiv.

42. Quoted by Berdan, in the introduction to his edition of *The Poems of John Cleveland*, p. 32.

43. For example, in *The Mennonite Preacher* (1641), *Bathsheba* (1654), *Titus* (1655), and *Sampling Officials of the Amsterdam Drapers' Guild* (1662), we see the edges of papers, letters, books, but generally not anything that would let us read the writing.

44. Cf. Alpers, *Art of Describing*, pp. 188–92: "while other Dutch artists offer us visible texts, Rembrandt insists that it is the Word within and not the surface of the texts that must be valued." She concludes that Rembrandt "deserts the surface of things to plumb human depths" and "settles for the materiality of his medium itself" (p. 224). Slive, *Dutch Painting*, p. 78, asserts that "Rembrandt opened up a new field in the history of painting. It is the world which lies behind visible appearances, but is, at the same time, implied. It is the sphere of the spirit, of the soul."

Chapter 8. Metal and Flesh in The Merchant of Venice

1. Weber, *The Protestant Ethic*.

2. Marx, *Early Writings*, p. 239; quoted by Thomas, *Man and the Natural World*, p. 23.

3. Hawkes, *Idols of the Marketplace*, p. 5, suggests that Protestants found in Scripture a warning that "the replacement of nature by custom is called 'idolatry'."

4. Donne's "Canonization" certainly raises some of the same questions in observing the ways people—mistaking in various ways the real locus of value—observe "the King's real, or his stamped face" (line 7).

5. Rabb, *Struggle for Stability*, p. 91. This may have been especially vivid to those who worked the land: "the real wages of an average agricultural labourer steadily declined until in the 1620s his or her daily wage bought only half what it had in the late fifteenth century"; Bending and McRae, introduction *The Writing of Rural England*, p. xvi.

6. Rabb, *Struggle for Stability*, p. 54, observes that "Azpilcueta, Bodin, Gresham, Laffemas, the mercantilists—all in their own ways were trying to secure a grip on the bewildering economic torrents of their day," without any more success than was achieved in politics, science, philosophy, or religion.

7. McNally, *Political Economy*, p. xii, is among those who argue that "changes in agrarian economy, which drove rural producers from their land, forced them onto the labour market as wage labourers for their means of subsistence, and refashioned farming as an economic activity based upon the production of agricultural commodities for profit on the market, established the essential relations of modern capitalism." By the early

seventeenth century "more and more, the market dictated the internal organization of the English farm. . . . Thus emerged the classic capitalist structure of English farming characterized by the tripartite relationship of landlord, capitalist tenant, and wage labourer" (p. 8). This notion is fairly standard among economic historians. For a recent localized refinement that affirms the general pattern, see Whittle, *Development of Agrarian Capitalism*, which finds important and unique characteristics to the economic history of the English countryside running from the early fifteenth century, with the vanishing of serfdom, to the seventeenth, with the emergence of landless workers as a social class. Thirsk, *Agrarian History*, shows that—especially in the highly populated Midlands plains—English tenants increasingly found themselves landless. So, although Tawney and Hobsbawm may have exaggerated the burdens of emergent capitalism on the average small farmer, significant structural changes were evidently taking place, changes that (along with the feverish growth of London) alienated Englishmen from the land. Hawkes, *Idols of the Marketplace*, p. 8, citing Dobb, *Studies in the Development of Capitalism*, pp. 55–56, states that "early modern England . . . displays the capitalistic world system in embryonic form. This system first took shape in fifteenth-century England, with the beginnings of the mass expropriation of the peasantry, a process which was not completed for three hundred years. Expropriated peasants became proletarians, at first rural and later urban, who sold the commodity of their labor power on the market in exchange for money."

8. Hawkes, *Idols of the Marketplace*, pp. 66–67. Though the term may seem anachronistic, Gerard de Malynes's *Consuetudo* (1622) describes credit-paper as a functional though imaginary form of money.

9. Bending and McRae, *Writing of Rural England*, p. xix.

10. Siemon, *Word Against Word*, pp. 119–36, provides an excellent summary of the role of enclosures in the transition from a feudal to capitalist system in Shakespeare's England and Shakespeare's history plays; Siemon notes that "with remarkable consistency, variations on the theme of nostalgia and loss concerning the human costs of agricultural change characterize a chain of anti-enclosure utterances from the sixteenth century to the present" (p. 122).

11. Schama, *Landscape and Memory*, p. 154; Arthur Standish's *The Commons Complaint* (1611) asks the king to rescue woodlands.

12. In 1597, John Gerard observed that though goldenrod had been expensive not long ago, "since it was found in Hampstead Wood . . . no man will give half a crown for an hundredweight of it . . . esteeming no longer of anything, how precious soever it be, than whilst it is strange and rare." Quoted by Thomas, *Man and the Natural World*, p. 232. In this sense, goldenrod began to be valued in the manner of gold itself.

13. Wayne, *Penshurst*, p. 23.

14. Schama, *Landscape and Memory*, p. 13.

15. Quoted by Bate in a justly admired book of ecocriticism, *The Song of the Earth*, p. 78.

16. Williams, *Country and the City*, p. 96, argues that enclosures "reached a first peak in the fifteenth and sixteenth centuries. . . . [T]hat very powerful myth of modern England in which the transition from a rural to an industrial society is seen as a kind of fall, the true cause and origin of our social suffering and disorder. . . . But it is also a main source for that last protecting illusion in the crisis of our own time: that it is not capitalism which is injuring us, but the more isolable, more evident system of urban industrialism."

17. Reiss, *Discourse of Modernism,* pp. 130–31.

18. Shell, *Money, Language, and Thought,* p. 39. Foucault, *Order of Things,* p. 169, sees a similar awkward ambiguity in the nature of both money and language as sign systems, as the Renaissance gives way to what he calls the Classical period.

19. Goux, *The Coiners of Language,* p. 17; quoted by Hawkes, *Idols of the Marketplace,* p. 21. Cf. Goux, p. 4 (cited in Hawkes, p. 236 n. 53): "What had previously been analyzed separately as phallocentrism (Freud, Lacan), as logocentrism (Derrida), and as the rule of exchange by the monetary medium (Marx), it was now possible to conceive as part of a unified process."

20. E.g., Derrida, "Racism's Last Word"; a comparable supposition appears to underlie the otherwise very different work of Michel Foucault and Jacques Lacan, and of their followers. The liberationist poses of these works may partly reflect the struggles of their authors against the extraordinarily structured and traditionalist academic institutions of France. Though Hawkes does not cite these instances in *Idols of the Marketplace,* he makes clear his perceptive mistrust of the assumption that the defeat of *telos* and *logos* will necessarily usher in some more humane and ethical structure of consciousness and society (p. 22).

21. Hawkes, *Idols of the Marketplace,* p. 10.

22. Ibid., p. 12.

23. Marcuse, *One-Dimensional Man,* passim.

24. Hawkes, *Idols of the Marketplace,* p. 14.

25. See Winstanley's 1649 tract "The True Levellers Standard Advanced": "every one that comes to work, shall eate the Fruit of their own labours, one having as much Freedom in the Fruit of the Earth as another. Another Voice that was heard was this, *Israel shall neither take Hire, nor give Hire.* And if so, then certainly none shall say, This is my Land, work for me, and I'le give you Wages. For, The Earth is the Lords, that is, Mans, who is Lord of the Creation. . . . Another Voice that was heard in a Trance, was this, *Whosoever labours the Earth for any Person or Persons, that are lifted up to rule over others, and doth not look upon themselves, as Equal to others in the Creation: The hand of the Lord shall be upon that Laborer: I the Lord have spoke it, and I will do it.* This Declares likewise to all Laborers, or such as are called Poor people, that they shall not dare to work for Hire, for any Landlord, or for any that is lifted up above others; for by their labours, they have lifted up Tyrants and Tyranny; and by denying to labor for Hire, they shall pull them down again. He that works for another, either for Wages, or to pay him Rent, works unrighteously, and still lifts up the Curse; but they that are resolved to work and eat together, making the Earth a Common Treasury, doth joyn hands with Christ, to lift up the Creation from Bondage."

26. Shapiro, *Probability,* p. 272.

27. Stillingfleet, *Origines Sacrae,* pp. 110–12.

28. Lucking, "Standing for Sacrifice," hears in Gobbo's complaint the era's marketplace system of value "emphasized to the point of self-parody." Harris, *Sick Economies,* builds from Shylock's remarks a compelling argument that Shakespeare shared with other Renaissance condemners of usury "an anxiety about the impossibility of innate, immutable value" (p. 82).

29. Cf. Foucault, *Order of Things,* p. 194: "Agriculture is the only sphere in which the increase in value due to production is not equivalent to the maintenance of the producer. This is because there is really an invisible producer who does not require any remuneration."

30. Vickers, "The Idea of Exchange in *The Merchant of Venice*," rightly perceives Bassanio struggling here to distinguish "*res* from *voluntas*" (p. 46)—a struggle I see replicated across late-Renaissance culture.

31. Barber, "Wealth's Communion and an Intruder," provides an illuminating discussion of these alternative functions of wealth.

32. Bruster's well-observed *Drama and the Market*, p. xi, comments that "Consciously or unconsciously, playwrights connected identity with ownership" during the Renaissance.

33. Pascal, *Pensées*, no. 688, p. 245.

34. That mistake is understandable: Lorenzo's courtship of Jessica suggests that, outside of the enchantment of Belmont, sometimes a casket is (*pace* Dr. Freud) just a casket—a piece of surplus value lowered from her window along with her body and devoid of positive moral significance (2.6.33).

35. Shakespeare cannot quite leave it there, however. Instead he gives Portia a quick scene-ending couplet in which (as so often in this play) a supposedly heroic character implicates herself in the very superficiality that defeats the supposedly unworthy. "Draw the curtains, go. / Let all of his complexion choose me so" (2.7.78–79). This not only bespeaks racism—scholarly efforts to rescue Portia from this taint by defining "complexion" as a term of character rather than color seem to me too ingenious in the aftermath of the earlier discussion of his skin—but also suggests how quickly she reverts to the concealments and surfaces for which she will find redemptive use only much later.

36. Arragon rejects the lead casket because it should "look fairer," yet claims to see past the triangulated desire that would "jump with common spirits" such as "the fool multitude that choose by show, / Not learning more than the fond eye would teach, / Which pries not to th' interior" (2.9.32, 26–28). His onomastically apt arrogance, like Morocco's greed, sets him against the Christian (and especially Protestant) mistrust of claims to any outwardly visible "stamp of merit." In case we missed the theologically charged term the first time, Shakespeare has Arragon wish "that clear honor / Were purchas'd by the merit of the wearer" (2.9.39–43). Even a mild Calvinist would have known it was damnable to "assume desert"—a word that turns up in each of his four lines leading up to the reading of the enclosed scroll, which comments dismissively, "Some there be that shadows kiss" (2.9.51, 66).

37. Levin, "A Garden in Belmont," p. 18, briefly summarizes the main evidence, though he rather cavalierly dismisses it in service of his unusually optimistic reading of the play as a whole.

38. For an important exposition of these signals, see Lewalski, "Biblical Allusion and Allegory." For a more freewheeling reading of the myths to which the play may allude, see Fiedler, " 'These Be the Christian Husbands.' "

39. Danson's classic *Harmonies of "The Merchant of Venice*," p. 64, and Vickers, "Idea of Exchange," p. 44, take notice of this sermon's relevance.

40. Portia's speech on behalf of mercy echoes a nature-loving passage from Isaiah that invites anagogic reading, as a prophecy of the Incarnation that would take the world from the old dispensation to the new: "Surely as the raine cometh downe and the snowe from heaven, and returneth not thether, but watereth the earth and maketh it to bring forthe and budde, that it maie give sede to the sower, and bread unto him that eateth, So shal my worde be . . ." (Isaiah 55: 10–11, Geneva Bible, 1560).

41. Coryat, *Coryats Crudities*, p. 232.

42. Adelman, "Her Father's Blood," articulates and historicizes the play's unresolved conflict about whether to read Jessica's identity by the race into which she was born or the religion into which she converts. Cf. 5.1.81–82: "nought so stockish, hard, and full of rage / But music for the time doth change his nature."

43. On Portia and Antonio as Christ figures, see J. A. Bryant, "Bassanio's Two Saviors" p. 72. For further permutations, see Dobbins and Battenhouse, "Jessica's Morals," which identifies Jessica with Jacob, Rachel, and the Israelites generally. Fortin, "Launcelot and the Uses of Allegory," p. 265, agrees with Lewalski's argument that "Jessica may figure forth the filial piety relationship of the New Dispensation to the Old"; Fortin acknowledges that this theory leaves a gap "between the 'real' Jessica and the allegorical Jessica," but suggests that the problem can be solved by sophisticating the allegory. See also Cunningham and Slimp, "Less into the Greater," p. 232: "Both Old Gobbo and Old Shylock are like and unlike Isaac; Launcelot and Jessica like and unlike Jacob."

44. Fortin believes that Gobbo provides "an allegorical counter-statement to the major allegorical statement of the play" ("Launcelot," p. 259); Fortin's conclusion is that the fifth act offers "a world far too complex for naïve allegory to be given full credit."

45. If you are most blessed "when men revile you, and persecute you," especially for your religious "righteousness," then isn't Shylock blessed? Do the Christians carry out the Sermon's admonition to "love your enemies," or more specifically, to conciliate on the way to court "lest thine adversarie deliver thee to the judge"? Doesn't the Sermon specify that those who hate their fellow man—which is what Shylock points out he is—violate in their hearts the commandment not to kill, no less than Shylock does in plotting actually to kill Antonio? Aren't the Christians the ones obsessed with fine clothes and feasts and drinking, three things Jesus here warns against? And aren't the Christians guilty of what Jesus describes as hypocritical evildoing when they make a public display of their religious zeal instead of enforcing it in the privacy of their rooms and the privacy of their hearts? As Portia says in her first scene, "It is a good divine that follows his own instructions; I can easier teach twenty what were good to be done, than to be one of the twenty to follow mine own teaching" (1.2.14–17).

46. Onstage we see both of them clutching keys to precious caskets. Where Shylock refuses a payoff of three thousand ducats and demands Antonio's flesh instead, the disguised Portia refuses that same sum of money, demanding instead the ring that Bassanio says is virtually part of his body. When Shylock offered the bond, he said, "If he will take it, so; if not, adieu; / And for my love I pray you wrong me not" (1.3.169–70), and threatened to walk away. The disguised Portia says almost the same thing while also threatening a walk-out: "For your love I'll take this ring from you . . . And you in love shall not deny me this" (4.1.427–29). Portia then threatens eye-for-an-eye (or at least ring-for-ring) justice, vowing to trade infidelity for infidelity, rather than forgiveness for the hope of forgiveness; and even when she relents, she makes Antonio offer his soul as the collateral on the gold wedding ring, just as Shylock made Antonio's body the collateral on the golden ducats. Danson, *Harmonies*, pp. 191–92, takes note of some of these correlations.

47. E.g., Deuteronomy 10:16, Leviticus 26:41, Ezekiel 44:7, Acts 7:51, and Romans 2:29. Shapiro, *Shakespeare and the Jews*, pp. 113–30, provides an excellent summary of the issues surrounding circumcision and their applicability to this play.

48. Benjamin, *Origin of German Tragic Drama*, p. 235; in this summary I am drawing on several of Benjamin's writings, all of which remain somewhat obscure to me, but the cluster of associations nonetheless seemed worth mentioning.

49. Fowler, *Renaissance Realism*, p. 101. Roland Frye, *Shakespeare and the Christian Doctrine*, pp. 34–35, questions the allegorization of Antonio into Christ.

50. Rabkin, "Meaning and Shakespeare," p. 121; on p. 103, Rabkin describes this play as a "test case" for the problem of meaning.

51. Lucking, "Standing for Sacrifice," p. 373, observes that "Paradoxically enough, it is only the Shylocks of this world who can be undeviatingly consistent in their moral conduct, and Portia in contriving a situation in which her husband is doomed to fail would seem to be manifesting a new awareness of the irresolvable contradictions challenging the serene certitudes of Belmont."

52. Krier, "Psychic Deadness in Allegory," pp. 48–49, explores this intriguing correlation between allegory and greed in the Mammon episode.

53. Lucking, "Standing for Sacrifice," p. 366, hears the implication that Portia thus "represents" sacrifice, which may also be another cue for Bassanio to associate her with the lead casket.

54. Marx, *Capital*, vol. 1, part 1, chap. 2.

55. Martin, *Baroque*, p. 120, citing Kepler's *Gesammelte Werke*, 1:9 *(Mysterium Cosmographicum)* and 7:258 *(Epitome Astronomiae Copernicae)*.

56. Watching Bassanio approach, Portia says, "This night methinks is but the daylight sick,/It looks a little paler"; and his first words to her are "We should hold day with the Antipodes,/If you would walk in absence of the sun" (5.1.124–28).

57. Blake, "Annotations to Wordsworth's Preface to *The Excursion*," p. 784.

58. Cf. Locke, *Essay Concerning Human Understanding*, bk. 2, chap. 8, sec. 17: "let not the eyes see light or colours, nor the ears hear sounds; let the palate not taste, nor the nose smell, and all colours, tastes, odours, and sounds, as they are such particular ideas, vanish and cease, and are reduced to their causes." So Portia's bird takes on the mysterious presence of the soul-bird in Marvell's "Garden."

59. Donne, *Devotions Upon Emergent Occasions*, Nineteenth Expostulation, p. 99.

60. Engle, *Shakespearean Pragmatism*, offers many insights—including some about usury in *Merchant*—about Shakespeare's resistance (as himself a marketer of theater) to principles of epistemic certainty.

61. For a broader perspective on the socio-political dangers of contractual absolutism, see Atiyah, *Rise and Fall of Freedom of Contract*.

62. Cf. Netzloff, "The Lead Casket," p. 166: "*The Merchant of Venice* is situated within a contemporary debate that attempted to justify England's entrance into a colonial economy by uniting the heroic dimension of colonial expansion, a chivalric discourse appealing to England's gentry, with the interests of commerce and capital." For one of the countless characterization's of Christian salvation as "Man's *Redemption* by a *Mediator*," see Sprat, *History of the Royal Society*, p. 82.

63. For a brief but perceptive discussion of similarities between the *Laws* and a Shakespeare play, see Young, "Shakespearean Tragedy in a Renaissance Context."

64. Hooker, *Works*, bk. 2, chap. 7, sec. 5.

65. Danson, *Harmonies*, p. 178, takes Lorenzo's remarks here as a much more convincing exposition of true love than I do.

66. E.g., Hooker, *Works*, 1:161; bk. 1, chap. 4, sec. 5, of the *Laws*: "God alone excepted, who actually and everlastingly is whatsoever he may be, and which cannot hereafter be that which he is not; all other things besides are somewhat in possibility, which as yet they are not in act. And for this cause there is in all things an appetite or desire,

whereby they incline to something which they may be. . . . All things therefore coveting as much as may be to be like unto God in being ever, that which cannot hereunto attain personally doth seek to continue itself another way, that is by offspring and propagation." The comic competition for progeny that closes *The Merchant of Venice* may be degrading, but it matches the downgraded version of immortal divinity that the play as a whole keeps suggesting we must accept.

67. In fact, for Hooker, "the absolute perfection of Scripture is seen by relation unto that end whereto it tendeth"; *Works*, bk. 2, chap. 8, sec. 5.

68. Cf. Hooker, *Works*, 1:317, *Laws* 3.10.1: "The nature of every law must be judged of by the end for which it was made." Again relativism and teleology are made mutually dependent rather than mutually exclusive.

69. See similarly 2.7.5.

70. Hamill, "Poetry, Law, and the Pursuit of Perfection," p. 230, compares this last passage from Hooker's *Laws* (bk. 1, chap. 5) to Portia's ideas on how "true perfection" may be approached (5.1.108).

71. Cunningham and Slimp, "Less into the Greater," p. 229, observe that, because mercy constitutes "participation" in the divine nature, Portia demonstrates a way to become what 2 Peter (1:4) calls "partakers of the divine nature." This seems to me a helpful word: the Christians take parts in the Christian script and partake of Christ's essence, both of which suggest the complicated ways they simultaneously are and are not the holy figures, in spirit and in body.

72. Netzloff, "Lead Casket," p. 161.

73. Porter, *Flesh in the Age of Reason*, p. 73. For another version of this concession, see Richard Kroll's highly perceptive *The Material Word*, on the way Pierre Gassendi led an attack on direct certainties, reminding us that we navigate a universe of representations; language and even thought—perhaps even perception—"inevitably intervene between us and the world, which is itself only partially known by indicative signs. . . . We only know an object by some partial, external indication of its nature, whose totality or essence is hidden from us" (p. 123). Thus, "The development of a distinctively neoclassical ideology of contingency" (contrasted to "a dogmatic epistemology such as Aristotle's") "accompanies a remarkably coherent theory of *mediation, accommodation,* or *incarnationalism.* A skeptical epistemology not only admits but also welcomes the infusion of signs into our mental economy. It may deny an immaculate access to spirit, the mind of God, the individual conscience, and the essential properties of bodies, but it does not dismiss any of these as working postulates if supported on sufficient evidentiary grounds. Signs, in short, mediate between us, the world, God, and others, and even our own cognitive processes. Seen from another angle, for us to know any of these things, representation must accommodate itself to our partial ways of knowing" (pp. 62–63).

Chapter 9. Thomas Traherne

All quotations from Traherne's *Centuries* and his *Thanksgivings* in this chapter and elsewhere in the text are based on *Centuries, Poems and Thanksgivings*, ed. H. M. Margoliouth. All other quotations from Traherne's poetry—except those poems found in Margoliouth and not in Dobell—are based on *The Poetical Works of Thomas Traherne*, ed.

Bertram Dobell. I have favored the Dobell manuscript version of the poems because the Burney collection used by Margoliouth shows clear and (though plausible) often misguided interventions by Traherne's brother Philip.

1. E.g., Salter, *Thomas Traherne, Mystic and Poet*, p. 24; Johnston, "Thomas Traherne's Yearning Subject," p. 378, observes that, to many commentators, the writings "seem ecstatic and childlike."

2. Dobell, introduction to Traherne, *Poetical Works*, lxxxii–iv. Marcus, *Childhood and Cultural Despair*, p. 182, insists rightly that "Traherne was no Berkeleian—he never denies the existence of things in themselves, independent of the human mind."

3. Marks, introduction to *Christian Ethicks*, p. lxiv; also in Marks's "Thomas Traherne and Cambridge Platonism." On the relationship between Traherne's resolution of this dichotomy and Leonardo's resolution of it in his theory of perspective, see Johnston, " 'Heavenly Perspective,' " pp. 331–32. Johnston writes with remarkable subtlety and scope about Traherne's engagement with the inventions of perspective in the visual arts and sciences.

4. Lewalski, *Protestant Poetics*, p. 361.

5. "Thanksgivings for the Body" celebrates "The spacious Room / Which thou hast hidden in mine Eye, / The Chambers for Sounds / Which thou hast prepar'd in mine Ear, / The Receptacles for Smells / Concealed in my Nose; / The feeling of my Hands, / The taste of my Tongue. / But above all, O Lord, the Glory of Speech whereby thy / Servant is enabled with Praise to celebrate thee" (lines 92–101).

"Thanksgivings for the Soul" adds that "To create an endless unsensible Body, / Is not the way to Celestial Greatness. / A Body endless, though endued with Sense, / Can see / Only visible things, / Taste / The Qualities in Meat and Drink, / Feel / Gross or tangible Bodies, / Hear / The harshness or melody of Sounds, / Smell / The things that have Odours in them. / But those things which neither Sight, nor Smell, nor Taste, can discern . . . Are all Nullities to such a Creature" (lines 187–215).

6. Eliot, "Mystic and Politician," p. 590; see similarly Wilson, "A Neglected Mystic."

7. *Centuries*, 1.41. It works the other way around also: Christ's wounds become visual apertures, "Orifices too small to let in my Sight, to the vast Comprehensions of thine Eternal Lov" (1.64). This respect for the very discontinuities, the apparent gaps and dark spots of the perceivable world, is what distinguishes Traherne's love of the world from George Wither's devotion to the Protestant divine voice heard within, emanating from "a Place (if Place we call it may) / Within the Concave of whose wondrous Orb, / The Eye of Contemplation may survay / Sights, which no Bounds, or Shaddowes, do disturb." *Vox Pacifica*, quoted by Norbrook, *Writing the English Republic*, p. 143.

8. Johnston, "Heavenly Perspectives," p. 379, observes that Traherne "attempts to devise a poetic middle ground between subjective and objective representation that maintains what he sees as desirable qualities in each."

9. Western alchemy was largely built on the *Emerald Table* of Hermes Trismegistus, which begins by making simile the key to understanding a profoundly analogical world: "That which is beneath is like that which is above: & that which is above is like that which is beneath"; Roger Bacon, *The Mirror of Alchimy*, p. 16.

10. For a classic primitivist view of the noble savage, see *Centuries*, 3.12: "By this you may see who are the Rude and Barbarous Indians: For verily there is no Salvage Nation under the Cope of Heaven, that is more absurdly barbarous than the Christian World. They that go Naked and Drink Water and liv upon Roots are like Adam, or Angels in comparison of us." See also 3.46 on country life as Edenic.

11. Dobell, introduction to Traherne, *Poetical Works*, p. lxiii.

12. Traherne, *Roman Forgeries*, sigs. B6r–B7r. Wade, *Thomas Traherne*, p. 116, notes that people bemoan Traherne spending his time on polemic in *Roman Forgeries*, because they focus on the man who "sentimentalized prettily over green fields." My point is that the polemical and sentimental Trahernes are united in their quest for a pure original truth into which the human spirit can rightly and comfortably settle.

13. The final stanza of "The Recovery" again disdains conventional markers of richness: "All gold and silver is but empty dross, / Rubies and saphires are but loss" (lines 64–65). Similarly in "Thoughts (IV)," "The stable Earth which we beneath behold, / Is far more precious than if made of gold" (lines 45–46). There was "No Gold, nor Trade, nor Silver there" in Eden ("Adam," line 14). See also *Centuries* 1.13, 25, 29; 2.7, 12; 3.18, 72; and 4.7, 89.

14. Johnston, " 'Heavenly Perspective,' " p. 7.

15. E.g., *Centuries*, 2.66: "That Violence wherewith som times a man doteth upon one Creature, is but a little spark of that lov, even towards all, which lurketh in His nature."

16. Hawkes, *Idols of the Marketplace*, p. 196. cf. Hill, *World Turned Upside Down*, p. 414: "Traherne's communism, unlike Winstanley's, was in the imagination only."

17. The anticapitalist emphasis is not very persistent and hardly ever analytic; furthermore, in the *Christian Ethicks*, Traherne has God speak to humanity practically like a modern stockbroker: "You think your interest is abated, and your fruition endangered by the communication of your Treasures to many, I know they are increased and multiplied by the number of the Enjoyers" (p. 249).

18. Nicolson, *Breaking of the Circle*, p. 196.

19. Deneef, *Traherne in Dialogue*, p. 19. Day, *Thomas Traherne*, p. 21, argues that "Traherne held a strict monist view." Contrast this implication of a dominant intellect with Clements, *Mystical Poetry of Thomas Traherne*, p. 59, on the "direct, immediate, intuitive, open-eyed" expression of Traherne's verse. There is arguably a similarity between Traherne's phenomenology and the argument of Foster, *The Nature of Perception*, that physical reality is mind-dependent but real nonetheless.

20. Webber, *The Eloquent "I,"* p. 253.

21. Dickson, *Fountain of Living Waters*, pp. 172–73. For similar reasons I resist the conclusion of Martz, *The Paradise Within*, p. 39, that "Paradise, for Traherne, as for Peter Sterry, has always been essentially inward and spiritual." The inward and the outward are not distinguishable for Traherne, nor the spiritual from the physical—Traherne is emphatic that neither of these can have meaning, or can even exist, without its counterpart. Salter, *Mystic and Poet*, p. 81, argues that Traherne resembles the Cambridge Platonists in "their shared conviction that knowledge of God is not to be reached by abstract theoretical discourse but by immediate experience"; cf. John Smith, *Discourse*, and Salter, pp. 81–85. Traherne is distinguishable from the Cambridge Platonists, however—as from the Gnostics—by his refusal to relegate matter to an inferior status.

22. Hawkes, *Idols of the Marketplace*, p. 196.

23. Ibid., p. 196.

24. Lewalski, *Protestant Politics*, p. 356, observes in Traherne's poems "much naming of beauties or joys or glories (often in long incantatory lists whose terms re-echo in poem after poem) as if such naming will call forth the essence of the thing." Johnston, "Heavenly Perspectives," p. 380, suggests that "Traherne claims invention of an idealized unity between objects and the words that describe them."

25. A less sanguine poet might have noticed—as the opening provokes readers to consider—the same possibility after death. Some of the poetic epitaphs Traherne wrote do hint that the dead see God and truth more clearly, more wakingly, than those who struggle to sustain the ego do in life. The motif of non-being before birth appears also in "The Salutation": "When silent I, / So many thousand thousand yeers, / Beneath the dust did in a chaos lie, / How could I smiles or tears, / Or lips or hands or eyes or ears perceiv? / Welcome ye treasures which I now receive" (lines 7–12). As in Montaigne (and perhaps in Shakespeare's *Tempest*, 1.2.272–96 and 354–63), this question seems to be a way of comprehending death by staring into a temporal mirror.

26. Montaigne, "Apology for Raymond Sebond," p. 322.

27. Salter, *Mystic and Poet*, p. 56, offers but then rejects the Bacon comparison. The key distinction for me is that Bacon sees religion and science as necessarily separate worlds, whereas Traherne sees them as necessarily identical.

28. Bacon, *The Advancement of Learning*, bk. 1, in Warhaft, *Francis Bacon*, p. 202.

29. I believe that Hawkes, *Idols of the Marketplace*, pp. 205–6, may have turned the terms the wrong way around when he writes that "The Vision" advises us "not to adore the 'fountain' but the 'spring' of which it is the visible sign"; though Hawkes speaks of "the empirical world (symbolized by the 'fountain')," it seems to me that Traherne here places "the fountain" as God working in subterranean mode, with the stream as its phenomenal manifestation. But in "The Circulation," lines 59–60, Traherne appears to have it Hawkes's way around. Contemporary uses are also ambiguous; cf. Comito, *Idea of the Garden*, p. 101: "Physis herself, in Bernard Sylvester's epic, *De mundi universitate*, first sees the approach of the divine Urania reflected in the fountain of matter."

30. Cf. the opening lines of "The Anticipation": "My contemplation dazzles in the End / Of all I comprehend, / And soars above all heights."

31. Marvell, "The Garden"; see similarly, in this regard, Robert Southwell, "Looke Home," and the final stanza of Traherne's "The Circulation," which identifies God as the only being that can exist "Without original . . . Which mortal man can take delight to know. / He is the primitive eternal spring / The endless ocean of each glorious thing" (lines 74–78).

32. Johnston, " 'Heavenly Perspective,' " p. 335, aptly compares this passage to Arcimboldo's paintings.

33. Levao, *Renaissance Minds*, p. 56, observes that "in *De coniecturis* . . . the ascent of the *intellectus* to silence is juxtaposed with the necessity of its descent. It may be perched on a high tower in the *Apologia*, but here it must come down to the realm of the senses, even against its desire, in order to be itself most fully (2.16)."

34. Blake, *Complete Writings*, p. 431; cf. Traherne's *Centuries* 1.27 ("You never Enjoy the World aright, till you see how a Sand Exhibiteth the Wisdom and Power of God") and 2.67 ("O what a Treasure is evry Sand when truly understood!").

35. Lines 64–72 of "The Anticipation" also attribute to God the capacity to want, so that he can enjoy receiving.

36. For a condensed instance of this argument, see "The Review," which begins, "Did I grow, or did I stay? / Did I prosper or decay? / When I so / From *Things* to *Thoughts* did go?" (lines 1–4). Traherne adds that, compared to thoughts, "I *Things* as *Shades* esteem" (line 19).

37. Vives, *Opera omnia*, 3:143–44; cf. Donawerth, *Shakespeare and the Sixteenth-Century Study of Language*, p. 4.

38. This preference for things over words persists even into the attack on the papacy in *Roman Forgeries*, sig. A6.

39. "Thanksgivings for the Glory of God's Works," lines 398–404; see similarly "Thanksgivings for God's Attributes": "Such is the Glory of thy exquisite Presence, that is at once wholly in millions of persons. / Wholly in them all, like the Sun in a Mirrour, in a thousand thousand Mirrours, that maketh by its Beams the Heavens also to be present there, / And me, like a Mirrour, the entire possessor of all thy Glories" (lines 127–32). On the link between Traherne and Plato's suggestion in the *Phaedo* that the mirror offers knowledge of essences, see Johnston, " 'Heavenly Perspective'," p. 306; on Ripa's more equivocal and instrumental view of that possibility, see her p. 309; on Augustine's notion of the mind as a mirror which holds a thing beyond the capacity of immediate sensation, see her p. 313.

40. On the link between childhood and transparency, cf. "The World": "My virgin-thoughts in Childhood were / Full of Content, / And innocent, / Without disturbance, free and clear, / Ev'n like the Streams of Crystal Springs" (lines 29–33).

41. John Rowland, a close contemporary of Traherne's, proposes something similar in his dedicatory epistle to the 1658 edition of Topsell's *History of Four-Footed Beasts*, accepting kinship (even, remarkably enough, in mortal annihilation) with other animals "ordained by God to live upon the same earth, and to be Fellow-commoners with Man" (sig. A4r).

Conclusion

Note to epigraph: Milosz, *New and Collected Poems*, p. 569.

1. Hughes, review of Max Nicholson's *The Environmental Revolution*; quoted by Bate, *Song of the Earth*, p. 27.

2. Thomas, *Dictionarium linguae Latinae et Anglicanae*, sig. PP2v.

3. As Harrison, *Forests*, p. 28, points out, Aristotle's word for the material (as opposed to form) of an object is *hyle*—a word that originally meant "forest." Though the Romans decline to translate this, as sound and etymology would urge, as *sylva*, they chose the next best thing: *materia* meant the core usable wood of a tree (as opposed to its bark or leaves).

4. Jackson, *Treatise Containing the Originall*, pp. 456–59.

5. Willey, *Seventeenth-Century Background*, p. 33, argues that "in spite of such harbingers as Petrarch, we may perhaps take the later fifteenth and the sixteenth centuries as the epoch of the rebirth of confidence in 'Nature'. In encountering such men as More, Montaigne and Bacon we find ourselves at the beginning of a process which continues for about three centuries." Keith Thomas, *Man and the Natural World*, notes the disdain of the English in the sixteenth century for their British neighbors who lived closely with their livestock (p. 94), but notes also the affectionate (if non-human) names the English began to give that livestock (p. 96), and mentions that Queen Elizabeth gave animal nicknames to her courtiers (p. 99). Thomas's opening pages explore the theological insistence on a sharp and hierarchical distinction between the human and other animals.

6. Maus, *Inwardness and Theater*, p. 8.

7. Rorty, *Philosophy and the Mirror of Nature*, p. 223.

8. Shuger, "Civility and Censorship," makes a convincing argument that this fear of socially destructive misrepresentations was the top priority of censorship, though often overlooked by modern readers who anachronistically associate censorship primarily with broad ideological repressions.

9. Evett, *Literature and the Visual Arts*, pp. 155–57.

10. It may also have been deemed politically and culturally risky; Bacon's *Great Instauration*, repeatedly attempts to make the premises of a standard conservative ideological campaign appear to arise independent of any distorting human agency. The idea that reality itself lacked a stable identity even if perfectly perceived—which I understand as Niels Bohr's answer to Heisenberg on this issue—does not seem to have been much explored in this theocentric culture.

11. Bacon's *New Organon*, bk. 1, aphorism 126, in Warhaft, *Francis Bacon*, p. 370.

12. Hanson, *Discovering the Subject*, p. 148, sees in Bacon a recognition that "to reclaim such objectified power, men must identify with it, acquire its properties, become themselves objectified."

13. Ibid., p. 146.

14. Derrida, *Of Grammatology*, p. 158.

15. Koerner, *Reformation of the Image*, p. 282.

16. Nuttall, *A New Mimesis*, p. 10, wittily notes that Jonathan Culler puts "text" ontologically ahead of " 'the real world' " by the magical application of one extra set of quotation marks.

17. Lacan, *Écrits*, p. 65.

18. Spolsky, *Satisfying Skepticism*, p. 8, citing Wittgenstein, Austin, and (in limited ways) Cavell.

19. Michaels, "Doubt Is Their Product," pp. 96–101.

20. On the environmental costs of Christian anthropocentrism based in Genesis, see Lynn White, Jr.'s brief but influential "The Historical Roots of Our Ecological Crisis," pp. 1203–7.

21. Thomas, *Man and the Natural World*, p. 250.

22. Ibid., pp. 256–57.

23. Ibid., p. 193.

24. See ibid., pp. 243–55, including reports indicating that other English cities were already badly polluted as well.

25. See ibid., p. 135, discussing horrified stories of children born with tails or hooves: "It was because the separateness of the human race was thought so precarious, so easily lost, that the boundary had been so tightly guarded." This book has been tracing the counter-movement, which found the boundary between humanity and nature guarded, like the gates of Eden, against our will and only too well.

26. Thomas, *Man and the Natural World*, p. 23, briefly documents this tyranny, and quotes Lynn White Jr.'s characterization of Christianity as "the most anthropocentric religion the world has seen." Again conservative doctrine contained the seeds of its own destruction: as Thomas notes (p. 278), the assumption of a divine plan in nature and even the argument for God's existence by the evidence of that design offer a framework on which twenty-first-century attitudes toward the preservation of species-diversity could be hung quite neatly. And even in a conservative seventeenth-century society, a radical transformation from tyranny to benevolence (or at least a shift in the distribution of tyranny and benevolence) was evidently possible: apparently because he had

been born in 1646, a Year of the Dog, the shogun Tokugawa Tsunayoshi established (in 1687, the year before England's "Glorious Revolution") several "Laws of Compassion" by which "somewhere between sixty thousand and two hundred thousand people were either put to death or exiled for animal-welfare violations"; MacFarquhar, "Bark," discussing Stanley Coren and Andy Bartlett's *Pawprints of History*. Though this story may seem at once quaint and horrible, it should not disguise what was actually a remarkably systematic and rational conservation program this shogunate established to control soil erosion and deforestation on the ecologically delicate islands of Japan. See Grove, *Green Imperialism*, p. 62.

27. Spolsky, *Satisfying Skepticism*, pp. 10–11.

28. Martin Heidegger, in his 1934–35 seminars on Hölderlin's hymns "Germany" and "The Rhine," quoted by Bate, *Song of the Earth*, p. 257; see also Heidegger's 1953 lecture "The Question Concerning Technology."

29. A few years ago I drafted a light metacritical article called "Can We Still Say 'We'?" The argument was legible in the ironies of the title: daunted by critiques of universalizing gestures as complicit in essentialism, racism, imperialism, and sexism, literary commentators became censorious against the use of the first-person plural—even though they still meant it, found ways to imply it, and were often entitled to use it for the remarkably narrow demographic that actually reads books such as this one. As generalizations go—and, without them, thinking can't go anywhere—the critical "we" tended to be more valid that many other generalizations that found an easier reception in such scholarship. But, in the wide and sometimes foamy wake of prominent scholars preaching disjunction and difference in cultural studies, these pronouns—like characterological psychology, authorial biography, gender difference, or gender sameness, in other phases of critical fashion—became a kind of alarm bell that set off reflexive historicist admonishments.

Certainly as someone studying the skeptical arguments that perceptions differ and that other minds are inaccessible, I must remain alert to the problem. But radical skepticism also provokes the corrective recognition that we nonetheless find many ways to communicate and to navigate the same terrain. So—while hoping to oppress no one, including my readers, with my deployment of the category of the human—I find myself stubbornly sustaining the notion of a functionally collective reality. I use "us" to signal in most cases the normative audience of plays, viewer of paintings, or reader of books (including this one) with whom I am aspiring to share some perceptions—and to signal in some cases experiences and conflicts shared by the vast majority of human beings living in the modern Western culture running from Shakespeare's world to mine, and doubtless well beyond. As someone arguing for ecological consciousness, I must strive to defend the possibilities of collectivity that confer obligations across differences of time and species.

Bibliography

Achinstein, Sharon. *Literature and Dissent in Milton's England*. New York: Cambridge University Press, 2003.

Adamson, Joni, Mei Mei Evans, and Rachel Stein, eds. *Environmental Justice Reader*. Tucson: University of Arizona Press, 2002.

Adelman, Janet. "Her Father's Blood: Race, Conversion, and Nation in *The Merchant of Venice*." *Representations* 81 (2003): 4–30.

———. *Suffocating Mothers*. New York: Routledge, 1992.

Agrippa, Henry Cornelius. *Of the Vanitie and Uncertaintie of Artes and Sciences*. 1530. Edited by Catherine M. Dunn. Northridge: California State University, 1974.

Alpers, Paul J. *What Is Pastoral?* Chicago: University of Chicago Press, 1996.

Alpers, Svetlana. *The Art of Describing*. Chicago: University of Chicago Press, 1983.

Anderson, Judith H. *Words That Matter: Linguistic Perception in Renaissance English*. Stanford, Calif.: Stanford University Press, 1996.

Anderson, Linda. "The Nature of Marvell's Mower." *Studies in English Literature, 1500–1900*, 31 (1991): 131–46.

Anon. *Hic Mulier* and *Haec Vir*. London, 1620.

Anselment, Raymond A. *Loyalist Resolve: Patient Fortitude in the English Civil War*. Toronto: Associated University Presses, 1988.

Ariès, Philippe. *L'enfant et la vie familiale sous l'Ancien Régime*. Paris: Plon, 1960.

Aristotle. *The Nicomachean Ethics*. Translated with an introduction and notes by W. D. Ross. Revised by J. L. Ackrill and J. O. Urmson. Oxford: Oxford University Press, 1998.

———. *The Art of Rhetoric*. Translated by H. C. Lawson-Tancred. New York: Penguin, 1992.

Ashton, Peter, Alice I. Davies, and Seymour Slive. "Jacob van Ruisdael's Trees." *Arnoldia* 24 (1982): 2–31.

Atiyah, Patrick S. *The Rise and Fall of Freedom of Contract*. Oxford: Clarendon Press, 1979.

Auerbach, Erich. *Mimesis: The Representation of Reality in Western Literature*. Translated by Willard R. Trask. Princeton, N.J.: Princeton University Press, 2003.

Aughterson, Kate. "Redefining the Plain Style." *Studies in Philology* 97 (2000): 96–143.

Augustine of Hippo. "On the Profit of Believing." In *On the Holy Trinity; Doctrinal Treatises; Moral Treatises*, Chapter 20. Edited by Philip Schaff. New York: Christian Literature Publishing, 1890.

———. *Seventeen Short Treatises of St. Augustine*. Translated by C. L. Cornish. Oxford: J. H. Parker, 1847.

———. *The Trinity*. Translated by Stephen McKenna. Washington, D.C.: Catholic University of America Press, 1963.

Bacon, Francis. *Francis Bacon: A Selection of His Works*. Edited by Sidney Warhaft. Indi-
anapolis: Bobbs-Merrill, 1982.
————. "The Clue to the Maze." In *Selected Writings*. Introduction and notes by Hugh
G. Dick. New York: Modern Library, 1955.
————. *The Works of Francis Bacon*. 14 vols. Collected and edited by James Spedding,
Robert Leslie Ellis, and Douglas Denon Heath. London: Longman, 1857–74.
Bacon, Roger. *The Mirror of Alchimy*. Edited by Stanton J. Linden. New York: Garland,
1992.
Baines, Richard. British Library, Harley MS 6853, ff. 3078.
Baker, Herschel. *The Wars of Truth*. Cambridge, Mass.: Harvard University Press, 1952.
Barber, C. L. "Wealth's Communion and an Intruder." In *Modern Critical Interpretations:
William Shakespeare's "The Merchant of Venice,"* edited by Harold Bloom, pp. 37–61.
New York: Chelsea House, 1986.
Barbour, Reid. *Literature and Religious Culture in Seventeenth-Century England*. Cam-
bridge: Cambridge University Press, 2002.
Barkan, Leonard. "Diana and Actaeon: The Myth as Synthesis." *English Literary Renais-
sance* 10 (1980): 317–59.
Bartlett, Andy, and Stanley Coren. *The Pawprints of History*. New York: Free Press, 2002.
Bate, Jonathan. *The Song of the Earth*. London: Picador, 2000.
Baudrillard, Jean. *Simulations*. Translated by Paul Foss, Paul Patton, and Phillip Beitch-
man. New York: Semiotext(e), 1983.
Beale, John. *Herefordshire Orchards*. London, 1657.
Bending, Stephen, and Andrew McRae, eds. *The Writing of Rural England, 1500–1800*.
New York: Palgrave Macmillan, 2003.
Benjamin, Walter. *The Origin of German Tragic Drama*. Translated by John Osborne.
London: Verso, 1985.
Berdan, John M. *The Poems of John Cleveland*. New Haven, Conn.: Yale University Press,
1911.
Berger, Harry, Jr. "The Ecology of the Mind." *Centennial Review* 8, no. 4 (1964): 409–34.
————. *Second World and Green World*. Berkeley: University of California Press, 1988.
Berkeley, George. *New Theory of Vision*. Dublin: Aaron Rhames, 1709.
Berry, Edward. *Shakespeare and the Hunt*. Cambridge: Cambridge University Press, 2001.
Blake, William. *Complete Writings*. Edited by Geoffrey Keynes. London: Oxford Univer-
sity Press, 1969.
Boehrer, Bruce. *Parrot Culture: Western Art, Literature, and the World's Most Talkative
Birds*. Philadelphia: University of Pennsylvania Press, 2004.
————. *Shakespeare Among the Animals: Nature and Society in the Drama of Early Mod-
ern England*. New York: Palgrave/St. Martin's Press, 2002.
Bonaventure, Saint. *The Breviloquium*. Vol. 2 of *The Works of Bonaventure: Cardinal,
Seraphic Doctor, and Saint*. Translated by José De Vinck. Paterson, N.J.: St. Anthony
Guild Press, 1963.
Bramwell, Anna. *Ecology in the Twentieth Century: A History*. New Haven, Conn.: Yale
University Press, 1989.
Browne, Sir Thomas. *Religio Medici*. In *The Major Works*, edited by C. A. Patrides, pp.
59–161. New York: Penguin, 1977.
Bruno, Giordano. *The Heroic Frenzies*. Translated by P. E. Memmo, Jr. Chapel Hill: Uni-
versity of North Carolina Press, 1964.

Bruster, Douglas. *Drama and the Market in the Age of Shakespeare.* Cambridge: Cambridge University Press, 1992.

Bruyn, Josua. "Toward a Scriptural Reading of Seventeenth-Century Dutch Landscape Paintings." In *Masters of the Seventeenth-Century Dutch Landscape Painting,* edited by Peter C. Sutton, pp. 84–103. Boston: Museum of Fine Arts, 1987.

Bryant, J. A. "Bassanio's Two Saviors." In *Shakespeare's Christian Dimension,* edited by Roy Battenhouse, pp. 71–76. Bloomington: Indiana University Press, 1994.

Calderwood, James L. *Forms of Drama.* Englewood Cliffs, N.J.: Prentice-Hall, 1969.

Calvin, Jean. *Institutes of the Christian Religion.* Edited by John McNeill and translated by Ford Lewis Battles. Philadelphia: Westminster Press, 1960.

———. *Institution de la religion chrestienne.* Vol. 1. Edited by Jean-Daniel Benoît. Paris: J. Vrin, 1957.

Carew, Richard. *The Survey of Cornwall,* 1602. Exeter: Devon and Cornwall Record Society, 2004.

Carey, John, ed. *Andrew Marvell: A Critical Anthology.* Baltimore: Penguin, 1969.

Carroll, Lewis. *Alice's Adventures in Wonderland and Through the Looking-Glass.* New York: Modern Library, 2002.

Carroll, William C. *The Great Feast of Language in "Love's Labour's Lost."* Princeton, N.J.: Princeton University Press, 1976.

Cartmill, Matt. *A View to a Death in the Morning: Hunting and Nature Through History.* Cambridge, Mass.: Harvard University Press, 1993.

Carver, Marmaduke. *A discourse of the terrestrial paradise, aiming at a more probable discovery of the true situation of that happy place of our first parents habitation.* London, 1666.

Cassirer, Ernst. *The Individual and the Cosmos in Renaissance Philosophy.* Translated by Mario Domandi. Philadelphia: University of Pennsylvania Press, 1963.

Catholic Encyclopedia. Edited by Charles G. Herbermann, Edward A. Pace, Condé B. Pallen, Thomas J. Shahan, and John J. Wynne. 15 vols. London: Robert Applegate, 1910.

Cavalcanti, Guido. *The Poetry of Guido Cavalcanti.* Translated and edited by Lowry Nelson, Jr. New York: Garland, 1986.

Cavell, Stanley. *Disowning Knowledge.* Cambridge: Cambridge University Press, 1987.

Cavendish, Margaret. *Duchess of Newcastle, Poems, and Fancies.* London, 1653.

Cawdry, Robert. *A Treasurie or Storehouse of Similes.* London, 1609.

Cervantes Saavedra, Miguel de. *Don Quixote.* Translated by J. M. Cohen. Harmondsworth: Penguin, 1952.

Chagall, Marc. *My Life.* New York: Orion Press, 1960.

Charles I, King of England. *Eikon Basilike: The Portraiture of His Majesty King Charles 1st.* 1648–49. Reprint, London: D. Stewart, 1879.

Charron, Pierre. *De la sagesse.* 1601/1604. Edited by Barbara de Negroni. Paris: Fayard, 1986.

Chong, Alan. *Still-life Paintings from the Netherlands, 1550–1720.* Zwolle: Waanders, 1999.

———. "The Market for Landscape Painting in Seventeenth-Century Holland." In *Masters of the Seventeenth-Century Dutch Landscape Painting,* edited by Peter C. Sutton, pp. 104–20. Boston: Museum of Fine Arts, 1987.

Clarkson [Claxton], Laurence. *Look About You.* London, 1659.

Clements, A. L. *The Mystical Poetry of Thomas Traherne.* Cambridge, Mass.: Harvard University Press, 1969.

Cleveland, John. *The Poems of John Cleveland.* Edited by John M. Berdan. New Haven, Conn.: Yale University Press, 1911.

Comenius, John Amos. *The Great Didactic.* Edited and translated by M. W. Keatinge. London: A & C Black, 1896.

Comito, Terry. *The Idea of the Garden in the Renaissance.* New Brunswick, N.J.: Rutgers University Press, 1978.

Cook, Elizabeth. *Seeing Through Words.* New Haven, Conn.: Yale University Press, 1986.

Cooper, Thomas. *An Admonition to the People of England.* 1589. Edited by Edward Arber. English Scholar's Library of Old and Modern Works, no. 15. Birmingham, 1878.

Copenhaver, Brian P. "Natural Magic, Hermetism, and Occultism." In *Reappraisals of the Scientific Revolution,* edited by David Lindberg and Robert Westman, pp. 261–302. New York: Cambridge University Press, 1990.

———. "A Tale of Two Fishes: Magical Objects in Natural History from Antiquity Through the Scientific Revolution." *Journal of the History of Ideas* 52 (1991): 373–98.

Corbett, Richard. *The Poems of Richard Corbett.* Edited by J. A. W. Bennett and H. R. Trevor-Roper. London: Oxford University Press, 1955.

Corns, Thomas N. *The Cambridge Companion to English Poetry, Donne to Marvell.* New York: Cambridge University Press, 1993.

———. "Thomas Carew, Sir John Suckling, and Richard Lovelace." In *The Cambridge Companion to English Poetry, Donne to Marvell,* edited by Thomas N. Corns, pp. 200–220. New York: Cambridge University Press, 1993.

Coryat[e], Thomas. *Coryats Crudities Hastily Gobled Up in Five Moneths Travells.* London, 1611.

Cosin, Richard. *An Apologie for Sundrie Proceedings by Jurisdiction Ecclesiasticall.* London: C. Barker, 1593.

Cowley, Abraham. *The English Writings of Abraham Cowley: Essays, Plays, and Sundry Verses.* Edited by A. R. Waller. London: Cambridge University Press, 1905.

Crane, Mary Thomas. *Shakespeare's Brain: Reading with Cognitive Theory.* Princeton: Princeton University Press, 2001.

Crewe, Jonathan. "The Garden State." In *Enclosure Acts: Sexuality, Property, and Culture in Early Modern England,* edited by Richard Burt and John Michael Archer, pp. 270–89. Ithaca, N.Y.: Cornell University Press, 1994.

Croll, Morris W. *"Attic" and Baroque Prose Style: The Anti-Ciceronian Movement.* Edited by J. Max Patrick, Robert O. Evans, with John M. Wallace. Princeton, N.J.: Princeton University Press, 1969.

Cruttwell, Patrick. *The Shakespearean Moment.* London: Chatto & Windus, 1954.

Cunnar, Eugene R. "Names on Trees, the Hermaphrodite, and 'The Garden.'" In *On the Celebrated and Neglected Poems of Andrew Marvell,* edited by Claude J. Summers and Ted-Larry Pebworth, pp. 121–38. Columbia: University of Missouri Press, 1992.

Cunningham, John, and Stephen Slimp. "The Less into the Greater: Emblem, Analogue, and Deification in *The Merchant of Venice.*" In *The Merchant of Venice: New Critical Essays,* edited by John W. Mahon and Ellen Macleod Mahon, pp. 225–82. London: Routledge, 2002.

Cusanus, Nicholas. *De visione Dei.* 1453.

Daley, A. Stuart. "The Midsummer Deer of *As You Like It*, II.i." *Philological Quarterly* 58 (1979): 103–6.

Danson, Lawrence. *The Harmonies of "The Merchant of Venice."* New Haven, Conn.: Yale University Press, 1978.

Davis, J. C. "Religion and the Struggle for Freedom in the English Revolution." *Historical Journal* 35 (1992): 507–30.

Day, Malcolm M. *Thomas Traherne*. Boston: Twayne, 1982.

Dear, Peter. "Method and the Study of Nature." In *The Cambridge History of Seventeenth-Century Philosophy*, edited by Daniel Garber and Michael Ayers, 1:147–77. Cambridge: Cambridge University Press, 1998.

De Jongh, Eddy. *Questions of Meaning: Theme and Motif in Dutch Seventeenth-Century Painting*. Edited and translated by Michael Hoyle. Leiden: Primavera Pers, 2000.

De Malynes, Gerard. *Consuetudo, vel Lex Mercatoria, or The Antient Law-Merchant*. London, 1622.

De Man, Paul. "Intentional Structure of the Romantic Image." In *Romanticism and Consciousness*, edited by Harold Bloom, pp. 65–77. New York: Norton, 1970.

Demetz, Peter. "Defenses of Dutch Painting and the Theory of Realism." *Comparative Literature* 15 (1963): 91–115.

Deneef, A. Leigh. *Traherne in Dialogue: Heidegger, Lacan, and Derrida*. Durham, N.C.: Duke University Press, 1988.

Denham, Sir John. "Coopers Hill." In *The Penguin Book of Renaissance Verse, 1509–1659*. Selected by David Norbrook, edited by H. R. Woudhuysen. London: Penguin, 1992.

Derrida, Jacques. *Of Grammatology*. Translated by Gayatri Chakravorty Spivak. 1976. Reprint, Baltimore: Johns Hopkins University Press, 1997.

———. "Racism's Last Word." *Critical Inquiry* 12 (Autumn 1985): 290–99.

Descartes, René. *The Philosophical Writings of Descartes*. 3 vols. Translated by John Cottingham, Robert Stoothoff, and Dugald Murdoch. Cambridge: Cambridge University Press, 1985–91.

Dickson, Donald R. *The Fountain of Living Waters: The Typology of the Waters of Life in Herbert, Vaughan, and Traherne*. Columbia: University of Missouri Press, 1987.

Dillenberger, John. *Images and Relics: Theological Perceptions and Visual Images in Sixteenth-Century Europe*. Oxford Studies in Historical Theology. Oxford: Oxford University Press, 1999.

———. *Protestant Thought and Natural Science*. London: Collins, 1961.

Dionysius the Areopagite. *Dionysius the Areopagite on the Divine Names and the Mystical Theology*. Translated by C. E. Rolt. 1920. Reprint, New York: Macmillan, 1951.

Dobb, Maurice. *Studies in the Development of Capitalism*. London: Routledge, 1946.

Dobbins, Austin C., and Roy W. Battenhouse. "Jessica's Morals: A Theological View." *Shakespeare Studies* 9 (1976): 107–20.

Dobson, Andrew. *Green Political Thought*. 3rd ed. London: Routledge, 2000.

Donawerth, Jane. *Shakespeare and the Sixteenth-Century Study of Language*. Urbana: University of Illinois Press, 1984.

Donne, John. *Devotions Upon Emergent Occasions*. Edited by Anthony Raspa. New York: Oxford University Press, 1987.

———. *John Donne*. Edited by John Carey. Oxford: Oxford University Press, 1991.

———. *The Sermons of John Donne*. Edited by Evelyn M. Simpson and George R. Potter. 10 vols. Berkeley: University of California Press, 1953–62.

Donno, Elizabeth Story, ed. *Andrew Marvell: The Critical Heritage*. London: Routledge, 1978.

Doody, Margaret. *The Daring Muse: Augustan Poetry Reconsidered*. New York: Cambridge University Press, 1985.

Douglas, Mary. *Cultural Bias*. London: Royal Anthropological Institute, 1978.

Drayton, Michael. *The Works of Michael Drayton*. 5 vols. Edited by J. William Hebel. Oxford: Blackwell, 1961.

Dryden, John. "Discourse Concerning the Original and Progress of Satire." 1693. In *Of Dramatic Poesy, and Other Critical Essays*. Edited by George Watson. 2 vols. London: J. M. Dent, 1962.

Duffy, Eamon. "The Cradle Will Rock." *New York Review of Books* (December 19, 2002): 61–63.

Eden, Richard. *The Decades of the New World . . . Written in . . . Latin*. 1555.

Edwards, Karen. *Milton and the Natural World*. Cambridge: Cambridge University Press, 1999.

Elam, Keir. *Shakespeare's Universe of Discourse: Language-Games in the Comedies*. Cambridge: Cambridge University Press, 1984.

Elder, John. *Imagining the Earth: Poetry and the Vision of Nature*. Urbana: University of Illinois Press, 1985.

Eliot, T. S. "Andrew Marvell." In *Andrew Marvell*, edited by John Carey, pp. 46–58. Baltimore: Penguin, 1969.

———. "The Metaphysical Poets." In *Homage to John Dryden: Three Essays on Poetry of the Seventeenth Century*. London: Hogarth Press, 1927.

———. "Mystic and Politician as Poet." *Listener* 3 (1930): 590–91.

Elizabeth I, Queen of England. In *Queen Elizabeth's Defence*. Edited by W. E. Collins. London: SPCK, 1958.

Empson, William. *Some Versions of Pastoral*. London: Chatto & Windus, 1935.

Engle, Lars. *Shakespearean Pragmatism: Market of His Time*. Chicago: University of Chicago Press, 1993.

Estok, Simon C. "Teaching the Environment." In *Shakespeare Matters*, edited by Lloyd Davis, pp. 177–90. Cranbury, N.J.: Associated University Presses, 2003.

Evans, Malcolm. *Signifying Nothing: Truth's True Contents in Shakespeare's Text*. Athens: University of Georgia Press, 1986.

Evett, David. *Literature and the Visual Arts in Tudor England*. Athens: University of Georgia Press, 1990.

Ex, Sjarel. Foreword to *Pieter Saenredam, the Utrecht Work*, edited by Liesbeth M. Helmus, pp. 4–5. Los Angeles: Getty Museum, 2002.

Fabian, Bernhard, ed. *Collected Works of Ralph Cudworth*. Vol. 1. New York: Georg Olms Verlag, 1977.

Ficino, Marsilio. *Opera omnia*. Basel, 1576.

Fiedler, Leslie A. "'These Be the Christian Husbands.'" In *Modern Critical Interpretations: William Shakespeare's "The Merchant of Venice,"* edited by Harold Bloom, pp. 63–90. New York: Chelsea House, 1986.

Finch, Anne. *The Poems of Anne, Countess of Winchilsea*. Edited by Myra Reynolds. Chicago: University of Chicago Press, 1903.

Fish, Stanley. *How Milton Works*. Cambridge, Mass.: Harvard University Press, 2001.

———. *Surprised by Sin*. New York: St. Martin's Press, 1967.

Fitter, Chris. *Poetry, Space, Landscape: Toward a New Theory.* New York: Cambridge University Press, 1995.

Fortin, René. "Launcelot and the Uses of Allegory in *The Merchant of Venice.*" *Studies in English Literature, 1500–1900,* 14 (1974): 259–70.

Foster, John. *The Nature of Perception.* Oxford: Clarendon Press, 2000.

Foucault, Michel. *The Order of Things.* 1966. Reprint, New York: Random House, 1970.

Fowler, Alastair. "Genre and Tradition." In *The Cambridge Companion to English Poetry, Donne to Marvell,* edited by Thomas N. Corns, pp. 80–100. New York: Cambridge University Press, 1993.

———. *Renaissance Realism: Narrative Images in Literature and Art.* Oxford: Oxford University Press, 2003.

Frank, Joseph, ed. *Hobbled Pegasus: A Descriptive Bibliography of Minor English Poetry.* Albuquerque: University of New Mexico Press, 1968.

Frye, Roland Mushat. *Shakespeare and Christian Doctrine.* Princeton, N.J.: Princeton University Press, 1963.

Fuchs, Rudolph Hermann. *Dutch Painting.* New York: Oxford University Press, 1978.

Fudge, Erica. *Perceiving Animals: Humans and Beasts in Early Modern English Culture.* New York: St. Martin's Press, 2000.

———. "Saying Nothing Concerning the Same: On Dominion, Purity, and Meat in Early Modern England." In *Renaissance Beasts: Of Animals, Humans, and Other Wonderful Creatures,* edited by Erica Fudge, pp. 70–86. Urbana: University of Illinois Press, 2004.

Fuller, Thomas. *Abel Redevivus; or, The Dead Yet Speaking: The Lives and Deaths of the Modern Divines.* London, 1651.

Galilei, Galileo. *The Assayer.* In *Discoveries and Opinions of Galileo.* Translated by Stillman Drake. New York: Anchor, 1957.

———. Letter to the Grand Duchess Christina of Tuscany, 1615.

Gardiner, Stephen. *An Explication and Assertion of the True Catholique Faith.* Rouen, 1551.

Gardner, Helen, ed. *The Metaphysical Poets.* 1957. Reprint, London: Penguin, 1972.

Gascoigne, George. *Works.* Edited by J. W. Cunliffe. Cambridge, 1910.

Gassendi, Pierre. *Dissertations en forme de paradoxes contre les Aristotéliceins, Livres I et II.* Edited and translated by Bernard Rochot. Paris: Librairie philosophique J. Vrin, 1959.

———. *Opera omnia.* Lyon, 1658.

Georgel, Pierre, and Anne-Marie Lecoq. *La peinture dans la peinture.* Dijon: Musée des Beaux-Arts, 1983.

Gibbons, Brian. "Amorous Fictions and *As You Like It.*" In *Fanned and Winnowed Opinions: Shakespearian Essays Presented to Harold Jenkins.* Edited by John Mahon and Thomas Pendleton, pp. 52–78. London: Methuen, 1987.

Gilman, Ernest B. *The Curious Perspective: Literary and Pictorial Wit in the Seventeenth Century.* New Haven, Conn.: Yale University Press, 1978.

———. *Iconoclasm and Poetry in the English Reformation: Down with Dagon.* Chicago: University of Chicago, 1986.

Giordano Bruno. *The Heroic Frenzies.* Translated by P. E. Memmo, Jr. Chapel Hill: University of North Carolina Press, 1964.

Glacken, Clarence J. *Traces on the Rhodian Shore: Nature and Culture in Western Thought from Ancient Times to the End of the Eighteenth Century.* Berkeley: University of California Press, 1973.

Goldberg, Jonathan. "Fatherly Authority." In *Rewriting the Renaissance.* Edited by Margaret W. Ferguson, Maureen Quilligan, and Nancy J. Vickers, pp. 3–32. Chicago: University of Chicago Press, 1986.

Goldmann, Lucien. *The Hidden God: A Study of Tragic Vision in the Pensées of Pascal and the Tragedies of Racine.* Translated by Philip Thody. New York: Humanities Press, 1964.

Goux, Jean-Joseph. *The Coiners of Language.* Translated by Jennifer Curtiss Gage. Norman: University of Oklahoma Press, 1994.

Gowing, Laurence. *Vermeer.* London: Faber and Faber, 1952.

Grafton, Anthony. *The Transmission of Culture in Early Modern Europe.* Philadelphia: University of Pennsylvania Press, 1990.

Greenblatt, Stephen J. *Shakespearean Negotiations: The Circulation of Social Energy in Renaissance England.* Berkeley: University of California Press, 1988.

Greene, Thomas M. *The Light in Troy: Imitation and Discovery in Renaissance Poetry.* New Haven, Conn.: Yale University Press, 1982.

Greg, W. W. "Pastoral: A Literary Inquiry." In *Pastoral and Romance,* edited by Eleanor T. Lincoln, pp. 7–11. Englewood Cliffs, N.J.: Prentice-Hall, 1978.

Gregerson, Linda. *The Reformation of the Subject: Spenser, Milton, and the English Protestant Epic.* Cambridge: Cambridge University Press, 1995.

Gregory, Henry Duval V. "Tabletop Still Lifes in Haarlem, c. 1610–1660: A Study of the Relationships Between Form and Meaning." Ph.D. diss., University of Maryland, 2003.

Greville, Fulke. *A Treatie of Humane Learning.* London, 1633.

Gross, Kenneth. *The Dream of the Moving Statue.* Ithaca, N.Y.: Cornell University Press, 1992.

Grove, Richard H. *Green Imperialism: Colonial Expansion, Tropical Island Edens and the Origins of Environmentalism, 1600–1860.* New York: Cambridge University Press, 1995.

Guibbory, Achsah. *Ceremony and Community from Herbert to Milton: Literature, Religion, and Cultural Conflict in Seventeenth-Century England.* New York: Cambridge University Press, 1998.

Habington, William. *Poems.* Edited by Kenneth Allott. London: University of Liverpool Press, 1948.

Haller, William. *Foxe's Book of Martyrs and the Elect Nation.* London: J. Cape, 1963.

Hamill, Monica J. "Poetry, Law, and the Pursuit of Perfection." *Studies in English Literature, 1500–1900* 18 (1978): 229–43.

Hammond, Paul. "Marvell's Sexuality." *The Seventeenth Century* 11 (1996): 87–123.

Hannaford, Renée. " 'Express'd by Mee': Carew on Donne and Jonson." *Studies in Philology* 84, no. 1 (1987): 61–79.

Hanson, Elizabeth. *Discovering the Subject in Renaissance England.* New York: Cambridge University Press, 1998.

Hariot, Thomas. *A Briefe and True Report of the New Found Land of Virginia.* London, 1590.

Harris, Jonathan Gil. *Sick Economies: Drama, Mercantilism, and Disease in Shakespeare's England.* Philadelphia: University of Pennsylvania Press, 2004.

Harrison, Peter. *The Bible, Protestantism and the Rise of Natural Science.* Cambridge: Cambridge University Press, 1998.

Harrison, Robert Pogue. *Forests: The Shadow of Civilization.* Chicago: University of Chicago Press, 1992.

Hartman, Geoffrey. *Beyond Formalism.* New Haven, Conn.: Yale University Press, 1970.

Hawkes, David. *Idols of the Marketplace.* New York: Palgrave, 2001.

Haydn, Hiram. *The Counter-Renaissance.* New York: Scribner's, 1950.

Healy, John. *Pliny the Elder on Science and Technology.* New York: Oxford University Press, 2000.

Hegel, G. W. F. *Aesthetics: Lectures on the Fine Arts.* 2 vols. Translated by T. M. Knox. Oxford: Clarendon Press, 1975.

Heidegger, Martin. *Basic Writings.* 2nd ed., revised and expanded. 1964. Reprint, San Francisco: Harper, 1993.

Helgerson, Richard. "Soldiers and Enigmatic Girls: The Politics of Dutch Domestic Realism, 1650–1672." *Representations* 58 (1997): 49–87.

Helmus, Liesbeth M., ed. *Pieter Saenredam, the Utrecht Work: Paintings and Drawings by the Seventeenth-Century Master of Perspective.* Los Angeles: Getty Museum, 2002.

Herbert, Edward, Lord of Cherbury. *De Veritate.* Translated by Meyrick H. Carré. Bristol: J. W. Arrowsmith, 1937.

Herbert, George. *The English Poems of George Herbert.* Edited by C. A. Patrides. Rutland, Vt.: Everyman's Library, 1991.

Hermes Trismegistus. *Hermetica; The Ancient Greek and Latin Writings Which Contain Religious or Philosophic Teachings Ascribed to Hermes Trismegistus.* Edited by Walter Scott. 4 vols. Oxford: Clarendon Press, 1924.

Herrick, Robert. *The Complete Poetry of Robert Herrick.* Edited by J. Max Patrick. New York: New York University Press, 1963.

Heydenreich, I. H. *Leonardo da Vinci.* London: Allen and Unwin, 1954.

Hickeringill, Edmund. *The History of Whiggism.* London, 1682.

Hill, Christopher. *Puritanism and Revolution.* London: Secker and Warburg, 1958.

———. *The World Turned Upside Down: Radical Ideas During the English Revolution.* New York: Viking Press, 1972. Reprint, London: Penguin, 1991.

Hirst, Derek. "The Failure of Godly Rule in the English Republic." *Past and Present* 132 (1991): 33–66.

Hirst, Derek, and Steven Zwicker. "Andrew Marvell and the Toils of Patriarchy: Fatherhood, Longing, and the Body Politic." *ELH* 66, no. 3 (1999): 629–54.

Hobbes, Thomas. *The Elements of Law, Natural and Politic.* 2nd ed. Edited by Ferdinand Tönnies. London: Frank Cass, 1969.

Hollander, Martha. *An Entrance for the Eyes: Space and Meaning in Seventeenth-Century Dutch Art.* Berkeley: University of California Press, 2002.

Hooker, Richard. *Works: Laws of Ecclesiastical Polity.* 2 vols. Oxford: Oxford University Press, 1850.

Hugh of St. Victor. *De tribus diebus.* Turnhout: Brepols, 2002.

Hughes, Ann. *The Causes of the English Civil War.* London: Macmillan, 1991.

Hughes, Ted. "The Environmental Revolution." *Your Environment* 1 (1970): 81–83.

Hyman, Lawrence. *Andrew Marvell.* New York: Twayne, 1964.

Innes, John. "Students to Preserve Human DNA in Trees." *Scotsman* (May 26, 2003).

Jackson Thomas, *Treatise Containing the Originall of Unbeliefe.* London, 1625.

Jenkyns, Richard. *Virgil's Experience.* Oxford: Clarendon Press, 1998.

John, Saint of the Cross. *The Complete Works of Saint John of the Cross.* Edited and translated by E. Allison Peers. London: Burns and Oates, 1964.

Johns, Karl. "The Jesuits, the Crèche and Hans von Aachen in Prague." *Umění* 46, no. 4 (1998): 189–97.

Johnson, Samuel. *Lives of the English Poets.* Edited by George Birkbeck Hill. Oxford: Clarendon Press, 1905.

Johnston, Carol Ann. " 'Heavenly Perspective': Thomas Traherne and Seventeenth Century Visual Traditions." Ph.D. diss., Harvard University, 1992.

———. "Heavenly Perspectives, Mirrors of Eternity: Thomas Traherne's Yearning Subject." *Criticism* 43 (2001): 377–405.

Jonson, Ben. *Epicoene.* Edited by Edward Partridge. New Haven, Conn.: Yale University Press, 1971.

———. *Volpone.* 2nd ed. Edited by Robert N. Watson. London: A & C Black, 2003.

Kalstone, David. "Marvell and the Fictions of Pastoral." *English Literary Renaissance* 4 (1974): 174–88.

Karlstadt, Andreas. *On the Removal of Images.* 1522. In *Karlstadt, Emser, and Eck on Sacred Images: A Reformation Debate, Three Treatises in Translation,* 2nd ed., edited by Bryan Mangrum and Giuseppe Scavizzi. Ottawa: Dovehouse Editions, 1991.

Kepler, Johannes. *Gesammelte Werke.* Edited by M. Caspar. Munich: C. H. Beck. 20 vols. 1937–2002.

Kermode, Frank. "The Argument of Marvell's *Garden.*" In *Andrew Marvell,* edited by John Carey, pp. 250–65. Baltimore: Penguin, 1969.

Kernan, Alvin B. "The Shakespearean Conception of History." In *Modern Shakespearean Criticism,* edited by Alvin B. Kernan, pp. 245–75. New York: Harcourt Brace, 1970.

Kettering, Alison McNeil. *The Dutch Arcadia: Pastoral Art and Its Audience in the Golden Age.* Totowa, N.J.: Allanheld & Schram, 1983.

Koerner, Joseph Leo. *The Reformation of the Image.* Chicago: University of Chicago Press, 2004.

Kousnetsov, I. "Sur le symbolisme dans les paysages de Jacob van Ruisdael." *Bulletin du Musée National de Varsovie* (1973): 31–41.

Krier, Theresa M. "Psychic Deadness in Allegory." In *Imagining Death in Spenser and Milton,* edited by Elizabeth Jane Bellamy, Patrick Cheney, and Michael Schoenfeldt, pp. 46–64. Houndmills, Basingstoke, Hampshire: Palgrave Macmillan, 2004.

Kroll, Richard W. *The Material Word: Literate Culture in the Restoration and Early Eighteenth Century.* Baltimore: Johns Hopkins University Press, 1991.

Kronenfeld, Judy Z. "Shakespeare's Jaques and the Pastoral Cult of Solitude." *Texas Studies in Literature and Language* 18 (1976): 451–73.

Kunzle, David. *From Criminal to Courtier: The Soldier in Netherlandish Art, 1550–1672.* Leiden: Brill, 2002.

Lacan, Jacques. *Écrits.* Translated by Alan Sheridan. New York: Norton, 1977.

Lake, Peter. "Puritan Identities." *Journal of Ecclesiastical History* 35 (1984): 112–23.

———. "Religious Identities in Shakespeare's England." In *A Companion to Shakespeare,* edited by David Scott Kastan, pp. 57–84. Oxford: Blackwell, 1999.

La Rochefoucauld, François de. *Maximes.* Paris, 1678.

Legouis, Pierre. *Andrew Marvell.* 2nd ed. Oxford: Oxford University Press, 1968.

Leigh, Richard [?]. *The Transproser Rehears'd.* Oxford, 1673.

Leonardo da Vinci. "Linear Perspective." In *The Theory of the Art of Painting*, vol. 1 of *The Notebooks of Leonardo Da Vinci*. Compiled and edited by Jean Paul Richter. 1883. Reprint, New York: Dover, 1970.

———. *Treatise on Painting*. 2 vols. Translated by A. Philip McMahon. Princeton, N.J.: Princeton University Press, 1956.

Lerner, Laurence. "Essay on Pastoral." *Essays in Criticism* 20 (1970): 275–97.

Levao, Ronald. *Renaissance Minds and Their Fictions: Cusanus, Sidney, Shakespeare*. Berkeley: University of California Press, 1985.

Levesque, Catherine. *Journey Through Landscape in Seventeenth-Century Holland: The Haarlem Print Series and Dutch Identity*. University Park: Penn State University Press, 1994.

Levin, Harry. "A Garden in Belmont: *The Merchant of Venice*, 5.1." In *Shakespeare and Dramatic Tradition: Essays in Honor of S. F. Johnson*. Edited by W. R. Elton and William B. Long, pp. 13–31. Newark: University of Delaware Press, 1989.

———. *The Myth of the Golden Age in the Renaissance*. New York: Oxford University Press, 1969.

Lewalski, Barbara K. "Biblical Allusion and Allegory in *The Merchant of Venice*." *Shakespeare Quarterly* 13 (1962): 327–43.

———. *Protestant Poetics*. Princeton, N.J.: Princeton University Press, 1979.

Lloyd, Christopher. *Enchanting the Eye: Dutch Paintings of the Golden Age*. London: Royal Collection, 2004.

Locke, John. *An Essay Concerning Human Understanding*. In *The Works of John Locke in Nine Volumes*. Vol. 1. 1690. 12th ed. London: Rivington, 1824.

———. *Of the Conduct of the Understanding*. In *The Works of John Locke in Nine Volumes*. Vol. 2. 1706. 12th ed. London: Rivington, 1824.

Loewenstein, David. "Politics and Religion." In *The Cambridge Companion to English Poetry, Donne to Marvell*, edited by Thomas N. Corns, pp. 3–30. New York: Cambridge University Press, 1993.

Lovelace, Richard. *The Poems of Richard Lovelace*. Vol. 2. Edited by C. H. Wilkinson. London: Oxford University Press, 1925.

Low, Anthony. *The Georgic Revolution*. Princeton, N.J.: Princeton University Press, 1985.

Low, Lisa. "Ending in Eden: Mind and Nature in Milton, Marvell, Wordsworth, and Wallace Stevens." Ph.D. diss., University of Massachusetts, 1986.

Lucking, David. "Standing for Sacrifice." *University of Toronto Quarterly* 58 (1989): 355–75.

Luther, Martin. "The Babylonian Captivity of the Church." 1520. Translated by A. T. W. Steinhäuser, revised by Frederick C. Ahrens and Abdel Ross Wentz. In *Luther's Works*. 55 vols. Vol. 36. Edited by Helmut Lehmann. Philadelphia: Muhlenberg Press, 1959.

———. *Commentary on Galatians*. In *Luther's Works*, vols. 26–27. Edited by Jaroslav Jan Pelikan and Helmut Lehmann. 1535; reprint, St. Louis: Concordia, 1955–86.

MacFarquhar, Larissa. "Bark." *New Yorker* (February 3, 2003): 88–92.

Mackenzie, Donald. *The Metaphysical Poets*. Hampshire: Macmillan, 1990.

MacLeish, Archibald. *Collected Poems, 1917–1982*. Boston: Houghton Mifflin, 1985.

Madsen, William G. *From Shadowy Types to Truth: Studies in Milton's Symbolism*. New Haven, Conn.: Yale University Press, 1968.

Maimonides. *Guide of the Perplexed*. Translated by S. Pines. Chicago: University of Chicago Press, 1963.

Malcolmson, Cristina. "The Garden Enclosed/The Woman Enclosed." In *Enclosure Acts: Sexuality, Property, and Culture in Early Modern England*, edited by Richard Burt and John Michael Archer, pp. 251–69. Ithaca, N.Y.: Cornell University Press, 1994.

Mangrum, Bryan and Guiseppe Scavizzi, eds. *A Reformation Debate: Karlstadt, Emser, and Eck on Sacred Images*. Toronto: University of Toronto Press, 1991.

Manley, Lawrence. *Convention 1500–1700*. Cambridge, Mass.: Harvard University Press, 1980.

Manwood, John. *A Brefe Collection of the Lawes of the Forest*. London, 1592.

Marcus, Leah Sinanoglou. *Childhood and Cultural Despair*. Pittsburgh: University of Pittsburgh Press, 1978.

Marcuse, Herbert. *One-Dimensional Man*. Boston: Beacon Press, 1964.

Margoliouth, H. M. Introduction to *Centuries, Poems and Thanksgiving*, by Thomas Traherne, edited by H. M. Margoliouth, pp. ix–xli. Oxford: Clarendon Press, 1958.

Marks, Carol L. Introduction to *Christian Ethicks*, by Thomas Traherne. Edited by George Robert Guffey and Carol L. Marks, xi–l. Ithaca, N.Y.: Cornell University Press, 1968.

———. "Thomas Traherne and Cambridge Platonism." *PMLA* 81 (1966): 521–34.

Martin, John Rupert. *Baroque*. New York: Harper and Row, 1977.

Martyr, Peter. *The Decades of the New World Written in Latin*. London, 1555.

Martz, Louis L. *The Paradise Within: Studies in Vaughan, Traherne and Milton*. New Haven, Conn.: Yale University Press, 1964.

Marvell, Andrew. *Andrew Marvell: The Complete Poems*. Edited by Elizabeth Story Donno. London: Penguin Books, 1985.

Marx, Karl. *Capital: A Critique of Political Economy*. 1867. Edited by Frederick Engels and translated by Samuel Moore and Edward Aveling. Chicago: Charles H. Kerr, 1906.

———. *Early Writings*. Translated by Rodney Livingstone and Gregor Benton. Harmondsworth, Middlesex: Penguin, 1975.

Maus, Katharine Eisaman. *Inwardness and Theater in the English Renaissance*. Chicago: University of Chicago Press, 1995.

Maycock, Alan L. *Nicholas Ferrar of Little Gidding*. Grand Rapids, Mich.: Eerdmans, 1938.

Mayor, A. Hyatt. "The Photographic Eye." *Metropolitan Museum of Art Bulletin* 5 (Summer 1946).

McColley, Diane Kelsey. "Milton and Nature." *Huntington Library Quarterly* 62 (1999–2001): 423–44.

McDermott, Patricia. "Eternal Triangles: The Secularization of the Sacred in the Art of Francisco Goya." In *Leeds Papers on Symbol and Image in Iberian Arts*, edited by Margaret A. Rees, pp. 221–48. Leeds: University of Leeds, 1994.

McFarland, Thomas. *Shakespeare's Pastoral Comedy*. Chapel Hill: University of North Carolina Press, 1972.

McNally, David. *Political Economy and the Rise of Capitalism*. Berkeley: University of California, 1988.

McRae, Andrew. "Satire and Sycophancy: Richard Corbett and Early Stuart Royalism." *Review of English Studies* 54 (2003): 336–64.

Melanchthon, Philip. "On the Soul." In *A Melanchthon Reader*, translated by Ralph Keen, pp. 239–89. New York: Peter Lang, 1988.

Merchant, Carolyn. *The Death of Nature: Women, Ecology, and the Scientific Revolution.* San Francisco: Harper & Row, 1980.

———. *Earthcare: Women and the Environment.* London: Routledge, 1995.

Michaels, David. "Doubt Is Their Product." *Scientific American* (June 2005): 96–101.

Middleton, Thomas and Samuel Rowley. *The Changeling.* Edited by George W. Williams. Lincoln: University of Nebraska Press, 1966.

Milosz, Czeslaw. *New and Collected Poems, 1931–2001.* New York: Ecco, 2001.

Milton, John. *Complete Poems and Major Prose.* Edited by Merritt Y. Hughes. Indianapolis: Bobbs-Merrill, 1976.

Montagu [Mountague], Richard. "Letter of Ju. 28, 1624." In *The Correspondence of John Cosin.* Publications of the Surtees Society, Vol. 52. Edinburgh: Blackwood & Sons, 1869.

Montaigne, Michel de. "Apology for Raymond Sebond." In *The Complete Essays of Montaigne,* translated by Donald M. Frame, pp. 318–457. Stanford, Calif.: Stanford University Press, 1948.

———. *The Complete Essays of Montaigne.* Translated by Donald M. Frame. Stanford, Calif.: Stanford University Press, 1948.

Montias, Michael. *Art at Auction in Seventeenth Century Amsterdam.* Amsterdam: Amsterdam University Press, 2003.

More, Henry, *Conjectura Cabbalistica.* London, 1653.

———. "Cupids Conflict." In *Philosophical Poems.* Cambridge, 1647.

Morris, Brian, and Eleanor Withington. Introduction to *The Poems of John Cleveland.* Oxford: Clarendon Press, 1967.

Morris, Harry. "*As You Like It: Et in Arcadia Ego.*" *Shakespeare Quarterly* 26 (1975): 269–75.

Moschus. *Last Flowers: A Translation of Moschus and Bion.* Translated by Henry Harmon Chamberlain. Cambridge, Mass.: Harvard University Press, 1937.

Moxey, Keith P. F. *Pieter Aertsen, Joachim Beuckelaer, and the Rise of Secular Painting in the Context of the Reformation.* New York: Garland, 1977.

Murphy, Stephen. "The Death of Actaeon as Petrarchist Topos." *Comparative Literature Studies* 28, no. 2 (1991): 137–55.

Myers, Anne. "The Man in the London Street." Unpublished essay.

Neckam, Alexander. *De Naturis Rerum.* Edited by T. Wright. London: Longman, 1863.

Netzloff, Mark. "The Lead Casket." In *Money and the Age of Shakespeare,* edited by Linda Woodbridge, pp. 159–76. New York: Palgrave Macmillan, 2003.

Nicolson, Marjorie Hope. *The Breaking of the Circle.* Rev. ed. New York: Columbia University Press, 1960.

Norbrook, David. *Writing the English Republic.* Cambridge: Cambridge University Press, 1998.

Norgate, Edward. *Miniatura or the Art of Limning.* London, 1627–28.

Normand, Lawrence. "*What Passions Call You These?*" *James VI and Edward II in Christopher Marlowe and English Renaissance Culture,* edited by Darryll Grantley and Peter Roberts, pp. 172–97. Aldershot: Scolar Press, 1996.

Nuttall, A. D. *A New Mimesis.* New York: Methuen, 1983.

Oelschlager, Max. *The Idea of Wilderness: From Prehistory to the Age of Ecology.* New Haven, Conn.: Yale University Press, 1991.

Orgel, Stephen. *The Illusion of Power.* Berkeley: University of California Press, 1975.

Orme, Nicholas. *Medieval Children.* New Haven, Conn.: Yale University Press, 2001.

Ortner, Sherry Beth. "Is Female to Male as Nature Is to Culture?" In *Woman, Culture, and Society,* edited by Michelle Zimbalist Rosaldo and Louise Lamphere, pp. 67–87. Stanford, Calif.: Stanford University Press, 1974.

Ovid. *Metamorphoses.* Translated by Arthur Golding. 1567. Reprint, London: Centaur Press, 1961.

Ozment, Steven. *Ancestors.* Cambridge, Mass.: Harvard University Press, 2001.

Panofsky, Erwin. *Meaning in the Visual Arts.* New York: Doubleday, 1955.

———. *Perspective as Symbolic Form.* Translated by Christopher Wood. New York: Zone Books, 1997.

Pascal, Blaise. *Pensées.* Translated by A. J. Krailsheimer. Baltimore: Penguin, 1966.

Patterson, Annabel. *Pastoral and Ideology: Virgil to Valéry.* Berkeley: University of California Press, 1987.

Pearlman, E. "George Herbert's God." *English Literary Renaissance* 13 (1983): 88–112.

Perkins, William. *The Workes of that Famous and Worthy Minister of Christ in the Universitie of Cambridge.* 3 vols. London, 1612.

Phillips, John. *The Reformation of Images: Destruction of Art in England, 1535–1660.* Berkeley: University of California Press, 1973.

Plato. *Cratylus.* In *The Dialogues of Plato.* Translated by Benjamin Jowett. 2 vols. New York: Random House, 1937.

Pliny the Elder, *Natural History: A Selection.* Translated by John F. Healy. London: Penguin, 1991.

Plomp, Michiel C. "Pieter Saenredam as a Draughtsman." In *Pieter Saenredam, The Utrecht Work,* edited by Liesbeth M. Helmus, pp. 51–72. Los Angeles: Getty Museum, 2002.

Plumwood, Val. *Feminism and the Mastery of Nature.* London: Routledge, 1993.

Popkin, Richard Henry. *The History of Scepticism from Erasmus to Spinoza.* Revised and expanded ed. Berkeley: University of California Press, 1979.

Porter, Roy. *Flesh in the Age of Reason.* London: Penguin, 2003.

Post, Jonathan. *English Lyric Poetry: the Early Seventeenth Century.* London: Routledge, 1999.

Potter, Lois. *Secret Rites and Secret Writing.* Cambridge: Cambridge University Press, 1989.

Powicke, Frederick J. "The Reverend Richard Baxter's Last Treatise." *Bulletin of the John Rylands Library* 10 (1926): 182–97.

Puttenham, George. *The Arte of English Poesie.* 1589. Edited by Gladys Doidge Willcock and Alice Walker. 1936. Reprint Cambridge: Cambridge University Press, 1970.

Pyle, Cynthia. "The Art and Science of Renaissance Natural History." *Viator* 27 (1996): 265–321.

Quarles, Francis. *Argalus and Parthenia.* London, 1629.

———. *Emblemes.* London, 1635.

Quint, David. *Origin and Originality in Renaissance Literature: Versions of the Source.* New Haven, Conn.: Yale University Press, 1983.

Quintilian. *Institutio Oratoria.* Translated by H. E. Butler. Cambridge, Mass.: Harvard University Press, 1920.

Rabb, Theodore K. *The Struggle for Stability in Early Modern Europe.* New York: Oxford University Press, 1975.

Rabkin, Norman. "Meaning and Shakespeare." In *The Merchant of Venice: Critical Essays,* edited by Thomas Wheeler, pp. 103–25. New York: Garland, 1991.

Rale[i]gh, Walter. *Discoverie of . . . Guiana,* 1596. Reprint, New York: Da Capo Press, 1968.

———. "The Sceptic." In *The Works of Sir Walter Ralegh,* edited by William Oldys and Thomas Birch. 8 vols. New York: Burt Franklin, 1954.

Raspa, Anthony. "Crashaw and the Jesuit Poetic." *University of Toronto Quarterly* 36 (1966): 37–54.

Ray, John. *Observations topographical, moral, & physiological; made in a journey through part of the Low-countries, Germany, Italy, and France.* London, 1673.

Read, Kirk D. "Poolside Transformations: Diana and Actaeon Revisited by French Women Renaissance Lyricists." In *Renaissance Women Writers,* edited by Anne D. Larsen and Colette H. Winn, pp. 38–54. Detroit: Wayne State University Press, 1994.

Rees, Christine. *The Judgment of Marvell.* London: Pinter, 1989.

Reiss, Timothy J. *The Discourse of Modernism.* Ithaca, N.Y.: Cornell University Press, 1982.

Reynolds, Myra, ed. *The Poems of Anne, Countess of Winchilsea.* Chicago: University of Chicago Press, 1903.

Ricks, Christopher. "Allusion: The Poet as Heir." *Studies in Eighteenth Century Literature III,* edited by R. F. Brissenden and J. C. Eade, pp. 209–40. Toronto: University of Toronto, 1976.

Roberts, Jeanne Addison. *The Shakespearean Wild: Geography, Genus, and Gender.* Lincoln: University of Nebraska Press, 1991.

Rogers, John. *The Matter of Revolution: Science, Poetry, and Politics in the Age of Milton.* Ithaca, N.Y.: Cornell University Press, 1996.

Ronk, Martha. "Locating the Visual in *As You Like It.*" *Shakespeare Quarterly* 52 (2001): 255–76.

Rorty, Richard. *Philosophy and the Mirror of Nature.* Princeton, N.J.: Princeton University Press, 1979.

Rosenberg, Jakob, and Seymour Slive. *Dutch Art and Architecture, 1600–1800.* New York: Penguin, 1966.

Ross, Alexander. *Mel heliconium; or, Poeticall honey gathered out of the weeds of Parnassus.* London, 1643.

———. *Mystagogus Poeticus.* London, 1648.

Ross, Susan. "Gerard David's Models for Motherhood." *Rutgers Art Review* 17 (1997): 2–15.

Rowland, John. "Epistle Dedicatory." In *History of Four-Footed Beasts,* 1658, by Edward Topsell. Reprint, New York: Da Capo Press, 1967.

Salter, K. W. *Thomas Traherne, Mystic and Poet.* London: Edward Arnold, 1964.

Sambucus, Johannes. *Emblemata.* Leiden, 1564.

Sandys, George. *Ovid's Metamorphoses Englished.* Oxford, 1632.

Saussure, Ferdinand de. *Course in General Linguistics.* Edited by Charles Bally, Albert Sechehaye, and Albert Riedlinger. Translated by Roy Harris. London: Duckworth, 1983.

Sawday, Jonathan. *The Body Emblazoned: Dissection and the Human Body in Renaissance Culture.* London and New York: Routledge, 1995.

Schama, Simon. "Dutch Landscape: Culture as Foreground." In *Masters of Seventeenth-Century Landscape Painting,* edited by Peter C. Sutton, pp. 64–83. Boston: Museum of Fine Arts, 1987.

———. *The Embarrassment of Riches.* New York: Knopf, 1987.

———. *Landscape and Memory.* New York: Vintage, 1995.

Schleiner, Winfried. " 'Tis Like The Howling of Irish Wolves Against the Moone': A Note on *As You Like It* 5.2.109." *English Language Notes* 12 (1974): 5–8.

Schwartz, Gary, and Marten Jan Bok. *Pieter Saenredam: The Painter and His Time.* The Hague: SDU Publishers, 1990.

Scoufos, Alice-Lyle. "The *Paradiso Terrestre* and the Testing of Love in *As You Like It.*" *Shakespeare Studies* 14 (1981): 215–27.

Sedinger, Tracey. " 'If Sight and Shape Be True': The Epistemology of Crossdressing on the London Stage." *Shakespeare Quarterly* 48, no. 1 (1997): 63–79.

Selden, Raman. "Hobbes and Late Metaphysical Poetry." *Journal of the History of Ideas* 35 (1974): 197–210.

Sessions, W. A. "Marvell's Mower: The Wit of Survival." In *The Wit of Seventeenth-Century Poetry,* edited by Claude J. Summers and Ted-Larry Pebworth, pp. 183–98. Columbia: University of Missouri Press, 1998.

Sextus Empiricus. *Outlines of Pyrrhonism.* Translated by R. G. Bury. Buffalo, N.Y.: Prometheus Books, 1990.

Shakespeare, William. *The Riverside Shakespeare.* 2nd ed. Edited by G. B. Evans et al. Boston: Houghton Mifflin, 1997.

Shapiro, Barbara J. *A Culture of Fact: England, 1550–1720.* Ithaca, N.Y.: Cornell University Press, 2000.

———. *Probability and Certainty in Seventeenth-Century England: A Study of the Relationships Between Natural Science, Religion, History, Law, and Literature.* Princeton, N.J.: Princeton University Press, 1983.

Shapiro, James. *Shakespeare and the Jews.* New York: Columbia University Press, 1996.

Sharpe, Kevin, and Steven N. Zwicker, eds. *Politics of Discourse: The Literature and History of Seventeenth-Century England.* Berkeley: University of California Press, 1987.

Shell, Marc. *Money, Language, and Thought: Literary and Philosophic Economies from the Medieval to the Modern Era.* Berkeley: University of California Press, 1982.

Shuger, Debora, "Civility and Censorship in Early Modern England." In *Censorship and Silencing: Practices of Cultural Regulation,* edited by Robert Post, pp. 89–110. Los Angeles: Getty Research Institute, 1998.

———. "Conceptions of Style." In *The Cambridge History of Literary Criticism: The Renaissance,* edited by Glyn Norton, pp. 176–86. New York: Cambridge University Press, 1999.

Sibscota, George. *The deaf and dumb man's discourse, or, A treatise concerning those that are born deaf and dumb, containing a discovery of their knowledge or understanding.* London, 1670.

Sidney, Philip. *The Countesse of Pembroke's Arcadia.* Vol. 4. 1598. Edited by Albert Feuillerat. London: Cambridge University Press, 1926.

———. *The Defence of Poesie.* London, 1595.

————. *Sir Philip Sidney's Defense of Poesy*. Edited by Lewis Soens. Lincoln: University of Nebraska Press, 1970.

Siemon, James. *Shakespearean Iconoclasm*. Berkeley: University of California Press, 1985.

————. *Word Against Word: Shakespearean Utterance*. Amherst: University of Massachusetts Press, 2002.

Simmons, I. G. *Environmental History: A Concise Introduction*. Cambridge, Mass.: Blackwell, 1993.

Sinfield, Alan. *Literature in Protestant England, 1560–1660*. London: Croom Helm, 1983.

Slaughter, Mary. *Universal Languages and Scientific Taxonomy in the Seventeenth Century*. Cambridge: Cambridge University Press, 1982.

Slive, Seymour. *Dutch Painting: 1600–1800*. New Haven, Conn.: Yale University Press, 1995.

————. *Jacob van Ruisdael*. New York: Abbeville Press, 1981.

————. *Jacob van Ruisdael: A Complete Catalogue of His Paintings, Drawings and Etchings*. New Haven, Conn.: Yale University Press, 2001.

Smith, A. J. "Sacred Earth: Metaphysical Poetry and the Advance of Science." *Proceedings of the British Academy* 71 (1985): 251–66.

Smith, Hallett. "Elizabethan Pastoral." In *Pastoral and Romance*, edited by Eleanor T. Lincoln, pp. 12–24. Englewood Cliffs, N.J.: Prentice-Hall, 1978.

Smith, John. *Discourse, Concerning the True Way or Method of Attaining to Divine Knowledge*. Cambridge, 1660.

Smith, Nigel. *Literature and Revolution in England, 1640–1660*. New Haven, Conn.: Yale University Press, 1994.

Snyder, Susan. *Pastoral Process*. Stanford, Calif.: Stanford University Press, 1998.

Sommerville, C. John. *The Secularization of Early Modern England: From Religious Culture to Religious Faith*. New York: Oxford University Press, 1992.

Soper, Kate. *What Is Nature?* Oxford: Blackwell, 1995.

Southwell, Robert. *Complete Poems*. Edited by Alexander Grosart. London, 1872.

————. *Epistle of Comfort*, 1587–88. Edited by Margaret Waugh. Chicago: Loyola University Press, 1966.

Sparke, Michael. *Crumms of Comfort*. London, 1627.

Specter, Michael. "The Extremist." *New Yorker* (April 14, 2003): 52–67.

Spenser, Edmund. *Poetical Works*. Edited by J. C. Smith and E. de Selincourt. London: Oxford University Press, 1970.

Spolsky, Ellen. *Satisfying Skepticism: Embodied Knowledge in the Early Modern World*. Burlington: Ashgate, 2001.

Sprat, Thomas. *History of the Royal Society*. 1667. Facsimile edited by Jackson I. Cope and Harold Whitmore Jones. St. Louis: Washington University Studies, 1958.

Stempel, Daniel. "Marvell's Cartesian Ecstasy." *Journal of the History of Ideas* 28 (1967): 99–114.

Sterry, Peter. *A Discourse of the Freedom of the Will*. London, 1675.

Stewart, Stanley. *The Enclosed Garden*. Madison: University of Wisconsin Press, 1966.

Stillingfleet, Edward. *Origines Sacrae*. London, 1662.

Stone, Gregory B. "The Philosophical Beast." In *Animal Acts: Configuring the Human in Western History*, edited by Jennifer Ham and Matthew Senior, pp. 23–40. New York: Routledge, 1997.

Stone, Lawrence. *The Causes of the English Revolution, 1529–1642.* 2nd ed. London: Ark, 1986.

———. *The Family, Sex, and Marriage, 1500–1800.* New York: Harper & Row, 1977.

Strier, Richard. *Love Known: Theology and Experience in George Herbert's Poetry.* Chicago: University of Chicago Press, 1983.

Stubbes, Philip. *Anatomie of Abuses.* London, 1583.

Studing, Richard. "Shakespeare's Bohemia Revisited: A Caveat." *Shakespeare Studies* 15 (1982): 217–26.

Sullivan, Garrett A. *The Drama of Landscape: Land, Property, and Social Relations on the Early Modern Stage.* Stanford, Calif.: Stanford University Press, 1998.

Sutton, Peter C. "Introduction." In *Masters of the Seventeenth-Century Dutch Landscape Painting,* edited by Peter C. Sutton, pp. 1–63. Boston: Museum of Fine Arts, 1987.

Sutton, Peter C., ed. *The Age of Rubens.* Boston: Museum of Fine Arts in association with Ludion Press, 1993.

———. *Masters of Seventeenth-Century Dutch Landscape Painting.* Boston: Museum of Fine Arts, 1987.

Swan, James Morrill. "History, Pastoral and Desire: A Psychoanalytic Study of English Renaissance Literature and Society." Ph.D. diss., Stanford University, 1974.

Swillens, P. T. A. "The Paintings." In *Catalogue Raisonné of the Works by Pieter Jansz. Saenredam, Published on the Occasion of the Exhibition [of] 15 September–3 December 1961.* Utrecht: Centraal Museum, 1961.

Targoff, Ramie. *Common Prayer: Models of Public Devotion in Early Modern England.* Chicago: University of Chicago Press, 2001.

Tasso, Torquato. *Jerusalem Liberated [Godfrey of Bulloigne].* 1581. Translated by Edward Fairfax. London, 1600.

Tayler, Edward. *Nature and Art in Renaissance Literature.* New York: Columbia University Press, 1964.

Thirsk, Joan, ed. *The Agrarian History of England and Wales.* Vol. 4. 1500–1640. Cambridge: Cambridge University Press, 1967.

Thomas, Keith. *Man and the Natural World: Changing Attitudes in England, 1500–1800.* New York: Pantheon, 1983.

Thomas, Thomas. *Dictionarium linguae Latinae et Anglicanae.* London, 1587.

Todorov, Tzvetan. *The Conquest of America.* Translated by Richard Howard. New York: Harper, 1992.

Toliver, Harold. *Marvell's Ironic Vision.* New Haven, Conn.: Yale University Press, 1965.

Traherne, Thomas. *Centuries, Poems and Thanksgivings.* Edited by H. M. Margoliouth. Oxford: Clarendon Press, 1958.

———. *Christian Ethicks.* Edited by George Robert Guffey and Carol L. Marks. Ithaca, N.Y.: Cornell University Press, 1968.

———. *The Poetical Works of Thomas Traherne.* 2nd ed. Edited by Bertram Dobell. London: Published by editor, 1906.

———. *Roman Forgeries.* London, 1673.

Trimpi, Wesley. *Muses of One Mind: The Literary Analysis of Experience and Its Continuity.* Princeton, N.J.: Princeton University Press, 1983.

Tryon, Thomas. *The Good House-Wife.* London, 1657.

Turner, James. *The Politics of Landscape.* Oxford: Blackwell, 1979.

Tyndale, William. *The Obedience of a Christian Man.* 1528. Reprint, London: Penguin, 2000.

Uhlig, Claus. "The Sobbing Deer." In *Renaissance Drama,* new series 3, edited by S. Schoenbaum, pp. 79–109. Evanston, Ill.: Northwestern University Press, 1970.

Underdown, David. *Revel, Riot, and Rebellion: Popular Politics and Culture in England, 1603–1660.* Oxford: Clarendon Press, 1985.

Van Haute, Bernadette. *David III Ryckaert: A Seventeenth-Century Flemish Painter of Peasant Scenes.* Turnhout, Belgium: Brepols, 1999.

Van Heemstra, Geraldine. "Space, Light and Stillness." In *Pieter Saenredam, The Utrecht Work,* edited by Liesbeth M. Helmus, pp. 73–90. Los Angeles: Getty Museum, 2002.

Van Os, Henk, Jan Piet, Filedt Kok, Get Luijten, and Frits Scholten, eds. *Netherlandish Art in the Rijksmuseum, 1400–1600.* Zwolle, Netherlands: Waanders, 2000.

Van Regteren Altena, I. Q. *Jacques de Gheyn, Three Generations.* 3 vols. Translated by Mary Charles. The Hague: M. Nijhoff Publishers, 1983.

Vaughan, Henry. *The Works of Henry Vaughan.* Edited by L. C. Martin. London: Oxford University Press, 1957.

Vickers, Brian. "The Idea of Exchange in *The Merchant of Venice.*" In *L'image de Venise au temps de la Renaissance,* edited by M. T. Jones-Davies, pp. 17–49. Paris: Jean Touzot, 1989.

Vives, Juan Luis. *Opera omnia, distributa et ordinata in argumentorum classes praecipuas.* Edited by Gregorio Mayans y Siscar. 3 vols. London: Gregg Press, 1964.

Vlieghe, Hans. *Flemish Art and Architecture 1585–1700.* New Haven, Conn.: Yale University Press, 1998: 297–304.

———. "Een pastorale door Gerard Seghers." *Jaarboek van het Koninklijk Museum voor Schone Kunsten-Antwerpen* (1976): 299–304.

Wade, Gladys I. *Thomas Traherne.* Princeton, N.J.: Princeton University Press, 1946.

Walford, E. John. *Jacob van Ruisdael and the Perception of Landscape.* New Haven, Conn.: Yale University Press, 1991.

Walker, George. *The History of the Creation.* London, 1641.

Walpole, Horace. *Anecdotes of Painting in England.* London, 1762–1795.

Walsh, John, Jr. "Vermeer." *Metropolitan Museum of Art Bulletin* 31 (Summer 1973): Reproduction 75 (unpaginated).

Warhaft, Sidney, ed. *Francis Bacon: A Selection of His Works.* Indianapolis: Bobbs-Merrill, 1982.

Warnke, Frank, ed. *European Metaphysical Poetry.* New Haven, Conn.: Yale University Press, 1961.

Waswo, Richard. *Language and Meaning in the Renaissance.* Princeton, N.J.: Princeton University Press, 1987.

Watson, Robert N. "As You Liken It: Simile in the Wildness." *Shakespeare Survey* 56 (2003): 72–92.

———. Introduction to *Volpone* by Ben Jonson. New Mermaids Series. 2nd ed. London: A & C Black, 2003.

———. "*Othello* as Reformation Tragedy." In *In the Company of Shakespeare,* edited by Thomas Moisan and Douglas Bruster, pp. 65–96. Madison, N.J.: Fairleigh-Dickinson University Press.

———. *The Rest Is Silence: Death as Annihilation in the English Renaissance.* Berkeley: University of California Press, 1994.

———. *Shakespeare and the Hazards of Ambition.* Cambridge, Mass.: Harvard University Press, 1984.

———. "Tragedy." In *The Cambridge Companion to English Renaissance Drama,* edited by A. R. Braunmuller and Michael Hattaway, pp. 301–51. New York: Cambridge University Press, 1990.

Webb, John. *An Historical Essay.* London, 1669.

Webber, Joan. *The Eloquent "I": Style and Self in Seventeenth-Century Prose.* Madison: University of Wisconsin Press, 1968.

Weber, Max. *The Protestant Ethic and the Spirit of Capitalism.* 1904. Reprint, New York: Scribner's, 1930.

Webster, Charles. *The Great Instauration: Science, Medicine, and Reform, 1626–1660.* New York: Holmes and Meier, 1976.

Wedgwood, C. V. *Poetry and Politics Under the Stuarts.* Cambridge: Cambridge University Press, 1960.

Wheelock, Arthur, Jr., with Alison McNeil Ketterina, Arie Wallert, and Marjorie E. Wieseman. *Gerard ter Borch.* Washington, D.C.: National Gallery of Art, 2004.

White, Lynn, Jr. "The Historical Roots of Our Ecological Crisis." *Science* 155 (1967): 1203–7.

Whitney, Geffrey. *Choice of Emblemes.* Leiden, 1586.

Whittle, Jane. *The Development of Agrarian Capitalism: Land and Labour in Norfolk, 1440–1580.* Oxford: Oxford University Press, 2000.

Wiegand, Wilfred. "Ruisdael-Studien: Ein Versuch Ikonologie der Landschaftsmalerie." Ph.D. diss., Hamburg, 1971.

Willet, Andrew. *Hexapla in Genesin.* London, 1608.

Willey, Basil. *The Seventeenth-Century Background.* 1934. Reprint, London: Chatto and Windus, 1950.

Williams, A. M., ed. *Conversations at Little Gidding.* London: Cambridge University Press, 1970.

Williams, Raymond. *The Country and the City.* New York: Oxford University Press, 1973.

Willis, Paul J. " 'Tongues in Trees': The Book of Nature in *As You Like It." Modern Language Studies* 18, no. 3 (1988): 65–74.

Wilson, A. Doris L. "A Neglected Mystic: Thomas Traherne." *Poetry Review* 16 (1925): 11–22, 97–104, 178–82.

Wilson, Thomas. *The Arte of Rhetorique.* London, 1560.

Winstanley, Gerrard. "The True Levellers Standard Advanced." 1649.

Wither, George. *A Collection of Emblemes.* London, 1635.

———. *The Shepheards Hunting.* London, 1615.

Wittgenstein, Ludwig. *Philosophical Investigations.* 1953. Translated by G. E. M. Anscombe. Oxford: Blackwell, 1986.

Wolters, Margreet. "The Well Stocked Kitchen." In *Still Lifes: Techniques and Style,* edited by Arie Wallert, pp. 41–43. Amsterdam: Rijksmuseum, 1999.

Young, Bruce W. "Shakespearean Tragedy in a Renaissance Context." In *Approaches to Teaching Shakespeare's "King Lear,"* edited by Robert H. Ray, pp. 98–104. New York: MLA, 1986.

Young, David. *The Heart's Forest.* New Haven, Conn.: Yale University Press, 1972.

Zwicker, Steven N. *Lines of Authority: Politics and English Literary Culture, 1649–1689.* Ithaca: Cornell University Press, 1993.

———. "Lines of Authority." In *Politics of Discourse: The Literature and History of Seventeenth-Century England,* edited by Kevin Sharpe and Steven N. Zwicker, pp. 230–70. Berkeley: University of California Press, 1987.

Index

Acknowledgments

Among the many colleagues and students to whom I owe gratitude, particular thanks to those who read drafts and pursued research for me: Emily Bartels, Amy Bruinooge, John Carriero, Kristine Chong, Brian Copenhaver, Stephen Dickey, Robert Dorit, Bonnie Foote, William T. Hendel, David Kunzle, Margaret Lamont, Lilian Lee, Margaret Maurer, Russ McDonald, Claire McEachern, Ruth Morse, Anne Myers, Kris Pangburn, William Phelan, Holly Crawford Pickett, Jonathan Post, Alan Roper, Michael Salzman, Chris Sellin, Debora Shuger, Julia Sue Wai, Barbara Bellow Watson, and Dana Cairns Watson.

Special thanks to the Guggenheim Foundation, for the time and encouragement bestowed by a fellowship, and for the generous subvention that helped keep this large book relatively affordable. Thanks to the UCLA Faculty Senate for annual research grants, to the Center for Medieval and Renaissance Studies and the Clark Center for Seventeenth- and Eighteenth-Century Studies at UCLA for providing research assistants, and to the UCLA Friends of English for helping with the acquisition of illustrations. Thanks to the many libraries—especially UCLA and the Bibliothèque Nationale in Paris—that were indispensable for my research.

Thanks, finally, in loving memory, to Janet Field-Pickering, for launching this book by requesting a lecture on *As You Like It*, and for bringing Shakespeare to life for so many teachers and their students.